THE ILLUSTRATED

ENCYCLOPEDIA

OF THE SECURITIES INDUSTRY

THE ILLUSTRATED
ENCYCLOPEDIA
OF THE SECURITIES INDUSTRY

Allan H. Pessin

Vice President, Compliance Department
Salomon Brothers, Inc.

New York Institute of Finance

229838

Library of Congress Cataloging-in-Publication Data

Pessin, Allan H.
  The illustrated encyclopedia of the securities industry
Allan H. Pessin.

  ISBN 0-13-450306-6: $59.95
  1. Securities—Dictionaries.   2. Investments—Dictionaries.
3. Stock-exchange—Dictionaries.   I. Title.
HG4513.P463   1988
332.63'2'0321—dc19   87-27864
                                           CIP

R
332.63
P 475

This publication is designed to provide accurate and authoritative information in
regard to the subject matter covered. It is sold with the understanding that the
publisher is not engaged in rendering legal, accounting, or other professional service. If legal advice or other expert assistance is required, the services of a competent professional person should be sought.

*—From a Declaration of Principles jointly adopted by a Committee of the
American Bar Association and a Committee of Publishers and Associations*

Printed in the United States of America
10   9   8   7   6   5   4   3   2   1

New York Institute of Finance
(NYIF Corp.)
70 Pine Street
New York, NY 10270

THE ILLUSTRATED
ENCYCLOPEDIA
OF THE SECURITIES INDUSTRY

A

ABC Agreement. Memberships in the NYSE must be owned by individuals exclusively and not by firms or other venture groups. Many persons unable or unwilling to commit an impressive amount of money for a seat frequently purchase one under a special contract with funds advanced by their partnership (or corporation) instead. In this manner, too, the risk of seat-value fluctuation is greatly minimized for the individual member, because it is spread among all the principals in proportion to their financial interest in that concern. The contract arrangement is called an *ABC Agreement*, and, among other things, it determines (1) the disposition of that seat if the member dies or resigns from the firm; and (2) the extent of that member's participation in the organization's (a) capital structure, (b) profits and losses, and (c) net assets on dissolution. (In the event of resignation, there are three options available; hence the name "ABC." The member can (A) retain the seat, but buy another one for the firm; (B) sell the seat and remit the proceeds to the firm; or (C) transfer the seat for a nominal consideration to a person designated by the firm and approved by the exchange's board of directors.)

See also New York Stock Exchange, Inc.

Accounting Equation. This formula is used in totalling balance sheets:

Total Assets = total liabilities + shareholders' equity

The formula may be restated in terms of shareholders' equity or in terms of total liabilities as follows:

Total Assets – total liabilities = shareholders' equity
or
Total assets – shareholders' equity = total liabilities.

See also Balance Sheet.

Accounts Receivable. The part of a corporation's current assets consisting of money owed it by its customers. Most manufacturing companies sell to wholesalers or distributors, and goods are usually shipped with payment expected within fifteen to ninety days. The total amount of billings outstanding represents the amount of money due the company for goods already shipped. Since the entire amount of the billings will probably not be collected for various reasons (such as bankruptcy of the buyer), an estimate of bad debts is made. This allowance for bad debt is deducted from the total accounts receivable, and the leftover figure is shown on the balance sheet. This net figure represents an estimate of the amount that will be eventually collected.

See also Balance Sheet (Assets).

Account Record. *See* Broker/Dealer Organization (Margin Department).

1

Accumulation Area. In technical analysis, this lateral move in the market price of a security indicates that buyers are willing to purchase at the current price.

See also Support and Resistance Levels; Technical Analysis (Vertical Line Chart).

Accumulation Unit. *See* Variable Annuity.

Accretion. The adjustment of the tax cost basis in equal annual amounts over the life of the bond.

Accrued Interest

Itemizing Accrued Interest. An important piece of information peculiar to transactions in most debt issues and essential for both comparisons and confirmations is the addition of accrued interest to the principal amount in the contract. Only contracts for income bonds, issues in a default status, or regular-way transactions in municipal or corporate bonds effected five business days prior to an interest payment date are exceptions. For purchasers, accrued interest represents another transaction expense, and for sellers, more proceeds. It must be shown as a separate item on the execution statement because of its taxable status as ordinary income for the recipient. It can never be entitled to favorable treatment for tax purposes in capital gains or loss transactions.

This out-of-pocket expense for the purchaser is only temporary. When the corporation next pays interest on its debt, the purchaser collects the entire amount, part of which is reimbursement for the earlier payment to the former bondholder and part is payment for the current holder's status as a creditor of that concern.

Calculating Accrued Interest. Because most issuers of debt securities pay interest only semiannually, a precise method has been developed by the NASD and securities exchanges for determining amounts of accrued interest as-

sociated with transactions effected in the interim period.

Interest dollars accrue to the debt holder's benefit from the date the issuer last paid interest and continue up to, but not including, the settlement date of the regular-way or cash sale. In the case of seller's-option contracts, accrued interest is handled the same way it is with regular-way contracts, even though the purchaser may not anticipate receiving certificates until some future date. Thus, interest will not accrue for the seller through:

1. The fifth business day after trade date for corporate and municipal bonds executed regular way. Interest ceases to accrue after the day before the fifth business day. That is, if the trade day is May 9, the fifth business day falls on May 16 and interest ceases after May 15.

			MAY			
S	*M*	*T*	*W*	*T*	*F*	*S*
1	2	3	4	5	6	7
8	9	10	11	12	13	14
15	16	17	18	19	20	21
22	23	24	25	26	27	28
29	30	31				

2. The next business day after trade date for U.S. government obligations executed regular way. Interest ceases to accrue after the day before the next business day. That is, if the trade date is May 13, the next business day falls on May 16 and interest ceases after May 15.

3. The day of the trade for a debt obligation executed as a cash contract. Interest ceases to accrue after the day before trade date. That is, if the trade date is May 16, interest ceases after May 15.

For calculation procedures: (1) in the case of corporate and municipal bonds, there are thirty days in each month and 360 days in the year; and (2) in the case of U.S. government obligations, consideration is given to the actual number of days in each calendar month (365 days each year and 366 in leap years).

Example: Regular-way corporate bond. What are the interest dollars due the seller of a $10,000, 6.5% corporate bond traded regular way on Wednesday, October 13, with interest dates of January and July 1 (interest last paid on July 1)?

```
                     OCTOBER

     S     M     T     W     T     F     S
                                   1     2
     3     4     5     6     7     8     9
     0    11    12   [13]   14    15    16
    17    18    19    20    21    22    23
    24    25    26    27    28    29    30
    31
```

30 days in July
30 days in August
30 days in September
19 days in October   (not including the fifth busi-
___   ness day after October 13)
109 *total days of interest*

The formula for calculating interest is:

principal × rate × time = interest $(P \times R \times T = I)$

Thus,

$$\frac{\$10,000}{1} \times \frac{6.5}{100} \times \frac{109}{360} = \frac{\$7,085,000}{36,000} = \$196.81 \text{ due the seller}$$

Example: Regular-way U.S. government bond. What are the interest dollars due the seller of a $5,000, 3% U.S. Treasury bond traded regular way on Friday, July 14, with interest dates of February and August 15 (interest last paid on February 15)?

```
                      JULY

     S     M     T     W     T     F     S
                                         1
     2     3     4     5     6     7     8
     9    10    11    12    13   [14]   15
    16    17    18    19    20    21    22
    23    24    25    26    27    28    29
    30    31
```

14 days in February   (15 days in a leap year)
31 days in March
30 days in April
31 days in May
30 days in June
16 days in July
___
152 *total days of interest* (153 days in a leap year)

Before calculating the interest in this example, we must take into consideration two points about the $P \times R \times T = I$ formula. In calculating interest dollars for a U.S. government bond, a somewhat modified application of the usual formula is needed for greater accuracy. Although $P \times R \times T = I$ is still used (1) the rate is expressed as a percentage for that particular 6-month period alone, rather than as an annual percentage requirement; and (2) the time is expressed as the actual number of interest days related to the actual number of calendar days in that 6-month period under consideration.

In Example 2, therefore, interest dollars are calculated thus:

$$P \times R \times T = I$$

$$\frac{\$5000}{1} \times \frac{1.5}{100} \times \frac{152^a}{181^b} = \frac{\$1,140,000}{18,100} = \$62.98 \text{ due the seller}$$

[a] 153 days in a leap year.
[b] 182 days in a leap year and $63.05 total interest.

Example: Seller's-option corporate bond. What are the interest dollars due the seller of a

$2,000, 5% corporate bond traded "sellers 21" on March 16, with interest dates of May and November 1 (interest last paid on November 1)?

```
                    MARCH

     S    M    T    W    T    F    S
                    1    2    3    4    5
     6    7    8    9    10   11   12
     13   14   15  [16]  17   18   19
     20   21   22   23   24   25   26
     27   28   29   30   31
```

    30 days in November
    30 days in December
    30 days in January
    30 days in February
    22 days in March
    142 *total days of interest*

Despite the fact certificate delivery may be expected on April 5 (21 calendar days after March 16), interest accrues up to, but not including the fifth business day after trade date. Interest calculation is:

$$\frac{\$2,000}{1} \times \frac{5}{100} \times \frac{142}{360} = \frac{\$1,420,000}{36,000} = \$39.44 \text{ due the seller}$$

Example: Regular-way corporate bond traded five business days before interest date. What are the interest dollars due the seller of an $8,000, 4.25% corporate bond traded regular way on thursday, September 24, with interest dates of April and October 1 (interest last paid on April 1)?

    30 days in April
    30 days in May
    30 days in June
    30 days in July
    30 days in August
    30 days in September
    180 *total days of interest*

```
                  SEPTEMBER

     S    M    T    W    T    F    S
                    1    2    3    4    5
     6    7    8    9    10   11   12
     13   14   15   16   17   18   19
     20   21   22   23  [24]  25   26
     27   28   29   30
```

Interest dollars are calculated thus:

$$\frac{\$8,000}{1} \times \frac{4.25}{100} \times \frac{180}{360} = \frac{\$6,120,000}{36,000} = \$170.00 \text{ due the seller}$$

Because the calculation procedure entitles the seller to the full six months of interest, the comparison/confirmation will appear "flat" this means that when the seller delivers the certificates, they will be ex coupon for a bearer security; ex-interest for a registered issue.

Example: Cash transaction municipal bond. What are the interest dollars due the seller of a $5,000, 5.875 municipal bond traded for "cash" on Monday, January 19, with interest dates of March and September 1 (interest last paid on September 1)?

```
                   JANUARY

     S    M    T    W    T    F    S
                         1    2    3
     4    5    6    7    8    9    10
     11   12   13   14   15   16   17
     18  [19]  20   21   22   23   24
     25   26   27   28   29   30   31
```

30 days in September
30 days in October
30 days in November
30 days in December
18 days in January   (through the day before trade date)

138 *total days of interest*

The interest calculation is as follows:

$$\frac{\$5,000}{1} \times \frac{5.875}{100} \times \frac{138}{360} = \frac{\$4,053,750}{36,000} = \$112.60 \text{ due the seller}$$

Example: Cash transaction on a U.S. government bond. What are the interest dollars due the seller of a \$20,000, 7.70% U.S. government bond traded for cash on Tuesday, April 6, with interest dates of June and December 1 (interest last paid on December 1)?

			APRIL			
S	M	T	W	T	F	S
				1	2	3
4	5	6	7	8	9	10
11	12	13	14	15	16	17
18	19	20	21	22	23	24
25	26	27	28	29	30	

31 days in December
31 days in January
28 days in February (29 days in leap year)
31 days in March
5 days in April

126 *total days of interest* (127 days in a leap year)

The interest calculation is:

$$\frac{\$20,000}{1} \times \frac{3.85^a}{100} \times \frac{126^b}{182^c} = \frac{\$9,702,000}{18,200} = \$533.08 \text{ due the seller}$$

[a] See Example 2 above for modification of the $P \times R \times T = I$ formula.
[b] 127 days in leap year.
[c] 183 days in a leap year and \$534.37 total interest.

Account Statement. *See* Trading Policies.

Acid Test Ratio. *See* Balance Sheet (Quick Asset Ratio).

Active Bonds. Corporate debt instruments expected to trade frequently on the trading floor of the NYSE are assigned privileges in the active category. Included are most convertible bonds and substantial issues of well-known corporations. Brokers receiving orders to buy or sell such bonds step into the ring and make their bids or offerings *verbally,* provided they equal or improve on the price terms of the prevailing quotation. Such information is furnished to them by a quotations clerk, a NYSE employee who maintains a record of best bids and offerings and posts them on a uotation board just outside the ring.

Orders to buy or sell fifty bonds or more may permissibly be entered as "all or none," thereby enabling a broker verbally to qualify this order in the trading crowd. This sharply contrasts with the manner in which all-or-none stock orders are handled, regardless of quantity involved in that order.

Acceptance of a bid or offering to consummate a transaction is accomplished within the confines of the ring by the statements, "Take it" or "Sold" in precisely the same fashion that stock orders are executed.

If no member accepts the vebal bid (or offering), that broker is free to use market judgement and withdraw from the trading ring. In other words, the broker can use personal discretion (but still be subject to the risk of missing the market). A broker is not bound to state or even restate the terms and conditions specified in an order if confident that the order can be executed at a better price. This is the origin and appliation of the expression "free crowd" for active bonds.

See also Corporate Bond Transaction; Inactive Bonds

Active Box. Securities held by a brokerage firm that are eligible for use as collateral in financing arrangements are maintained collectively in a physical location known as the "open box" or "active box." Such securities include the following: (1) issues in proprietary accounts (securities owned by the firm itself, and those in its principals' accounts if pledged as their capital contribution to the organization; (2) issues purchased in customer cash accounts not yet paid for and those past settlement date; (3) issues in customer margin accounts whose value is necessary to finance debit balances in those accounts.

The Margin Department of the brokerage firm values each customer account in consideration of market price fluctuations and continously advises the Box Section which securities to segregate and which to place in the active box.

See also Broker/Dealer Organization; Segregation.

Addendum to the Uniform Application for Approval of Registration (NYSE). *See* Registration of Personnel (NYSE)

Adjusted Exercise Price. *See* Evaluating Options (Cash Dividends and Stock Splits).

Adjustment Bond. *See* Income Bond.

Administrators of Estates. *See* Fiduciary Accounts.

Advance-Decline Theory. Market averages and indexes include a limited number of components. Although averages are useful in many ways, some market analysts are more concerned with the *number* of stocks that advance in relation to the number that decline in order to gain a more detailed picture of market direction. It is not at all unusual for declines to exceed advances on a day on which other market indicators are pointing upward. This is a signal to the advance-decline theorist that the market will soon follow

downward. Naturally, there is more to this theory than watching each day's picture. The follower of this theory keeps daily totals of advances and declines, subtracts the smaller from the larger figure to arrive at a net balance, and watches for pertinent changes.

The figures are often plotted on graph paper, as illustrated in the following figure, and analyzed in conjunction with the number of issues actually traded that day. This is known as *the breadth of the market*. The breadth index is computed by taking the net of the advance-decline figure and dividing it by the total number of issues traded that day. If, on a given day, there are 1,350 different issues traded, and, of these, 712 advanced, 464 declined, and 174 remain unchanged:

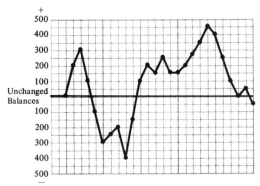

Advances and Declines

$$(712 - 464)/1{,}350 = +18.4\%$$

If the day's results are:

374	issues up
598	issues down
426	issues unchanged
1,398	total issues traded

Then $(+374 -598/1{,}398 = -16.0\%$

The market as measured by other indicators may be approaching a low point. However, if the advance-decline net balance is cumulatively showing positive signs, the analyst concludes that the market will hold and reach for higher ground. A sell signal, on the other hand, occurs if, in a rising market, net declines continually surpass net advances.

Many sophisticated approaches have developed from the advance-decline theory. These have proved to be useful tools in judging market timing.

The following table labeled "Market Diary," shows the number of issues advancing, declining, and remaining unchanged each day for the preceding six trading sessions. It includes the number of issues setting new highs and lows for the year during those sessions. This kind of overview should prove sufficient for followers of this theory to gauge market direction and spot changes in trends as soon as they occur.

Market Diary

	Wed	Tues	Mon	Fri	Thur	Wed
Issues traded	1,943	1,961	1,954	1,948	1,943	1,980
Advances	985	826	523	690	647	896
Declines	509	661	1,004	782	851	636
Unchanged	449	474	427	476	445	448
New highs, 1987	120	92	77	110	106	156
New lows, 1987	4	11	12	5	5	4

See also Confidence Theory; Dow Theory; Odd-Lot Theory; Short-Interest Theory; Technical Analysis.

Advance Refunding. Occasionally, a municipality may desire to refund an outstanding issue but cannot do so because of call protection written into the bond's indenture. In this situation, the issuer might attempt an *advance refunding.* This maneuver, also known as *prerefunding,* is a method for virtually retiring bonds while still outstanding. A new bond issue is sold, and the proceeds of the sale are immediately invested in U.S. government securities whose maturity dates closely correspond to the call dates and/or maturity dates of the outstanding issue. The government securities are set aside in an escrow ac-

count for the *sole purpose* of redeeming the outstanding municipals. Thus the bonds may be considered as virtually redeemed, as there is no possibility of default on the government issues pledged to redeem them. By this procedure, the old issue is *defeased* (eliminated) from the calculation of the municipality's debt limit. The *debt limit* is the legal maximum amount of debt that a municipality may issue.

See also Municipal Securities.

Advertising.

NASD Rules of Fair Practice. The NASD Rules of Fair Practice state that any communication designed for public consumption may not contain false or misleading statements of any material facts. Nor may such a communication purposely omit information if, in so doing, it distorts the subject matter or confuses the reader. The scope of this interpretation includes newspaper and magazine publications and reprints as well as other public media, such as radio, television, telephone recordings, and motion pictures.

In advertising material, consideration must be given to inclusion of the following specific elements and their pertinent questions:

1. *Necessary data:* Does the issuer's name appear herein? Is the material dated?

2. *Recommendations:* Is there a reasonable basis for any recommendation made in the material? Are prices of securities given as of the time the material was prepared? Has the firm disclosed its market-making activities in the securities they discuss? Do they own any rights, warrants, or options to purchase these securities in the future? Do they have a substantial interest in the securities already?

3. *Claims and opinions:* Does the material contain exaggerated claims or superlatives or express unreasonable opinions? Does it contain promises of specific results or forecast future events without identifying them as only predictions?

7

4. *Testimonials:* Has a specialist or a well-known personality expressed an opinion or provided supplementary material for this communication? If so, are there disclosures both of that person's qualifications and of any compensation, direct or indirect, being paid for these services?

5. *Offers of free service:* Are there any visible or hidden charges, conditions, or obligations levied on the recipient of the material?

6. *Claims for research facilities:* Does the material make unwarranted claims about the member's research facilities?

7. *Hedge clauses:* Have any caveats or warning statements been used that may be termed misleading?

8. *Recruiting advertising:* Are specific earnings figures or compensation ranges exaggerated, unwarranted, or unreasonable under the prevailing circumstances?

9. *Periodic investment plans:* Does the material disclose that these types of plans do not assure profits or protect against losses in declining markets? Moreover, if it discusses the principle of dollar-cost averaging, it must stress to investors that the system requires continuing purchases through periods of low-price levels to be most effective.

10. *References to regulatory organizations:* Do communications with the public state or imply approval, sponsorship, or endorsement by any regulatory body or any security or membership in any trade association? Such implications are illegal and references to membership in the NASD or in SIPC must comply with each organization's bylaws and rules.

11. *Identification of sources:* If not prepared by that member, do statistical tables, charts, graphs, and other illustrations used in public communications disclose the source of that information?

Each item of advertising, be it market letter, sales literature, or research report, must be approved via signature or initial by a registered principal of the firm that issues it. The approved material must be maintained in a separate file for at least three years from the date of first use.

In addition, if that communication pertains to registered investment companies or to options it must be filed with the NASD's Advertising Department in Washington, D.C., in accordance with the following time parameters: (1) investment companies: within ten days of first use or publication; and (2) options: at least ten days prior to use.

All other advertising and sales literature is subject to a routine spot-check procedure. The NASD in Washington may request submission of these communications for review purposes, about once annually, to determine whether that member's materials comply with the Association's standards dealing with truthfulness and taste. Other self-regulatory bodies, such as stock exchanges, have similar examination requirements. The NASD inspection procedure will not be applied (except for municipal securities, direct participation programs and investment company materials) if that member has been subjected to a spot check review by another self-regulatory organization within the past year.

See also National Association of Securities Dealers; Rules of Fair Practice.

Advertising (NYSE Policies). The Member Firm Regulation and Surveillance Division of the NYSE becomes involved in advertising and public communications practices used by member organizations. The policies it administers in this respect may be summarized as follows:

1. *Each market letter and all sales literature* prepared and issued by member organizations for distribution to customers or to the general public must be approved in advance by a member, allied member, or authorized employee. Authorized employees are generally branch office managers but could also include any designated employee familiar with the rules

and ethical standards of the exchange. Furthermore, the term *sales literature* is interpreted to mean controlled and selected mailings to describe a member firm's capabilities, special talents, or the availability of published materials.

2. *Each research report or statistical analysis* prepared and issued by a member organization for distribution to customers or to the general public must be approved in advance by (a) a member, allied member, or authorized employee; *and* (b) a supervisory analyst qualified as such with the NYSE.

3. *All other forms of advertising* (except for tombstone ads announcing nondescript underwriting participations, business cards, and announcements of internal reorganizations, officers, employees, which events have already been approved by various departments of the exchange), including newspaper, magazine, radio, television, and telephone market reports must also be approved in advance by a member, allied member, or authorized employee. Before giving this approval, member firm principals or designated employees must assure themselves that the material meets the exchange's high standards of acceptability for completeness, truthfulness, and accuracy. The NYSE enforces compliance with these standards by scrutinizing copies of sales literature, research reports, broadcast scripts, and other documents used in communications with the public. Once a year, on a random-month basis, each member firm submits its advertising materials to the Member Firm Regulation and Surveillance Division for examination. For purposes of this study they choose materials published by the firm during a single month.

See also National Association of Securities Dealers; New York Stock Exchange; Rules of Fair Practice.

Advisement Fee. *See* Management Groups.

Advisor's Client Account. This type of account, a fully disclosed relationship, is estab-

lished when separate customer accounts are introduced to a brokerage firm and maintained in the names of each of the investment advisor's clients. Under the circumstances, federal and exchange regulations require the carrying firm to obtain all the essential information about each of these people in order to exercise proper supervision and control.

When advisors open an advisor's client account, they must furnish the executing firm with the following: (1) information for a new account report form for each customer; (2) the supplementary documents that apply to the specific account category into which each of the advisor's clients falls (individual, joint tenancy, corporation, association, and so on); and (3) a trading authorization or power of attorney giving sufficient authority to the investment advisor.

INVESTMENT ADVISOR ATTESTATION

(date)

Broker/dealer
Address
City, State, Zip Code

Dear Sirs:

Instructions for clients of our firm are given by the Trading Department of our concern, an investment advisor registered with the SEC.

In light of New York Stock Exchange Educational Circular #273, for your records, a copy of the usual form of authority granted by our clients is printed on the back of this letter. We confirm, in accordance with that circular, that we will be responsible for the financial integrity of the account.

We also confirm that we maintain detailed records concerning the financial background and investment objectives of our clients, and that we comply with the provisions of Regulation T issued by the Board of Governors of the Federal Reserve System, to the extent we are subject to such provisions.

Very truly yours,

Investment Advisor

CLIENT/INVESTMENT ADVISOR AGREEMENT

(date)

Investment Advisor
Address
City, State, Zip Code

Gentlemen:

I hereby authorize you at any time and from time to time to issue to the custodian of my securities,

XYZ Bank

or to any borker I may designate, or you may select, instructions for the sale, purchase, deposit in connection with any plan of reorganization, recapitalization or other like plan, or exchange, of stocks or bonds, or other securities or investments, for my account. This shall not authorize you to receive any of my stocks, bonds, other securities, investments or cash or to authorize any disposition thereof except to me or against countervalue. While I naturally expect you will exercise diligence and care in acting on my behalf, I agree that you shall not be held liable for any losses sustained by reason of transactions executed upon your instructions or by reason of any failure on your part to issue instructions.

This authority shall be effective whether or not you usually first discuss with me the action you propose to take, and will remain in force until you receive written notice of revocation. To induce you to act under it, I hereby agree that, in the event of my death or other termination of this authority, you will be held harmless from any loss or liability incurred as a result of any action taken by you after such termination and before you have received noticed of it.

Very truly yours,

A. Customer

It is not always possible to secure this last document from a client of an investment advisor. However, it is permissible to substitute an attestation from the investment advisors that they have obtained a signed power of attorney that is current and on file in their office.

This representation must be accompanied by a blank power typically employed by that advisor.

See also Special Omnibus Account; Trading Authorization.

Affiliated Person. Normally, affiliated persons, with their ability to influence management policies, can distribute their controlling securities only: (1) if a registration statement has become effective; (2) via a secondary private placement; or (3) if a special exemption can be found, such as contained in SEC Rule 144.

Registered representatives of brokerage firms exercise extreme caution in dealing with customers who can be classified as affiliated persons. Questionable situations about control, restriction, or marketability should be referred to legal counsel before executing any sell order. A good checklist to use in making this determination is to obtain answers to the following questions: (1) Is the issuing corporation or trust closely held? (2) Does the proposed sale involve a large amount of stock in relation to the number of shares outstanding? (3) Did the seller acquire these securities via an option plan, merger, reorganization, or conversion of a privately placed debt security? (4) Is the seller an officer, director, trustee, beneficiary, or principal stockholder of the issuer? (5) Is the seller a relative by birth or marriage of an officer, director, trustee, beneficiary, or principal stockholder of the issuer? (6) Is the seller an estate of a deceased person who was an officer, director, trustee, beneficiary, or principal stockholder of the issuer? Or, is the seller related to someone who is? (7) Is there a restriction relating to the transfer of ownership for these certificates? (8) Is this sale part of a distribution registered with the SEC? (9) Has the seller participated in any distribution of these securities within the past year? (10) Is the seller a participant in a group that may be classified as an affiliated person? (11) Are there any other circumstances related to this sale that would lead you to suspect a control relationship exists? If the answer to *any* of these questions is yes, the registered representative should contact legal counsel immediately.

See also SEC Rule 144; Securities Act of 1933.

Aftermarket. *See* Stabilizing the Aftermarket.

Agency Transaction. As *agent,* the securities firm reports to its customer that it executed an order in the capacity of a *broker.* That is, the firm acted as a middleman between the customer and the market-maker.

Example: A firm might report, "As your agent, we bought for your account and risk 100 shares of Connecticut General Insurance Company at 64¾." In addition to this price, the firm generally charges a commission, a fee for the services rendered. The commission must be shown as a separate item on the customer's report and must not be included or disguised in the execution price. Under NASD rules, the commission amount must be fair and reasonable. There is no minimum schedule of commission rates for OTC transactions. All commissions are negotiated between customer and broker.

See also Principal Transaction.

Aggregate Exercise Price (AEP). This price is the product of multiplying the unit of trading by the exercise price. This is the amount that is exchanged between the buyer of the option and the seller of the option on exercise.

See also Exercise Price; Options; Unit of Trading.

All or None (AON). An all-or-none qualification may be given by customers intent on purchase (or sale) of *more* than one round lot (100 shares), but who stipulate that *all must be executed at the same time.* A member acting in behalf of this customer is prohibited from announc-

ing this qualification *orally* in the trading area. In fact, an all-or-none specification requires use of a unique strategy to execute the order if at all possible.

Without revealing the terms or conditions of this customer's order, the member must inquire about the *quotation and size* for that stock (*see* Bid and Offer). This means that the member requests information about the prevailing highest bid and lowest offering prices (quotation) as well as the number of shares wanted and offered at those respective levels (size). If the prevailing price is unsatisfactory or the size insufficient to accommodate the customer's instruction to execute at one time, the member stands by silently, doing nothing. The member has no status in the trading area. Market conditions must be watched carefully until both price and quantity available can completely satisfy that order. If it happens, *then,* and only then, does the member act to execute this order. While the member is waiting, that stock may trade at fluctuating prices and in various quantities because, after all, the exchange is a continuous auction marketplace. This member cannot participate until, and if, that stock becomes available in sufficient quantity and at the proper price(s) to satisfy the terms of the customer's instructions. It may take all day to do it, or it may never happen at all.

See also Fill or Kill (FOK); Immediate or Cancel.

All-or-None Bond Order. *See* Active Bonds.

All-or-None Offering. When a corporation is offered a best-efforts underwriting (that is, one in which the investment banker does not guarantee distribution of the offering), the corporation can counter a best-efforts proposition with, "If you can't sell it all, cancel the entire offering, including the portion already distributed." This type of agreement, sometimes linked to a best-efforts offering, is called an *all-or-none offering.*

The corporation may choose this approach because it may simply be uneconomical to complete such a distribution unless the entire amount of capital required can be financed. No customer purchases can be finalized until the issuer determines that the entire offering was marketed successfully. This can take several days, weeks, or even months. (A registration statement relating to an offering may continue to be effective for two years thereafter, provided no material changes occur in the affairs of the corporation. If an offering is not attempted within three days after the effective date, the SEC must be notified immediately.

See also Best-Efforts Offering; Underwriter; Underwriting.

Alternative Requirement. *See* Financial Protection Requirements (NYSE).

Alternative Order (Either/Or). This order is used by a customer who is wary of price movements in a particular issue and is interested in protecting an interest or position if the issue fluctuates in an unexpected fashion. It involves entry of a limit order *and* a stop order on the same ticket for the same security at different prices.

The execution of *either* of these orders causes cancellation of the other.

Example: With a stock trading at 24, a customer can enter an order to either *buy at 23 or 25 stop.* If the price drops down to 23, the limit order is executed and the stop order cancelled. But if the price moves up to 25 (or above), the stop order is elected, causing purchase at the best available price, and the limit order to buy at 23 is cancelled. If there is a partial execution of one of these orders for a multiple number of round lots, an identical quantity is automatically cancelled in the other order.

Example: If an investor owns XYZ Corporation stock presently trading at 46 and is interested in selling it at a slightly higher price, the following order can be entered: Sell long 100 XYZ at 50 *or* 43 stop. If the price moves up to 50, the limit order is executed and the stop order cancelled. However, if the price drops instead to 43 (or below), the stop order is elected, causing sale at the best available price and cancellation of the limit order to sell at 50. Thus, the holder is automatically able to salvage some proceeds when the market acts contrary to expectations.

See also Limit Order; Stop Order.

American Depository Receipt (ADR). Receipts evidencing the shares of a foreign corporation on deposit or under the control of a U.S. banking institution are called American Depositary Receipts (ADRs). ADRs are designed to facilitate transactions and expedite transfers of ownership of selected foreign securities in the United States. When a foreign company's transfer agent is located in the country of origin, which is the usual practice, an ordinary reregistration of certificates from old owner to new owner initiated from the United States can take weeks to effect. This is an unacceptable situation for our highly liquid securities markets.

Therefore, to accommodate investors and brokerage firms in this country, a U.S. bank with overseas offices and foreign correspondents creates this new security to represent shares of the underlying foreign stocks physically held in its possession, either in the United States or overseas. Morgan Guaranty Trust Company, N.A., and Citibank Corporation, N.A., both headquartered in New York City, are typical of such banking institutions. Each bank acts as an intermediary between the foreign company's transfer agent and the U.S. investor. Each is empowered to transfer ownership of the ADRs on its own books and records but continues as the official holder of record on the company's stockholder list. The actual foreign shares remain registered in the name of the bank while under the control of that bank. Of course, inves-

An American Depository Receipt

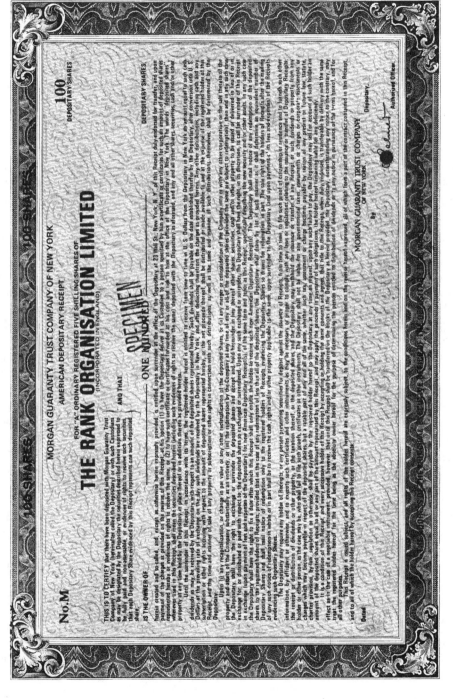

tors can always exchange ADRs for the underlying common stock (or vice versa) if they choose to do so, but this is rarely the case except among international traders who often need the comparable security to satisfy contractual sale commitments here or abroad. In any event, a nominal certificate fee is levied on the party requesting an exchange into or out of an ADR.

ADRs are available in various denominations and may represent the foreign stock on a share-for-share basis; however, in the case of Japanese securities, one ADR generally is equal to ten underlying shares. These certificates are subject to SEC regulation within the United States. For this reason, holders of ADRs are entitled to full protection under our laws as well as most advantages of stock ownership accorded to investors in domestic securities. With cooperation from the foreign corporation and through essential agency efforts of the U.S. bank, ADR investors are accorded the following privileges of ownership:

1. They receive current financial information about the company, including an audited annual report containing a balance sheet and income statement.

2. They are accorded voting privileges by means of proxies transmitted promptly to the registered ADR holders on the bank's records.

3. They receive cash dividends when paid by the foreign corporation. The bank converts the foreign currency into dollars, deducts a processing fee, and remits the balance to the ADR holder. If a tax was withheld at the source, in accord with the laws of the issuer's country, the bank notifies the ADR investor of the amount, thus enabling the party to claim it as a credit on his or her U.S. tax return.

4. They receive stock dividends or stock splits as distributed by the foreign corporation. The bank converts the additional shares into new

ADRs and delivers those certificates to the registered holders listed on its own records.

5. They receive subscription rights for new stock to be issued by the foreign corporation. However, this occurs only if the corporation decides to raise new capital via this method and only if it complies with the registration provisions of the Securities Act of 1933 and other applicable laws of the U.S. for the new stock. Otherwise, the rights will be sold by the bank (if they have a market value) and a check for the dollar proceeds, after currency conversion, sent to the ADR holder.

See also Over the Counter (OTC).

American Stock Exchange Market Value Index. The American Stock Exchange computes an index that is similar to that used by the NYSE, NASDAQ, and Standard & Poor's in that it measures the aggregate market value changes in all common shares, American Depository Receipts (ADRs) and warrants listed on the AMEX.

It totals the market values of those securities (price times shares outstanding), divides it by the market value at the close of the previous day, and then multiplies that figure by the previous closing index. Thus a percentage change in the index is equal to the percentage change in market value. This index always expresses a relative change in the total value of all shares, never an absolute change. A report of the index might read 50.98 up .13.

A new issue admitted to dealings is included in the index after it trades for one hour. The number of issues used as a divisor is then increased by one for the next computation.

The index is first prepared at 10:15 and then at 10:30 A.M. (New York time); and then half-hourly from 11:00 A.M. to 3:30 P.M. It is shown again at the close. Changes are from the previous close, not from the previous half-hour.

See also Averages and Indexes; Dow Jones Averages; NASDAQ-OTC Price Index; New

York Stock Exchange Index; Standard & Poor's Index.

Annuity Contract. An *annuity* is an investment contract between a life insurance company and a subscriber. The insurance company agrees to make periodic payments to that party, as long as he or she lives, in exchange for the deposit of a specific sum of money. The deposit required depends on the amount of periodic payment to be made as well as the individual's age and sex. The insurance company's mortality tables play a key role in this determination. Annuities are sold only by life insurance companies because only those companies can guarantee the annuity mortality risk. That is, payments are guaranteed for the lifetime of the annuity holder regardless of mortality tables of that insurance company.

An annuity contract, classified according to its mode of operation, is either fixed or variable. A *fixed annuity* is one in which the life insurance company pays a set amount to the annuitant periodically (*see* Fixed Annuity). For a *variable annuity* a life insurance company makes periodic distributions that vary in amount according to the investment securities in a special portfolio created for such contracts (*see* Variable Annuity). Annuity contracts that are combinations of both fixed and variable portions are known as *hybrid* (*see* Hybrid Annuity).

Annuity Payments. There are two programs regarding the *time* when payments will begin. These two programs, immediate or deferred, may apply to either a fixed or variable annuity contract. Under the *immediate program* the subscriber pays a single premium for the investment contract, and annuity distributions commence right away. In the *deferred program* the subscriber's deposit may be in a lump sum or paid in installments over a period of years. Whether in lump sum or in installments, the life insurance company's distributions to the contract holder are not scheduled to begin until some specified date in the future, usually at least ten years hence. Most investors choose the installment procedure under a deferred program. This is because most annuity contracts are bought for future retirement income while the investor is still working. Such contracts can be, and often are, incorporated into an investor's Keogh plan or Investment Retirement Account (IRA).

In choosing the *method* for payment, the investor has several options. One of these options must be selected by the annuitant at the time the contract matures. They are:

1. A *lump-sum distribution* in lieu of an annuity.

2. *Life annuity* payments that are made monthly or periodically during the contract holder's lifetime and that terminate only on death, no matter how long that person lives.

3. *Life annuity with payments certain*—monthly or periodic payments are made to the annuitant during that person's lifetime. However, if the contract holder dies before a specified number of payments have been made (that is, ten or fifteen years' worth), the insurance company guarantees that the distributions continue and will be paid to the decedent's beneficiary. The beneficiary's payments will cease only after the minimum number of such payments has been reached.

4. *Unit refund annuity*—monthly or periodic payments are made to the annuitant during the subscriber's lifetime. However, if death occurs before that person receives payments equivalent to the contract's original purchase cost, the difference between those payments and the amount invested is refunded to the decedent's beneficiary in a lump-sum distribution.

5. *Joint and survivor annuity*—payments are made monthly or periodically during the lives of two people and continue until both have died. These contractual distributions are appealing to married couples because they are assured of an income for life for as long as either one lives.

When a variable annuity matures and payments are about to begin, the value of the accumulation units is used to purchase a fixed number of annuity units. An *annuity unit* is an accounting symbol that is used to measure the value of the contract holder's account during the distribution period. The annuity payments are based on the value of the annuity units. Because the annuity units are invested in a separate account with an interest in a portfolio of equity securities, the investment results, and consequently the annuitant's payments, will vary up and down.

Taxation of Annuities. Deposits into an annuity contract, like purchases of mutual fund shares, are usually made with an investor's after-tax dollars. That is, the investor uses personal income remaining after payment of income taxes. Yet it need not always be that way. Because mutual funds, as well as fixed and variable annuities, are acceptable investments under the Employees Retirement Income Security Act of 1974 (ERISA) they can be an integral part of a formal retirement plan program approved by the Internal Revenue Service (IRS). If this is the case, those contractual deposits are tax deductible. This means that they are made from the purchaser's pretax income. Annuity contracts included in IRS-approved pension, profit-sharing, Keogh, or IRA retirement plans are usually identified as qualifying annuities. Those purchased independently are called nonqualifying annuities. Because most annuity contracts are of the nonqualifying variety, let us focus on their tax characteristics.

Unlike a mutual fund investor, the individual annuitant pays no income tax on dividends or capital gains from realized appreciation or unrealized appreciation (paper profits) that are credited to the nonqualifying contract during the accumulation period. Income tax is handled in the same fashion as it is with IRS-approved retirement plans. All tax liabilities are deferred until payments or withdrawals begin.

(The IRS has ruled that the privilege of postponing tax liability does not apply to certain annuities. Investment contracts affected are those in which the insurance company permits policyholders to make purchase and sale decisions for securities in their personalized separate accounts. In those instances, the investor must pay taxes on income received into that account in the year in which it is received.) Mutual fund shareholders, on the other hand, must pay tax on distributions made by the fund in the year in which paid even though such distributions may be automatically reinvested in additional shares. (The only exception would be if those mutual fund shares were incorporated into the individual's tax-exempted pension, profit-sharing, Keogh, or IRA plan.) This apparent heavier tax burden borne by a mutual fund investment plan participant as compared with an annuity purchaser has a counterbalance. The mutual fund itself pays no tax as a regulated Subchapter M company, whereas the separate account of the life insurance company is fully liable for whatever income or gain is realized from equities in its portfolio. That tax liability is taken into full consideration when the value of accumulation units is determined and credited to an annuitant's account.

Payments to holders of fixed or variable annuity contracts are taxed as ordinary income. This means that persons receiving payments must pay federal tax at their regular tax bracket rate on those payments. At retirement, most persons are in a lower tax bracket than when they were fully employed. Regular periodic payments are treated as earned income and are subject to a maximum tax, if appropriate. But if a lump-sum payment is chosen, it is classified as preference income and can subject the recipient to a higher tax. In determining the amount of tax-reportable income, the annuitant first subtracts the amount of money personally deposited in that contract. Then the annuitant pays tax on the portion of the payment in excess of that amount.

Regulation of Variable Annuities. As is the case with all insurance companies, those insurance companies selling annuities are registered with, and regulated by, the state insurance department of each state in which they do business. In addition, the individual agent must also be registered as a life insurance agent in each state in which annuity contracts will be sold. When variable annuities are to be marketed by the life insurance company and its agents, the registration and regulation function becomes a multi-responsibility because those annuity contracts are subject to SEC jurisdiction, too. The variable annuity represents an interest in a separate account of securities, and such interest is defined as a security under the law. Consequently, as a publicly owned security, it must be registered with the SEC under the Securities Act of 1933.

This registration of the annuity is preceded by registration with the SEC of the separate account itself. Because it offers accumulation and annuity units in a changing portfolio of securities, the separate account is an investment company as defined in the Investment Company Act of 1940. Thus, it must be registered pursuant to this Act and classified as a unit investment trust.

The variable annuity sales arm of the life insurance company, making a continuous public offering of a registered security, must also register with the SEC. It meets the registration requirement contained in the Securities Exchange Act of 1934 and must qualify as a broker/dealer organization. It must meet the capital, filing, and reporting responsibilities associated with that form of registration. Once this is accomplished all of its sales agents must register, too, and must complete a qualifying written examination to prove their capabilities.

Moreover, because most insurance company annuity sales affiliates have elected to join the NASD, these persons are also subject to the association's rules and standards for proper conduct. This means that the firm and its agents are subject to the terms of the NASD's Rules of Fair Practice, including the sections dealing with the terms and conditions for offering investment company shares.

Annuity Unit. *See* Annuity Contract.

Arbitrage. This is the simultaneous purchase and sale of the same (or equivalent securities to take advantage of price differences prevailing in separate markets. An arbitrage can include: (1) the purchase of a security on one exchange (or over-the-counter market) and its immediate sale on another exchange (or over-the-counter market); or (2) the purchase of a convertible bond and immediate sale of the underlying stock; or (3) the purchase of a convertible preferred stock and immediate sale of the underlying common stock; or (4) the purchase of warrants or rights to subscribe in a company followed by immediate sale of the stock that is acquired by subscription; or (5) the purchase of stock in a company to be acquired and immediate sale of comparable shares in the company making the acquisition, using its own stock as payment.

Example: If a convertible bond can be purchased for $1,000 when 25 shares of comparable stock are selling at $45 per share, it would be profitable for a trader to buy it, convert it quickly into 25 shares of stock, and sell the stock immediately.

Gross sale proceeds	$ 1,125
Cost to purchase bond	$ −1,000
Gross profit (before transaction expenses)	$ 125

A critical factor to consider with the purchase of a convertible bond is the amount of accrued interest to be added to the market price. A significant amount of interest could destroy a "profitable" arbitrage by raising total acquisition expenses above net sale proceeds of the underlying stock.

The professional trader (*arbitrageur*), alert to such profit possibilities no matter how minute, quickly makes purchases and sales to close those gaps that develop from aberrations between supply and demand. Consequently, the average investor does not have an opportunity to participate in a *bona fide arbitrage* (locked-in profit). More likely, if such an investor participates at all it will be in the form of a *risk arbitrage,* which also involves purchase and sale transactions, but not necessarily at the same time. The designation is derived from the fact that a participant exposes his/her capital to market risk until, and if, the positions can be closed out.

Because profit is not readily apparent in prevailing prices, risk arbitrageurs either: (1) buy the convertible security and hold it, hoping the underlying security is about to move sharply higher, at which point the underlying stock can then be sold to lock up the profit; or (2) sell the underlying stock short if it is believed that the stock has peaked and the convertible security is trading too close to parity with the stock itself. If the convertible security subsequently declines, they will then buy it, convert it, deliver it off to close out the short position, and lock up the profit.

Many risk arbitrages also occur with proposed corporate mergers prior to ratification by their stockholders. Uncertainty about the success of these arrangements creates wide differences in market value between the shares of the two companies. Good profits can result if the merger is completed under the announced terms and conditions. But if the proposals are altered or abandoned, a participant usually suffers heavy losses. Invariably, the security that was purchased declines sharply while the stock sold short skyrockets in value.

In futures, arbitrage consists of the simultaneous purchase and sale of similar financial instruments or comodity futures in order to benefit from an anticipated change in their price re-lationship. Arbitrage helps futures markets stay in line with cash markets.

See also Arbitrage Account; Conversion; Futures.

Arbitrage Account. In an arbitrage, a customer purchases a security and, at about the same time, either (1) sells short the same security in a different market; or (2) sells short an equal security in the same or different market to take advantage of a difference in prices (*see* Arbitrage).

Example: A person purchases XYZ stock at $71 on the NYSE and simultaneously sells it short on the Pacific Stock Exchange at $73.

Example: A person purchases an ABC convertible bond for $1,300 then simultaneously sells short the underlying stock into which the bond is convertible for more than $1,300 of market value. Such transactions and similar activities are referred to as *bona fide arbitrages.*

Under Regulation T, bona fide arbitrage transactions require no limitation to the amount of credit the broker is permitted to extend to the customer. However, the major stock exchanges do require their members, while the dual position exists, to (1) obtain a deposit equal to 10% of the value of the long security; and (2) keep the short position marked to the current market price (that is, the short position should be closely watched so that changes in market price will be reflected in changes in margin demands).

It should be kept in mind that, while most arbitrage sale transactions are usually short sales, long sales may also be made. However, in the event the long security is convertible into the security you are selling, conversion instructions must be issued *prior* to the long sale.

See also Arbitrage; Margin Account; Regulation T; Short Sale.

Arbitration (NYSE). Although arbitration does not function as a *department* within the organization of the NYSE, its purpose and responsibilities are significant. The rules and policies of arbitration are administered by the Office of the Secretary of the exchange; therefore they fall within the jurisdiction of the executive staff in the organizational scheme of the NYSE (see New York Stock Exchange, Inc).

Arbitration facilities have been provided by the NYSE to resolve disputes involving money or securities. Disputes between members of the NYSE must be presented to arbitration for settlement under terms of the exchange's constitution and rules. Intermember controversies may not be brought before the public court system.

Although it is not mandatory to do so, the exchange's arbitration facilities are also made available to settle disputes between (1) members and allied members; (2) allied members and allied members; and (3) registered representatives and member organizations, or allied members therein.

Because these parties are registered and approved by the exchange and have signed specific agreements to achieve such status (*see* Registration of Personnel), any of them can be compelled to resolve a controversy before the arbitrators at the request of another party to the dispute. However, if the disputants agree otherwise, they may seek satisfaction in court instead.

New York Stock Exchange arbitration is also available to nonmembers, such as customers, in disagreement with a member, member organization, or a registered representative concerning money or securities.

While the nonmember cannot be required to use these facilities, the nonmember *can* compel the member, member organization, or registered representative to go to arbitration. The initiative belongs to the nonmember, who need merely sign an agreement to abide by the decision without further recourse in a public court, to activate arbitration machinery.

Many irate customers (as well as members,

allied members, and registered representatives) prefer to use this procedure because (1) the arbitrators are fair and impartial; (2) the dispute is heard and resolved in a reasonable time after filing notice with the Office of the Secretary (as compared to the public court system); and (3) hearing costs are reasonable (between $25 and $550 per hearing, depending on the amount in dispute as well as the classification of the parties involved) and borne by the party initiating the proceedings.

Each year, the *chairperson* of the NYSE Board of Directors appoints a Board of Arbitration comprised of members and allied members who serve in this capacity at the pleasure of the exchange's governing body. From time to time, as need be, the chairperson of the exchange also appoints two panels of arbitrators: (1) one panel is comprised of persons engaged in the securities business; (2) one panel is comprised of persons *not* engaged in the securities business.

Controversies between members, allied members, or member organizations, are heard and resolved by (1) one person from the Board of Arbitration if the amount in dispute is less than $10,000; or (2) three or five persons from the Board of Arbitration if the amount in dispute is $10,000 or more.

Controversies involving any nonmember, at the request of the nonmember, are heard and resolved by either: (1) five arbitrators comprised of (a) one person from the Board of Arbitration, (b) one person from the panel of persons engaged in the securities business, and (c) three persons from the panel of persons not engaged in the securities business; (2) three arbitrators from the Board of Arbitration if the amount in dispute is less than $100,000 or more; or (3) five arbitrators from the Board of Arbitration if the amount in dispute is $100,000 or more.

In all controversies brought to arbitration, the decision of the majority of the arbitrators is final and binding on all parties without right of appeal to the NYSE Board of Directors or to the public courts.

See also National Association of Securities Dealers.

At-the-Close Order. For tactical or other reasons, a customer can request that an order be executed at the end of a particular day. This instruction necessitates processing as as ordinary market order, but only at the time a bell begins ringing to signal the end of trading that day. The bell is rung for thirty seconds, and within that time frame a member with an *at-the-close order* completes the transaction at the best available price. There is no assurance that this will be the final trade in that security. Another member, perhaps with a similar instruction, may be more fortunate with his or her timing within those thirty seconds.

See also At-the-Close Odd-Lot Order.

At-the-Close Odd-Lot Order. Some customers prefer to buy or sell their stock as near as possible to the end of the trading day, probably on the supposition that they can get a more favorable execution price. The specialist is prepared to satisfy this eccentric belief without questioning the customer's motives, provided that this instruction is received before trading on the stock exchange ceases for the day. However, an at-the-close order to buy or sell is not executed on the last round-lot sale of the day. Rather, it is bought (or sold) on the final quotation of the day. (Short sales at the close are prohibited.)

When the closing bell (signaling the end of the trading that day) stops ringing, the prevailing highest bid and lowest offering prices become the closing quotation. This quotation is the determinant for executing at-the-close orders. Those customers will buy at the offering price plus the differential or sell long at the bid price minus the differential.

Some investors even attempt to hedge their instructions by entering limit orders with an "or at-the-close" stipulation. If their limit price cannot be satisfied during the normal trading session, they request an execution on the closing quotation, *at whatever price prevails.* This approach assures completion of their investment program that day.

See also Differential; Odd-Lot Stock Execution.

At-the-Opening Order (Opening Only). This qualification for a market or a limit order necessitates execution on the initial transaction for the stated security that day or the order is automatically cancelled. Obviously then, it must be entered prior to the first transaction for that stock, although not necessarily prior to the opening of the NYSE at 9:30 A.M., New York City time. For one reason or another, a stock may not *open* until later in the day, if at all.

Auction Market. On the exchange floor, traders bring their orders to *trading crowds*, that is, posts on the floor designated for the trading of certain securities.

Example: IBM, among other securities, may be traded at one post, while General Motors is traded at another post.

Once in the crowd, the traders announce the number of shares they have to buy or sell and the price that the order calls for. If another trader in the crowd has an order that permits him or her to buy or sell at that price, a trade is made. If no one else in the crowd wishes to buy or sell at that price, then the trader must wait until someone is willing. Thus securities are traded by means of *open outcry* in what is known as an *auction market.*

By contrast, over-the-counter transactions are made in what is considered a negotiated market, since the trades are consummated between two broker/dealers, either over the phone or by means of electronic data links.

See also Bid and Offer; Over the Counter (OTC).

Authorized Stock. This is the maximum number of shares that the state secretary permits a corporation to issue.

See also Common Stock; Preferred Stock.

Automatic Reinvestment of Distributions. *See* Voluntary-Accumulation Plans.

Automatic Withdrawal. *See* Voluntary-Accumulation Plan.

Average and Index. An average and an index differ as to the number of components used. An average is based on a small number of securities, whereas an index uses a broader sampling. However, there isn't any clear line of demarcation between the two, and so, in some instances, one analyst's average may be another analyst's index.

An average adds the market value of selected stocks and divides either by the number of issues or by a divisor that allows for stock splits or other changes in capitalization. Criticism of averages is based on the small number of issues included in the sample and the resultant disproportionate effect that one company can have on the average. Also, the securities chosen are not always representative of the purpose of the average.

Example: American Telephone & Telegraph, which is clearly a utility corporation, is a component of the Dow Jones *industrial* averages. Averages are, nonetheless, widely accepted and have provided a reliable market indicator for many years.

See also American Stock Exchange Market Value Index; Dow Jones Averages; NASDAQ-OTC Price Index; New York Stock Exchange Index; Standard & Poor's Index.

Award Ceremony. With debt issues in particular, the bidding and award ceremony may be an extremely complex affair. Not only must the syndicate contend with price, but interest rate expenses as well. Although one group's bid may be higher than the others, it may still lose the award because the interest rate proposal would cost the company more money over the life of the issue than the rates proposed by its competitors. The *net interest cost (NIC)* to the issuer is the principal factor influencing an award of bonds to an underwriter.

Example: On a $20 million bond issue maturing in thirty years with the bidding as shown below, you would lose to your competitor because the issuer's NIC is higher in your case though your bid price offers the corporation more initial money:

Bidding on a $20,000,000 Bond Issue

Corporation Receives and Pays	*Your Syndicate's Bid*	*Competitor's Bid*
Corporation receives	101 ($20,200,000)	100½ ($20,100,000)
	Your Interest	**Competitor's Interest**
Corporation pays	**Rate Proposal**	**Rate Proposal**
annually	7% ($1,400,000)	6¾% ($1,350,000)
Corporation's expense over 30 years	**$41,800,000**	**$40,400,000**

In the case of competitive underwritings, when it becomes obvious that bidding will be keen, each group usually submits its bid with a *tail* attached, hoping to gain a slight advantage. This means that it dislikes bidding in round numbers or round fractions and will instead submit a bid something like 98.4361 for a bond issue or 18.9752 for a stock. The bid is often carried to four decimal places, although there is no rule preventing them from extending it even further.

B

Backing Away. *See* National Association of Securities Dealers Automated Quotations; Rules of Fair Practice (Section 1; Section 6).

Back-Door Subscription Conduit. *See* Hot Issue.

Backwardation. A condition where the nearby futures months and spot prices are at a premium to the deferred months (a British term).
    See also Futures.

Balanced Investment Company. These investment companies strive to minimize market risks while earning reasonable current income. They hope to achieve long-term growth of principal and income through moderate investment practices. Balanced companies are so named because they maintain varying percentages of bonds, preferred stocks, and common stocks in their portfolios. The term *balance* does not refer to equal amounts of security class when, in fact, most balanced companies maintain 60 to 75% of their assets in common stocks alone. The remainder is invested in the senior securities (bonds and preferred stocks) of better quality companies. A balanced company tends to decline less in value than common stock companies do in falling markets and to be less volatile in bull markets.
    In recent years the number of balanced companies as a percentage of all registered investment companies has been steadily declining while the number of diversified common stock companies has been increasing.

    See also Bond and Preferred Stock Company; Diversified Common Stock Company; Formula Investing; Income Company; Investment Company.

Balanced Mutual Fund. *See* Balanced Investment Company.

Balance Sheet. Periodically, a corporation needs to demonstrate to its shareholders what the company is worth. The company simply lists everything it owns (assets) and everything it owes (liabilities). *Assets* are items of value—things that a company *owns* or *has owed to it*; assets are a corporation's possessions, or its pluses. *Liabilities* are the company's obligations—its debts, what the company *owes*. The difference between assets and liabilities represents the company's net worth or the stockholders' net ownership, called *stockholders' equity*. This tabulation of assets, liabilities, and net worth is known as a *balance sheet*. Traditionally, the balance sheet is arranged as follows:

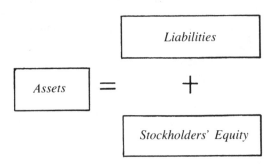

Both sides "balance," of course, because a corporation's stockholders have a stake in their corporation equal to the amount by which the corporation's assets exceed its liabilities. Expressed, another way, what a company owns (its assets) minus what it owes (its liabilities) is equal to its net worth. The net worth (stockholders' equity) represents the value of the shareholders' investment in the corporation: It is the amount of money invested in the business by stockholders, plus the profits that have *not* been paid out as dividends. The basic balance sheet (or accounting) equation is:

Total assets = Total liabilities + Stockholders' equity

Since a firm's financial state is continually changing, the balance sheet must be dated. The balance sheet's date shows on what day the tabulations were made. The assets, liabilities, and stockholders' equity are listed at their values *at the close of business* on the date shown at the top of the statement. A *simplified* balance sheet appears to the right.

The value of the items owned—of the assets—can be figured many different ways. In actuality, the amount of money received from buyers, should all the assets be sold (liquidated), may differ dramatically from the values shown on the balance sheet. The shareholders' (stockholders') equity therefore represents the amount of money that *would* go to the preferred and common stockholders if all the company's assets were sold at the values at which they are carried on the balance sheet and if all liabilities were paid off as well. Thus, in another form, the balance sheet equation is:

Shareholders' equity = Total assets −Total liabilities

Balance Sheet
Roxbury Manufacturing Company
December 31, 1978

Assets	
Cash	$ 75,000
Marketable securities	150,000
Accounts receivable	375,000
Inventory	400,000
Total current assets	$1,000,000
Property, plant, and equipment	$ 605,000
Prepayments	20,000
Intangibles	10,000
Total assets	$1,635,000

Liabilities	
Accounts payable	$ 200,000
Accrued expenses	150,000
Accrued taxes	50,000
Total current liabilities	$ 400,000
Bonds—8%, due 1995	500,000
Total liabilities	$ 900,000

Stockholders' Equity	
Preferred stock—6% ($100 par)	$ 75,000
Common stock ($10 par)	300,000
Capital surplus	100,000
Retained earnings	260,000
Total stockholders' equity	$ 735,000
Total liabilities and stock holders equity	$1,635,000

Assets. These are all the things of value that a company owns or has due: cash, buildings, machinery, patents, and good will. A corporation's assets are traditionally listed, by type, in the following order: (1) current assets (cash, marketable securities, accounts receivable, inventory); (2) fixed assets (property, plant, and equipment); (3) sundry assets (prepaid expenses and deferred charges); and (4) intangible assets (patents, franchises, good will).

1. *Current assets* are items that a company owns or has owed to it and that, in the normal course of business, will be converted into cash within a year or less. This category includes: (a) cash, (b) marketable securities, (c) accounts receivable, and (d) inventory.

See also Accounts Receivable; Cash; Inventory; Marketable Securities.

The sum of these four types of current assets is the corporation's *total current assets*. Compare the following section with the first section in the Roxbury balance sheet:

Current Assets:

Cash	$ 75,000
Marketable securities at cost	
(Market value – $156,000)	150,000
Accounts Receivable	
($390,000 less $15,000 allowance	
for bad debt)	375,000
Inventory (first-in/first-out)	400,000
Total current assets	$1,000,000

(Some corporate balance sheets might show such additional items as "notes receivable" and/or "prepaid expenses." The bookkeeping method here treats prepaid expenses as a sundry asset rather than as a current asset. This variation is just one example of the methods used by modern-day accountants. *See also* Sundry Asset.)

Current assets are in constant motion. When a company sells its products, an appropriate amount is deducted from inventory and goes into accounts receivable. When buyers pay their bills, accounts receivable become cash and the cash may then be used to pay debts. Or a company may add to inventory and thus repeat the cycle.

Also, when an item is sold for more than its inventoried value, the difference (that is, the *gross profit*) automatically increases the total current assets by the amount of the profit. (We shall demonstrate how this profit is reflected on

the *other* side of the balance sheet later.) Since both sides must balance, this profit is reflected by a corresponding increase in shareholders' equity. The company has made a profit, and the shareholders are therefore better off.

See also Quick Asset.

2. *Fixed assets* are items of value that can be used in current operations and that can be expected to generate revenue. Included in this category are such items as improved land, buildings, furniture and fixtures, machinery, tools, and transportation equipment—sometimes referred to collectively as *property, plant, and equipment*. These assets are normally not considered as items to be sold but rather as "tools of the trade" with which the manufactured product is produced, displayed, and transported. Most fixed assets are listed on the balance sheet at cost minus accumulated depreciation. To determine the value of a corporation's fixed assets, look at the entry under assets labeled "Property, plant, and equipment." This figure represents what the company paid to acquire the asset (cost), less an annual allowance for "wear and tear" on the asset (depreciation).

See also Depreciation.

Liabilities. On the *right* (debit) side of the balance sheet are listed the corporation's debts and, further down, the stockholders' equity. The liabilities section contains: (1) current liabilities (obligations that fall due within a year) and (2) fixed liabilities (long-term obligations).

See also Current Liability; Fixed Liability.

Stockholders' (Shareholders') Equity. The difference between the corporations' total assets and total liabilities is referred to as *stockholders' equity* or *net worth*. The final section of the balance sheet represents the stockholders' equity, which is the stake that the stockholders, both common and preferred, have in their corporation. This section itemizes the amount of equity or *ownership* by the *true owners* of the corporation, the shareholders. It might be thought of as the money that the corporation "owes" the owners. The items in this category are: (1) preferred stock, (2) common stock, (3) paid-in capital (capital surplus, or the amount of money the company received from the sale of shares of common stock, in addition to its par value), and (4) retained earnings (earned surplus, or the amount of profit that the company retains in the business after paying dividends on common stock).

See also Common Stock (Balance Sheet); Paid-In Capital; Preferred Stock (Balance Sheet); Retained Earnings.

In the following figure, dollar amounts have been entered for the various entries in all three sections of the balance sheet. Note that the "Total assets" amount on the left equals the "Total liabilities and stockholders' equity" figure on the right.

The common stockholders' stake in the company can be found by adding together the common stock listing ($500,000), paid-in capital ($0), and retained earnings ($150,000). The sum of these three figures shows the common stockholders' equity.

On the other hand, let us assume the company decides to continue operations for future profits. To reward the stockholders, it decides to distribute a dividend. Since the term "retained earnings" means earnings retained in the business, any distributed earnings in the form of dividends *decreases* retained earnings.

See also Dividends.

Capitalization Ratios. A company's *capitalization* is simply the sum of the balance sheet values for the corporation's bonds, preferred stock, and common stock. All three elements of

Assets		Liabilities	
Cash	$ 80,000	Accounts payable	$ 60,000
Accounts receivable	135,000	Accrued expenses	+ 40,000
Inventory	+ 140,000	Total liabilities	$100,000
Total current assets	$355,000	*Stockholders' Equity*	
Property, plant and equipment	470,000	Preferred stock $100 par	100,000
Prepaid expenses	+ 25,000	Common stock $1 par	500,000
		Retained earnings	+ 150,000
		Total liabilities and stockholders' equity	
Total assets	$850,000	equity	$850,000

The balance sheet balances. If this company decides to liquidate, it realizes $850,000 in cash from the sale of the assets, at least in theory. If it next pays off all obligations ($100,000 for all liabilities), it would have a total of $750,000 to be distributed to the owners of the company, its shareholders. The preferred stockholders are entitled to receive par for their stock ($100,000), leaving $650,000 for the common stockholders.

the common stock are added: common stock, paid-in capital, and retained earnings. Thus capitalization represents the monies invested in the company by the original purchasers of the bonds, preferred stock, and common stock. It also reflects retained earnings, which is the capital that has not been paid out as dividends but that rather has been reinvested in the company. Capitalization tells us how a company got its funds and, secondarily, how it is handling them.

Capitalization is expressed in terms of three ratios, one each for bonds, common, and preferred stock. Each of these capitalization ratios represents the proportion of money collected through each vehicle to the total capitalization amount, assuming the total amount is equal to 100%.

Example: Here is a typical manufacturing company's balance sheet:

Balance Sheet
Roxbury Manufacturing Company
December 31, 198X

Assets	
Cash	$ 75,000
Marketable securities	150,000
Accounts receivable	375,000
Inventories	+ 400,000
Total current assets	$1,000,000
Property, plant, and equipment	605,000
Prepayments	20,000
Intangibles	+ 10,000
Total assets	$1,635,000

Liabilities	
Accounts payable	$ 200,000
Accrued expenses	150,000
Accrued taxes	50,000
Total current liabilities	$ 400,000
Bonds 8%—Due 1995	500,000
Total liabilities	$ 900,000

Stockholders' Equity	
Preferred stock—6% ($100 par)	$ 75,000
Common stock ($10 par)	300,000
Capital surplus	100,000
Retained earnings	260,000
Total stockholders' equity	$ 735,000
Total liabilities and stockholders' equity	$1,635,000

Roxbury's capitalization is $1,235,000, calculated as follows:

Bonds	$ 500,000
Preferred stock	75,000
Common stock	300,000
Capital surplus	100,000
Retained earnings	260,000
Capitalization	$1,235,000

The *bond ratio* is derived by dividing total capitalization into the bonded debt, usually outstanding bonds maturing five years or more in the future.

$$\text{Bond ratio} = \frac{\text{Bonds}}{\text{Total capitalization}}$$

$$\text{Bond ratio} = \frac{\$\ 500,000}{\$1,235,000} = 0.405 \text{ or } 40.5\%$$

The *preferred stock ratio* is found by dividing total capitalization into the par value of the preferred stock.

$$\text{Preferred stock ratio} = \frac{\text{Preferred stock}}{\text{Total capitalization}}$$

$$\text{Preferred stock ratio} = \frac{\$75,000}{\$1,235,000} = 0.061 \text{ or } 6.1\%$$

The *common stock ratio* is found by dividing total capitalization into all three parts of the common stock account.

$$\text{Common stock ratio} = \frac{\text{Common stock} + \text{Capital surplus} + \text{retained earnings}}{\text{Total capitalization}}$$

$$\text{Common stock ratio} = \frac{\$300,00 + \$100,000 + \$260,000}{\$1,235,000}$$

$$= 0.534 \text{ or } 53.4\%$$

All three capitalization ratios add up to 100%, as shown in the following figure:

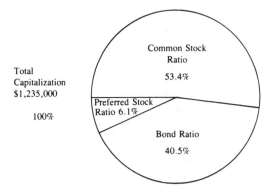

Total
Capitalization
$1,235,000

100%

There are certain capitalization ratio "yardsticks."

Example: If the combined bond and preferred stock ratios exceed 50% of the total capitalization, an industrial company is generally considered by industry standards to have a leveraged capital structure. This condition may be considered speculative.

Book Value. The net tangible assets backing each share of common stock is known as *book value.* Calculating book value is easy: Since the balance sheet always shows the theoretical value of the common stockholders' equity (common stock plus paid-in capital plus retained earnings), just subtract the intangible assets (if any) and divide by the number of outstanding common shares.

Example: The formula, applied to the Roxbury balance sheet, is as follows:

		Common Stock	+	Capital surplus	+	Retained earnings
Book value	=					
−	Intangibles	÷	Number of shares of common stock outstanding			

Book value = ($300,000 + $100,000 + $260,000

− $10,000) ÷ $30,000 = $21.67
per share

The book value per common share represents the amount of cash that would be available for each share of common stock (1) if all the assets (excepting intangibles) are sold at the values at which they are carried on the balance sheet and (2) if all liabilities, bondholders, and preferred stockholders are also "paid off." For our purposes, assume that the company must pay the bondholders and preferred stockholders the total par value of their securities as shown on the balance sheet. (Accountants would probably use the higher value between the total par value as shown on the balance sheet and the total market value based on the call price of their securities.)

A company's book value can be of great significance, despite the fact that, in the real world, liquidating the company at balance sheet values is virtually impossible. An increasing book value is generally considered to be a healthy sign for a company; a decreasing book value may indicate a weakening financial situation. To the securities analyst, whether a company's book value is increasing or decreasing is especially significant. While normally a company's book value and its market value bear no correlation (with some exceptions mostly for financial service companies, such as insurance firms), these values usually move in concert.

Example: The "bid" shown in the newspaper for mutual funds is actually the book value of a share of the fund.

Summary. The balance sheet reflects the company's financial position at a particular point in time—what it owns, what it owes, and what the shares are worth. It is like a snapshot of a subject "on the run"—the action is frozen, and the values are reflected as of the close of business on the balance sheet date.

While one balance sheet can be very revealing, a *series* of balance sheets, possibly covering the previous five or six years of operations, can be of even greater significance. The *trends* are extremely important. Is this year's current ratio better or worse than it has been over the last several years? Is the book value per common share going higher or lower? A study of the ratios over a period of a few years can reveal much about the company's future prospects.

Bank Credit. The amount of credit generated by bank loans far exceeds the sum of actual currency received in the form of deposits. This interesting phenomenon is founded on the fact that currency is not the primary medium used in financing and supporting the economy. Most businesses function by drawing on currency if necessary, although they seldom make use of this privilege. Instead, a commercial bank extends a line of credit to a business enterprise in the form of a loan, while maintaining the "proceeds" in a demand-deposit account. Then, as needed, the business organization requests its bank (in the form of a check) to transfer portions of this artificial balance to the accounts of its creditors, either at the same bank, or at other banks within the nation. At the same time, checks the business receives as payment from its own customers are used to offset and reduce any borrowing reflected by the balance in its demand deposit account. In this fashion, very few currency exchanges ever take place. Substantially all details are handled as bookkeeping items between the commercial banks involved, who act as agents and who use the facilities of the district Federal Reserve Bank to: (1) sort and return the checks to the original bank; (2) transfer underlying balances between them within one to four days thereafter; or (3) wire immediate balances to a particular bank the same day payment is required, if doing so is specified as a condition of a contractual agreement. (The Fed also services nonmember banks for processing checks.)

The success of the nation's economy depends on the acceptance of those pieces of paper called *checks*. If people demanded the underlying currency as sole payment for debts, the whole banking system would be severely handicapped in its ability to provide credit to its customers. It would only be able to lend out dollar for dollar of cash assets and cash deposits received. However, because of the universal acceptance of checks, a commercial bank effectively "manufactures" credit by depositing its own check in a borrower's demand deposit account. The fundamental backing behind the "business" of a commercial bank is the bank's own promise, pledging its general assets as collateral. A commercial bank is successful insofar as it is able to maneuver its currency demand deposits and loan demand deposits in a fashion that permits it to meet its customer obligations.

The penalty for failing to do so is to face a "run on the bank" without sufficient collateral to meet those demands. This juggling is obviously somewhat risky due to the difficulty in gauging both depositor intentions and customer loan requirements. To promote confidence in the banking system and to ensure soundness of operation, both Federal Reserve and state banking authorities have imposed reserve requirements on the activities of the commercial institutions that they regulate.

See also Federal Reserve System; Multiplier Effect of Credit Power.

Bank Deposits. Banks manufacture credit by means of loans to finance a variety of private businesses and other commercial enterprises. Customer loans are contingent on a bank's willingness to commit its own capital and its ability to attract money from depositors, either passively, or through purchase. (When a bank offers to pay attractive rates of interest for long-term deposits, it is said to be *purchasing money*. It hopes to lend it to borrowers at much higher rates.) A bank's accounts are classified as either: (1) demand deposits; (2) time deposits; or (3) savings deposits.

See also Demand Deposits; Federal Reserve System; Savings Deposits; Time Deposits.

Bank Float. When a purchase is paid for by check, the seller's bank, on receipt of the payment check, immediately credits its deposit records and thereby creates additional loan power (*see* Multiplier Effect of Credit Power). The check, however, may take one to four days to clear. During the clearing period, the seller's bank pays no interest to the depositor, that is, to the seller.

The financial advantage for banks, realized from this delay in transferring ordinary funds between banks for typical commercial transactions is called *bank float*. In annual transactions aggregating billions of dollars, banks earn significant sums of money in additional interest revenue as a result of the "float."

Bankers' Acceptances. These credit instruments are designed to finance shipment and/or storage of merchandise by manufacturers, both domestically and abroad. They are drafts (bills of exchange) that have been accepted (guaranteed) by a bank or trust company for payment on a specific date in the future (one to six months). Bankers' acceptances provide manufacturers and exporters with capital liquidity during the period between the time of manufacture (or export) and payment by the purchasers of the goods. These short-term, guaranteed drafts may be marketed several times before maturity by the relatively few securities dealers who maintain a market for them. Bids and offerings are reflected at discounted prices from face value, the method used in the trading of U.S. Treasury bills. The rate of interest, calculated on an annual basis and adjusted for the exact number of days involved, is reasonably low, reflecting the relative safety of this investment. Profits earned and interest received on a bankers' acceptance are taxable for American investors.

See also Money Market Instrument.

Banks for Cooperatives. Under supervision of the Farm Credit Administration, Banks for Cooperatives (Co-op) make and service loans for farmers' cooperative associations and issue debt instruments to arrange for this financing. The federal government does not guarantee these obligations, but they are secured by banks organized under federal charter operating under government supervision. The bearer securities issued by the Co-op pay interest that is fully taxable to the recipient under federal regulations but exempted from state and municipal taxes. They are legal investments for, and are most popular with, other banks and state and local governments.

See also U.S. Government-Sponsored Corporation or Agency Obligation.

Barron's Confidence Index. *See* Confidence Theory.

Basis Price. *See* Odd-Lot Stock Executions.

Basis Price Odd-Lot Order. Executing an odd-lot order on a quotation may be inequitable for some investors who deal in relatively inactive stocks with a wide spread between their bid and offering prices. On request, the specialist will establish and permit execution of odd-lot orders at a *basis price*.

A basis price is an artificial round-lot transaction created at a price somewhere between the prevailing bid and offering if (1) that issue did not trade throughout the day; and (2) the spread between bid and offering prices equals at least two full points.

Example: 141-143, 86½-89, 107-112.

The price is set by the specialist at a level believed to be where that stock will eventually next trade. It is not necessarily directly between the prevailing quotation. It could be on or close to the current bid or offering price. The specialist's judgment is influenced by such factors as the trend of prices in the rest of the market and knowledge of a large buy or sell interest overhanging this particular stock or industry. Each basis price, although established by the specialist, is subject to approval by a floor official to ensure fairness for the customer in view of market conditions.

Basis price executions are available only to customers who (1) deal in stock assigned 100-share trading units by the exchange; (2) enter their orders at least thirty minutes before the market closes; and (3) instruct their orders be marked "on basis." The following table lists some sample basis price odd-lot executions.

Sample Basis Price Odd-Lot Executions

	Basis Price*	Execution Price
Buy on basis	147	147⅛ (147 + ⅛)
Sell long on basis	87¾	87⅝ (87¾ − ⅛)
Buy at 111 or on basis**	113½	113⅝ (113½ + ⅛)
Sell long at 130 or on basis**	131	130⅞ (131 − ⅛)
Sell long at market or on basis	95⅝	95½ (95⅝ − ⅛)

*Short sales are prohibited on a basis price.

**Because it is unknown at the time of entry whether the security will trade that day, most basis price orders include a provision for execution on an effective sale, too.

See also Differential; Odd-Lot Stock Execution; On-the-Quotation.

Bearer Bond Certificate. This type of bond does not have its owner's name imprinted on it and comes with interest coupons attached. When an interest payment is due, the holder merely clips off a coupon with the appropriate date inscribed on it and dposits it in a bank (as would also be necessary with the deposit of an ordinary check). Bearer securities are as freely interchangeable between investors as the money in an individual's pocket.

See also Registered Bond.

Beneficial Owner. Those customers whose securities are held by the brokerage firm but registered in the brokerage firm's name for reasons of convenience are called the *beneficial owners* of those shares. The issuing corporation does not know who they are, but the brokerage firm, acting as their agent, has a fiduciary responsibility to accord them full privileges of ownership.

Allocation of Money and Securities. The distribution of money and/or securities, allocated pro rata to the beneficial owners, must, of course, be equal to the amount received from the company.

Example: If the Dividend Department receives a $1,500 check from an issuer for a payment rate of $.50 per share, and its position list shows the following beneficial owners and quantities on the record date, the pro rata allocation is:

	Holdings	Allocation
Customer A	250 shares	$ 125
Customer B	1,000 shares	500
Customer C	1,300 shares	650
Customer D	50 shares	25
Customer E	400 shares	200
	3,000 shares	$1,500

Similar pro rata calculation and apportionment is needed when a corporate distribution is a stock dividend or a split-up.

Example: Using the record of customer holdings depicted above:

1. If the company pays a 2% stock dividend (two shares of new stock for each 100 shares owned), the brokerage firm receives one certificate of 60 shares (2% of 3,000) and must allocate it accordingly.

	Stock Dividend	New Holdings
Customer A	5 shares	255 shares
Customer B	20 shares	1,020 shares
Customer C	26 shares	1,326 shares
Customer D	1 share	51 shares
Customer E	8 shares	408 shares
	60 shares	3,060 shares

2. If, *instead,* the company splits up its shares four for three (four new shares for every three old shares), the brokerage firm receives 1,000 additional shares. (The firm already has 3,000 shares, and ⅓ × 3,000 = 4,000.) The 1,000 additional shares are allocated accordingly.

	Old Holdings	Stock Dividend	New Holdings
Customer A	250 shares	83⅓ shares	333⅓ shares
Customer B	1,000 shares	333⅓ shares	1,333⅓ shares
Customer C	1,300 shares	433⅓ shares	1,733⅓ shares
Customer D	50 shares	16⅔ shares	66⅔ shares
Customer E	400 shares	133⅓ shares	533⅓ shares
	3,000 shares	1,000 shares	4,000 shares

If fractional shares result, the company, at its predetermined, stated option, may (1) pay cash in lieu of the fraction; (2) allow the holder to subscribe to the next highest full share; or (3) redeem the fraction at prevailing market values. Thus, if the fractional shares in the illustration were redeemed at a time when the stock was valued at 36, all but Customer D would be credited with $12 (⅓ of 36). Customer D would be paid $24 (⅔ of 36).

In this illustration, because a brokerage firm often receives a full number of shares from the company, it credits its customer accounts with their full shares and acts as a dealer for the resolution of fractions per customer request.

3. If, *instead* of a stock split up, the company reorganizes by splitting down (a reverse split), and if it decides on a ratio of one for five (one new share for every five shares), the brokerage firm must adjust its customer holding records for that issue accordingly.

	Old Holdings	New Holdings
Customer A	250 shares	50 shares
Customer B	1,000 shares	200 shares
Customer C	1,300 shares	260 shares
Customer D	50 shares	10 shares
Customer E	400 shares	80 shares
	3,000 shares	600 shares

Proxy. Generally at least once a year, corporations distribute to stockholders an advisory and voting solicitation, giving the stockholder a right to elect directors and decide on other important matters brought before an annual or special meeting of the company. Beneficial owners cannot cast their votes directly, however, because the corporation recognizes only the brokerage firm as its stockholder from its street name registration of certificates. The Proxy Department of the brokerage sends a request form to each of the beneficial owners, soliciting instructions regarding casting of this ballot. This form is called a proxy. Proxies are also solicited by the Reorganization Department in cases of redemption calls on convertible issues, exchange and tender offers, and certain purchases pursuant to a rights offering.

When the beneficial owners notify the Proxy Department about their preferences, the brokerage firm reflects their votes in the total cast in behalf of all of its customers at the company's meeting. It is as valid a participation in the company's affairs as if the customers had personally attended the meeting and cast their own votes. As a result of its customers' diverse opinions, brokerage firms usually submit split votes to reflect their instructions. Thus, if a broker was a stockholder of record of 7,180 shares, it might vote 4,130 shares for, and 3,050 shares against, a particular proposal (or some other such split vote). Sometimes, the beneficial owners do not bother to advise the Proxy Department about their preference, and, under certain conditions, that voting privilege may be wasted. In significant matters affecting the financial interest of stockholders in a public company, exchange regulations preclude members from voting unless specific instructions are received from the rightful owners of those shares. If routine matters are submitted to holders for a vote, in the absence of customer instructions, the brokerage firm is allowed to reflect its own judgment. It normally sides with management of the company, accepting its voting recommendations.

Solicitations. The Proxy Department of the brokerage acts as agent for dissident shareholders or any other group anxious to communicate with, or solicit, the beneficial owners whose shares are in firm custody, if (1) that group has registered its proxy statement or solicitation with the SEC, per Section 14 of the Securities Exchange Act of 1934; and (2) the group agrees to reimburse the brokerage firm for postage and other out-of-pocket expenses.

A stockholder solicitation may be a simple plea for a vote to effect a reform or to overthrow the company's present management. Or, it may be a request for the beneficial owners to tender their shares in response to a purchase proposition.

See also Broker/Dealer Organization; Exchange Offer; Proxy; Redemption Call; Tender Offer.

Best-Efforts Offering. Realistically, a young corporation with no proven *track record* (experience) is unable to negotiate a firm commitment underwriting arrangement, that is, one in which the underwriter guaranties the distribution of the offering. Usually, in such cases, the investment banker firm agrees merely to devote its best efforts in making this offering a success but will not guarantee the corporation payment for any unsold portion of the issue. In a *best-efforts offering*, the investment banker acts only as an agent of the corporation. (This is different from a firm commitment underwriting, in which, by virtue of the absolute guarantee, the investment banker assumes status as a principal.) The unsold portion of a best-efforts offering is returned to the issuer without further liability for the investment banker firm. It pays the corporation only for those shares it has managed to distribute.

See also All-or-None Offering; Underwriter; Underwriting.

Beta. *See* Index Options.

Bid and Offer. When a commission house or two-dollar broker accepts an order from a telephone clerk (*see* Order Transmission), that person must proceed to the specific trading post assigned by the exchange for all activity in that issue. Without revealing any terms of the order, a member always asks first for the *current market* for that security.

Example: The broker might say, "How is Motors?" (General Motors Corporation), or "What's the market for Big Steel?" (U.S. Steel Corporation), or "How are you making Ma Bell?" (American Telephone and Telegraph Corporation). (Experienced brokers playfully refer to some issues by slang or amusing designations commonly accepted by the community.)

Requesting Quotation and Size. This is recognized as a request for a quotation and size. It refers to the *highest bid price* existing with the number of shares so represented, and the *lowest offering price* available with the number of shares reflected also at that level.

Examples: "46½ to 46¾, 300 by 100," means there are 300 shares wanted at 46½ and 100 shares available at 46¾.

"57⅞ to 58⅛, 2 up," means there are 200 shares wanted by someone at 57⅞ and 200 shares offered for sale by someone at 58⅛.

Although it may not be a personal bid or offering price, the specialist, acting as a coordinator, assumes responsibility for furnishing the quotation on request. Brokers who are unwilling to accept these prevailing prices may verbally express their own proposals, but only if their price is *equal to, or better than*, the price in the existing quotation. Thus, if a quotation is 31⅜ bid, offered at 31¾, a broker with an order to buy stock can compete verbally in the trading area only if able to bid 31⅜ or higher. Even if that broker wants to purchase enormous amounts of stock at a lower price, a member is forbidden to interfere with anyone willing to pay a higher price and must, therefore, remain silent. An identical rule exists for sellers, prohibiting them from offering stock for sale unless their price is *equal to, or lower than*, the prevailing offering.

What is the Range? To plan strategy more effectively, a broker may request the *range* as well as the quotation and size. The range refers to the opening sale, high sale, low sale, and latest sale for that particular issue.

Example:

12¼,	13,	12,	12⅝
open	high	low	last

The first three prices are furnished by the specialist. The latest or last sale appears on an indicator at the trading post that is manually operated by the specialist or a clerk.

The Language of Bidding and Offering. Brokers who want to participate actively in the auction process by stating their own bids or offers must use the phraseology prescribed by the exchange to avoid confusion and misunderstanding. To *bid* for stock, a member must first state the intended purchase price followed by the number of shares desired.

Example: "86¼ for 100," "17 for 1,000," or "48⅝ for 600" are typical of bids on the floor of the exchange.

To *offer* stock for sale, a member must first state the number of shares to be disposed of, and then the price desired.

Example: "200 at 21," "10,000 at 37⅞," or "700 at 45¼" are typical of offerings on the floor of the exchange.

Accepting a Bid or Offer. When a contra broker makes a bid for stock that is agreeable to the terms of the customer's order, a member shows acceptance of that bid at this price by saying, "Sold!"

This declaration consummates a transaction and leads immediately to a new series of bids and offerings for other shares of that security.

If the quantity on a member's order is insufficient to satisfy the entire bid, the member shows partial acceptance by saying, "Sold 100," "Sold 400," and so forth, as the case may be.

When a contra broker makes an offering of stock that is agreeable to the terms of the customer's order, a member shows acceptance of that offer at that price by saying, "Take it!" This statement, too, consummates a transaction and necessitates a new auction for other buyers and sellers of that security. Partial acceptance of an offering is indicated by, "Take 200," "Take 800," and so forth, as the case may be.

In this manner, price and volume fluctuate continuously, with brokers and traders accepting bids and/or offerings made by other members of the exchange.

From time to time, a member organization may receive a customer's order that is simply too big to be handled by the normal market procedures. To accommodate that customer, the firm may turn to certain unique methods described in the New York Stock Exchange's *Constitution and Rules.* Because they are unorthodox, a member organization must first obtain approval from the NYSE before employing any of these measures (*see* Exchange Distributions and Acquisitions; Secondary Distribution; Special Offering).

See also Crossing Stock; Errors in Execution; Stopping Stock; Super DOT System; Ticker Tape.

Bid Wanted (BW). *See* National Quotation Bureau, Inc.

Blanket Fidelity Bond. Each NASD member organization that meets three requirements—(1) has employees; (2) is required to join the Securities Investor Protection Corporation (SIPC), a nonprofit membership corporation organized by act of Congress in 1970 to ensure customer assets at broker/dealers who become insolvent), and (3) is subject to SEC net capital rules—must purchase and maintain fidelity bond insurance to protect the firm against financial loss sustained (a) by means of fraud (including fraudulent trading activities); (b) on premises (including misplacement of securities); (c) in transit (including misplacement of securities); and (d) through forgery or alteration.

Required coverage ranges from $25,000 to $5,000,000 based on the broker's required net capital. Self-insurance up to the greater amount of $5,000 or 10% of the necessary minimum coverage is permissible, but the deductible provision counts as a direct charge against that firm's net capital computation. A deductible provision in excess of this amount is allowed only if the firm can show that it was unable to obtain a lower provision. In any event, that degree of excess self-insurance must be eliminated as soon as possible. The NASD must be notified within ten business days if a member's coverage declines below the minimum required by this rule, if the policy is cancelled, or if the insurance will not be renewed.

See also Financial Protection Requirements (NYSE).

Block Size. This term describes the size of a transaction involving 10,000 or more shares or $200,000 or more of market value.

See also SEC Rule 144.

SEC Rule 144

The broker/dealer may purchase the securities for its own account only if it is a marketmaker in that security or if the quantity involved is of *block size* (10,000 or more shares or $200,000 or more in value). It may subsequently solicit buy orders from its customers to dispose of these shares.

1. Allows the sale of restricted securities (investment letter) or unrestricted but unregistered securities.
2. By affiliated and nonaffiliated persons.
3. Within any ninety-day period.

4. But the sale is limited to the greater of (a) 1% of shares outstanding, or (b) average weekly volume for previous four weeks.
5. Filing and reporting details are inapplicable for nonaffiliated persons holding unregistered or restricted stock for three or more years.

Blue List. The primary source of information for offerings in the municipal secondary market is the *Blue List*. Bonds are listed by state and the basic information given includes the: (1) number of bonds offered, (2) issuer, (3) maturity date, (4) coupon rate, (5) price, and (6) dealer firm making the offering.

Bond ratings are not included in these listings. Other information of interest in the Blue List includes settlement dates on recent offerings of new issues, a separate section on prerefunded bonds, and also miscellaneous offerings including a scattering of U.S. government and agency obligations, railroad equipment trust certificates, corporate bonds, and even preferred stocks. The total number of listings gives an indication of the size and liquidity of the market and is referred to as the *floating supply*.

See also Daily Bond Buyer.

Blue Room. *See* Trading Floor NYSE).

Blue-Skying the Issue. Most state governments have their own securities laws that are separate and distinct from federal regulations. Engaging in securities activities within their borders requires compliance with their laws as well as with the federal statutes.

While a security is in the process of being registered with the SEC (during the cooling-off period), the managing underwriter's attorneys try to qualify that issue for sale under the laws of the various states in which the offering will be attempted. Some states permit public offerings of securities simply on the basis of an effective SEC registration statement. Other states require qualification through submission of an effective registration statement filed with their own securities commissioners. This is what the lawyers want to ascertain before the underwriters irrevocably commit themselves to the corporation. The practice of analysis, investigation, and qualification with these state laws is known as *blue-skying the issue.* (This expression stems from the enactment day of the nation's first state securities law, in Kansas, in the early 1900s. At that time, a legislator reputedly quipped, "Now Kansas citizens will have more of a basis for making investment decisions than merely by the shade of blue sky.")

If the lawyers find that the security cannot qualify for sale in too many of the "big money" states, they advise the investment bankers either to defer or cancel their plans to underwrite this issue. After all, why should they jeopardize their capital and potential success in an offering because of legal restraints prohibiting solicitation of significant investors?

Securities salespeople who deal with purchasers residing in these states must also be registered with the securities commissioners. Failure to comply with this particular blue-sky provision enables customers to rescind the transaction anytime in the future. Such failure also can subject the representatives and their firms to civil and criminal penalties by those states.

See also Twenty-Day Cooling-Off Period; Underwriting.

Board of Governors. *See* Federal Reserve System; National Association of Securities Dealers.

Boiler Room Operations. A boiler room is a high-pressure sales organization usually employed in the promotion of securities of little value, such as those issued by assetless *shell* corporations. Boiler room sales are outlawed under federal law and industry rules.

See also Manipulation of Security Prices and Deceptive Devices; Rules of Fair Practice; Securities Exchange Act of 1934.

Bona Fide Arbitrage. *See* Arbitrage.

Bond and Preferred Stock Companies. These investment companies as a type are in the minority but are growing. Preferred stock companies are few and are often classified as income-type companies. Bond funds have been growing in popularity primarily because of the unique characteristics associated with the securities in their portfolios.

Example: Some bond companies provide excellent stability of principal together with a good current yield by investing exclusively in short-term debt instruments. Their portfolios hold U.S. Treasury bills, government agency notes, bankers' acceptances, CDs, and high-quality commercial paper, all with maturities ranging up to one year. These "money market" funds are designed for persons seeking current income and minimal risk with investment capital available for relatively brief periods. Some bond companies invest exclusively in municipal securities and provide shareholders with interest that is exempted from federal income taxes. Most other bond company portfolios, however, are composed of many different corporate debt instruments that offer investors diversification and a good return as well as the stability of income that characterizes all bond funds.

See also Income Company; Investment Company; Money Market Fund.

Bond Broker. Members who execute orders in the bond room of the NYSE as a matter of continuing practice are called *bond brokers.* Actually, any member of the exchange is permitted to transact business in the bond room, but because this room is physically separated from the rooms where stocks are traded and competitive floor brokerage rates are nominal per $1,000 face value bond, relatively few members bother to participate there.

Bond Power. *See* Good Delivery of Securities.

Bonds. Bonds of all issuers have had appeal throughout U.S. history for two major reasons:

1. *Ready marketability.* They are more liquid than real estate and most other investment media. This is due to the fact that (a) they can be bought or sold at minimum expense; (b) they pledge to pay a fixed amount of interest over their lifetime; (c) they must be redeemed at face value on a specific date; (d) they can be maintained in a portfolio without annual carrying charges or maintenance fees; and (e) they command a determinable investment value because of their senior securities status and the creditworthiness of their issuer.

2. *Ready negotiability.* Bonds are easily transferred from seller to buyer.

As securities, bonds differ from stock in that they represent debt, not ownership (or equity) as stock does. Therefore, a corporation may issue bonds (debt instruments) and/or stock (shares in equity/ownership), whereas governments may issue only debt securities.

See also Bearer Bond Certificate; Corporate Bond; Municipal Securities; Registered Bond; U.S. Government Securities.

Interest. An important price consideration in making a securities contract is any distribution of money contemplated or pending by the issuing corporation. As a creditor, the holder of a bond receives interest on this loan to the company, while a stockholder receives dividends from the net profits or surplus if declared by the company's board of directors. But those payments are not made on a daily basis. So market prices and contract expenses are influenced by the trade date's proximity to the usual distribution dates.

Most corporations pay interest on their bonds only semiannually (every six months). This is usually accomplished on the first or fifteenth days of the two months involved, as stated in the indenture.

Examples:

> January 1 and July 1 (J and J 1)
> February 15 and August 15 (F and A 15)
> March 1 and September 1 (M and S 1)
> April 15 and October 15 (A and O 15)
> May 1 and November 1 (M and N 1)
> June 15 and December 15 (J and D 15), and so forth.

Thus, if a bondholder sells that security in the interim period between payment dates, the seller cannot collect from the corporation the interest that has been accruing. However, because a bondholder has senior status as a creditor, the seller is still entitled to interest for each day spent as a creditor. The interest amount that accrues from the company's last payment date is advanced by the purchaser of the bond at the time the certificates are delivered on settlement date.

Example: Assume interest dates of March 15 and September 15 for a 6% debenture sold for settlement on June 15. On the June 15 settlement date, the purchaser pays the seller $15 interest, which has accrued since March 15, in addition to the contract price agreed on. Then, on September 15, the purchaser as a new bondholder receives $30 from the corporation—$15 for reimbursement of the initial out-of-pocket payment of interest to the former holder and $15 for interest due as a creditor of the corporation. A simplified diagram of this example appears in the following figure.

Interest Payment Cycle for 6% Debenture [$60 annual interest per $1,000 bond]

March 15		Settlement of Sale		September 15
($30)	$15	June 15	$15	($30)
		Seller entitled to 3 months of accrued interest equal to $15		Purchaser entitled to 3 months of accrued interest equal to $15 for a period of time as a creditor

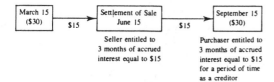

March 15 ($30)		Settlement of Sale June 15		September 15 ($30)
	$15 →		$15 →	

Seller entitled to 3 months of accrued interest equal to $15

Purchaser entitled to 3 months of accrued interest equal to $15 for a period of time as a creditor

Not all bond transactions are as simple as the one in this example. Because the transactions in our active and precise marketplace are complex, the Uniform Practice Committee has provided NASD members with details for determining the exact interest amount due the seller in various situations.

To make the necessary calculations, you must remember that interest accrues on a day-by-day basis and that (1) for calculation purposes in the case of corporate and municipal bonds, there are thirty days in each month and 360 days in the year; whereas (2) in the case of U.S. government obligations, there are always an actual number of days to count in each calendar month under consideration (365 days each year and 366 in leap years.

Furthermore, interest will accrue up to, *but not including* (1) the fifth business day after trade date for all corporate and municipal bonds executed regular way or seller's option; (2) the next business day after trade date for all U.S. government obligations executed regular way or seller's option; (3) the day of the trade for any debt obligation executed as a cash contract.

Example: $10,000 Pacific Telephone and Telegraph 6½% bonds due January 1, 2003, traded on Wednesday, September 13, at 90½. How much must the purchaser pay the seller?

Step 1: Calculating accrued interest days.

With a stated maturity of January 1, 2003, this company pays interest on January 1 and July 1 of each year until the year 2003, when the bond must be redeemed. Because this is now September 13, the company obviously last paid interest on July 1. Therefore, interest began accruing for the seller on July 1 and ceased on the fifth business day after the September 13 trade date:

30 days in July
30 days in August
19 days in September (up to but not including the fifth
—   business day after September 13)
79 days of accrued interest

Step 2: Calculating interest dollars.

The formula for calculating interest is:

Principal $\times$ rate $\times$ time $=$ interest or $P \times R \times T = I$

Thus,

$$\frac{\$10,000^a}{1} \times \frac{6.5}{100} \times \frac{79}{360} = \$142.64 \text{ accrued interest}$$

[a]Note that the principal is always $1,000 per bond regardless of market price because that sum represents the company's obligation to its creditors at maturity. The company is not concerned with fluctuations in the market price in the interim.

Step 3: Calculating total amount.

$142.64 is added to the contract value of $9,050 (90½) and is shown as a separate item on the customer's confirmation. The accrued interest amount is an added expense for the purchaser and additional proceeds for the seller. The total amount due the seller is $9,192.64.

Example: $7,000 Norton Simon Industries 4¾% bonds due May 1, 1990, traded on Thursday, October 20, at 71¼. How much must the purchaser pay the seller?

Step 1: Calculating accrued interest days.

With a maturity date set at May 1, 1990, the company's semiannual interest payments are paid on May 1 and November 1 each year until 1990. It pays a total of $47.50 (4¾% of $1,000) per bond each year, or in actuality, $23.75 per bond at six-month intervals. Since the transaction occurred on October 20, it is obvious that the last interest distribution was made on May 1 of that year. Thus, accrued interest days are:

30 days in May
30 days in June
30 days in July
30 days in August
30 days in September
26 days in October (up to but not including
___ the fifth business day after October 20)

176 days of accrued interest

Step 2: Calculating interest dollars.

The formula for calculating interest is:

$$P \times R \times T = I$$

Thus:

$$\frac{\$7,000}{1} \times \frac{4.75}{100} \times \frac{176}{360} = \$162.56 \text{ accrued interest}$$

Step 3: Calculating total amount.

$162.56 is added to the contract value of $4,987.50 (price of 71¼ = $712.50 per $1,000 bond; there are seven bonds); this amount is shown as a separate item on the customer's confirmation. The accrued interest amount is an added expense for the purchaser and additional proceeds for the seller. The total amount due the seller is $5,150.06.

Example: $5,000 U.S. Treasury bond, 3%, due February 15, 1998, traded on Friday, July 14, at 81.8. How much must the purchaser pay the seller?

Step 1: Calculating accrued interest days.

With a stated maturity of February 15, 1998, the government pays the semiannual interest of $15 (one-half of $30, or 3%) per $1,000 bond on February 15 and August 15 of each year until 1998. The accrued interest days involved in this transaction begin counting on February 15 and stop on the *calendar* day prior to July 17 (July 17 is the next business day after the July 14 trade date). Therefore, the interest days are:

14 days in February (15 days if a leap year)
31 days in March
30 days in April
31 days in May
30 days in June
16 days in July

152 days of accrued interest (153 days if a leap year)

Step 2: Calculating interest dollars.

In calculating interest dollars for a U.S. government bond, a somewhat modified application of the usual formula is used for greater accuracy. Although $P \times R \times T = I$ is still honored and the principal amount remains $1,000 per bond (1) the *rate* is expressed as a percentage for that particular six-month period alone, rather than an annual percentage requirement; and (2) the *time* is expressed as the actual number of interest days related to the actual number of calendar days in that six-month period under consideration.

Thus, interest dollars are calculated as:

$$P \times R \times T = I$$

$$\frac{\$5,000}{1} \times \frac{1.5}{100} \times \frac{152\,(153 \text{ in leap year})}{181\,(182 \text{ in leap year})} = \begin{array}{l}\$62.98 \\ (\$63.05 \text{ in} \\ \text{leap year})\end{array}$$

Step 3: Calculating total amount.

$62.98 is added to the contract value of $4,062.50 (price of 81.8, or 81⁸/₃₂, = $812.50 per $1,000; multiply by 5 since this is a $5,000 bond); this amount is shown as a separate item on the customer's confirmation. The accrued interest amount is an added expense for the purchaser and additional proceeds for the seller. The total amount due the seller is $4,125.48.

Example: $50,000 U.S. Treasury bond, 8¼%, due May 1, 1990, traded Tuesday, March 23, at 108⅞ cash contract settlement. How much must the purchaser pay the seller?

Step 1: Calculating accrued interest days.

With a maturity set for May 1, 1990, the government pays interest on this bond on May 1 and November 1 each year until 1990 when the issue will be redeemed. Thus, in this problem, because interest was last paid on November 1 of the previous year, the days of accrued interest are figured from last November 1.

30 days in November
31 days in December
31 days in January
28 days in February (29 days if a leap year)
22 days in March (interest accrues up to but not including the trade day for cash contracts)
142 days of accrued interest (143 days if a leap year)

Step 2: Calculating interest dollars.

The formula for calculating interest is:

$$P \times R \times T = I$$

Thus:

$$\frac{\$50,000}{1} \times \frac{4.125^a}{100} \times \frac{142^b}{181^c} = \$1,618.09^d$$

[a] ½ of 8¼%.
[b] 143 in leap year.
[c] 182 in leap year.
[d] $162.05 in leap year.

Step 3: Calculating total amount.

$1,618.09 is added to the contract value of $54,437.50 (price of 108⅞ = $1,088.75 per $1,000; multiply by 50 since this is a $50,000 bond; this amount is shown as a separate item on each customer's confirmation. The total amount due the seller is $56,055.59.

Example: $2,000 Albany County, New York, general obligation bonds, 7.60%, due October 1, 1988, traded " sellers 18" on Monday, August 22, at 100⅜. How much must the purchaser pay the seller?

Step 1: Calculating accrued interest days.

With a maturity stated to be October 1, 1988, this issuer pays semiannual interest of $38.00 (½ of $76, or 7.60%) per $1,000 per

bond on April 1 and October 1 until October 1, 1988, when the bond will be redeemed. Although the certificates will be delivered eighteen calendar days after August 22, interest accrues for the seller's benefit only from April 1 (when the county *last* paid interest) until, but not including, August 29 (the fifth business day after trade date). The accrued interest days are therefore:

30 days in April
30 days in May
30 days in June
30 days in July
28 days in August
148 days accrued interest

Step 2: Calculating interest dollars.

The formula for calculating interest is:

$$P \times R \times T = I$$

Thus:

$$\frac{\$2,000}{1} \times \frac{7.60}{100} \times \frac{148}{360} = \$62.49$$

Step 3: Calculating total amount.

When the seller delivers the certificates on September 9 (eighteen calendar days after August 22) a check for $2,069.99 will be waiting; $2,007.50 for the contract price (price of 100⅜ = $1,003.75 per $1,000 bond; there are two bonds) plus $62.49 worth of accrued interest. From August 29 onward, accrued interest is the property of the new bondholder.

Trading Plus Accrued Interest and Trading Flat. Most bonds trade in the marketplace at a price *plus accrued interest.* Bonds that do not usually trade in this manner, such as income bonds, are traded *flat.* Most income bonds and all obligations of issuers for which interest has been deferred normally trade flat. That is, the contract price does not entail the addition of accrued interest. If such bonds are in coupon form, all unpaid coupons must be delivered to the new purchaser of the certificate. If they are detached from the certificate when delivered, great care should be exercised to ensure that the serial numbers on the coupon match the serial numbers of the certificate itself.

Pricing. Equity securities customarily trade in the market in values reflected in dollars and cents. For example, a stock priced at 75 is really $75 per share and a round lot (100 shares) is worth $7,500.

However, corporate (and U.S. government) bond prices are not normally reflected in this way.

1. *In percentages.* Bonds are priced at a percentage of face (par) amount.

Example: A bond represented at 75 is valued not at $75, but rather at 75% of the par value appearing on the bond certificate. (Keep in mind that a *stock* quoted at 75 would be valued at $75 per share!)

Other examples are:

75% of $500 par = $375 market value
75% of $1,000 par = $750 market value
75% of $5,000 par = $3,750 market value
75% of $10,000 par = $7,500 market value

Unless otherwise specified, it is safe to assume that the face amount of a bond is $1,000 per bond. This is the traditional *par* of an overwhelming number of outstanding debt securities. It is the company's principal obligation to the holder for repayment at maturity. On order tickets, trade reports, and other memoranda used within the securities industry, the $1,000 par value is often abbreviated by the Roman numeral "M." Thus an order for one bond is written as 1M, five bonds as 5M, ten bonds as 10M, and so forth. The interest requirement is also specified as a percentage of the same par value.

Any bond that trades in the marketplace below its face amount is commonly called a *discount bond*, whereas one that sells above face amount is referred to as a *premium bond*. In any

event, at maturity, the holder of either security may expect to receive only its face value from the issuing company.

See also Discount; Premium.

2. *In whole numbers.* Whole number bond prices are easily translated into dollar figures merely by adding a zero to the last numeral represented.

Examples:

$$91 = \$ \ 910 \text{ per bond}$$
$$83 = \$ \ 830 \text{ per bond}$$
$$108 = \$1,080 \text{ per bond}$$

3. *In whole numbers and fractions.* To understand what a fraction means in a bond quotation, you must know the decimal equivalent of the fraction. Most corporate bonds fluctuate in variations of one-eighth (⅛% of $1,000). The decimal equivalents are as follows:

⅛ = .125 or $1.25 per bond (.125 of 1% of $1,000)
¼ = .250 or $2.50 per bond (.250 of 1% of $1,000)
⅜ = .375 or $3.75 per bond (.375 of 1% of $1,000)
½ = .500 or $5.00 per bond (.500 of 1% of $1,000)
⅝ = .625 or $6.25 per bond (.625 of 1% of $1,000)
¾ = .750 or $7.50 per bond (.750 of 1% of $1,000)
⅞ = .875 or $8.75 per bond (.875 of 1% of $1,000)

Determining the dollar value for a bond priced with a whole number and fraction can be calculated by either: (1) placing the decimal equivalent of the fraction next to the last whole number and then moving the decimal one place to the right; or (2) adding the dollar value of the fraction to the dollar value of the whole number.

Examples:

91⅛	=	91.125 =	911.25 or	$ 910.00
				+ 1.25
				$ 911.25
83½	=	83.50 =	835.00 or	$ 830.00
				+ 5.00
				$ 835.00
108⅞	=	108.875 =	1,088.75 or	$1,080.00
				+ 8.75
				$1,088.75

4. *In whole numbers and decimal points.* Some bond issues, particularly obligations of the U.S. government, have such good marketability in a keenly competitive market that they trade in variations as small as thirty-seconds or sixty-fourths rather than eighths. In practice, these fractional designations are separated from the whole number by means of a decimal point, and the denominator is dropped completely. The decimal value equivalents of these fractions are listed in the following table:

32nds	64ths	per $1,000	32nds	64ths	per $1,000
+	1	.15625	16+	33	5.15625
1	2	.31250	17	34	5.31250
1+	3	.46875	17+	35	5.46875
2	4	.62500	18	36	5.62500
2+	5	.78125	18+	37	5.78125
3	6	.93750	19	38	5.93750
3+	7	1.09375	19+	39	6.09375
4	8	1.25000	20	40	6.25000
4+	9	1.40625	20+	41	6.40625
5	10	1.56250	21	42	6.56250
5+	11	1.71875	21+	43	6.71875
6	12	1.87500	22	44	6.87500
6+	13	2.03125	22+	45	7.03125
7	14	2.18750	23	46	7.18750
7+	15	2.34375	23+	47	7.34375
8	16	2.50000	24	48	7.50000
8+	17	2.65625	24+	49	7.65625
9	18	2.81250	25	50	7.81250
9+	19	2.96875	25+	51	7.96875
10	20	3.12500	26	52	8.12500
10+	21	3.28125	26+	53	8.28125
11	22	3.43750	27	54	8.43750
11+	23	3.59375	27+	55	8.59375
12	24	3.75000	28	56	8.75000
12+	25	3.90625	28+	57	8.90625
13	26	4.06250	29	58	9.06250
13+	27	4.21875	29+	59	9.21875
14	28	4.37500	30	60	9.37500
14+	29	4.53125	30+	61	9.53125
15	30	4.68750	31	62	9.68750
15+	31	4.84375	31+	63	9.84375
16	32	5.00000	32	64	10.00000

Examples:

94.8 $= 94 + $ $^8/_{32}$% of $1,000 $= 940+2.50,$
or $942.50 per bond

71.12 $= 71 + $ $^2/_{32}$% of $1,000 $= 710+3.75,$
or $713.75 per bond

89.23 $= 89 + $ $^{23}/_{32}$% of $1,000 $= 890+7.19,$
or $897.19 per bond

97.30 $= 97 + $ $^{30}/_{32}$% of $1,000 $= 970+9.38,$
or $979.38 per bond

The fraction is always reflected in terms of thirty-seconds unless it is followed by a plus sign (+), which signifies that it is denominated in sixty-fourths. In this situation, double the fraction and add one. The decimal value equivalents of these fractions are listed in the preceding table.

Examples:

85.8 $+ = 85 + $ $^{17}/_{64}$% of $1,000 $= 850+2.66,$
or $852.66 per bond

79.20 $+ = 79 + $ $^{41}/_{64}$% of $1,000 $= 790+6.41,$
or $796.41 per bond

93.3 $+ = 93 + $ $^7/_{64}$% of $1,000 $= 930+1.09,$
or $931.09 per bond

98.11 $+ = 98 + $ $^{23}/_{64}$% of $1,000 $= 980+3.59,$
or $983.59 per bond

Retirement of Debt Securities. On the maturity date, the corporation must redeem the obligation by paying holders the principal amount due plus any interest accrued from the last interest date. The issuer may retire its debt in a number of ways:

1. In a *refunding*, the corporation uses the proceeds from a new bond issue to retire the existing bond issue.

2. With a *sinking fund*, the company sets aside a dollar amount annually, often in cash or government securities, for the purpose of retiring the debt.

3. In an *open market purchase* (prior to maturity), the issuer simply buys up the bonds in the market at a price that is below par value.

4. By *exercising a call* (also prior to maturity), the corporation requires bondholders to redeem their bonds prior to maturity.

5. In a *conversion*, holders may exchange their bonds for shares of stock.

More often than not, the corporation uses several of these methods to retire a particular bond before maturity. For example, it might issue a partial call for redemption with monies available from a sinking fund or might force conversion of an exchangeable issue via full or partial calls for redemption.

The various ways of retiring a bond issue are summarized in the following table.

Refunding	New bond issue to redeem an older one
Sinking Fund	Annual reserve set aside, often in cash or in government securities
Open Market Purchase	Purchase bonds in the market below par value
Exercising a Call	Corporation requires bondholder to redeem prior to maturity
Conversion	Exchange bond for shares of stock

See also Yields.

Major Factors Affecting Bond Values. Although the aggressive forces of supply and demand play a role in determining values of debt securities, these are only two of several factors influencing bond fluctuation in the marketplace. The availability of credit and the issuer's ability to pay interest and repay principal in accordance with the terms of its indenture are equally important considerations governing movement in corporate bond prices.

As for the *availability of credit,* in the course of regulating money and credit in the United States, the Federal Reserve Board exerts a definite influence on the secondary market for all debt instruments. When the amount of available funds is reduced, competition for these monies increases capital borrowing costs. But what about long-term debt, issued under the older and cheaper terms, that has 10,15,20, or even 25 years remaining until maturity? Obviously, such a security is no longer as attractive at face value as it was before. This is especially true if lenders can employ their money at higher cur-

rent rates. Therefore, the older bond with the lower fixed interest rate must invariably decline in value until its yield is comparable to the newly prevailing financial conditions.

Example: A 4.5% coupon rate bond that was issued at $1,000 five years ago and that has 25 years from today remaining until maturity is not worth as much money as a comparable quality 6.5% coupon rate bond issued today to mature in 25 years. The former bond should theoretically decline in value to the level at which it yields the going rate of 6.5%. (We say "theoretically" because other factors influence bond prices.)

$$\frac{.045}{.065} = \frac{x}{\$1,000}$$
$$.065x = (.045)(\$1,000)$$
$$= \$45.00$$
$$x = \$692.31$$

Proof:

$$\frac{\$45 \text{ (interest)}}{\$692.31 \text{ (cost)}} = .06499, \text{ or } 6.50\% \text{ yield}$$

Conversely, a 7.25% rate coupon bond issued at $1,000 two years ago, with 23 years to maturity, should be more valuable if current rates declined to 6.50% for comparable quality bonds issued today with a similar maturity. The bond with the 7.25% coupon should theoretically appreciate in value to a level where it would yield the going rate of 6.50%.

$$\frac{.0725}{.065} = \frac{x}{\$1,000}$$
$$.065x = (.0725)(\$1,000)$$
$$= \$72.50$$
$$x = \$1,115.38$$

Proof:

$$\frac{\$72.50 \text{ (interest)}}{\$1,115.38 \text{ (cost)}} = .06500, \text{ or } 6.50\% \text{ yield}$$

The *issuer's ability to pay* is another major influence on bond prices. Three advisory services—Fitch, Moody's, and Standard & Poor's—render ratings on bonds, in accordance with confidential criteria focusing on the issuer's financial strength and management.

See also Ratings.

Other Factors Influencing Bond Prices. The market values of bonds also depend, to one degree or another, on: (1) a call feature; (2) the existence of a sinking fund, and (3) convertible features. A *call feature* tends to put a ceiling on the price of a bond; it is senseless for someone to pay more for a bond than the price at which the issuer could buy it back from the holder. A *sinking fund* puts a floor on the bond's price because the fund plays the role of a "buyer in the wings," with which the corporation can repurchase its debt in the open market if the price drops to a low enough level. A *conversion feature* enables the issuer to assign a slightly lower-than-normal coupon rate to the bond, inasmuch as the convertibility permits bondholders to participate in the success of the company's common stock.

See also Call Features; Convertible Bonds; Sinking Fund.

Types of Protection for Bondholders. The various kinds of protection available to holders of the four types of bonds are summarized briefly in the following table.

Type of Bond	Protection Available to Bondholder
Mortgage	Pledges real assets, such as real estate
Collateral Trust	Pledges portfolio of corporation's securities in another company
Equipment trust	Pledges machinery, such as railroad cars and planes
Debentures	*Unsecured;* pledges only the general assets, which are intangible assets such as goodwill and reputation

If the corporation is unable to pay interest on the date prescribed in the bond's indenture or if it is unable to repay the principal at maturity, the trustees, in behalf of the holders of the instruments, can, through judicial process under Chapter X of the Bankruptcy Act, lay claim to the assets securing these loans. This action often forces the management of the company to counterclaim with its own suit in a Chapter XI petition, asking continuing control and protection from its creditors.

If management's appeal is denied, it has only two options: (1) liquidation of the assets to salvage what is left; or (2) continuance of the corporation through reorganization and deferral of debt repayments or, in general, holding all creditors' immediate claims in abeyance.

Bond Ratio. *See* Balance Sheet (Capitalization Ratios).

Bond Room. *See* Trading Floor (NYSE).

Book Value. *See* Balance Sheet (Book Value).

Borrowing Restrictions for Broker/Dealers. *See* Securities Exchange Act of 1934 (Section 8).

Bottom Line. *See* Income Statement (Primary Earnings per Share).

Breadth Index. *See* Advance-Decline Theory.

Breakaway Pattern. *See* Double Tops and Bottoms (Climaxes).

Break-Even Point. At this price (or prices), a particular strategy of transaction neither makes nor loses money. In options, the term refers to the result of the strategy at the expiration date. A *dynamic* break-even point changes as time passes.

Breakout. In technical analysis, a breakout is the rise through a resistance level or the decline through a support level by the market price of a security.

See also Support and Resistance Levels; Technical Analysis (Vertical Line Charts).

Breakpoint. *See* Sales Load.

Breakpoint Sales. It is contrary to equitable principles of trade to solicit mutual fund orders in dollar amounts just below the level at which the sales charge will be reduced on quantity transactions. Such practice is unfair because it forces investors to bear the burden of a maximum load, when for a little more money deposited over a thirteen-month period they can enjoy a lower sales charge. As a rule of thumb, the NASD will look with suspicion on investments made within $1,000 of a mutual fund's breakpoint.

Although the use of a breakpoint is encouraged by the authorities, the practice of breakpoint sales is not! The former benefits investors, but the latter does not.

See also Investment Companies.

Broker. This term refers to any person or firm in the business of effecting transactions in securities for someone else's account.

Broker's Blanket Bond. Blanket insurance covers all employees, officers, and partners of NYSE member organizations and protects investors against misplacement, fraudulent trading, and check forgery. Such coverage is required by the NYSE Constitution.

See also Financial Protection Requirements (NYSE).

Broker's Broker. An agent who locates municipal bonds for other municipal bond traders.

Broker's Collateral Loan. When using the loan facilities of a bank to finance customer activities, a broker/dealer assumes the role of *debtor* by borrowing money to carry customer debit balances. The firm is obliged to deposit securities as the bank's protection in what is known as a *broker's collateral loan*. It is also sometimes referred to as a *call loan* because either party has the privilege of terminating the loan on 24-hour notice. Naturally, the bank requires more in securities value than the amount they are lending to the firm. The general practice of the major banks is to obtain securities worth at least $133\frac{1}{3}$ of the money borrowed by that organization. Thus, if a broker/dealer wants to borrow $300,000 to carry customer debit balances, it must deposit customer securities worth at least $400,000 ($300,000 \times 133\frac{1}{3}\%$) and pay interest to the bank on the money received.

See also Hypothecating Customer Securities.

Broker/Dealer Organization. Within a brokerage firm, entry and execution of an order to buy or sell a security is only the beginning of the complex chain of events that is necessary to complete a transaction. Other ancillary activities behind the scenes at an average broker/dealer organization may employ more people in the concern than registered representatives who solicit and trade securities for customer and firm accounts.

Details and departmental structure may vary widely from firm to firm, depending on business/product mix and sophistication of its clientele. It is unlikely that a retail firm's operations would be organized identically to those of a wholesale firm that does no business with public customers. A firm that clears its trade activities through another member's facilities would be structured still differently. But the basic operations concept and work flow is found throughout the industry. After execution of an order, certificate shuffling, payments, record keeping, and supervisory control procedures must prevail to some extent at all brokerage firms.

Order Department. The people concerned with the actual execution of orders to buy and sell securities are members of the Order Department. If they are situated together in the same physical area, this section of the brokerage firm is likely to be called the *order room* instead. (This area may also be called the *wire room* because it serves as an electronic communications center between the firm's main office and its branch sales offices.) However, that arrangement is not too practical for a large firm, and, in all likelihood, the Order Department may be located in different rooms, floors, or even buildings. The separation is determined on the basis of execution locale and/or security type. That is, handling of exchange transactions may take place in one area and over-the-counter transactions in another area. Or, corporate debt activities may be ministered to in one place, government and municipal securities in another, and equity issues in still another area.

Location is of relatively minor importance because of technological advances in modern data communication facilities. Many large brokerage firms use a technique known as *message switching*. It links sales, operations, and trading locales by computer, so that each order can be (1) routed from a sales office to a particular trader in the Order Department or directly to

the trading floor of a designated stock exchange; (2) examined, following execution, as to trade details in order to ensure compliance with its terms and conditions; and (3) automatically relayed back to the appropriate sales office and to the firm's other operations departments for processing.

In a nonautomated firm, each buy or sell instruction is written on an order form, time-stamped per SEC rule, and telephoned or teletyped to the appropriate exchange for execution (or directed to the firm's traders in the over-the-counter market). After execution, the order form is time-stamped again to indicate the approximate minute of completion, noting price, quantity, and perhaps information on the contra broker, (SEC Rule 17a-3 necessitates both entry and execution times on order tickets so that, in the event of a dispute or inquiry, the problem can be pinpointed accurately in time. Computerized communication facilities are capable of making these time notations automatically.) Such information is then transmitted to the Purchase and Sales (P & S) Department for the start of operations departmental activity.

In summary, an Order Department (1) accepts customer instructions prepared by registered representatives; or (2) prepares its own order form for dealer-to-dealer trades initiated in behalf of the firm's account and risk (see the following sample order forms).

Purchase and Sales (P & S) Department. This department has two principal responsibilities: (1) to compare the terms and conditions of each transaction with the contra brokerage firm (the firm that is on the opposite side of the transaction), or firms involved; (2) to prepare a customer's confirmation notice (the bill for payment of a purchase or the advice for proceeds due the customer when selling).

Multiple copies of each comparison/confirmation are prepared by the P & S Department.

The actual number varies with the work flow peculiar to that brokerage concern and the preference of some customers to direct duplicates to an agent bank, accountant, or attorney. Often, upwards of five copies are prepared, one each to the registered representative, Margin Department, Cashiering Department, Controller's Department, and to the firm's files. In addition to a comparison for the contra dealer, and a confirmation for the customer, a detailed trade manifold is prepared for the Cashiering Department.

See also Accrued Interest; Comparison Procedures Between Broker/Dealers; Confirmations.

Margin Department. In some brokerage firms, a special credit unit serves in an advisory capacity as an agency of the Cashiering Department, and in others it is a separate entity known as the Margin Department.

This Margin Department (or credit unit) monitors all trade activities and ensures that payment and delivery are satisfied in accord with federal, exchange, and firm requirements. It advises cashiering *when* to complete its responsibilities—that is, after proper payment or acceptable delivery is accomplished.

The Margin Department's attention is focused principally on customer activity because customers tend to be unfamiliar with, or rather casual about, regulations and customs of the securities industry. It is interesting and important to note that when the firm acts in an agency capacity, although customer payment for a purchase may be delayed, the Margin Department must still authorize its own firm's payment for the security certificate as soon as it is received from the contra firm. The sacredness of a contract between members must be upheld despite the tardiness, or even the default, of a customer who precipitated the event.

In any event, the Margin Department maintains an account record for each customer and posts each activity on that card on a trade (activity) date basis. Informal entries are made in pencil and are sometimes posted on separate cards for each customer's specialized account, be it cash, margin, subscription, miscellaneous, and so on (see the following sample account record). In highly automated firms, this record may be a computer printout or even tiny, computer-generated images on microfilm or microfiche.

In the case of a cash account, many customers want possession of their certificates instead of leaving them in care of the brokerage firm. After full payment is made for each purchase, the Margin Department gives the Cashiering Department instructions to "transfer and ship." This authorizes Cashiering to send that security to the issuer's transfer agent to have the customer's name inscribed on a new certificate and on that company's shareholder records. When this is done, the brokerage firm delivers the certificate to the customer, completing this transaction.

Some knowledge of elementary bookkeeping is helpful for anyone employed in this area, because debits and credits are used to reflect securities positions and money balances. Thorough familiarity with Regulation T of the Federal Reserve Board is more than important; it is critical to compliance with securities laws and to the preservation of firm assets. Margin clerks must be able to analyze account postings and initiate corrective action if contra brokers or customers default in any aspect of their contracts.

Example: Note in the sample account record that Mr. Harris Berg bought 100 U.S. Steel Corporation at 36¼ on August 12, in a cash account for a total cost of $3,685.09. However, his check for payment did not arrive until August 26, thus necessitating an approved extension of time to defer mandatory liquidation proceedings. The Margin Department prepares these extension request forms after communicating with the registered representative to ascertain the customer's reason for failure to pay by the seventh business day after trade date. It must determine if approval was obtained for Harris Berg's extension. (If this were a margin account, the inquiry and request for extension would be submitted on the fifth business day following trade activity.) Furthermore, in margin accounts particularly, when sufficient collateral is not deposited on the trade date itself, the details of this deficiency must be posted in a separate firm ledger identified as *Federal Calls for Margin*. This record, available for New York Stock Exchange inspection for at least one year, indicates when and how customer margin calls are met (that is, by deposit of money or other securities, or by liquidation). No further action need by initiated in the customer's account until the fifth business day.

Note that Mr. Berg's check amounted to $3,625.00, $60 short of the total due; this $60 represents the commission fee. Because the account is delinquent by less than $500, no further federal action is necessary under Regulation T. However, the margin clerks should not issue instructions to register the certificate and send it to Mr. Berg until the additional money is deposited. Observe, too, that Harris Berg sold 200 U.S. Steel at 34¾ on September 4, 1988, for net proceeds of $6,828.83. One hundred shares are already in the account from the purchase in August. But where are the other 100 shares? If these are in Mr. Berg's possession, they must be deposited in this account by the fifth business day after trade date, and certainly not later than the seventh business day. If he procrastinates past the tenth business day following settlement date, Mr. Berg will run afoul of SEC Rule 15c3-3, which requires the brokerage concern to buy in that 100-share default. Competent and efficient margin clerks do not wait for this to occur. They communicate with the registered representative immediately after trade date to inquire about the 100-share deficiency, asking when they may expect to receive the certificate. Often enough, the clerks discover that the extra 100 shares was a mistake, or that this 100-share unit was a short sale and should be processed in the customer's margin account instead.

The point of the preceding discussion is merely to highlight the role of the Margin Department, underscoring its importance as (1) a liaison between registered representative sales efforts and cashiering responsibilities; and (2) the source of technical expertise in the subject of compliance with credit regulations governing securities transactions.

Cashiering Department. This department (commonly known as the *cage*), which finalizes all transactions for the brokerage concern, is subdivided into three major sections: (1) the Receive and Deliver Section, where money and securities come into or go out of the firm; (2) the Box Section, where certificates are stored for a while; (3) the Transfer Section, where arrangements are made to reregister certificates from one name to another, and/or provide desired certificate denominations.

See also Cage.

Receive and Deliver Section. The Receive and Deliver Section (R & D) accepts certificates directly from customers, broker/dealers, and various securities depositories in the United States. It makes immediate payment for receipt of customer securities only if it is specifically instructed to do so by the Margin Department. This instruction is generally accomplished by means of a validated transaction manifold (comparison/confirmation) or via a specially prepared debit memorandum notice.

Receive and Deliver must first determine that securities are in transferable form (that they meet the specifications for good delivery outlined in the NYSE Constitution or in the NASD Uniform Practice Code) and, in the case of customers particularly, that they are accompanied by supporting documentation. This function is especially pertinent when certificates are registered in the name of a corporation, legal trust, estate of deceased person, incompetent, guardian, or person holding power of attorney over the owner of that issue. In the absence of a contingent comparison/confirmation of a trade, securities received free are usually given to the transfer section to reregister in the firm's own name. When they are returned from the transfer agent, the new certificates go to the Box Section for storage pursuant to regulatory requirements.

When the Receive and Deliver Section needs securities to deliver versus a sales transaction, it withdraws them from the Box or from a securities depository, wherever they may be held. It dispatches them to the contra broker/dealer or bank against payment. The proceeds are then credited to the proper account or paid to the customer, as directed by the Margin Department. Securities to be delivered free, such as to a customer who paid for them and wants possession, normally go to the Transfer Section first. They should be reregistered into customer name before being sent out of the firm. (An important exception may be for delivery to a bank or to a sophisticated financial institution that can effect prompt registration out of street name.) Otherwise, there is a danger that the certificates may be lost or stolen and the broker may continue to receive interest or dividends without any evident justification for this money on the firm's records. The firm's bookkeeping, then, is likely to get bogged down with the need to maintain a suspense account. The firm must then wait for someone to claim those dollars or eventually surrender them to the state under prevailing escheat laws (laws that deal with a state's claim to abandoned property).

Box Section. The term *Box*, which is used to identify the section of the cage where securities are temporarily stored, originated many years ago when certificates were actually kept in portable metal receptacles. Although boxes are not completely outmoded, many firms now use on-premises vaults, cabinets, and even desk drawers to serve the same purpose. More than ever before, brokerage firms are encouraged to store their securities in various industry-owned and industry-operated depositories. This lessens the risk of theft and, correspondingly, reduces the firm's fidelity insurance premiums. New

York Stock Exchange member firms utilize the services of Depository Trust Company (DTC), (a member bank of the Federal Reserve System, at present wholly owned by the NYSE), whereas NASD firms can turn to National Securities Clearing Corporation (NSCC).

Box clerks are responsible for the storage of securities in firm custody. They act on orders issued by the Margin Department and the Receive and Deliver Section. Fully paid issues in cash accounts and excess collateral securing debit balances in margin accounts must be isolated from securities used by the firm in the conduct of its own business. This storage of securities held in cash accounts and registered in a customer's name is called *safekeeping.* The same situation for customer margin account securities registered in the broker's name is known as *segregation.* The two classifications demand almost identical physical treatment. The Box Section stores those protected securities in a bank vault, identifying the true owners by means of separate folders containing each customer's securities held in safekeeping; and by either bulk or individual identification for segregated securities.

The vault in which these securities are held is sometimes referred to as the "free box," indicating that the securities held within are owned by the underlying customers free and clear of encumbrances. Securities in which the brokerage firm has an interest are maintained in the "active box" and can be used as collateral in financing arrangements. The Margin Department values each customer account and continuously advises the Box Section which securities to segregate and which to place in the active box.

See also Active Box; Segregation.

Transfer Section. The Transfer Section of the cage is responsible for reregistering securities into a more desirable title of ownership and/or certificate denomination. This is accomplished by submitting the old certificate to the issuing corporation or to its authorized transfer agent, accompanied by written instructions as to the type of change required. Transfer is completed when the corporation or its agent cancels the old certificate, issues a new one, adjusts its ownership records accordingly, and returns the new document to the same brokerage firm.

Normally the Transfer Section of the cage is given all registered securities received by its firm to reregister into either firm name, for segregation purposes, or into customer name, for safekeeping or delivery purposes, per instruction from the Margin Department or the Box Section.

Sometimes, securities are in proper form for delivery but the available denominations are all wrong. In this case, the Transfer Section must request from the company's agent the right-sized pieces to make good delivery to the contra firm.

See also Reregistering Securities; Segregation.

There are, depending on the particular firm, several other departments that offer ancillary, or auxiliary, services to customers. These are the Dividend, Proxy, Reorganization, Stock Record, and Controller's Departments.

Dividend Department. The title Dividend Department, something of a misnomer, refers to the area responsible for accepting, allocating, paying, and/or claiming dividends and interest distributions associated with securities in the firm's custody.

The clerks in this department must be sure the firm receives all interest and dividends to which it is entitled. This involves reconciling a single check the firm receives from the corporation or its disbursement agent to the rate applicable for the number of shares or bonds registered in the firm's own name on the day the company closes its record book for payment purposes. Although this procedure sounds routine, it occasionally does not work out that way. Strange as it seems, the firm sometimes receives more than it should. This can be explained by (1) an error on the part of the company's disbursement agent; or, more likely, (2) a security, delivered to a contra firm or customer prior to the record date, that

was not registered promptly by that party. In the second case, the dividend clerk will hold the extra money or security in a suspense account waiting for the proper party to submit proof of claim for rightful payment. After an appropriate number of years have elapsed (the number varies from state to state), the broker must surrender unclaimed funds and securities to its own state of domicile.

Underpayments can be attributed to (1) an error on the part of the company's disbursement agent; (2) a mistake by the firm's own record keeping department, an error which can now be corrected; or (3) failure by the firm's Transfer Section promptly to reregister certificates received by the firm before the record date. In the third situation, the Dividend Department must claim the distribution from the delivering firm. The issuing corporation cannot be held at fault for sending a distribution to a party not technically entitled to it. After all, as far as the corporation is concerned, recognition was properly extended to the holder appearing on its ledger at the close of business on the official record date.

Occasionally, the selling firm is the cause of underpayment problems because it fails to deliver certificates promptly on settlement date. If this happens, the Dividend Department immediately notifies the Receive and Deliver Section of the cage to impose a condition of settlement to the contract in order to qualify as a good delivery (*see* Due Bill).

The Dividend Department must also allocate monies and/or securities received among the underlying owners entitled to them.

See also Beneficial Owner; Distribution Dates.

Proxy Department. Closely related to the work of the Dividend Department and frequently allied with that group in a typical brokerage concern is the Proxy Department. The Proxy Department distributes corporate publications, including financial reports, meeting notices, and voting information to the beneficial owner of shares. Because the corporation does not know the identity of these parties, the Proxy Department, acting under stock exchange and NASD regulations, obtains material sent directly to stockholders of record and mails it to customers for whom the firm holds securities in street name.

The Proxy Department must solicit instructions from the beneficial owners of securities, regarding casting of ballots for the election of directors and other important matters brought before an annual or special meeting of the company. The Proxy Department also acts as agent for dissident shareholders or other groups who wish to communicate with the beneficial owners.

See also Beneficial Owner; Proxy.

Reorganization Department. This service unit is responsible for the following functions:

1. It obeys corporate calls for redemption of issues in custody of the brokerage firm and solicits instructions from beneficial owners of called convertible issues (*see* Redemption Call).

2. It converts appropriate securities into common stock on request of their underlying owners.

3. It exchanges one class of security for another class of the same issuer, pursuant to a reorganization of the corporation and solicits instructions from beneficial owners of such securities (*see* Exchange Offer).

4. It exchanges one company's securities for another company's securities or money, pursuant to a merger ratified by the shareholders of both companies. In these circumstances, the Reorganization Department may submit shares held for its firm's customers for shares in the surviving company or in shares of a newly organized third company, according to terms of the merger agreement. Records of the holdings of the firm and its customers are adjusted subsequent to completion of the exchange. If the merger is an outright acquisition for cash, the customer's account will be credited with the funds received after the Reorganization Department submits the old shares and obtains payment.

5. It subscribes for new shares in a company, pursuant to a rights offering. When a company gives its holders preemptive rights to subscribe to new stock, the Reorganization Department uses these rights, along with supplementary funds from the customer's account, to acquire the new stock from the company. If additional rights are needed to satisfy the customer's written instructions, they, too, must be purchased, either from the company's agent or in the open market. Conversely, if certain customers decide not to subscribe or if they own rights in excess of the amount needed to subscribe for the number of shares they want to buy, the Reorganization Department disposes of the extra rights before they expire. It may either sell them to the company's agent bank or standby underwriter, or accept someone else's bid in the open market. Either way, the appropriate customer accounts are credited with the net proceeds of that sale.

Purchases via subscription warrants are handled in the same fashion as subscription rights. They, too, require written instructions from the beneficial owner before positive action may be taken by the Reorganizatiiton Department. They, too, require consideration of a ratio formula set by the company for purchase of the new shares.

Example: The company may declare with issuance of its rights (or warrants) that four rights are needed for each new share at $45, or that each warrant entitles the holder to subscribe to two new shares at $24.50, and so forth.

6. It transmits securities to an intended purchaser under terms of a proxy statement and on specific written instructions from its beneficial owner (*see* Tender Offer).

Stock Record Department. The position lists used by the Dividend, Proxy, and Reorganization Departments in performing their responsibilities are, in reality, documents prepared and maintained by the Stock Record Department. This unit serves as a control and easy reference department for monitoring securities under the brokerage firm's jurisdiction. Industry custom and tradition have bestowed on this department the title *Stock Record*, although it does, in fact, keep records of all securities, stocks and bonds alike. Individual records are maintained for each issue in alphabetical order. For financial reasons, these records must be unquestionably current and accurate. The stock record ledger shows (1) the name of a security; (2) the owner of that security; and (3) the location of that certificate.

In terms of location, the stock record clerk should be able to identify whether that security is in (1) safekeeping; (2) segregation; (3) a loan arrangement at a bank (hypothecation); (4) a loan to another broker/dealer; (5) reregistration proceedings at the transfer agent; (6) transit to the customer's agent bank or broker versus payment; or (7) fail-to-receive status from a contra broker/dealer or customer.

In the course of business each day, entries are processed by different operations departments that bear on the Stock Record Department's responsibilities. Changes in quantities and/or location are debited or credited to this group's records, and the daily totals must balance. A "break" in stock record balance figures indicates that a mistake was made in an entry somewhere along the way. Such a mistake must be corrected immediately before the problem compounds itself and defies resolution. An uncorrected break could ultimately lead to serious losses in firm capital and could jeopardize the assets of customers.

Controller's Department. A surface examination of the controller's function in a brokerage firm doesn't generally reveal its involvement with customer trade processing. Most people think of this area in terms of accounts payable, employee payroll records, financial reporting to regulatory bodies, interest control, general accounting, and so forth. Although all this is obviously true, the Controller's Department is also involved in the very last step in customer operations activity—preparation of the statements of account. This monthly or quarterly statement is a summary of all that has occurred on the customer's behalf during the period of time under consideration.

See also Statement of Account.

Bucket Shop. This type of brokerage concern accepts but does not immediately execute customer orders, hoping that market values will fluctuate against the customers' interests. This then enables those firms to bill the customer at the original, now unfavorable, price while they execute those orders at the prevailing price, pocketing the difference for themselves. This practice is outlawed by federal law (*see* Securities Exchange Act of 1934) and industry rules (*see* Rules of Fair Practice).

Bulk Identification. *See* Segregation.

Bunching. Some customers and/or registered representatives can avoid paying the odd-lot differential by combining two or more odd-lot orders for entry and execution as a round lot. This practice, known as *bunching*, is acceptable provided each of the interested customers gives approval to this activity prior to the transaction. Obviously, it can be attempted only when the terms and conditions of the odd-lot orders are identical, and the total quantity amounts to a round lot.

Bunched orders are executed on the floor of the exchange as a round lot, normally handled by a commission house broker, specialist, or two-dollar broker. However, once executed, the transaction must be split up into proper quantities and allocated among each of the participating customers. The odd-lot customer's saving is solely in avoiding payment of the odd-lot differential (⅛ point). Other expenses contingent to the transaction remain basically the same.

In an opposite vein, exchange regulations forbid customers from breaking up shares that make up round lots and entering them simultaneously as odd lots at identical prices. That practice is unfair to the specialist, who is obliged to execute all of them at the same time when a single effective sale occurs. Otherwise, the owner of several round lots of an issue subject to wide price fluctuation could be assured of a single favorable execution for the entire order (1) for the nominal fee of ⅛-point differential; and (2) to the tactical detriment of the specialist's inventory cost position.

See also Differential; Odd-Lot Stock Execution.

Business Day. *See* Delivery Dates.

Buyer of an Option. This person purchases an option contract, thus creating a long option position.

See also Options; Writer of an Option.

Buying Call Options. *See* Option Strategies.

Buying Power. *See* Margin Account (Long Account).

Buying Put Options. *See* Option Strategies.

Buy Minus. This instruction requests a member to purchase a security via market or limit order, as the case may be, but at a price lower than the previous different-priced transaction for that stock.

Example:

Previous different price   47⅞
Sale at this price qualifies   45

See also Sell Plus.

Buy-In Procedures. A person who lends stock certificates to a short seller retains the right to request that the certificates be returned at any time. If the short seller's firm cannot find another lender and does not return the certificates, it is placed in an unenviable position. The lender, holding the short seller's collateral, terminates the agreement and holds the firm in default. The process of termination is called a *buy-in* and, of course, is used only when all attempts at borrowing have proved futile. The lender arranges to buy that security in the marketplace, for guaranteed delivery, at whatever price is available. The lender holds the borrower financially responsible for any difference between the total cost of the purchase and the money held as collateral.

In a buy-in, there probably will not be much difference between the lender's purchase cost and the money held as collateral. The reason for this is that a collateral loan is continuously marked to the market to reflect any changes in the value of the security.

See also Borrowing Stock Certificates; Close-Out Procedures; Mark to the Market.

Buy-Stop Order. This order is entered with a memorandum price above present market levels because it is intended either to (1) curtail a loss on an existing short position; (2) preserve a profit on a short position previously established; or (3) purchase a security, but only if a transaction at the stated price level creates a technical buy signal.

Example: Assume that speculator Joe Smith sells a stock short (that is, a stock he doesn't own) at 35 anticipating a decline in value. He can suffer a substantial loss if the price rises contrary to his expectation. To protect himself against the possibility of unlimited loss, he can enter a buy-stop order at 40 (or some other price level above the present 35). Then, if the price rises to 40 or above (instead of trading exactly at 40, a price gap may occur; such penetration also activates the stop order—that is, 40⅛, 40¼, and so forth), his memorandum becomes a market order, and he purchases the stock immediately at the best available price. This (1) closes out the short position; and (2) curtails his loss at about $500 plus commissions and other incidental expenses ($4,000 purchase cost −$3,500 sale proceeds). It is impossible to determine the exact loss until the purchase is effected because the best available price is unknown until the stop order is activated to become a market order.

Example: If speculator Mary Brown sells a stock short at 46 and sees it decline to 38, as she anticipated, she will have a profit of approximately $800 after purchasing stock to close out her position. But the price might decline even further if she is patient. Then again, it might move up to 46 or even higher, eliminating what paper profits she now enjoys at 38. To protect this profit, Mary Brown, instead of purchasing stock at 38, can enter a buy-stop order at 41 (or some other price level above the present 38). Then, if the price of the security continues to decline, her short position will profit further. But if it rises to 41 (instead of trading exactly at 41, a price gap may occur; such penetration also activates the stop order—that is, 40⅞, 41⅛, and so forth), the memorandum becomes a market order and stock is purchased immediately at the best available price. This transaction (1) closes out the short position; and (2) establishes a profit

of about $500 less commissions and other incidental expenses ($4,600 sale proceeds −$4,100 purchase cost). Once again, the exact profit cannot be calculated until the actual purchase price is determined.

Example: Suppose the Ralph Babcock, a technician (someone who plots prices of securities on charts or watches price fluctuations without regard to underlying corporate fundamentals), observes over a period of time that a particular stock has fluctuated between 71 and 74. He might be inclined to enter a buy-stop order at 74½ or thereabouts. He believes that if and when this apparent accumulation of shares by informed sources is completed, the price will move up through the 74 level and may rise to 80, 90, 100, or even higher. Therefore, he wants to purchase that stock, but *only* if it does move convincingly above that 74 level. As a knowledgeable technician, Ralph Babcock also realizes that instead of accumulation, the minimal fluctuation thus far may be reflecting distribution.

If that is the case, the price may never move above 74 and may even soon drop below 71. Why should he waste his capital by acquiring stock somewhere between 71 and 74 under those circumstances? If it eventually trades at 74½ or above, the technician then establishes a long position. If it never trades up to that level, no purchase takes place.

See also Choosing Types of Stock Orders; Sell-Stop Order; Stop Order.

BW. *See* National Quotation Bureau, Inc.

C

Cabinet Crowd. *See* Inactive Bonds.

Cage. Collectively, the Receive and Deliver, Box, and Transfer Sections of the Cashiering Department of a Broker/Dealer Organization are commonly known as *the cage*, because they are physically situated in a locked-in area whose entrances and exits are continuously guarded. Strict security measures are necessary because of the presence and availability of money and of valuable stock and bond certificates.

> *See also* Broker/Dealer Organization (Cashiering Department).

Calendar Spread. *See* Option Strategies (Spreads).

Callable Preferred Stock. This type of preferred stock permits the corporation to retire the issue, at its option, by paying these preferred stockholders a specified value for their shares. If it recalls the stock in the first few years after issuance, the corporation also pays the holders a small premium for their inconvenience. But the size of the premium declines as the age of the stock increases until finally, after about nine or ten years, these preferred stockholders receive only the face value of their certificates if the company exercises its call privilege.

Exercise of a call is considered by the corporation only when: (1) the terms of an older issue are economically unsuitable for it and (2) it can obtain the same funds under more favorable terms and conditions in existing money markets.

Periodic partial calls of an issue are not unusual either; in this case, the certificates are selected for redemption in an unbiased lottery.

The recall value of a callable preferred stock may be (1) the *par*, or face, value appearing on each certificate (stated per share); (2) greater than par value; (3) somewhat higher than the existing market price prior to the call announcement if this action was unanticipated; or (4) lower than the existing market price prior to the call announcement if: (a) money market conditions warranted a somewhat higher market price and a call was unexpected, or (b) that stock was also convertible, and the present value of the preferred was comparable to the high market value of the common.

In this last situation (4b), the corporation can painlessly eliminate the preferred stock by exercising its call privilege, thereby forcing conversion into common with a minimal outlay of cash on its part. What little cash is needed will pay off those few holders who neglected to convert within the time period specified.

Example: A share of preferred stock is callable at $100 and convertible into two shares of common. When the common is selling at $60 per share,

$$2 \text{ shares of common} \times \$60 = \$120$$

Therefore, each share of preferred stock is also comparable to $120 in value. The corporation can call the preferred stock at $100, knowing that, unless the holders converted into two shares of common, they would "lose" $20 in market value for their investment—in effect, forcing them to convert.

Since the depression of the 1930s, most corporations insist on some call feature in their preferred stock offerings, even if they concede to making the issue noncallable for the first three or five years. Without a call feature, the corporation could be committing itself to paying comparatively high dividends on a particular issue for the rest of its corporate life.

See also Convertible Preferred; Cumulative Preferred; Participating Preferred; Prior Preferred.

Call Features of a Bond. The presence of a call feature in the indenture of a bond tends to establish a ceiling for the price of that security. After all, who would buy a bond significantly above its call price, knowing that the company can retire it at any time and pay holders only the redemption value specified? In fact, excluding consideration of bonds that are also convertible, the only time a bond trades significantly above face value is when interest rates are declining in the financial community. In such cases, responsible management would probably call that older, more expensive issue anyway and refinance the debt through refunding (unless, of course, the indenture stipulated that the bond was nonrefundable).

See also Refunding.

In periods of unsettled monetary conditions, investors may demand and receive "call protection" for the first five to ten years of a bond's lifetime. That is, the bonds are noncallable for the first five to ten years and then become redeemable at declining premium prices as the issue ages toward its maturation date. Consequently, if the cycle of interest rates within the economy should decline in the bond's early life, higher coupon bonds will rise above the future call price. But they never quite rise to the true level normally appropriate for a bond with that rate. The call feature looms like a spectre and to some extent restrains price advances.

Of course, on the other hand, if interest rates subsequently move higher, depressing the price of fixed debt issues, these bonds, never having experienced full appreciation, do not dramatically decline in value either. The moderating influence of a deferred call provision in combination with frequently changing interest rates, provides modern securities markets with "cushion" bonds. A *cushion bond* is a high current coupon debt instrument with a deferred call provision in its indenture; thus it offers a better return and minimal price volatility as compared to a bond without call protection. It has great appeal for the conservative investor seeking a somewhat higher yield on capital and is most often issued by well-rated industrial corporations and public utilities.

Exercising a Call. The exercise of a call by the corporation requires bondholders to redeem their bonds prior to maturity. This method is most frequently employed today for early debt retirement because the company enjoys the flexibility of making full or partial calls to suit its purpose. However, there is usually a clause in the indenture requiring payment somewhat above face value if the corporation inconveniences the bondholders by calling certificates in the first few years after issuance. It is known as the bond issue's *call premium*.

Example: The certificate pays $1,020 if called in the first five years, $1,010 in the next five years, and only face value, $1,000 thereafter. The dollar amount paid above par value is the call premium.

Call Loan. *See* Broker's Collateral Loan.

Call Money. *See* Hypothecating Customer Securities.

Call Option. This contract entitles its holder to buy an underlying security or other financial interest at a specified price and at or before a predetermined expiration date.

Buying. An investor generally buys calls for two basic reasons: (1) to participate in any price rise in the underlying security, or (2) to hedge a short stock position against a price increase.

Participating in price rise. The bullish call buyer seeks to benefit from an increase in the market price of the underlying security. This strategy gives the call buyer the ability to speculate with a limited amount of capital because the premium of the call is considerably less than the cost of purchasing the underlying security outright. By so leveraging the funds, the purchaser of calls has an opportunity to benefit more from any increase in the price of the security percentagewise, than if the stock itself had been bought. He or she might *lose* the entire investment should the stock decrease in market value.

Example: A customer purchases 1 CBA January 25 call when the market price of CBA is 24½, paying a premium of $200.

If CBA is above $25 at the option expiration date, the call holder (buyer) has a choice of either exercising the call or liquidating the option on the exchange. Assuming CBA is trading at $30 near expiration and the January 25 call is trading at intrinsic value of $5, the call holder may realize a $300 profit ($500–$200) by closing out the long call position. By liquidating the call, the customer has earned a 150% return ($300 ÷ $200). On the other hand, the stock itself has increased by only 22½%. Of course, the return could have been greater if the call option was selling for more than intrinsic value.

If CBA is below $25 at the option expiration date, the call option will expire worthless and the customer will lose the entire $200. However, this is the *maximum loss* no matter how low the stock declined.

The break-even point for a call purchaser is the exercise price plus the premium paid for the call. In the above example, the break-even point is $27 ($25 + $2). When the stock is above that price at or near expiration, the position will be profitable.

Protecting short stock position. A second reason to purchase a call is to protect a short stock position against a price increase. If the stock price remains the same, the customer will lose the amount of the call premium. If it declines, any profit made in the short position is reduced by the amount of premium. However, should the price of the security rise, the short seller is protected against substantial loss.

Example: A customer sells short 100 shares of XYZ at $35 per share and simultaneously purchases 1 XYZ May 35 call for a premium of $300.

Should XYZ decline to $20 per share, the investor will make a profit of $1,500 ($3,500 – $2,000) from the short stock position but will lose $300 by the call expiring worthless at expiration date. The net profit is $1,200 ($1,500 – $300).

If XYZ remains the same, the call option will expire worthless for an investor loss of $300.

If XYZ increases above $35 near the option expiration date, the call buyer may decide to exercise the call option and acquire 100 shares at $35 to cover the short position. Thus the customer has no loss in the stock short sale but incurs a loss of $300 from the call purchase. In this example, the short seller with a long call has a maximum risk of $300. In the latter two instances, the price paid for the call might be considered to be insurance.

In summary, a speculator may purchase calls for possible profit potential, for the limitation of loss, for leverage, or for the protection of a short stock position.

Writing Covered Call Options. An investor generally writes calls covered by an underlying stock he or she owns for two basic reasons: (1) to realize option premium income; and (2) to provide downside protection for ownership of an underlying security.

Realizing option premium income.

Example: An investor purchases 100 shares of RST at $60 and at the same time writes 1 RST November 60 call receiving a premium of $400.

Should RST increase to any price above 60 by expiration date, the call writer will be assigned an exercise notice and will sell 100 shares of RST at $60. The investor earns the $400 premium but does not participate in any of the stock's increase above $60, although the object of receiving premium income was achieved. Even if the stock went to 74, the writer would be paid only the $60 agreed on in the option contract.

The covered call writer who owns the underlying security has, in return for the premium, given up the opportunity for profit in the underlying security from a price rise above the exercise price. Of course, in this example, had the investor purchased the stock below the exercise price, say at 58½, he or she would have realized a profit of $550 ($400 + $150) on exercise.

However, had the investor purchased the stock above the exercise price, say at 60¾, he or she would have had a profit of only $325 ($400 − 75) on exercise.

Downside protection. Should RST decline to $55 prior to the expiration date (assuming stock purchased at $60), the option writer will not be assigned an exercise notice. The investor keeps the $400 premium and has a paper loss of $500 in the stock. If the investor sells the stock, the $400 premium will partially offset the realized loss of $500, reducing the overall loss to $100. Thus, the premium provides the covered call writer with some downside protection. The break-even point is the stock's purchase price minus the premium. In the above example, it would be $56 ($60 − $4).

The covered call writer has no control over

when delivery may be required for the underlying stock, since the assignment of an exercise notice may be made any time prior to the expiration of a writer's obligation.

Writing Uncovered Call Options. A person generally writes uncovered (naked) calls for the purpose of realizing option premium income. Someone who is bearish toward the underlying stock can write a naked call to realize a profit from a call option's decline in value.

Example: A speculator writes an uncovered CBA May 85 call when the market price of CBA is $90 and receives a premium of $700.

If CBA is below $85 at the option expiration date, the option writer will not be assigned an exercise notice. Since the option expires worthless, the writer keeps the $700 premium as his profit.

If CBA is above $85 at expiration date, the option writer will be assigned an exercise notice. The writer is obligated to deliver (sell) 100 shares of stock at $85 per share. The speculator must then purchase (or borrow) 100 shares in the open market at the current market price in order to make delivery. Assuming the underlying stock increased to 94 at expiration, the call writer could purchase 100 shares of stock at 94 and deliver (sell) them at $85. He would thus experience a $900 loss in the stock transaction, offset, however, by the $700 premium which would reduce the net loss to $200.

The break-even point for the naked call writer is the exercise price plus premium received. In the previous example, it would be $92 ($85 + $7). Obviously, a naked call writer can still profit even when the stock goes against him as long as it does not rise by more than the amount of the premium received.

Of course, the naked call writer may close out the position prior to exercise and realize either a profit or loss depending on the price paid to buy back the option.

The price of the underlying security could theoretically rise indefinitely which would, in turn, cause the uncovered call writer unlimited loss. Therefore, such transactions are suitable only for very knowledgeable investors with the financial capacity to sustain large losses.

The uncovered call writer has no control over when he or she may be required to deliver (sell) the underlying stock, since the assignment of an exercise notice may be made any time prior to the expiration of his or her obligation as a writer.

See also Options; Option Strategies.

Cancellation. Although a *cancellation* is not really a type of order or even a qualification for execution of an order, its role can significantly influence trading activities on the floor of the exchange.

Officially, prior to an actual execution of the transaction, a person entering an order on the New York or American Stock Exchange is privileged to change any of the terms or conditions of that order. That person can direct the broker to modify or negate any previous instructions and may, in fact, terminate the entire order itself.

After execution, cancellation of a transaction requires approval (and such approval is hard to get) from (1) the other party to that trade; and (2) a floor official (a member of the exchange appointed by the Chairman of the Board of Directors to represent and assist the exchange in the equitable conduct of business on the trading floor).

Can Crowd. *See* Inactive Bonds.

Capitalization (and Capitalization Ratios). *See* Balance Sheet (Capitalization Ratios).

Capital Shares. *See* Dual Purpose Investment Company.

Capital Stock. This term refers to a corporation's total equity capital. This is often used (er-

roneously) as a synonym for the more popular term, "common stock."

See also Common Stock; Preferred Stock.

Capital Surplus. *See* Paid-In Capital.

Cash. The part of a corporation's current assets consisting of bank deposits, along with bills and coins in the corporate "till." Such deposits are usually of the demand type, such as checking account balances.

See also Balance Sheet (Assets).

Cash Account. A new account report form is required for cash accounts of individual customers. When instructions are to be given by someone other than the customer personally, a trading authorization form, limited or full, must be signed by that customer and filed with the firm before that agent's instructions can be accepted. A joint account agreement form is also required for cash accounts of joint customers.

See also Corporate Accounts; Fiduciary Accounts; Joint Customers; New Account Report Form; Trading Authorization; Unincorporated Associations.

Basic Rules and Requirements. Regulation T states that a customer may execute in this account "bona fide" cash transactions in securities. Simply stated, a customer may trade any kind of security in this account, whether it be listed or unlisted, equity or debit, or corporate or government security. A bona fide cash transaction for purchases is deemed to be one in which a customer makes prompt payment in full and does not sell the security before it is in fact paid for. For long sales, the term means that the customer is selling a security that is owned. If the security is not on deposit with the broker, the customer must make prompt delivery of the security. No short sales are permitted in a cash account.

Regulation T requires that all purchases in a cash account be paid within seven business days. Extensions of time for good reason are permitted. Most brokers encourage their customers to pay for their trades by settlement date, which is normally five business days after trade date. Settlement date is the date brokers settle trades with each other (street-side settlement). It is a good business practice for brokers to settle customer side at the same time or sooner.

If a customer sells a security that is owned but that is not long in the account and if a customer does not make delivery by settlement date, SEC Rule 15c3-3 permits ten additional business days for the delivery to be made. If the customer fails to deliver the security by that date, the broker is obligated to buy in the security in order to settle the transaction. It is also possible for the customer to obtain an extension to prevent the buy-in if unusual circumstances are preventing the delivery from being made.

Regulation T provides a penalty for any customer who buys a security and then sells it without making payment first. (This does not preclude a client from selling a security before the purchase of that same security has settled. The client can still comply with both the spirit and letter of the law by paying for the security in full, on or before settlement date, using funds other than those generated by the sale.) When this occurs, the broker must immediately restrict the account to a funds-on-hand basis for a period of ninety calendar days after the sale. Such an account is commonly referred to as a frozen account. During this time the customer may not make any additional purchases unless sufficient funds are already on deposit with the broker to cover the full purchase cost.

Other Important Points. 1. A purchase of a when-issued security is subject to the NYSE 25% minimum maintenance requirement (but not the $2,000 minimum equity requirement) while that security is being traded on a when-issued basis.

Example: If customer Joe Smith purchases $10,000 worth of ALM stock when-issued, he must deposit at least $2,500 (25% of market value) to meet the NYSE requirement. Full payment is required within seven business days of the date the security is actually issued.

2. Cash-on-delivery (C.O.D.) transactions may be executed in a cash account. A *C.O.D. transaction* is one in which customers do not pay for the purchase until the actual security is delivered either to them or their fiduciary agent. A C.O.D. transaction of which a party says "Don't know (DK) about this transaction" must be resolved within two business days. If a DK'd transaction is not so resolved, then the trade is liquidated. As soon as the DK occurs, in order to further delay settlement, the broker must formally request an extension of time from a national securities exchange or the NASD.

3. In trying to settle a C.O.D. transaction, if the broker is unable for good reason to obtain the security for delivery to the customer or the customer's agent within 35 calendar days of the trade date, then the broker must formally request an extension of time from a national securities exchange or the NASD.

4. Rule 387 of the NYSE provides the following requirements for C.O.D. transactions: (a) each order must bear the notation that it is a cash-on-delivery (C.O.D.) or receive-versus-payment (R.V.P.) transaction; (b) the broker must receive from the customer, prior to, or at the time of, entering the order, the name and address of the agent and the account number of the customer on file with the agent; (c) the broker must deliver to the customer the confirmation (bill) containing all trade facts no later than the close of business on the business day following execution of the order; (d) the customer must agree to deliver instructions to his or her agent by the fourth business day for C.O.D.s to the broker and by the third business day for R.V.P.s from the broker.

5. A *regular-way sale* is a sale transaction that settles in five business days. A customer must wait until settlement date to withdraw the proceeds.

6. A *cash sale* is a sale transaction that normally settles the same day. Proceeds can be withdrawn on the same day. This is the purpose of a cash sale. In making a cash sale, the customer incurs a slight penalty by having to sell at a price a bit below the prevailing market price. (Note the distinction between a cash *account* and a cash *sale*.)

See also Margin Account; Regulation T; SEC Rule 15c3-3.

Cash Contract. When a security transaction is made for "cash," delivery of certificates to the purchaser's office is due on the same day as the trade. A *cash contract* is stipulated in the bid or offer. The terms are equally applicable to corporate, municipal, or U.S. government securities. In particular, trades effected before 2:00 P.M. (New York City time) must be settled by 2:30 P.M., whereas those executed after 2:00 P.M. must be settled within thirty minutes.

See also Cash Sale; Corporate Bond Transaction; Delivery Dates; Delivery Option Contract; Next-Day Contract; Regular-Way Contract; Seller's-Option Contract; When-Issued/When-Distributed Contract.

Cash Dividends. A board of directors announces a cash dividend payment of $0.50 per common share approximately two months before the dividends are actually paid out to the stockholders. As a result, the Doktabessie Corporation balance sheet (page 61) undergoes changes between the time the corporation declares a cash dividend and the time it actually pays it.

The declaration of a cash dividend creates a current liability of $6,000 ($0.50 × 12,000 common shares). Current liabilities must be adjusted to include this new obligation, which must be paid out within the next year. An item (probably labeled "dividends payable") is added to current liabilities, raising the total by $6,000 to $477,000. Where does this $6,000 come from? From the accumulated retained earnings. Retained earnings may be thought of as unpaid dividends. Management has now decided to pay some of this accumulated value to the common stockholders. So we now reduce retained earnings by $6,000 (from $290,000 to $284,000). The overall "change" on the balance sheet is an increase in current liabilities and a decrease in retained earnings.

Since current assets remain the same while current liabilities have increased, several ratios are adversely affected. The dividend reduces: (1) the working capital (net current assets), (2) the quick asset ratio (acid test ratio), (3) the current ratio, and (4) the book value.

Logically, the dividend also reduces the common stockholders' stake in the company, because part of their accumulated profits is paid out to them. Understandably, the value remaining after they receive their dividends is reduced by the amount of such dividends.

See also Stock Dividends; Stock Splits.

When the Doktabessie Corporation actually pays out the cash dividends, the company is actually dispersing cash in the amount of the current liability established for such payment. The following changes occur: (1) *cash* decreases and (2) *dividends payable* disappears.

Cash is now $159,000 ($165,000 – 6,000), and total current assets decreases to $892,000. The total current liabilities entry goes back to $471,000. Note where the ultimate change occurs: Cash is reduced, and the payment comes from retained earnings. The shift was done in two stages: (1) When the dividend is *declared*, retained earnings decrease and current liabilities increase; (2) When the dividend is *paid*, cash decreases and that particular current liability disappears.

Cash Flow. Realizing that one of the operating expenses — depreciation — is "artificial," we

DOKTABESSIE CORPORATION
BALANCE SHEET
June 30, 1979

Assets		*Liabilities*	
Cash	$165,000	Accounts payable	$166,000
Marketable securities	18,000	Accrued taxes	70,000
Accounts receivable	260,000	Notes payable	84,000
Inventory	455,000	Accrued expenses	151,000
Total current		Total current liabilities	471,000
assets	$898,000	First mortgage bonds: 7½% due 1/1/94	500,000
		Total liabilities	$971,000
Property, plant, and equipment:		*Stockholders' Equity*	
Land	$ 75,000	Preferred stock ($100 par,	
Buildings	506,000	1,000 shares authorized,	
Equipment	89,000	issued, and	
Machinery	164,000	outstanding)	100,000
	834,000	Common stock ($25 par,	
Less: Accumulated		12,000 shares authorized,	
depreciation	−217,000	issued, and	
Net property, plant,		outstanding)	300,000
and equipment	$617,000	Paid-in capital	58,000
		Accumulated retained	
		earnings	290,000
		Total stockholders' equity	$748,000
Intangibles	204,000	Total liabilities and stockholders'	
Total assets	$1,719,000	equity	$1,719,000

might ask how much actual cash the company has available before it pays out any monies on preferred or common stock cash dividends. Depreciation is not actually "spent," at least not in the current year, and therefore cash flow is equal to the sum of net income and annual depreciation.

Cash flow = net income + annual depreciation

Example:

Cash flow = $105,525 + $56,000 = $161,525

See also Income Statement.

Cashiering Department. *See* Broker/Dealer Organization.

Cash Sale. This type of securities sale transaction normally settles the same day. Proceeds can be withdrawn on the same day. This is the purpose of a cash sale. In making a cash sale, the customer incurs a slight penalty by having to sell at a price a bit below the prevailing market price. (A cash sale should not be confused with a cash account.)

See also Cash Account; Regular-Way Sale.

Cash Transaction. *See* Cash Account.

Certificate of Beneficial Interest. *See* Real Estate Investment Trust.

Certificate of Deposit (CD). Substantial amounts, often in excess of $100,000, entail issuance of a negotiable certificate to the depositor evidencing the bank's written obligation to pay interest and repay principal at maturity. This instrument is a *certificate of (time) deposit (CD)* and may be sold to another investor at a negotiated price in the secondary market if the holder wants to recover his or her money before the maturation date.

These negotiable securities are issued by commercial banks against money deposited with them for a definite period of time. A time deposit cannot be withdrawn until the end of the specified period, in contrast with the privilege of a demand or savings deposit.

If the depositors want to convert their certificates to cash before the maturity date, they must sell them in the secondary market to other people or institutions. Actual interest realized by

resale of a CD in the secondary market depends on prevailing monetary conditions. When short-term money rates are higher than the fixed percentage specified in the CD, realized interest will be less than the stated rate. If short-term money was available at a lower percentage, that CD's resale would result in higher realized interest. The maximum interest paid by commercial banks on CDs of less than $100,000 is fixed by the Federal Reserve Board and is usually set somewhat higher than that paid on savings deposits. The interest rate varies, depending on the size of the deposit and the length of time involved.

See also Demand Deposit; Savings Deposit; Time Deposit.

Certificate of Incorporation. *See* Charter.

Certificate of Indebtedness. (1) A receiver, in immediate need of working capital to keep a bankrupt corporation operating during the inquiry, can satisfy this urgency by issuing receivers' certificates of indebtedness. These are short-term debt obligations of the bankrupt corporation that assume a priority for payment of interest and repayment of principal over all other outstanding creditors of the company. Within the 90- to 120-day lifetime of these certificates, the receiver, with the support of the courts, must decide on and implement a solution to the problem. If the receiver liquidates the assets, the holders of other types of bonds might be fortunate to get back 50 cents for each dollar of investment. Forced liquidations, like fire sales, never command top prices on an auction block.

See also Income Bond.

Appointment of a Receiver in Bankruptcy. One of these options is chosen by the presiding judge in the Chapter X proceedings. Before making this decision, the judge seeks the advice of an expert in the industry and gives that expert the necessary authority to direct the corporation while investigating the causes and alternatives in this predicament. The court-appointed administrator of a failed corporation is called a *receiver in bankruptcy.* The receiver is granted remuneration by the court from the remaining assets of the company.

The receiver can raise capital in a number of ways: For short-term (90- to 120-day) operating capital, until a decision is made on liquidation or reorganization, the receiver can have issued *certificates of indebtedness.* In the event of reorganization, *income* (or *adjustment*) *bonds* can be issued with maturities often of 150 to 200 years.

U.S. Treasury certificates of indebtedness are bearer obligations with maturities ranging up to one year in duration and in denominations of $1,000 through $500 million. They differ from Treasury bills in that they carry a fixed rate of interest, usually in the form of coupons. They are quoted and traded at a price reflecting the *average rate of return* for an investor holding them until maturity (yield-to-maturity). Their yields are computed in the same way as corporate bond yields. Because of legal restrictions and conditions prevailing in the money market, Treasury certificates have not been offered domestically since the mid-1970s.

Example: The bid and asked prices of a one-year certificate with a 4.25% coupon may appear in this form:

Bid	Asked	Yield-to-Maturity
97⅛	97¼	7.20%

See also Marketable Security; U.S. Treasury Bill; U.S. Treasury Bond; U.S. Treasury Note; Yield.

Charter (Certificate of Incorporation). This document is written by the founders of a corporation and filed with a state. The state approves the articles and then issues a certificate of incorporation. Together, the two documents become the charter and the corporation is recognized as a legal entity. The charter includes such information as the corporation's name, purpose, amount of shares, and the identity of the directors. Internal management rules are written by the founders in the bylaws.

See also Corporation.

Churning. *See* Discretionary Account.

Class of Options. Options of the same type (put or call) that cover the same underlying security are of the same class.

Example: All Exxon calls or all GM puts.

See also Listed Options; Series of Options.

Clearing House. An adjunct to a futures exchange through which transactions executed on the floor of the exchange are settled using a process of matching purchases and sales. A clearing organization is also charged with the proper conduct of delivery procedures and the adequate financing of the entire operation.

See also Futures.

Clearing Member. A member firm of the clearing house. Each clearing member must also be a member of the Exchange. Not all members of the exchange, however, are member of the clearing organization. All trades of a nonclearing member must be registered with, and eventually settled through, a clearing member.

See also Futures.

Climax. *See* Double Tops and Bottoms.

Close, The. The period at the end of the trading session, sometimes used to refer to the closing price.

Closed-End Investment Company. *See* Management Company.

Closed-End Management Company. *See* Management Company.

Close-Out Procedures. When a contra broker/dealer defaults on a bona fide transaction created under provisions of the Uniform Practice Code, a member can close that contract. This limits its capital exposure to further market fluctuations in that security. If a contra member fails to deliver the certificate, the purchasing firm can implement *buy-in* procedures. Conversely, if a contra member refuses to pay on the seller's good delivery of certificates, the seller can implement *sell-out* procedures.

Buy-In Procedures. On any day subsequent to the settlement date of the contract, the purchasing firm that has failed to receive its certificates may give written notice to the selling firm of its intent to consider that contract in default; and (1) on the second business day following such notice, purchase that security in the marketplace for guaranteed regular-way delivery or for cash settlement; and (2) hold that seller financially responsible for any money difference from terms of the original contract.

If the seller is unable to deliver the certificate because it in turn has failed to receive the certificates from another member, the seller may immediately transmit the buy-in notice to its contra dealer in default. This procedure may be extended further by additional retransmittals in a kind of chain reaction.

Postponing execution of a buy-in for at least seven days is also necessary if the seller gives written notice to the purchasing firm that the securities are in transit or at the transfer agent for reregistration purposes. Such a notice must cite the certificate numbers and cannot be further extended without specific consent from the district NASD Uniform Practice Committee.

Once a buy-in is executed, the purchaser is obliged to give an immediate report of this action via telegram or other comparable written media to the delinquent seller, informing that firm of the quantity purchased and the price paid. The formal confirmation notice is then prepared and distributed by the usual channels of communication.

Sell-Out Procedures. If the purchasing firm fails to accept delivery of the security without adhering to official NASD rejection procedures, the seller can, *without further notice,* dispose of that security in the marketplace at the best available price. The seller holds the original buyer responsible for any monetary loss resulting from the default.

When a sell-out is executed, the selling firm is obliged to send an immediate report of its action via telegram or other comparable written media to the dealer who reneged, informing that firm of the quantity sold and the price received. Formal confirmation notice is then prepared and distributed by the usual channels of communication.

See also Good Delivery of Securities; Rejections and Reclamations.

Closing Range (or Range). The high and low prices, or bids and offers, recorded during the period designated as the official close.

See also Futures.

Closing Transaction. Any transaction that decreases an investor's position is said to be a closing transaction. A *closing sale transaction* liquidates the position of an investor who is long an option. In a *closing purchase transaction,* an investor who is short buys back the short option, thus eliminating a short option position.

See also Opening Transaction; Option.

Code of Arbitration. *See* National Association of Securities Dealers.

Code of Procedure. *See* National Association of Securities Dealers.

C.O.D. Transaction. *See* Cash Account.

Collateral Trust Bond. To back these bonds, the corporation pledges a portfolio of securities held in trust by a commercial bank, as protection for the holders of these debt instruments. This arrangement might be used by a corporation having a substantial interest in another valuable, perhaps subsidiary, corporation. Thus, if Gulf & Western industries wanted to issue a collateral trust bond, it could do so by pledging the shares of Paramount, a subsidiary.

The credit rating of this type of bond is quite good because the indenture usually requires additional collateral to be deposited or immediate repayment of the loan if the pledged security value declines to a level that may jeopardize the creditors' protection.

See also Debentures; Equipment Trust Bond; Mortgage Bond.

Combination. A *combination* is a call and a put on the same underlying security with different exercise prices and/or expiration dates. As with a straddle, an investor can buy or write a combination and therefore be either long or short a combination.

Example: A long combination might be the purchase of 1 WXY August 35 call and the purchase of 1 WXY August 30 put.

Example: A short combination might be the sale (writing) of 1 ABC July 45 call and the sale of 1 ABC April 40 put.

The straddle and the combination options are similar except that straddles have the same exercise and same expiration dates, whereas combinations have different exercise prices and/or expiration dates. The break-even points and profit zones for combination options may be determined by the same methods as for straddles (the combined premium plus the call striking price and put striking price less the combined premiums).

Commercial Paper. When a Federal Reserve Bank lends a portion of its excess reserves to cor-porations in need of short-term financing to conduct operations, the (uncollateralized) loan agreement is known as commercial paper.

This type of security represents unsecured short-term corporate obligations with maturities ranging up to nine months (270 days, to be precise) in duration. It is nine months because a debt instrument for public distribution redeemed more than nine months later requires time-consuming, expensive registration proceedings with the SEC, under terms of the Securities Act of 1933. Therefore, extended maturities for commercial paper offerings are unique. Typical denominations range from $100,000 to $1 million, in bearer form.

Corporations issue this paper to satisfy monetary requirements in connection with their current operations, and this "IOU" efficiently serves this purpose. Finance companies and commercial factors in particular find this means an effective way to raise money. The issuers of commercial paper tailor the maturities to the needs of the investors. Therefore, most investors hold commercial paper to maturity and no secondary market is required.

See also International Securities.

Commingling of Securities. *See* Hypothecation of Customer Securities; Securities Exchange Act of 1934 (Section 8); Segregation.

Commission (or Round-Turn). In futures trading, the one-time fee normally charged by a broker to a customer when a futures position is liquidated either by offset or delivery.

See also Futures.

Commission House Broker. Exchange members executing orders in behalf of their own organizations and its customers are known as *commission house brokers.* Whether the firm's principals include as many as 23 members of the exchange, such as Merrill Lynch, Pierce, Fenner &

Smith Inc. (the largest U.S. member organization), or as few as one seatholder, the minimum qualification for a member firm, there is usually a time each day when a commission house broker is unable to handle the volume of orders received. Two orders received at the same time in different securities can be enough to create a problem. If a member tries to execute both, the member may miss the market in one of those issues. To avoid this risk, members use the services of a two-dollar broker.

See also Two-Dollar Broker.

Commitment. This trade establishes a position (purchase transaction).

See also Margin Substitution.

Committee on Corporate Financing (NASD). *See* National Association of Securities Dealers.

Committee on Uniform Security Identification Procedures (CUSIP). This agency of the NASD is responsible for issuing identification numbers for stock and bond certificates. CUSIP developed and implemented a nine-digit number and/or letter system for identifying most publicly owned security issues.

Example: "066050105" is the unique number that has been assigned to Bankamerica Corp. common stock.

See also Reporting Requirements of the SEC (Periodical and Other Reports).

Committees/Conservators for Incompetents. *See* Fiduciary Accounts.

Commodities. *See* Futures.

Commodity Futures Trading Commission (CFTC). This Federal agency was created by Congress to regulate futures trading. The CFTC Act of 1974 became effective April 21, 1975. Previously, futures trading had been regulated

by the Commodity Exchange Authority of the USDA.

See also Futures.

Common Stock. A corporate charter can authorize two distinct forms of capital stock: preferred and common. Although common stock is always found in the capital structure of a corporation, the same is not true for preferred stock.

Both types of stock are assigned *par values.* Common stock par value is an arbitrary figure, which should soon lose relevance as the stock begins to trade in the marketplace and thereby acquire a different (and usually higher) market price. For preferred stock, however, par value is more important, because it is the basis on which dividends are calculated.

See also Par Value.

Common stock is a unit of equity ownership in a corporation. Owners of this kind of stock exercise control over corporate affairs and enjoy any capital appreciation. They are paid dividends only after preferred stock. Their interest in the assets, in the event of liquidation, is junior to all others.

Types. The amount of common stock permitted by the corporate charter is known as *authorized stock.* The directors of the corporation enjoy a good deal of flexibility with authorized stock because they rarely distribute all of it when initiating the firm's operation. In exchange for their capital, the investors are allocated only a portion of that authorized stock; this is then called *issued-and-outstanding stock.* In accordance with their judgment, the directors may further utilize the authorized but unissued stock any time in the future for any worthwhile corporate purpose. They can, for example: (1) sell it to raise more capital; (2) distribute it to already existent shareholders as a stock dividend or stock split; (3) present it to key employees as supplementary compensation or bonuses for their good work; or (4) use it as payment for shares of another corporation they want to acquire, be it a merger or merely an investment.

Treasury stock is a third type of common stock. The market price for equity securities is influenced by public psychology, often without regard to underlying basic value. When business news is uninspiring or pessimistic, the price of these shares can be depressed partly by the distress sales of the holders. At this time, the directors of the corporation may consider using some of the corporation's cash surplus to repurchase the shares in the open market. Shares that have been issued and that are reacquired through purchase, and occasionally by donation, are identified as *treasury stock.*

Example: A new corporation has one million shares of authorized stock, distributed as follows:

Issued stock		700,000
Issued-and-outstanding stock	650,000	
Treasury stock	50,000	
Unissued stock		300,000
Total authorized stock		1,000,000

When reacquired by the corporation, treasury stock loses some basic privileges and gains a unique accounting characteristic in the process. Treasury stock is not considered by the corporation as outstanding stock when the accountants calculate the company's earnings performance on a per-share basis. It is certainly issued stock, but it is treated for accounting purposes as if the stock were unissued. Thus the same amount of net income is apportioned among fewer shares *outstanding*, giving an illusion of increased earnings to the less knowledgeable, and often unwary, investor. Although stock exchange and Securities and Exchange Commission rules require financial statements to inform investors about the existence of treasury stock, few corporations explain the *effect* of treasury stock ownership to the average investor receiving this report.

Example: What is the effect on earnings for our illustrative corporation when it has a net income of $2,500,000?

$$\frac{\$2,500,000 \text{ net income}}{700,000 \text{ shares issued}} = \$3.57 \text{ earnings per share}$$
(*including* treasury stock)

$$\frac{\$2,500,000 \text{ net income}}{650,000 \text{ shares issued}} = \$3.85 \text{ earnings per share}$$
and outstanding only (*excluding* treasury stock)

Treasury stock does not receive dividend distributions or voting privileges. It would be foolish and inefficient to pay dividends on this stock when no actual distribution ever occurs, nor would it be practical to allow voting privileges. If this practice were permissible, the present management could use the corporation's money to acquire sufficient voting control to keep themselves in power forever.

Properly employed, treasury stock is a valuable tool of management to be utilized in the interest of all stockholders. The directors can use this stock in several ways: (1) They may exchange it for the shares of another corporation with whom they wish to merge; (2) they may use it to fulfill commitments they have made with respect to pension plans, profit-sharing plans, and employment contracts with key personnel; or (3) they may reoffer it for sale in the marketplace—they hope at a profit. If this can be arranged, the shareholders gain another interesting advantage. Ordinarily, the profit on such transactions is not taxable to the corporation.

When and if released or distributed by the corporation, treasury stock regains all lost privileges and once again is identified as outstanding stock of the company.

Benefits. Unless otherwise specified, in accordance with state law, common stockholders in a corporation receive certain advantages in re-

Types of Common Stock

Authorized Stock

Issued Stock | Unissued Stock

Issued *and* Outstanding Stock

Treasury Stock: Issued but reacquired by corporation (issued but *not* outstanding)

turn for their capital contribution via purchase of issue-and-outstanding stock.

1. *Voting privilege.* This privilege is the right to decide on matters of essential interest in the affairs of the corporation. It includes mergers, reorganizations, recapitalizations, and so on, as well as the annual election of directors. Votes on such matters may be cast either directly by stockholders or through the use of proxies or voting trusts, either of which empowers a third party to cast the vote in behalf of the stockholders.

Two types of voting are associated with common stock ownership, both of which permit the holder to cast one vote for each share of stock held. In *statutory voting*, the shareholder may cast one vote per share for each proposal on the agenda or for each nominee for directorship. In *cumulative voting*, however, the number of votes cast is multiplied by the number of issues or nominees.

2. *Dividends.* These are distributions to stockholders when earned and declared by the board of directors. Although dividends are usually normally associated more with preferred than with common stock, distributions may also be made on common stock.

See also Dividends.

3. *Limited access to books and records.* All publicly owned corporations registered with the SEC must provide their stockholders with an annual, audited copy of their financial statements prepared by an independent public accountant. Some stock exchanges also require distribution of internally prepared interim statements by the corporation to keep stockholders continuously apprised of the financial condition of their companies. To probe any deeper than the typical balance sheet and income statement usually requires either a court order and/or a close examination of the company's Forms 8K and 10K on file at the SEC. These quarterly and annual reports contain more detailed information than is normally distributed to shareholders. Management is obviously wary about revealing information that can: (1) give competitors an advantage, or (2) be used by dissident groups to unseat it.

4. *Ready transferability of shares.* Changes in ownership may be accomplished at your instruction as the present stockholder. You may give your shares away or sell them to anyone you choose without prior consultation with the directors of the company. Legal restrictions exist in a few instances, usually because of previous distributions of stock not registered with the SEC. However, those occasions are infrequent, last for a relatively short period, and affect very few shareholders.

5. *Proportionate share of the assets in liquidation.* If the stockholders or the public courts elect to dissolve the corporation and supervise the liquidation of its assets, creditors and principals are reimbursed in a definite order of priority. After employees' wages have been paid and federal, state, and local tax authority judgments have been satisfied, all of the corporation's secured and general creditors must be paid in full.

What monies remain are made available for distribution to the stockholders according to their proportionate interest in the company. If the company's capital structure includes preferred stock as well as common stock, the preferred stockholders must be paid their liquidation rights in the corporation before the common holders can participate. Finally, with no one else left, the common stockholders share in what remains of the assets.

6. *Subscription privilege (preemptive right)*. This is a right, issued by a corporation to its shareholders, to purchase newly issued shares (before the public offering). It must be exercised within a fixed period, usually thirty to sixty days, before the privilege expires and becomes worthless.

See also Preferred Stock; Theoretical Value.

Balance Sheet. In the stockholders' (shareholders') equity section of the balance sheet is the number of shares of common stock outstanding and their par value. Historically, par value represented the price at which the shares were first sold by the corporation. After the initial offering, however, par value has very little real significance. For purposes of illustration, the amount shown on the balance sheet as "common stock" to represent the company's "seed money"—the amount of money, at par value, that the company first received from the sale of stock. In recent years, because stock transfer taxes are based on par values, corporations are assigning par value well below the price at which the shares are sold. Today, par value has little or no meaning in terms of the value of the shares.

Example:

Common stock $10 par $300,000
Authorized, issued, and outstanding
30,000 shares

See also Balance Sheet (Liabilities).

Common Stock Ratios. *See* Balance Sheet (Capitalization Ratios).

Comparison. Comparison procedures between participating broker/dealers vary somewhat, by exchange locale and over-the-counter transactions. For New York Stock Exchange transactions, comparisons are arranged through Securities Industry Automation Corporation (SIAC), a computerized facility processing transactions in behalf of Stock Clearing Corporation (SCC), a wholly owned subsidiary of the NYSE. It also processes transactions on behalf of the American Stock Exchange Clearing Corporation (ASECC), a wholly owned subsidiary of the AMEX. Over-the-counter transactions are usually compared through the National Securities Clearing Corporation (NSCC), a subsidiary of the NASD. For exceptional reasons, with approval of both buying and selling firms, a trade may be processed "ex clearing house" (XCH) without clearing house participation. "Exceptional reasons" include in-house arranged "crosses," a need to obtain a new security certificate for tax-loss purposes, or a contract for other than regular-way settlement, but, by and large, round-lot activity is handled through the appropriate clearing facility.

On trade date plus one (that is, the next business day), each broker submits a list of its previous day's trades to SIAC. Such lists include: (1) buy or sell; (2) quantity; (3) description of issue; (4) price; and (5) name of contra firm.

SIAC then sorts the information and prepares a *contract sheet* that itemizes the information by issue on separate purchase and sales blotters (see the following figure). By means of this computerized system, SIAC contract sheets are able instantly to identify, and advise each firm of, a break in information on the second business day after the trade. The system isolated differences in trade details submitted by participating firms, such as price or contra-party discrepancies. The computer even offers "good name" suggestions when a problem is caused by a mismatch in contra brokers. That is, when there is a mismatch, the computer will suggest the name of

69

a firm that is possibly the correct one because that firm, too, is involved in a similar mismatch. Any disagreement must be resolved by the firms through direct communication or else promptly deleted from the contract sheets. This procedure allows sufficient time for adjustments and preparation of final notices to facilitate settlement on the fifth business day. New York Stock Exchange final notices are net balance summaries to receive from, or deliver to, the clearing corporation for deposit in that member organization's account, thus effecting a net settlement for each member. The National Securities Clearing Cor-

poration, employing a similar settlement procedure, advises each firm what its security balance or deposit requirement will be at the clearing house on settlement day. For ease in settling transactions, both SIAC and NSCC interpose themselves into each intermember transaction, becoming the contra principal for receipt, delivery, and payment. The actual securities may then conveniently be maintained on account at Depository Trust Co. (DTC) for safekeeping purposes.

Let us briefly examine three settlement procedures in terms of a single day's activities in

Purchase Contract Sheet

one issue—American Motors Corporation—that is traded both on the NYSE and via NASDAQ in the over-the-counter market.

SIAC's Net Balance Settlement. First, let us look at how SIAC prepares a net balance settlement.

Example: Suppose that on a single day, Broker A at different times:

Bought	Sold
100 shares @ 8 from Broker L	200 shares @ 7⅞ to Broker R
200 shares @ 8⅛ from Broker O	300 shares @ 8 to Broker T
300	500

Each member firm's activity per issue, including Broker A's trades in American Motors, is netted out by SIAC based on fully compared information. That is, if there are no price or trade differences between the participating firms, SIAC prepares a written notice to receive or deliver a net amount of shares. (Each price or trade difference is commonly called a "DK," meaning, literally, "Don't know." If the disagreement cannot be resolved by the close of business on trade date plus two, the transaction must be deleted from the contract sheets and eventually satisfied ex clearing house.)

Example: With Broker A's trade in American Motors, the 300 shares bought would be offset by the 500 shares sold, resulting in a net balance to deliver of only 200 shares. Instead of receiving 300 from Brokers L and O and delivering 500 to Brokers R and T, Broker A will (1) pair off 300 shares of its own sales with 300 of its purchases during the day; and (2) deliver the excess 200 shares of sales to its continuous settlement account at SIAC where it will be automatically transferred and credited to the appropriate purchasing member's account.

That firm may not even be Brokers R or T, the original trade participants. After all, due to the netting procedure, Brokers R and T may have completely paired off their purchases and sales internally. Nevertheless, because trading is conducted only with a small community of member firms, some broker(s) will need those shares and will be readily identified by the computerized facilities of SIAC. Money balances are determined, netted out, and settled via SIAC, too, from trade details submitted by each firm on the day after execution. A single check will be issued by SIAC if a member's credits exceed purchase costs, or by the firm to SIAC if the costs exceed sale proceeds (see the following figure, SIAC's CNS Accounting Summary).

NSCC's Net Balance Settlement. The second comparison procedure is NSCC's net balance settlement. The comparison mechanics for the NSCC are virtually identical to SIAC's procedures. Here, too, we find submission of trade details, contract sheets, DKs, and receipt/delivery advisories. No contra firm is cited in a balance notice because here, too, the DTC is always named as the contra party in the settlement process. Accordingly, each member firm's security account, by issue, is debited or credited with an appropriate number of shares from its net balance on settlement date. And, because this is accomplished on a cumulative basis (1) the number of fail-to-receive or fail-to-deliver contracts for each member declines sharply; and (2) physical handling of securities certificates between firms is similarly curtailed.

The cumulative receipt and delivery of securities feature of DTC and SIAC is known as *continuous net settlement (CNS)*; it can be exemplified by using the American Motors situation cited previously. After arriving at a net balance to deliver 200 shares to the DTC to satisfy its trade contracts for the day, Broker A may (1) deliver 200 shares to the DTC on settlement day and thus complete its commitment; (2) reduce by 200 shares its long position in the DTC certificate depository (if it has such a position large enough to do so); or (3) be unable to deliver 200 shares on settlement date for various reasons and thus fail to meet its obligation as promised.

In the last situation, Broker A's account at

SIAC's CNS Accounting Summary

| STOCK CLEARING CORPORATION American Stock Exchange Clearing Corporation | | CNS ACCOUNTING SUMMARY | | | | | | SIAC |

MEMBER NUMBER *0002* MEMBER NAME *ACME SECURITIES INC.* SETTLEMENT DATE *06-28-74* PAGE *001*

CUSIP NUMBER	SECURITY DESCRIPTION	OPENING POSITION LONG/SHORT (-)	SETTLING TRADES BOUGHT/SOLD (-)	STOCK DIVIDENDS AND MISC ACTIVITY REC/DEL (-)	RECEIPTS AND DELIVERIES REC/DEL (-)	CLOSING POSITION LONG/SHORT (-)	CURRENT MARKET PRICE	CURRENT MARKET VALUE LMV/SMV (-)
963150107 000	WHEELING PITTSBURGH STEEL CORP.	175	1,000		1,000 -	175	14.000	2,450.00
964066104 000	WHITE MOTOR CORPORATION	565 -	800	1,000 -	200	565 -	13.500	7,627.50 -
966323107 001	WHITING CORPORATION	220	25 -			195	15.750	3,071.25
980881106 000	WOOLWORTH F.W.	1,363 -	200 -		1,000	563 -	24.250	13,652.75 -
984121103 000	XEROX CORPORATION	898 -			500	398 -	114.000	45,372.00 -
989399100 000	ZENITH RADIO OF DELAWARE	373				373	28.000	10,444.00

YESTERDAY'S CLOSING BALANCE	121,847.50 -	SETTLING TRADES	21,537.50	YESTERDAY'S CLEARING DEPOSIT		LONG MARKET VALUE	15,965.25	TODAY'S CNS SETTLEMENT	
YESTERDAY'S SETTLEMENT	5,210.00	STOCK DIVIDENDS EARNED/PAYABLE	100.00	TODAY'S CLEARING DEPOSIT		SHORT MARKET VALUE	66,652.25 -	44,313.00 -	
TODAY'S OPENING BALANCE	116,637.50 -	MISC ACTIVITY		TODAY'S CLOSING BALANCE	95,000.00 -	NET MARKET VALUE	50,687.00 -	OWED BY MEMBER = DR DUE TO MEMBER = CR (-)	

CNS

DTC is set up as short 200 shares and marked to the market daily until the delinquency is eliminated. Furthermore, it becomes subject to the buy-in provisions of the NASD Uniform Practice Code if enough firms with long positions on DTC records want to withdraw their certificates physically from the depository. Each day of subsequent trading in American Motors by Broker A and its customers prompts an automatic adjustment in the firm's position record for that issue at DTC. Thus, on the following settlement date, if Broker A buys 600 shares and sells 300 shares of American Motors, its resulting 300-share act balance to receive will eliminate the 200-share short position and create a 100-share long position at DTC without ever making physical delivery to the depository.

Over-the-Counter Physical Comparison. The third settlement procedure is the over-the-counter physical comparison. When one or both of the firms involved in a trade is not a member of the NSCC or DTC, the participants cannot make use of the corporation's clearance facilities. They must prepare and exchange a written comparison no later than trade date plus one. This form, containing exact transaction details, may be mailed or hand delivered. It must be signed by the contra firm to evidence its acceptance and then returned to the sender prior to settlement date. Each transaction is a separate contract between the broker/dealers.

With this firm-by-firm procedure, a participating broker is unable to pair off its daily purchases and sales in the same issue so as to arrive at a net balance. This situation thus generates far more interfirm certificate shuffling on settlement date than results from a formal clearance system. (Clearance has been able to reduce the number of physical receipts and deliveries by as much as 75%.) Items to be handled with this procedure as well as noncleared items from a formal clearance system are settled in the office of the purchasing firm by means of delivery versus payment. The practice is known as a *window settlement* because the seller's messenger presents the security to a cashiering clerk through a barred teller's cage (similar to those found in a bank) and waits for payment.

This laborious procedure can delay physical settlement of contracts past the fifth business day and may create serious fail problems for the brokerage firms involved. Steps are underway to compel all NASD members to clear through NSCC in New York or via several of its satellite clearing facilities in major cities throughout the United States. When completed and coordinated with a national depository system, the program will allow for immediate nationwide electronic clearance and securities delivery.

See also Confirmation; Confirmations (Comparisons).

Competitive Bidding. Unlike the underwriting in which terms and conditions are negotiated between the corporation's officials and its investment bankers, a *competitive* underwriting involves more than one underwriting group. Under the terms of their by-laws, or because of governmental regulation in certain industries, some corporations are prohibited from making public offerings on a negotiated basis. In a *competitive* offering underwriting contracts are awarded

after competitive bidding by separate groups of investment bankers formed for this purpose.

The issuer announces its intent to issue a security and requests bids from the various syndicates to guarantee it a price for the privilege of reoffering the issue publicly at a somewhat higher level. The mechanical processes are identical in both negotiated and competitive deals; they differ only in the manner of determining prices. Meetings of the due-diligence type are held with all the competing groups, but they are referred to as *information meetings* instead.

No price discussions are conducted with the corporation for fear of providing an advantage to one group in preference over the others. Prices are certainly discussed within the separate groups themselves in order to reach agreement on a bid to be submitted to the company. Final prices by the individual syndicates are generally not decided until an hour or so before presentation to the corporation. Each syndicate wants to bid high enough to win the award but not too high, lest they overprice the issue and discourage investors. Interestingly, when the group later contacts institutional investors to solicit their orders, the prospective buyers ask for the next highest competitive bid. If that bid is close to the winning bid, the issue will sell out quickly. But if the winners top the next highest bid by a wide margin, the professional investor believes the security has been overpriced and often balks at buying at those levels.

The bids must be submitted promptly at a designated hour and location in sealed envelopes, with all interested parties in attendance. True and tragic stories can be told about a representative of an underwriting group who arrived a few minutes too late for consideration and discovered subsequently that his bid would have won the award. When the bids are opened by the corporation's officials, their attorneys and accountants are usually present to advise on the legality and the economics of the bids before making an award to any of the candidates. As has happened, if these advisors rule against the form or the prices of the bids that have been submitted, the corporation may refrain from selling the issue to anyone at that time.

Most general obligation (municipal) bonds are offered via competitive bid. The prospective issuer publishes an *official notice of sale* in the financial press and sometimes even mails a copy to underwriters who previously bid for securities offerings by the issuer. The official notice of sale gives details of the contemplated offering, such as type, size, date for the bids to be delivered, paying agent, purpose of the issue, bond attorney, maturity dates, amount of good faith deposit, and the statement declaring the right to reject any and all bids. It also invites interested parties to submit bids. The municipality examines the bids at the appointed time and awards the bonds to the underwriting group who has the bid for the *lowest net interest cost (NIC)* to the municipality.

If more than one underwriter submits a bid for an equal lowest net interest cost, then whoever's bid has the highest immediate dollars receives the bond issue.

Example: The offering consists of $370,000 of municipal bonds, for which a price of 100.50 has been bid:

Amount	Coupon Rate	Maturity	Bond Years		Calculations:		
$ 10,000	4.0%	1 Year	10	Bond	Annual Interest		
15,000	4.0	2 Years	30	Years	per bond		
20,000	4.0	3 Years	60	100	× $40	=	$4,000
25,000	4.5	4 Years	100				
30,000	4.5	5 Years	150				
35,000	4.5	6 Years	210	460	× 45	=	20,700
40,000	5.0	7 Years	280				
45,000	5.0	8 Years	360				
50,000	5.0	9 Years	450	1090	× 50	=	54,500
100,000	5.5	10 Years	1000	1000	× 55	=	55,000
$370,000							

Total Bond Years	Total Interest
2650	$134,200
Less premium	1,850
Net Interest cost	$132,350

$$\frac{\$132,350}{2,650} = \$49.9433 \text{ Net interest cost per bond}$$

$$\frac{\$49.9433}{10} = 4.9943\% \text{ Net interest cost rate}$$

See also Negotiated Offering; Underwriting Agreement.

Competitive Market-Maker. Exchange members who are willing and able to buy and/or sell stock in any NYSE listed issue at the request of a Floor Official or another broker holding a customer's order are called *competitive market-makers.* The ability to deal in any stock differentiates them from specialists who are limited in their activities to a limited number of issues. The requirement for them to provide market depth and narrower spreads in prevailing quotations to accommodate public orders distinguishes them from competitive traders. Competitive market-makers may also act as two-dollar brokers to earn brokerage fees when their services are not needed. But, they are restricted in this capacity to acceptance of only market or limited price orders. They may not handle stop orders or any orders which direct their use of discretion in the execution process. Moreover, they may not act as a competitive market-maker and a two-dollar broker or even act as a competitive market-maker and as a competitive trader in the same stock during the same trading day.

See also Competitive Trader; Two-Dollar Broker.

Competitive Trader. Members who buy and sell stock for a personal account and risk are known as *competitive traders.* They are registered with the exchange to act in this manner and must meet certain financial, trading, and reporting requirements. Restrictive regulations have been formulated to prevent competitive traders from conflicting with transactions initiated by customers of member organizations. In complying with the rules and attempting to buy and sell profitably, competitive traders frequently assist specialists in providing liquidity for listed stocks. They often satisfy aggressive customer supply or demand by acting for their own accounts on the opposite sides of these transactions. With certain limitations, competitive traders may also act as two-dollar brokers to earn brokerage fees when trading opportunities are not available.

See also Specialist; Two-Dollar Broker.

Conduct of Broker/Dealers. Section 15 of the Securities Exchange Act of 1934 obliges all registered brokers and dealers to adhere to the following standards:

1. They are obliged to "observe high standards of commercial honor and just and equitable principles of trade in the conduct of...business."

2. They must supervise and review the securities activities of all principals, employees, and associated people.

3. They may make recommendations to customers only if suitable to the customer's needs and objectives.

4. They are directed to maintain proper books and records, including a new-account investigation report for each customer (*see* Reporting Requirements of the SEC).

5. They must refrain from exercising discretionary authority in customer accounts unless suitable written authorization is on file from the customer. (Overtrading in these accounts is also prohibited).

6. They are prohibited from demanding or requiring reciprocal brokerage business from a mutual fund in exchange for soliciting orders for that fund's shares from its public customers. This admonition applies as well to rebating or sharing of commissions by broker/dealers from order executions by mutual funds.

7. They must, when responsible for customer securities and/or money, protect those assets in the following ways: (a) They must take physical possession of fully paid, cash account securities and excess margin account securities (defined as all securities in the account with a market value exceeding 140% of the customer's debit balance) and then place the certificates into safekeeping/segregation, as the case may be. Under SEC Rule 15c3-3, this means a mandatory buy-in must be initiated if the securities haven't been received from a contra broker/dealer by the thirtieth calendar day following the settlement date. If it is a customer who is delinquent in a sale transaction, the firm must buy-in that security immediately after the tenth business day following settlement date. (b) They must deposit excess customer monies such as free credit balances into a "special reserve bank account for the exclusive benefit of customers." In this way, broker/dealers cannot jeopardize these funds by using them in personal trading or underwriting activities. Customer funds may be used only to offset other customer activities, such as those that necessitate some form of financing (margin accounts, and so forth). SEC Rule 15c3-3 sets forth a formula for determining that amount of customer assets (credits) versus customer activity liabilities (debits). The calculation in accord with that formula must be done weekly by most broker/dealers. The resulting net credit is then immediately deposited in full into the special reserve bank account. Some firms, with minimal customer assets under their control, are permitted to make the calculation monthly instead of weekly. However, they must then deposit 105% of the net credit into that reserve bank account instead of on a dollar-for-dollar basis.

8. They shall maintain minimum net capital of $25,000 *or* $\frac{1}{15}$ of aggregate indebtedness (loosely defined as adjusted liabilities; adjusted to the extent of including only customer-related liabilities and those senior to customer claims in the event the firm is forced to liquidate itself), whichever is the larger dollar amount of those two figures (Rule 15c3-1), if they carry customer monies or securities on their premises. An alter-

native formula, less complicated in the calculation process, is the greater of $100,000 or 4% of the aggregate debit items in the Rule 15c3-3 formula used for protection of customer monies and securities.

9. They must protect customer assets by using proper safekeeping and hypothecation procedures. *See* Securities Exchange Act of 1934 (Section 8).

10. They must carry prescribed minimum amounts of fidelity bond insurance. This helps to ensure that, in the event of fraud by an officer or employee of the broker/dealer, the firm will remain viable and will preserve its customers' assets.

11. They should have current knowledge of background and financial information of corporations for which they act as market-makers and must also transmit this information to investors or contra dealers who request it (Rule 15c2-11).

12. They are urged to avoid use of fictitious quotations or prices.

13. They must prepare confirmation/comparison notices of transactions, revealing essential terms and conditions, including the extent of interest in, or control of, that issuer by the executing brokerage firm.

14. They are directed to send customers a statement of account at least once every three months, provided that (a) there is a money balance or security position at the end of the quarter, or (b) there has been any trading or financial activity in the account during the quarter.

The first major amendment to the Securities Exchange Act of 1934 was legislated in 1938. It expanded on the provisions of Section 15 and led to the registration of the national Association of Securities Dealers with the SEC. The amendment is commonly referred to as the Maloney Act, and it provided for registration of any association that establishes standard operating rules and trading procedures for its members to abide by in the conduct of its securities business.

Registered associations are accorded self-regulatory and disciplinary powers similar to those accorded registered securities exchanges. However, the SEC retains the right of review and denial of new rules and regulations and may exercise its authority to uphold, increase, reduce, or cancel any measure of discipline proposed by the association against a member.

The 1975 amendments to the 1934 Securities Exchange Act mandated the SEC to appoint a Municipal Securities Rulemaking Board (MSRB). The purpose of the MSRB is to formulate entry standards, operating rules, and procedures appropriate for municipal securities concerns that are obliged to register with the SEC under the 1934 Act.

See also Blanket Fidelity Bond Insurance; Maloney Act; Municipal Securities Rulemaking Board; Reporting Requirements of the SEC; Securities Exchange Act of 1934 (Section 8); SEC Rule 15c2-11; SEC Rule 15c3-1; SEC Rule 15c3-3.

Conduit Theory. *See* Subchapter M (Internal Revenue Code).

Confidence Theory. Two old and completely erroneous cliches are often used to explain sharp rises or falls in stock market prices: "more buyers than sellers" or "more sellers than buyers." Because every transaction requires both a buyer and a seller, one side can never outnumber the other. However, it would be correct to say that often one side becomes more anxious than the other. The double auction market employed by exchanges is built on the premise that competition among buyers and sellers will create the price. In the presence of competitors, potential buyers must raise their bids to fill their orders; hence, a market rise. If we measure this emotion, we have the basis of an interesting market technique.

The *Confidence Theory* proposes that price movements are based on an increase or decrease in the investor's confidence in the future trend of prices. Fundamentals are of little importance, because they do not reflect what the buyer is willing to pay.

Example: In 1965, General Motors reported earnings or $5.25 per share, a five-year high, yet the stock did not trade higher than fifteen times those earnings during that year. Contrast this to 1961 when a nineteen-times multiple was reached and to 1970 when GM traded as high as 39 times earnings. Followers of the Confidence Theory hold that the investors' feeling for the future matters much more than their analysis of the present.

The difficulty with this theory is the method of measurement. How do we recognize the early signs of an increase or decrease in the emotions of the market movers? Can confidence be charted the way we chart earnings, volume, or prices? Some interesting answers to these questions have been advanced.

Barron's Confidence Index uses yields on bonds to measure the investor's willingness to take risks. This may seem a strange way to forecast stock prices, but bond yields have an excellent record for leading other indicators by many months. We hope to read the trend by comparing the yields on high-quality, lower-yield bonds with the yields of more speculative debt securities. (Yields on all bonds move in the same *direction*. It is the comparative yield movements between high-quality and low-quality bonds on which this theory is founded.) If the yield on lower-grade bonds declines, it shows that investors are leaving the safe harbor of high quality and speculating a bit more. An increase in yield on high-grade bonds tends to show that their attraction has diminished. This means that buyers have confidence; that is, they will take their chances with the higher-yielding, less-protected security. This confidence indicates a trend on which investors can base their decisions, hopefully months before those who read facts rather than emotions.

Many proponents of the Confidence Theory apply their study to public interest in speculative stocks. Low-priced issues, both listed and over the counter, as well as new securities offerings of untested companies, are the yardstick. When speculation in these securities reaches a fever pitch—beware! Confidence is reaching its peak and is probably spending its final energy seeking profit in the least likely areas. Because fundamentals have been put aside and emotions are ruling the marketplace, the bubble will burst, and new opportunities will soon be available—at much lower prices. Although not measured as formally as the Barron's Index, this method is followed by many professional traders and investors.

All market theories, in one way or another, are attempts to measure confidence. Although they take different paths, they seek an answer to one question: What will the investing public do next? Stock prices do not go up or down on their own; investor confidence reflects the eagerness to buy and sell, and prices move accordingly.

See also Advance-Decline Theory; Dow Theory; Odd-Lot Theory; Short Interest Theory; Technical Analysis.

Confirmation. The P & S Department of a brokerage firm prepares customer confirmation notices from information furnished by the Order Department on an execution report. Most of the details are identical to those included in comparisons, and it is not surprising to see many brokers employing a confirmation model that is similar to, or even a duplicate of, their comparison forms. The information on a comparison form, along with each broker's transfer, reclamation, and delivery form, was standardized by BASIC in 1972. (BASIC is an acronym for Banking and Securities Industry Committee, a trade association of bankers and brokers dedicated to promoting economy in operating procedures by standardizing widely used industry forms.) It is to the firm's financial advantage to incorporate as many of these duplicated features as possible into the same illustrative scheme (see the following figures).

Three items that *may* appear on a customer's confirmation but never on a broker/dealer comparison are (1) an SEC registration fee; (2) transfer taxes; and (3) commission charges. They are inapplicable for a contra broker/dealer transaction because your firm does not act as its *agent*, and payment of appropriate transfer taxes and an SEC fee, if required, is fundamental with a brokerage firm's good delivery of securities anyway. "May" is stressed for customer transactions because some or all of those charges do not even apply for customers under certain circumstances. For instance:

1. An SEC registration fee is paid normally by the seller of an equity security tradable on a national securities exchange whether the order is executed on the exchange or over the counter.

However, the SEC has exempted the following sales transactions from imposition of that fee: (a) sales of stock offered pursuant to an effective registration statement (spot secondaries and listed options sales remain liable for the SEC fee); (b) private placements of stock by the issuing corporation; (c) the sale of securities pursuant to, and in consummation of, a tender or exchange offer; (d) the exercise of a warrant or subscription right or the conversion of a convertible security; and (e) transactions executed outside the United States that are not reported, or required to be reported, to the Consolidated Tape Association. There is no fee charged to sellers of debt securities.

2. Florida tax is paid by *sellers of equity or debt securities*, but only when sale execution occurs within Florida's borders.

See also Confirmations (Comparisons); Comparison; Rules of Fair Practice (Section 12).

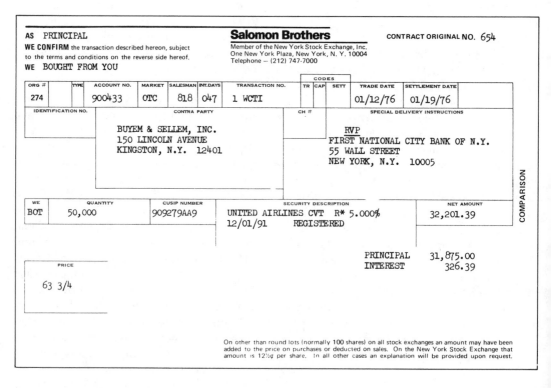

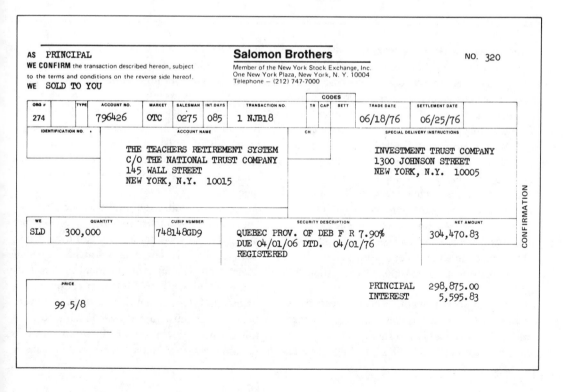

AS PRINCIPAL
WE CONFIRM the transaction described hereon, subject
to the terms and conditions on the reverse side hereof.
WE BOUGHT FROM YOU

Salomon Brothers
Member of the New York Stock Exchange, Inc.
One New York Plaza, New York, N. Y. 10004
Telephone – (212) 747-7000

CONTRACT ORIGINAL NO. 774

ORG #	TYPE	ACCOUNT NO.	MARKET	SALESMAN	INT.DAYS	TRANSACTION NO.	TR	CAP	SETT	TRADE DATE	SETTLEMENT DATE
274		B00502	OTC	458		1 WFY1				02/05/76	02/13/76

IDENTIFICATION NO.

CONTRA PARTY
STOCKUMBOND CORP.
200 WALL STREET
NEW YORK, N.Y. 10005

CH # 502

SPECIAL DELIVERY INSTRUCTIONS

COMPARISON

WE	QUANTITY	CUSIP NUMBER	SECURITY DESCRIPTION	NET AMOUNT
BOT	127	170880108	CHRISTIANA SECURITIES	19,431.00

PRICE
153

PRINCIPAL   19,431.00

On other than round lots (normally 100 shares) on all stock exchanges an amount may have been
added to the price on purchases or deducted on sales. On the New York Stock Exchange that
amount is 12½¢ per share. In all other cases an explanation will be provided upon request.

AS PRINCIPAL
WE CONFIRM the transaction described hereon, subject
to the terms and conditions on the reverse side hereof.
WE SOLD TO YOU

Salomon Brothers
Member of the New York Stock Exchange, Inc.
One New York Plaza, New York, N. Y. 10004
Telephone – (212) 747-7000

NO. 320

ORG #	TYPE	ACCOUNT NO.	MARKET	SALESMAN	INT.DAYS	TRANSACTION NO.	TR	CAP	SETT	TRADE DATE	SETTLEMENT DATE
274		796426	OTC	0275	085	1 NJB18				06/18/76	06/25/76

IDENTIFICATION NO.

ACCOUNT NAME
THE TEACHERS RETIREMENT SYSTEM
C/O THE NATIONAL TRUST COMPANY
145 WALL STREET
NEW YORK, N.Y. 10015

CH

SPECIAL DELIVERY INSTRUCTIONS
INVESTMENT TRUST COMPANY
1300 JOHNSON STREET
NEW YORK, N.Y. 10005

CONFIRMATION

WE	QUANTITY	CUSIP NUMBER	SECURITY DESCRIPTION	NET AMOUNT
SLD	300,000	748148GD9	QUEBEC PROV. OF DEB F R 7.90% DUE 04/01/06 DTD. 04/01/76 REGISTERED	304,470.83

PRICE
99 5/8

PRINCIPAL   298,875.00
INTEREST   5,595.83

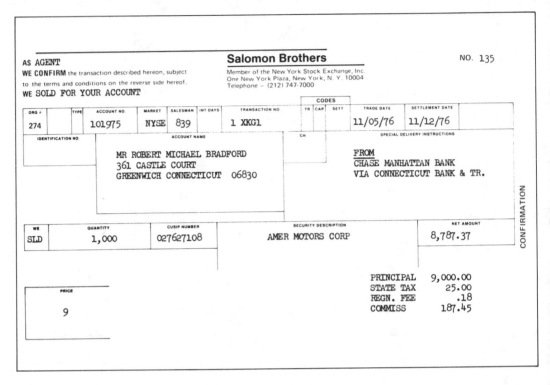

Confirmations (Comparisons). Unless the members use the facilities of a national clearing corporation, each party to an over-the-counter transaction must send written notice to the contra broker/dealer on or before the first business day following that trade. This confirmation (or comparison, as it is generally called) must cite pertinent details of the transaction. Any discrepancies must be corrected promptly by the party in error. If the terms stated on these written notices concur, each party must sign a copy and return it to the confirming member. This officially binds that member to acceptance of the transaction. This legal contract now demonstrates a willingness to perform as agreed upon on the settlement date.

Should a writen notice be received by a member who denies even participating in that transaction, that party must signify refusal of the trade by stamping it *DK (Don't Know)*, signing it, and returning it to the confirming dealer. It is then the responsibility of the confirming dealer to furnish proof of this claim. This is one good reason why it is essential for members to have assurance of the integrity of contra broker/dealers. In a volatile securities marketplace, where many thousands of dollars may be committed on the strength of a telephone call, there can be no substitute for the confidence of honor between members.

Under certain circumstances a member may choose to treat another member as a customer rather than as the contra dealer on a particular transaction. This is especially so when the other dealer is not a member of a national clearing corporation and insists that this transaction be settled C.O.D. (collect on delivery). In that event the member must first receive assurance from this customer that, if settlement will be made to or through that firm's agent (that is, a bank or another dealer), (1) confirmations will be presented no later than trade date plus one; (2) the agent is readily identified and given prior written instructions to accept and settle even partial deliveries.

Moreover, if that agent or contra firm is a member of a SEC-registered securities depository, with few exceptions, confirmation, acknowledgment and book entry settlement must take place via the facilities of that depository.

Consolidated Tape System. As a prelude to the much discussed and highly automated National Market System (NMS) of the future, a computerized system was implemented in 1974 to promptly report securities transactions effected in various marketplaces on a single ticker tape. The participants include all regional stock exchanges. Instinet, "third market" NASD member dealers as well as the New York and American Stock exchanges, both of whose ticker-tape facilities are utilized for this arrangement.

Under the Consolidated Tape System, all transactions in NYSE-listed securities are reported on the NYSE ticker tape as they occur (Network A), whereas those issues listed on the AMEX, or traded exclusively on the regional exchanges, are published on the AMEX ticker tape (Network B).

See also Ticker Tape.

Constant-Dollar Plan. *See* Formula Investing.

Constant-Ratio Plan. *See* Formula Investing.

Construction and Development REIT. *See* Real Estate Investment Trust.

Consumer Credit. Credit extended to the ultimate users of goods and services.
See also Federal Reserve System.

Contango. A condition whereby the deferred futures months are at a premium to the nearby futures months and spot price (a British term).
See also Futures.

Contemporaneous Reserve Requirement. *See* Federal Reserve System.

Contingent Order. *See* Switch Order.

Continuing Commissions. In spite of NASD restrictions against influencing or rewarding employees of other firms, it should be borne in mind that the Board of Governors of the NASD has held that the payment of continuing commissions is not necessarily improper. *Continuing commissions* refers to a practice of paying commissions to (1) registered representatives no longer in that member's employ; or (2) the spouse or other beneficiaries of deceased registered representatives formerly employed by that member.

In the first instance, the practice is permissible without a formal agreement only if that person remains a representative registered with another member of the NASD. But if that person is no longer registered or if the second instance described above is applicable instead, a bona fide contract must have been drawn and signed to that effect while the registered representative was employed by that member organization.

Two further important points to remember about continuing commission payments are the following: (1) although such payments may be made for consideration of any type of securities transaction, they must not include payment for solicitation of *new* business or *new* customer accounts; and (2) under no circumstances can payments be made to someone who is not eligible for membership in the NASD or to someone who has been disqualified from associating with a member due to disciplinary action taken by the NASD's Board of Governors.

Continuous Existence. *See* Corporation.

Continuous Net Settlement (CNS). This procedure is used by all clearing corporations to simplify processing daily transactions and correspondingly to reduce the number of certificate deliveries required. The clearing corporation interposes itself on each transaction, crediting or debiting each member's total holdings in each issue. The net balance is carried forward from day to day.

See also Comparison.

Contra Broker. This firm is the one on the opposite side of the transaction. If your firm buys, then the contra firm is the seller; if your firm sells, the contra firm is the buyer.

See also Broker/Dealer Organization.

Contract Month. The month in which futures contracts may be satisfied by making or accepting a delivery.

See also Futures.

Contract Sheet. This complete list of each member's daily transactions is arranged by issue and prepared by the clearing house for members to check for accuracy of detail and approval of settlement terms.

See also Comparison.

Contractual Periodic-Payment Plan. This investment accumulation plan is far more formalized in operation than the voluntary-accumulation plan. Under this program, the participant agrees to invest a fixed sum of money at specified time intervals over a ten- or fifteen-year period. This plan often stipulates deposits of as little as $10 or $20 monthly over that time span with no initial down payment required.

This investment program is more popularly referred to as a *contractual plan* because of the implied commitment in the agreement to participate. Still, it is flexible enough to allow for late,

or even deferred, payments as well as to permit advance or accelerated deposits if the investor chooses. Deferred payments extend the duration of the plan by the number of deposits omitted. Accelerated payments merely shorten the effective life of the contract. No particular consequence or advantage is attached to either action.

The typical contractual periodic-payment plan is set up to function as a unit investment trust of the "participating" variety. The payments actually purchase trust units, and the money is then invested in shares of the mutual fund. Because the distinction is strictly technical in nature, contractual plan purchases are usually thought of as direct investments in mutual funds rather than as an intermediary arrangement. Exact mechanical details vary from mutual fund to mutual fund, and a copy of the offering prospectus should be carefully scrutinized by interested parties.

Sales Charges. The Investment Company Act of 1940 and its subsequent amendments in 1970 limit the sales charge for periodic payment plans to 9% of the total investment. Thus, a $10,000 ten-year plan with a maximum load would entail $900 in sales charges deducted from deposits over that period of time.

The use of a sales charge with offerings of mutual funds is rather commonplace. But the application of that sales charge in the case of contractual periodic-payment plans is what has made these plans historically controversial. The sales load is not deducted from investor deposits in equal increments. Most of the sales charge borne over the life of the contract is deducted from payments during the early years of operation. This front-end load effect, or *prepaid-charge plan,* as it is sometimes called, places it in sharp contrast with the *level-loaded* voluntary-accumulation plan and the single payment purchase arrangement.

The contractual planholders who default voluntarily and redeem their shares purchased during the first few years probably lose a sizable amount of their deposited dollars. Dollars used in payment of sales charges for contractual plans are not always refundable for early redemption of shares from the investors' accounts. In past years, this consequence led some critics to identify these programs as *penalty plans.* The Investment Company Amendments Act of 1970 legislated regulations to blunt or avoid such penalties for investors withdrawing from such plans in a reasonable period of time.

Under this law, there are two distinct methods by which sales charges can be levied in an offering of periodic- payment plans. In either instance the maximum load cannot exceed 9% of the total investment. The offering prospectus must clearly state which of the two methods has been officially elected for use by the company and its sales agents. In both instances, the custodian bank servicing these contracts must send the investor (within sixty days) a notice of initiation of the plan and a statement of total charges to be incurred. The bank must also inform the subscriber about the availability of a cancellation privilege and its advantages if utilized within 45 days from the date of this notification. If the participant exercises such privilege within the 45-day period, the investor can obtain (1) the then current value of the shares in the contractual account; plus (2) *a full refund* of all sales charges and other ancillary charges such as custodial fees, insurance premiums, and so on.

To summarize, in the case of cancellation within 45 days of notification:

Refund = current value of shares
+ full refund of all charges

The 1970 law also requires the initial payment in any contractual plan to be at least $20 with minimum deposits thereafter of $10.

Method 1 for levying a sales charge. As much as 50% of the first twelve monthly pay-ments may be deducted in equal increments and applied toward the total requirement due on the plan contract. The remaining 50% load will then be deducted in equal proportionate increments from the balance of payments due on the contract over the remaining nine or fourteen years.

Example: An analysis of a $10,000 ten-year plan with a 9% load, using this method is as follows:

Annual payments for 10 years			=	$1,000.00
First year's payment	=	$1,000.00		
Less sales charge @ 50%	=	$ 500.00		
Total load for 10 years (9% of $10,000)			=	$ 900.00
Amount of money invested in fund's shares in first year			=	$ 500.00
R emaining dollars necessary to satisfy total load requirement in next 9 years			=	$ 400.00
Approximate sales charge deductions over remaining annual payments ($400.00 ÷ 9 years)			=	$ 44.44

If this method is used, the investment company, its underwriter, or the custodian bank must give written notice to investors (1) who have missed three or more payments within fifteen months after issuance of the plan certificate; or (2) who have missed one or more payments between the fifteenth and eighteenth month after initiation of the plan, advising them of their right to cancel the plan before expiration of the eighteenth month, and to receive (1) the current value of the shares in the account; plus (2) a refund of all sales charges paid that exceeded 15% of total deposits in the contract thus far.

Even investors who have kept current in their plan deposits are entitled to the cancellation privileges providing they act before the end of the eighteenth month.

To summarize, in the case of cancellation between 45 days and eighteen months of notification under method 1:

Refund = current value of shares
+ (amount deducted for sales
charges −15% of total invested)

To illustrate this point about cancellation, let us assume that a plan subscriber cancels the program using method 1 after depositing $100 the first month. Because the decision is within the first 45-day *full reimbursement period*, the investor will receive a refund payment of $50 worth of sales charges and the value of the shares in the account.

On the other hand, let us assume that the subscriber withdraws from the plan after a full year after depositing $1,000 (of which $500 was for sales charges). The investor will receive the redemption value of shares owned plus $350 of the sales charge expense. The sales charge refund is calculated this way:

(1) $1,000 (total deposited)
       ×   .15
       $ 150 (15% of deposits)

(2) $ 500 (deducted for sales charges)
       −   150 (15% of total deposits)
       $ 350 (sales charge refund)

With this method, the investor is not entitled to a refund of ancillary expenses that may have been imposed—custodial fees, insurance premiums, and so on—when termination of the contract is at this late date.

Method 2 for levying a sales charge. This method, introduced in 1970, attempts to apportion the front-end sales charge more equitably than the 50% first-year load procedure. In this second method, as much as 20% may be deducted from annual payments to cover the sales charge expense. But the deduction may not average more than 16% from each annual deposit based on the first four years of operation of the plan. Let us express this rule another way: As much as 64% of the first year's deposits may be subtracted as sales-charge expense, but the amount must be apportioned over the first four years' required payments into this plan. Furthermore, the amount of sales charge subtracted from monthly payments during this time must

also be in equal proportion to each other, calculated on a year-by-year basis.

Example: If the annual sales charge requirement is determined to be $120, the fund cannot deduct it all from the first two monthly payments and take nothing more for the rest of that year. For the monthly payments to be in equal proportion to each other, the $120 requirement must be taken at the rate of $10 per month during that year. This *spread-load* application avoids concentration of sales charge deductions from any single payment and ensures that relatively similar amounts of money will be invested in fund shares with each deposit in the early years. It also gives rise to the designation of this kind of periodic investment program as a *spread-load contractual plan*.

Example: An analysis of a $10,000 ten-year contractual plan with a 9% load, using a typical spread-load option, is as follows:

Annual payments for each of 10 years	= $1,000.00
Total load for 10 years (9% of $10,000)	= $ 900.00
Maximum deduction of sales charges in first 4 years (16% of $4,000, which is also equal to 64% of an annual payment)	= $ 640.00*
First year's payment = $1,000.00 Less 20% sales charge = $ 200.00	
Amount of money invested in fund's shares in first year	= $ 800.00
Remaining dollars necessary to satisfy load requirement in next 3 years ($640–$200)	= $ 440.00
Sales charge deductions over remaining 6 years ($900–$640)	= $ 260.00
Or, $\dfrac{\$260}{72 \text{ months for 6 years}}$	= 3.61 per month**

*Can be subtracted in equal or unequal annual increments so long as each monthly deduction per year is equal. For example, $200, $200, $200, and 40; or $200, $200, $120, and $120, and so on.
**Equal amounts of $3.61 per month must then be deducted from payments.

The opportunity for recovery of a major portion of the sales charge within the first eighteen months is *not* available when this method is used by the company or its underwriter. But the

45-day full-refund-of-load privilege *is* effective with use of this method.

To summarize, in the case of cancellation between 45 days and eighteen months of notification under method 2:

Refund = current value of shares only (includes *no* portion of load charges)

Cancellation Privilege After Notification of a Contractual Periodic Payment Plan's Initiation.

Refund Under:

Cancellation Occurs:	Method 1, Law of 1970	Method 2, Law of 1970
Within first 45 days	Value of shares plus full refund of charges	Value of shares plus full refund of charges
Within period between 45 days to 18 months	Value of shares plus amount of sales charge paid that is more than 15% of total money deposited	Value of shares only
After 18 months	Value of shares only	Value of shares only

The foregoing table shows a summary of the cancellation privileges under method 1 and method 2 for levying sales charges according to the Investment Company Amendments Act of 1970.

Advantages and Services

Self-explanatory advantages. The conveniences available to the contractual periodic-payment planholder generally overlap with those available to the voluntary-accumulation plan investor. The ones that need no explanation include: (1) professional management; (2) diversification of investment portfolio; (3) ease of operation of investment; (4) dollar-cost averaging; (5) ability to purchase full and/or fractional shares with each deposit; (6) automatic reinvestment of distributions (and at net asset value, too); (7) conversion privileges (8) automatic withdrawal programs; (9) advantageous breakpoint privileges on purchases.

In fact, contractual plan investors frequently enjoy additional services not generally provided in the case of other mutual fund investment programs.

Redemption. Contractual plan investors may redeem as much as 90% of their share holdings at current value and then redeposit these monies before expiration of the plan at the then prevailing net asset value. No sales charge is levied on the reinvestment of withdrawn funds. Thus, the planholder can withstand temporary financial emergencies without terminating the investment contract and losing sales charge expenses previously borne.

Declaration of trust. Under the contractual plan, an investor may create a Declaration of Trust agreement. On the death of the investor, this agreement can provide for immediate distribution of these mutual fund shares to specified beneficiaries without subjecting those assets to time-consuming probate court proceedings.

Insurance. The planholder also has an opportunity to purchase plan-completion insurance and thus guarantee a fully paid contract if the planholder should die before total payments have been deposited. Plan-completion insurance is declining-term life insurance whose premium, computed at group rates, is paid for by the investor as an additional monthly charge. There is no cash value in such policies. Each year the investor lives to make payments in the plan means that much less coverage on that person's life. When the contract is completed, the insurance policy is terminated.

The purpose of the insurance is to ensure satisfaction of the contractual plan in the event of the planholder's untimely death. Thus, it tempers the possibility of principal loss for the beneficiaries because of front-end load expenses in the early years. The insurance company deposits the unpaid balance due in the plan immediately on notification of the planholder's death. The proceeds are not paid directly to the estate or to any beneficiary. Rather, they are paid to the mutual fund's custodian or plan trustee to purchase as many full and/or fractional shares at the current price, thus completing the plan. Although the details vary from company to company, maximum coverage is available from $30,000 to $45,000, despite the possible subscription to a larger-sized contractual plan.

Medical examinations are also required on most contracts above $10,000. A few states prohibit the sale of life insurance on a tie-in arrangement for mutual fund purchases. Other states, because of their blue-sky laws, will not even permit offerings of contractual plans using the terms and conditions just described.

See also Investment Company Act of 1940 and 1970 Amendments; Mutual Fund; Unit Investment Trust Company; Voluntary-Accumulation Plan.

Controller's Department. *See* Broker/Dealer Organization.

Conversion. Conversion is a retirement privilege initiated by the bondholder that benefits the corporation at the same time. A conversion feature in a bond indenture allows the holders to exchange their certificates for a specific number of shares of stock in the corporation. Thus the company eliminates its debt by acquiring more stockholders. When this feature is included in a bond issue, it tends to be a very attractive incentive for investors because it permits them seniority as creditors and the advantage of potential price appreciation in the common stock at the same time.

Advantages to Issuer. The conversion privilege, while considered to be the prerogative of the bondholder, is also advantageous to the issuing corporation. Because this form of dual status (creditor/stockholder) is an attractive feature for investors, a corporation can issue this obligation with a somewhat lower interest rate

than is necessary for ordinary straight debt securities. Furthermore, if the company prospers, thereby experiencing appreciation in the value of its underlying stock, this debt can be eliminated with a minimal outlay of cash. The corporation merely calls the issue, thus forcing the bondholders to convert into equity or lose the economic advantage of the stock's prevailing market price. That is when the minimal outlay of cash is required. Somewhere between 1 to 5% of all convertible bondholders neglect to act in time to effect the exchange and can subsequently claim only redemption value from the corporation.

Example: A $1,000 bond is convertible into thirty shares of stock when the underlying shares are trading at $50. Bondholders will "lose" $500 in paper value if they fail to convert in the time allowed following distribution of the call notice.

Shares	30
Market price	× $50
Paper value versus $1,000 redemption value	$1,500

The bondholders usually receive thirty to sixty days' advance notice to arrange conversion. Call announcements, both partial and full, are published in most major newspapers in the United States as well as in all the financial services media. If the bonds are registered in the name of the owner (as most corporate bonds are), the trustee sends each holder an announcement of the redemption decision, citing applicable certificate serial numbers in cases of partial calls.

Conversion Price. A convertible feature in a bond can have a dramatic effect on the market price of that issue. This is especially true when the underlying stock reaches a price level at which it becomes economically feasible for a holder to convert into that stock. It is called a *conversion price* and is set in the indenture by the issuing corporation at the time the bond is offered for sale.

Example: A conversion price of $40 means that the bondholders will not benefit financially if they convert into stock until the underlying stock begins trading at $40 and above.

See also Conversion Price; Conversion Ratio.

Conversion Ratio. The conversion price is also a means by which a corporation informs its bondholders how many shares they will receive if they decide to convert or if they are "forced" to convert. This information can be computed by dividing the face value (par of the bonds by the conversion price. The formula is called the *conversion ratio.*

To protect the bondholders from dilution of their interest in the underlying equity, the conversion price is adjusted downward to reflect stock dividends, stock splits, subscription rights, or warrants to be distributed to the stockholders during the lifetime of that bond. In the illustration that follows, the conversion price would be adjusted to $20 to reflect a two-for-one split, to $36.36 for a 10% stock dividend, and so forth. Further protection against dilution is given to the bondholders when the indenture forbids primary distributions of additional stock by the corporation below the conversion price.

Example:

$$\frac{\$1,000}{\$40} \quad \text{(conversion price)} = 25 \text{ shares of stock}$$

Thus the holders of this bond can, at their option, exchange each bond for 25 shares of stock. It would not be sensible for them to do so, however, if the stock is trading below $40—say at $35. They would be changing a senior security worth about $1,000 for a junior security worth $875 (25 shares × $35). But if the stock price rises to $45, then 25 shares are worth $1,125, and, unless the price of the bond appreciates to at least that value at the same time, there is a financial advantage in converting that security.

(Unless the corporation calls their bonds for redemption, the holders are under no obligation to convert into stock at any time. An important

factor for them to consider is the difference in current yield between the convertible security and the underlying stock. The holders must weigh that distinction in light of their financial circumstances and objectives. Generally speaking, the bondholder is better off owning the convertible security, even after the stock begins trading above the conversion price. The convertible security normally trades above the value of the underlying stock and offers the better current yield.)

Parity. The ideal situation, simple in theory, is for the bond and its comparable stock to sell continuously at equal money values after the stock reaches its conversion price. Below that price, the bond should trade at its appropriate value for a debt instrument. Above that price, it would fluctuate directly with the movement of the underlying stock.

The term "should" is used because in reality it does not happen that way. In fact, the conversion feature acts as a lure for investors, causing the bond to trade above its theoretical value. Even when the stock is below its conversion price, the bond usually sells higher than a comparable straight debt security with the same credit rating and maturity. (Except when the stock is trading *far below* its conversion price, such as $16 when the conversion price is $45.)

As the stock approaches and exceeds the conversion price, the bond begins trading at a premium value over the market value of the stock.

Example:

Stock			Convertible Bond	
Shares		25	Actual bond market value	$ 1,100
	×	$40	Theoretical value	−1,000
Stock market value	$ 1,000	=	(A 10% premium)	$ 100

The textbook relationship of "equal money value" for a convertible security and its comparable stock is called *conversion parity.* The mathematical formula for conversion parity is:

$$\frac{\$1,000 \text{ par value of bond}}{\text{conversion price}} = \frac{\text{market price of bond}}{\text{market price of stock}}$$

The following examples illustrate this concept.

Example: What is the parity price of a bond convertible into common stock at $20 when the common stock is selling at 35?

$$\frac{\$1,000 \text{ (par)}}{\$20 \text{ (conversion price)}} = \frac{x}{35}$$
$$20x = (35)\ (\$1,000) = \$35,000$$
$$x = \$1,750$$

That is, when this bond is trading at 175 ($1,750), it is worth the same amount of money as the underlying stock selling at 35.

Example: What is the parity price of 80 shares of common stock receivable on conversion of a bond presently trading at 115 ($1,150)?

$$\frac{\$1,000}{\$12.50} = \frac{\$1,150}{x}$$
$$1,000x = (12.50)(\$1,150) = \$14.375$$
$$x = 14.375, \text{or} \$14\tfrac{3}{8}$$

(The conversion price of $12.50 is calculated by dividing $1,000 par value of the bond by the number of shares receivable. That is, $1,000 / 80 shares = 12½, or $12.50.) At $14⅜ per share, 80 shares of common stock are worth $1,150, the same value as the bond itself.

Example: What is the market price of a stock selling two points below parity when the bond has a *conversion ratio* (number of shares receivable) of 20 and is selling at 90 ($900)?

$$\frac{\$1,000}{\$50} = \frac{\$900}{x}$$
$$1,000x = (\$50)(\$900) = \$45,000$$
$$x = \$45$$

However, because the stock is selling two points *below* parity, the current price must be *$43!*

Example: What is the market value of a bond selling 20% above conversion parity if its conversion ratio is 45 and the underlying stock is at $53?

First, translate the conversion ratio into the conversion price, adapting it to the parity formula by dividing $1,000 par value by the ratio.

$$\frac{\$1,000}{45 \text{ shares}} = \$22.22 \text{ conversion price}$$

Then,

$$\frac{\$1,000}{\$22.22} = \frac{x}{\$53}$$
$$22.22x = \$53,000$$
$$x = \$2,385.24, \text{ or a bond price}$$
$$\text{of } 238.52$$

But that price is "parity." If the bond is actually trading 20% above that price it must be selling at a value equal to:

$$\$2,862.29\ [(\$2,385.24 \times .20) + \$2,385.24]$$

See also Arbitrage (Bonds); Conversion Price.

Quotations. Bond prices can be quoted in: (1) percentages, (2) whole numbers, (3) whole numbers and fractions, and (4) whole numbers and decimal points.

Conversion Price. To avoid the cumbersome fractions sometimes involved with conversion ratios, some corporations express convertibility in terms of a conversion price. The *conversion price* is simply a market value level for underlying common stock at which the preferred holder *may* find it economically feasible to convert into common stock. At the time of a preferred stock offering, the initial conversion price is often set from 10 to 15% above the prevailing market price of the common stock. This higher price helps to avoid the prospect of immediate or near-term conversion by the preferred stockholders, which would defeat the whole purpose of the offering.

The conversion price indirectly reveals the conversion ratio of the issue. When divided into the par value of each preferred share, the conversion price discloses the number of common shares receivable on exchange. The formula for determining the conversion ratio based on the conversion price and par value is:

$$\frac{\text{Common shares receivable}}{\text{upon conversion}} = \frac{\text{par value of preferred stock}}{\text{conversion price}}$$

This formula resolves the problems of dilution and the resulting cumbersome fractions. Even with adjustments, the conversion price figure rarely extends beyond the fourth decimal place. Moreover, investors relate easily to dollar prices in making value judgments regarding conversion feasibility.

Example: XYZ Industries issues a convertible preferred stock with a $100 par value and a $40.50 conversion price. Apply the conversion ratio formula:

$$\text{Common shares receivable} = \frac{\$100}{\$40.50}$$

$$\text{Common shares receivable} = 2.4691$$

To carry this example further, assume that, with the common stock at $36, the board of directors votes to split the common stock two for one. Because its preferred holders are protected against dilution, the conversion price must be halved to enable those investors to obtain twice as many shares as before, on conversion. To determine that price, first multiply the former shares receivable by the number of shares to be received for each share now held. Then divide the par value of the stock by that new number.

Step 1: $2.4691 \times 2 = 4.9382$

Step 2: $\dfrac{\$100 \text{ par value}}{4.9382} = \$20.25 \text{ conversion price}$

In an arithmetically efficient marketplace, the trading level of the old stock will also be adjusted. It should revise itself to a level where the total shares now receivable on conversion are worth the same amount of money as the old share package was worth at $36 per share. Thus:

Step 1: $\$36 \times 2.4691 = \$88.887$

Step 2: $\dfrac{\$88.887}{4.9382} = \$18 \text{ revised market price per share}$

Now assume that the board of directors votes to pay a 10% stock dividend soon after this with the common stock price still at $18 per share. Both the conversion price and the conversion ratio must be adjusted again. Using the same approach, the new conversion ratio is:

$4.9382 \times (\frac{1}{10} \text{ share per new share}) = 5.4320$ new shares obtainable upon conversion

The new conversion price becomes:

$$\frac{\$100 \text{ par value}}{5.4320} = \$18.409$$

The adjusted market level per share after the distribution is effective should be:

Before: $\$18 \times 4.9382 = \$88.887$

After: $\dfrac{\$88.887}{5.4320} = \$16.36 \text{ new market level per share}$

Determining a preferred stock's conversion ratio from its conversion price used to be a relatively simple chore; it was generally set at $100. Then, for certain sales and marketing reasons, increasing numbers of corporations began issuing $50 and $25 par value preferred stock. Since then, although the formula still works, it is difficult to calculate an accurate conversion ratio without knowing the specific par value of that particular issue.

When to Convert. Theoretically, the conversion price is a market level for common stock at which the convertible preferred stockholder may find it economically feasible to convert into common. In practice, it doesn't often work out that way unless the preferred issue is being retired by the corporation under an option it normally reserves for that purpose. Generally, convertible preferred stockholders are better off holding their shares or selling them in the open market. The reason is that, as the price of common stock rises near and through the conversion price, the convertible preferred stock invariably trades at a premium price, that is, at a value above the worth of the underlying common shares. This is caused by the preferred stock's usually higher dividend rate, its status as a security senior to the common stock, and its overall ability to enjoy the best features of both securities concurrently. It is important, however, to be able to determine the extent of premium at which the preferred sells above parity at any time. The premium is a critical basis on which value judgments are made in our efficient marketplace.

See also Conversion Ratio; Convertible Preferred Stock; Parity.

Conversion Ratio. The terms of convertibility are set at the time the corporation offers the issue in exchange for capital. It may state that this preferred stock shall always be convertible into two shares of common stock at the holder's option— or into 3.3 shares or 4½ shares or some other number that management deems necessary to make the preferred sale a success. When expressed in this fashion, the ratio of underlying common stock available for each share of convertible preferred is called the *conversion ratio*.

Not all corporations present conversion features in such terms. The conversion terms can become complicated in the event the corporation subsequently issues more common shares in the form of stock dividends or reorganizes its capital structure through a stock split. To provide for these and other potential maneuvers involving common stock, the corporation invariably guarantees the convertible preferred stockholders against dilution of their equity interest in the concern. The terms therefore guarantee that, in

such cases, preferred stockholders will be entitled to a proportionately larger number of common shares. This enables them to maintain the same percentage of underlying ownership in the company if and when they convert into common. As a result, the conversion ratio may become unwieldy, perhaps extending to as many as five or six decimal places, such as 3.21647 shares.

See also Conversion Price; Convertible Preferred Stock; Parity.

Convertible Bonds (Margin Trading). Convertible securities eligible for margin transactions are defined as margin debt securities. Specifically, convertible bonds eligible for margin are: (1) listed convertible bonds; (2) OTC convertible bonds on the list prepared by the Federal Reserve and approved for margin; and (3) listed and approved OTC bonds with warrants attached (often times referred to as a *unit*). Convertible bonds are eligible for trading on a margin basis in the margin account under the same conditions and rules as stocks. However, the initial Regulation T Margin requirements for convertible bonds and stocks may differ, even though both are classified as equity securities. As a matter of information, the requirements for convertible bonds and stocks have been the same (50%) since January, 1974. However, it should be kept in mind that the Federal Reserve has the authority to put different requirements into effect.

NYSE Minimum Maintenance Requirements. Long positions in convertible bonds are subject to the same requirements as common stocks, which is 25% of the current market value. This requirement for convertible bonds is calculated in exactly the same way as for common stocks.

Since both the convertible bonds and the common stock have the same requirements, both are treated the same for initial as well as minimum maintenance requirements.

See also Margin Account; Margin Transaction.

Convertible Preferred Stock. This type of preferred stock enables the stockholders to exchange their shares for a predetermined number of shares of common stock in the company any time they choose to do so. It is understandable that the value of this type of preferred stock is influenced by the fluctuations in price of the common stock because the holder enjoys the best features of both preferred and common stock at the same time. It is a very attractive feature and enables the corporation's directors to pay a lower fixed dividend on this issue than they would without it.

Although the common shares may be split up or down, stock dividends paid, or other distributions accomplished, the par value of preferred stock remains fixed for its entire lifetime. Any adjustments necessitated by those distributions are effected through changes in the preferred issue's conversion ratio and conversion price.

See also Callable Preferred Stock; Conversion Price; Conversion Ratio; Cumulative Preferred Stock; Parity; Participating Preferred Stock; Prior Preferred Stock.

Convertible Security. A convertible security is one that can be converted into another security.

Example: A convertible bond or convertible preferred stock may be converted into the underlying stock of the same corporation at a fixed rate. The rate at which the shares of the bond or preferred stock are converted into the common is called the conversion ratio.

Cooling-Off Period. *See* Twenty-Day Cooling-Off Period.

Corner. Although such instances are rare in modern times, situations have developed where one party (or a group of people) has acquired a substantial quantity of the available shares of a particular issue and, as a result, exerted influential pressure on its market price. This effect is particularly pronounced when that issue has built up a large short interest, and the borrowers suddenly find the certificates can be obtained only under exorbitant terms and conditions. The party or group who exercises such control establishes a powerful corner in the market. The premiums demanded are outrageous, and, often as not, the certificates are unavailable for any fee. It is the cornerer's intention to drive up the price by forcing the short seller to cover at any cost and at values determined arbitrarily. The classic corner created in Northern Pacific Railroad shares in the early twentieth century is recounted in the autobiography of the late Bernard Baruch.

See also Borrowing Stock Certificates; Lending at a Premium.

Corporate Accounts.

Cash Account. The following documents are required for cash accounts of corporate customers: (1) new account report form; (2) a copy of the charter or an excerpt from the bylaws giving the corporation authority to engage in securities transactions; and (3) a resolution from the board of directors authorizing specific people to act in behalf of the corporation (see the following figure).

In recognition of the fact that a trading resolution is not always obtainable for corporate cash accounts, especially when securities transactions are conducted on a C.O.D. basis. (C.O.D. stands for *cash on delivery.* Most institutional investors do not maintain continuing accounts at brokerage firms. Payments are made on delivery of certificates, and there are seldom either money or security balances on deposit at the firm in their behalf.) The NYSE recommends as a substitute measure (1) that a memorandum be signed by a member or allied member of the brokerage firm citing reasons for belief that the people named in the new account report form are authorized to do business in behalf of the corporation; and (2) that this memorandum be in-

Corporate Resolution, Full Authority [Page 1]

SIA form 105(a)

CORPORATION ACCOUNT

(AUTHORIZING TRADING IN SECURITIES AND COMMODITIES AND PERMITTING MARGIN TRANSACTIONS AND SHORT SALES)

Gentlemen:

The undersigned Corporation, by.. its President, pursuant to the resolutions, a copy of which, certified by the Secretary, is annexed hereto, hereby authorizes you to open an account in the name of said Corporation; and the undersigned also encloses herewith your Customer's Agreement and Consent to Loan of Securities duly executed on behalf of the Corporation. This authorization shall continue in force until revoked by the undersigned Corporation by a written notice, addressed to you and delivered at your office at...

Dated, ...

....
      (City)   **(State)**

Very truly yours,

....

By..
                                     President

I, ..., being the Secretary of ...., hereby certify that the annexed resolutions were duly adopted at a meeting of the Board of Directors of said Corporation, duly held on the............................... day of ...., at which a quorum of said Board of Directors was present and acting throughout and that no action has been taken to rescind or amend said resolutions and that the same are now in full force and effect.

I further certify that each of the following has been duly elected and is now legally holding the office set opposite his name:

                        , President
                        , Vice-President
                        , Treasurer
                        , Secretary

I further certify that the said Corporation is duly organized and existing and has the power to take the action called for by the resolutions annexed hereto.

IN WITNESS WHEREOF, I have hereunto affixed my hand this .... day of ...., 19.......

....
                                     Secretary

CERTIFIED COPY OF CERTAIN RESOLUTIONS ADOPTED BY THE BOARD OF DIRECTORS WHEREBY THE ESTABLISHMENT AND MAINTENANCE OF TRADING ACCOUNTS HAVE BEEN AUTHORIZED

RESOLVED—

FIRST: That the President or any Vice President of this Corporation, or   or   be and they hereby are, and each of them hereby is, authorized and empowered, for and on behalf of this Corporation (herein called the "Corporation"), to establish and maintain one or more accounts, which may be margin   accounts, with   (herein called the "Brokers") for the purpose of purchasing, investing in, or otherwise acquiring, selling (including short-sales), possessing, transferring, exchanging, pledging, or otherwise disposing of, or turning to account of, or realizing upon, and generally dealing in and with (a)* any and all forms of securities including, but not by way of limitation, shares, stocks, bonds, debentures, notes, scrip, participation certificates, rights to subscribe, option warrants, certificates of deposit, mortgages, choses in action, evidences of indebtedness, commercial paper, certificates of indebtedness and certificates of interest of any and every kind and nature whatsoever, secured or unsecured, whether represented by trust, participating and/or other certificates or otherwise; and (b)* any and all commodities and/or contracts for the future delivery thereof, whether represented by trust, participating and/or other certificates or otherwise.

The fullest authority at all times with respect to any such commitment or with respect to any transaction deemed by any of the said officers and/or agents to be proper in connection therewith is hereby conferred, including authority (without limiting the generality of the foregoing) to give written or oral instructions to the Brokers with respect to said transactions; to borrow money and securities and if transactions in commodities are authorized hereby to borrow commodities and/or future contracts in commodities, and to borrow such money, securities, commodities and/or future contracts in commodities from or through the Brokers, and to secure repayment thereof with the property of the Corporation; to bind and obligate the Corporation to and for the carrying out of any contract, arrangement, or transaction, which shall be entered into by any such officer and/or agent for and on behalf of the Corporation with or through the Brokers; to pay in cash or by checks and/or drafts drawn upon the funds of the Corporation such sums as may be necessary in connection with any of the said accounts; to deliver securities, contracts and/or commodity futures to the Brokers; to order the transfer or delivery thereof to any other person whatsoever, and/or to order the transfer of record of any securities, or contracts, or titles, to any name selected by any of the said officers or agents; to affix the corporate seal to any documents or agreements, or otherwise; to endorse any securities and/or contracts in order to pass title thereto; to direct the sale or exercise of any rights with respect to any securities; to sign for the Corporation all releases, powers of attorney and/or other documents in connection with any such account, and to agree to any terms or conditions to control any such account; to direct the Brokers to surrender any securities to the proper agent or party for the purpose of effecting any exchange or conversion, or for the purpose of deposit with any protective or similar committee, or otherwise; to accept delivery of any securities, contracts and/or commodity futures; to appoint any other person or persons to do any and all things which any of the said officers and/or agents is hereby empowered to do, and generally to do and take all action necessary in connection with the account, or considered desirable by such officer and/or agent with respect thereto.

SECOND: That the Brokers may deal with any and all of the persons directly or indirectly by the foregoing resolution empowered, as though they were dealing with the Corporation directly.

THIRD: That the Secretary of the Corporation be and he hereby is authorized, empowered and directed to certify, under the seal of the Corporation, or otherwise, to the Brokers:

(a) a true copy of these resolutions;
(b) specimen signatures of each and every person by these resolutions empowered;
(c) a certificate (which, if required by the Brokers, shall be supported by an opinion of the general counsel of the Corporation, or other counsel satisfactory to the Brokers) that the Corporation is duly organized and existing, that its charter empowers it to transact the business by these resolutions defined, and that no limitation has been imposed upon such powers by the By-Laws or otherwise.

Note: If either (a) or (b) in the first paragraph is not applicable please strike out the inapplicable part.

Corporate Resolution, Margin Account Authority
[Page 1]

ASEF—Form 105(b)—As of February, 1956—Printed May, 1960

CORPORATION ACCOUNT
(SECURITY CASH ACCOUNTS ONLY—FULL AUTHORITY)

Gentlemen:

The undersigned Corporation, by   its President, pursuant
to the resolutions, a copy of which, certified by the Secretary, is annexed hereto, hereby
authorizes you to open an account in the name of said Corporation; and the undersigned
represents that no one other than the undersigned has any interest in such account. The
undersigned also encloses herewith your Customer's Agreement duly executed on behalf
of the Corporation. This authorization shall continue in force until revoked by the undersigned Corporation by a written notice, addressed to you and delivered at your office at

....

Dated,...

....
            (City)   (State)

                                        Very truly yours,

                                        ....
                                        By...
                                                                    President

    I,   , being the Secretary of
                    , hereby certify that the annexed resolutions were duly adopted at a
meeting of the Board of Directors of said Corporation, duly held on the ....
day of ...., at which a quorum of said Board of Directors was present and
acting throughout and that no action has been taken to rescind or amend said resolutions
and that the same are now in full force and effect.

    I further certify that each of the following has been duly elected and is now legally
holding the office set opposite his name:

                                        , President
                                        , Vice-President
                                        , Treasurer
                                        , Secretary

    I further certify that the said Corporation is duly organized and existing and has the
power to take the action called for by the resolutions annexed hereto.

    IN WITNESS WHEREOF, I have hereunto affixed my hand this   day
of   , 19

                                        ....
                                                                    Secretary

Corporate Resolution, Margin Account Authority
[Page 2]

ASEF—Form 105(b)—*Continued*—As of February, 1956

CERTIFIED COPY OF CERTAIN RESOLUTIONS ADOPTED BY THE BOARD OF DIRECTORS WHEREBY THE ESTABLISHMENT AND MAINTENANCE OF SECURITY CASH ACCOUNTS HAVE BEEN AUTHORIZED

RESOLVED—

FIRST: That the President or any Vice-President of this Corporation, or   or   be and they hereby are, and each of them hereby is, authorized and empowered, for and on behalf of this Corporation (herein called the "Corporation"), to establish and maintain one or more accounts, with   (herein called the "Brokers") for the purpose of purchasing, investing in, or otherwise acquiring, selling, possessing, transferring, exchanging, or otherwise disposing of, or turning to account of, or realizing upon, and generally dealing in and with any and all forms of securities including, but not by way of limitation, shares, stocks, bonds, debentures, notes, scrip, participation certificates, rights to subscribe option warrants, certificates of deposit, mortgages, choses in action, evidences of indebtedness, commercial paper, certificates of indebtedness and certificates of interest of any and every kind and nature whatsoever, secured or unsecured, whether represented by trust, participating and/or other certificates or otherwise; but such authorization shall not include the opening of marginal accounts or the making of short sales.

The fullest authority at all times with respect to any such commitment or with respect to any transaction deemed by any of the said officers and/or agents to be proper in connection therewith is hereby conferred, including authority (without limiting the generality of the foregoing) to give written or oral instructions to the Brokers with respect to said transactions; to bind and obligate the Corporation to and for the carrying out of any contract, arrangement, or transaction, which shall be entered into by any such officer and/or agent for and on behalf of the Corporation with or through the Brokers; to pay in cash or by checks and/or drafts drawn upon the funds of the Corporation such sums as may be necessary in connection with any of the said accounts; to deliver securities to, and deposit funds with, the Brokers; to order the transfer or delivery of securities to any other person whatsoever, and/or to order the transfer of record of any securities to any name selected by any of the said officers or agents; to affix the corporate seal to any documents or agreements, or otherwise; to endorse any securities in order to pass title thereto; to direct the sale or exercise of any rights with respect to any securities; to sign for the Corporation all releases, powers of attorney and/or other documents in connection with any such account, and to agree to any terms or conditions to control any such account; to direct the Brokers to surrender any securities to the proper agent or party for the purpose of effecting any exchange or conversion, or for the purpose of deposit with any protective or similar committee, or otherwise; to accept delivery of any securities; to appoint any other person or persons to do any and all things which any of the said officers and/or agents is hereby empowered to do, and generally to do and take all action necessary in connection with the account, or considered desirable by such officer and/or agent with respect thereto.

SECOND: That the Brokers may deal with any and all of the persons directly or indirectly by the foregoing resolution empowered, as though they were dealing with the Corporation directly.

THIRD: That the Secretary of the Corporation be and he hereby is authorized, empowered and directed to certify, under the seal of the Corporation, or otherwise, to the Brokers:

    (a) a true copy of these resolutions;

    (b) specimen signatures of each and every person by these resolutions empowered;

    (c) a certificate (which, if required by the Brokers, shall be supported by an opinion of the general counsel of the Corporation, or other counsel satisfactory to the Brokers) that the Corporation is duly organized and existing, that its charter empowers it to transact the business by these resolutions defined, and that no limitation has been imposed upon such powers by the By-Laws or otherwise.

FOURTH: That the Brokers may rely upon any certification given in accordance with these resolutions, as continuing fully effective unless and until the Brokers shall receive due written notice of a change in or the rescission of the authority so evidenced, and the dispatch or receipt of any other form of notice shall not constitute a waiver of this provision, nor shall the fact that any person hereby empowered ceases to be an officer of the Corporation or becomes an officer under some other title, in any way affects the powers cluded in the customer's account file for at least six years following termination of this relationship with the firm.

Margin Account. The following documents are required for margin accounts of corporate customers: (1) new account report form; (2) a copy of the charter or an excerpt from the bylaws giving the corporation authority to engage in securities transactions on a credit or margin basis; (3) a resolution from the board of directors authorizing specific people to engage in margin credit transactions in behalf of the corporation (see figures on pages 94–95); (4) customer's agreement; (5) loan-consent agreement; and (6) a signed credit agreement.

In this instance, it is advisable not to engage in margin account transactions for any corporation until a specific resolution authorizing such activity is in hand.

See also Credit Agreement; Customer's Agreement; Loan-Consent Agreement; New Account Report Form; Unincorporated Associations.

Corporate Bond. Corporations employ various means, such as issuing stock, to raise capital. Their short-term requirements (five years or less) may be satisfied by bank loans, promissory notes, or certificates offered privately or publicly. For long-term borrowing of capital involving significant sums of money, corporations must turn to debt financing through an offering of bonds.

Bond offerings require considerable investor trust and confidence in the issuer's ability to honor an obligation over many years. As a result, small, relatively unknown, or asset-poor companies can be denied the ability to finance themselves by selling b₍

Sometimes, howev₍ ₎hese small, unknown corporations are affiliates or subsidiaries of much larger businesses that may be willing to pledge their own reputation or assets to secure such loans. The resulting debt instruments of the

subsidiary are then referred to as guaranteed bonds. Interest payments and/or principal repayments are backed or assured by the parent concern, a corporation other than the issuer. Using this technique, many local railroads were able to develop extensive trackage in the early years of the twentieth century.

Stocks Versus Bonds. The basic differences between stock and bonds are as follows:

Stock	*Bond*
A share of stock represents fractional *ownership* in the corporation	A bond certificate represents *creditorship* in a corporation.
An owner receives *dividends*, as earned and declared by the corporation.	A creditor receives *interest* that must be paid when due.
The *lifetime* of stock is *continuous* with the existence of the corporation.	The *lifetime* of a bond is *limited* to a specific maturity date when that obligation must be repaid.

Broadly speaking, it is frequently more advantageous for a corporation to borrow money than to obtain funds through the issuance of stock. In a period of continuing economic inflation, capital procured under current terms and conditions can be repaid at maturity in "cheaper dollars." Furthermore, interest requirements payable on debt instruments are fully deductible from the corporation's taxable income, whereas dividend distributions to stockholders represent after-tax, nondeductible earnings. For corporations in the 36% tax bracket, this means that the federal government is bearing 36% of the corporation's interest burden.

(Most bonds mature on a particular date twenty to thirty years after issuance. On rare occasions, a corporation may issue debt instruments without a maturity date. These are called perpetual bonds. Canadian Pacific 4% consolidated debentures are an example.)

These reasons do not necessarily mean that corporations with a borrowing capability should exercise this privilege. Only companies with an opportunity to generate greater income than the cost of issuing and carrying debt securities (excluding state and local tax requirements, if any) should use this measure as a means of *leveraging* their capital.

A company that borrows in this manner, hoping to increase significantly the return for the common stockholder, is said to be *trading on the equity*. This practice may prove to be perilous in declining cycles of the economy. The corporation continually faces a significant amount of preferential fixed charges that must be satisfied from current income before any stockholders can participate. It has literally traded for capital at the expense of its stockholders.

Types. Because bonds are debt securities, they are classified by the *type of protection* extended to creditors:

1. *Mortgage bonds* are backed by the pledge of the issuing corporation's real assets, such as real estate (*see* Prior Lien Bonds).

2. *Collateral trust bonds* are secured by the corporation's portfolio of securities, held in trust by a commercial bank.

3. *Equipment trust bonds* pledge machinery or equipment of the company.

4. *Debentures* are unsecured debt, backed only by the general assets of the firm.

Corporate Bond Transactions. Most bond transactions take place over the counter; that is, away from the trading floor of the registered securities exchanges in the United States. This is only partly due to the fact that comparatively few debt issues are listed for trading there. The NYSE's lenient application of trading regulations has enabled most bond activity to take place over the counter. Nevertheless, those bonds that are listed represent a significant amount of dollar value and importance in the marketplace.

With some exceptions, NYSE member firms with orders for listed stock traditionally execute those orders on the floor of the exchange. Listed bond orders have never been sub-

ject to that historical custom. This circumstance prevails because many bond traders and market-makers have always been nonmembers of the NYSE. Consequently, they have no ties to any exchange rules or traditions. Moreover, the NYSE never really promoted itself as a bond marketplace for general public participants because, until recent years, the bond market was strictly for professionals whereas the stock market was principally for the less-sophisticated, smaller investor able to assume financial risk.

As might be expected in light of its position in the securities industry, the NYSE does have a rule designed to protect the interests of the small bond investor. It requires members to provide these investors with the advantages of the exchange's centralized marketplace and prompt trade publicity (*see* Nine-Bond Rule).

Bond orders are sent to the floor of the exchange under different conditions and procedures than those used to handle stock orders. The physical facilities are much smaller than any of the stock trading areas and lack the recognizable presence of a trading post. All trading activity must take place within the outline of an octagonal diagram imbedded into a rubberized flooring in the center of the room. It is generally referred to as a *trading ring*.

Listed bonds are assigned trading privileges by either of two systems on appropriate determination by the Floor Department of the NYSE (*see* Active Bonds; Inactive Bonds).

Bond contracts on the NYSE settle in a number of ways (*see* Cash Contract; Next-Day Contract; Regular-Way Contract; Seller's-Option Contract; When-Issued/When- Distributed Contract).

The final consideration in any bond contract concerns payment of interest. Interest is not included in the contract price. Unless specified to the contrary, all bonds trade in the marketplace "and interest." The amount of applicable accrued interest associated with a debt obligation constitutes an additional expense to the purchaser and additional proceeds for the seller of that security. The issuing corporation normally pays interest only twice each year. So, if the bond is traded in the interim period, the new owner must advance the interest accruable from the last payment and expect reimbursement with the usual semiannual distribution.

Those bonds that are in default of interest payments or that promise to pay interest only when and if earned (that is, income bonds), trade flat in the marketplace. (On two days each year, even bonds that normally trade "and interest" will be traded flat—ex interest. This peculiarity occurs when the settlement date for a bond contract falls on the same day as the issuer's semiannual payment date for interest. The seller is then entitled to the interest accruable for the entire preceding period and will receive it from the corporation itself, instead of from the purchaser of that bond.) The contract price on these bonds is the only consideration exchanged between purchaser and seller. A purchaser has no future obligation to the former owner if the corporation eventually decides to make an interest distribution, either currently or cumulatively.

Corporation. There are three principal types of business organizations in the United States today: proprietorship, partnership, and corporation. the corporation developed because of the shortcomings and disadvantages associated with proprietorships and partnerships (*see* Individual Proprietorships; Partnerships). A corporation is a chartered association of individuals in a business enterprise.

If you form a corporation with other individuals, you gain two significant advantages: (1) Continuous existence of your business organization: On the retirement or death of a shareholder, the corporation's existence is unaffected. The corporation continues to function in legal perpetuity. Transferability of ownership is simple. (2) Limited financial liability for all investors:

Normally, as a shareholder (principal) in your corporation, you can be held financially liable and can suffer losses only to the extent of your investment in the corporation. Your personal assets and possessions are not subject to the claims of the creditors of your business.

These privileges are granted to the corporation and its principals by state statutes. The state's secretary validates the issuance of a charter to this association and permits it to exist as a recognized legal institution. As a result, corporations can obtain long-term, more permanent forms of capital through offerings of securities, with relative ease.

The corporate form of organization has its disadvantages too. They include: (1) increased record keeping and voluminous paper work: (2) many more taxes to be paid (and at higher rates) than other forms of business enterprise; and (3) closer governmental supervision. However, these shortcomings are outweighed by the corporation's important advantages.

Establishing the Corporation. The laws of incorporation vary from state to state, but many procedures are common to all fifty states. For instance, after the state Secretary approves the incorporation, a *certificate of incorporation* (or *charter*) is filed with the county clerk within the state and becomes a matter of public record. At least one petitioner for incorporation must be a citizen of the United States, although not necessarily a citizen or resident of the state in which incorporation is petitioned for.

Although the information required within the charter also varies according to individual state laws, important features, are, once again, common to all states. All states require the following:

1. *Name of the corporation.* The corporate name must be original and precise because, once approved by the state secretary, no other corporation in that state will be permitted to operate

using that name or a similar one in the same or similar line of endeavor.

2. *Names and addresses of the incorporators.* The number of persons necessary as incorporators can vary widely; it is as few as one in some states. In any event, this petition is generally filed by an attorney who represents the organizers and who frequently is cited as the principal founder in order to simplify and expedite proceedings. After approval, the lawyer assigns the stock to the true principals in proper proportion to their equity interest.

3. *Location of an office in the state of incorporation.*) Although it is not required to engage in business activities from this office, a corporation must maintain an official location within the state of incorporation to receive correspondence and/or subpoena. For simplicity and for tax reasons, many corporations in this country are chartered within the state of Delaware, where they use local concerns to represent them even though they are headquartered and actually do business thousands of miles away.

4. *Purpose of incorporation.* As a legal entity, a corporation may participate only in activities specifically approved by the state Secretary. In the securities industry, brokerage firms are particularly affected by this feature. To avoid almost certain litigation, they must not permit a corporation to use their services in arranging unauthorized purchases or sales of securities.

5. *Amount of capital stock authorized and issued.* The state Secretary permits the corporation to issue a maximum number of shares representative of its capital. It is identified as authorized stock in the charter. Otherwise, if the corporation had an unlimited, unrestricted privilege, they could dilute or "water" the participation of the already existent shareholders. Any increase in the number of authorized shares necessitates a petition to the state Secretary to amend the charter. This petition must be accompanied by evidence of overwhelming support for this proposal among the voting stockholders.

The corporate form of business and the issuance of securities to raise capital make the securities possible.

See also Bonds; Common Stock; Preferred Stock.

Coupon Rate. *See* Nominal Yield.

Court Review of SEC Orders. *See* Securities Exchange Act of 1934 (Section 25).

Cover. The purchase of a futures contract to offset a previously established short position.
See also Futures.

Covered Call Options. *See* Call Option.

Cover Short Transaction. *See* Margin Account (Short Account).

Credit Agreement. Under SEC Rule 10b-16, any broker/dealer extending credit to a customer in a margin account must disclose the terms and conditions under which such financing will be maintained. Most firms secure a signed credit agreement from customers to evidence their understanding and acceptance of these arrangements. The following figure shows a suggested agreement style; specific wording may vary markedly from firm to firm.
See also Customer's Agreement; Loan-Consent Agreement.

Credit Balance. The credit balance reflects the money held in the customer's margin account after all commitments have been paid in full. The abbreviation for credit balance is *Cr.*
See also Margin Account (Short Account).

Crossing Stock. Brokerage firms frequently receive orders in the same securities at the same

Members of the New York Stock Exchange, Inc.

One New York Plaza
New York, N.Y. 10004 (212) 747-7000

Salomon Brothers

_____
(Date)

Securities & Exchange Commission Rule 10b-16 requires brokers and dealers to furnish, and update as necessary, information concerning interest
charges to their customers. This letter is sent to you in compliance
with the requirements of that Rule and to acquaint you with the conditions
governing interest charges to your margin or other credit account by
Salomon Brothers.

Salomon Brothers charges you interest on the net debit balance in your
margin-type accounts. The net debit balance is the cost of securities
purchased less money deposited to finance these transactions. Accordingly, the net debit balance will vary with subsequent deposits or withdrawals of money and/or additional purchases and sales of securities.
In determining the net debit balance we also give you credit for free
cash balances in any other type of account you maintain with us. Those
cash balances are applied first against the debit balance in the margin-
type account bearing the highest rate of interest. Any excess is then
applied against the debit with the next highest rate, and so forth, until those cash balances are fully employed.

We do not charge interest on a short sale in your account because no
debit balance is created. However, if the margin requirement for the
short sale is satisfied by a deposit of securities, a debit may be
created by the need to give lenders our cash to collateralize the
borrowing of certificates required to settle the short sale transaction.
In any event, a subsequent adverse mark-to-the market in connection
with your short sale will lead to or increase a debit balance upon
which interest will be charged.

The rate of interest charged by Salomon Brothers is determined daily.
This Firm does not employ a fixed interest rate, and different methods
are used depending upon the type of security being financed. The
rates and methods are as follows:

-      In the case of U. S. Government and Government Agency securities,
       the interest rate charged will be 1/2% more than our highest ac-
       tual interest rate cost to borrow on U. S. Government and Govern-
       ment Agency securities collateral for that day;

-      In the case of corporate bonds and equities, the interest rate
       charged is dependent upon the amount of the debit balance and
       is based upon the highest Broker Call Loan rate printed in the
       Wall Street Journal for that day, plus a percentage as shown below:

Debit Balance	Percentage Premium Over Broker Call Loan Rate
Under $250,000	2 %
$250,001 - $500,000	1 1/2%
$500,001 - $1,000,000	1 %
Over $1,000,000	1/2%

Salomon Brothers

Therefore, the rate of interest charged on any particular day is subject to various factors and may rise or fall at any time without prior notice to you.

The formula used in calculating the interest dollars charged is the net debit balance for each day multiplied by the applicable rate of interest as described above, on the basis of a 360-day year.

Interest charges do not become a part of the debit balance until posted in the account toward the end of the calendar month, on a date that may vary from month to month. The posting date, the rates applied in the interim period between posting dates and the days on which they were applied will be identified on the monthly statement of account. We suggest you retain copies of these statements to enable you to verify our interest charges and your debit balances.

Unless payment for the interest charge is made promptly upon posting, further interest will be imposed upon this amount. The unpaid interest will be added to your debit balance so that this results in a compounding of the interest charged to you. There are no other charges as a result of our extension of credit to you.

If we extend credit to you in the form of a Reverse Repurchase Agreement, whether made on a day-by-day or a term basis, the above provisions are applicable; except that the interest rate we charge will be negotiated on a transaction-by-transaction basis. The formula for calculating the interest charge on the Agreement is the money paid to you for the actual number of days multiplied by the negotiated rate on the basis of a 360 day year. Unless the Agreement calls for installment payments during the term of the transaction, the interest is payable in full immediately upon completion of the transaction.

As a part of your Customer's Agreement or Reverse Repurchase Agreement with us, you have given us a general lien on all money, securities, commodities, or other property which we may at any time be carrying for you, or which may at any time be in our possession either for safekeeping or otherwise. They can be used to secure any and all of your obligations to us without regard to the accounts in which your property may be held. We may at any time require you to deposit cash or such additional collateral as, in our sole discretion, we determine is necessary as security for your obligation to us.

We believe that the foregoing fully sets forth the details of our policies and charges to you. If you have any questions, please do not hesitate to contact us.

Very truly yours,

SALOMON BROTHERS

time from different customers on opposite sides of the market.

Example: Customer Y wants to buy 100 shares of General Motors at the same time that Customer Z enters an order to sell 100 shares of General Motors.

Because all orders are transmitted to a centralized location on the floor of the stock exchange, it appears likely that the executing broker can pair off the buy order with the sell order in that security at the same time and price. This is known as a *cross*. However, before this is accomplished, several important conditions must prevail.

1. The transaction must be effected at the trading post assigned for activity in that security, within the framework of the existing quotation.

2. There must be at least a ¼ point *spread* (spread is the difference between the bid and offering prices) in the quotation at the time the broker enters the trading area. (When a spread is greater than ¼ point, the broker attempts to cross stock as close as possible to the price of the last sale in order to avoid charges of discrimination from either party to the transaction.) A ⅛ spread prevents a member from pairing off those orders because of inability to displace others represented at those prices (that is, brokers, representing other customers, who were in the trading area first).

Example: A quotation of 21–21⅛ leaves no room in between the bid and offering prices to arrange a cross. But a quotation of 21–21¼ provides an opportunity to pair off the orders at 21⅛.

3. The executing broker in a cross must give *either* the buyer or the seller a brief opportunity to improve on the price at which the broker can pair off those orders. This is done by momentarily either bidding ⅛ point lower or offering ⅛ point higher than the price at which the cross will be arranged.

Example: To illustrate the mechanical features of this procedure, assume that a quotation is 70–70¼ in General Electric Corp. shares when Broker A enters the trading area intent on crossing 100 shares of stock at 70⅛. After inquiring about the current quotation, Broker A can achieve this objective by announcing *either* (1) "70 for 100,...100 at 70⅛, take it;" or (2) "100 at 70¼...70⅛ for 100, sold."

In (1), the broker attempts to improve on price for the buyer by momentarily bidding 70 for 100 shares. If another broker had a multiple round-lot sell order in the crowd, the broker could have interrupted that cross and sold the stock at 70 to the buyer represented in the trading area before the entry of Broker A and to Broker A, as well.

In (2), Broker A offers 100 shares momentarily at 70¼, trying to do better for the seller before accepting the bid at 70⅛. If a substantial buyer of that stock was in the trading crowd, that broker could have interrupted the cross by purchasing stock from the offeror represented first at 70¼, as well as from Broker A's customer.

By observing this last rule, at least one customer can enjoy a price benefit derived from a bona fide open auction market. That customer does not rely entirely on an arbitrary price set by the broker, as would otherwise be the case.

See also Bid and Offer.

Cum Rights. This term is applied to a stock trading in the marketplace "with subscription rights attached," which are reflected in the price of that security.

See also Theoretical Value.

Cumulative Preferred Stock. This type of preferred stock permits a stockholder to lay claim to any dividends that were omitted by the corporation in previous years. "Cumulative" means that any deferred dividends will accumulate, and it requires that this arrearage be paid in full before any distribution is permitted to the common stockholder. A noncumulative preferred stock offers no such assurance to its holders. Any dividends passed are gone forever and no longer represent a commitment by the corporation to those stockholders.

See also Callable Preferred Stock; Convertible Preferred Stock; Participating Preferred Stock; Prior Preferred Stock.

Cumulative Voting. In this type of voting, you as a stockholder are allocated one vote for each share you hold. But each share is then multiplied by the total number of proposals on the agenda or the total number of vacancies to be filled on the board of directors, as the case may be. You may then apportion your total vote as you desire.

Example: As the owner of 100 shares, you can apportion 500 votes any way you want among the five nominees for the five directorships to be filled at that election.

Sample Voting Combinations for a Stockholder Owning 100 Shares

	Nominee A	Nominee B	Nominee C	Nominee D	Nominee E
Choice 1	500	0	0	0	0
Choice 2	100	300	0	100	0
Choice 3	0	400	100	0	0
Choice 4	200	100	0	0	200

Any such combinations of vote placement are acceptable in cumulative voting as long as you do not cast more than 500 votes for a single nominee or the entire slate of directors as a whole. It is possible, therefore, for minority holders to concentrate their votes, cast them for just a few proposals (directors) that they favor, and significantly increase the probability of passage (election) for their choices.

See also Statutory Voting; Voting Trust.

Currency in Circulation. *See* Money.

Current Liability. Current liabilities are debts of the corporation that are scheduled for payment within one year. A quick comparison of current liabilities with current assets determines, as accountants do, whether the company has enough money to stay in business: Since current assets, at least in theory, represent the source from which current liabilities are paid, we want to know how the debts compare with the assets.

Current liabilities might include: (1) *accounts payable*, the amount the company owes to its business creditors; (2) *accrued expenses*, amounts owed to its salespeople in salaries and wages, interest on debt, and all other unpaid items; (3) *accrued taxes*, federal, state, and local taxes owed, social security (FICA) deductions, and local government levies withheld from employees; (4) *notes payable*, monies owed to banks, to other lenders, or on outstanding bonds that are due to be paid within the year.

Example: The current liabilities section of the balance sheet of a typical manufacturing corporation reads:

Accounts payable	$200,000
Accrued expenses	150,000
Accrued taxes	+ 50,000
Total current liabilities	$400,000

See also Balance Sheet (Assets); Fixed Liability.

Current Market. *See* Bid and Offer.

Current Ratio. Working with a dollar figure for working capital is rather difficult, especially when comparing one company with another. Dollars alone do not tell the whole story. A company may have only a modest amount of current liabilities, requiring a relatively small amount of working capital. Or its current liabilities may be very large, requiring many more dollars of working capital for safety's sake. Of primary importance, therefore, is the proportion by which current assets exceed current liabilities. To arrive at this ratio, called the *current ratio*, divide current assets by current liabilities:

$$\text{Current ratio} = \frac{\text{Current assets}}{\text{Current liabilities}}$$

Example: Using the figures from the previous section on working capital:

$$\text{Current ratio} = \frac{\$1,000,0000}{\$\ \ \ 400,000} = 2.5$$

The current ratio, 2.5, means that this corporation can cover its current liabilities two and a half times over. In other words, for every dollar of current liabilities, it has 2.5 dollars of current assets.

The current ratio may be expressed in a variety of ways:

2.5 or 2½ or 2.5 × or 2½ times
or 2.5 to 1 or 2½ to 1 or 2½/1

A "good" current ratio, for the typical manufacturing company, is 2 to 1 or higher. For a company with easily collectable receivables, like a public utility, a current ratio as low as 1 to 1 may be acceptable.

See also Balance Sheet.

Current Yield. Bonds do not trade in the marketplace at par value. Almost all trade at either a discount or premium. As a result, comparing nominal yields does not permit investors to compare the return on one bond with other bonds issued previously under different rates and money market conditions. To provide a means of valid comparison despite price fluctuations, most public investors rely on calculation of current yield.

The *current yield* gauges the return on an investment by relating the stated interest rate to the actual number of dollars needed to purchase that security. Current yield is calculated by the following formula:

$$\frac{\text{Annual interest payment}}{\text{current market price}} = \text{current yield (in decimal equivalent)}$$

Example: A bond with a nominal yield of 5% (paying $50 annually) and a market value of $990 would have a current yield of 5.05%.

$$\frac{\$50}{\$990} = 0.0505 \text{ (decimal equivalent), or } 5.05\%$$

If that same bond were trading at a value of $1,100, the current yield would only be approximately 4.55%.

$$\frac{\$50}{\$1,100} = .0505 \text{ (decimal equivalent), or } 5.05\%$$

See also Bonds (Quotations); Discount; Nominal Yield; Premium; Yield to Maturity.

Cushion Theory. *See* Short Interest Theory.

Customer Assistance Program. *See* New York Stock Exchange, Inc.

Customer's Agreement. This document sets forth the privileges and conditions under which the firm will finance customer credit transactions. Federal law requires that this document, signed by the customer, be secured before a margin account can be established. The customer's agreement is also known as a *hypothecation agreement* or *margin agreement* (*see* the following figure).

See also Credit Agreement; Loan-Consent Agreement.

Customer-Side Settlement. *See* Cash Account.

CUSTOMER'S AGREEMENT

Gentlemen:

In consideration of your accepting one or more accounts of the undersigned (whether designated by name, number or otherwise) and your agreeing to act as brokers for the undersigned in the purchase or sale of securities or commodities, the undersigned agrees as follows:

1. All transactions under this agreement shall be subject to the constitution, rules, regulations, customs and usages of the exchange or market, and its clearing house, if any, where the transactions are executed by you or your agents, and, where applicable, to the provisions of the Securities Exchange Act of 1934, the Commodities Exchange Act, and present and future acts amendatory thereof and supplemental thereto, and the rules and regulations of the Federal Securities and Exchange Commission, the Board of Governors of the Federal Reserve System and of the Secretary of Agriculture in so far as they may be applicable.

2. Whenever any statute shall be enacted which shall affect in any manner or be inconsistent with any of the provisions hereof, or whenever any rule of regulation shall be prescribed or promulgated by the New York Stock Exchange, the Federal Securities and Exchange Commission, the Board of Governors of the Federal Reserve System and/or the Secretary of Agriculture which shall affect in any manner or be inconsistent with any of the provisions hereof, the provisions of this agreement so affected shall be deemed modified or superseded, as the case may be, by such statue, rule or regulation, and all other provisions of the agreement and the provisions as so modified or superseded, shall in all respects continue and be in full force and effect.

3. Except as herein otherwise expressly provided, no provision of this agreement shall in any respect be waived, altered, modified or amended unless such waiver, alteration, modification or amendment be committed to writing and signed by a member of your organization.

4. All monies, securities, commodities or other property which you may at any time be carrying for the undersigned or which may at any time be in your possession for any purpose, including safekeeping, shall be subject to a general lien for the discharge of all obligations of the undersigned to you, irrespective of whether or not you have made advances in connection with such securities, commodities or other property, and irrespective of the number of accounts the undersigned may have with you.

5. All securities and commodities or any other property, now or hereafter held by you, or carried by you for the undersigned (either individually or jointly with others), or deposited to secure the same, may from time to time and without notice to me, be carried in your general loans and may be pledged, repledged, hypothecated or re-hypothecated, separately or in common with other securities and commodities or any other property, for the sum due to you thereon or for a greater sum and without retaining in your possession and control for delivery a like amount of similar securities or commodities.

6. Debit balances of the accounts of the undersigned shall be charged with interest, in accordance with your usual custom, and with any increases in rates caused by money market conditions, and with such other charges as you may make to cover your facilities and extra services.

7. You are hereby authorized, in your discretion, should the undersigned die or should you for any reason whatsoever deem it necessary for your protection, to sell any or all of the securities and commodities or other property which may be in your possession, or which you may be carrying for the undersigned (either individually or jointly with others), or to buy in any securities, commodities or other property of which the account or accounts of the undersigned may be short, or cancel any outstanding orders in order to close out the account or accounts of the undersigned in whole or in part or in order to close out any commitment made in behalf of the undersigned. Such sale, purchase or cancellation may be made according to your judgment and may be made, at your discretion, on the exchange or other market where such business is then usually transacted, or at public auction or at private sale, without advertising the same and without notice to the undersigned or to the personal representatives of the undersigned, and without prior tender, demand or call of any kind upon the undersigned or upon the personal representatives of the undersigned, and you may purchase the whole or any part thereof free from any right of redemption, and the undersigned shall remain liable for any deficiency; it being understood that a prior tender, demand or call of any kind from you, or prior notice from you, of the time and place of such sale or purchase shall not be considered a waiver of your right to sell or buy any securities and/or commodities and/or other property held by you, or owed you by the undersigned, at any time as hereinbefore provided.

8. The undersigned will at all times maintain margins for said accounts, as required by you from time to time.

9. The undersigned undertakes, at any time upon your demand, to discharge obligations of the undersigned to you, or, in the event of a closing of any account of the undersigned in whole or in part to pay you the deficiency, if any, and no oral agreement or instructions to the contrary shall be recognized or enforceable.

10. In case of the sale of any security, commodity, or other property by you at the direction of the undersigned and your inability to deliver the same to the purchaser by reason of failure of the undersigned to supply you therewith, then and in such event, the undersigned authorizes you to borrow any security, commodity, or other property necessary to make delivery thereof, and the undersigned hereby agrees to be responsible for any loss which you may sustain thereby and any premiums which you may be required to pay thereon, and for any loss which you may sustain by reason of your inability to borrow the security, commodity, or other property sold.

11. At any time and from time to time, in your discretion, you may without notice to the undersigned apply and/or transfer any or all monies, securities, commodities and/or other property of the undersigned interchangeably between any accounts of the undersigned (other than from Regulated Commodity Accounts).

Customer's Agreement [Back]

12. It is understood and agreed that the undersigned, when placing with you any sell order for short account, will designate it as such and hereby authorizes you to mark such order as being "short", and when placing with you any order for long account, will designate it as such and hereby authorizes you to mark such order as being "long". Any sell order which the undersigned shall designate as being for long account as above provided, is for securities then owned by the undersigned and, if such securities are not then deliverable by you from any account of the undersigned, the placing of such order shall constitute a representation by the undersigned that it is impracticable for him then to deliver such securities to you but that he will deliver them as soon as it is possible for him to do so without undue inconvenience or expense.

13. In all transactions between you and the undersigned, the undersigned understands that you are acting as the brokers of the undersigned, except when you disclose to the undersigned in writing at or before the completion of a particular transaction that you are acting, with respect to such transaction, as dealers for your own account or as brokers for some other person.

14. Reports of the execution of orders and statements of the accounts of the undersigned shall be conclusive if not objected to in writing, the former within two days, and the latter within ten days, after forwarding by you to the undersigned by mail or otherwise.

15. Communications may be sent to the undersigned at the address of the undersigned given below, or at such other address as the undersigned may hereafter give you in writing, and all communications so sent, whether by mail, telegraph, messenger or otherwise, shall be deemed given to the undersigned personally, whether actually received or not.

16. Any controversy between you and the undersigned arising out of or relating to this contract or the breach thereof, shall be settled by arbitration, in accordance with the rules, then obtaining, of either the Arbitration Committee of the Chamber of Commerce of the State of New York, or the American Arbitration Association, or the Board of Arbitration of the New York Stock Exchange, as the undersigned may elect. If the undersigned does not make such election by registered mail addressed to you at your main office within five (5) days after receipt of notification from you requesting such election, then the undersigned authorizes you to make such election in behalf of the undersigned. Any arbitration hereunder shall be before at least three arbitrators and the award of the arbitrators, or of a majority of them, shall be final, and judgment upon the award rendered may be entered in any court, state or federal, having jurisdiction.

17. This agreement and its enforcement shall be governed by the laws of the State of New York and its provisions shall be continuous; shall cover individually and collectively all accounts which the undersigned may open or re-open with you, and shall enure to the benefit of your present organization, and any successor organization, irrespective of any change or changes at any time in the personnel thereof, for any cause whatsoever, and of the assigns of your present organization or any successor organization, and shall be binding upon the undersigned, and/or the estate, executors, administrators and assigns of the undersigned.

18. The undersigned, if an individual, represents that the undersigned is of full age, that the undersigned is not an employee of any exchange, or of any corporation of which any exchange owns a majority of the capital stock, or of a member of any exchange, or of a member firm or member corporation registered on any exchange, or of a bank, trust company, insurance company or of any corporation, firm or individual engaged in the business of dealing, either as broker or as principal, in securities, bills of exchange, acceptances or other forms of commercial paper. The undersigned further represents that no one except the undersigned has an interest in the account or accounts of the undersigned with you.

Very truly yours,

Witness...

Dated, ...

....
(Signature)

....

....
(City)   (State)

D

Daily Bond Buyer. An important source of information to the municipal bond professional is the *Daily Bond Buyer*. Besides news of specific importance to the municipal trade, information about pending offerings and official notices of sale are also found. Some of the most important statistical measures found in the *Bond Buyer* are:

1. 20-Bond Index: A sampling of medium-quality (Baa) to high-quality (Aaa) bonds with twenty-year maturities, indicating a hypothetical composite "bid" by a dealer. if the index was at 6.25% it would give an indication of the rate *new* issues would have to be offered in order to compete with *outstanding* issues.

2. 11-Bond Index: Contains only high-grade (Aa, Aaa) issues drawn from the 20-bond index and thus has a lower yield than the 20-bond index. (Lower quality equals high yield, while higher quality equals low yield.)

3. Placement Ratio: The number of bonds sold to the public compared to those offered for sale as new issues during that week. A high placement ratio (90% or more) indicates successful reception by the investing public of the new offering compiled as of Thursday's figures each week. The placement ratio is sometimes referred to as the *acceptance ratio*.

4. 30-Day Visible Supply: Anticipated new offerings announced for sale within the next thirty days. It gives an idea of the supply "overhanging" the market at a given time. The amount excludes short-term offerings.

The *Bond Buyer* also provides a subscription wire service geared to the municipal bond trade. This service, *Munifacts*, is similar to the Dow Jones or Reuter News services, but is aimed at the corporate securities and commodities professional.

Currently there are four independent municipal bond rating services: (1) Moody's Investors Service, (2) Standard & Poor's Corporation, (3) Fitch's Investor Service, and (4) White's Tax-Exempt Bond Market Ratings.

Bonds rated Baa or higher by Moody's and BBB or higher by Standard & Poor's are considered *investment grade*. The top four ratings are also known as *bank quality*, due to the fact that federal law permits commercial banks to purchase these investment-grade bonds for their own portfolio. White's Tax-Exempt Bond Market Rating reflects the value of municipal bonds based on a numbering system.

Example: If a 6.00% bond has a rating of 100, then a bond rated 94 yields 6.30%. Each point on the White's scale represents five basis points (A basis point is 1/100 of 1% [.01%].)

Daisy Chains. These patterns of continuous buying and/or selling activity in the same issue by the same customer, or with the same broker, and at successively higher or lower prices are typical of the repurchase agreements prohibited by the SEC.

See also Manipulation of Security Prices and Deceptive Devices.

Dated Date. *See* Municipal Security (Organization of the Syndicate).

Day Order. This order is one that remains valid only for the remainder of the trading day on which it is entered. Unless specified to the contrary, all orders are automatically regarded as day orders. The New York Stock Exchange accepts only day orders or good-til-cancelled orders.

See also Good-Til-Cancelled Order.

Dealer. Any person or firm buying and selling securities for a personal account as part of a regular business.

Debenture. This is an *unsecured* debt offering of a corporation. It promises only the general assets (sometimes referred to merely as "goodwill and reputation") as protection for the holders of these securities. Debentures are most often offered as subordinated debt instruments by corporations. This means that, although they are classified as liabilities of a given corporation, they are junior in ranking (or subordinate) to the claims of all other creditors in the event of dissolution. Holders of a subordinated debenture realize that, as unsecured creditors of the corporation, they have a claim-to-asset priority only over stockholders in the company.

Only companies with superior credit ratings or corporations that are fixed-asset-poor are capable of marketing debentures successfully. The corporation with a high credit rating is able to borrow at lower rates of interest than one with no rating or no assets at all. The rate of interest on any loan is directly related to the degree of risk involved. High risk equals high interest expense for the borrower to compensate the creditors for their financial exposure.

See also Collateral Trust Bond; Equipment Trust Bond; Mortgage Bond.

Debit Balance. In a margin account the broker holds the customer's securities as collateral in street name so that they are readily negotiable. This enables the broker to promptly liquidate or sell the securities in the event the customer fails to maintain a proper level of margin in the account. The customer's loan, or debit balance, is an open-ended collateralized loan. This means that there are no specific time limits on the loan nor are specific installments or dollar payments required. The customer may leave the loan open for as long as he or she chooses, provided the broker remains satisfied with the condition of the customer's account. Specifically, the broker continually follows the securities in the customer's account and compares their market value to the loan (debit balance). As long as the market value of the collateral exceeds the amount of the loan by a sufficient amount the broker will permit the loan to remain open. In short, *debit balance* is the amount of money owed to the broker by the customer as a result of transactions in an account. The abbreviation for debit balance is *Dr.*

See also Credit Balance; Margin Account.

Declaration Date. On this date a corporation's board of directors convenes a meeting, decides on a distribution, and makes a public announcement of the distribution.

See also Distribution Dates.

Deferred Futures. The most distant months on a futures market.

See also Futures.

Deficiency Letter. If the SEC finds omissions or misrepresentations in a registration statement, it sends the corporation a *deficiency letter* explaining its position on the matter. The *effective date* of a registration statement is delayed or postponed indefinitely until that deficiency has been corrected. No distribution may proceed prior to the effective date, and even subtle offers to sell the issue to be offered before that time constitute a violation of the law.

Despite its vigilance and conscientiousness, the SEC never guarantees the adequacy or accuracy of any registration statement. The public's assurance of protection is found under sections of the Securities Act of 1933 regarding civil liability. The law gives an investor the opportunity to bring suit for reimbursement of financial losses sustained. The investor has authority to collect from: (1) the officers of the corporation; (2) the directors of the corporation; (3) the principal stockholders in the corporation (holders of 10% or more of the outstanding common stock); (4) the investment bankers who act as underwriters; and (5) anyone whose name voluntarily appears in the registration statement.

Purchasers must be prepared to prove that they lost money because of the incomplete or distorted material information presented in this solicitation. Omission of material fact and/or misrepresentation of fact are the two bases under which purchasers of a public offering can recoup their investment. Disgruntled investors cannot collect on "paper losses" (unrealized), nor can they collect under this Act unless purchase was effected from this particular distribution. Transactions in the open market after the offering are not usually subject to the terms of the Securities Act of 1933, but may fall instead within the jurisdiction of the Securities Exchange Act of 1934.

See also Effective Date; Public Offering; Registration Statement; Securities Act of 1933; Securities Act of 1934.

Delivery. In futures trading, the tender and receipt of an actual commodity or financial instrument or cash in settlement of a futures contract.

See also Futures.

Delivery Dates (Settlement Dates). Four basic contracts are recognized in the Uniform Practice Code of the NASD: the regular-way contract, the Seller's Option contract, the cash contract, and the when-issued or when-distributed contract. Each one calls for a different settlement date (delivery of certificates from selling firm to purchasing firm). If a previously established settlement date is declared a holiday, delivery is postponed until the following business day. The term "business day" is used throughout the UPC, and in particular when referring to settlement and delivery, to mean any day on which the securities industry is open and conducting business. However, on several days during the year, the banking system is closed and the securities industry is open. Those days are good business days for purposes of the Code, although they cannot be contract settlement dates for transaction purposes.

Example: The Columbus Day holiday is a prime illustration of this occurrence. Although the stock market is open, the banks in New York City and most other sections of the country are closed. Consequently, if ordinary settlement-day calculations would result in a delivery on this day, settlement will be deferred until the following business day.

Note, too, that the Federal Reserve Board, through its Regulation T, recognizes such bank holidays to be good business days for determining when payments for purchases are due, when extensions of time may be requested or will expire, and, if necessary, when liquidation of a securities position should take place.

See also Cash Contract; Seller's Option Contract; Regular-Way Contract; When-Issued or When-Distributed Contract.

Delivery Notice In futures trading, the written notice given by the seller of his intention to make delivery against an open, short futures position on a particular date.

See also Futures.

Delivery Options Contract.

Seller's Option. Delivery of the certificates to the purchaser's office is due on the date specified in the terms of the contract. The delivery period is normally expressed as a number of calendar days following the day of the trade and would not be shorter than the period prescribed for a regular-way contract in a given security.

Example: "Seller's 24," "seller's 39."

A contract marked "seller's 25" and transacted on March 11 is due April 5 (there are twenty days left in March plus the 5 in April).

		MARCH				
S	M	T	W	T	F	S
		1	2	3	4	5
6	7	8	9	10	11	12
13	14	15	16	**17**	18	19
20	21	22	23	24	25	26
27	28	29	30	31		

		APRIL				
S	M	T	W	T	F	S
					1	2
3	4	5	6	7	**8**	9
10	11	12	13	14	15	16
17	18	19	20	21	22	23
24	25	26	27	28	29	30

The Uniform Practice Code does not set a maximum number of days on a seller's-option contract, but the New York Stock Exchange limits its members to a sixty-day calendar period. This limit has become commonly accepted by most NASD members, too.

The Code provides the means to shorten the number of days for settlement after an option contract has been established. All the seller need do is give the purchasing firm one business day's written notice that delivery of the certificate is scheduled for the following day and full payment from the purchaser is expected at that time. However, written notice cannot be given before the fifth business day after the trade.

Example: A corporate security traded "seller's 20" can be delivered to the purchaser on the sixth business day after the trade date, but no earlier. This is accomplished simply by giving written notice to the purchasing firm on the fifth business day and making physical delivery the next day.

Buyer's Option. Delivery of the certificates is expressed as a number of calendar days following the trade date. Delivery is due on the date specified in the terms of the contract at the time of the transaction.

Example: "Buyer's 10," "buyer's 17."

If the seller delivers the certificates before that time, the purchaser may refuse to accept and pay for them without prejudicing any rights in the contract.

See also Cash Contract; Delivery Dates; Regular-Way Contract; When-Issued or When-Distributed Contract.

Delivery Points. In futures trading, those points designated by futures exchanges at which the financial instruments or commodity covered by a futures contract may be delivered in fullfillment of the contract.

See also Futures.

Delivery Price. In futures trading, the price fixed by the clearing house at which deliveries on futures are invoiced; also the price at which the futures contract is settled when deliveries are made.

See also Futures.

Demand Deposit. In this type of account, the owner retains the ability to withdraw funds at any time, without giving prior notice of his or her intention to do so. All business and personal checking accounts, as well as commercial and individual loans are, in fact, demand deposits. Loans are recognized as demand deposits because the borrower is either given a negotiable check for the proceeds or has a deposit account created with power to draw checks on the credit balance as money is needed.

See also Certificate of Deposit (CD); Savings Deposit; Time Deposit.

Depository Trust Company. This member bank of the Federal Reserve System was founded specifically to safeguard securities and facilitate delivery between participating broker/dealers and banks. Although it is now wholly owned and organized by the New York Stock Exchange, it is expected that equity interest and control will eventually be divided as follows: 60% by the banking community members, 20% by the New York Stock Exchange, and 20% by the American Stock Exchange.

Currently operating as an independent entity reporting to the executive vice-president of the NYSE, Depository Trust Company, Inc. (DTC) is a quasi-cashiering department for members of the SCC. Its services extend into several areas:

1. DTC holds on deposit in its vault many stock and bond certificates of issues listed on the NYSE and AMEX as well as selected over-the-counter securities, thus reducing the potential for loss and theft; and lowering the incidence of bookkeeping errors resulting from the inevitable shuffling of certificates within and between firms in the course of daily activity. (All certificates are registered in the name of CEDE, a nominee partnership entity, with contingent stock or bondholder privileges, such as interest, dividends, proxies, subscription rights, and so on, apportioned among members according to their contributions of certificates to this pool.)

2. DTC arranges for collateral loan service on request without actually surrendering physical possession of the certificates to the lending institution. Credit is extended to those firms based on appropriate bookkeeping entries on the records of DTC.

3. DTC automatically and electronically arranges for "delivery" of securities to satisfy contracts by debiting the seller's account records

and crediting the recipient's records with quantity figures obtained from the volume clearance process. The certificates remain physically immobilized in the DTC vault throughout the entire transaction.

See also Broker/Dealer Organization (Cashiering Department); New York Stock Exchange, Inc.; Stock Clearing Corporation.

Depreciation. As fixed assets grow older, they decrease in value due to ordinary wear and tear, action of the elements, or obsolescence. Since a company's balance sheet attempts to list everything owned by the corporation at current value, the value at which fixed assets are shown declines as the assets get older. When a fixed asset is acquired by the corporation, it is not charged as a business expense in the year it is purchased. Since a fixed asset is expected to last quite a few years, the company charges it as an expense a little at a time, spread over the years it is supposed to be usable to the company. By way of analogy, assume that you as an individual (were it legal!) could spread out a deductible personal expense of $5,000 for a car. Instead of taking the full $5,000 deduction in the year in which you incurred the actual expense, you might instead deduct $1,000 a year for five consecutive years, thus spreading out the expense. Such spreading out of the expense is legal for the corporation. The amount by which the fixed assets are lowered each year is the portion of the cost of fixed assets charged as an expense for a given year; that portion is called *annual depreciation* and is listed as such.

Net Cost. When a fixed asset is purchased, the company determines how long the asset is expected to be used; this is its *useful life.* It also determines the value that it expects to receive when the asset is scrapped; this is its *salvage value.* The cost of the asset is considered to be the initial price minus the salvage value, because the salvage value will be received some time after the item is purchased. In most cases, this net cost figure is the amount depreciated over the item's useful life, not the full price paid. The simple equation is:

Net cost = Actual cost – Salvage value

Example: In each of the following examples for determining the amount of depreciation, the fixed asset is purchased for $40,000; it is expected to have a useful life of five years and a salvage value of $10,000.

$$Net cost = Actual cost - Salvage value$$
$$= \$40,000 - \$10,000$$
$$= \$30,000$$

(A practice that is accepted by the Internal Revenue Service is to ignore any salvage value of less than 10%. Since both depreciation and salvage value are estimates anyway, the practice makes sense. In our examples, we will always use salvage values.)

Fixed assets may be depreciated by two principal methods; (1) straight-line and (2) accelerated cost recovery system.

Straight-Line Depreciation. This is the simplest and most commonly used method. To determine the amount of each year's depreciation, divide the net cost of the item (actual cost — salvage value) by the number of years of useful life.

$$Annual depreciation = \frac{Net cost}{Years of useful life}$$

Example:

$$Annual depreciation = \frac{\$30,000}{5} = \$6,000$$

Fixed assets are carried at cost less accumulated depreciation. At the end of the item's first year of use, the fixed asset section of the balance sheet shows:

Fixed Assets

Cost	$40,000
Accumulated depreciation	–6,000
	$34,000

The annual write-off (depreciation) is the same in years 2 through 5. At the end of the second year, the accumulated depreciation is $12,000 ($6,000 from year 1 plus $6,000 form year 2), and the balance sheet shows:

Fixed Assets

Cost	$40,000
Accumulated depreciation	–12,000
	$28,000

By year 5, accumulated depreciation totals up to $30,000, and the asset has been "written down" to a carrying value of $10,000, its salvage value. The total picture in chart form is shown in the following figure:

Straight-Line Depreciation Illustration

Year	Annual Depreciation	Accumulated Depreciation	Asset's Balance Sheet Value
1	$30,000 ÷ 5 = $6,000	$6,000	$34,000
2	30,000 ÷ 5 = 6,000	12,000	28,000
3	30,000 ÷ 5 = 6,000	18,000	22,000
4	30,000 ÷ 5 = 6,000	24,000	16,000
5	30,000 ÷ 5 = 6,000	30,000	10,000

Note that each year's depreciation is 20% of the net cost of the fixed asset since we are working with a useful life of five years (100% ÷ 5 = 20%).

Accelerated Cost Recovery System. A change in the tax law has effectively replaced the sum-of-years' digits and double declining balance depreciation methods with the accelerated cost recovery system.

Comparing Methods for Determining Depreciation. The effect of each method for calculating annual depreciation is different. With the straight-line method, you even out profits over several years, and you list a high remaining value for the asset in the later years. With the accelerated system, you take a large write-off in early years, thus lowering your early profits as well as your early taxes. With this method, you consequently list a lower remaining value in the later years. Since the accelerated method accelerates depreciation more than straight-line, it is used when your chief concern is to lower taxes in the early years of an asset's useful life.

It is permissible to use one method of depreciation for reporting to stockholders and another for purposes of filing a tax return. Very often a company reports to its stockholders on a straight-line basis and files its tax return on an accelerated basis, since it produces a higher expense and therefore a lower tax.

Designated Order Turnaround (DOT). This computerized system is used by the New York Stock Exchange to match and automatically execute small sized market orders.

See also Differential.

Differential. The specialist must accept every odd-lot order transmitted in proper form for execution. *The specialist must always buy when a customer wants to sell, and sell when a customer wants to buy, at the first possible opportunity following receipt of each odd-lot order.* The prospect of continually trading contrary to public activity places the specialist at an obvious economic disadvantage, particularly because principal transactions preclude charging a commission to buffer potential losses. To counter balance this inequity, the NYSE permits the specialist to levy a special charge for service on each transaction. This charge, officially called a *differential*, is added to the effective sale on a customer's purchase and deducted from the effective sale on a customer's sale.

The differential is not shown as a separate item on the trade confirmation that the customer receives from the broker. The differential has already been taken into consideration in the execution report. Therefore, if a customer is notified that an odd lot was purchased at 23¼, then the customer should realize that the 23¼ price includes the differential charge for the specialist's service ($23\frac{1}{8} + \frac{1}{8} = 23\frac{1}{4}$). Similarly, an odd-lot seller notified of an execution price of 85⅞ should realize that the 85⅞ amount is the transaction price after deducting the differential ($86 - \frac{1}{8} = 85\frac{7}{8}$). In each instance, a customer may also be charged a commission by the member firm transmitting this order to the specialist for execution. The commission is shown as a separate item on the trade confirmation received by the customer.

The amount of differential charged by the specialist depends on the price of a round-lot transaction in that security executed on the floor of the New York Stock Exchange after receipt of the odd-lot order. This qualifying round-lot transaction is called an *effective sale*. An effective sale may, therefore, be defined as a round-lot transaction on which a customer's odd-lot execution price is determined (see the following table).

Differentials on the NYSE

If the effective sale is…	The differential is…
⅛ point or below	One-half the price of the effective sale
5/32 point	3/32 point for sell orders, ⅛ point for buy orders
above 5/32 point	⅛ point

Almost all round-lot transactions occur on the NYSE above 5/32 point so that for practical purposes, the differential on the big board is ⅛ point for both buyers and sellers of odd lots. This means that an odd-lot buyer purchases at ⅛ point more, and an odd-lot seller sells at ⅛ point less, than the round-lot customer.

The American Stock Exchange generally uses a split differential for execution of odd-lot orders on its premises (see the following table).

Differentials on the AMEX

If the effective sale is...	The differential is...
Below $40 per share	⅛ point
At $40 or above	¼ point

The exceptions to this basic rule about differentials relate to odd-lot executions (1) at the opening; (2) via the NYSE DOT (designated order turnaround) system, if entered as part of a round-lot order; and (3) through off-the-trading-floor facilities of a few large member organizations.

There is no differential charged to odd-lot orders entered before daily trading begins if those orders are executed on the opening transaction in that issue. Because the specialist receives these instructions in plenty of time to aggregate all odd lots, pair them off, and arrange inventory position adjustments, the customer is accorded the benefit of saving ⅛ point.

Although the DOT system is designed as an automated communications facility for processing small round-lot orders, it also accommodates odd-lot orders of up to 99 shares entered alone or as part of a round-lot order (such as an order to buy or sell 499 shares). The individual odd-lot order and a round lot with an accompanying odd lot are all executed by the specialist. A single odd-lot order is subject to the differential charge (except on opening transactions). However, if an odd-lot order is entered in the DOT system as part of a round-lot order, the round lot is executed without a floor brokerage

fee and the odd lot without a differential. In fact, that entire order is executed at one price.

See also At-the-Close Odd-Lot Order; Basis Price Odd-Lot Order; Bunching; Limit Order (Odd-Lot); Market Order (Odd-Lot); Odd-Lot Execution Transactions; Odd-Lot Stock Execution; On-the-Quotation; Short- Stop and Short Stop-Limit Orders; Stop-Limit Order (Odd-Lot); Stop Order (Odd-Lot).

Digest of Earnings Reports. In addition to daily quotations and transaction prices, the *Wall Street Journal* also publishes financial news that influences values of these securities. Such information includes earnings reports released by corporations publicly owned and registered with the SEC. Admittedly, these reports are just thumbnail sketches of the actual financial statement. Nevertheless, they do serve an important function for stockholders and potential investors. The announcements are simple to read and understand. Without comment or excuse, they are published quickly and gain wide circulation. Moreover, they are isolated in the *Wall Street Journal* each day in a section called "Digest of Earnings Reports" (see the following table) and therefore can't easily be overlooked. When used in conjunction with dividend and transaction news, which is also in this newspaper, these reports can be employed as a basis for making certain fundamental analyses about a company's stock.

The typical earnings report compares the previous year's and the current year's net sales (revenues), net income (or loss), per share earnings (primary and fully diluted), and extraordinary items taken into consideration during these fiscal periods.

Information Listed. Concentrate on the figure and see how much pertinent information can be recognized or gleaned from a typical Digest of Earnings Report. Next to the corporate title is a letter designation indicating the princi-

Digest of Earnings Reports

ALTAMIL CORP. (A)

Quar Nov 30:	1976	1975
Sales	$12,995,751	$10,155,316
Net income	546,418	391,292
Avg shares	1,535,000	1,670,000
Shr earns (primary):		
Net income	.34	.22
Shr earns (fully diluted):		
Net income	.30	.20

ARGUS CORP. (T)

Year Nov 30:	1976	1975
Net income	$11,380,000	$12,138,000
aShr earns:		
Income	1.16	1.25

a-Based on common and Class C shares.

BASSETT FURNITURE INDS (O)

Year Nov 30:	1976	1975
Sales	$226,447,812	$160,882,934
Net income	17,259,619	9,891,935
Shr earns:		
Net income	2.26	1.30

BOC INT'L LTD. (F)

Year Sept 30:	1976	1975
Sales	$1,024,100,000	$817,600,000
Income	45,500,000	30,200,000
Ext cr	500,000	500,000
Net inco	46,000,000	30,700,000

The above results have been computed at the pound's current rate.

BOMBARDIER-MLW LTD. (Mo)

9 mo Oct 31:	1976	a1975
Sales	$180,010,000	$172,386,000
Income	53,000	1,216,000
Extrd cred	113,000	446,000
Net income	116,000	1,662,000
Shr earns:		
Income	.01	.31
Net income	.04	.43

a-Restated to reflect the acquisition of MLW-Worthington.

BRODY (B.) SEATING CO. (A)

Quar Nov 30:	1976	1975
Sales	$4,754,200	$4,325,000
Net income	45,700	31,000
Shr earns:		
Net income	.06	.04

BROOKS FASHION STORES (O)

Quar Nov 27:	1976	1975
Sales	$15,694,115	$13,434,755
Net income	1,312,790	1,086,948
Shr earns:		
Net income	.35	a.29
9 months:		
Sales	44,973,063	35,773,447
Net income	3,273,251	2,926,327
Shr earns:		
Net income	.87	a.78

a-Adjusted for a 50% stock dividend in April 1976.

COMMONWLTH HOL INNS-CAN (T)

Year Oct 31:	1976	1975
Revenues	$156,374,200	$120,694,700
Income	425,100	412,900
Extrd chg	a3,500,000	
Net loss	3,074,900	b412,900
Shr earns:		
Income	c	c
Net loss	c	c

a-Write-down of investment in Caribbean. b-Income. c-No earnings for common shares after deduction of preferred dividend requirements.

COOPER LABS INC. (N)

Year Oct 31:	1976	1975
Sales	$95,170,000	$88,256,000
Income	4,631,000	2,025,000
Extr credit	a4,771,000	
Net income	9,402,000	2,025,000
Shr earns (primary):		
Income	.70	.31
Net income	1.43	.31
Shr earns (fully diluted):		
Income	.70	....
Net income	1.35	....
Quarter:		
Sales	26,092,000	24,134,000
Income	1,812,000	800,000
Extrd credit	a4,265,000	
Net income	6,077,000	800,000
Shr earns (primary):		
Income	.28	.12
Net income	.93	.12
Shr earns (fully diluted):		
Income	.28	....
Net income	.85	....

a-Consists of a gain from a debenture exchange and tax-loss carryforwards.

FORUM RESTAURANTS (O)

Year Aug 29:	1976	a1975
Sales	$22,878,000	....
Loss cnt op	201,000	....
Loss dis op	b388,000	....
Net loss	589,000	....

a-Comparable figures unavailable; company changed its fiscal year ending from May 31 to the last Sunday in August. b-Includes loss of $409,000 on disposal of discontinued operations.

GILBERT-ROBINSON INC (O)

Quar Nov 27:	1976	1975
Sales	$7,164,322	$5,472,943
Net income	334,165	261,459
Avg shares	1,548,878	a1,376,000
Shr earns:		
Net income	.22	a.19
6 months:		
Sales	14,684,456	10,966,684
Net income	799,029	487,769
Avg shares	1,491,209	a1,394,000
Shr earns:		
Net income	.54	a.35

a-Adjusted for a 20% stock dividend in April 1976.

HY-GAIN ELECTRONICS (O)

Quar Nov 27:	1976	1975
Sales	$12,311,655	$18,617,986
Net loss	2,034,598	a4,409,409
Shr earns:		
Net loss	....	a1.41

a-Income.

IMPERIAL INDUSTRIES (A)

Quar Sept 30:	1976	a1975
Sales	$8,488,000	$6,551,000
Loss cnt op	141,000	257,000
Loss dis op	....	147,000
Net loss	141,000	404,000
9 months:		
Sales	22,721,000	19,868,000
Loss cnt op	458,000	603,000
Loss dis op	....	489,000
Net loss	458,000	1,092,000

a-Restated to reflect discontinued operations.

PACESETTER BUILDING SYS (O)

Year Oct 31:	1976	1975
Sales	$18,342,833	$14,522,432
Net income	1,338,010	988,377
Shr earns:		
Net income	1.40	1.01
Quarter:		
Sales	5,434,453	4,355,662
Net income	402,224	362,125
Shr earns:		
Net income	.42	.37

PAY'N PAK STORES INC. (O)

Quar Nov 30:	1976	1975
Revenues	$22,577,874	$20,183,015
Net income	894,525	746,979
Shr earns:		
Net income	.55	a.45
9 months:		
Revenues	62,414,299	57,792,126
Net income	2,357,565	2,082,372
Shr earns:		
Net income	1.46	a1.25

a-Adjusted to reflect 10% stock dividend in May, 1976.

PROCHEMCO INC. (O)

Year Oct 31:	a1976	1975
Revenues	$42,375,000	$40,306,000
Net income	b780,000	d150,000
Shr earns:		
Net income	.54	...

a-Includes a new cotton machinery division, acquired July 1, 1976. b-Includes a nonrecurring gain of $225,000 on the sale of ranch property in Mississippi. d-Loss.

REAL EST INV TRUST (A)

Year Nov 30:	1976	1975
Income	$1,861,072	$2,201,770
Cap gain	21,702	130,988
Net income	1,882,774	2,332,758
Shr earns:		
Income	1.14	1.35
Net income	1.15	1.43
Quarter:		
Income	413,562	515,220
Cap loss	....	2,136
Net income	413,562	513,084
Shr earns:		
Income	.25	.32
Net income	.25	.32

SHONEY'S INC. (O)

Year Oct 31:	1976	1975
Revenues	$95,290,593	$70,018,911
Net income	5,446,786	3,906,696
Shr earns (com & com equiv):		
Net income	1.40	1.03

SILVER KING MINES (O)

Quar Oct 31:	1976	1975
Net loss	$211,205	$517,182
6 months:		
Net loss	480,009	666,992

SOUTHWEST FACTORIES (O)

Year Sept 30:	1976	1975
Revenues	$21,300,000	$22,600,000
Net income	263,423	536,037
Shr earns:		
Net income	.04	.11

pal marketplace where this issue is traded. In referring to the legend at the base of the figure, we realize that Altamil Corp. is traded primarily on the American Stock Exchange (A), Argus Corp. is on the Toronto Stock Exchange (T), Bassett Furniture Industries is over-the-counter (O), and so forth.

The earnings reports are for varying fiscal periods, and so care should be taken before impetuous conclusions are drawn. Some reports are annual, but many are just semiannual or for the preceding quarter, or even for the last nine months or thirty weeks. Note, too, that comparisons between 1975 and 1976 are facilitated because the figures for both fiscal periods are positioned side by side. Footnotes are kept to a minimum but play an important role. They help in making a worthwhile analysis, should the company's report contain extraordinary and nonrecurring income or write-offs. Commonwealth Holiday Inns of Canada, Forum Restaurants, and Prochemco Inc., among others, masde such announcements in their reports.

A company may report its earnings both on a primary and on a fully diluted basis. This double reporting means that the company has convertible securities outstanding and may also have securities classified as common stock equivalents. Under present accounting regulations, corporations with convertible securities outstanding are required to state their earnings both before and after consideration for conversion of those issues into common stock. Altamil Corp., Cooper Labs, Inc., and Shoney's Inc. fall into this category.

Determinations to Be Made. A number of other information items can be determined from these reports.

Net profit margin (after-tax). To calculate the percentage of net income available for stockholders from net sales, simply divide net income by net sales. In the case of Pacesetter Building Systems, the after-tax profit margin for fiscal 1976 was about 7.3% ($1,338,010 ÷

$18,342,833). If a company reports a loss, there is, understandably, no profit margin.

Approximate number of common shares outstanding. To determine the common shares outstanding, divide net income by the per-share earnings figure presented. As long as the share earnings are not fully diluted or adjusted for common stock equivalents, the result will be a good approximation of common stock outstanding. In the case of Prochemco, Inc., divide $780,000 by .54 to find that there are about 1,444,444 shares outstanding.

Percentage increase in per-share earnings. To calculate the percentage increase in per-share earnings subtract last year's per-share earnings from this year's figure. Then divide the difference by last year's earnings per share. For Bassett Furniture Industries, the percentage increase is almost 74%.

$$\frac{(2.26 - \$1.30)}{1.30} = \frac{\$\ .96}{\$1.30} = .738, \text{rounded to } .74, \text{or } 74\%$$

If the company projects the same percentage increase over each of the next three years, the same arithmetic formula can determine those earnings for those years.

Example:

Year 1

$$\frac{(x - \$2.26)}{\$2.26} = \frac{.74}{1}$$
$$x - \$2.26 = .74(2.26)$$
$$x - \$2.26 = 1.6724$$
$$x = 1.6724 + \$2.26$$
$$x = \$3.93$$

Year 2

$$\frac{(y - \$3.93)}{\$3.93} = \frac{.74}{1}$$
$$y - \$3.93 = .74(3.93)$$
$$y - \$3.93 = 2.9082$$
$$y = 2.9082 + \$3.93$$
$$y = \$6.84$$

Year 3

$$\frac{(z-\$6.84)}{\$6.84} = \frac{.74}{1}$$

$$z-\$6.84 = .74(6.84)$$

$$z-\$6.84 = 5.0616$$

$$z = 5.0616 + \$6.84$$

$$z = \$11.90$$

At that percentage rate of increase, earnings will have moved spectacularly in a short period of time.

Sales growth. To calculate sales growth, subtract last year's sales from this year's sales. Then divide the difference by last year's sales. For Imperial Industries the percentage increase is almost 30%.

$$\frac{\$8.488.000 - \$6,551,000}{\$6,551,000} = \frac{\$1,937,000}{\$6,551,000} = \begin{array}{l}.295, \text{rounded to } .30, \\ \text{or } 30\%\end{array}$$

The increase is notable despite the fact the company reported a net loss of capital from unprofitable operations. This type of analysis is really more relevant over a longer period of time, say five to ten years, than it is over a two-year period. The longer period is better because on a short-term basis management is capable of temporarily inflating sales revenues or deferring them to a succeeding fiscal period. A brief comparison is meaningful only when it signals a departure from a well-established pattern of growth (or lack of it). It thus alerts the prospective investor to look deeper into the situation for valid reasons.

Price-earnings ratio. The calculation of a price-earnings ratio from an earnings report can be done only in conjunction with the price of the issue appearing in the stock transaction tables. Just divide the price per share by the earnings per share. The result is a ratio often used by investors as an indicator of value.

Example: For Cooper Labs, Inc., use the fully diluted annual net income per share of $1.35 and its current price of 11. The price-earn-

ings ratio (P/E) is about 8.1 ($11 ÷ $1.35). However, a few months ago the stock was trading at five. Its P/E at that time (predicated on current earnings) was therefore only 3.7 ($5 ÷ $1.35). An analyst who realized that this was an inordinately low ratio could have bought the stock and profited handsomely today as a result.

Knowledge of this formula and a little arithmetic can also enable an investor to solve for any one of the components, given two of the three basic ingredients: ratio, price, and earning per share.

Example: Given a P/E ratio of fifteen for Argus Corp., its price must be about 17¼. The formula and procedure is as follows:

$$\frac{x\,(\text{price})}{\$1.16\,(\text{earnings})} = \frac{15\,(\text{ratio})}{1}$$

$$x = \$15\,(\$1.16)$$

$$x = \$17.40$$

Or, given a P/E ratio of 7.97 for Bassett Furniture Industries and a bid price $18, its annual earnings must be $2.26 per share.

$$\frac{\$18.00\,(\text{price})}{x\,(\text{earnings})} = \frac{7.97\,(\text{ratio})}{1}$$

$$7.97\,x = \$18.00$$

$$x = \frac{\$18.00}{7.97}$$

$$x = \$2.26\,(\text{rounded})$$

Dividend payout ratio. To determine the dividend payout ratio you must also refer to another information source in conjunction with the Digest of Earnings Reports. That source can be the stock transactions tables in the newspaper, if the issue is on an exchange. It can be the Over-the-Counter Markets tables, if the stock is registered in NASDAQ. If the stock is traded elsewhere, the source of supplementary information used can be the Dividend Record, published by Standard & Poor's Corporation. The additional information needed is the indicated annual dividend payment. If the stock is listed in the newspapers, the figure appears next to the name of the issue in the stock tables.

The dividend payout ratio is calculated by dividing the annual dividend distribution per share by the net income per share. Thus, for Bassett Furniture Industries, with an 80¢ indicated annual dividend, the payout ratio is 35%.

$$\frac{\$.80}{\$2.26} = .35, \text{ or } 35\%$$

In other words, this company paid out 35% of what it had available from current earnings in dividends to its common stockholders. The remainder of its earnings was reinvested in the business. Industrial corporations in a growing stage of development generally have low percentage dividend payout ratios, if any at all. Their profits are primarily plowed back into the company. Mature corporations, such as well-established electric and gas utilities concerns, have high-percentage dividend payouts. Some are even in the neighborhood of 80–90% of their net earnings each year.

See also Newspaper Financial Reports; New York Times Market Indicators; Standard & Poor's Stock Reports.

Direct Participation Programs. This term refers to investments in (1) oil and gas drilling ventures; (2) real estate syndicates (except REITs, that is, real estate investment trusts); (3) citrus grove development; (4) cattle breeding programs; and (5) other items of similar nature and intent, individually or in combination.

NASD rules set standards by which these programs must abide to ensure adherence to NASD principles of fairness and reasonableness. These standards relate to: (1) compensation paid to sponsors and underwriters for distribution of subscription units and for continuing supervision; (2) possible conflicts of interest for the sponsors; (3) the financial condition of the sponsors; (4) minimum subscription commit-

ments; (5) liquidation or exchange of units held by investors; (6) future assessment possibilities; (7) reinvestment of revenues derived from operation of the program; (8) rendering periodic operational financial reports; and (9) investor suitability.

Tax-Sheltered Programs. Specifically, member investigations of tax-sheltered programs shall include the following: (1) investigation to determine that the management of a tax-sheltered investment program has experience and a working knowledge of tax-sheltered investments sufficient for the proper handling of investment monies and the maintenance of the tax-sheltered program; (2) physical inspection of all properties described in the prospectus as being acquired by the tax-sheltered program, a review of all documents pertaining to such acquisitions, and an examination of the facilities of any servicing function performed by the tax-sheltered management; (3) examination of applicable partnership agreements; and (4) review of available information with respect to the issuer's position within its industry, including: (a) examination for proper disclosure of all conflicts of interest of the sponsor of the tax-sheltered program, and (b) examination of all records submitted by appraisers, engineers, financial consultants, and other independent consultants, with special attention paid to the procedures they used in analyzing the tax-sheltered investment, and study of all tax aspects of the tax-sheltered program to ensure that the described or anticipated tax benefits will, in fact, accrue to the investor.

Discount Rate. *See* Federal Reserve System.

Discount Window. A member bank's application for reserve credit is made at a special teller's cage at the Federal Reserve Bank; hence, the origin of the expression "discount window" to designate that area. When strict controls are in effect, that window may even be closed completely, necessitating a search for alternate credit sources.

See also Discount Rate; Federal Reserve System.

Discretionary Account. When employees or principals of a member organization have authority to create activity in a customer's account on their own initiative, that account must be defined and identified as a *discretionary account.* Such discretion, when utilized improperly, can be harmful both to the customer's capital and the firm's reputation. If the employee's or principal's compensation from the firm depends on the commissions they earn from transactions in a discretionary account, there may be an overwhelming temptation to churn (needlessly overtrade) the account just to generate commissions. Experience has shown that a customer's money is rapidly depleted under those circumstances. Quite often, the outcome is litigation against both the firm and the person exercising discretion for engaging in activity prejudicial to the customer's financial circumstances and investment objectives. Therefore, orders for this type of account should not be excessive in size or frequent in number in view of the customer's financial resources.

Several brokerage concerns prohibit discretionary accounts entirely. They allow power in a customer's account to be held only by a person not associated with a brokerage firm. Regulations of the NYSE and AMEX do not forbid discretionary accounts, but recognizing the pitfalls of such accounts, the exchanges mandate the following precautions:

1. A signed trading authorization must be obtained from the customer and accepted by an authorized principal or officer of the brokerage concern. The form is retained by the firm in its files for at least six years after the account is closed.

2. Each order ticket entered for a transaction in which this authorization is used must be marked *discretionary* and initialed promptly by a registered principal.

3. Discretionary accounts must be reviewed frequently by a person delegated with supervisory responsibility *other* than the one who is exercising discretion. This is necessary to ensure that there is no excessive and improper activity. (A list of all discretionary accounts should be maintained at control locations with a written statement of the firm's supervisory procedures.)

Verbal or written instructions from a customer for an employee or principal to use judgment regarding (1) time of execution and/or (2) price of execution do not constitute discretion as defined by the regulatory authorities. The customer must specify buy or sell, quantity, and issue.

See also Trading Authorization.

Distribution Area. *See* Support and Resistance Levels.

Distribution Dates

Cash Distribution Dates. Both investors and brokerage concerns must understand and act within the framework of four essential dates associated with corporate distributions. In chronological sequence, for cash dividends, these dates are:

1. Date of declaration. The day on which a corporation's board of directors convenes a meeting, decides on a distribution, and makes public announcement of this fact.

2. Ex-dividend (interest) date. The day on which a security begins trading in the marketplace without the value of the dividend/interest distribution belonging to a purchaser of that issue. Because an overwhelming number of corporate securities contracts are created regular way, the ex-dividend date consequently is normally the fourth business day prior to the record date.

119

If the company's sole transfer agent is a significant distance from the major marketplaces, or the corporation makes a late dividend announcement, the Uniform Practice Committee of the NASD may arbitrarily fix an ex-date earlier than the fourth business day before record date. To do so gives entitled purchasers sufficient time to effect a reregistration and avoid the problem of subsequent dividend claims. The NYSE and AMEX require listed companies to maintain transfer agents, or their representatives, within the vicinity of the exchanges themselves; listed companies must be able to effect a reregistration within 24 hours, if necessary.

An exception to that rule of thumb involves certain foreign issues. This occurs when the transfer agent's principal office is located in the company's country of origin and there are definite communication difficulties. Interesting, too, is the fact that most mutual funds are also in the exceptional category. Because they don't really trade in the open market, their boards of directors set the ex- dividend date as well as all the other dates pertinent to a distribution.

3. Record date. The day on which a corporation closes its register of securities holders to determine the recipients of an announced distribution. This date is set by the directors of the issuing corporation.

4. Payment date. The day on which a corporation or its disbursement agent makes payment of a distribution to its previously determined holders of record. (A *holder of record* is a party whose name is inscribed in the corporation's register of stockholders, or creditors, as the case may be. these holders receive a distribution from the company if their names still appear on this list at the close of business on the record date.)

Example: Assume a declaration of a distribution payable to holders of record on January 16 and realize that, technically speaking, a purchaser should become a holder of record on the settlement date of the contract. ("Technically

speaking," because, in reality, it may be physically impossible to accomplish this feat. The contract may settle in California and the company's transfer agent may have its office in New York.) The following conclusions may be drawn:

			JANUARY			
S	M	T	W	T	F	S
		1	2	3	4	5
6	7	8	9	10	11	12
13	14	15	16	17	18	19
20	21	22	23	24	25	26
27	28	29	30	31		

1. A regular-way contract made as late as January 9 settles on January 16, the record date, and entitles a purchaser of that security to the announced distribution.

2. Regular-way contracts made beginning on January 10 settle after January 16 and entitle sellers of that security to the announced distribution. Therefore, on January 10, the security begins trading ex dividend. A look at the calendar shows that January 10 is the fourth business day prior to the January 16 record date. (Note that for an atypical transaction—such as a cash contract that settles on the same day as the trade itself—the ex-dividend date would be the day after the record date. Persons buying that stock in a cash contract on any day up to, and even including, the record date can have their names recorded on the company's books to get that dividend distribution.)

To remember who gets the cash distribution, use the following rule of thumb: First, compare the settlement day of the contract to a company's record date. If the settlement day falls on any day up to and including the record date, the distribution belongs to the buyer. If the settlement day falls after the record date, it belongs to the seller.

Stock Distribution Dates. Stock dividends and stock splits may cause unique trading problems for the securities industry. The chronological sequence of dividend dates for cash distributions is inapplicable. The ex-dividend date, now called the "ex-distribution date," is positioned after the payment date instead of after the date of declaration. Thus, the chronological sequence for a stock distribution is as follows: (1) date of declaration; (2) record date; (3) payment date; and (4) ex-distribution date. The rule of thumb is that the ex-distribution date will be the next business day following payment by the corporation. (The procedural rules for handling subscription rights are identical to that for stock distributions and splits. It goes "ex" on the day after trading in them commences, which is also the day after payment.) Due bills are redeemable beginning on the fifth business day after the issuer's payment date.

Example: Using the foregoing calendar, if the company declared a 5% stock dividend on January 2 for payment on January 24 to holders of record on January 10, the following analysis can be made: (1) All regular-way contracts in the marketplace will, therefore, trade with due bills attached from January 4 (settlement date is January 11) through January 24; (2) Commencing on January 25, that issue will trade "ex distribution" and all outstanding due bills may be redeemed for the additional stock on January 31; (3) Any delivery of stock to a purchasing firm after January 10 (through January 31) must be accompanied by a due bill for the stock dividend.

Illustrative Dividend Synopsis. Statistical information about dividends and dividend-payment policies of publicly held corporations can be found in the *Dividend Record*, a publication of Standard & Poor's Corporation (S&P), New York City. Typical of the service provided by S&P is the following brief history of dividends paid by Georgia-Pacific Corporation, a large company listed principally on the New York

Stock Exchange. That fact is noted by the identifying symbol (■) preceding its name.

Divd $	Declared	Ex-date	Stk Record	Payable
■Georgia-Pacific—Com. p$0.80				
Rate— 0.20Q Pd '76 — new — 0.40: old — 0.50				
& stk '75 — old — 0.80 & stk.				
0.20	Jan 26	Jan 30	Feb 5	Mar 25
2% Stk	Jan 26	Jan 30	Feb 5	Mar 25
0.30	Apr 7	May 17	May 21	Jun 21
3 for 2 Split		Aug 13	Jun 25	Aug 12
(After 3 for 2 Split)				
0.20 Init	Jul 26	Aug 23	Aug 27	Sep 27
0.20	Oct 25	Nov 5	Nov 12	Dec 13

This detailed synopsis sets forth essential dates for cash and stock distributions made by the company in 1976, as well as its total payments in the preceding year. Next to the corporate title is a notice that the common stock of this issuer has an indicated dividend policy of $.80 per share annually (com. p$0.80). In the following two lines it presents the following information: (1) The company's quarterly rate payment of $.20 per share Rate—0.20Q); 2) What it actually paid in 1976, both in terms of old shares and new shares owned by an investor (Pd '76—new—0.40: old— 0.50 & stk.). This dual presentation is necessary because Georgia-Pacific split its stock 3 for 2 during the year. This notice reveals that the corporation in 1976 paid $.40 per share on the "new" or split-up shares and $.50 per share plus a stock dividend on the "old" or pre-split shares of common stock. What it paid in 1975 by comparison to 1976 ('75—old—0.80 & stl). It was $.80 per share on the pre-split shares plus a stock dividend.

If we read down column 1, titled "Divd $" we recognize that the corporation made six distributions in 1976; four cash payments; one stock dividend, and one stock split. Those distributions were declared by the board of directors on the dates shown in column 2. They were actually made on the dates shown in column 5 ("payable") to holders whose names were inscribed on the company's books on the record dates (column 4). Column 3 reflects the dates on which the stock began trading in the marketplace on a regular-way basis without the value of the distributions attached to the transaction price.

Example: Assume you were a holder of 100 shares of Georgia-Pacific at the beginning of 1976. Now let's see what you received from the company for your investment:

1. On March 25, you received $.20 per share, or $20 for your 100 shares.

2. On the same date you received two additional shares of stock as a stock dividend.

3. On June 21, you received $.30 per share and because you now owned 102 shares your check was for $30.60.

4. On August 12, the company split its stock 3 for 2 (three new shares for every two old shares already owned). This ratio is also known as a 50% split because, when expressed on a per-share basis, it results in ½ of an additional share for each share currently held. Because you owned 102 shares before, you were entitled to 51 additional shares ($102 \times .50 = 51$). Another way to formulate the result of this distribution is to multiply the shares already owned by the terms of the ratio. Thus, $102 \times \frac{3}{2} = 153$ shares.

5. On September 27, Georgia-Pacific paid $.20 per share as an initial ("Init") dividend following the split. Because you now owned 153 shares your check amounted to $30.60.

6. The final distribution in 1976 was $.20 per share on December 13, and your payment was the same as the preceding one, $30.60.

As a result of the cash distributions during the year the company reported to the Internal Revenue Service payments to you of $111.80. The cash dividends are fully taxable to the shareholders, whereas the stock distributions serve merely to reduce the investor's per-share acquisition cost.

District Bank. *See* Federal Reserve System.

District Business Conduct Committee. *See* National Association of Securities Dealers.

District Uniform Practice Committee. *See* National Association of Securities Dealers.

Diversified Common Stock Company. A *diversified management company* is one that has at least 75% of its assets represented by (1) cash and cash items (receivables); and/or (2) government securities; and/or (3) securities of other investment companies; and/or (4) other securities, limited to (a) all securities of one issuer having a value not greater than 5% of the management company's total assets, and (b) no more than 10% of the voting securities of the issuing corporation.

Example: If a diversified management company has total assets of $100,000, it must invest at least $75,000 of these assets in such a way so as not to acquire $5,000 worth (5% of total assets) in any one company's stocks and bonds combined. In addition, such monies may not purchase more than 10% of the voting stock of the corporation. However, the remaining 25% of the assets may be invested without regard to the 10% limitation. Thus, the diversified company could acquire full control of other corporations.

A management company will not lose its status as a diversified company if the mixture or value of its securities and other assets subsequently changes to such an extent that it no longer conforms to the formula. This statement assumes, of course, that the discrepancy did not result from a voluntary acquisition by the investment company.

See also Management Company; Nondiversified Company.

This type of investment company represents an overwhelming percentage of investment companies in the industry today. These companies invest virtually all their assets in a portfolio of common stocks in a wide variety of industries. But they have sufficient maneuverability to permit their officials to shift into debt securities or even into a cash position if, in their opinion, market conditions warrant it. Stated objectives are worded to stress appreciation of capital as the paramount concern. Investment income is of relatively minor importance to these companies. the more conservative common stock companies try to obtain reasonable current income from invested capital whereas the "gogo" variety (companies whose investing philosophy is oriented toward frequent trading in stocks subject to dramatic price fluctuation) emphasize capital gains without regard for dividend or interest income. As a result, the performance records of those aggressive companies have proved to be more volatile than those of any other type or subcategory.

See also Investment Company.

Divided Account. *See* Underwriting Agreement.

Dividend. Dividends are distributions to the stockholders when earned and declared by the board of directors. The directors are not compelled to pay out any or all of a corporation's earnings in the form of cash dividends—not even to preferred stockholders. They may have other more important plans for these monies to facilitate the company's growth. The only prior claim preferred stockholders have to corporate dividends is that they must be completely satisfied, including arrearages, before any distribution of cash or stock can be made to common stockholders.

If a dividend is declared and paid to the investors, it is distributed equally per share to holders whose names appear on the company's records on a date set by the board of directors.

To conserve cash, the board of directors may decline to distribute anything, or they can pay dividends in the form of stock. In the latter case, shares may be distributed from the corporation's authorized but unissued stock or from treasury stock, if need be, each common shareholder's percentage of ownership is unaffected, because each shareholder's proportionate interest in the company remains unchanged.

Example: On declaration of a 10% stock dividend but before its payment, a common stockholder's proportionate interest is:

$$\frac{100 \text{ shares owned}}{1,000,000 \text{ shares issued and outstanding}}$$
$$= 1/10,000 \text{ interest in the corporation}$$

After payment, percentage ownership in the corporation is:

$$\frac{110 \text{ shares owned}}{1,100,000 \text{ shares issued and outstanding}}$$
$$= 1/10,000 \text{ interest in the corporation}$$

See also Common Stock; Preferred Stock.

Selling Dividends. It is unfair and unethical for any NASD member or employee to solicit purchase orders for mutual fund shares solely on the basis of an impending distribution to be made by that company. No advantage is gained by the investor under those circumstances for the following reasons:

1. The price of the shares is reduced by the exact amount of the distribution on the day the shares begin selling ex-dividend. The ex-dividend date is set by the mutual fund's board of directors, trustees, or underwriter and does not follow the usual NASD rules for such procedure. It is often fixed after the record date instead of prior to it.

2. The investor is liable for taxes on the distribution received from the company.

3. The salesperson's compensation will be higher because it is based on the offering price— the price that includes the dividend amount prior to the ex date.

Effect on Option. When a corporation pays a cash dividend, there is no adjustment to the strike price of the listed option contract. This is significant because the writer of a covered call option (if the option is not exercised) retains both the dividends and the premium, increasing the rate of return and the appeal of the strategy. If, however, the corporation pays a stock dividend or splits the stock, there will be an adjustment in contract terms for both the number of shares and the strike price.

There are two rules for stock splits or dividends: First, if a stock dividend or split creates an even multiple of 100 (200 and so forth), then the adjustment will "split" the contract.

Example: A person owns one XYZ April 50 call, and the company declares a 2-for-1 stock split. The necessary adjustment provides that the option holder now owns two 100-share contracts for April 25 calls. As can be seen, the aggregate exercise amount did not change. Before the split, the aggregate exercise price was \$5,000 ($100 \times \$50$). After the split, the aggregate exercise price is also \$5,000 (200 shares $\times$ \$25). The formula for the adjustment is:

$$\frac{\text{Old Exercise Price}}{\text{Split ratio}} = \text{Adjusted Exercise Price}$$

$$\frac{\$50}{(2 \div 1)} = \$25$$

Second, if the stock split or stock dividend results in an odd lot and a round lot, then the adjustment increases the number of shares in the unit of trading and decreases the exercise price.

Example: A holder of a January 60 put, on a 3-for-2 split in the underlying stock, would have the terms of the put option adjusted to represent one contract for 150 shares at an exercise price of \$40. Once again, the aggregate exercise price is the same after the split as before the split.

The formula for the adjustment in the exercise price is:

$$\frac{\text{Old Exercise Price}}{\text{Split Ratio}} = \text{Adjusted Exercise Price}$$

Example:

$$\frac{\$60}{(3 \div 2)} = \frac{60}{1.5} = \$40$$

The formula for the adjustment in the unit of trading is:

$$100 \times (\text{Split Ratio}) = \text{Adjusted unit of trading}$$

Example:

$$100 \times (3 \div 2) = 100 \times 1.50 = 150$$

The terms of the new contract are:
One January 40 put representing 150 shares

If a corporation declares a 5% stock dividend, the same process takes place. An outstanding January 50 call option is converted into one contract representing 105 shares at an exercise price of 47⅝.

The formula for adjustment in the exercise price is:

$$\frac{\text{Old Exercise Price}}{(+\text{Decimalized dividend percentage})} = \text{Adjusted Exercise Price}$$

Example:

$$\frac{\$50}{1 + .05} = \frac{\$50}{1.05} = \$47.619 = \$47⅝$$

The formula for adjustment in the unit of trading is:

$$100 \times (1 + \text{decimalized Dividend Percentage}) = \text{Adjusted Unit of Trading}$$

Example:

$$100 \times (1 + .05) = 100 \times 1.05 = 105$$

Any adjustment in the exercise price is rounded to the nearest ⅛ of a dollar and any adjustment in the number of shares is rounded down to the lowest full number of shares. Remember that options premiums are quoted on a per-share basis. Hence if a contract has been adjusted to 105 shares, a bid of $4 commits the customer to $420, not $400 (105 shares × $4).

The formula for aggregate premium is:

$$\frac{\text{Adjusted Unit}}{\text{Of Trading}} \times \text{Option Price} = \text{Aggregate Premium}$$

Example:

$$105 \times \$4 \quad = \$420$$

If a corporation spins off a subsidiary or issues rights or warrants, the exchange determines the value of such distribution so that appropriate adjustments can be made to the contract. The adjustments for the respective changes are made on the ex-distribution date.

Effect of Settlement Date. The OCC settlement date is the business day following the trade date. This means that clearing member firms must make their margin deposits on that day. The customers of the members will make payment to the member firms according to firm policy, but in no event later than Regulation T requirements (seven business days for both cash and margin accounts). Even if the writer receives an assignment a day or two after the date of exercise, the stock transaction settles five business days from exercise date. Thus, the writer of a naked call may be required to purchase the stock for cash or next-day settlement to satisfy the exercise.

Once an exercise notice has been assigned to the writer of an option, the writer cannot effect a closing purchase transaction on the exercised option, but must purchase (in the case of a put) or sell (in the case of a call) the underlying security pursuant to the exercise.

Trade dates and settlement dates via option exercises determine who is entitled to a dividend or other distribution. Dividends belong to those stockholders who are holders of record on the record date. Holders of record are determined by settled trades. Thus, to receive a dividend, the holder of a call option must exercise it prior to the ex-dividend date, which is normally four business days prior to the record date. Since the exercise of a call is equivalent to buying the stock, an exercise notice tendered more than four business days from the record date will entitle the new owner (the exerciser of the call option) to the dividend. If a put option holder exercises a put before the ex-dividend date, the put writer is entitled to the dividend because the writer would then be the recorded owner of the stock.

See also Aggregate Exercise Price; Dividend Distributions; Ex-Dividend Date; Intrinsic Value; Time Value; Regulation T; Volatility.

Dividend Distributions. An important price consideration in making a securities contract is any distribution of money contemplated or pending by the issuing corporation. A stockholder receives dividends from the net profits or surplus if declared by a company's board of directors, but those payments are not made on a daily basis. So market prices and contract expenses are influenced by the trade date's proximity to the usual distribution dates.

Payment of dividends to stockholders is not obligatory; the payment of interest to bondholders is. Stockholder dividends are paid at the discretion of the corporation's board of directors. In fact, the board of directors is generally responsible for setting three of the four essential dates associated with any payments to the stockholders. These are: (1) the date of declaration. The board determines the time of its meeting to announce the distribution. (2) the date of payment. The board determines when distribution will actually be made. (3) the date of record. The board determines when the company's transfer agent and registrar will close their books for the purpose of identifying the recipients of the distribution.)

The one important date the directors normally do not set is the date on which that stock will begin trading in the marketplace without the value of the dividend included in the contract price. That date is established by the Uniform Practice Committee of the NASD and is called the ex-dividend date (The ex-dividend date for open-end investment company shares—mutual funds—is designated by the issuer or its principal underwriter, not by the NASD.) It is closely related to, and dependent on, the record date itself.

SEC Rule 10b-17 requires directors of corporations issuing publicly traded securities to make timely announcements of distributions so that appropriate action can be taken by the Uniform Practice Committee. With few exceptions, this means that they must notify the committee at least ten days prior to the record date so that the NASD membership has current information essential to its trading activities. The rule applies to distribution of rights and warrants as well as to dividends of cash and additional stock because they are treated in a similar fashion in the marketplace.

Normally, a stock will commence trading ex dividend (for cash distributions), ex rights, or ex warrants, as the case may be, on the fourth business day prior to the record date. If the record date is a nondelivery date (that is, a bank holiday), the security will be trading "ex" on the fifth business day prior to the record date.

Occasionally, a cash dividend will not be paid in a multiple equal to the monetary value in which that security is traded, that is, ⅛ (12½¢), ¹⁄₁₆ (6¼¢), or ¹⁄₃₂ (3⅛¢) of a dollar (or in lower-priced stocks, pennies). When this occurs on the ex-dividend date, the bid prices prevailing and all pending buy orders on the books of a member organization are reduced in value by the next highest variation for that security rather than by the exact amount of the distribution.

Examples: For stocks trading in variations of eighths:

A   4¢ dividend will reduce bids by ⅛ of a point.

A 55¢ dividend will reduce bids by ⅝ of a point.

A 91¢ dividend will reduce bids by 1 point.

For stocks trading in variations of sixteenths:

A   4¢ dividend will reduce bids by ¹⁄₁₆.

A 55¢ dividend will reduce bids by ⁹⁄₁₆.

A 91¢ dividend will reduce bids by ¹⁵⁄₁₆.

See also Dividends; Due Bills and Due Bill Checks.

Dividend Department. *See* Broker/Dealer Organization.

Dividend Payout Ratio. *See* Digest of Earnings Reports.

DK. *See* Cash Account.

Dollar Cost Averaging. This program is followed by large and small investors alike. The client who purchases mutual funds on an accumulation or contractual basis or who uses a personal investment plan program is following this theory. Investment companies and other large institutions also apply it to their portfolios. It is based on investing fixed dollar amounts at periodic intervals, regardless of price. Over a period of time, the average cost per share" will be less than the average of the purchase prices, providing an opportunity for profit over a long term. This program is not designed for short-term trading, and when opting for it, an investor chooses an amount he or she can continue to invest for five years or more.

Example: This example of a dollar cost averaging program, of necessity, covers only a short period, but it demonstrates the inherent quality of dollar cost averaging—reducing average cost per share below the average of purchase prices.

	Amount Invested	Market Price per share	Number of Shares Purchased
January 1988	$100	$ 50	2
February 1988	$100	$ 40	2½
March 1988	$100	$ 30	3⅓
April 1988	$100	$ 40	2½
May 1988	$100	$ 50	2
	$500	$210	12⅓
	Total investment	Aggregate market prices	Shares owned

$$\text{Average price of investment} = \frac{\text{aggregate market price of shares}}{\text{number of monthly investments}}$$

Therefore, $\dfrac{\$210}{5}$ = $42.00 average price of investment

$$\text{Average cost per share} = \frac{\text{total money invested}}{\text{total shares and fractions owned}}$$

Therefore, $\dfrac{\$500}{12.33}$ = $40.55 average cost per share

Our example also shows a nice profit for the client, as the most recent price is $50. This is not necessarily true in all cases. If we switch the order of prices and put $30.00 last, the average cost would still be $40.55. However, the investor will sustain a loss if the stock is sold at this time because the stock is now selling at $30 rather than at $50.

The average cost is lower than the average price because fewer shares are bought at the higher levels; many more shares are purchased when the price is low.

To get the true insight into dollar cost averaging, compare the periodic investment of equal-dollar amounts with the periodic purchases of equal-share amounts. The investment of equal-dollar amounts gives a decided advantage over the investment of equal-share amounts. To do so, use the information from the example above, except that this investor will buy 2.467 shares of stock, regardless of price, instead of depositing $100 monthly. In the example, 2.467 shares is the average number of shares purchased each time. It is determined by dividing the total

shares owned (12.33) by the total number of investments (5).

	Number of Shares Purchased	Market Price Per Share	Amount Needed For Investment
January 1988	2.467	$50	$123.35
February 1988	2.467	40	98.68
March 1988	2.467	30	74.01
April 1988	2.467	40	98.68
May 1988	2.467	50	123.35
	12.33 Shares		$518.07

The investment of equal-dollar amounts gives a decided advantage over the investment of equal-share amounts. In the latter instance, the exercise resulted in the investment of more dollars and a higher average cost per share ($518.07 ÷ 12.33 = $42.02).

Doing Business. *See* SEC Rule 147.

Don't Know (DK). *See* Cash Account.

Double Tops and Bottoms. These technical patterns offer an excellent method of determining the levels of major supply and demand so as to avoid false signals. These two patterns are often referred to as *M* and *W* formations because they take the shape of those letters in a plotted chart (see the following graphs). In each case, a price has been reached twice but supply (tops) or demand (bottoms) caused a reversal. Chartists who see these patterns are alerted by them to determine if existing supply or demand has been satisfied. Does the price find support at the bottom? If so, a rise in price is indicated. Is resistance encountered at the top? If so, a decline will occur. Penetration of these levels leads to the conclusion that the price will continue in the upward or downward direction, and the chartist can make investment decisions accordingly.

Perfectly shaped *M*s and *W*s are rare. It is not uncommon to find triple or even quadruple tops or bottoms instead of doubles before the breakout takes place. A technician's consolation

Double Top, "M"

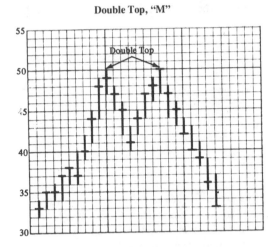

Double Bottom, "W"

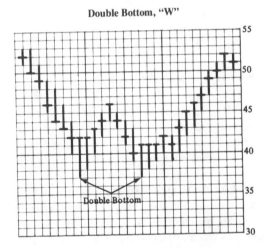

in these cases is that when the subsequent movement in that issue does occur, it is significant.

Double tops and bottoms are based on support and resistance techniques and can be further analyzed to estimate the duration of a trend. Here, volume also becomes an important factor because it enables you to predict how much "steam" is left in the move. When volume contracts as prices rise, the forecast is for an imminent decline because the rally is apparently beginning to starve for want of anxious buyers. Conversely, if prices continue to fall as volume declines, be ready for a rally in the near future.

This situation is indicative of a situation where those who wanted to sell have done so already and all who are left are holders with strong positive convictions about that stock's future. Consequently, the path of least resistance will soon point toward higher prices. On the other hand, rises or declines in prices of an issue, accompanied by high or increasing volume, signal a continuation of that upward or downward movement, as the case may be. The following grid summarizes forecasts based on price and volume:

		VOLUME	
		Contracts	Increases
PRICE	Rises	Imminent decline	Continued rise
	Falls	Rally in near future	Continued fall

Climaxes. An expansion of the previous charting approach, which is also dependent on a study of volume in conjunction with a continuing price trend, often results in what is known as a *climax.* (Climaxes can happen on the buy side as well as the sell side. However, climaxes, or breakaway patterns, are more prevalent on the sell side of the market.) A climax usually arises when, after a slow but persistent trend in one direction, important news is announced affecting a company's fortunes. Maybe it is a large new business contract, or perhaps it is a dividend omission or a poor earnings statement. Sometimes there is no news at all. In any event, a high volume of trading suddenly develops to accelerate the decline (or rise) to such an extent that (1) a price gap is created between the previous low (or high) sale and the next transaction; and/or (2) the vertical line chart illustrates an unusually large range between high and low prices for that

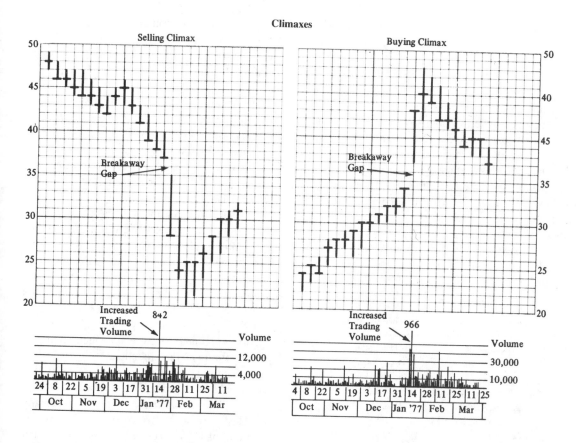

Climaxes

period. (See the graphs above for illustrations of selling and buying climaxes.) When the increased selling (or buying) has been quickly completed, a reversal invariably and inevitably occurs. That is, prices rise (or decline) to the earlier level to close that gap.

See also Support and Resistance Levels; Technical Analysis (Vertical Line Charts).

Dow Jones Averages.

The Dow Jones Industrial Average. Three separate averages are prepared by Dow Jones. The *Industrial Average*, based on thirty stocks, is the most widely quoted market average or index. If one hears the phrase, "The market was up four today," it means that this relatively small average has shown a rise of four points for the

trading session in relation to the present overall total of about 2,500 points.

The Dow Jones Industrial Average (DJIA) is computed by totaling the market prices of all component issues and dividing the sum by a comparatively constant number to produce the arithmetic DJIA. The divisor is "comparatively constant" only in relation to the prices of the included securities. It, too, is adjusted (although only downward) from time to time to reflect stock splits and stock dividends that will affect the average by five or more points. That divisor is currently .784. If each security in the average moved one point in the same direction on a given day, the effect on the DJIA would be about 34 points up or down, as the case may be. Note that the DJIA is not expressed in terms of dollars and cents. Rather, the DJIA is expressed only in points plotted against an overall numerical figure.

Despite competition from larger indexes, the popularity of the Dow remains undiminished. Its wide usage is due in part to the fact that its founder, Charles Dow, began his computations back in 1884, thus giving it the longest continuity in its field. The Dow Theory is also based on this average. The following thirty common stocks included in the Dow Jones Industrial Average as of Fall 1987 (the companies change from time to time):

Allied Corporation	International Business Machines Corp.
Aluminum Company of America	Navistar, Inc.
Primemerica Corp.	International Paper Co.
American Express Company	McDonalds Corp.
American Telephone & Telegraph Co.	Merck & Co., Inc.
Bethlehem Steel Corp.	Minnesota Mining & Manufacturing Corp., Inc.
Boeing Co. Inc.	Phillip Morris Co.
Chevron Corp.	Procter & Gamble Co.
Coca Cola Co.	Sears Roebuck & Co.
E.I. Du Pont de Nemours & Co.	Texaco, Inc.
Eastman Kodak Co.	Union Carbide Corp.
Exxon Corp.	USX Corp.
General Electric Co.	United Technologies Corp.
General Motors Corp.	Westinghouse Electric Corp.
Goodyear Tire & Rubber Co.	F.W. Woolworth Co.

The Dow Jones Transportation Average. This average contains twenty common stocks. Once known as the Rail Average, diminishing interest in and declining growth of railroads, together with a desire to reflect the importance of other forms of transportation, prompted the change. The list now includes six airlines and three trucking companies.

The Dow Jones Utility Average. This average is made up of fifteen major utility companies that service all parts of the United States.

The Dow Jones Composite Average. This average consists of the 65 stocks included in the industrial, transportation, and utility indexes.

See also American Stock Exchange Market Value Index; Averages and Indexes; NASDAQ-OTC Price Index; New York Stock Exchange Index; Standard & Poor's Index.

Dow Theory. This theory is based on the writings of Charles Dow, an editor of the *Wall Street Journal* early in the twentieth century. His ideas on stock-price movements were later elaborated on by S. A. Nelson, who also wrote for the *Journal.* It was Nelson who named Dow's hypotheses the Dow Theory.

Using the Dow Jones averages as its base, the theory proposes that these market averages rise or fall in advance of similar changes in business activity. By properly reading the averages, you get a prediction of things to come and can accurately plan investments based on prior price movements. Although it was never considered a get-rich-quick scheme by its originators, the theory is claimed to be a reliable method of predicting future market direction.

The three basic movements in the market are listed here in order of importance:

1. The *primary movement* is long term and may last from one to five years. This is the overall trend of the market and the most important reading. You must be able to differentiate between brief reversals of the major trend and reversals from a bull to a bear market and vice versa.

2. *Secondary movements* reverse the primary movement and last for short periods, perhaps one to three months. As many as three to five of these shifts may occur during a bull or bear market before a trend reversal is indicated. The secondary movements provide information for medium-term trading decisions. More important, they help you to anticipate the life expectancy of the primary movement. Experienced technicians measure the percentage of variance from the primary movement, correlate it with the time it takes to reach that level and, using historical precedent for that issue, project the duration potential of the primary movement.

The graph below represents both primary and secondary movements. Note the primary movement illustrated between points *A* and *B* (upward), and then between *B* and *F* (downward). The temporary, short-lived reactions between *A* and *B* are secondary movements, as are the short rallies between *B* and *F*. The Dow theorists believe that an upward trend is not reversed until one of those secondary reactions penetrates the bottom of a previous reaction, such as that which occurred at point *D* in relation to *C*. Conversely, the downward trend is reversed when a secondary movement rally penetrates the top of a previous rally, such as what happened when point *G* rose above *E*. Analogies are often drawn between primary and secondary movements and the seas. Primary movements are comparable to the incoming and ebb tides, whereas secondary movements represent ocean waves influenced by those flows.

3. *Daily fluctuations* are of little consequence to longer-term market movements. They are not indicative of primary or secondary movements and are often emotional reactions. They are like ripples that appear on the waves of the sea, to use the analogy referred to earlier. Propo-

**Dow Jones Primary and
Secondary Movements**

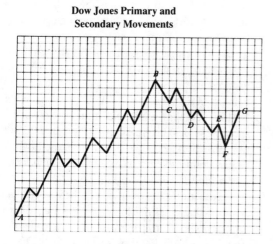

nents of the Dow Theory hold that all factors concerning market conditions are built into the averages. It is unnecessary, therefore, to consider sales, earnings, dividends, production costs, or the hundreds of other factors included in fundamental analysis. These elements are implicit in the averages, and their effects can be clearly read.

See also Advance-Decline Theory; Confidence Theory; Dow Jones Averages; Odd-Lot Theory; Short Interest Theory; Technical Analysis.

Dual Purpose Investment Company. These companies are closed-end companies and are also known as *leveraged companies.* They publicly distribute two classes of securities in equal amounts in a single offering, with each class having different objectives and privileges.

One class is comparable to preferred stock and is identified as *income shares.* This class is entitled to receive the net dividends and interest earned by the company from the entire portfolio, with a minimum dollar amount assured. The other class is comparable to common stock and is identified as *capital shares.* This class is entitled to any appreciation in value and all established net gains from transactions effected in the securities of the entire portfolio. Conversely however, any decline in the value of those securities, up to 50%, is a risk experienced exclusively by the capital shareholders. Further declines involve both income and capital shareholders alike.

A leverage factor is enjoyed by the holders of each class of security because each dollar of investment actually receives a benefit from $2 worth of portfolio. If either class of shares is purchased on a stock exchange or in the over-the-counter market at a discount from net asset value, the degree of leverage for those holders is further intensified. The typical leverage factor has been approximately an effective 2.5 to 1 ratio based on transaction prices of capital shares. (Investment Companies—Mutual Funds and Other Types [*New York: Weisenberger Financial Services, Inc., 197*1], *p. 22.*)

At the time of the initial offering, the dual purpose company fixes a call date (ten or fifteen years later), at which time the income shares must be redeemed by the company. Then, with abolition of those particular shares, the company is able to turn open-end subject to approval of the capital shareholders. Thus the company can begin issuing fully redeemable securities.

See also Investment Company; Management Company.

Due Bill (Due Bill Check). When a security is sold before the ex-dividend date but delivered to the purchaser after the record date, the seller receives a distribution from the corporation to which the seller is not legally entitled. The transfer agent and registrar have no way of knowing that this has occurred, simply because the seller failed to deliver the certificate promptly. The tardy seller prevents the purchaser from reregistering it by the close of business on the record date. It is not the transfer agent's responsibility to rectify this situation.

The Uniform Practice Code stipulates that when a tardy seller eventually delivers the certificate to the purchasing member, the certificate must be accompanied by an instrument evidencing the transfer of title to the distribution, if it is to be considered a good delivery. This document is officially called a *due bill.* Once the due bill is created, it becomes the seller's obligation to pay this I.O.U. at the first opportunity after the payment date. Failure to do so enables the purchaser to initiate buy-in proceedings immediately thereafter.

A due bill for a cash dividend or for accrued interest on registered bonds is a post-dated check (due-bill check) depositable on the corporation's payment date (see the following figure).

The transfer of title to a right, warrant, stock dividend, stock split, or other stock distribution (such as a *spin off;*—a distribution of stock in a company that is owned by another corporation and is being allocated to the holders of stock in the latter corporation) is a simple, legal document redeemable on a date set by the Uniform Practice Committee. This date is related to the company's issue date for the stock (see the figure on page 133).

Because of the additional time it takes to print, register, and distribute new stock rights, or warrant certificates, the issuing corporation provides for a considerable amount of time to elapse between record and payment dates. Recognizing this, and yet still anxious to permit trading in the "old" stock in the meantime, the Uniform Practice Committee usually decrees that (1) all settlements of transactions after the record date, until the due-bill redemption date, must carry the due bills attached to the stock certificate; (2) the security will commence trading "ex distribution" on the first business day after the payable date for the stock, a date set by the corporation's directors; and (3) due bills will be redeemable on the fifth business day after the payable date of the stock distribution.

Sometimes, the delay in reregistering certificates is the fault of the purchaser instead of the seller. If the buyer holds the certificates in negotiable form beyond the record date and neglects to reregister them, the buying firm may lose its claim against the seller for the distribution. This will occur unless those certificates were registered in the selling firm's name rather than that broker's customer's name or some other NASD member's name. Nevertheless, the seller should use best efforts in assisting collection of that distribution for the buyer. It is the buyer's responsibility to present substantiating evidence of this claim.

Sometimes it is an action of the issuing corporation that gives rise to the use of a due bill in a typical transaction, particularly, in the case of a sizable stock dividend or any stock split. Extra time is needed for printing so many additional

Due Bill Check

Due Bill Check

Consider this check as due bill until payable date as shown below

NEW YORK ...., 19 .... No. 1999

X Y Z BANK

1-2

210

Pay
To
The
Order
Of ....$ ....

....DOLLARS

In Payment of Dividend or Interest   Dividend Account
                                              Interest Account

On ....

NOT PAYABLE BEFORE ....

Record Date ....

**Due Bill for Stock Dividend
or Stock Distribution**

Due Bill for Stock Dividend or Stock Distribution

For value received, the undersigned hereby assigns, transfers and sets over
to..the stock distribution
of .... (   ) shares of ....
stock of ....to be issued on
...................to the registered holder of ....
(   ) shares of...................stock of ....
represented by certificate number ...., to which the
undersigned is entitled as a stock dividend, and hereby irrevocably constitutes
and appoints ....attorney
to transfer the shares representing said stock dividend on the books of said
corporation, with full power of substitution in the premises.

Dated.............................

....
(Official Signature)

133

certificates and preparing for personalized registration and denomination requirements. In such a case, the corporation provides for a significant number of days between the time its entitled stockholders are identified and the time the distribution commences. But in the interim period, stock market trading continues in the old shares and at prices that include the value of the forthcoming distribution. Thus, to satisfy contracts made after the company has recorded the names of holders to whom the new shares will be directed and before those new shares are actually distributed, the seller's broker must deliver the old certificates, accompanied by a due bill, to the purchasing firm.

If a customer is the underlying seller and delivers the old securities registered in his/her name, the Margin Department must withhold payment of sufficient proceeds from the transaction until the new shares are distributed and sent to the broker to complete the obligation.

Example: The Margin Department might withhold 50% of the proceeds for a 2-for-1 split or 100% stock dividend, 33⅓% of the proceeds for a 3-for-2 split or 50% stock dividend, and so forth.

Because they are unable to understand the record keeping complexities involved in this corporate exercise, many customers erroneously believe that shares received from the company after the original sale automatically belong to them, not to the new purchaser. Withholding a portion of the sale proceeds guarantees the integrity of the transaction. Registered representatives should explain to these customers that the value of shares was included in the original contract price.

See also Dividend Distributions.

Due-Diligence Meeting. Some time during an underwriting, before the effective date, a meeting is arranged between the corporation's officials and the members of the underwriting group. Attendance by all syndicate participants is mandatory. Awareness of personal liability, as set forth in the Securities Act of 1933, stimulates a willingness and a necessity for the participants to pay serious attention to the arrangements under discussion. Hence, this convention is often identified as a *due-diligence meeting.* An investment banker who is dissatisfied with any terms or conditions discussed at this forum still has sufficient time to withdraw from the meeting and from the underwriting group with no financial or legal liability.

The purposes of this meeting are: (1) to discuss and review pertinent information for inclusion in, or as an amendment to, the registration statement; (2) to prepare a final prospectus (a condensation of the effective registration statement) for later use in solicitation of orders; and (3) to begin negotiation for a formal underwriting agreement between the corporation and the investment bankers.

One of the few items in the formal agreement not fixed at this meeting is the payment price to the corporation and the price at which the public offering will be attempted. These values are usually set the night before, or even in the early morning hours of, the effective date. It is done at this time in order to adjust to market conditions prevailing at the time of the offering. To be sure, price ideas can be discussed at a due-diligence meeting, but they are not truly binding for any of the participants.

See also Effective Date; Final Prospectus; Preliminary Prospectus; Registration Statement.

E

Early Warning System. *See* Financial Protection Requirements (NYSE).

Earned Surplus. *See* Retained Earnings.

Earnings Available for Common Stock. *See* Net Earnings.

Earnings Before Interest and Taxes (EBIT). *See* Income Statement (Total Income).

Earnings per Share. *See* Income Statement (Primary Earnings per Share).

Eastern (Undivided) Account. The typical municipal syndicate, called an *Eastern* account, has undivided selling and underwriting liabilities.

Example: If a participant agrees to underwrite and sell $1,000,000 of bonds in a $10,000,000 syndication, its participation is 10%. If that participant completes the sale of all $1,000,000 of its allotment, but $800,000 remain unsold by the rest of the syndicate members, that firm still has a 10% ($80,000) liability for the unsold portion.

While this arrangement might seem unfair to the diligent syndicate member, remember that most large general obligation issues are *serial* bonds with varied maturities and yields. Thus certain maturities move more slowly. It would be unfair to allocate all the easy sales to some syndicate members and all the tough ones to others. So the whole syndicate must pull together to complete the distribution.

See also Underwriting Agreement; Western (Divided) Account.

Effective Date. In the absence of a deficiency letter, a registration statement automatically becomes effective on the twentieth calendar day after filing (the twenty-day cooling-off period). SEC rules allow for an earlier effective date if requested by the issuer or its underwriter and approved by the SEC's staff. Approval of an earlier effective date generally depends on such factors as: (1) whether the issuer has been a reporting company under the Securities and Exchange Act of 1934 for at least three years (well-known and significant issuers of securities to public investors may, under the proper circumstances, be permitted to begin their public offerings as soon as 48 hours after filing of its registration statement with the SEC); (2) whether the issuer is up-to-date in its reporting requirements to the SEC; (3) the type and amount of publicly owned securities of the same issuer already outstanding; and (4) the extent of information furnished in the registration statement.

See also Deficiency Letter; Registration Statement.

Effective Sale. This term refers to a round-lot transaction consummated on the floor of the New York Stock Exchange after entry of an odd-lot order by a customer. Its price is used to determine the execution price for the odd-lot order after consideration of the dealer's fee.

See also Differential; Odd-Lot Stock Execution.

Electing Sale. This round-lot transaction activates (triggers) a stop order. The electing sale is *not* the same as the effective sale.

See also Effective Sale; Odd-Lot Stock Execution; Stop Order (Odd-Lot).

Emancipated Minor. *See* New Account Report Form (Age).

Equipment Trust Bond. For this type of bond, the corporation pledges machinery, such as the working equipment normally employed in everyday operation, as collateral for the loan. Railroads, truckers, airlines, and oil companies typically turn to this means of financing for their purchases of locomotives, freight carriers, trucks, aircraft, oil-drilling rigs, and so forth.

Principal Amount	Maturity	Interest Rate (%)	Yield Price (%)*
$400,000	1973	4¼	3.00
400,000	1974	4¼	3.25
395,000	1975	4¼	3.50
395,000	1976	4½	3.75
400,000	1977	4½	3.90
410,000	1978	4½	4.00
405,000	1979	4¾	4.10
405,000	1980	4¾	4.20
405,000	1981	4¾	4.25

*Accrued interest to be added.

See also Collateral Trust Bond; Debenture; Mortgage Bond; Philadelphia Plan; Serial Bond.

Equity. The net worth in a customer's margin account is referred to as the customer's equity in the account. In a long account, equity equals the current market value of the securities less the debit balance. (Equity = LMV – Dr).

See also Margin Account.

Equity REIT. *See* Real Estate Investment Trusts.

Errors in Execution. As trades occur, the two members involved in the transaction approach each other to determine the name of the firm each party represents. Each member announces the name of the principal organization represented on that transaction. This is known as a *floor give-up.* The participants cannot assume the firm name that often appears on a member's white oblong identification badge is the firm represented in a specific transaction because the member may be acting as a two-dollar broker. Even with these precautions, surrounding noise and continuous psychological pressures occasionally lead to an error in execution. The member or the

Equipment Trust Serial Bond

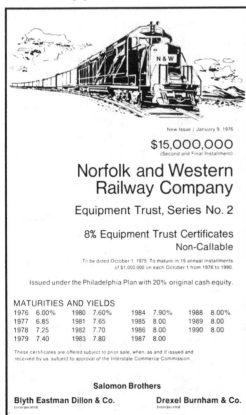

New Issue / January 9, 1976

$15,000,000
(Second and Final Installment)

Norfolk and Western Railway Company

Equipment Trust, Series No. 2

8% Equipment Trust Certificates
Non-Callable

To be dated October 1, 1975. To mature in 15 annual installments of $1,000,000 on each October 1 from 1976 to 1990.

Issued under the Philadelphia Plan with 20% original cash equity.

MATURITIES AND YIELDS

1976	6.00%	1980	7.60%	1984	7.90%	1988	8.00%
1977	6.85	1981	7.65	1985	8.00	1989	8.00
1978	7.25	1982	7.70	1986	8.00	1990	8.00
1979	7.40	1983	7.80	1987	8.00		

These certificates are offered subject to prior sale, when, as and if issued and received by us, subject to approval of the Interstate Commerce Commission.

Salomon Brothers

Blyth Eastman Dillon & Co.
Incorporated

Drexel Burnham & Co.
Incorporated

firm must bear the financial consequences of that mistake. The customer may not suffer a loss as a result of a broker's blunder.

It is not always easy to identify the broker who errs on a transaction. Sometimes the problem involves the number of shares actually executed. (Broker A asserts purchase of 400 shares, but Broker B claims sale of only 300 shares.) If neither member admits fault, the smaller number of shares will be binding in the contract unless that broker's original order was larger than this amount. In that case, the dispute must be submitted to a floor official for resolution.

Sometimes it may be that the price of execution is contested. (Broker C asserts purchase price of $12\frac{3}{8}$, but Broker D claims sale of stock at $12\frac{5}{8}$.) This kind of misunderstanding is usually resolved by researching the exchange's official record of transactions. If it cannot be easily resolved because of the activity and price fluctuation at that approximate time (1) a compromise may be agreed to or sharing financial liability between these members; or (2) the matter must be submitted to a floor official for settlement.

Sometimes it may be the participating brokers' executing capacity at question. (Broker E claims to be the buyer, while Broker F asserts title to the purchase.) If the specialist, or some other witness in the trading area, cannot positively recall which of those members was verbally represented as the buyer, the problem must be submitted to a floor official for satisfaction.

Exchange Acquisition. *See* Exchange Distributions and Acquisitions.

Exchange Distributions and Acquisitions. An order that is too large to be handled by normal market procedures may be handled (with the approval of the NYSE) by an exchange distribution or acquisition procedure. In the following discussion, only the seller's viewpoint is emphasized, simply because these situations are usually initiated by a customer intent on disposing of a large block of stock. The characteristics and procedures associated with the sale also apply to purchases.

After considering such relevant factors as (1) the range of prices and volume of transactions in that issue on the floor of the exchange in the preceding month, (2) attempts to dispose of the security in question in the regular auction market, (3) amounts and prices of bids in the specialist's records and in the current auction market, (4) past and current public and member interest in that security on the floor of the exchange, and (5) the quantity of stock to be disposed of, concurrent approval by the Floor Department and a floor official permits a member firm to attempt an *exchange distribution*.

In an exchange distribution, the selling customer must first give written certification to the NYSE (1) of ownership of all the shares offered for sale (short sales are prohibited because announcement and distribution of a large amount of stock for sale is likely to cause the price to decline, thus benefiting a short seller to the detriment of other investors); and (2) that this represents all the specific security to be offered for a reasonable period of time.

Then the member firm may ask a few other member organizations to canvass their clients and solicit offsetting buy orders to accommodate this customer. (Ordinarily, only one large firm—two at most—is asked to determine confidentially whether its extensive branch office network and corresponding large number of customer accounts can develop enough interest to make the offering worthwhile. Be aware that as yet the seller has not officially entered a noncancellable order. The customer is merely reflecting an indication to become binding only if enough offsetting buy orders are accumulated.)

In return for this service, the seller agrees to pay the participating firms a *special commission*, a commission large enough to (1) satisfy the member firm's commission requirements for both its own and the buyer's transactions; (2) attract potential purchasers who can thereby trade *net* (no commission); and (3) encourage registered representatives in these firms to work a little harder.

Full information must be revealed to potential buyers at the time of solicitation, including the total number of shares being offered for sale.

During the time of offering and solicitation, neither the seller nor participating member organization may bid for or purchase any of that security in the marketplace for any account in which they have a direct or indirect interest. Stabilization in any form is prohibited.

When sufficient offsetting orders are accumulated by the firm coordinating the distribution, the large sell order and all of the buy orders are sent to the floor of the exchange where they are officially crossed at the current market price (*see* Crossing Stock); that is, within the prevailing quotation.

Exchange distributions are printed on the ticker tape as the sales are executed and identified by the letters *DIST* before the security symbol and volume.

Example:

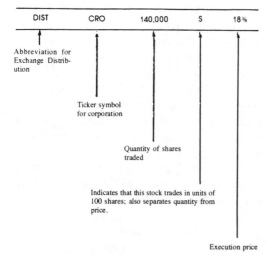

The comparable purchase of a large amount of stock with these characteristics is called an *exchange acquisition* and is identified on the ticker tape by the letters *ACQ* before security symbol and volume.

Example:

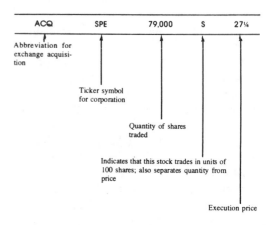

Sometimes, to facilitate the transaction and assure success for the seller of a large block of stock, a participating member organization may decide to act in a principal capacity. It can buy the stock from the seller and attempt to distribute those shares to its own customers while assuming market risk for any unsold portion. Here, too, the firm must notify potential buyers at the time of solicitation about the size of the offering; the fact that it is acting as principal; and that it may, nevertheless, be charging the buyer a commission or, if it chooses to do so under the circumstances, no commission at all.

See also Bid and Offer.

Exchange Offer. Sometimes, with a corporation in dire financial straits, bondholders may be willing to accept an equity security in exchange for their debt instruments to avoid prolonged and expensive bankruptcy proceedings. Or, such an exchange may be directed as a result of judicial decision in a bankruptcy court. Either way, the

Reorganization Department of the brokerage submits the old certificates on behalf of its owners and accepts the new security in satisfaction. A voluntary exchange request needs written instructions from the beneficial owner to accomplish this, whereas an involuntary exchange does not.

Example: The figure on p. 140 is an advertisement announcing a voluntary exchange of convertible debentures for convertible preferred stock in the same company. The brokerage must therefore communicate with the beneficial owners of the 5¾% debentures held in custody by its firm to solicit instructions concerning the disposition of those securities. The offering circular and letters of transmittal must be sent promptly to those persons so that they can respond and appropriate action be taken before the offer's expiration date on January 14, 1977.

See also Beneficial Owner; Broker/Dealer Organization.

Exchange-Type Investment Company. These companies were created to take advantage of a tax loophole that existed prior to 1967. Until that date, an individual with a large paper profit in a security could swap those shares for an equal value of shares in this type of investment company and be able to defer payment of capital gains taxes on the transaction. The capital gains tax liability was officially established for the investor only when the shares received from this investment company were disposed of. In the meantime, however, the investor was able to convert this single security investment into a diversified portfolio of securities and lessen the risk of market price volatility. Of course, any subsequent payments of investment income or trading profits made by the investment company subjected the holder to a tax liability on that particular distribution.

That loophole was closed by the IRS in July 1967, effectively barring "swap funds" from offering such an advantage without future congressional legislation. However, in 1975 it was discovered that the IRS ruling pertained only to exchange-fund *corporations*, and the concept was revived for limited partnership forms of organization. The exchange-type company was barred again in late 1976 with passage of the Tax Reform Act of that year. Any exchange-type corporation or partnership, founded when the concept was legitimate, can continue to function but cannot offer the tax-deferred swap privilege for securities received after the appropriate cut-off dates.

See also Investment Company.

Ex-Dividend Date. This term refers to a date set by the Uniform Practice Committee or by the appropriate stock exchange, on which a given stock will begin trading in the marketplace without the value of a pending dividend included in the contract price. It is closely related to and dependent on the date of record. It is often represented as "X" in the stock listing tables in the newspapers.

See also Distribution Dates.

Executors (Executrixes) of Estates. *See* Fiduciary Accounts.

Exempted Security. This type of issue is exempted from registration under the Act of 1933. Exempted securities include: (1) obligations of, or guaranteed by, the U.S. government; (2) obligations of, or guaranteed by, any state or municipality of that state; (3) issues of domestic banks or trust companies (securities issued by a bank holding company are not exempted from the registration requirement); (4) commercial paper or bankers' acceptances maturing within 270 days of issuance; (5) issues of building and loan associations; (6) securities of farmers' cooperative associations; (7) securities of a common or contract carrier (rails, airlines, truckers,

This announcement is neither an offer to sell nor a solicitation of an offer to buy or exchange these securities. The Exchange Offer is made solely by the Offering Circular.

Notice of Exchange Offer to Holders of
5¾% Convertible Subordinated Debentures Due 1996

of

HALLCRAFT HOMES, INC.

Hallcraft Homes, Inc. ("Hallcraft") is offering to the holders of its 5¾% Convertible Subordinated Debentures due 1996 ("Debentures"), subject to the terms and conditions set forth in the Offering Circular dated December 10, 1976, to exchange for such Debentures, shares of newly authorized Series A Convertible Preferred Shares in the ratio of

**66⅔ Series A Convertible Preferred Shares for each
$1,000 principal amount of 5¾% Debentures
(without payment of accrued interest)**

**This Exchange Offer expires at 5:00 P.M., Phoenix Time,
on January 14, 1977, unless extended.**

Hallcraft is not obligated to accept any Debentures unless at least 90% of the $15,000,000 Principal Amount of the Debentures outstanding are validly tendered, and the other conditions of the Exchange Offer, as described in the Offering Circular, are met.

The Offering Circular (together with the Annual Report of Hallcraft) contains important information which should be read before any decision is made with respect to the Exchange Offer. Debentures may be tendered by delivering, before the Expiration Date, such Debentures and a properly executed Letter of Transmittal to the Exchange Agent: United States Trust Company of New York, Corporate Agency Department, 130 John Street, (20th Floor), New York, New York 10038.

Questions or requests for assistance or for additional copies of the Offering Circular (together with the Annual Report of Hallcraft) and the Letter of Transmittal may be directed to Hallcraft at (602-956-8440, collect) or the Information Agent:

The Carter Organization, Inc.
55 Liberty Street, New York, New York 10005
(212) 962-6117 (collect)

The Exchange Offer is being made by Hallcraft in reliance on the exemption from the registration requirements of the Securities Act of 1933 afforded by Section 3(a)(9) of the Act. In accordance with the conditions of such exemption, no commission or other remuneration will be paid or given directly or indirectly for soliciting exchanges pursuant to the Exchange Offer.

December 13, 1976

and so on); (8) receivers' or trustees'certificates issued with court approval; (9) issues of small business investment companies (SBIC); (10) securities offered and sold exclusively intrastate; (11) issues of religious, educational, charitable, or nonprofit institutions; and (12) insurance policies or mixed annuity contracts (variable annuities and variable life insurance policies are not exempted).

Also exempted are offerings that qualify under Regulations A and D of the Securities Act of 1933.

Regulation A permits offerings under an abbreviated statement when the value of all securities issued by that corporation in the preceding year does not exceed $1,500,000. Offerings by an affiliated person must not exceed $100,000 to qualify for the privilege offered under Regulation A. Although Regulation A does grant a qualified registration exemption to securities offerings of limited value, it requires the use of an offering circular containing much of the same information presented in a full registration statement. However, it does take less time and costs considerably less money in legal and SEC filing fees to accomplish a distribution under Regulation A.

SEC Rules 501-506, under *Regulation D*, set forth terms and conditions within which issuers can offer unregistered securities for sale in limited dollar amounts to a limited number of investors and/or to defined "accredited persons." For the most part these unregistered offerings are called private placements.

See also Private Placement; Registered Security.

Any obligation issued by a governmental entity after 1968 that specifically relates to property leased to, loaned to, or owned by a commercial enterprise whose payments are securing the debt is not an exempted security unless the monies build or improve facilities from which the general public can be expected to realize a communal benefit. These exempted facilities in-

clude airports, waterways, harbors, mass transit, and pollution-control proficiencies. That stipulation ended a special tax privilege previously enjoyed by purchasers of industrial revenue bonds other than those listed in the foregoing— namely, the ability to avoid federal taxation of the interest received from them.

In accordance with this criterion and by special order of the Secretary of the Treasury, the following agencies are also classified as exempted securities: (1) District of Columbia Armory Board, (2) Export-Import Bank (EX-IM), (3) Farmer's Home Administration (FHA), (4) Federal National Mortgage Association (FNMA) "Fannie Mae," (5) General Services Administration (GSA), (6) Government National Mortgage Association (GNMA) "Ginnie Mae," (7) Maritime Administration (Title XI of the Merchant Marine Act), (8) Small Business Administration (SBA), (9) Student Loan Marketing Association (SLMA) "Sallie Mae."

"Exemption" means that securities of the foregoing governmental entities and agencies are not subject to compliance with requirements imposed on other issuers, brokers, dealers, and public investors in sections of the 1934 Act having to do with (1) regulation of margin and credit; (2) restrictions regarding certificate borrowing and lending; (3) SEC registration and procedures for reporting financial information; (4) proxy solicitations; (5) filing of beneficial ownership notices for public information and inspection; and (6) SEC intervention in matters involving trading, clearance, and settlement practices for those securities. Bear in mind, however, that the exemption does not extend to deceitful practices concerning those issues. Where it can be ascertained that a fraud was perpetrated on public investors, brokers, and dealers, the SEC does have authority to initiate civil and/or criminal proceedings against the guilty parties.

The Securities Reform Act of 1975 amended the 1934 law to exclude from its exemptive privileges obligations of states, commonwealths, and municipalities, but only with regard to Sections 15 and 17 of the statute. Those sections now mandate SEC registration for brokers, dealers, and municipal departments of banks trading in these securities. They also allow registration of a national association for self-regulation purposes and creation of a national system for clearance and settlement of such exempted securities transactions. As a result, a Municipal Securities Rulemaking Board (MSRB), composed of industry, banking, and public representatives, was created and now formulates rules and procedures for brokers, dealers, and municipal trading departments of banks. As an official body, it is empowered to establish regulations for participants in municipal securities activities as the NASD does for its membership in the case of corporate securities.

See also Industrial Revenue Bond; Municipal Securities Rulemaking Board; Securities Exchange Act of 1934.

Margin Requirements. Rules and requirements for U.S. government and municipal securities and certain nonconvertible corporate bonds. Any direct obligation or security guaranteed as to payment of principal and interest by the federal government, a state government, or a local government is commonly referred to as an exempt security because it is not subject to the usual margin rules under Regulation T. There is no Reg T initial requirement on these securities. Consequently, the only requirements that apply are those of the various exchanges and the broker's own house requirements.

In this category too are corporate nonconvertible debt securities and mortgage pass-through securities not guaranteed by an agency of the U.S. government—but only if they meet the following criteria: (1) the aggregate amount of its original par value at issuance was at least $25 million; (2) the issue was SEC registered under the 1933 Act and current reports are filed with the Commission; and (3) the issuer is not in default on any interest, principal, or other distribution mandated under the indenture.

The NYSE requirements on these securities, which in effect serve as both initial and maintenance requirements, are listed below:

Security	NYSE Requirement
U.S. government obligations	5% of principal amount
State and municipal obligations	15% of principal amount or 25% of market value* whichever is less. (Above price of 60 use the former; below 60 use the latter.)
Eligible nonconvertible bonds	25% of market value

*On trade date purchase cost is considered the market value. After trade date, closing prices of the preceding business day are used for market value.

Example:

Long Positions

100 U.S. Treasury bonds @ 80	= $80,000
50 Chicago municipal bonds @ 70	= $35,000
30 U.S. Steel nonconvertible bonds @ 60	= $18,000
Long balance = $100,000 Dr.	
Calculated data for this account:	
NYSE initial and maintenance requirement	= $17,000

We calculate this amount as follows:

Security	LMV	NYSE Requirement
U.S. Treasury bonds	$ 80,000	$ 5,000 (5% × $100,000)
Chicago municipal bonds	$ 35,000	$ 7,500 (15% × $ 50,000)
U.S. Steel nonconvertible bonds	$ 18,000	$ 4,500 (25% × $ 18,000)
	$133,000	$17,000

This $17,000 total for NYSE margin requirement serves as the initial and maintenance requirement. It is also the figure we use below in calculating Reg T excess. (We use the terms Reg T excess and Reg T call, though technically with exempt securities Regulation T requirements aren't in effect. Reg T accepts the requirements set by the NYSE.)

LMV = $133,000
Equity = $33,000 (LMV − Dr)
Reg T excess = equity − margin required
= $33,000 − $17,000
= $16,000

How much cash must the customer owning the account just described deposit after a purchase of 500 U.S. Treasury notes @ 90 (cost $450,000)?

Calculations:

Reg T call   =   margin required – Reg T excess
               =   (5% × 500,000) – $16,000
               = $25,000 – $16,000
               = $9,000

Note here that the $16,000 Reg T excess was used to meet part of the $25,000 margin requirement on the purchase. Also, we calculate the Reg T call required by taking 5% of the principal of the Treasury notes rather than the cost, as required by the NYSE.

See also Margin Account; Reg T Call; Reg T Excess.

Exempted Transaction. To avoid burdensome paperwork and expense, certain transactions are exempted from registration requirements of the Securities Act of 1933. They include: (1) transactions by anyone other than the issuer, a dealer, or an underwriter; (2) brokers' transactions executed on the unsolicited request of customers; (3) transactions by an issuer that do not involve a public offering (such as a private placement, which is an offering to a limited number of purchasers); and (4) transactions by securities dealers, except for: (a) those pursuant to an effective registration offering of securities that are traded within 90 days of an initial public offering of securities by the issuer and 40 days of subsequent public offerings of securities by that issuer; (b) those representing an unsold allotment or subscription by a dealer participating in a distribution by an issuer or underwriter. Note carefully that the transactions in subitems (a) and (b) are exceptions to exemption from registration. In other words, transactions that fall within these parameters must be qualified with the SEC. Generally, this means that purchasers and expected purchasers must be furnished with a prospectus for that issue before settlement of their transaction, even after the underwriter's group has been dissolved and most participants have disposed of their commitment.

See also Private Placement; Securities Act of 1933.

Exemption. *See* Exempted Security.

Exercise Cutoff Time. In order to exercise an option, a customer must so instruct his or her broker prior to the exercise cutoff time. For brokers who are members of the NASD or of an exchange, the exercise cutoff time is 5:30 P.M. eastern time, on the business day immediately preceding the expiration date. The exercise cutoff time should *not* be confused with the expiration date.

See also Expiration Date.

Exercise Limits. *See* Regulation of Options Trading.

Exercise Price. The exercise price (or striking price) is the price per share at which the holder of an option may purchase or sell the underlying security on exercise of the option.

An important feature of the listed options market is the standardization of "striking prices." The exchange or NASD sets the exercise prices, depending on the market value of the underlying securities.

Exercise prices are generally fixed at 2½-point intervals for securities trading below 25; five-point intervals for securities trading between 25 and 200; ten-point intervals for securities trading at 200 or above. A few exceptions, which are based on the degree of volatility of the underlying securities, may permit additional strike price levels other than the ones just mentioned.

When trading is to be introduced in a new expiration month, an exchange or NASD ordinarily selects the two exercise prices surrounding the market price of the underlying security on the day of selection.

Example: If the underlying security trades at 37 during the day exercise prices are being selected for a new expiration month, two new series of options will ordinarily be selected with exercise prices at 35 and 40, such as XYZ July 35 calls and XYZ July 40 calls.

However, if the market price of the underlying security is at, or very close to, a standard exercise price, three prices might be selected: that nearest the market price and the two surrounding exercise prices.

When significant price movements take place in an underlying security following the introduction of a new expiration month, additional series of options with exercise prices reflecting such price movements may be opened for trading in the expiration months that are already trading.

Example: XYZ October 30 puts have previously been opened for trading. An exchange or NASD will ordinarily open XYZ October 25 puts, as well as XYZ 25 puts for the other two expiration months then trading, when the underlying security price reaches 27½.

See also Aggregate Exercise Price; Listed Options.

Expense Ratio. Also known as the *operating ratio*, this ratio is an excellent measure of corporate efficiency and should therefore be compared with the results of prior years. An increasing expense ratio could indicate a company's loss of control over cost. The formula is:

$$\text{Expense ratio} = \frac{\text{Operating costs}}{\text{Net sales}}$$

Or,

$$\text{Expense ratio} = \frac{\text{Cost of goods sold} + \text{selling, general and administrative expenses} + \text{depreciation}}{\text{Net sales}}$$

Example:

$$\text{Expense ratio} = \frac{\$1,590,000 + 154,000 + 56,000}{2,000,000} = 0.9 \text{ or } 90\%$$

See also Management Group.

Expiration Date. An unexercised option expires worthless after its expiration date. For listed options, which have standardized expiration dates, the expiration time represents the latest time by which notice of exercise must be received in proper form at the Options Clearing Corporation. The expiration time is 11:59 P.M. eastern time, on the Saturday immediately following the third Friday of the expiration month. The expiration time should not be confused with the earlier exercise cutoff time. In order to exercise an option, a customer must so instruct his or her broker prior to the exercise cutoff time. For brokers who are members of the NASD or of an exchange, the exercise cutoff time is 5:30 P.M. eastern time, on the business day immediately preceding the expiration date. If an outstanding option is not exercised prior to its expiration, it becomes worthless.

Should an option holder wish to exercise on any business day other than the one immediately preceding the expiration date, the latest time is 8:00 P.M. eastern time.

Under present practices all equity options on the same underlying security are assigned to one of three expiration month cycles: the January-April-July-October cycle; the February-May-August-November cycle; or the March-June-September-December cycle.

Example: If February, May, and August options are opened for trading, the November series will be introduced on the Monday following expiration of the February options.

See also Listed Option.

Extension of Time to Defer Mandatory Liquidation Proceedings. *See* Broker/Dealer Organization (Margin Department).

Extension Request Form. *See* Broker/Dealer Organization (Margin Department).

F

Face-Amount Certificate Company. This type of investment company issues a debt instrument obligating itself to pay a stated sum of money (face amount) on a date fixed more than 24 months after issuance. The certificate is offered in consideration of deposits made by an investor, usually in periodic installments. The total money deposited is less than the face amount redeemed at maturity. The difference represents compound interest and is taxable to the individual as ordinary income. The rate of interest is predetermined and is represented on a yield-to-maturity basis. This means that the percentage is an average return and is accurate only if the investor holds the certificate until it matures.

The company provides a formula of cash surrender values that apply to each certificate annually should the holders decide to redeem their shares prior to maturity. Normally, investors have to hold their certificates for at least eight years before the cash surrender value is equal to the money deposited during that time period. If, of course, redemption is chosen after this period but prior to maturity, the rate of return is lower than the yield-to-maturity specified. To encourage the investor to continue making installment payments, the issuing corporation may grant additional credits of perhaps 1 to 2% each year that are then added to the cash surrender value of the certificate. These credits enable investors to reach a break-even point that much sooner and to increase the effective yield if they leave the face amount on deposit with the company until maturity.

In lieu of early surrender for cash value, a certificate holder can discontinue installments and merely retain what is owned until maturity. The company will provide a paid-up certificate representing the cash surrender value plus compound interest thereon. No additional credits are granted on paid-up certificates, however.

Face-amount certificates may be issued in consideration of a single lump-sum payment as well as installment-type deposits. The advantage of the former procedure is that investment money is employed immediately, and the schedule of cash surrender values is arranged to reach the break-even point at the end of the fourth year instead of the eighth year. The break-even point is reduced even further if the company grants additional credits, as it is privileged

To ensure the integrity of the financial arrangements required with face-amount certificates, federal and state authorities dictate the type and quality of investments employed by the issuing company. Generally speaking, this means that face-amount companies may invest in U.S. government and municipal obligations, prime real estate and mortgages, and some equity securities of the highest quality only. In fact, the nature of face-amount certificates is so similar to insurance that some states have assigned supervision of these companies to the insurance commissioner rather than to their securities regulators.

See also Investment Company; Management Company; Unit Investment Trust Company.

Failed Contract. A fail-to-receive or fail-to-deliver is a contract between two brokerage concerns that is not fulfilled by certificate delivery and payment on settlement date. Each day such contracts remain open interferes with that issue's market liquidity and, in prolonged instances, penalizes the responsible member firm's net capital position. The fail situation is often brought about by certificates registered in such a way, or in such denominations, that they do not qualify as a good delivery.

See also Rules of Fair Practice (Section 31).

Federal Funds. A commercial bank in a deficit reserve position can generally borrow money from commercial banks with excess reserve positions. These short-term (usually overnight) loans are called federal funds. Reserve balances are transferred the same day between members of the Federal Reserve System by means of the District Bank's internal telegraphic facilities. The rate of interest associated with such borrowing, known as the *federal funds rate*, is determined by supply-and-demand relationships in the money market. If the quantity of money available is limited, the rate may rise sharply, particularly on Wednesday afternoon when reserves are calculated and there is great demand by member banks. If supplies of money are readily available or if commercial loan demand ebbs, the federal funds rate declines and may even experience no significant demand whatsoever.

There is also competition for federal funds from sources other than commercial banks eager to satisfy reserve requirements.

Example: It is customary for professional dealers in U.S. government securities to settle their contracts in federal funds, because it is "instant money," that is, immediately usable by the seller.

In addition to being somewhat riskier for a seller to accept, a personal check normally takes from one to four days to clear through the banking system before it becomes good money. In the interim, the seller cannot make use of the proceeds. (The seller's bank, however, promptly credits its own deposit records and immediately creates new loan power. The advantage to banks of this delay is called *bank float*.

Borrowing federal funds is not always the cheapest source of money available to member banks of the Federal Reserve System (*see* Prime Rate). However, its chief advantages are: (1) convenience, (2) promptness, (3) no collateral needed as security, and (4) minimal restraints on its use. (When its loan demand is high, a bank may be tempted to borrow federal funds and simply lend them to customers instead of reserving them for federal requirements.)

See also Federal Reserve System.

Federal Home Loan Banks. Federal Home Loan Banks (FHLB) operate as a credit reserve system for savings and loan associations, homestead associations, savings banks, and insurance companies that qualify and apply for membership. FHLB issues obligations to finance the home building industry in the United States by granting mortgage loans with the monies generated from the offerings. Such debt is a legal investment for fiduciary, trust, and public funds. It is issued in bearer form with interest payable to holders subject to federal taxation but exempted from state and municipal taxes.

See also U.S. Government-Sponsored Corporation or Agency Obligation.

Federal Intermediate Credit Banks. Federal Intermediate Credit Banks (FICB), under supervision of the Farm Credit Administration, make loans to agricultural credit corporations and production associations through issuance of debt obligations maturing within five years. Interest paid to the holders of FICB obligations is fully taxable to them under federal regulations but exempted from state and municipal taxes.

See also U.S. Government-Sponsored Corporation or Agency Obligation.

Federal Land Banks. Federal Land Banks (FLB) arrange loans secured by first mortgages on farm or ranch properties for general agricultural purposes. The obligations of these banks are created from an offering of bonds. They provide the holder with exemption from state and municipal taxes on interest received, but the interest is subject to full federal tax liabilities. The bonds are not guaranteed by the U.S. government but are backed by participating banks organized under federal charter operating under government supervision. They are lawful investments for fiduciaries, trust funds, federal credit unions, federal savings and loan associations, savings banks, and commercial banks organized under a national charter. Denominations of certificates range from $1,000 to $100,000.

See also U.S. Government-Sponsored Corporation or Agency Obligation.

Federal National Mortgage Association. Federal National Mortgage Association (FNMA, Fannie Mae) is a publicly owned, government-sponsored corporation established to provide liquidity for mortgage investments in the marketplace. The corporation purchases and sells mortgages insured by the Federal Housing Administration (FHA) or Farmers Housing Administration (FHDA) or guaranteed by the Veterans Administration (VA), using monies generated in part from short-term notes and debenture obligations offered publicly. The balance of its funds is realized from direct purchase of its capital stock by qualified buyers and sellers with whom it deals in these mortgages. Institutional investors whose names appear on an approved list are obligated to subscribe to FNMA common stock pursuant to a prescribed formula. The

stock as well as the association's bonds are readily marketable. The debentures are issued only in bearer form with interest coupons attached. The interest paid on the association's bonds is fully taxable to investors despite the fact that its common stock and bonds are clearly defined as an "exempted security" under the Securities Exchange Act of 1934.

See also U.S. Government-Sponsored Corporation or Agency Obligation.

Federal Open Market Committee (FOMC). *See* Federal Reserve System.

Federal Reserve System. Unlike the situation in most western European countries, the idea of a government-operated central bank never sat well with the American public. Attempts were made to conform to the European system, as evidenced by the abortive First and Second Banks of the United States in the early 1800s. The booms and subsequent financial busts in the nation affected relatively small segments of the population. After all, the country was still in its infancy, and its economy was largely agrarian. However, in the decade following the American Civil War, the situation changed dramatically. Large-scale immigration and industrialization added to the

**Chain of Command in the
Federal Reserve Banking System**

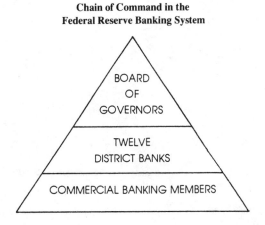

Federal Reserve Banks and Branches

Legend

——— Boundaries of Federal Reserve Districts ——— Boundaries of Federal Reserve Branch Territories

★ Board of Governors of the Federal Reserve System

◉ Federal Reserve Bank Cities • Federal Reserve Branch Cities

Federal Reserve Banks and Branches

DISTRICT	FEDERAL RESERVE BANK	ADDRESS
1	BOSTON	30 Pearl Street (Boston, Massachusetts 02106)
2	NEW YORK	33 Liberty Street (Federal Reserve P.O. Station, New York, New York 10045)
	Buffalo Branch	160 Delaware Avenue (P.O. Box 961, Buffalo, New York 14240)
3	PHILADELPHIA	925 Chestnut Street (Philadelphia, Pennsylvania 19101)
4	CLEVELAND	1455 East Sixth Street (P.O. Box 6387, Cleveland, Ohio 44101)
	Cincinnati Branch	105 West Fourth Street (P.O. Box 999, Cincinnati, Ohio 45201)
	Pittsburgh Branch	717 Grant Street (P.O. Box 867, Pittsburgh, Pennsylvania 15230)
5	RICHMOND	100 North Ninth Street (P.O. Box 27622, Richmond, Virginia 23261)
	Baltimore Branch	114-120 East Lexington Street (P.O. Box 1378, Baltimore, Maryland 21203)
	Charlotte Branch	401 South Tryon Street (Charlotte, North Carolina 28201)
	Culpeper Communications Center	P.O. Drawer 20 (Culpeper, Virginia 22701)
6	ATLANTA	104 Marietta Street N. W. (Atlanta, Georgia 30303)
	Birmingham Branch	1801 Fifth Avenue, North (P.O. Box 2574, Birmingham, Alabama 35202)
	Jacksonville Branch	515 Julia Street (P.O. Box 929, Jacksonville, Florida 32203)
	Nashville Branch	301 Eighth Avenue, North (Nashville, Tennessee 37203)
	New Orleans Branch	525 St. Charles Avenue (P.O. Box 61630, New Orleans, Louisiana 70161)
	Miami Office	P.O. Box 847 (Miami, Florida 33152)
7	CHICAGO	230 South LaSalle Street (P.O. Box 834, Chicago, Illinois 60690)
	Detroit Branch	160 Fort Street, West (P.O. Box 1059, Detroit, Michigan 48231)
8	ST. LOUIS	411 Locust Street (P.O. Box 442, St. Louis, Missouri 63166)
	Little Rock Branch	325 West Capitol Avenue (P.O. Box 1261, Little Rock, Arkansas 72203)
	Louisville Branch	410 South Fifth Street (P.O. Box 899, Louisville, Kentucky 40201)
	Memphis Branch	200 North Main Street (P.O. Box 407, Memphis, Tennessee 38101)
9	MINNEAPOLIS	73 South Fifth Street (Minneapolis, Minnesota 55480)
	Helena Branch	400 North Park Avenue (Helena, Montana 59601)
10	KANSAS CITY	925 Grand Avenue (Federal Reserve Station, Kansas City, Missouri 64198)
	Denver Branch	1020 16th Street (P.O. Box 5228, Terminal Annex, Denver, Colorado 80217)
	Oklahoma City Branch	226 Northwest Third Street (P.O. Box 25129, Oklahoma City, Oklahoma 73125)
	Omaha Branch	102 South Seventeenth Street (Omaha, Nebraska 68102)
11	DALLAS	400 South Akard Street (Station K, Dallas, Texas 75222)
	El Paso Branch	301 East Main Street (P.O. Box 100, El Paso, Texas 79999)
	Houston Branch	1701 San Jacinto Street (P.O. Box 2578, Houston, Texas 77001)
	San Antonio Branch	126 East Nueva Street (P.O. Box 1471, San Antonio, Texas 78295)
12	SAN FRANCISCO	400 Sansome Street (P.O. Box 7702, San Francisco, California 94120)
	Los Angeles Branch	409 West Olympic Boulevard (P.O. Box 2077, Terminal Annex, Los Angeles, California 90051)
	Portland Branch	915 S. W. Stark Street (P.O. Box 3436, Portland, Oregon 97208)
	Salt Lake City Branch	120 South State Street (P.O. Box 780, Salt Lake City, Utah 84110)
	Seattle Branch	1015 Second Avenue (P.O. Box 3567, Seattle, Washington 98124)

complexity, dimensions, and duration of the nation's business cycles, culminating in the financial panic of 1907.

As a result, Congress was pressured into finding a solution intended to forestall, or at worst, temper the effects of business recessions. It came up with the Federal Reserve Banking System, a compromise between traditional independent banking and a strong central regulatory banking authority.

District Bank. The Act of 1913 and its modifications of 1935 provide for a partitioning of the United States into twelve banking districts. Within each district, a Federal Reserve Bank (also referred to as a District Bank) is established to: (1) service the financial needs of commercial banks in the area; (2) supervise the safety and soundness of local commercial banks; and (3) manage the nation's supply of money and the amount of credit extended by commercial banks under its jurisdiction. In other words, the District Federal Reserve Bank, acting together ("in concert") with its satellite branches, is responsible for monitoring and regulating commercial banking activities within its geographic locale.

Organization. Each District Bank is an autonomous agency managed by its own officials. Six of its nine-member board of directors are elected by the commercial banks subscribing to membership in the Federal Reserve network from that district. The remaining three directors, including its chairman, are appointed by the Board of Governors of the entire system. The Board of Governors exercises nationwide jurisdiction and approval over the policies and mechanisms of Federal Reserve banking. For instance, the important operating positions of president and first vice-president of each District Bank are filled through appointment by the bank's own directors. But the appointments depend on approval by the Board of Governors of the Federal Reserve System. This chain of command allows flexibility for decentralized, independent banking and still provides for effective governmental control when needed.

The Federal Reserve Board of Governors. The Federal Reserve Board of Governors is a governmental institution headquartered in Washington, D.C. Its principal duty is to supervise the workings of the Federal Reserve System.

The Board's functions include: (1) formulating and interpreting regulations affecting monetary policies of Reserve banks on the national, rather than on the district, level; (2) directing bank examinations; (3) issuing economic-research, and related, publications; (4) compiling and releasing a weekly statement of assets and liabilities of all twelve Federal Reserve Banks (District Banks); and (5) surveilling international operations of District Banks.

The Board also has official power to: (1) establish credit requirements for loans involving securities as collateral (these rules and procedures are contained in its Regulations T, U, and G); (2) regulate and enforce consumer credit rules (Regulation W). Overall, the Board of Governors formulates national credit policies, interprets them for specialized circumstances, and oversees their execution.

Whereas the Board is created by act of Congress, its members are appointed by the President of the United States with consent of the Senate. It is comprised of seven members chosen from various walks of life to serve fourteen-year terms of office. Terms are arranged so that a vacancy develops every two years. In practice, since 1913, governors have included respected industrialists, farmers, lawyers, accountants, economists, educators, and others. There is one important legal proviso concerning membership: No two members of the Board may come from the same Federal Reserve District at the same time.

The financial affairs of the Federal Reserve System are self-sustaining. This means that Congress does not support it with allocations of money. Even the expenses of the Board, which is obviously not a revenue-generating center, are paid from assessments levied on the twelve District Banks. At the end of its fiscal year, the Fed generally remits a surplus to the Secretary of the Treasury to help support the government.

Federal Reserve Membership. Of some 14,500 commercial banks in the United States at the end of 1986, 5,613 (a total comprised of 4,604 national banks and 1,009 state banks) were members of the Federal Reserve System. This number represents only 38% of eligible banks, but these members have 75% of all deposits. They therefore provide the Fed with significant control over bank credit activities. In the early 1980s, both the number and percentage of member banks declined due to mergers and voluntary resignations. In fact, all national banks, chartered by the Controller of the Currency, are obliged to join the system. Only state-chartered banks have a choice of belonging, after weighing the advantages against the disadvantages of federal control. Savings banks and savings and loan associations do not belong to the Federal Reserve System; they have their own regulatory organizations.

An important requisite of membership is for each commercial bank to subscribe 6% of its capital and surplus in stock of its District Bank. there is no public market for this issue, and the purchase cost is fully refundable if the member bank resigns from the system. However, if the District Bank fails, ownership of stock does not yield to the member commercial bank a percentage of the underlying net assets of the District Bank. The assets revert to the United States in the event of liquidation. However, ownership does entail certain advantages.

Ownership entitles the member bank to the following: (1) an annual 6% cumulative dividend; (2) a vote in the election of two-thirds of the directors of its District Bank; (3) the privilege of borrowing from the District Bank; (4) the right to transfer funds to other cities by means of Federal Reserve wire facilities; and (5) the privilege of acquiring currency as it is needed.

The disadvantages of membership center primarily on the Fed's stringent regulation of member-bank deposit, reserve, and loan arrangements. Although state controls are similar in nature to federal powers, state authorities are not as severe or aggressive in exercising their abilities over state-chartered, nonmember banks.

The Federal Reserve Board may exercise specialized controls accorded it by legal statute. These controls are: (1) setting reserve requirements, (2) influencing the discount rate, and (3) conducting direct open market operations.

Reserve Requirements. Each commercial bank, whether a member of the Federal Reserve System or not, is obliged to set aside a percentage of its deposits, thereby restricting the amount of potential credit available to borrowers and protecting the financial interests of currency depositors. Federal Reserve members must keep these funds lying fallow, while most state-regulated banks are allowed to invest them in interest-bearing U.S. Treasury and municipal obligations. The Federal Reserve percentage requirements depend on: (1) the quantity and type of deposits held by the bank (that is, dollars' worth of demand, time, and savings deposits); and (2) whether or not a bank qualifies as a Reserve City Bank.

Percentage requirements over the years can and do vary widely, as the Federal Reserve Board of Governors exercises this major power to influence the credit-making ability of commercial banks under its jurisdiction. The Board can act arbitrarily as long as it operates within a framework of limitations set by law.

	Minimum (%)	Maximum (%)
Demand deposits, Reserve City Banks	10	22
Demand deposits, other banks	7	14
Time deposits	3	10

151

State reserve requirements tend to be more lenient than federal rules, but total bank deposits are generally lower, too, thus tempering the significance of this inequity.

Each Federal Reserve member bank is obliged to calculate its requirement each day. But it "settles up" and segregates the necessary funds only at the end of the banking week (which ends on Wednesday afternoon); it segregates funds equal to its average requirement during the previous two weeks, for the period ending that Monday. It is called that bank's *contemporaneous* reserve requirement.

The result is a ceiling on credit, a limitation for member banks determined by the Federal Reserve Board of Governors after careful analysis of the economy. When business activity slackens, the Board may lower reserve requirements, provide member banks with more lending power, and, it is hoped, encourage an expansion in borrowing by commercial and agricultural interests. Conversely, to combat an overexpansive and inflationary cycle, the Board may arbitrarily increase the percentage figures, thereby forcing member banks to reconsider and curtail lax lending practices. Such an increase might even necessitate cancelling some outstanding loans to bring reserves into compliance with requirements.

The Reserve regulates the country-wide availability of credit through reserve requirements by means of a mechanism called the *multiplier effect*. Specifically, since the amount of total credit is a multiple of bank reserves, the adjustment of reserves has a *multiplier effect* on general credit.

As a result of customer deposits and withdrawals during the week, the money segregated as a federal reserve must be adjusted. Some banks calculate that they are in a deficit position, while others find that they have reserves in excess of the requirement.

Example: A bank has $100,000,000 in deposit balances and, with a 10% reserve requirement, makes loans of $82,000,000. Assuming no other activity during the week, the bank lends an additional $50,000,000 to its customers. Its position is then:

($00,000)

Checking Account Deposit Balances	Money Loaned	Money Set Aside As Reserves
$150 ($100 + $50)	$132 ($82 + $50)	$18

With demand deposits of $150,000,000, an 18% requirement necessitates $27,000,000 in reserve. The bank has a $9,000,000 deficit to be resolved immediately.

The following week, after satisfying that obligation, the banks customer may draw the $50,000,000 check on his or her account and pay a creditor, who may then deposit it in another bank. This creates an unusual situation in the original bank.

($00,000)

Checking Account Deposit Balances	Money Loaned	Money Set Aside as Reserves
$100 ($150 − $50)	$132	$27

The deposit balances are less than the money loaned to customers. This unbalanced condition cannot be allowed to prevail for very long, or it will jeopardize the assets of the bank itself. The bank must either: (1) attract new cash deposits of at least $32,000,000 (In fact, the shuffling of deposits and withdrawals by various customers during the week usually enables it to easily cover this deficiency. New deposits can take the form of additional savings and demand deposits or even CDs. Banks highly regarded in the financial community can easily "purchase" deposits through sale of negotiable and nonnegotiable CDs. All they need do is promise to pay a somewhat higher rate of interest than that prevailing for savings deposits.); (2) call for repayment of some outstanding loans to reduce its loan total; or (3) sell off some of its own assets to cover the shortage. (This could be a prelude to insolvency if all other actions fail and the bank's real assets are insufficient to meet the call for payment of the check.)

Whichever course of action is chosen, after the $5,000,000 withdrawal, the bank's figures should have the correct percentages. Let's assume the bank attracts new cash deposits of $32,000, the first of the options listed above:

($00,000)

Checking Account Deposit Balances	Money Loaned	Money Set Aside as Reserves
$132	$132	$27

Now, however, with deposits of $13,200,000, only $2,376,000 is needed as reserves (18% of $13,200,000 = $2,376,000). So the bank actually has an excess in reserve of $3,240,000 ($2,700,000 − $2,376,000 = $324,000). This amount represents money that can be invested or loaned to customers.

Now let us examine how the member bank handles both the deficit and the excess reserve situations as they arise.

On Wednesday afternoon, if a bank finds itself in a deficit reserve position, it can do one of two things: (1) It can liquidate some of its own securities assets to cover the deficit (which is obviously distasteful and used as the last choice); (2) It can arrange to borrow the necessary money immediately, usually from another member bank. (*See* Federal Funds.)

On Wednesday afternoon, if a bank finds itself in an excess reserve position, it again has two options: (1) It can invest the money in high-quality, interest-bearing securities. Quite often this means purchases of U.S. government and government-agency bills and notes, although it does not necessarily mean restriction to those instruments. The bank can also buy municipal and corporate securities and thus diversify its portfolio. (2) It can lend the excess reserves to corporations in need of short-term financing to conduct current operations. These uncollateralized, working-capital loans are known as *commercial paper*. Generally, however, excess reserves are most often loaned to other banks with deficit reserve positions or to dealers in government securities who customarily settle their obligations with such *federal funds*.

Discount Rate. When money supplies are tight and rates begin to climb, member banks turn to the District Federal Reserve Bank for assistance in meeting the weekly reserve requirement. The District Bank stands ready and able to lend reserves to member banks in need of them. But this assistance must be considered a privilege and not a right of membership in the Federal Reserve System. This means that the District Bank can and does impose restrictive conditions on such borrowing arrangements. For instance, it insists: (1) that borrowing be confined exclusively to meeting the reserve requirement, precluding speculation in securities, commodities, or real estate transactions; (2) that a deposit of collateral be pledged to secure the credit extended (the only collateral ordinarily deemed eligible is U.S. government obligations and certain government-agency obligations from the bank's portfolio); and (3) on the right of review of the member bank's investment portfolio and the quantity and character of its customer loans.

For the service and accommodation of lending funds, the District Bank charges interest to its members. The rate at which interest is charged is called the *discount rate* because the borrowing bank does indeed receive credit discounted from the market value of the securities pledged as its collateral. The discount rate is a relatively fixed rate of interest compared to federal funds, commercial paper, CDs, and the like, which are subject to competitive market conditions. Officially, the board of directors of each District Bank is empowered to set this rate level, although it is strongly influenced by the policies of the national Board, which has overriding authority for approval or denial. It is often alleged that the Board of Governors of the Federal Reserve System instigates a District Bank's request to alter its rate, because it uses this method to voice opinion about the desirability of credit expansion or contraction. In fact, the Board of Governors' presence here is so visible that changing the discount rate is sometimes considered to be one of its functions rather than that of the District Banks.

An increase in the discount rate is taken as a signal of the banks' intent to tighten credit control and discourage borrowing. A rate adjustment downward reflects the Federal Reserve Board's intention to open the so-called "discount window" wider and stimulate borrowing.

The discount rate, in turn, affects the so-called *prime rate,* which is the rate that banks charge on loans to their best customers.

Open Market Operations. The borrowing attitudes of member banks are only minimally affected by changes in the discount rate. As long as credit remains available, its cost is subordinate to its potential for generating higher revenues and profits. The discount rate should be viewed as a minor factor in the overall banking picture. It is merely a clue to the Federal Reserve Board's opinion of the country's near-term financial prospects and a prelude to more significant measures to induce changes in the economic cycle.

The most important factor in provoking such changes is an adjustment in bank reserve requirements, but this measure can bring about serious long-term consequences due to its inflexibility. Once a trend has become established (either up or down), it isn't easy to reverse it by using this passive method of control. Nor does this method of adjusting the reserve requirement allow for consideration of seasonal business factors or for temporary distortions in the money supply.

Therefore, since changes in the discount rate are not very effective and adjustments of the reserve requirement are relatively inflexible, the Board implements short-term monetary policy through the use of *open market operations.* This term refers to the purchase and sale of U.S. government and government-agency securities as a means of directly controlling the nation's money supply.

This activity also provides the Federal Reserve with significant revenues needed to continue as a self-sustaining agency. Revenues are also realized in the form of interest from the government and government-agency securities in the system's own portfolio and from the discount rate paid by member banks to finance deficient reserves.

Federal Open Market Committee. The purpose of buying and selling securities for the Fed's portfolio account is to enable it to exercise control over the size of bank reserves and, in so doing, influence the amount of money and credit made available by the banking community. If undesirable monetary conditions exist due to an overabundance or lack of credit, the Federal Open Market Committee (FOMC) arranges to buy or sell eligible securities outright in the open market. This committee is permanently comprised of the seven governors of the Federal Reserve Board and the president of the New York District Bank. Four other District Bank presidents serve too, but their participation is temporary because these positions are rotated annually among the eleven other District Bank presidents. The twelve members of the FOMC officially direct all open market operations, although the day-to-day mechanical responsibilities are assigned to a senior officer of the New York District Bank, through which all transactions are conducted. This individual is the manager of the system's open market account and abides by the overall credit policy of the FOMC, subject to prevailing market conditions.

Restricting Credit. The Federal Reserve

Board has been granted official authority to regulate credit used to purchase, carry, or trade securities. It does not have authority to regulate credit in exempted securities transactions. Its specific powers in these matters are described in detail in Regulations T, U, G, and X.

The manager's staff restricts its unconditional purchases and sales to transactions with dealer banks and nonbank dealers that act as market-makers in U.S. government and selected government-agency notes and bonds. (Nonbank dealers are securities firms recognized by the Federal Reserve Board for maintaining continuous bids and offerings in all the issues eligible for inclusion in open market activity. Each firm must be financially capable and willing to deal in sizable quantities over an extended period.) Since same-day or next-day settlement is traditional, prompt payment produces the desired effect on the banking system.

If the FOMC buys securities from a dealer bank, it pays for them simply by increasing the number of reserve dollars on deposit at the District Bank for that institution for the full amount of the purchase. Thus that bank suddenly has an opportunity to expand its credit-making capability. Even if it doesn't immediately expand the availability of credit, this is enough to stimulate demand for outstanding debt issues. This, in turn, raises prices and lowers yields on those investments. If the purchase is accomplished from a nonbank dealer, the same result is achieved at the member bank in which the nonbank dealer deposits the Fed's check. When you consider that the FOMC deals in considerable quantities and uses the financial capabilities of several banks and nonbank dealers concurrently, you can appreciate the impact of this maneuver on the entire system.

On the other hand, if the FOMC sells securities to dealer banks, it promptly debits the reserve balance held on deposit for those banks. Or, if the sale is to nonbank dealers, FOMC debits the reserve balance of those commercial banks on which the nonbank dealers have drawn their checks for payment. The affected banks, with a smaller reserve base, must terminate some loans, restrict new credit, or use available currency to satisfy reserve obligations. Undoubtedly, banks and other investors will also sell off some debt issues in their portfolios. Such action consequently lowers prices and correspondingly increases prevailing interest rates for securities investment purposes. Prices and yields on fixed-interest investments always move in opposite directions.

These outright transactions are often supplemented or replaced by matched sale-purchase contracts. These are FOMC sales of Treasury bills for immediate cash settlement that include a provision for their repurchase by the Fed at the same price on a specified date (normally within one to three days after the original transaction). Their purpose is to temporarily absorb (withdraw) and then replace bank reserves without upsetting the financial equilibrium created by Federal Reserve basic policy. The Fed uses such contracts as a tactic for fine-tuning the system rather than as a strategic tool for influencing longer-term objectives. The rate of interest associated with such arrangements is determined competitively among participating dealers.

Expanding Credit. In a somewhat similar but opposite fashion, the manager of the Federal Reserve account can temporarily supply reserves by initiating *repurchase agreements. Repos*, as they are popularly referred to, are Federal Reserve contracts to purchase a specific government issue, government-agency security, or even banker's acceptance from a nonbank dealer at a fixed price, with provision for resale to that dealer (1) at the same price, (2) within an agreed period of up to fifteen days, and (3) at a rate of interest determined competitively.

Repurchase agreements are made only with nonbank dealers, because dealer banks can borrow from the District Bank as necessary at the advantageous discount rate. Since the nonbank dealers deposit the money they receive from the Fed in their local banks, the Fed purchase has the effect of increasing reserves at those comercial banks. The resale of the repos by the Fed to the nonbank dealers subsequently reduces reserves because the dealers withdraw money from their accounts to pay the Fed.

Dealing in repos is advantageous to the nonbank dealers because it enables these firms to finance their securities inventories at a lower rate of interest than is otherwise available. The initiative for this privilege, however, rests solely with the manager of the Federal Reserve account and is used as another fine-tuning tactic.

In summary, therefore, open market operations of the Federal Reserve System can assume any or all of three identities: (1) outright purchases and sales of U.S. Treasury and government-agency securities; (2) matched sale-purchase transactions in Treasury bills; and (3) repurchase agreements.

These marketing arrangements are so powerful, yet so flexible, that they permit the manager of the Federal Reserve account to effectively and immediately reverse financial policy objectives if directed to do so by the FOMC. Its impact on the banking system is a significant one, because the Fed has an ability to deal in government and agency issues outstanding currently valued in excess of hundreds of billions of dollars.

Other controls. To underscore its credit objectives and policies, the Federal Reserve Board may also exercise specialized controls accorded it by legal statute. They are: (1) moral suasion; (2) regulating margin requirements; and (3) influencing consumer credit.

1. *Moral suasion:* The first of these other specialized controls is the Board's ability to pressure bank credit activities merely by threatening to implement any of the above three primary powers. This control is facetiously referred to as the Board of Governors' "open-

mouth policy." It directs attention to the fact that member bank practices are subject to regular examination by the Fed and that available sanctions include removing uncooperative officers or closing the offending bank itself. The Fed is, therefore, in an advantageous position to enforce compliance with its directives.

2. *Margin requirements:* Delegated with authority to regulate credit when the purpose of a loan is to purchase, carry, or trade corporate securities, the Federal Reserve Board fixes the minimum margin requirement to be imposed by: (1) brokers (that is, people who serve as agents between sellers and buyers) and dealers (that is, people who sell and buy on their own behalf) (Regulation T); (2) banks (Regulation U); and (3) all other creditors (Regulation G).

At present, these rules are stricter for credit extension by brokers and dealers than for credit extension by banks or by other grantors of securities-related loans.

3. *Consumer credit:* By Presidential order, the Federal Reserve Board has authority to regulate the installment loans consumers arrange for goods and services. Under Regulation W, the Board can decide on minimum down payments and loan maturities for such items as automobiles, household appliances, and charge accounts. The Board tries to curb demand and accompanying inflationary pressures on the economy in this fashion. This power has been used only during wartime and for a short period immediately after World War II.

Concluding Comments. The growth of international banking and the less-than-unanimous membership in the Federal Reserve System by U.S. commercial banks prevent the Board of Governors of the Federal Reserve System from exercising absolute control over the American economy. However, the Board retains sufficient influence and ability to cushion the effect of swings in business cycles by dealing with the major financial institutions just as soon as those tendencies appear to act contrary to national economic policy. In the late seventies and eighties, the duration of each cycle has been shorter, but the cycles also recur more frequently than ever before in history. Perhaps this is due to Federal Reserve Board influence, or perhaps it is the result of better worldwide communication and cooperation by executive governmental authorities. In the years ahead, the Federal Reserve System will certainly be called on to develop new procedures and controls to accomplish its purposes in this country's increasingly complex finances. The only certainty is that—whatever its action—it will inspire controversy. Economists have never been able to agree whether the Board of Governors' policies affecting money supply are inflationary, deflationary, or even appropriate to the conditions that prevail.

Fidelity Bond Insurance. *See* Blanket Fidelity Bond Insurance; Financial Protection Requirements (NYSE).

Fiduciary. *See* Fiduciary Accounts.

Fiduciary Accounts. A *fiduciary* is a person to whom property is entrusted for the benefit of another; the generic term includes administrators, executors, trustees, guardians, receivers-in-bankruptcy, and committees for incompetents. They are either court appointed or legally validated to act in this capacity and may not, under normal circumstances, delegate their authority to another person. Margin accounts for most fiduciaries are prohibited by law. But this is not always the case. Many recently written trust instruments empower their fiduciary to utilize the leverage factor associated with margin accounts if that party deems it suitable in light of prevailing conditions. Therefore, if a fiduciary presents an authorization for such an account, the registered representative should contact general counsel for advice. Many fiduciaries are also restricted to activity in securities specifi-

cally prescribed under state statutes. These securities may be selected from a published document and are described simply as *legal investments* (legals). More lenient states permit fiduciary investments under "prudent man" rules, meaning that fiduciaries are charged with acting as conservative persons would in managing their own affairs, without further qualifying restrictions.

Registered representatives must be particularly alert when doing business with fiduciaries. Aiding in an impropriety can result in financial liability for the registered rep and the firm. Questions about which securities are on the legal list in various states should be referred to general counsel.

Administrators of Estates. An *administrator* is a court appointee directed to settle the final affairs of a deceased person. Such a procedure is necessary if a person dies without leaving a valid will specifically designating somebody to pay outstanding obligations and estate taxes, to liquidate assets, and/or make distributions to beneficiaries. The following documents are usually required for a brokerage account in the disposition of securities for these estates: (1) new account report form; (2) a court order or certificate appointing the administrator (must be dated within the past six months); (3) inheritance tax waivers if required by the transfer agent (for securities to be reregistered); (4) affidavits of domicile (for securities to be reregistered); and (5) affidavit of death satisfaction (for securities to be distributed to beneficiaries).

Executors (Executrixes) of Estates. An *executor* (*executrix*, if a female) is a person named in a valid will to minister to the final affairs of a deceased person. The executor/executrix is responsible for paying outstanding obligations of the decedent and estate taxes, if applicable. An executor/executrix is also empowered to sell assets of the estate and/or to make distributions to beneficiaries named by the decedent in the will. The following documents are usually needed in connection with a brokerage account for these estates: (1) new account report form; (2) a certified copy of the will and all codicils to it; (3) a court order or certificate recognizing the executor (dated within the past six months); (4) inheritance tax waivers if required by the transfer agent (for securities to be reregistered); (5) affidavits of domicile (for securities to be reregistered); and (6) affidavit of death satisfaction (for securities to be distributed to beneficiaries).

Trustees. A trustee is a person or an institution appointed under terms of a legal instrument to perform a specific function. The trustee's authority is spelled out in the trust document itself. A trust created by people to operate during their lifetime is called a *living*, or *inter-vivos*, trust. A legal agreement effective on its creator's death is called a *testamentary* trust. Its terms and objectives are explained in the decedent's will. The following documents are needed for a brokerage account: (1) new account report form; and (2) a certified copy of the trust agreement.

Guardians. The following documents are needed for a brokerage account in the case of guardians: (1) new account report form; and (2) a guardian appointment certificate issued by a court.

Receivers-in-Bankruptcy. The following documents are needed for a brokerage account in the case of receivers-in- bankruptcy: (1) new account report form; and (2) a court order evidencing appointment of the receiver.

Committees or Conservators for Incompetents. The following documents are needed for a brokerage account in the case of committees or conservators for incompetents: (1) new account report form; (2) a court order evidencing appointment of a committee or conservator to manage the assets of someone declared legally incompetent.

A trading authorization or power of attorney may not be accepted from any fiduciary customer. Prevailing laws prohibit a fiduciary from delegating authority to someone else.

See also Living Trust; New Account Report Form; Prudent Man; Registered Representative (Responsibilities); Rules of Fair Practice (Section 9).

Fill or Kill (FOK). This qualification is a variation of the all-or-none instruction except that it necessitates *immediate* execution or cancellation of the order. A fill-or-kill order also requires a *complete* execution, although not necessarily at one price. (If an order was entered to buy 1,000 at 36 FOK, the customer would surely be satisfied to buy 400 at 35⅞ and 600 at 36 immediately). It does not permit the stock exchange member to wait until it is possible to execute this order if it cannot be done promptly. When entering the trading area, the member simply requests a quotation and size. If the existing market precludes immediate satisfaction of the entire order, the member leaves the area and reports to the customer that nothing was done and the order is thereby cancelled.

See also All or None (AON); Immediate or Cancel.

Final Prospectus. When an underwriting is permitted to begin, (at the end of the cooling-off period), the underwriters first contact customers who gave indications of interest and now solicit bona fide orders from them. Unless the offering is a very popular one, it is unlikely that all those "circles" will turn into orders. Some customers may be unhappy with the final price of the issue and others may have experienced a change in financial circumstances during the cooling-off period. Furthermore, it is probable that the underwriters and members of the selling group will also solicit parties who never expressed indications of interest and who never even received or read the red herring.

If for no other reason, this is why the SEC requires that a final prospectus be presented to *all* subscribers to a registered distribution of securities no later than with confirmation of their purchase. The final prospectus, which is a condensation of material information appearing in the amended registration statement, is the only means of order solicitation recognized as acceptable by the SEC. It provides purchasers and prospective purchasers with information about the security and the issuer necessary for making an intelligent investment decision. In fact, if the customer is not given a red herring prior to the effective date, and the first opportunity to become informed about the issue occurs on the receipt of a prospectus with the trade confirmation, the purchaser may cancel the transaction within a reasonable time thereafter without loss or penalty.

Delivery of a prospectus is considered to be so important that the SEC requires it to be used by: (1) the underwriters when they offer any portion of their commitment; (2) the selling group members when they offer any portion of their allotment; and (3) any broker/dealer acting as principal in a transaction involving a security highlighted in an effective registration statement, if that transaction occurs: (a) within forty days after the effective date (or commencement of the public offering, whichever is the later date) if the issuer had previously distributed other securities under another registration statement and has not been filing current reports with the SEC, or (b) within ninety days after the effective date (or commencement of the public offering, whichever is the later date) if the issuer has never filed a registration statement for any class of securities before and has not been filing current reports with the SEC. Care must be taken by the underwriters and the members of the selling group to ensure they extend no credit (margin) to purchasers of this issue if it is defined as a new issue (that is, a primary distribution by an issuer as opposed to a secondary offering of securities by affiliated persons). The Securities Exchange Act of 1934 prohibits such extensions of credit to customers during the offering and for up to thirty days after the distribution is terminated.

See also Indication of Interest; Twenty-Day Cooling-Off Period; Underwriting.

Financial and Operational Combined Uniform Single Report (FOCUS). The NYSE requires member firms to subject themselves to an annual audit. Supplementing the annual audit is a mandated series of internal examinations performed by the member firm itself. The results of these examinations are reportable to the exchange and to various other supervisory bodies in a document known as the Financial and Operational Combined Uniform Single Report (FOCUS). It is actually comprised of two reports: an abbreviated form prepared monthly; and a more detailed analysis to be filed quarterly (see the following figure). The FOCUS reports probe deeply into the component parts of a member firm's capital structure, aggregate indebtedness, operating activities, profitability, and, in general, its continuing efficiency. Although the statistics presented in these reports are unaudited, they nevertheless enable the Surveillance Coordination Department of the NYSE to monitor trends within each firm and to take appropriate remedial action prior to a financial catastrophe. The FOCUS reports serve also to require the officials of each member firm to employ proper financial controls in their accounting systems and to remain alert to the customary signals of operating deterioration (see the figure on the following page).

See also New York Stock Exchange, Inc.

Financial Principal. *See* National Association of Securities Dealers.

Financial Protection Requirements (NYSE). Of paramount importance both to the board of directors and to the Member Firm Regulation and Surveillance Division of the NYSE is the assurance that a customer's financial interests are properly safeguarded at all times when dealing with a member organization. The exchange

Monthly Focus Report

NAME OF BROKER-DEALER

NAME AND TELEPHONE NO. OF PERSON COMPLETING THIS REPORT

ID NO.

SEC FILE NO.
98

ITEM	FOR MONTH ENDS 19___ (IN THOUSANDS—$000's OMITTED)						
	JAN	FEB	MAR	APR	MAY	JUN	JUL
1. Total Tickets							
2. Markets							
a. NASDAQ							
b. Other							
c. Capital Requirement							
3. Total Fails							
a. To Deliver							
b. To Receive							
4. Aged Fails							
a. To Deliver							
b. To Receive							
5. Clearing Agency Balances							
a. Long							
b. Short							
6. Unrestricted Cash							
7. 15c3-3 Reserve							
a. Account Balance							
b. Requirement/Exemption							
c. Deposit							
8. Customer Accounts							
a. Secured Debits							
b. Total Credits							
9. Inventory Positions							
a. Long							
b. Short							
10. Securities Borrowed							
11. Allowable Assets							
12. Deficits in Unsecured and Partly Secured Accounts							
13. Unsecured Loans and Advances							
14. Subordinated Loan Agreements							
a. Cash							
b. Securities							
c. Repayment Value							
15. Secured Demand Notes							
a. Face Amount							
b. Collateral Value							
16. Unconsolidated Income/Expense							
a. Gross Income							
b. Total Expenses							
17. Trading and Investment Account Gains or Losses							
18. Ownership Equity/Partnership Capital							
a. Additions							
b. Withdrawals							
19. Debt-Equity Total							
20. Current (Working) Capital							
21. Total Haircuts							
22. AI/Reserve Formula Debits							
a. Aggregate Indebtedness or,							
b. Aggregate Debit Items Under Reserve Formula							
23. Net Capital							
24. Ratio and Excess Net Capital							
a. AI/NC Ratio (%)							
b. Net Capital in Excess of:							
(1) Greater of 6⅔% of AI or Minimum; or,							
(2) Greater of $100,000 or 4% of Aggregate Debit Items Under Reserve Formula							
c. Net Capital in Excess of:							
(1) Greater of 10% of AI or 120% of Minimum; or,							
(2) Greater of $120,000 or 7% of Aggregate Debit Items Under Reserve Formula							
25. Charges to Capital							
a. Operational Charges							
b. Potential Charges							
c. Scheduled Capital Withdrawals Within 6 Months							
26. Securities Concentrations							
a. Proprietary Accounts							
b. Customers' Accounts Under 15c3-3							

community offers its customers several forms of such monetary protection.

Fidelity Bond Insurance and Broker's Blanket Bond Coverage. Each member organization that does business with the public is obliged to carry policies to protect itself from loss of money or securities resulting from fraudulent practices or misplacement caused by any official or employee of that firm. The insurance policy covering a member firm's partners, officers, and employees for losses stemming from criminal activity is called *fidelity bond insurance.* The policy insuring the firm against fraudulent trading, check and/or securities forgery, and unexplained shortages of money and securities is known as a *broker's blanket bond.* The specific minimum coverage levels necessary depend on the capital of the member organization and the type of customer relationship established. In general, the minimum coverage ranges from $200,000 to $5 million per firm.

Substantial Net Capital. In addition to fidelity insurance, each member of the NYSE is required to maintain a minimum net capital. The amount of net capital required is prescribed in SEC Rule 15c3-1 which applies to all brokers, not only members of the NYSE. Members of the NYSE occasionally have higher requirements based on exchange rules which can be more restrictive.

Since the rules are designed to protect the public, the amount of capital required is based on the amount of public business a broker does. A broker may choose between what is called the basic formula or the alternative requirement.

The *basic formula* is based on total liabilities relating to the broker's business with the public. These liabilities are called *aggregate indebtedness.* Under the basic rule, a broker's net capital available to support its customer business must not be less than $\frac{1}{15}$th of its aggregate indebtedness.

Further, the rules state that if its net capital is less than $\frac{1}{10}$th of its aggregate indebtedness, the broker may not expand its business. If a broker's net capital is less than $\frac{1}{12}$th of its aggregate indebtedness, then it must take steps to either increase its net capital or reduce its aggregate indebtedness, so that its net capital position improves to at least $\frac{1}{10}$th of aggregate indebtedness. (The broker must not allow the ratio to exceed 8:1 during its first year of business.)

Under the *alternative requirement,* a broker's net capital requirements are based on total receivables related to its customer business, called aggregate debit items. Under this rule, a broker's net capital available for its customer business must be at least 4% of its aggregate debit items.

Further, if a broker's net capital is less than 7% of its net debit items, then it cannot expand its business. If its net capital is 6% or less, it must take positive steps to increase the percentage to 7%.

Minimum Capital. In addition to the foregoing ratio requirements, the NYSE imposes minimum dollar requirements on members dealing with the public.

The minimum dollar requirement is $100,000. In addition, if the broker's net capital is less than 150% of the above ratio requirements, then the broker may not expand its business. If net capital is less than 125% of the above ratio requirements, then the broker must take positive steps to increase it to at least 150%.

Early-Warning System. The NYSE has implemented an early-warning system to forestall the possibility of dissolution. When a member organization's ratio of net capital to aggregate indebtedness for fifteen consecutive business days is (1) more than 1:10, or its net capital is less than 150% of its minimum dollar requirement, the firm cannot expand its business activities until it declines below that ratio; or if it is (2) more than 1:12, or its net capital is less than 125% of its minimum dollar requirement, it must reduce its business at least to a level resulting in a 1:10 ratio.

Furthermore, if a computation of net capital at the end of any month reveals that a firm's (1) aggregate indebtedness is larger than twelve times its capital, or (2) net capital is less than 120% of the capital required, a special report disclosing this fact must be filed promptly with the SEC and continued for each month thereafter until this deficiency in financial condition has been reduced below that level for three consecutive months.

Financial Statement Analysis. Intelligent investment decisions are made after careful consideration of available information: facts about world events, domestic news, industry reports, and corporate announcements. Most investors also rely on financial information released by the company to aid them in their judgments to buy or sell.

Information that comes from the corporation itself is subject to an individual investor's interpretation, despite the well-known axiom that "figures don't lie." A corporation with $1 million in total assets and at least 500 stockholders is obliged to register with the Securities and Exchange Commission under the Securities Exchange Act of 1934. (Exempt from this rule are banks and insurance companies regulated by state or federal authority, whose rules parallel the SEC's anyway. Also excluded from reporting requirements are corporations engaged in religious, education, fraternal, or other eleemosynary enterprises.) These corporations must report significant events and changes as they occur periodically and must file an audited financial statement with the commission annually. At about the same times, similar information is distributed to the company's shareholders. However, the information is "raw," without explanation or analysis. Shareholders and prospective purchasers are expected to know and understand the techniques the company uses to keep the investment community informed. This is often a difficult task because accounting is not a precise science. It is a sophisticated art, using various methods to present the same basic information and arrive at different conclusions. Accounting practices vary from company to company, even within the same industry. Frequently, the difference in approach depends on management's judgment; sometimes it depends on the preferences of the auditor who prepares the statements. In any case, anyone who analyzes such information should realize that these documents are only part fact and part opinion.

Nevertheless, valuable insight into the health and wealth of a corporation is often readily apparent from careful examination of that institution's financial reports. A shareholder or registered representative need have only fundamental knowledge of accounting terms, procedures, and analysis in order to interpret such data competently.

See also Balance Sheet; Income Statement.

Fingerprinting. *See* Reporting Requirements of the SEC (Brokers and Dealers).

Firm Commitment Underwriting. *See* Underwriting.

Firm Market. *See* National Quotation Bureau, Inc.

First Notice Day. The first day, varying by contracts and exchanges, on which notices of intention to deliver actual notices of intention to deliver actual financial instruments or physical commodities against futures are authorized.

Five-Percent Guideline Policy. *See* Markup and Markdown.

Fixed Annuity. This type of annuity contract (also called a *guaranteed-dollar annuity*) is one in which the life insurance company pays a set amount of money to the annuitant periodically.

This sum can be increased somewhat by extra payments if the contract is also a "participating" type of agreement. That is, a participating annuity agreement functions exactly like participating preferred stock (*see* Participating Preferred Stock). If the insurance company's investments that secure this annuity generate more money than anticipated, the contract holder will share in the excess income.

The insurance company's reserves, backing all payments to the annuitant, are invested in a portfolio comprised of fixed debt securities and real estate mortgages. In these respects the fixed annuity resembles the operation of a face-amount-certificate company. The subscriber's risk in owning a guaranteed-dollar annuity is that inflation may erode the purchasing power of the fixed payments. Consequently, buyers of these contracts are advised not to rely on this income exclusively for survival in their retirement years.

Fixed annuities are subject to the exclusive jurisdiction of state insurance commissioners; they are not regulated by the SEC.

See also Annuity Contract; Hybrid Annuity; Variable Annuity.

Fixed Liabilities. The fixed liabilities appear below current liabilities on the right-hand side of the balance sheet. The major item, ordinarily, is the corporation's funded debt, usually outstanding bonds maturing five years or more in the future. This category may also include long-term promissory notes, bank loans, and other obligations.

Bonds are carried on the balance sheet at their par value. Keep in mind that the actual market prices of the company's own bonds could be either at a premium (above par) or at a discount (below par). The coupon rate and maturity date are usually indicated for each bond outstanding.

Example: The liabilities section of the balance sheet of a typical manufacturing corporation looks like this:

Liabilities

Accounts payable	$200,000
Accrued expenses	150,000
Accrued taxes	+ 50,000
Total current liabilities	$400,000
Convertible debentures	+ 500,000
8% interest, due 1995	
Total liabilities	$900,000

See also Balance Sheet (Liabilities); Current Liability.

Fixed Trust. A fixed trust issues shares reflecting units of participation in a packaged portfolio of securities, such as U.S. government or tax-exempt obligations. Municipal bond funds are often represented in this fashion and were sold exclusively in this manner prior to the Tax Reform Act of 1976. Now, new funds of this type are generally organized as corporate entities and classified as management companies. In a fixed trust, investors can purchase an interest in a prearranged but risk-diversified portfolio composed of many municipal bonds (mostly revenue type) geared to their personal requirements. Because the portfolio is fixed for the life of the trust, there is no trading or management activity or expenses for investors to bear after the start-up costs are satisfied.

The fixed trust municipal bond funds provide subscribers with interest exempted from federal income taxes and are characterized by the following unique features:

1. The fund inevitably must decline from its original size as its component issues are retired pursuant to maturation or to exercise of sinking fund provisions in their indentures. Holders electing to redeem shares in the fund by tendering them back to the trustees also cause the fund's size to diminish.

2. When the fund's asset value declines to a predetermined level (by means of issuer- or subscriber-directed redemptions), the trustees

liquidate the trust and distribute the value of its net assets pro rata among the remaining shareholders.

See also Investment Company; Participating Trust; Unit Investment Trust Company.

Flat. *See* Bond Interest (Trading Plus Accrued Interest and Trading Flat).

Floating Debt. *See* Municipal Security (Assessing Debt).

Floor Broker. A member who is paid a fee for executing orders for Clearing Members or their customers. A Floor Broker executing customer orders must be licensed by the CFTC.

Floor Brokerage Fee. This fee is paid to a broker on the floor for executing a trade.

See also Specialist.

Floor Give-Up. *See* Errors in Execution.

Floor Ticket. *See* Order Ticket.

Floor Trader. A member who generally trades only for his own account, for an account controlled by him or who has such a trade made for him. Also referred to as a "Local".

Flower Bond. Prior to April 1971, from time to time the Treasury Department issued bonds with a special provision in their indentures designed to make them attractive to wealthy individuals with sizable estates. Those issues, when owned by decedents at the time of their death, could be redeemed by heirs at face value in satisfaction of federal estate taxes, even though they had a current market value at the time substantially below face value.

The Treasury Department's purpose was well served because, as a result of this feature, it was able to arrange financing at interest rates below those prevailing or similar issues without

it. A provision of the tax code eliminated this tax advantage from bonds issued after April 1971, but previous issues of these so-called "flower bonds" will be available with this privilege until 1998.

Flow of Funds Provision. *See* Municipal Security (Types of Indenture).

FOCUS. *See* Financial and Operational Combined Uniform Single Report.

FOK. *See* Fill or Kill.

Foreign Securities Exchanges. *See* Securities Exchange Act of 1934 (Section 30).

Form 144. *See* SEC Rule 144.

Forms Required by SEC. *See* Reporting Requirements of the SEC.

Formula Investing. Although there are many approaches to formula investing, the basic tenets are the same: Devise a formula that reduces the guesswork of investing and stick with it. Many such plans are offered; their advantage is that they relieve the investor from the continual decision making and interpretation required by other methods.

Constant-Ratio Plan. A constant-ratio plan simply requires an investor to maintain a percentage balance between stocks and bonds in his or her portfolio. The selection of the ratio would depend on the investment aim; the more conservative, the higher the percentage of bonds. Once established, the position is reviewed periodically and changes made as necessary to adjust the balance.

Example: If an investor wishes to maintain a constant ratio of 50% stocks and 50% bonds, an initial investment of $100,000 will be $50,000 in bonds and $50,000 in stocks. Assume that after a period of time the portfolio has increased in value by 10% but the entire increase has taken place in the stock portion. The value of the position now reads: stocks $60,000, bonds still $50,000. The investor now sells $5,000 of the stocks and purchases $5,000 of bonds. The result is a 50% constant ratio of $110,000, invested $55,000 each in stocks and bonds.

The concept of the constant ratio is at the heart of the balanced mutual fund. These investment companies state that they will maintain a ratio between their investments in comon and preferred stocks and bonds. The ratio usually has a built-in option for variation, but the basic concept is the same.

Constant-Dollar Plan. Similar to the constant ratio plan is the constant-dollar plan. Here the measuring device is not a percentage but a dollar value.

Example: Perhaps you as an investor set a maximum of $75,000 in stocks. When the value of your holdings exceeds this figure, you sell the necessary amount and purchase more bonds. Should stock values decline, you put in additional funds to increase your holdings to the predetermined level. This method prevents staying too long with a rising market; of course, it may force you out long before a rally reaches its peak. It also requires you to purchase at low prices to keep your formula in operation.

Many major institutions have developed their investment programs with variations of the constant-dollar plan. It can be adapted to meet individual needs, too, and it has many enthusiastic followers.

Forward Contract. A cash market transaction in which delivery of the commodity is deferred until after the contract has been made. It is not standardized and is not traded on organized exchanges.

Forward Pricing. *See* Mutual Fund.

Fourth Market. *See* Over the Counter.

Fractional Discretion. Some limit orders are occasionally entered by customers at specific prices but with an ⅛ or ¼ fractional point discretion to be used by the broker if necessary for consummation of the order.

Example: Buy 100 V at 74¾ plus ¼ discretion, or sell 100 Q at 10 less ⅛ discretion.

These orders are always accepted on the floor of the exchange, but only at the maximum price permissible for buy orders and the minimum price permissible for sell orders. The V buy order in the example would be entered at 75 or better, while the Q sell order would be entered at 9⅞ or better. This type of discretion does not absolve a broker from financial responsibility for choosing not to utilize this leeway and, as a result, missing the market.

Free Account Net Settlement (FANS). This securities depository is organized and promoted by the NASD for use by its members in OTC transactions. Its purpose is to immobilize certificate movement and reduce opportunities for theft of these valuable documents.

See also Comparison Procedures.

Free Crowd. *See* Active Bonds.

Free-Riding. As used in credit activities within the securities industry, this term refers to the illegal practice of purchasing and selling an issue without showing ability and intent to pay for the transaction. The penalty for this practice is to freeze the account for ninety days.

See also Hot Issue.

Frozen Account. *See* Cash Account.

Full Disclosure Act. *See* Securities Act of 1933.

Full-Refund-of Load Privilege. *See* Contractual Periodic-Payment Plan.

Full Reimbursement Period. *See* Contractual Periodic-Payment Plan.

Fully Diluted Earnings per Share. A corporation may have convertible bonds and/or convertible preferred stock outstanding. Investors realize that earnings per common share would be affected if such securities were to be converted. Fully diluted earnings reflect the per-share results as they would be if all potential common shares were added to the outstanding common stock. Under this method all warrants, stock options (options issued privately by the corporation), and convertible issues are considered as exchanged for additional common stock.

The following figure contains the same basic figures as those in the original Roxbury statement, but they have been recalculated on the assumption that the outstanding bonds are convertible and that they have been converted. The bonds are convertible into 20,000 additional shares of stock, and the corporate tax rate is assumed to be 37%.

Balance Sheet
Roxbury Manufacturing Company
December 31, 198X

Assets

Cash	$	75,000
Marketable securities		150,000
Accounts receivable		375,000
Inventory		400,000
Total current assets	$	1,000,000
Property plant, and equipment	$	605,000
Prepayments		20,000
Intangibles		10,000
Total assets	$	1,635,000

= Liabilities

Accounts payable	$	200,000
Accrued expenses		150,000
Accrued taxes		50,000
Total current liabilities	$	400,000
Bonds—8%, due 1995		500,000
Total liabilities	$	900,000

+ Stockholders' Equity

Preferred stock—6% ($100 par)	$	75,000
Common stock ($10 par)		300,000
Capital surplus		100,000
Retained earnings		260,000
Total stockholders' equity	$	735,000
Total liabilities and stockholders' equity	$	1,635,000

Income Statement
Roxbury Manufacturing Company
January 1–December 31, 198X

Net sales	$	2,000,000
Cost of goods sold	–	1,590,000
Selling, general, and administrative expenses	–	154,000
Depreciation	–	56,000
Operating income	$	200,000
Other income	+	7,500
Total income (EBIT)	$	207,500
Interest on bonds	–	40,000
Taxes (37% rate)	–	61,975
Net income	$	105,525
Preferred dividends	–	4,500
Net earnings (earnings available for common stock)	$	101,025

Income Statement
(Fully Diluted)
Roxbury Manufacturing Company
January 1–December 31, 198X

Net sales	$	2,000,000
Cost of goods sold	–	1,590,000
Selling, general, and administrative expenses	–	154,000
Depreciation	–	56,000
Operating income	$	200,000
Other income	+	7,500
Total income (EBIT)	$	207,500
Taxes (37% rate)	–	76,775
Net income	$	130,725
Preferred dividends	–	4,500
Net earnings (earnings available for common stock)	$	126,225

Assuming that these are exchanged for common stock, the Interest on bonds entry disappears. With that deduction of $40,000 gone, the income before tax rises from $167,500 to

$207,500. At a tax rate of 37%, the tax burden under fully diluted conditions is $76,775 instead of $61,975, thus raising net earnings from $101,025 to $126,225. Again assuming that the bonds are converted, we must take into account the additional shares thus created. If 30,000 shares were outstanding before the conversion, then the fully diluted earnings figure is calculated by dividing the "new" net earnings by 50,000 shares of common stock (30,000 outstanding + 20,000 after conversion). Of course, all these changes affect the "ordinary" earnings per share of the corporation:

$$\text{Fully diluted earnings per share} = \frac{\text{net earnings}}{\text{Number of Shares of Common Stock Outstanding after Conversion}}$$

$$= \frac{\$126,225}{50,000} = \$2.52$$

See also Primary Earnings per Share.

Fundamental Analysis. This method of stock market analysis examines the prospects of a security through the observation of accepted accounting measures such as earnings, sales, assets, and so on.

See also Technical Analysis.

Fundamental Short Sale. *See* Short Sale.

Funded Debt. *See* Municipal Security (Assessing Debt).

Futures. To the layperson, "Wall Street" is typically tantamount to the securities business, and the terms "securities" and "futures" are generally viewed as synonymous. That view, however, is erroneous. For some time, a sizable portion of

Wall Street's product mix has consisted of futures, and, perhaps to the chagrin of some, the percentage is increasing. Futures, however, are still generally viewed as a speculative trading medium from which few winners emerge, not as proper vehicles for the sophisticated investor. It's a questionable impression; indeed, today's futures trader is apt to be highly sophisticated — a risk taker — but generally capable of assuming risk both financially and psychologically, and also well aware of the economic functions that futures markets provide. Futures markets now appeal to a broad spectrum of participants, but that does not minimize the need for knowledge and the experience in order to trade successfully. Still, futures trading is not suitable for many. Many brokerage firms feel that with leanings towards futures concentrate their efforts accordingly. It's a valid approach.

The Forward Contract. When farmers and ranchers first wondered how to lessen the risk they take in raising a crop or a herd, they took the first step toward today's futures contracts. Historically, farmers planted, raised, harvested, and took their crops to a central market for public sale. Cattle ranchers bred and fed their livestock, then herded them to a stockyard or railroad depot. These markets, which still exist for the purchase and sale of commodities, are now referred to as *cash,* or *spot, markets.*

Until the commodity — the harvest or the herd — could be taken to market, the producer was exposed to risk. Essentially, the risk was that the market price would be too low for the producer to make a profit. How could the producer reduce that risk?

One means was the *forward contract,* by which a producer guaranteed future delivery of the commodity to a buyer, who in return guaranteed the price. The contract could be for so many bushels of corn or for so many head of cattle. The price could be whatever the producer and buyer agreed on, and delivery took place at the normal harvest or market time.

Example: A wheat farmer might anticipate that, as a result of an oversupply, the price of wheat probably would be very low at harvest time. To earn a profit on the crop, he needs a price of $1.70 a bushel. Yet he cannot know the price at harvest time, six months away. So he sells a forward contract, which obligates him to deliver the crop in six months at $1.70 per bushel. With such a contract, the farmer receives a guarantee of the price and, therefore, of his profit.

The Futures Contract. The futures contract is similar to the forward contract. Both relate to an underlying commodity (or, as we shall see, some other financial interest). Both guarantee a price. Both specify that delivery is to take place at a certain time.

Futures and forward contracts differ, however, in one important respect: A forward contract is negotiated between a particular buyer and seller. Futures contracts for a given commodity are interchangeable, having common specifications for such terms as size of contract, commodity grade, delivery months, and so on. The futures contract is standardized by the exchange on which it trades and is therefore easily traded. A *futures contract* is therefore a legal commitment for the seller to make delivery of a standardized quantity and quality of the underlying commodity at a specified time.

The value of a futures contract depends on the market price of the underlying commodity in the *spot*, or *cash*, market. To determine the value of a contract, multiply the spot market price by the size of the contract.

Example: If gold is quoted at $305 per ounce on COMEX, one contract of gold is worth

Specifications of the Standard Contract

Specification	Example
Commodity name	Gold
Exchange name	Commodity Exchange, New York (COMEX)
Size of contract	100 troy ounces
Grade	.999 fine or .95 fine
Delivery months	Current calendar month, the next two months, and Feb/Apr/June, Aug/Oct/Dec $0.10 per ounce ($10)
First delivery date	First Friday of the delivery month; this is the first day on which delivery may be made.
First notice date	Two business days before the first delivery date; this is the first day on which a seller may issue notice of intention to deliver.
Expiration date	Second Friday before delivery of the futures contract; this is the last day on which an option may be exercised.
Minimum price fluctuation (basis points)	$0.10/per ounce; this is the smallest change allowable in the price movement of a contract.

$30,500 ($305 per ounce times 100). A minimum price movement of $0.10 in the price of gold is therefore equal to a $10 change in the price of the contract ($0.10 per ounce times 100 ounces in a contract).

Over the years the underlying interests of futures contracts have changed and increased in number. For many years, contracts traded exclusively on agricultural commodities, such as corn, wheat, pork bellies, and soybeans, as well as on precious metals. In the early 1980s, futures contracts became available on oil and gasoline, debt instruments, and even stock indexes. The figure on the next page presents a sampling of the many types of contract available today.

Representative Futures Contracts

Underlying	Trading Months	Contract Size	Minimum Price Fluctuation	Exchange
Wheat (hard red winter)	Mar/May/July Sept/Dec	5,000 bushels	$0.0025 per bu. ($12.50)	Kansas City Board of Trade
Cattle, Live	Feb/Apr/Jun Aug/Oct/Dec	20,000 pounds	$.00025 per lb. ($5)	Mid-America Commodity
U.S. Treasury Bonds	Mar/June Sept/Dec	$100,000 face value 8% coupon	1/32 point ($31.25)	Chicago Board of Trade
Standard & Poor's 500 Stock Index	Mar/June Sept/Dec	500 X S&P stock index value	5 points ($25)	Chicago Mercantile Exchange/Index and Options Division
U.S. Dollar	Mar/June Sept/Dec	$100,000 U.S. dollars	$0.0001 ($10)	Toronto Futures Exchange
No. 2 Heating Oil (New York)	All months	42,000 gallons	$0.0001 per gal. ($4.20)	New York Mercantile Exchange
Japanese Yen	Jan/Mar/Apr Jun/July/Sep Oct/Dec, and spot month	12,500,000 Japanese yen	$0.000001 per Japanese yen	Singapore International Monetary Exchange

Opening and Closing Transactions. A transaction in futures contracts must be identified as either "opening" or "closing" a position. The initial buying or seing of a futures contract results in an *open position* for the buyer or seller, respectively. The seller's position is "open" because it is considered *short* — the seller has sold a commodity that he or she does not own. The buyer's position is considered *long* because the contract is for a future purchase of the commodity. As a result, the buyer's position is also "open."

A closing transaction is one that offsets a position. A commitment may be closed in two ways: (1) By an *offsetting* (liquidating) *transaction:* To close or offset, a short position, a *seller* buys a comparable contract (a *closing purchase transaction*). A buyer closes a long position by selling a comparable contract (a *closing sale transaction*). All but a small percentage of positions are closed this way. (2) By *delivering* or *receiving* the commodity. A seller may close a position by delivering the commodity, a buyer by receiving it.

Role of the Exchanges. A futures exchange provides the trading arena for standardized futures contracts. As in the case of stock exchanges, only members may trade on futures exchanges.

Each exchange has a board, which might be called the board of directors, board of governors, or board of members. This body, elected by the exchange membership, governs its activities very much as stock exchanges are self-regulated. Serving under the board are appointed committees that are concerned with various operations of the exchange.

Role of the Clearing Houses. The clearing house is an exchange-affiliated agency that clears trades, guarantees performance, and handles fulfillment through delivery.

Clearing. After every trade, the buyer's and seller's firms submit the data on the trade to the clearing house. The Figure below illustrates what happens there. At the clearing house data from the buying and selling firms are compared. If the data match, the trade is *cleared.* If not, the data are sent back to the firms for correction. Should the trade data still not match up, the trade is handled on an *out trade* — that is, as a special case.

Guaranteeing Performance. The clearing house thus acts as a third party to all trades (as it does in options clearing. During the course of a trading day, Smith may sell a contract to Jones, Jones to Doe, and Doe to someone else. Once the trade is made, however, the contract no longer exists between the last buyer and seller. The clearing house becomes the *contra* (or "other" party) to each transaction — a buyer to every seller and a seller to every buyer. Purchasers and sellers of the contracts create financial obligations not to one another but to the clearing corporation or to the exchange through its member firms.

Example: When customer Smith trades through her brokerage house to Jones, who trades through his brokerage house, Smith's legal and financial obligation is to her brokerage house. In turn, her firm has an obligation to the clearing corporation, which is the ultimate guarrantor on the trade.

Delivery. Although fewer than three percent of all futures contracts result in physical delivery, clearing corporations have to provide the mechanism for delivery of the underlying commodity.

Long Position Report. Usually just before the delivery month, holders of short positions (the sell side), who have the actual commodity and wish to make delivery, file a *notice of intention to deliver* to the clearinghouse. With this notice, holders state their intention to deliver on the next business day before the first delivery day of the expiring contract month. That's the short side. As for the long side, clearing corporations require members to submit, two days before the first delivery day, a *long position report*, which shows the open long positions that they hold. The next day (the day before the first deliv-

ery day), the clearinghouse assigns deliveries to its firms on the basis of the length of time that they have held open positions. Those with the oldest open long positions get the notices first. All deliveries and payments take place on the next business day, which is the first *delivery day* of the month.

Retail clients who are long and who have not offset their positions by delivery day will be sent warehouse receipts notifying them where the commodity is being held and demanding payment.

Quotations. Look at the figure on page 171. Futures contract quotations are typically listed alphabetically by commodity, with the expiration dates grouped below each commodity. Corn, for example, is listed before soybeans, soybeans before wheat, and so on. Notice also that these commodities all fall under the heading of "Grains and Oil Seeds." Other categories are "Livestock and Meat," "Metals and Petroleums," "Wood," and "Financial," among others. When a commodity is traded on more than one exchange, it is repeated with the abbreviation for the exchange in parentheses after the commodity name. Wheat, for instance, is listed three times because it trades on the Chicago Board of Trade (CBT), the Kansas City Board of Trade (KC), and the Minneapolis Grains Exchange (MPLS). These abbreviations are explained in a key at the bottom of the quotation section. Next to the commodity names are the standard contract sizes, such as 5,000 bushels for corn, and the unit of quotation, such as cents per bushel.

At the top of the columns of quotations are the following headings:

- *Open:* The price at which each contract first traded.
- *High/Low:* The high and low prices of the day.
- *Settle:* The price at which the contract closed.

Operations of the Clearing Corporation

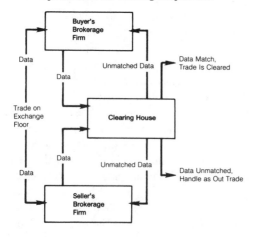

FUTURES PRICES

Thursday, April 10, 1986.

Open Interest Reflects Previous Trading Day.

	Open	High	Low	Settle	Change	Lifetime High	Low	Open Interest
GRAINS AND OILSEEDS —								
CORN (CBT) 5,000 bu.; cents per bu.								
May	228½	229½	227	228	— ¼	291¼	222½	33,049
July	220¼	221¾	218½	219¼	— 1½	286	218½	30,339
Sept	204¼	205¼	202¾	203	— 1¾	270	202¾	8,086
Dec	200½	201¼	199	199¼	— 2	235½	199	37,218
Mar87	209½	210¼	207¾	207¾	— 2	242½	207¾	5,283
May	213½	213¾	212	212¼	— 1½	242	212	1,423
July	215	215	212¾	212¾	— 1¾	222	212¾	175
Est vol 49,000; vol Wed 46,044; open int 115,573, +4115.								
SOYBEANS (CBT) 5,000 bu.; cents per bu.								
May	525	529¼	521½	524¾	+ 1¾	657	489	23,833
July	521½	527¼	518½	522¾	+ 2¾	658	497	27,993
Aug	519½	526	517½	521¼	+ 2	609	498½	3,898
Sept	510½	514	508½	510	....	555½	496	3,265
Nov	509	511¾	504½	507¾	— 1	556½	498	19,093
Jan87	516¼	521	514	516¾	— ½	565	509	1,512
Mar	524½	529	522½	526	— ½	576	519½	1,367
May	531	533¼	527½	530½	— 1½	556	527¾	142
Est vol 29,500; vol Wed 28,643; open int 81,115, +1,330.								
SOYBEAN MEAL (CBT) 100 tons; $ per ton.								
May	154.40	156.00	153.50	154.90	+ 1.00	163.90	134.00	15,674
July	153.90	155.40	152.80	154.40	+ 1.00	167.00	134.00	13,588
Aug	153.20	154.80	152.30	154.10	+ 1.20	163.50	135.50	4,603
Sept	151.00	152.60	149.50	151.10	+ .60	159.30	137.50	3,306
Oct	148.10	149.00	146.50	148.50	+ .50	156.00	136.00	4,017
Dec	149.20	150.50	147.50	149.60	+ .40	157.00	136.00	6,910
Jan87	....	....	....	150.70	+ .50	157.50	136.00	820
Mar	....	....	....	151.00	....	159.00	149.00	275
Est vol 12,000; vol Wed 11,530; open int 49,193, —30.								
SOYBEAN OIL (CBT) 60,000 lbs.; cents per lb.								
May	17.50	17.64	17.41	17.43	+ .02	27.45	16.76	16,734
July	17.77	17.97	17.72	17.75	+ .04	25.25	17.05	16,469
Aug	17.85	18.05	17.80	17.88	+ .06	25.15	17.16	5,659
Sept	17.95	18.07	17.95	17.95	....	24.05	17.10	2,959
Oct	18.05	18.15	17.95	17.97	....	22.80	17.25	3,666
Dec	18.45	18.55	18.35	18.40	....	22.50	17.51	7,714
Jan87	18.60	18.65	18.50	18.50	— .05	22.35	17.70	1,127
Mar	19.00	19.05	18.85	18.90	....	20.25	18.20	398
Est vol 12,000; vol Wed 20,055; open int 54,762, +170.								
WHEAT (CBT) 5,000 bu.; cents per bu.								
May	295½	298	285	286¾	— 9¼	350	274	5,224
July	250½	251	246	246¼	— 4½	310	246	16,154
Sept	252	253	248½	249	— 3½	299	248½	6,627
Dec	260¾	260¾	256	256	— 4½	308¼	256	5,442
Mar87	261½	261¾	257	257	— 4¾	287	257	614
Est vol 11,000; vol Wed 8,921; open int 34,105, —269.								
WHEAT (KC) 5,000 bu.; cents per bu.								
May	280	281	272	273¼	— 8½	301	263½	3,898
July	242	242¾	239½	239½	— 2½	298½	239½	8,425
Sept	245½	245¾	243½	243½	— 2	281½	243½	1,633
Dec	253½	253½	253	252½	— 2	283	253	799

	Open	High	Low	Settle	Change	Lifetime High	Low	Open Interest
Dec	38.95	39.15	38.80	38.81	— .35	59.25	38.45	9,459
Mar87	40.00	40.10	39.85	39.85	— .35	49.50	39.50	692
Est vol 3,000; vol Wed 4,119; open int 20,426, —297.								
ORANGE JUICE (CTN) — 15,000 lbs.; cents per lb.								
May	94.55	95.00	94.20	94.50	— .95	162.50	82.60	1,706
July	94.40	94.80	93.70	93.70	— 1.00	157.50	83.50	1,823
Sept	93.70	93.90	92.60	92.60	— 1.40	127.25	82.00	1,020
Nov	93.60	93.60	92.50	92.50	— 1.35	125.00	82.50	467
Jan87	93.00	93.00	92.10	92.10	— 1.00	113.00	83.75	270
Mar	93.25	93.25	92.90	92.85	— .80	122.00	83.90	948
May	94.00	94.00	94.00	93.20	— 1.20	94.75	84.50	665
July	....	....	....	93.70	— 1.10	95.00	84.75	306
Est vol 650; vol Wed 743; open int 7,205, —122.								
SUGAR — WORLD (CSCE) — 112,000 lbs.; cents per lb.								
May	9.45	9.45	8.85	8.91	— .46	9.58	3.58	31,072
July	9.45	9.45	8.65	8.74	— .61	9.50	3.79	27,053
Sept	9.39	9.42	8.83	8.83	— .50	9.42	4.05	357
Oct	9.38	9.40	8.80	8.80	— .50	9.40	4.02	42,446
Jan87	9.50	9.50	9.50	8.80	— .50	9.50	5.65	169
Mar	9.61	9.64	9.06	9.10	— .45	9.64	6.03	14,198
May	9.80	9.82	9.25	9.27	— .41	9.82	6.75	3,520
July	9.85	9.90	9.32	9.34	— .44	9.92	7.77	1,500
Est vol 28,688; vol Wed 23,784; open int 120,315, +314.								
— METALS & PETROLEUM —								
COPPER (CMX) — 25,000 lbs.; cents per lb.								
Apr	....	....	64.30	+ .40	65.25	63.00		0
May	64.00	64.75	64.00	64.55	+ .40	74.00	60.00	34,680
July	64.75	65.40	64.70	65.25	+ .40	72.55	60.25	26,994
Sept	65.35	65.85	65.35	65.80	+ .40	70.90	60.90	8,197
Dec	65.90	66.60	65.90	66.45	+ .40	70.30	61.60	6,976
Mar87	67.15	67.15	67.15	67.10	+ .40	70.00	62.55	1,558
May	....	....	....	67.45	+ .40	70.00	62.90	437
July	....	....	....	67.85	+ .40	69.95	63.25	197
Est vol 7,700; vol Wed 13,440; open int 79,141, +929.								
GOLD (CMX) — 100 troy oz.; $ per troy oz.								
Apr	337.50	339.50	337.50	338.90	— .40	496.80	314.70	1,721
June	339.80	342.80	339.00	341.70	— .50	433.50	320.50	60,368
Aug	343.00	346.00	343.00	345.10	— .50	427.50	328.00	17,586
Oct	347.00	348.60	346.30	348.30	— .50	395.70	331.50	7,271
Dec	349.00	353.00	349.00	351.70	— .50	392.00	336.50	13,538
Feb87	354.50	355.00	354.40	355.20	— .50	397.50	337.30	11,716
Apr	357.00	357.00	357.00	358.30	— .50	405.00	346.30	8,147
June	360.00	360.70	360.00	361.60	— .50	409.00	350.50	7,368
Aug	....	....	....	365.10	— .50	408.50	356.00	6,472
Oct	368.00	366.70	366.70	368.70	— .50	420.00	361.00	4,973
Dec	372.00	372.00	372.00	372.60	— .50	399.40	367.00	1,666
Feb88	....	....	....	376.70	— .50			230
Est vol 27,000; vol 33,678; open int 141,056, +3,142								

May	1,835	1,840	1,818	1,828	+ 13	2,422	1,792	5,480
July	1,880	1,889	1,865	1,878	+ 17	2,429	1,844	7,833
Sept	1,930	1,935	1,915	1,925	+ 17	2,430	1,891	3,373
Dec	1,972	1,974	1,960	1,965	+ 15	2,425	1,934	4,720
Mar87	2,004	2,014	2,000	2,003	+ 18	2,385	1,978	1,320
Est vol 3,064; vol Wed 2,547; open int 22,824, —49.								
COFFEE (CSCE) — 37,500 lbs.; cents per lb.								
May	224.50	231.75	233.25	227.96	+ 3.74	272.62	131.00	5,031
July	229.25	237.00	228.25	232.49	+ 3.77	278.38	135.50	5,451
Sept	234.50	239.28	233.00	238.76	+ 5.48	282.78	137.50	3,233
Dec	244.75	247.00	237.00	243.58	+ 4.83	287.10	138.00	1,600
Mar87	243.00	247.00	241.00	246.00	+ 4.10	290.33	156.75	700
May	251.00	251.00	251.00	249.50	+ 4.50	291.83	188.00	206
Est vol 2,987; vol Wed 2,139; open int 16,242, +182.								
COTTON (CTN) — 50,000 lbs.; cents per lb.								
May	62.05	62.35	61.60	61.65	— .90	70.00	58.80	2,647
July	62.90	63.10	62.57	62.65	— .48	70.05	56.05	5,787
Oct	39.05	39.20	38.80	38.85	— .30	65.50	38.50	1,705

ACC—Amex Commodities Corp.; CBT—Chicago Board of Trade; CME—Chicago Mercantile Exchange; CMX—Commodity Exchange, New York; CRCE—Chicago Rice & Cotton Exchange; CSCE—Coffee, Sugar & Cocoa Exchange, New York; CTN—New York Cotton Exchange; IPEL—International Petroleum Exchange of London; IMM—International Monetary Market at CME, Chicago; KC—Kansas City Board of Trade; LIFFE—London International Financial Futures Exchange; MCE—MidAmerica Commodity Exchange; MPLS—Minneapolis Grain Exchange; NYFE—New York Futures Exchange, unit of New York Stock Exchange; NYM—New York Mercantile Exchange; PBOT—Philadelphia Board of Trade; WPG—Winnipeg Commodity Exchange.

- *Change:* The difference in the closing prices between this day and the previous day.
- *Lifetime High/Low:* The highest and lowest prices at which the contract has traded in its lifetime to date.
- *Open Interest:* The total number of futures contracts that have not been offset by an opposite transaction or fulfilled by delivery.

Example: In the figure, you see that the size of a corn contract on the CBT is 5,000 bushels and that the price quotes represent cents per bushel. Five yearly corn contracts settle in the same months: May, July, September, December, and March. As soon as a March contract for one year expires, a new contract begins trading for July of the next year on the CBT.

The May contract opened at 228½ ($2.285) per bushel. During the trading day, the highest price was 229½ ($2.295), and the lowest was 227 ($2.27). It closed at 228 ($2.28), which represents a ½-point change from the previous day's close. Since the contract began trading, the highest price has been 291¼ ($2.9125) and the lowest, 222½ ($2.225). There are 33,049 positions sells) in the May contract that have not been offset by an opposite transaction or by delivery.

Expiration months tend to be standardized, from one exchange to another.

Example: Silver, which is traded on the CBT and COMEX, has identical expiration months on both exchanges.

Open Interest and Volume. After the listing for each commodity are figures for volume and open interest.

Volume is the number of contracts that were traded during the day, whether the transactions opened or closed positions. The previous day's volume is included as a point for comparison of the current day's trading.

Open interest is the total number of open contracts, whether buys or sells, *as of* the close of trading.

Volume and open interest do not necessarily increase or decrease in relationship to each other. Heavy volume during a trading day, for example, could leave open interest almost unchanged from the previous day if the opening and closing transactions are roughly equal in number. Or volume could increase from one day to the next — but decrease open interest if most of the trades closed positions.

Margin. To ensure that member firms have enough funds to cover their positions in the market, clearing corporations require members to deposit and maintain margin against their posi-

tions. Margin in futures trading is roughly analogous to margin in stock trading.

But only roughly. The two types of margin differ in several ways. Whereas margin for most stock transactions is 50 percent, for a futures trade it is typically less than 10 percent (it varies from one exchange to the other). In securities, buying on margin is optional, but all futures trades are on margin. Perhaps the most crucial difference is in the purpose of margin. In the purchase of a stock or bond, margin is partial payment; the remainder of the purchase is financed by the brokerage firm. In futures transactions, margin is a *performance bond* or "earnest money," insuring that purchasers and sellers will live up to their contractual obligations. Because the margin is not partial payment, the brokerage firm makes no loan and no interest is paid, as in the case of margin purchases of securities.

There are two kinds of margin in futures trading: initial margin and maintenance margin.

Initial Margin. Initial (or original) margin is the money deposited for each contract upon the purchase or sale of the contract, usually 10 percent of the total worth of the contract. The exchanges set initial margin, depending on the volatility of the commodity and of the futures market itself. Brokerage houses usually ask their customers for a slightly higher margin than that set by the exchange.

Example: If an exchange requires initial margin of 10 percent on its orange juice contracts, a member brokerage firm might require 15 percent. If the cash price of orange juice is $0.9500 per pound and a contract consists of 15,000 pounds, then the value of the contract is $14,250 (15,000 pounds times $0.95). The brokerage firm will require an initial margin deposit of $2,137.50 (15 percent of $14,250).

Original margin can be posted in any of the following ways — or in any combination of them: (1) Cash (usually in the form of bank-issued margin certificates). (2) Stock in the clearing corporation. (3) Interest-bearing obligations of the federal government (T bills, T bonds, T notes, and the like). (4) Letters of credit from an approved commercial bank.

Maintenance Margin. Maintenance (or variation) margin is additional margin required on an established long position as a result of a decline in the value of the contract. It is calculated by the exchange clearinghouse at the end of the trading day. The clearinghouse requires variation margin from the member firms, and retail clients are asked by their brokerage houses to put up more margin or have their positions sold out.

Most exchanges set the total amount of margin required in relation to the net short or long position that each member holds in each contract.

Example: A member holds a long position (the buy side) in 15 silver contracts and a short position (the sell side) in 10 silver contracts, and delivery for all the contracts is in the same month. The total margin required is for the net long position of 5 silver contracts.

Some exchanges and many independent clearing corporations seek additional protection by requiring maintenance margin on all long and short positions even when they can be offset by other contracts held by other members.

Futures trading is highly leveraged with, either long or short done on margin, only a small portion of the contract's face value is actually required. Margin is not a down payment, but a deposit of good faith money — technically, a performance bond. The implication is that, if a physical transaction of the actual commodity takes place at delivery time, the balance of the money due will be forwarded. Initial margin requirements are set by the exchange and subject to change. Brokerage firms can — and often do — require a higher margin, but not less than the exchange minimum. Typically, the margin required is 5% to 10% of the value of the contract; thus 100 ounces of gold at $400 per ounce may require $4,000 in margin. No other money is due, and there is no financing cost on the differ-

ence between the contract's value and the margin. Indeed, the margin deposited might be placed in Treasury bills, and the interest accrues to the customer.

However, there is a risk. Leverage works both ways. If the price of gold falls, the customer has to be prepared to forward additional margin if the position is to be maintained or the brokerage firm has the legal right to liquidate the position at the market price. On the other hand, if gold's price strengthens, the equity over the required margin can be withdrawn. This procedure is known as *marking to the market.* The commission charge is generally minimal relative to the value of the contract and paid only once, when the position is liquidated. Commissions are negotiable. A $40 roundturn cost for a contract that has a face value of $40,000 reflects a cost of a tenth of one percent. Relative to the securities markets, the cost of commodities transactions is considerably less expensive.

Markets. Futures markets are similar to the securities markets in many ways. There are exchanges, whose purpose is to provide a physical site for trading and on which only exchange members can execute orders. The exchanges have a fixed number of seats (members), whose price is function of supply and demand at any given time. Each exchange has self-regulatory committees whose purpose is to maintain fair and equitable floor trading practices. There are definitive opening and closing times. Order entry is analogous to any stock exchange, and confirmation of execution is generally provided within minutes. The types of orders are similar to the stock exchanges; indeed, the array is even broader.

There are also some important differences. Daily futures price swings can have limits, in either direction, whereas no such restraints exist in securities. Moreover, much of the trading done in securities is on cash settlement basis while virtually all trading in futures is on margin.

The CFTC can impose limits on the maximum number of contracts that a speculator can have in a particular futures market, and such limits are closely monitored. There are no specialists on the various exchange floors as there are on the stock exchanges. Floor brokers may be in the employ of a brokerage firm or be independent, but no floor member has the implied responsibility of helping to support a sliding market or brake a rising market as is the case for a specialist. The daily price limits on most exchanges tend to offset the specialists' function.

Note: A misconception persists in respect to terminology. Futures are not options and options are not futures. A futures contract implies that the seller (the short) is willing and capable of tendering the actual physical commodity, whereas the implication for the buyer (the long) is a willingness to take delivery at the time the futures contract reaches expiration. In actuality, very few transfers of the physical commodity from seller to buyer take place. Options, however, have no such implied responsibility. Options will expire if not exercised, and there will be no transfer of the physical commodity.

Market Participants. Those who trade commodities may be categorized as either hedgers or speculators.

Today the typical consumer of commodities, if not as large as, say, General Mills, is considerably larger than the local miller of yesteryear. This consumer-processor must figure out its commodity costs months in advance. Like the farmer in our example, the corporate food processor can fix its commodity costs by *hedging* — that is, by buying a number of contracts equal to its consumption need. The processor is thereby hedged against an unexpected price rise caused by crop shortages.

The main interest of hedgers is therefore to protect their business against sudden adverse price fluctuations. In traditional agricultural futures, the hedger is usually a producer or proces-sor. Financial futures are traded by large financial institutions, such as banks or insurance companies. Large portfolio managers deal in stock index futures.

The speculator may also trade any or all of these futures. *Speculators,* assuming the hedgers' risk, hope to profit through the astute buying and selling of contracts prior to expiration.

Speculators may be either position traders or scalpers. *Position traders* sometimes use fundamental analysis but more often rely on charting an other forms of technical analysis to figure out near-term market movements. Position traders may be either on the exchange floor or an "upstairs traders." An *upstairs trader* watches quote screens and stays in touch with a floor broker by phone. A *scalper*, often referred to as a *local*, is always on the floor, attempting to profit from small one-tick moves in the market and usually taking and eliminating positions within minutes. Rather than trying to discern the direction of the market, as the position trader does, the scalper tries to profit from minor intraday fluctuations that are not important to the position trader.

The distinction between hedgers and speculators, however, is not always hard and fast. Today's producer/consumers may "lift" (that is, offset) their hedge positions by buying or selling other futures contracts to close their initial purchase or sale. Eliminating the hedge entails risk, even though the large producers have the resources to estimate the size and future price of yearly crops more accurately than most speculators. When they lift their hedge positions, producer/consumers temporarily assume the role and risk of speculators. (As a result, futures exchanges also function as alternate cash marketplaces, because many producers and consumers prefer to deliver or take delivery over risking lifting their hedges at what seems to be a profitable time.)

Both hedgers and speculators benefit the futures marketplace. One of the biggest benefits of hedging is that it results in lower prices for the ultimate consumer. Without hedging, both producers and processors would have to add an extra amount to the product price to counterbalance the risk of adverse price change.

Contrary to popular opinion, speculators create neither volatility nor risk in futures markets. In fact, they lessen volatility and *assume* the risk that is already inherent in futures markets and that would otherwise be borne by the producer/consumer. Speculators also enhance liquidity by concentrating risk capital at a central location and putting it at the service of producers and consumers.

On balance, the mechanics for futures trading are fairly straightforward, but it is important to be fully aware of the brokerage firms requirements and procedures.

The trading requirements for bona fide hedgers are less stringent than for speculators, reflecting the fact that hedgers are dealing with a physical commodity somewhere along the line. Margin requirements are lower, thus reducing a hedger's capital needs.

Theoretically, hedgers use futures only for price protection, but in reality a portion of their trading often tends to be speculation under the cloak of hedging. A perfect hedge is difficult to obtain since it implies that all facets of the cash transaction perfectly match the futures position in respect (1) the size of the transaction, (2) delivery times, (3) location, and (4) quality.

Example: A gold dealer seeking 225 ounces of gold for July delivery in St. Louis cannot obtain such a hedge in the New York market. What would have to be considered is two contracts of 100 ounces each for June or August delivery in a New York approved vault. If the dealer elects to obtain three contracts, then 75 ounces of the trade is, in effect, a speculation.

Similarly, many participants overtrade. An important facet of successful futures trading is humility — the recognition that the market is bigger than the individual. Humility requires the

trader to recognize that his or her position in the market is wrong and/or the necessary capital to carry the position is lacking. Even hedgers are subject to margin calls, and there are times when hedging may not be appropriate.

Example: Let's look at a gold hedge. A jewelry fabricator anticipates a need for 200 ounces of gold for the Christmas period. It is now July and cash spot gold is selling at $400 per ounce. The dealer could (1) buy his inventory needs now and pay the financing costs, (2) elect to do nothing and in effect speculate on gold's price being the same near year-end, or (3) establish a long position in futures. Assume that December futures are selling at $425:

July 1:	December futures at $425
Spot gold at $400	2 contracts of 100 ounces each
200 ounces needed	are purchased
December 1:	
Spot gold is at $450/oz.	December futures at $450.
Additional cost for spot	2 December futures *sold* 450,
gold purchase at $450/oz.	profit 5,000. Futures position now 0.
or $10,000 more	

The hedge has enabled the dealer to hold his additional capital requirements to $5,000 instead of $10,000 if the hedge had not been employed. Moreover, if the dealer had difficulty sustaining physical gold from his normal suppliers, the delivery could be accomplished via the futures market, in effect transferring the futures position into a spot transaction.

This example is known as a *long hedge* since futures were purchased. The futures position can be liquidated any time prior to its formal expiration. If the dealer's needs changed to the extent that gold was not going to be needed, the long futures position is then sold.

A *short hedge* is the opposite, that is, futures are sold initially.

Example: A gold producer who is long 1,000 ounces of inventory but unsure of the demand from fabricators, sells an equivalent amount of futures — 10 contracts. The purpose is to protect the value of inventory if prices retreat. Moreover, the seller can always deliver the short futures position to the buyer. Remember, futures trading implies a willingness to tender delivery by the seller and buyer to take delivery.

Price Analysis. A commodity future exchange does not set prices. It simply affords a physical location at which buyers and sellers have orders executed by members of the exchange.

There are two basic approaches for evaluating futures prices — that is, what buyers are willing to pay and what sellers are seeking to obtain: (1) statistical analysis and (2) technical analysis. Each approach can be refined further for example, seasonal statistical analysis or computer applications in technical analysis. To a price purist, the statistical (supply/demand fundamental) approach is supreme as a forecasting method; the technician believes that a market's prevailing price action's all that's needed to determine the market's outlook. Theoretically, the latter approach is more objective on the analyst's part, whereas the former is more subjective since interpretation of statistical data is required.

In actually, the two approaches often overlap. Proper price evaluation typically requires drawing upon a mix of price forecasting methods, which at times reinforce one another and at other times conflict. Futures traders — speculators or others (hedgers) — tend to evaluate the same data differently, often reflecting individual biases toward price. Psychology is an important market factor and cannot be measured quantitatively. In either case, a commodity's price at any given time reflects a multitude of diverse assessments of its economic worth. It is this diversity of opinion that makes the markets so dynamic and unpredictable.

Fundamental Analysis. Simply stated, does a commodity's supply exceed demand or vice versa? In the former case, downward pressure should be exerted on price, and the reverse in the latter case. For an agricultural product, the fun-

damentalist attempts to develop a price projection by determining new crop production, coupled with existing inventory, and equate the total supply to expected domestic and foreign demand.

Seasonal considerations are important.

Example: U.S. soybeans are harvested in late summer/early fall and processed into oil and meal during the following months. Obviously, soybean supplies are large around harvest time and decline as the crop year progresses. Prices tend to be lower when supplies are greater and vice versa. The fundamentalist attempts to ascertain if the seasonal supply/demand imbalance has historical patterns from which price projections can be made.

Technical Analysis. Price data is interpreted, generally by analyzing the commodity's actual price performance as graphically shown on a bar or point and figure (P&F) chart. The technician looks for patterns that have historical tendencies, such as the ability of a commodity to hold above a certain price (*support level*) or its failure to penetrate a higher level (*resistance*). The longer that either of these opposite parameters holds, the further the market's momentum will carry prices, if the restraint gives way, reflecting the imbalance between buyers and sellers.

During the 1970s an increasing number of analysts used computers to determine a market's price bias, and such analysis has since developed into a broad-based forecasting approach.

- Widely used are *moving averages* — simply a way of determining a market's average price over a ten-or thirty-day period, for example, or some other combination of varying time frames — to assess whether the latest market price is above or below the cumulative average.

- *Relative strength indices* (RSIs) are widely used as a clue to whether a market is overbought or oversold. The rational for RSIs is somewhat similar to the contrary opinion approach in that the buyer seeks to establish a long position in a faling market, while the seller seeks clues to the top of the rising market.

Financial Instruments. Money is a commodity, subject to the laws of supply and demand. The price of money is interest, and to a large extent futures markets have evolved largely into financially related markets at the expense of the traditional agricultural markets. Moreover, the shift in emphasis is likely to harden, but the effect serves to strengthen the economic necessity for futures markets. This fact is being accepted by a broadening base of corporate structures seeking some protection against the uncertainties of interest rate swings. The speculative enthusiasm for financially related markets has increased almost geometrically; almost any trader can relate to interest rates, but may have difficulty determining or understanding the variables impacting on, for example, pork bellies.

Many factors influence the cost of money. In the macro sense, risk and time predominate: the greater the risk to principal (capital), the higher the rate of interest demanded by lenders, and vice versa. Moreover, the longer capital will be "tied up," the greater the uncertainty is as to the safety of principal, and typically money will cost more. Inflation, real or feared, impacts directly on the cost of money, reflecting the implied risk to money's purchasing power over time.

A working knowledge of basic economics is needed to assimilate, and attempt to interpret, the factors in influencing interest rates.

The key to interest rate swings is largely dependent on Federal Reserve actions, that is, monetary policy. Interpreting the Fed's actions and/or intent for the direction of interest rates is often a study in futility, but their actions filter through almost all the futures markets. The initial effect may be manifested in the Treasury bond and bill futures markets and quickly spread into the currency markets, stock indices, and metals. Also, if a major shift in rates seems to be unfolding, the agricultural markets will react as inventory financing costs change.

The Fed impacts on interest rates principally through the purchasing and selling of U.S. government obligations. These obligations, also known as Treasury securities, are marketable, interest-bearing obligations issued by the Treasury as a means of borrowing money to meet government expenditures not covered by taxes. The principal types of U.S. government securities are: T bills, T notes, and T bonds.

T bills are the type of security used most frequently in Federal Reserve open market operations. T bills are purchased by banks, corporations, and the public at prices lower than the face value of the bills. The interest received is basically the difference between the price paid for the bills and the amount received when they are sold or mature. T bills are issued in book entry form only, that is, the purchaser receives a statement rather than an engraved certificate which

U.S. Treasury Obligations

	T Bills	T Notes	T Bonds
Maturity range	3, 6, and 12 months	1 to 10 years	More than 10 years
Terms	Discount to face value	Coupon interest bearing	Coupon interest bearing
Controlling influences	Short term	Short to intermediate term	Long term
Futures contract unit value	$1,000,000 face	$100,000 face	$100,000 face

would typically reflect ownership. T bills are fully negotiable.

T notes are issued in demoninations of $1,000 or more, depending on the maturity of the issue, which can run from one to ten years. Notes pay interest semiannualy and are issued in registered or bearer form. A registered security has a specific name on the certificate, thus pinpointing ownership and making it difficult for stolen or lost notes to be transferred. Generally, registered obligations yield slightly less interest than bearer notes owing to the safety factor of specific ownership.

T bonds are longer-term debt obligations of the U.S. government, having initial maturities of more than ten years. There interest is paid semiannually, and the principal is paid at maturity. As in the case with T notes, bonds are issued in registered or bearer form.

The prices of these securities are directly related to interest rates. Basically, the price of the obligation is inversely related to the direction of change in interest rates. If interest rates decline, the value of the obligation goes up and vice versa.

Example: A T bond is issued at par $1,000 with 5 years remaining to maturity and a 12% coupon, which reflected market interest rates at the time of issue. Since then, however, prevailing interest rates have advanced to 15%. In order to remain competitive with the current market of 15%, the older 12% bond has to fall enough in price to provide a 15% return. Suppose the bond declines to about $900.

The new purchaser of the older 12% bond at $900 receives annual interest of $120, as opposed to the $150 on the new 15%. A $120 return on this $900 capital investment represents a yield to maturity of about 14.7%, fairly close to 15%, making the older obligation competitive with prevailing interest rates.

The initial buyer of the $1,000 bond might sell it at $900 for several reasons. The buyer may need immediate cash, and a T bond is a readily marketable security (at a price). The buyer may also feel that interest rates are going higher, perhaps to 18% from the prevailing 15%. Should that view prove valid, the 12% bond will decline even further, perhaps to $850, and the initial buyer wants to imit any further losses of capital.

On the other hand, the second buyer (at $900) may feel that interest rates are going not higher, but lower, and in his mind the 12% bond at $900 is a better investment than purchasing a new 15% obligation.

Finally, both initial and secondary buyer may have different ideas as to the trend of interest rates over different time frames. The first buyer may wish to move into short-term obligations — T bills, for example — while the second buyer shifts attention to longer-term securities — the T bond. Their attitudes toward inflation are likely to be the primary influences on how capital is committed.

As previously indicated, the rule of thumb is: the longer the maturity, the greater the interest return. A yield curve is a graphic representation of interest rates over varying time frames. A *normal (positive)* yield curve extends outward and slopes upward toward more distant maturities. An *inverted (negative)* yield curve sometimes develops and shows nearer-maturity obligations yielding higher returns than deferred maturities. This condition develops when inflationary concerns are more threatening in shorter time frames, relative to longer-term perceptions. The rate relationship rarely holds steady, thus enabling considerable opportunities for spreading within the futures complex. For example, if longer-term rates are viewed as too high relative to short-term rates, one might consider buying bond futures and shorting bill futures (Note: The contract sizes are different and a one-to-one contract may not be appropriate.)

Federal Reserve policies, administration fiscal policies and philosophy, wars or the threat of wars, inflationary psychology, and many other factors combine to make interest rate evels all but unpredictable. This unpredictability creates a need to minimize the risk of interest rate fluctuations, much like farmers sought a safety valve against the risk of grain prices in the mid-1800s. Just as the futures markets subsequently proved to be valuable and viable economic pricing media for segments of the agricultural industry, since the mid-1970s, they have also proven equally successful for the wide range of participants involved daily with financial instruments. In effect, interest rate swings can be greatly offset by hedging in the financial futures markets.

Example: (1) Six months hence, a corporation plans to raise $25 million through the sale of short-term obligations at a desired 12%. However, if interest rates trend higher during that time, to perhaps 15%, the note will have to bear the higher rate if they are to be marketed. Either way, the financing or marketing costs increase. To hedge in the futures market, the corporate treasurer sells the equivalent of $25 million T bills. Thus, if interest rates go up, the value of the bills sold will decline (remember the inverse relationship between rates and prices). At the time the corporate note is ready to be issued, the bill futures are repurchased at a lower price, leaving the corporation with no position in the futures market. However, the profit gained on the short T bill position helps to offset the costs of higher interest rates that the corporation will have to pay on its obligations.

The growth and acceptance of financially related futures since the mid-1970s has been phenomenal. Such markets now exist in the key financial trading centers of the free world and trading is round the clock. It is now easy to buy U.S. bond futures as easily in Singapore as on the Chicago Board of Trade; perhaps even more importantly, this broadening base of multinational futures markets may yet prove to be only in its early stages as the 1990s approach.

Floor Trading. Both hedgers and speculators must trade through floor brokers by using the *open outcry*. Traders on both sides of the trading pits buy and sell through shouts and hand signals. This method gives locals a large role because they facilitate liquidity and take advantage of opportunities not available to those who are not on the floor.

The open outcry auction allows any trader in the pit to bid or to take the other side of a trade. To do so, the trader shouts the bid or offer month, the number of contracts, and the price. This shouting is accompanied by finger signals.

Once a transaction is executed, the trader lists it on a trading card or order form. This card must show the number of contracts, the contract month, the price, the name of the contra clearing firm, and the other trader's initials. This information is then transferred to both the clearing corporation on the other side of the trade and to the exchange's price reporting system. (Unlike the information on the NYSE "tape," the time and the order of these trades are not exact.)

Normal and Inverted Markets. Refer again to the quotations figure on page 171, specifically the settle prices for copper. Notice that the prices for the near months are lower than those for the months farther out. The market for copper is said to be a *normal*, or *carrying charge*, market—that is, the distant months sell at a premium over near months. The premium is attributed to a carrying charge that is added to the value of the contract and that represents a collective value for insurance, warehousing, and cost of money to "carry" the commodity. The more distant months cost more because they entail greater carrying charges.

In a normal market, the maximum that a distant month can sell over a near month is the total of the carrying charges. If a price included more than these charges, professional traders would engage in what is known as *arbitrage*. That is, they would sell the distant month short and take delivery with the nearer, cheaper month, thus locking in a profit whether or not the more distant month's price rose or fell.

179

An *inverted market* is the opposite of a normal market; that is, the distant months sell at lower prices than near months. In the figure, the market for corn is inverted, with May contracts trading at a higher price than all others. The implication of an inverted market is that the commodity is in short supply. Buyers are bidding up the price of the near months to the extent that these months' prices more than offset the carrying charges included in the prices of contracts for the distant months.

In an inverted (or "discount" market, each contract that is further out in time trades at a lower price than one closer in. Whereas in a normal market the prices of the further-out contracts are limited by the carrying charges, *there is no limit to the amount that a near contract can trade over a more distant contract* in an inverted market. Inverted markets usually occur in periods of extreme bullishness.

Pricing in Futures Markets. Commodity futures markets exists because they provide a viable and proven economic function: price protection. For some basic commodities, the need for such protection goes back to the mid-1800s and still prevails. Agriculture provided the seed for futures markets. Farmers are persistently subject to price uncertainty, never quite knowing their ultimate production, that of their competitors, or the quality (marketability) of the crop. Similar uncertainties plague the agricultural user. The grain miller, for example, needs the assurance of steady supply and seeks ways to minimize the adverse effect that higher prices would likely have on profit margins. In short, all parties to the production, processing, and marketing chain are subject to the uncertainty of price and seek to minimize the risk of price swings in either direction.

Despite this common need, an outside factor is needed to absorb the diverse pricing objectives of the producer, who seeks higher prices, and the user, who obviously seeks lower prices.

The *speculator* is the binding force that gives the necessary liquidity to a futures market and makes the futures contract a viable pricing medium. The speculator's goal is price appreciation, not price protection. A futures market, however, can help to achieve both objectives at the same time.

Price is the common denominator of futures markets. Generally all the participants in a market have diverse views as to what is an equitable price for a given commodity at the moment (the *spot* or *cash* market) and at some time in the future. A price view is a judgment call that will prove correct for some and wrong for others. A unique feature of futures markets is that they enable both buyers and sellers to look well into the future and act upon their current judgment for what they feel prices may ultimately be.

As the future gradually becomes the present, the macro and micro supply/demand factors are persistently refined via the pricing mechanism of the futures markets. Commodities prices that ultimately settle into the present timeframe are likely to be well under or over initial price ideas of several months earlier. The approach works and its applicability to a wide range of nonagricultural interest has become a proven fact. Indeed, no other type of publicly available market structure offers such an economic opportunity.

This distillation of price-related motivations in the futures markets aids, among others: (1) multinational corporations and financial institutions to adjust to changes in foreign currency rates and the multifaceted interest rate structure, (2) agricultural producers and processors in their evaluation of production and inventory needs, and (3) speculative interests whose perception of prices and economic prospects may be contrary to the corporate view.

Futures markets, however, are not such simplistic pricing media, nor do they offer total price protection. The latter is virtually impossible within an economic structure that is oriented on a free market. What futures markets do provide is a working mechanism for projecting prices: for those market participants directly involved with the commodity, it's called *hedging*; for others it's *speculating*.

Influences on Price. For a futures market to be successful as a pricing medium, certain economic criteria must be realized:

1. *Price Volatility.* If a commodity's pattern calls for stable prices, it eases the apprehension of both producer and user as to what the future may bring. Such commodities have no need for a futures market. More importantly, speculative interest would be minimal, and the participation of speculators is needed to give a market liquidity. Accordingly, commodities whose prices are artificially controlled (administered) by government or monopolistic practices are not likely to have futures markets. Moreover, finished goods generally have less price volatility than raw (nonfinished) goods; very few of the former have had successful futures markets. For example, there is an active raw coffee bean futures market, but nothing for the processed product.

2. *Standardized Grades.* Regardless of the price objectives of futures market participants, certain assumptions apply to both buyers and sellers.

The purchase of a futures contract for a period of perhaps several months implies that the buyer is willing to take delivery of the commodity, at the original purchase price when the "present" catches up to the "future," even though prevailing prices may be lower. Conversely, selling a futures contract implies the willingness to deliver (tender) the specified commodity at the original selling price upon the expiration of the futures month, even if prevailing prices are higher. In actual practice, only a small percentage of futures contracts are settled by delivery.

Typically, buyers liquidate (sell) their earlier purchases before contract expiration, and sellers cover (buy), thus offsetting their initial positions.

Participants who are actually involved with the transfer of the physical commodity — from seller to buyer — must have prior knowledge that delivery will be satisfied by acceptable grades and that physical supplies will be at known locations approved only by the exchange where the futures contract was traded.

Example: A December 1986 gold futures contract, traded on the commodities exchange of New York (Comex), calls for the delivery in December of 100 ounces of fine gold (.999 purity). The buyer might have purchased the futures contract in January 1986, at the then prevailing price for the December 1986 delivery. Delivery to the buyer is made in New York by registered receipt issued by the exchange clearing house at a vault approved by the exchange. No other vault receipts are acceptable. (However, it is always the seller who selects the delivery site from those approved by the exchange.) The vault receipt represents ownership.

Price allowances can be made if, for example, the gold bar proves somewhat larger or smaller than the stipulated 100 ounces. What is important is that the buyer (who does not know, or need to know, the seller) knows exactly what a gold futures contract consists of, and the seller (who has no personal knowledge of the buyer) understands what the obligation to deliver entails.

The terms are legally binding. If exchange requirements did not exist, buyers and sellers would be reluctant to participate in futures. Thus, if a commodity is to develop a successful futures market, it must be assigned acceptable standards in grade and quality. Many commodities lack these requirements.

3. *Adequate Supply and Demand.* Successful futures markets also require broad buyer

and seller interest, the effect of which helps to minimize either side from dominating or controlling price swings. Although thousands of diverse commodities are traded daily throughout the world, only a handful do so on organized futures exchanges. A number of commodities do not lend themselves to public trading because demand is so limited that public interest in the product is minimal. For other commodities, supply may be so great that there is no concern about serious price swings; and, for example, governments may control the commodity or they may control the economy enough to offset the need for futures markets.

Example: Soybeans are widely grown in the U.S. and demand is worldwide. Rye, however, had a relatively narrow base of both producers and users, and futures trading in the grain lost its following several years ago. There is no futures market for diamonds, despite broad buyer interest, since the supply of gem-quality diamonds is tightly controlled by South African producers who can effectively influence price more than buyers. Likewise, there are no futures markets for goats and sheep, but very active markets in hogs and cattle. Both sides of the copper industry actively participate in futures, but the few U.S. aluminum producers have shown limited enthusiasm for aluminum futures.

4. *Acceptability.* A number of futures markets have failed as acceptable pricing medias. Success requires acceptance of futures as a viable economic necessity by those directly engaged with the commodity itself. Speculative interests do not make or break an established futures market, although at times this appears a debatable point.

Some producers/users of specific commodities shun futures, for several reasons of which a lack of knowledge of the markets' function appears foremost. Futures tend to be associated with speculation. In a free enterprise economy, however, price uncertainty tends to prevail, and failing to properly use marketing methods to minimize the unpredictability of prices is nothing more than speculation of a different kind. Still, publicly held corporations answer to their stockholders, most of whom are unfamiliar with futures, but who are generally aware of the sometimes adverse publicity the markets experience. Moreover, internal corporate politics may enter the picture as to who makes the decisions for pricing strategies used in the futures markets: corporate president, treasurer, purchasing agent? In either case, what is often missing is an understanding of futures and the analytical methods used in the markets.

The acceptability of a futures market as a pricing medium is reflected by its *open interest,* a statistical representation of the number of outstanding futures contracts in a specific market. The total is compiled daily by the exchange on which the commodity is traded and released to the news media and futures industry. Open interest shows the number of contracts long in each of the months being traded and, since for every buyer there is a seller's position, it can also be said to show the number of contracts short.

Example: If A buys a December 86 gold contract through brokerage firm XYZ, who is a clearing member of the exchange, and B sells a December 86 contract through member firm RST, the exchange reports as follows:

December 1986 Gold

Long	Short	Total open interest
XYZ 1 contract	RST 1 contract	1

If on the following day, C buys one contract through XYZ and D sells a contract through RST, the open interest is as follows:

XYZ 2	RST 2	2

On the third day, similar trades occur with market participants E and F, the open interest total is:

XYZ 3	RST 3	3

On the fourth day, customer A decides to sell her long position (*liquidate*), while customer D elects to cover his short (buy), the open interest is now:

XYZ 2   RST 2   2

The remaining participants:

C & E   B & F

Note: Customers offset their original positions with the same brokerage firm. If customer A, who bought gold through XYZ brokers, elects to sell a like gold contract through RST, she is then still long her original position and now also short one contract with RST, which is in contrast to her desire to be *flat*. While positions can be transferred to other brokerage firms, the usual practice is to initiate and liquidate positions through the same firm.

The higher the open interest, the greater the liquidity, which can facilitate ease of entry into and out of the market. Obviously, as a futures month nears the present time, the nearby positions' open interest contracts, as both buyers and sellers roll into more deferred futures months. Thus, if A wants to remain *net long gold* and is long a December 86 contract sometime prior to the contract's expiration, the December position will be liquidated and a long position will be established in, for example, August 87 futures.

Perhaps this procedure seems roundabout. Would it not be easier to simply buy 100 ounces of gold and avoid the seemingly time-consuming aspects of buying or selling and paying brokerage commission costs? The answer is no.

Consider the alternatives. If gold is selling at, say, $400 per ounce and one's analysis suggests a rise to perhaps $500 during the coming year, the purchase of 100 ounces in the spot market would require $40,000, generally paid at the time of delivery. If 90% of the purchase were financed at 10% per annum, one year's interest

would total $3,600, which effectively brings the price up to $436 over the year and reduces the profit potential. There may not be, however, any commission charge, but there could be a sales tax cost. Using the futures market could offer considerable alternative costs savings.

Example: Spot gold is now at $400 and the price for a year forward futures contract is selling at $440, the premium reflecting financing costs and estimated cost of storing 100 ounces of gold over a year. If, indeed, gold rises $100 during the year, the deferred futures contract purchased now will also appreciate to $500 so that its value equals spot gold. However, far less money is required than in the spot transaction.

Types of Orders. The *market order* the most commonly used, is be executed at the best possible price at the time the order reaches the trading pit. Using a market order generally means paying a higher price than if a limit order were used, but it assures the order giver of getting the contract, which limit order might never be executed.

Example: Buy 1 June live cattle at MKT.

A *limit order* places either a time or price limit on the execution. This type of order guarantees the price of execution if the order is executed.

Example: Given an order to "Buy 1 May sugar at 14.15," the floor broker *must* purchase the contract at 14.15 or a lower price.

To sell at the same price, the order would read, "Sell 1 May sugar at 14.15." In this case, the trader has to execute the order by selling at the price of 14.15 or higher.

Limit orders have one great disadvantage. A runaway market can quickly pass by the price on the limit order before the floor trader can execute the order. Often a broker is able to fill only part of a limit order at the designated price in a fast-moving market.

A *stop order* is a contingency order that is activated and executed only if the market reaches the price on the order. Sometimes called a *stop loss order*, this instruction is given to limit losses.

Example: A customer who is long a contract may enter an order as follows: "Sell 5 March silver at 615.70 stop." When any March silver contract trades—or is offered—at or below 615.70, the order becomes a market order to be sold at the best possible price at that time.

There is a crucial difference between stop orders in stock and those in commodities: In stocks, a trade must be made at or beyond the stop price for the stop order to become activated. In futures, there need be only a bid or an offer at or beyond the stop price.

If a stop is used with a purchase order, a purchase or bid at the designated price or higher activates it. Such an instruction is referred to as a *buy stop order.*

Example: "Buy 5 March silver at 615.70 stop." Thus, a trader who is short can limit losses by covering the short position.

The *stop limit order* combines elements of a stop and a limit order. Specifically, once the contract trades at or beyond the stop price, a stop limit order becomes a limit order.

A *buy stop order* becomes a limit order when a contract trades at or above the limit price.

Example: "Buy 10 gold at 320 stop limit." The trader has instructed the broker to buy 10 gold contracts if the gold contract trades or is bid for at, or above, 320—but not to pay more than 320.

A variation is, "Buy 10 June gold at 320 stop limit 320." The trader has instructed the broker to buy 10 June gold contracts if the price breaks out above 320 but not to pay more than 320.

A *sell stop limit order* becomes a limit order when the contract trades at or below the limit price.

Example: "Sell 8 July frozen orange juice contracts at 94.40 stop, limit 93.70." The broker has been instructed to sell 8 contracts if the price

goes down to or is offered at 94.40 but only if he can then get a price of 93.70 or better.

Sometimes called a *board order*, the market-if-touched order instructs the broker to buy at the market but only if the contract trades at a specified level. When used to buy, this order is placed below the currently trading price.

Example: With pork bellies trading at 60, an MIT order might look like this: "Buy 3 September pork bellies at 59.50 MIT." If the May contract trades at 59.50, the broker bids for it at that price. Because the instruction is now a market order, it might be filled at a higher price.

Although the MIT order seems the same as a stop or limit order, it differs in an important respect. The buy MIT, the buy limit, and the sell stop orders are all entered below the current market, but the buy MIT order could be eventually executed above the market. This cannot happen with the buy limit order and would probably not happen with the sell stop order. For the same reasons, although the sell MIT, the sell limit, and the buy stop orders are all entered above the current market, only the sell limit order can be assured of an *execution* above that market.

The *fill or kill order* has both a time and a price limit. It instructs the broker to execute the order at the limit price as soon as it is presented in the pit. If that cannot be done, the order is canceled.

Example: Buy 8 May bellies at 59.50 FOK.

See the following table for other types of order.

Other Types of Orders

Order	Instruction to Broker
Or Better (OB)	Execute at the designated price or better. Buy orders placed above the current market; sell orders placed below it.
Opening Order	Execute within the opening range, but not necessarily at the opening price, or cancel.

Open Order	An order to a broker that is good until it is cancelled or executed.
Closing Order	Execute within the closing range, but not necessarily at the closing price, or cancel.
Discretionary Order	Execute at the limit price, with a few points of discretion up or down.
Not Held Order	The broker has full discretion as to whether to execute the order and take the position. The broker cannot be held responsible if the order is not executed.
Limit or Market on Close Order	Execute, if possible, as a limit order during the trading session. If not possible, execute as a market order at the close.
Enter Day Stop EDS)	Enter a stop order at a specified price assuming that an earlier order cannot be filled. If the original order is a buy order, the EDS is a sell stop; for a sell order, a buy stop. *Example*: "Sell 6 December corn at 1.80, enter day stop at 1.90." The stop part of the EDS is cancelled at the end of the day.
Enter Open Stop	Same as EDS except that the stop remains good until cancelled rather than being cancelled at the end of the day.
Time Order	Execute within period specified. A good till cancelled (GTC) order is assumed to last for the life of the contract. A GTM is effective until the last trading day of the month in which it is entered. A GTW is good until the end of the week it is entered. A specific date or even time of day may be added after the price.
Scale Order	Execute either at a limit or at the market and then add more contracts to the position at specified price intervals. If the initial order cannot be filled at the specified price or better, more of the ensuing purchases are made.
Cancel Former Order	Enter a new order to change a limit, to change a stop, to change a day order to GTC, or even to cancel an order and enter another order for an entirely different month.
One Cancels the Other (OCO) Order	Execute one or the other of two orders, but not both. When one order is filled, the other is immediately cancelled.
Basis or Contingent Order	Execute if a contract in a different delivery month or even in another commodity attains a given price objective.
Spread	The simultaneous purchase and sale of contracts for the same commodity or instrument for delivery in different months or in different but related markets.
Buy on Opening	To buy at the beginning of a trading session at a price within the opening range.
Buy on Close	To buy at the end of the trading session at a price within the closing range.
Day Order	An order that is placed for execution, is possible, during the day's trading session. If the order cannot be executed that day, it is automatically cancelled.
GTC - Good Till Canceled	An order to buy or sell at a fixed price. It holds until executed or cancelled.
Switch Order	Switch a contract in a position to a different month or to a different exchange. Often used to offset a position in a delivery month and move the original position to a month that is further out.
Exchange for Physical or "Against Actuals" Order	In this "ex-pit" transaction, two hedgers meet by prior agreement outside the pit to exchange their cash and futures positions. One hedger, who is long the cash commodity and short the futures contract, delivers the commodity (or "actual") to the hedger who is short the cash commodity. In this way the hedgers close out their futures positions and consummate their transaction of the cash commodity.

Commissions. In futures trading, all commissions are negotiated. Purchasers of futures contracts pay one *round turn* commission when they first buy or sell, instead of two separate commissions, when they buy and sell contracts. This single fee covers both the initial purchase or sale and its subsequent offsetting transaction.

Limits. Trading on futures exchanges is conducted within the restraints of several types of limit:

1. Position limits.
2. Reportable positions.
3. Trading limits.

A *position limit* is the maximum number of contracts a trader may hold in a commodity. The limit is set by the exchange for the broker, depending on the broker's individual capital structure. The Commodity Futures Trading Commission (CFTC) approves the exchange's limits.

A *reportable limit* is the number of contracts specified by the CFTC at which traders must report their total positions by delivery month to the authorized exchange or the CFTC. In most commodities, the reportable limit is 25 contracts, a criterion set by the CFTC. Traders who hold 25 or more contracts, either long or short, are said to be *large traders.*

Both position and reportable limits apply only to large traders. Because of their economic needs, hedgers are not limited in the number of contracts that they may hold at one time. Note, however, that position limits are considerably higher than reportable positions. If a reportable position is 40 contracts, the position limit may be 400 or even 600, depending on the commodity.

A *trading limit* is the maximum price movement that an exchange allows for a commodity in one trading session.

Example: COMEX gold may move 2,500 points above or below the prior day's settlement.

(Sometimes the term *trading limit* is used to mean *position limit.)*

In a trading session, the market can be "limit up" or "limit down." When the market is *limit up* (or *bid limit*), all participants want to buy and no one wants to sell. In such a situation, the bids to buy are at the top of the daily allowable limit move, with no offers to sell at that price. In a *limit down* market, participants are looking to sell, and no one wants to buy.

The trading limit is established to prevent panic. On stock exchanges, trading may be suspended until catastrophic news has time to be accepted. On futures exchanges, there may be a series of limit up or limit down days, but losses are curtailed.

Other Types of Futures Contracts. Traditional commodities, such as soybeans or gold, form only a part of the futures marketplace. As for options, futures contracts are now traded on financial instruments, stock indexes, and even the inflation rate!

Financial Futures. Trading in financial futures started in this country in 1972, when the International Monetary Market (IMM) of the Chicago Mercantile Exchange started trading futures on the British pound sterling, Deutschemark, and Japanese yen. In 1975 the Chicago Board of Trade began trading GNMA futures, and one year later the rival Chicago Mercantile Exchange began trading T bill futures. In a time of currency fluctuations and huge budget deficits, trading in agricultural and precious metals futures has declined, while trading in financial futures has just as consistently grown.

Financial futures fall into two categories, both traded by speculators and hedgers: currencies and interest rate futures. Hedging is conducted primarily by *commercial*, which are large businesses and financial institutions seeking to protect themselves against radical swings in currency or interest rates.

Such institutions used to—and to some extent still do— hedge their currency needs by trading *forward contracts* in the foreign currency, or *forex*, market. Like its agricultural counterpart, the financial forward contract is tailor-made to the hedger's needs. It is not standardized, nor is there trading in a secondary market. Futures trading in foreign currencies represents a more standardized and liquid market than does forward contracting.

Stock Index Futures. The first stock index future was the Value Line Stock Index futures contract, which is based on the unweighted average of the *Value Line* 1600 and which began trading on the Kansas City Board of Trade in 1982. Having proved successful, it was followed in the same year by several others, such as the Standard & Poor's 500, which began trading on the Chicago Mercantile Exchange Index and Option Market Division. Other indexes have since followed. The stock index futures contract allows investors or speculators to play practically the whole market, through a single investment instrument, with great leverage.

Although similar, these contracts should not be confused with their near relatives, the stock index options. Both stock index futures and options contracts use the same or similar indexes and have been in use only since 1982. The stock index futures contract, however, far outdistances the stock index option in leverage. For this reason, experienced individual professional traders, investment banks, and the more sophisticated funds tend to trade the stock index futures contract (usually the Standard & Poor's 500 in preference to the index option. Retail clients are more attracted to the index option because, in buying an option, they can limit their risk to the amount of investment. Owners of futures contracts, on the other hand, are required to put up more margin if the index goes into a substantial decline. Similarly, investors who are short an index futures contract are required to put up more margin as the index rises.

Thus, although index futures offer greater leverage, the possible losses are also greater than with the index option. Unlike traditional commodity futures contracts, for index futures there is no underlying commodity in deliverable form. Instead, the underlying "commodity" is a cash amount that is based on the value of the index. For most index futures contracts, there is a daily cash settlement.

Example: The S&P 500 stock index futures contract is computed on the S&P 500 index. The *minimum fluctuation* (or *tick size*) is 0.05 point. Because the value of a contract is 500 times the value of the S&P 500 index, a change of 0.05 represents a $25 tick ($500 × 0.05). The S&P 500 futures contracts usually trade at a premium above the actual, or cash, index. Positions are revalued or "marked to the market" every night.

Conclusions. Generally, futures contracts are not recognized as securities, chiefly because their value is not determined by a party other than the buyer or seller. A stock goes up in price because of anticipated earnings, and those earnings depend ultimately on the success of the company's management. When you buy a share of IBM or Exxon, you may buy it from another shareholder rather than from the company. The stock's value depends neither on your own efforts nor on those of the previous shareholder but, rather, on the competence of a third party—the corporation's management.

Not so with futures contracts. Supply and demand, not managerial ability, ultimately determine the contract's price. If you buy stock in a gold mining company, you buy a security, because the company's earnings spring from management's abilities. If you buy either gold or a futures contract on gold, no management is involved.

Regulation. Early efforts to regulate futures trading were closely tied to the tremendous growth of commercial agriculture during the nineteenth and twentieth centuries in the United States. The Grain Standards Act of 1916 was aimed at standardizing grain quality as well as commercial and futures trading.

Shortly after World War I, a widespread depression brought about a great volume of speculation on futures markets. This brought about the passage of the Futures Trading Act of 1921, which was promptly declared unconstitutional by the U.S. Supreme Court. Congress quickly enacted the Grain Futures Act of 1922, which was upheld. This Act authorized the United States Department of Agriculture to regulate the exchanges. Although the Act gave the USDA the authority to conduct investigations, the powers authorized were not effective in controlling excessive speculation and price manipulation, as well as other abuses.

The Commodity Exchange Act of 1936 was more effective than any of the previous legislation. It authorized the regulation of commodities traded on futures markets other than just grains — such as cotton. This Act authorized the establishment of the Commodity Exchange Authority (CEA) which came under the supervision and control of the U.S. Department of Agriculture. The CEA was given broad powers to control market abuses, to prosecute price manipulation, to identify and controexcessive speculation. For the first time brokerage firms themselves came under the review of any regulatory body. The intention was to curb fraud, fictitious transactions, and other forms of abusive and unethical conduct.

The continued and aggressive growth of futures trading brought about real change in the regulation of the entire futures industry with enactment of the Commodity Futures Trading Commission Act of 1974. This Act truly changed the regulation of the futures industry by creating a freestanding commission called the Commodity Futures Trading Commission (CFTC). Although the CFTC chairman is appointed by the President of the U.S., as are the commissioners, the CFTC is a commission on a par with and of equal standing to the Securities and Exchange Commission. The personnel and records of the CEA were transferred to the CFTC. Contact with the USDA is maintained on a liaison basis. The chairman and the four commissioners are appointed by the president for a five-year period. The appointments are approved by the Senate.

The primary responsibilities of the Commission are: (1) designation of a board of trade as a contract market; (2) registration of futures commission merchants (FCMs), floor brokers, and associated persons (APs); (3) protection of an FCM's customer's funds; (4) audits of books and records of FCMs; (5) supervision of all trading on domestic contract markets; (6) establishment of position limits and trading limits for traders in order to control overspeculation; (7) investigation of unethical and questionable trad-

ing practices; (8) investigation of violations of Act; and (9) time stamping the receipt of customers' orders.

The 1974 Act gave the CFTC the authority to regulate all domestic contract markets. The CEA had authority over only certain agricultural commodities traded on futures exchanges. Such commodities as sugar, coffee, cocoa, and copper were not regulated. The term *contract market* applies both to a board of trade (exchange) and an individual commodity, such as gold, wheat, T bonds, Swiss francs, and so on.

Congress made certain amendments to the Commodity Exchange Act of 1936 in 1968 which established rules governing futures commission merchants (FCMs). These rules were adopted by the CFTC. These rules defined an FCM as any individual, association, partnership, or corporation that buys or sells futures contracts on commission. An FCM accepts and is responsible for customer funds. The CFTC also claimed authority over Associated Persons (AP). An AP is anyone associated with an FCM or an Introducing Broker. An AP is also anyone involved in the solicitation of acceptance of customer orders, and/or supervises people performing these functions. APs remain registered until they change sponsoring employees. The CFTC has recently discontinued the category of agency, replacing them with the category of *introducing broker* (IB). An IB is defined as any person, other than a person registered as an associated person of an FCM, (1) who is engaged in soliciting or in accepting for the purchase and sale of any commodity for future delivery on an exchange and (2) who does not accept any money, securities or property to margin, guarantee, or secure any trades or contracts that result therefrom. Agents were not required to register or demonstrate financial capacity. IBs must register and are required to post bonds with the CFTC. An IB must have an arrangement with a clearing member for the clearance of trades.

Commodity futures account executives

have to be formally tested (Series 3) and licensed by the Commodity Futures Trading Commission (CFTC), a division of the Department of Agriculture. Customers must meet more stringent financial requirements, relative to securities trading, and be made aware of the risks involved in futures trading. In some instances, one's age might prove a restraint on opening an account — the rational being that futures might not be in their best interests. A senior citizen is an example of such a client.

In addition to the FCMs, and IBs, the CFTC also requires the annual registration of: (1) floor brokers, (2) commodity trading advisors, (3) commodity pool operators, and (4) leveraged transaction merchants.

A *floor broker* is defined as any person who, in or surrounding any pit, ring, post, or other place provided by a contract market (exchange) executes for another person any orders for the purchase or sale of any commodity for future delivery.

A *commodity trading advisor* (CTA) is defined as any person who, for pay or profit, conducts a business of advising others, directly or indirectly, by publications or writing, of the value of futures contracts, or the advisability of trading in futures traded on contract markets. Excluded from this category because their services are considered incidental are banks or trust companies, newspaper reporters, floor brokers, or FCMs, publishers of bonafide newspapers, news magazines, business or financial publications of a general circulation and their employees, and any contract market. Any one who has not in the past 12 months offered trading advice to more than 15 persons, and does not hold himself out as a CTA is also exempt from registration.

Futures Commission Merchant. A firm or person engaged in soliciting or accepting and handling orders for the purchase or sale of futures contracts. Subject to the rules of a futures exchange, and who, in connection with such solicitation or acceptance of orders, accepts any money or securities to margin any money or securities to margin any resulting trades or contracts. The FCM must be licensed by the CFTC.

G

Garage. *See* Trading Floor NYSE).

General Obligation Bond. These bonds may be issued by either states, cities, towns, or counties. The taxing power of the issuer rests squarely behind such bonds, and thus they are also referred to as *full faith and credit bonds*. States have greater taxing powers than their political subdivisions and usually rely on personal and corporate income taxes as well as on sales, gasoline, or highway use taxes as security for such bonds. Defaults on such bonds are exceedingly rare, and so they have an outstanding record for safety of both payment of principal and interest.

Local issuers of municipal securities have, however, fewer taxing powers than states and usually rely on *ad valorem* (real property) taxes to back their GO bonds. Such taxes are often levied in mills per dollar of assessed valuation. (A mill is one-tenth of one cent.)

Example: If a property is assessed at $100,000 and the tax rate is 8 mills, the tax due is $800 ($100,000 $\times$ 0.008).

Sometimes a legal or constitutional limit is imposed on the taxing power of the issuer. General obligation bonds issued under such a limit are referred to as *limited tax bonds*, so that the purchaser understands that, unlike other GO issues, taxes may not be raised indefinitely to cover the debt service. Of course, bonds that are not limited as to rate or amount of tax are called *unlimited tax bonds*.

These bonds are usually issued in serial format.

See also Revenue Bonds; Serial Bond; Term Bond.

Give Up. An order executed by one brokerage house, but cleared by another house at the request of the customer.

Gold. There are four actively traded metal futures markets in the U.S.: gold, silver, copper, and platinum. Gold is the most active. Each metal responds to different supply/demand considerations with distinct and separate impact on their price structures.

Yet metal futures tend to move in unison. This interrelationship often develops despite little apparent justification for trending in a direction that is contrary to a specific metal's seeming fundamental worth. Psychology is therefore considered an important influence on the prices of the metals complex.

This is especially true of gold. Speculators have a dominant role in the gold futures market, and their attitude toward gold's price tends to be strongly biased, with seemingly little room at times for a middle-of-the-road approach. The confirmed "gold buy" generally sees the metal as undervalued regardless of its price, while the "purist" attempts to evaluate gold's value logically, viewing it as simply another commodity and probably overpriced. Either attitude tends to dominate the gold market for protracted periods.

Example: In 1979, inflationary fears triggered a buying spree that carried gold to a record high $850 per ounce and silver to $50 an ounce in early 1980. The gold bugs were anticipating $1,000 and higher, and, on the basis of the market's momentum at the time, the objective was not farfetched. It was also never seen. A precipitous price decline developed that persisted into much of 1981. To the purist, gold was heading back to $300 per ounce, if not lower. The bears' views were also not fully realized. In free markets, prices tend to ride a pendulum, but the extreme swings generally fail to reach expectations, partially because markets rarely perform as expected.

Psychology and pragmatism both impact on gold's price although not necessarily at the same time. The former appears more dominant when gold is rising (a bull market), while the latter seems to have greater impact in downward swings (a bear market). Gold's price at any given time tends to reflect a state of mind, relative to most other commodities. Accordingly, it is not difficult to rationalize price moves in either direction on a number or uncertainties, real or otherwise. It should be emphasized, however, that there is considerably more to gold's price than psychology. The fundamental setting can be important when not overshadowed by events that a purist would have nothing to do with gold per se. It should also be stressed that emotionalism and logic rarely complement each other.

The price of gold is the result of a matrix of diverse economic and psychological attitudes, most of which are not measurable for determining a specific price for the metal; at best, only a price range might be discernible. The futures market assimilates — and discards, if need be — the many variables impacting on gold at any given time, thus establishing an equilibrium price. The ability to forecast prices with some degree of success requires a constant awareness and some understanding of market dynamics as emphasized by futures.

Copper has certain seasonal price patterns, although their reliability has waned in recent years. Prices have shown a tendency to strengthen from December of one year to march of the following year. The seasonal strength reflects expectations of broadening demand for copper during the spring and summer from industries that might be described as "copper-intensive," notably automotive and construction. Generally, futures lead the economic setting, and copper users consider acquiring inventory before the actual need arises, unless interest rates are such that the cost of financing inventory proves prohibitive.

Example: The sharp contra-seasonal decline in prices during the first quarter of 1981 reflected alternate cost considerations, specifically inventory acquisitions versus financing costs. Typically, prices weaken after the first quarter as inventory needs subside. In either case, copper's seasonal tendency is primarily manifested via futures, enabling producers and users of the physical metal to adjust their pricing and marketing ideas to anticipated events, which may or may not actually materialize.

Good Delivery of Securities. The selling firm is expected to deliver the certificate on settlement date to the office of the purchasing firm during normal business hours in that community. Those certificates must be (1) negotiable; and (2) in units (denominations) considered acceptable under the Uniform Practice Code.

When both of these factors are present, the seller is making a *good delivery*. The seller is, therefore, entitled to payment, at the option of the seller (1) by company check; (2) by certified check; (3) by cashier's check; (4) by bank draft; or (5) in cash.

Partial Delivery and Payment of Expenses. If the seller is able to make only a partial delivery in units or multiples recognized by the Uniform Practice Code, then payment must be made for that portion tendered. The seller assumes responsibility for payment of (1) all expenses incurred in the shipment of the securities (such as insurance, postage, drafts); and (2) any transfer tax stamps necessary on the sale, delivery, or reregistration of certificates. In fact, if the securities are delivered without evidence of payment of these items by the seller, the purchaser may deduct from the purchase price the cost of any taxes the buyer would otherwise be forced to bear.

Negotiability. Most securities issued by U.S. corporations are in registered form. That is, the owner's name is imprinted on the face of the certificate and carried on the company's records. Consequently, a legal document appears on the back of the certificate to provide for its transferability. That legal document is officially called "an assignment and power of substitution" (see the following figure).

The registered owner of the security must sign this legal document exactly as the name appears on the face of the certificate to provide for its transferability. The signature on this contract makes the certificate virtually a fully negotiable instrument. If the registered owner finds it impossible or inconvenient to sign the back of the certificate, an assignment and power of substitution that is separate from the certificate can be endorsed and then attached to the security. This separate document, almost identical to the one imprinted on the certificate itself, is more popularly known as a *stock power* (or *bond power*). In endorsing this legal document, the registered owner literally assigns a personal interest in the corporation to a third party. This allows that party the right to substitute another name on the company's records in place of the one now recorded. Each signature on this assignment must be witnessed and dated as well as guaranteed by a broker/dealer or commercial bank acceptable to the transfer agent. Any alteration, erasure, correction, or modification on this document must also carry a guarantee acceptable to the agent in order to protect the agent against the possibility of litigation, alleging fraudulent transfer. The following figure shows the proper endorsements for specific certificate registrations.

Despite the relative ease in providing negotiability acceptable to the transfer agent, not all these registrations are considered as good deliveries to satisfy a transaction between broker/dealers. As a rule of thumb, good delivery between brokerage firms, at least in terms of negotiability, includes only registered certifi-

Certificate Registered in Name of:	Who Must Endorse the Assignment and Power of Substitution
1. Individual	That individual
2. Married woman	That woman*
3. Unmarried woman	That woman with the prefix Miss inscribed with her signature
4. Widow	That widow, with acknowledgement before a notary public
5. Custodian, under the Uniform Gifts to Minors Act.	That custodian
6. Guardian, infant, agent, attorney, or receiver in bankruptcy	The legally appointed official with evidence of authority accompanying the certificate
7. Two or more persons	All parties to this joint tenancy
8. Partnership	Any general partner
9. Company or firm (not a corporation)	Any general partner (the absence of Corp. or Inc. in the title is indicative of partnership organization)
10. Corporation	An officer of that corporation other than the one who must sign accompanying documentation.
11. Legal trust	One or more of the trustees, per terms of the accompanying trust agreement as official documentation
12. Estate of a deceased person	The duly appointed executor or administrator with official accompanying documentation

ªExcept in some foreign countries, which restrict the rights of married women to transfer securities.

cates that do not require accompanying documentation to satisfy the transfer agent's legal requirements. In addition, the securities must not be subject to special restrictions, as are certificates in the following list: (1) temporary certificates, when permanent ones are available; (2) mutilated certificates (or coupons) that have not been authenticated by the security's trustee, registrar, transfer agent, or issuer ("Mutilation" can be defined by many persons in many ways. Securities industry practice generally treats a certificate or a bond coupon that has been torn, cut, perforated, or altered in any way as a mutilation. So, too, is a security or coupon that has been scrawled on so that even a portion of the printed terms or authorized signatures are covered or obliterated); (3) certificates called for redemption (unless the entire issue has been called and this factor was specified under terms of the contract); or (4) certificates under government regulations (SEC black list, blocked list, license fees, affidavits, and so on, unless they can be accompanied by documents attesting to their acceptability through compliance with those regulations).

Certificate Denominations Acceptable for Delivery. Bond transactions: Coupon bonds are acceptable in denominations of $100, $500, or $1,000. Registered bonds are acceptable in denominations of $100, $1,000, or multiples thereof, but no larger than single certificates of $100,000. Bonds that are issued in either coupon or registered form without a specific charge for exchanging one for the other may be used in either form to settle transactions, unless otherwise specified at the time of the transaction.

Stock transactions in odd lots: Odd lots (less than 100 shares) are acceptable in any denomination as long as the total delivery is exactly equal to the contract amount. Partial deliveries are unacceptable.

Stock transactions in round lots: Partial deliveries of round lots (100 shares or multiples of 100 shares) are permissible if the amount ten-dered is equal to 100 shares or multiples thereof. There are three means by which round-lot contracts can be fully satisfied: (1) one certificate for the exact number of shares; (2) several certificates in denominations of 100 shares or in multiples of 100 shares; (3) certificates in odd-lot denominations, provided that 100-share pieces can be arranged from the combination.

Example: A 200-share contract can be satisfied with odd-lot certificates in denominations of 50, 50, 50, 50; or 70, 70, 30, 30; or 75, 75, 25, 25; or 60, 40, 50, 40, 10. Certificates for 90, 50, 60 shares do not constitute a good delivery, for although they total 200 shares, no combination of these certificates yields an even 100 shares.

Contracts involving round lots and odd lots must be satisfied as separate transactions with each delivery in accordance with the rules that apply to its category.

See also Close-Out Procedures; Rejections and Reclamations.

Good-til-Cancelled Order (GTC). This type of order is one that remains valid indefinitely, until executed or cancelled. It is also referred to as an *open order*, a name that reflects the permanency of its status. A day order changed to an open order or an open order changed to a day order loses any time priority it may have enjoyed in the specialist's book until then. Such changes require that the order be treated as a brand new instruction to buy or sell.

Most brokerage firms accommodate the preferences of some customers and accept orders good through the week, good through the month, or good through a specific day. Because those unique qualifications may not be entered on the NYSE trading floor, they must be entered as GTC instead. The member firm assumes responsibility for cancelling that order if it cannot be executed by the close of business on the specified date. If it fails to do so, it must also accept the financial liability associated with its error.

Lifetime of GTC Orders. The period designated by the term indefinitely can be an awfully long time. Technical adjustments are often implemented during this waiting period. To ensure the continued accuracy and validity of such orders on the records of each member organization, the NYSE requires these firms to compare and confirm their open orders with the specialist who holds them in the interim. Every six months or so on a day determined by the exchange, each member organization reenters its open orders under terms and conditions as they know them, resolving any differences before trading resumes the following day.

Reducing prices on Stocks Ex Dividend. One reason for potential differences is a mandatory price reduction for certain orders on the day that a stock first begins trading without the value of a pending dividend. Prior to the opening of trading activity on such an ex-dividend date, the following orders must have their price reduced: (1) limit orders to buy; and (2) stop orders to sell.

In other words, affected by this rule are those orders originally entered at a price below the then prevailing market.

Example: An open order to buy 100 shares at a limit of twelve when the stock is trading at fourteen will be reduced. So, too, will an open order to sell 100 shares at twelve stop.

The rationale behind this requirement is based on the fact there is usually about a one-month gap between the date the corporation closes its books to identify the recipients of that dividend and the date the dividend is actually distributed. During that interim period, it is unfair to oblige prospective purchasers to pay the same value for stock as before because the corporation will soon distribute a portion of its assets to other people, the former shareholders. After all, when those purchasers originally made their investment judgment, it was predicated on

a company whose assets included that distribution.

The logic behind the reduction of sell-stop orders is twofold. First, persons entering such orders are already shareholders and will therefore get that dividend from the company. Second, unless that memorandum level is lowered, sell-stop orders may be elected needlessly as a result of the automatic reduction in market value. This, in turn, negates the original intent behind entry of such orders. These customers want to sell only if supply-and-demand relationships necessitate it. They do not want to sell as a consequence of dividend distributions in which they will share anyway.

The price on pertinent orders is reduced by the exact value of a forthcoming cash distribution unless (1) the order is marked *do not reduce* (DNR) (Some investors are not concerned with the dissipation of assets brought about by dividend payments and are interested only in buying or selling at their predetermined price.); or (2) the value is not precisely divisible by the trading variation assigned to that security by the exchange. Ordinarily, that trading variation is ⅛ (12½¢). Thus, if a cash distribution is made that is valued at 25¢ per share, the price for appropriate orders is lowered by ¼, a 37½¢ distribution by ⅜, a 50¢ distribution by ½, and so forth. However, if the distribution is not precisely divisible by ⅛, the price for appropriate orders must be reduced by the *next highest* ⅛. Therefore, a 26¢ distribution requires a price reduction of ⅜; a 51¢ distribution, ⅝; a $1.20 distribution, 1¼; and so forth.

Adjusting Prices on Stocks with Forthcoming Stock Dividends. Forthcoming distributions of stock, such as stock dividends and stock splits, are treated in a different fashion, and the New York Stock Exchange and the American Stock Exchange each have their own practices regarding such distributions. In the case of a stock dividend or other stock distributions, NYSE limit orders to buy and stop orders to sell are adjusted on the ex-dividend (also called ex-distribution) date to more accurately reflect the customer's intention. That is, the prices of those appropriate GTC orders are always reduced, whereas the number of shares involved may be increased so as to maintain the same proportional transaction interest.

Example: If a customer had entered an open order to buy 100 shares of IBM at 270 just before it announced a 2-for-1 split (two new shares for each old share held), on the ex-distribution date the order will be adjusted as an order to buy 200 shares of IBM at 135. Because the customer's order indicated a desire to purchase $27,000 worth of IBM, after modification the customer's interest is maintained at the $27,000 level (200 × $135).

On the AMEX, all limit and stop orders have their prices reduced on the ex-distribution date, not just the buy-limit and sell-stop orders.

Calculating Price Adjustments for Stock Dividends. Price adjustments to NYSE or AMEX good-til-cancelled orders are made by dividing the price of the original order by 100% plus the percentage value of the stock dividend or stock distribution.

Example: In the case of a 50% stock dividend, an open limit order to buy 100 shares at 42 will be reduced in price to 28 (42 ÷ 150%) on the ex-dividend date. If the calculation results in a price and fraction not divisible by ⅛ (the usual variation on the NYSE and AMEX), the fraction is reduced to the *next lower* variation.

Example: Stock price adjustments based on a 3% stock dividend:

Old price	Calculated Value				New price at next Lower Variation
12	11.65	(12	÷	103%)	11⅝
23½	22.815	(23.50	÷	103%)	22¾
67⅞	65.895	(67.875	÷	103%)	65⅞
87¾	85.19	(87.75	÷	103%)	85⅛

Calculating Share Adjustments for Stock Dividends or Splits. Share adjustments to GTC orders on the NYSE conform to the following rules:

1. When a stock dividend or stock split results in one or more full shares for each share held, the appropriate order quantities are increased according to the exact percentage distribution. Thus, in the case of a 2-for-1 split, or 100% stock dividend, a 100-share GTC order is increased by 100% to 200 shares.

2. When a stock dividend or stock split results in less than 100 shares for each round lot held, the appropriate order quantities are increased but only up to the lowest full round lot. Odd lots are never tacked on to open orders when making a share adjustment. The calculation formula is:

old shares in the open order	×	the decimalized percentage stock distribution	=	new shares to be added to order (but only round lots)

Thus, with a 3-for-2 split, or 50% stock dividend, a 100-share order remains unchanged, whereas a 200-share order is increased to 300 shares.

3. When a stock dividend or stock split results in one or more round lots plus an odd lot for each round lot held, the appropriate order quantities are increased, but only up to the lowest full round lot. Odd lots are never tacked on to open orders when making a share adjustment. The calculation formula is:

old shares in the open order	×	the decimalized percentage stock distribution	=	new shares to be added to order (but only round lots)

Thus, in the case of a 6-for-5 split, or 20% stock dividend, a 300-share order remains unchanged, whereas a 600-share order is increased to 700 shares.

It is important to note that share adjustment rules do not pertain to AMEX open orders. American Stock Exchange GTC orders never have their share quantities increased. Order quantities remain the same, although price adjustments are always affected for stock distributions.

In the event the customer does not want the order automatically adjusted on the ex date, the order must be entered DNR (do not reduce). If the price is to be reduced but no adjustment is to be made to the quantity of a NYSE order, the customer must specify DNI (do not increase). A sample order guide for handling stock distribution on the NYSE is given in the following table.

Housing and Urban Development (HUD) to provide liquidity in home and federal agency mortgage financing. The corporation offers investors a participation in pools of qualified mortgages on private enterprises that are fully guaranteed by the U.S. government. These obligations, however, enjoy no specific tax exemption with respect to interest or repayment of principal thereon.

See also U.S. Government-Sponsored Corporation or Agency Obligation.

	Price of Order		Order Quantities and Adjustments		
Distribution	Divided by	100 Shares	300 Shares	500 Shares	1000 Shares
5 for 4	125%	100	300	600	1,200
4 for 3	133⅓%	100	400	600	1,300
3 for 2	150%	100	400	700	1,500
5 for 3	166⅔%	100	500	800	1,600
2 for 1	200%	200	600	1,000	2,000
5 for 2	250%	200	700	1,200	2,500
3 for 1	300%	300	900	1,500	3,000
4 for 1	400%	400	1,200	2,000	4,000

In any reverse split (that is, 1 for 2, 1 for 3, and so forth) all GTC orders, including all limit and stop orders, are cancelled.

See also Day Order.

Good Through the Week Month Specific Day. *See* Good-til-Cancelled Order.

Government National Mortgage Association GNMA, Ginnie Mae). This agency is an offshoot of the Federal National Mortgage Association (FNMA). It is a wholly owned government corporation operated by the Department of

Governments. *See* U.S. Government Securities.

Green Shoe. *See* Hot Issue.

Group Account Orders. *See* Municipal Security (Priority of Orders).

Guaranteed-Dollar Annuity. *See* Fixed Annuity.

Guardian. *See* Fiduciary Accounts.

H

Head-and-Shoulders Pattern. This pattern shows when a trend reversal has occurred. As shown in the following graph, a stock rises in price, then declines (left shoulder), and rises again far higher than before (head). Then the stock declines again to the neck. A third rise begins (right shoulder). The stock fails to reach the high achieved in forming the head, and it declines again. If the decline penetrates the neck line, it indicates an extended down trend in values. Although prices may return to the neck-line level before that happens, this reversal won't last long. A significant decline soon follows. Head-and-shoulder tops are bearish indicators.

Upward trends can also be forecast from this pattern of head and shoulders. The upward trend is seen when the pattern is upside down, as shown in the following graph. First comes the decline past the neck line and a rise back to the neck (left shoulder). This is followed by a decline to a much lower level (head) and a rally to the neck. Then comes another decline (right shoulder) but not as far. This upside-down head-and-shoulders pattern indicates an upward reversal. If the price manages to penetrate the neck-line level, an important trend reversal has occurred. Although a reaction sometimes drops prices back to the neck line, it is only temporary. A major rally soon commences to move market values appreciably higher. Head-and-shoulder bottoms are bullish indicators.

See also Double Tops and Bottoms; Support and Resistance Levels; Technical Analysis.

Hedger. One who purchases or sells a futures contract as a temporary substitute for a transactgion to be made at a later date. Usually it involves opposite positions in the cash market and the futures market at the same time.

Hedge Ratio. *See* Index Options.

Holder of Record. *See* Evaluating Options.

Holding Company. This type of investment company is formed to own a controlling interest in one or more subsidiary companies. Holding companies concentrate sizable investments in a few firms, hoping to gain control of those concerns or a significant voice in their management.

See also Management Company.

Hot Issue. A *hot issue* is a security in registration that is expected to trade at an immediate premium in the aftermarket (above the public offering price). This situation often creates a problem for the syndicate manager, although a happier one than stabilization.

Hot issues are conceived prior to the effective date when investor interest reaches such proportions that the underwriters cannot fully accommodate their customers' indications of interest. In fact, they cannot fully satisfy any of their customers. Demand spills over into the aftermarket, causing initial transactions there to trade higher than the price fixed by the underwriters in their offering.

In accepting an overabundance of indications of interest (many of them from favored customers), the syndicate manager may eventually allocate more certificates than available for distribution. In other words, the manager may decide to sell short a portion of that offering on behalf of the underwriters. *Overallocation* is a typical and acceptable practice in investment banking procedures, even if the issue merely appears to be "lukewarm." Who knows whether the public's enthusiasm will turn cold by the effective date? Who knows how many indications of interest may be cancelled because of disappointment about price, market conditions, and so forth?

The manager can use business judgment and, in accord with NASD rules, legitimately oversell the issue by up to 15% of the number of shares or bonds offered. If no cancellations are received when the offering commences, the manager can go into the aftermarket and purchase that security to cover (eliminate) the group's short position. This is not defined as stabilization, because more is paid than the syndicate's offering price.

Any loss sustained in this process is incurred by the manager on behalf of the members of the underwriting group and apportioned pro rata to their individual participation.

Another device that can be employed to cover the syndicate's short position is a method that does not cause aggressive buying in the aftermarket. The corporation can, and often does, grant the underwriters an option, or warrant, to purchase additional securities of the same issue below the public offering price, exercisable within a specific time. The privilege, known as a *green shoe* (named after the first issuer that used this technique), is generally exercisable within thirty days after the effective date at the same price as the underwriter's guarantee to the corporation. This new stock is registered with the SEC via amendment to the original registration statement. The manager then can exercise this option

and use the certificates received to close out the syndicate's short position. All profit in this case is distributed among the members, once again in proportion to their participation.

Free-Riding and Withholding Violations. An NASD member who participates in the public offering of securities is obliged to make a bona fide distribution of those securities. This directive is especially pertinent when the securities offered qualify as a hot issue. A member who declines to offer these securities publicly is instrumental in artificially establishing the premium by encouraging demand for the security while restricting the supply. Failure to make a bona fide distribution of an issue, known as *withholding*, is a violation of NASD Rules of Fair Practice. Furthermore, if the member subsequently sells that security in the aftermarket at a premium price, it is guilty of an additional unfair and unethical activity called *free-riding*. The two violations usually occur together because there is no benefit to withholding without the economic advantage of a free ride.

Allocating Hot Issues. The NASD Board of Governors further qualifies the conditions of a bona fide distribution. Their intent is to severely inhibit allocations of hot issues to persons associated with the offering and distribution process and to members of their immediate families as well. The restrictions are meant to preclude the temptation of free-riding for people who happen to be situated favorably.

For purposes of complying with the allocation interpretation, an issue will be "hot" only if it trades in the aftermarket on the first day above its fixed offering price. Thus, if the aftermarket price does not reach or exceed the fixed offering price a firm may allocate that issue to customers without regard to their occupational classification. This consideration, however, does not exempt that firm from its requirement to make a bona fide public offering of that security. Withholding is always prohibited, hot issue or not.

On the other hand, if the issue meets the

conditions set forth above and is considered to be "hot" a careful analysis of each subscriber's occupation and business affiliations must be made. Specifically, special attention must be paid to any subscription for a hot issue that is made by any of the following persons or groups: (1) any officer, partner, registered representative, other employee of any domestic broker/dealer organization, or members of such person's immediate family; (2) any domestic broker/dealer organization not a member of the underwriting or selling groups; (3) the managing underwriter's "finder" for this offering, its accountants, attorneys, financial consultants, or members of such person's immediate family; and (4) senior officers, securities department employees, or persons influencing securities activities in the following institutions (or members of such persons' immediate families): (a) a domestic commercial bank or trust company (including the domestic branch of a foreign bank); (b) a domestic savings bank or savings and loan association (including a credit union); and (c) an insurance company, registered investment company, registered investment advisor, pension or profit-sharing trust, or other financial institution.

Any person in category 1 must unequivocally be denied an allocation of a hot issue in any amount. (When the issuer is a financial institution or even a member firm itself "going public," it may allocate to its own employees and associates only if those persons agree to restrict sale of the certificates for at least twelve months thereafter. Bona fide gifts of those certificates during this period merely transfer the responsibility to the recipient.)

It is also obviously important to understand the NASD interpretation of the term "immediate family." As defined by the NASD immediate family includes (1) parents, (2) parents-in-law, (3) spouse, (4) children, (5) siblings, and (6) siblings-in-law. Also included is any relative to whom the person in a restricted category gives support directly or indirectly. These relatives must be accorded the same allocation treatment as the associated parties themselves, in line with the applicable category restriction.

The domestic broker/dealer described in category 2 is also precluded from subscribing to a hot issue at or above the public offering price, unless that organization furnishes the firm with a letter testifying that (1) this security will be allocated to bona fide public customers not included in the restricted categories, (2) at the fixed public offering price, and (3) without compensation for itself for this accommodation.

Persons described in categories 3 and 4 are not prohibited from purchasing a hot issue from a NASD member, but they are subject to certain limitations and conditions. For instance, they must have established an investment history with the particular firm intent on making the hot issue allocation to them. This means they must have made at least ten purchases there over three years with an average dollar value equal to the value of the intended allocation. Additionally, the firm's allocation to each of these persons must not be disproportionate in quantity as compared to bona fide nonrestricted public allocations. Such subscriptions will not be considered disproportionate if they are limited to no more than a single round lot (that is, 100 shares of stock or five $1,000 face value bonds). Moreover, the member firm is limited to an aggregate insubstantial quantity for allocation to these persons as a group. As explained by NASD officials, this means that regardless of the size of the member firm's underwriting or selling group's commitment, the quantity sold to these restricted categories collectively should be less than 2,000 shares or $25,000 par value for bonds.

Another problem encountered occasionally, but still one to beware of, is a request from the issuing company whose financing is being arranged to sell some of those securities to certain persons whose business affiliations place them in one of the restricted categories. If the offering is "hot," the member firm is nevertheless obliged by the NASD's directive to allocate those securities on the basis of consideration for investment history, disproportionate quantities, and insubstantiality. No partiality may be shown to an issuer's preferences. In fact, if the designated people fall in the first restricted category, they must be excluded from any allocation.

In its free-riding and withholding interpretation, the NASD also addresses itself to the possibility of a *back-door subscription* for a person in one of these categories through a financial institution acting as a conduit. (A *conduit* refers to a bank, trust company, investment advisory, or a similar omnibus type of account in which the underlying principal and/or business affiliations are not disclosed.) To permit an allocation to such an account domiciled in the United States, the firm must be certain the registered representative makes inquiry of the party authorized to place orders for the account and that he or she (1) makes certain that the underlying recipient of the security is not someone cited in those restricted categories; (2) notes the name of the party providing those assurances on an order ticket or some such similar document; (3) records the substance of what was said and done on the same document; and (4) has that document initialled by a registered principal of the firm.

If the conduit organization is a foreign broker/dealer or foreign bank, a slightly different approach must be employed. If it is participating in a distribution as an underwriter, there must be a provision in the agreement among underwriters prohibiting it from allocating those securities to people subject to NASD restrictions unless, of course, they can qualify under the considerations stated previously. If it is not participating as an underwriter, it must sign a blanket certification form such as NASD Form FR-1 see the following figure). This form advises the institution of the hot-issue restrictions. In completing it, the organization agrees not to violate these policies. The form is com-

pleted only once (the first time a participation is agreed on between the NASD member and the foreign broker/dealer or foreign bank) and stays in the member firm's files for the period of time prescribed under law. For each hot-issue allocation thereafter, the registered representative must prepare an order ticket or similar document that notes (1) the name of the official there who was questioned about the status of the underlying purchaser and the substance of his or her response to this query; and (2) the initialled approval by a registered principal of the firm.

The last and probably most difficult NASD hot-issue interpretation that must be complied with concerns investment partnerships and investment corporations. The difficulty is in recognizing those institutions for what they are and then securing specific information from them to permit a hot-issue allocation for those accounts. Let's look at the second aspect first. The NASD insists that before a hot issue is sold to an investment partnership or corporation (other than one registered under the Investment Company Act of 1940), the member firm must receive the names and business connections of all persons having a beneficial interest in the account. Beneficial interest includes not only ownership interests but financial interests, such as management and performance fees, as well. Consequently, if any of those persons named is employed in a capacity listed in previously mentioned restricted categories, this account must incur the same type of restriction as those do. Those partnerships or corporations prohibited by law from revealing the names of persons with a beneficial interest therein must, nevertheless, provide written assurance that no person restricted under the NASD interpretation has a beneficial interest in the account. Without this information or assurance, no hot issue should be allocated to that account.

As for the first part of the problem, the NASD defines an investment partnership or investment corporation as an institution whose primary function consists of investing in securities. It applies to such entities as hedge funds, investment clubs, and offshore management companies. But it can also pertain to several other concerns known by a variety of different names. That is what makes them so difficult to identify and regulate pursuant to NASD requirements. A well- managed NASD member firm should therefore insist that the registered representative determine and note on a new account information form the nature or principal business of any nonindividual client introduced to the firm. Particular attention in this regard should be directed toward any account established or maintained with a title containing any of the following key words: advisors, agency, associates, association, capital, club, company (if it is an unincorporated entity whose title does not reveal the principal business), counsellors, equity, family, fund, group, investors, investments, management, offshore, options, overseas, partners, pool, principals, proprietors, securities, society, syndicate, ventures. This list is not all inclusive, but it does serve as a guideline for suspicion. It is intended to alert the member firm and its registered representatives to the need to make a searching inquiry into the business affairs of their clients if they want to avoid NASD penalties.

Anyone who, as a person associated with a member organization, is subject to NASD jurisdiction should keep in mind that the District Business Conduct Committee will institute disciplinary proceedings against the purchaser and the seller of hot issues alike, should those issues be distributed contrary to NASD policies.

Remember, too, that this directive is pertinent to hot issues offered directly by the issuing corporation as well as to those that are underwritten by a member of the NASD.

See also National Association of Securities Dealers (Committee on Corporate Financing);

Short Sale; Stabilizing the Aftermarket; Syndicate; Underwriting.

Hybrid Annuity. Life insurance companies can and do offer annuity contracts for sale that are hybrids of basic fixed and variable programs. That is, these hybrids are part guaranteed-dollar and part variable; the appropriate percentage of each form in this customized annuity contract is predetermined by the individual subscriber. The annuity payments are then a combination of fixed dollars for a guaranteed base income and variable dollars for a possible hedge against inflation.

Example: If the annuitant chooses an investment contract that is 50% fixed and 50% variable, half of the premium deposit is applied for purchase of a fixed annuity and half for a variable one. Then, when payments commence, the holder is assured of a constant lifetime return from the fixed annuity, augmented by changing amounts of money from the variable contract. The specific amount receivable from a variable annuity depends on the investment performance of an underlying portfolio of securities in which deposit premiums are invested.

See also Annuity Contract; Fixed Annuity; Variable Annuity.

Hypothecating Customer Securities. The act of borrowing money to finance purchasing or carrying securities while using those securities as collateral for the loan is referred to as *hypothecation.* A broker/dealer has blanket written permission to hypothecate and to lend customers' margin securities, although this authorization is not unlimited. Federal, exchange, and NASD authorities do not permit a customer's securities to be used beyond the amount actually needed to cover the debt to the firm.

When a broker/dealer finances its customer's debit balances through bank loans, it complies with the banking community's requirements (*see* Broker's Collateral Loan). When financing is arranged by means of securities loans to dealers, it abides by the brokerage industry's customs.

For the purpose of financing margin account debit balances, the major stock exchanges and the NASD permit hypothecation of a customer's securities valued up to 140% of the debit balance. The cushion between the 133⅓% collateral required by the banks and the 140% in securities allowed by the authorities permits some flexibility for brokers in making and maintaining their arrangements. It is recognized that not all certificates are acceptable as collateral by the lending banks. Some banks will refrain from accepting odd-lot certificates, and some of them discourage loans having an unusual concentration in the securities of a single issuer.

Example: Assume that a customer has a $300,000 debit balance. The broker/dealer can place as much as $420,000 ($300,000 × 140%) worth of the collateral securities into a broker's collateral loan (call loan) to finance that debt. Thus, the extra allowable 6⅔% (140% − 133⅓%) yields $20,000 additional ($420,000 − $400,000) funds. That excess $20,000 value can serve to forestall the bank's call for more collateral should security prices decline. Or, it can be employed to help finance another customer's debit balance if appropriate certificate denominations or issues are not readily available.

Not all customer accounts have pledged collateral at the 140% level. Some customer accounts have pledged collateral below the 140% level because of the difficulty in arranging proper denomination and value from the particular issues in the account.

Example: If a customer had a $3,000 debit balance to be financed and only one certificate for 100 shares of IBM worth $27,000 available in the account, in all likelihood the firm would not deposit it into a call loan. It is impractical to break up round-lot certificates merely to arrange short-term financing. Instead, the firm would probably utilize some of the $20,000 excess from the customer to carry that $3,000 debit.

From an overall view of the situation there is no great advantage for the broker and no extensive jeopardy for the customers in these maneuvers. Furthermore, as the securities fluctuate in value, the broker/dealer must continuously substitute collateral to stay within the requirements. It must withdraw and segregate securities in some accounts and deliver certificates to the bank for others.

The rate of interest paid on this *call money* is influenced by (1) the prime rate charged to the bank's best customers; (2) the broker/dealer's past credit relationship with the bank; (3) the size of the loan itself; and (4) the quality and type of collateral pledged (stock versus bonds, corporate bonds versus U.S. government bonds, and so on).

Financing by Lending Certificates. When a broker/dealer finances its customer margin accounts by means of securities loaned to other broker/dealers, the firm becomes a creditor in these transactions. For its protection, the firm demands and receives 100% of the market value of the certificates being loaned.

It is generally advantageous to finance a customer's debit balance by lending certificates rather than by obtaining a bank loan. The catch is that it is not always possible to lend certificates; that is, there may be no demand for the certificate whereas bank financing is always available.

Example: Assume that a customer has a $5,000 debit in a margin account. The broker can finance this debit either by obtaining a bank loan or by lending certificates. If the broker finances the debit by a bank loan, then it deposits about $7,000 ($5,000 × 140%) worth of securities to serve as collateral for this account. On the other hand, if another firm is eager to borrow a $5,000 stock in that account to accommodate its own short-selling customer, the broker can lend the certificate to that firm. In exchange for the certificate, the lending broker receives

$5,000 in cash to hold as security. It then uses this money to finance its customer's $5,000 debit balance.

The lending broker clearly benefits by using this second method rather than obtaining a bank loan. The broker charges the margin customer regular interest to carry the $5,000 debit balance, but it incurs no interest expense to obtain these funds from the other broker. In the bank-loan method, the broker's profit is the difference between the bank's interest charge to the broker and the broker's interest charge to the customer. In the case of a stock loan between brokerage firms, the broker's profit is generally the entire interest amount paid to the broker by the margin-account customer.

Example: To see what this means in terms of monthly interest dollars on a $5,000 loan, let us use the following hypothetical notes:

	$5,000 Bank Loan	$5,000 Broker's Stock Loan
Broker charges customer 8% interest	$33.33	$33.33
Bank charges broker 6% interest	– 25.00	—
Broker's interest profit	$ 8.33	$33.33

This may not look substantial. However, if the total monthly debit balances in customer accounts are estimated at only $500,000, these dollars mean good profits for the broker.

See also Borrowing Stock Certificates; Securities Exchange Act of 1934 (Section 8); Segregation.

Hypothecation Agreement. *See* Customer's Agreement.

I

Immediate or Cancel (IOC). A qualification for *immediate or cancel* is a hybrid between the all-or-none and the fill-or-kill instructions. A customer entering this order wants the order executed promptly in accordance with quantity and price conditions specified but will accept consummation of *any portion* of the order, cancelling the unfilled balance immediately. Thus, this instruction gives the stock exchange member an opportunity to participate verbally in the trading area, albeit for a limited time period. The member can make the bid (or offering), and (1) if someone promptly responds but only partially fills this order, the member accepts, cancels the unsatisfied portion of the bid (offer), withdraws from the trading area, and reports partial success to the customer; or (2) if no one promptly responds, the member merely withdraws the bid (offer), retires from the trading area, and reports to the customer that the order has been cancelled.

See also All or None (AON); Fill or Kill (FOK).

Inactive Bonds. Inactive bonds are corporate debt instruments traded infrequently on the NYSE because of such factors as (1) limited quantities outstanding; (2) concentrated long-term holdings by institutional investors; or (3) lack of investor popularity for that issuer's industry, causing the Floor Department to assign that bond to inactive status.

Verbal bids or offerings would be futile in these instances, and so all bids and offerings are written on colored cards and filed in metal cabinets surrounding the trading ring. Hence, the significance of the expressions "cabinet" or "can" (a metal cabinet) crowd synonymous with inactive bonds.

Whereas only day or GTC orders may be entered on the floor in the stock trading room or active bond crowd, cabinet bond orders may also be entered as good-through-the-week or good-through-the-month as a convenience to investors that have an interest in dealing with them. Different colored cards indicate the effective lifetime of these orders.

Example:

White	= day orders
Blue	= good-through-the-week
Salmon	= good-through-the-month
Yellow	= good-til-cancelled

The absence of a specialist in the bond room precludes entry of stop orders in the active or inactive bond crowds. Normal market and limit orders, however, are acceptable and may be handled and executed in the fashion described.

Brokers with orders to buy or sell an issue assigned to the cabinets will first determine whether there is a contra order in the rack at an acceptable price. They inquire through a cabinet clerk (a NYSE employee responsible for maintaining the order cards in the proper cabinets). If no acceptable order is present, the brokers leave a card in the cabinet and go on about their business. If there is a satisfactory contra order card available, the card is removed from the rack and the original broker summoned. Both members step into the trading ring to consummate the transaction via verbal bid (offer) and acceptance.

Business is transacted in the cabinet crowd on a first-come, first-served basis. Priority belongs to each order in its entry time sequence. Although verbal bids or offers are permitted, any order in the cabinet at the same price has priority over a verbal competitor.

Members are held to terms and conditions specified on the order card and must consummate the transaction with the agreeable contra broker unless written cancellation is received by the cabinet clerk before preliminary acceptance by that broker.

In the final analysis, all NYSE bond transactions are completed within the trading ring. This is true for active and inactive bonds, even though the metal cabinets normally are used to facilitate entry and execution of inactive bond orders.

See also Active Bonds; Corporate Bond Transaction.

In-, At-, and Out-of-the-Money. *In-the-money* is an expression used to denote a securities option with a strike price that is profitable in comparison with the current market value of the underlying stock—that is, an option with intrinsic value. A *call option* is considered in-the-money if the underlying stock is higher than the striking price of the call. A put option is considered in-the-money if the stock is below the striking price.

Out-of-the-money is a term used to describe an option that has no intrinsic value. An option is out-of-the-money if the striking price is unprofitable in comparison with the current market value of the underlying stock. A *call option* is out-of-the-money if the underlying stock is below the striking price of the call. A *put option* is out-of-the-money if the stock is above the striking price.

Whether the investor is long or short the option has no bearing on this factor.

Options trading at parity (right at the intrinsic value) are said to be at-the-money; those whose exercise prices are substantially away from the market value of the underlying stock are referred to as deep-in- or deep-out-of-the-money.

See also Evaluating Options; Intrinsic Value; Premium; Time Value.

Income Bond. Reorganization of a bankrupt corporation can offer the company's creditors a better chance of recouping their investments over an extended period. Effecting a reorganization requires a greater amount of new, more permanent capital than that raised by receivers' certificates. At the same time, how can one acquire long-term financing for a corporation already in bankruptcy and besieged by its creditors?

The answer rests in the receiver's ability to eliminate the immediate claims of those creditors. The receiver attempts to do so by offering them a larger principal amount of higher- interest-bearing income bonds in exchange for their debt issues.

Example: The offer might be $1,300 of a 10% income bond for each $1,000 of a 6% mortgage bond in default.

Income bonds are long-term debt obligations that promise to pay interest only when, as, and if earned by the corporation. If the earnings of the corporation do not warrant current payment of the interest, the amount accrues (rather like missed dividends on cumulative preferred stock) without further legal difficulty. As a natural consequence of the uncertainty of interest payments, income bonds usually trade in the marketplace without accrued interest calculable as an addition to the contract price. Thus, they are said to be trading *flat*, unlike other debt securities, which normally trade on an *and interest* basis. The receiver and the successor management need not concern themselves about repayment of the principal amount because these bonds frequently carry maturity dates of 150 to 200 years after issuance.

If the corporation's bondholders agree to accept income bonds, permitting reorganization to proceed, they are, for the time being, receiving a bigger piece of nothing! Yet this recourse may represent their only chance of ever recovering their original investment. The corporation remains in bankruptcy under the control of a receiver until, and if, an agreement (adjustment) can be reached with those creditors, this is why income bonds are sometimes described as *adjustment bonds*. If the corporation can ever regain its former earning power, the creditors, now holding income bonds, not only receive more in interest dollars, but they also have more in principal amount as well.

See also Certificate of Indebtedness.

Income Company. These investment companies stress higher-than-average current income from investments without regard to quality or class of security in their portfolios. Capital gains are a minimal consideration, so that during inflationary periods in the economy the value of these shares tends to remain stable or even to decline. An exception exists only if the income-oriented company is fortunate in finding investment media able to improve on dividend payouts or to invest continuously in lower-quality securities. This latter possibility, however, would increase the risk factor for investors.

See also Investment Company.

Income Shares. *See* Dual Purpose Investment Company.

Income Statement. Most annual reports from a corporation contain in addition to the balance sheet, the income statement. The *income statement*, also known as the *profit and loss (P&L) statement*, is a statement of income and expenses usually over the *entire* year; it shows how much the company made or lost during the year. A typical, simplified, income statement appears in the following figure. (Assume 30,000 shares of common stock outstanding.)

Income Statement
Roxbury Manufacturing Company
January 1-December 31, 198X

Net sales	$ 2,000,000
Cost of goods sold	– 1,590,000
Selling, general, and administrative expenses	– 154,000
Depreciation	– 56,000
Operating income	$ 200,000
Other income	+ 7,500
Total income (EBIT)	$ 207,500
Interest on bonds	– 40,000
Taxes (37% rate)	– 61,975
Net income	$ 105,525
Preferred dividends	– 4,500
Net earnings (earnings available for common stock)	$ 101,025

Net Sales. This item shows the amount of money that the company took in as the result of its manufacturing activities. *Net* reflects the fact that returned goods and discounts have been taken into account. Were this a nonmanufacturing enterprise (such as an airline or utility), this item might be called *operating revenues.*

Cost of Goods Sold. Think of this item as "factory" cost. It includes such factors as the costs of maintaining the manufacturing facilities, raw materials, and labor.

Selling, General, and Administrative Expenses. This item includes the cost of running the sales office of the company: office payroll, salespersons' commissions, advertising, and other nonmanufacturing expenses.

Depreciation. The annual depreciation of the fixed assets appears in this category. You may consider this a noncash expense because the assets may have been paid for well in the past but are being "charged off" in small increments each year.

See also Depreciation.

Operating Income. Subtracting the operating costs from net sales gives operating income. It is "factory" profit, because we have not yet considered bond interest, taxes, or income from sources other than manufacturing.

Other Income. The income that the company receives as dividends and/or interest on the marketable securities it may own appears here. This item may also include other sources of income not related directly to the firm's operations, such as the sale of real estate (above book value) or rental income on unused land held for future use.

Total Income. Also known as earnings before interest and taxes (EBIT), this category is fairly self-explanatory.

Interest on Bonds. Almost as self-explanatory is the amount of money that the corporation pays out each year to service its outstanding bonds.

Taxes. This item includes federal and state income taxes, figured at the prevailing rates.

Net Income. This item is also known as *net profit.* All income and all expenses have now been weighed against each other. Only the stockholders remain to be satisfied.

Preferred Dividends. Note that the corporation deducted its bond interest payments before figuring its tax liability. Preferred dividend payments, however, are not a deductible item and do not lower taxes.

Net Earnings. Such earnings, also known as *earnings available for common stock,* may be reinvested in the company and/or paid out to the common stockholders as cash dividends. Any amount not paid out as dividends, at least in theory, increases the retained earnings account.

Just as balance sheet ratios measure a company's financial strength, so too do important income statement ratios reflect a company's state of affairs.

See also Cash Dividends; Inventory Turnover Ratio; Fully Diluted Earnings per Share; Payout Ratio; Price Earnings Ratio; Primary Earnings per Share; Retiring Debt; Return on Equity; Return on Invested Capital; Sale and Leaseback of Fixed Assets; Stock Splits; Yield on Common Stock.

Incompetents. *See* Fiduciary Accounts.

Individual Proprietorship. There are three principal types of business organization in the United States today: corporation, partnership, and proprietorship.

The simplest and most common form of business organization is known as an *individual proprietorship.* There are many advantages to a proprietorship. As the owner, you are your own boss and enjoy a great deal of freedom and flexibility in your business activities. You decide on the type of endeavor, the location, the quality and quantity of merchandise, and the hours during which you conduct your business, be it a service or manufacturer.

Some disadvantages, however, preclude the individual proprietorship from developing into a big business. Foremost among these handicaps is the lack of perpetuity. If you become incapacitated for an extended period, there is usually difficulty in continuing operation. Worse yet, on your death, your business, penalized without your guidance, ceases to exist too.

Still another deterrent to the individual proprietorship is the feature of unlimited liability. Under existing laws in most states, single proprietorships may be held personally accountable for the obligations incurred by their businesses. If your proprietorship fails, your creditors may lay claim to your *personal* assets as well as to those of the business itself.

Even in prosperity, additional obstacles prevail. To maintain or increase your competitive position in the industry, you need capital to improve and expand your business. As an individual, your personal resources are certainly limited, and you must therefore turn to outside sources for financing. Although your books and records may justify such borrowing, banks and commercial factors balk at granting credit for extended periods. In recognition of the shortcomings of an individual proprietorship, they might be willing to lend you capital, but for just a few years.

See also Corporation; Partnership.

Indenture. When dealing in debt securities, investors must understand the terms of the borrowing agreement. This agreement, referred to as an *indenture*, is merely a deed of trust established between the corporation and its creditors that specifies the full terms of the borrowing arrangement. Its provisions include such information as: (1) the rate of interest, with time and means of payment clearly stated; (2) the date of maturity and any terms or conditions for repayment of principal prior to maturity; (3) a detailed description of any collateral pledged, with priorities established for the bondholders in the event of default; and (4) the name and address of the party responsible for supervisory compliance with the terms of this agreement (the trustee).

Under the Trust Indenture Act of 1939 for public offerings of debt securities, an independent trustee must be appointed by the corporation to safeguard the interest of the creditors and ensure that the company abides by the terms of the borrowing agreement. The trustee is usually a commercial bank.

Indenture Qualification Statement. *See* Indenture Registration.

Indenture Registration. Most corporate debt issuers satisfy the Trust Indenture Act of 1939 by making a full disclosure in a formal registration statement submitted to the SEC for its scrutiny.

Thus both the security and its contingent indenture are fully registered commencing on the effective date. Debt securities exempted from the 1933 Act's registration requirement comply with the terms of the 1939 Act by presentation of an *indenture qualification statement* to the SEC. Although the issue itself is not registered, its indenture will be registered on the effective date. The effective date is generally the twentieth calendar day after the statement has been received by the SEC.

Whether the debt security is registered with the SEC or not, its indenture must set forth the full terms and conditions under which the loan will be maintained during its lifetime. Such facts include: (1) the amount, frequency, and method by which interest will be paid; (2) the maturation date and means by which the principal amount of the loan will be repaid; (3) earlier redemption privileges, if any, reserved for use by the issuer or the debt instrument holder; (4) convertibility features and terms, if any; (5) a full description of the collateral, if any, securing this loan; (6) the powers and responsibilities of the trustees in the event of a default by the issuer on any portion of the indenture agreement; (7) any agreements, concessions, or waivers that will be an integral part of the financing; (8) the duties and responsibilities of the trustees; (9) rights of the bondholders; and (10) obligations of the issuing corporation.

See also Securities Exchange Act of 1933; Trust Indenture Act of 1939.

Index. *See* Averages and Indexes.

Indication of Interest. Before investment bankers contractually commit themselves to the corporation, they seek assurance of reasonable opportunity for success. They are allowed under law to contact their customers and, with only preliminary information available at this time, solicit indication of interest from them. An *indication of interest* (referred to in slang as a *circle*) is merely an expression of consideration for that issue and is not a binding commitment on the customer or the investment banker. Prior to the effective date, customers may modify their indications any number of times without penalty as their investment monies or intentions change because of prevailing market conditions.

See also Investment Banker; Syndicate.

Individual Identification. *See* Segregation.

Industrial Development Bonds. *See* Municipal Securities; Revenue Bonds.

Inflation. Unlimited credit and unbridled willingness to use it lead to *inflation*. As its momentum increases, it is characterized by high employment and, paradoxically, a steadily declining standard of living for most people. This strange phenomenon is caused by spiraling prices of goods and services, for which demand exceeds production in the initial phase of the business cycle. Then two essential factors come into play: (1) More and more people compete for available goods and services, causing upward pressure on prices. (2) Because prices increase without too much difficulty and at a faster pace than personal income, it isn't long before consumers must apply for ever-increasing amounts of credit to acquire what they quickly become accustomed to in their living patterns.

Sooner or later, one or both of those factors essential to inflation begins to falter. Production catches, and then quickly exceeds, demand. This, in turn, causes business and agriculture to trim their needs for short-term credit for expansion purposes. Or perhaps banking management turns cautious about its loan activities, reevaluates its credit policies, and even demands repayment of some outstanding loans that are subject to short notice. As this "credit caution" develops, overproduction and debt-financing pressures lead to liquidation of inventories at below-cost prices. Increasing numbers of businesses take steps to curb costs and production and to bring supply more in line with demand. Then, as production halts and factories are closed, unemployment rises. People, already strapped with high consumer obligations, cut back in their demand for goods and services in order to afford necessities and repay their debts. This, in turn, leads to greater reductions in production and increasing unemployment. The snowballing effect of these defensive actions is frightening. As we have seen in the past, the result can be financial panic, recession, and even depression.

The ultimate objective of modern-day capitalism is moderate inflation in order to keep credit factors turned in a positive direction. Although agreeing on a definition of "moderate" might be difficult, moderation is the ideal goal. In a free society, a static economy cannot prevail for long, and the consequences of a significant drift in either direction are too objectionable. The problem, then, is how to regulate human nature and prevent sustained moves to either end of the business spectrum.

In the United States, we have approached this problem by monitoring and regulating the financial activities of the primary manufacturers of credit—commercial banks. The basic idea of such regulation was structured and implemented with legislation embodied in the Federal Reserve Banking Act of 1913.

See also Federal Reserve System.

Information Meetings. *See* Competitive Bidding; Due-Diligence Meeting.

Initial Margin Requirement. Regulation T establishes the initial margin requirement for a purchase on margin. The Regulation T initial requirement applies to the total cost of a purchase. The amount of margin a customer must deposit as the result of the initial requirement is commonly referred to as *Reg T call*. The following are some sample transactions that demonstrate the application of this rule. Assume each of the following purchases are initial transactions in newly opened margin accounts.

Account	Initial Requirement	Purchase	Reg T Call
Joe Smith	50%	100 shares of Stock A at $80 (cost *$8,000)	$4,000
Jane Doe	60%	100 shares of Stock B at $90 (cost *$9,000)	$5,400
John Edwards	75%	200 shares of Stock C at $60 (cost *$12,000)	$9,000

*In this table we use *net* cost to simplify our calculations. In reality calculations must be made on total cost and net proceeds (that is, with consideration for commissions and other fees).

According to the above sample transactions, Joe Smith must deposit $4,000 with his broker because there is a 50% initial margin requirement on his purchase of $8,000 worth of Stock A. Jane Doe, purchasing at a time when the initial margin requirement is 60%, has a Reg T call of $5,400. Similarly, John Edwards receives a Reg T call of $9,000 under a 75% initial margin requirement. With these purchases, Joe Smith, Jane Doe, and John Edwards have established long positions in their margin accounts.

All Reg T calls must be met within seven business days of the trade date.

Example: If Joe Smith executes his trade on Tuesday, January 10, his funds will be due no later than the following Thursday, January 19 (seven business days later). If funds are not deposited by that date, the broker will be obligated to liquidate the transaction or else apply to a registered stock exchange or district office of the NASD for an extension of time. (the Federal Reserve Board permits the waiving of a Reg T call of $500 or less at the broker's option.

See also Exempt Security (Margin Trading); Margin Account.

Inside Market. *See* National Association of Securities Dealers Automated Quotations; Rules of Fair Practice (Section 5).

Intangible Assets. Included in this category are items of value that have no physical existence, such as patents, franchises, and goodwill. Such items are very difficult to quantify. Traditionally, intangibles are the last item shown on the asset side of the balance sheet.

See also Balance Sheet (Assets).

Inter-American Development Bank (IADB). This bank, founded in 1959, is another international institution intent on promoting economic and social development and modernization by financing capital projects in its member countries. Only government members in the Western Hemisphere are eligible for such loans, although the bank's own borrowings are worldwide and denominated in various international currencies. Interest paid to holders of its debt obligations is fully taxable by federal, state, and local authorities.

Interest Coverage. When examining a company, we want to know how well it provides for the payment of interest coupons on its outstanding bonds. To find out, divide total income (EBIT) by the interest on the bonds:

$$\text{Interest coverage} = \frac{\text{total income (EBIT)}}{\text{interest on bonds}}$$

Example:

$$\text{Interest coverage} = \frac{\$207,500}{\$40,000} = 5.2 \text{ times}$$

Interest coverage of over four times is usually considered a safe margin for the protection of a company.

See also Income Statement.

International Bank for Reconstruction and Development (the World Bank). The International Bank for Reconstruction and Development is popularly known as the *World Bank* and often identified by professional dealers and traders simply as the *IB* (International Bank). The bank makes and guarantees loans to assist in the reconstruction and development of resources in countries that subscribe to its capital stock and play a role in the management of this institution. Through its sizable subscriptions, the United States controls about 25% of the voting power so that changes in the bank's Articles of Agreement (drawn and founded in July 1944) necessitate this nation's consent before they become effective. (Amendments to the Articles require 80-100% membership approval for adoption, the variance dependent on the nature of the change).

From the start of its operations in 1946, the bank's loans have been made to develop and modernize industry, agriculture, transportation, communications, education, electric power, and water supply facilities in over ninety member countries and territories.

The International Bank supplements its capital funds periodically through offerings of debt obligations to institutional investors in various countries. These obligations are denominated in various currencies throughout the world. Interest paid on World Bank bonds to U.S. residents is fully taxable by federal, state, and local authorities. However, it is exempted from federal taxation if paid to nonresident aliens and most foreign corporations, whether or not they are engaged in business in the United States.

See also International Securities.

International Securities. Various international institutions have been organized throughout the world to facilitate the pooling and investment of capital. Debt instruments issued by these institutions are characterized by principal and interest payments denominated in currencies of the country in which financing is arranged. Therefore, investors with specific currency preferences or requirements may choose from a variety of issues available in English pounds sterling, German marks, Dutch guilders, Swiss francs, and so forth. Consideration is further complicated by the variety of rates, maturities, and other terms and conditions specified in the indenture of those notes and bonds.

See also Inter-American Development Bank; International Bank for Reconstruction and Development.

Interpolation. The answers to both problems can be calculated by means of *interpolation*. Because two of the three quantities (nominal, or coupon rate and interest) are known and readily identifiable from the tables, a simple ratio solves the problem. The ratio is formulated on the fact that proportionate changes in yield-to-maturity will be comparable to proportionate changes in bond value. Once we have the ratio, we can determine the yield-to-maturity or the market value. The formula for computing the ratio for both situations is the same:

$$\frac{\text{amount of change from next lowest market value}}{\text{increment between next lowest and next highest market values}} = \frac{\text{amount of change from next highest yield-to-maturity}}{\text{increment between next lowest and next highest yield-to-maturity}}$$

Example of Finding Yield-to-Maturity by Interpolating: A bond is selling at 101½, is due in twelve years, six months, and has a coupon rate of 6.50%. Find the unknown yield-to-maturity.

$$\text{next highest yield-to-maturity} - \text{proportionate change} = \text{yield-to-maturity}$$

1. Computing the ratio:

Current price	101.50
Next lowest market value in bond tables	−100.85
Amount of change	.65
Next highest market value under 12 years, 6 months column	101.71
Next lowest market value under 12 years, 6 months column	−100.85
Increment in market value	.86

2. Finding the figures to plug into the ratio formula:

$$\frac{.65}{.86} = \frac{x}{.10}$$ (increment between 6.30 and 6.40 yield-to-maturity)

$$.86x = (.65)(.10) = .065$$
$$x = .07558$$

3. Using the ratio figure to compute the yield-to-maturity:

Next highest yield-to-maturity	6.40
Proportionate change	−.07558
Yield-to-maturity	6.32442 or 6.32%

Example of Finding the Market Value by Interpolating: A bond is selling at 7.23 basis, is due in exactly eleven years, and has a coupon rate of 6.50%. Find the market value.

$$\text{Next lowest Market price} + \text{proportionate change} = \text{market value}$$

1. Finding the figures to plug into the ratio formula:

Next highest yield	7.30
Basis yield	−7.23
Amount of change	.07
Yield	7.30
Yield	−7.20
Increment	.10

2. Computing the ratio:

(increment between 94.74 and 94.02 market value in the 11 year and 0 months column)

$$\frac{x}{.72} = \frac{.07}{.10}$$
$$.10x = (.07)(.72) = .0504$$
$$x = .504$$

3. Using the ratio figure to compute the market value:

Next lowest market value	94.02
Proportionate change	+.504
Market value, $945.24 per bond	94.524

See also Bond (Quotations); Current Yield; Discount; Nominal Yield; Premium; Yield-to-maturity (Professional Method).

Interpositioning. NASD members are not required to deal personally or exclusively with a market-maker in a security. There are times when it may prove tactically advantageous to use the services of a non-market-maker in the execution of an order to avoid disclosure of the firm's participation. This occurs when a firm has a reputation to favor buying or selling a particular security continuously. So, in order to avoid a change in price that others might impose on it because of the firm's reputation, a firm may find it advantageous not to contact a market-maker directly. Or, it may be wise to avoid the market-maker entirely if an offsetting order execution, that is, a cross, can be arranged with another member organization or within the firm itself. (A *cross* means to pair off a purchase order with a sell order in the same security at the same price for different customers.)

Nevertheless, an NASD member firm has the responsibility for ensuring that an order is executed at the most favorable price under prevailing market conditions. It must exercise reasonable diligence by considering (1) the size and type of transaction; (2) the number and character of primary markets checked; and (3) its own location and accessibility to the primary markets and quotation sources.

It is a violation of the Rules of Fair Practice for a member to interject a third party between itself and the best available market if doing so causes the customer to pay more on a purchase or receive less on a sale. This practice, called *interpositioning*, is unethical and unfair.

Example: A dealer firm reports this transaction to its customer: "As principal, we are selling to you for your account and risk 100 shares of Connecticut General Insurance Company at 65¾ net."

Suppose that instead of canvassing the market-makers to determine the best offering available (*see* National Quotation Bureau, Inc.), your firm contacted another member organization who was not a market-maker in that stock and transmitted the order to it. By canvassing the NQB and NASDAQ sources, this firm would undoubtedly uncover the primary market-maker, who is offering at 64¾, and purchase the stock from this market-maker. Then the firm might mark up the stock price and offer it to your organization at 65. You in turn would mark it up again, finally selling it to your customer at 66. The end result would be a double markup on a series of transactions stemming from a single buy order. The customer who initiated the original transaction ultimately pays more for that stock than would have been the case if the unnecessary third party had not been interposed into this situation.

Lack of facilities or lack or personnel in the firm's Order Department is not a valid defense for such an action. Channeling these orders to a non-market-maker as reciprocation for services or business received is not justification either.

If the member firm does not deal with a bona fide market-maker on the execution of an order for or with a customer, it must be prepared to prove that the total cost or net proceeds, as the case may be) is no higher (or lower in the case of net proceeds) than if the primary market is utilized directly.

See also Markup and Markdown; National Association of Securities Dealers Automated Quotations System; National Quotation Bureau, Inc.

Intervivos Trust. *See* Living Trust.

Intrinsic Value. This value is the immediate value of an option if it were to expire with the underlying stock at its current price, or the amount by which an option is in-the-money. For call options, it is the difference between the stock price and the striking price if that difference is a positive number. If the difference is not positive, it is considered zero. For put options it is the difference between the striking price and the stock price if the difference is positive, and zero otherwise.

Example: An investor purchases a January 30 call option for $300 when the stock is selling at 28. At that time the call is out-of-the-money (the underlying stock trading below strike price). Assume the stock then goes to 35. The option is now in-the-money. The investor has the choice of exercising the option or liquidating the option in the secondary market.

Another option buyer is willing to buy the January 30 call option for at least $500, because he or she can immediately exercise the option at $30 and sell the stock in the open market at $35. The amount, therefore, that is in-the-money is called the intrinsic value. A buyer would probably pay more than five points for the option, maybe $600 or $700, because of the time remaining until expiration. The excess amount over intrinsic value that he or she is willing to pay is called *time value.*

Thus every option price has two components: first is the intrinsic value (if any); second is the time value. The sum of these two components always equals the option price (premium).

A special term is used when the option is trading right at intrinsic value: *trading at parity*. Another special term is *deep-in- (or out-of-)* the-money. The word *deep* denotes that the market value of the stock is substantially away from the exercise price. The option may thus be either deep-out-of-the-money or deep-in-the-money.

See also Evaluating Options; In-, At- and Out-of-the- Money; Time Value.

Inventory. The part of the corporation's current assets consisting of raw materials, work in progress, and finished goods is called *inventory*. Like marketable securities, inventories are carried on the balance sheet at the lower of cost or market value. (*See also* Marketable Securities.) Except in very unusual situations, the market value of the inventory is expected to be higher than its cost: A manufacturing corporation makes its profit selling its finished goods for more than it costs to produce them. Cost accounting for inventory is based on two popular methods: (1) FIFO (first-in/first-out) and (2) LIFO (last- in/first-out). The method that a company chooses can have a dramatic effect on its earnings and on the value of the inventory remaining after a sale.

Example: Roxbury Manufacturing has three manufactured items in inventory, each one produced in successive months at successively higher costs. During inflationary periods, such a situation is the norm. The first item manufactured (the one longest in inventory) cost $100, the second item cost $110, and the last item cost $120. The company is now selling its products for $300 each. Under FIFO, the gross profit is $200, since the item sold is considered to be the first item produced at a cost of $100. The value of the inventory remaining after the sale totals $230. Under the LIFO method, the profit on the $300 sale is based on the last item produced (at a cost of $120), and the gross profit is therefore only $180. The remaining inventory valuation is $210.

Under FIFO (first-in/first-out), item No. 1—the first one produced—is paired against the sale at $300. Thus:

Under LIFO (last-in/first-out), item No. 3—the last one produced—is paired against the sale at $300. Thus:

During inflationary periods, therefore, the FIFO method yields higher profits (and higher taxes!) than LIFO. FIFO also results in higher inventory evaluation. During deflationary periods, the results are just the opposite. To remember the effects of LIFO over FIFO during inflationary periods, remember this:

LIFO =   Lower gross profits
          Lower taxes
          Lower inventory valuation

Inventory Turnover Ratio. We can measure how effectively the company is selling its products by determining how often its supply of inventory is manufactured and sold. Of the several methods for calculating this ratio, the simplest (and probably least professional) is as follows:

$$\text{Inventory turnover ratio} = \frac{\text{net sales}}{\text{year-end inventory}}$$

This method is presented because it is simple and workable. Other methods use the cost of goods sold, rather than net sales, as the numerator and the average inventory, rather than the year-end inventory, as the denominator. As a general guide, a "good" inventory turnover ratio for an average manufacturing company is six times per year.

Example: A corporation's annual report shows net sales of $14,000,000 (on the income statement) and an inventory of $2,682,000 (on the balance sheet). The inventory turnover is 5.2 times, determined as follows:

$$\text{Inventory turnover ratio} = \frac{\$14,000,000}{2,682,000} = 5.2 \text{ times}$$

Inverted Market. A futures market in which the nearer months are selling at premiums to the more distant months, generally reflecting a tightness of spot supplies.

Inverted Scale. *See* Scale.

Investment Advisor. These people or organizations are registered with the SEC to do business in that capacity under the Investment Advisors Act of 1940. A broker/dealer may process securities transactions for customers in this category in either a special omnibus account or an advisors' client account.

See also Advisor's Client Account; Special Omnibus Account.

Investment Banker. Ordinarily, in a public offering of securities by an issuer—especially one involving substantial amounts of certificates or dollars—the corporation employs the services of an investment banker. The investment banker, a broker/dealer registered with the SEC, plays an essential role in behalf of American industry. The investment banking firm is an important factor in the capital market because it arranges long-term financing for businesses. Commercial banks, on the other hand, are primarily involved in money market activities, that is, short-term financing.

Investment bankers do more than merely raise capital. Their many other services include: (1) counseling companies in the management of their money; (2) advising companies about merger and acquisition opportunities; (3) examining and analyzing corporate documents and financial statements with a view toward modernization of outdated practices; (4) providing marketability for corporate securities after public distribution; and (6) public relations work.

When a company finds itself in need of capital, it consults with an investment banker to establish a means of raising funds. Management often relies on the investment banker's expertise and experience in determining the means and type of financing to be employed. Important factors influencing the investment banker's judgment and recommendations are: (1) the amount of money needed by the corporation; (2) the availability of money in the marketplace; (3) the cost of money in the marketplace (interest rates and so on; (4) financial restrictions in the charter and/or bylaws; (5) existing capital structure of the corporation; (6) the popularity of that industry in the investment community; (7) recent experiences by the company's competitors in raising capital; (8) pending legislation or litigation having an important bearing on the company's (or industry's) immediate future; (9) the quality of management in that corporation; and (10) the purpose for which this capital is needed.

If the investment banker concludes that it is worthwhile to proceed, it enters into an agreement with the issuer to underwrite, or distribute, the securities. This means of distribution is known as a *negotiated underwriting*. Immediate decisions are reached about the type of security to be issued (common stock, preferred stock, or bonds). Then the corporation and investment banker must decide whether the offering will be attempted by means of private placement or public distribution.

See also Competitive Bidding; Primary/ Secondary Distribution; Private Placement; Public Offering; Syndicate; Underwriting.

Investment Company. These companies offer investors a convenient and professional approach to diversification. For the small investor in particular, the advantages of investing in an investment company are not easily matched by investing an equal amount of money in individual securities. This is an important reason why many people still own and continue to purchase shares in investment companies.

An *investment company* has been defined

as an institution primarily engaged in the business of investing and trading in securities. Within the meaning of this term as used in the securities industry, we must specifically exclude (1) a broker/dealer or underwriter; (2) a bank or savings and loan association; (3) an insurance company (but not its separate account for variable annuities); (4) a company regulated under the Public Utility Holding Act of 1935; (5) a religious, educational, or charitable institution; and (6) any organization dealing in oil, gas, or mineral royalties or leases.

The term "investment company" as expressed in the Investment Company Act of 1940 is employed to include only (1) a face-amount certificate company that offers discounted certificates redeemable at face value; (2) a unit investment trust company, organized under a trust indenture rather than a corporate charter and including both fixed and participating trusts; or (3) a management company, including both diversified and nondiversified companies as well as closed-end companies and open-end companies.

In addition to classification by organizational structure, another typecasting of investment companies is generally based on an examination of the objectives of those companies. However in many instances the statements of objectives are made in such broad language that it is often difficult to assign a company to a particular category. Furthermore, careful scrutiny of the policies employed to reach these objectives can lead to interesting debates. Nevertheless, for reasons of uniformity, the *NASD Training Guide* classifies investment companies as (1) diversified common stock companies; (2) balanced companies; (3) income companies; (4) specialized companies; (5) bond and preferred stock companies; (6) money market companies; (7) dual-purpose companies; and (8) exchange-type companies.

The potential for conflicts of interest and other associated inequities has been recognized by the federal government; therefore, investment companies are closely regulated.

Real estate investment trusts and annuities are also types of investment companies. They are not-so-distant relatives of well-known concepts embracing investment companies. They have many of the same characteristics and are subject to many of the same federal regulations. They, too, have stated objectives regarding the performance of investments in their portfolios. They also offer subscribers advantages and risks often associated with typical mutual fund investments.

See also Annuity Contract; Balanced Investment Company; Bond and Preferred Stock Company; Diversified Common Stock Company; Diversified Company; Dual-Purpose Investment Company; Exchange-Type Company; Face-Amount Certificate Company; Income Company; Investment Company Act of 1940 and 1970 Amendments; Management Company; Money Market Company; Nondiversified Company; Real Estate Investment Trust; Registration Statement; SEC Statement of Policy; Specialized Investment Company; Subchapter M (Internal Revenue Code); Unit Investment Trust.

The procedures and relationships created for continuous sales of open-end management company shares differ somewhat from an ordinary offering of securities. Their very uniqueness is responsible for labeling these open-end shares *mutual funds*.

The term *mutual fund* can technically be used to identify any investment company. It refers to a pooling of monies for investment purposes. Historically, however, it has been used to refer to open-end management companies. This is probably due to the effects of promotional advertising in the 1940s that was designed to acquaint the U.S. public with this blossoming investment medium.

There are four ways in which mutual fund

shares can be offered and distributed to the public—the direct-sale approach, the underwriter approach, the selling-group approach, and the plan-company approach.

Direct-Sale Approach. In the simplest approach, the mutual fund sells its shares directly, that is, without any sales force or organization for this specific purpose (see the following figure).

When such a relationship is established, those shares are offered at net asset value. The offering price and the bid price will be exactly the same price—net asset value. These companies are called *no-load mutual funds*, since there is no sales charge. Such companies rely on word-of-mouth advertising by satisfied shareholders and limited-budget media advertising to inform people of their existence. Understandably, these funds are in the minority compared to the funds with a *load* (sales charge). It is, however, a rapidly growing minority. More investors are becoming sophisticated enough to learn of and investigate the merits of mutual funds by themselves without relying solely on the word of a salesperson.

When this direct approach is chosen by a mutual fund none of the other sales methods about to be described may augment or supplement it.

Underwriter Approach. Most mutual fund shares are sold to or through a broker/dealer acting as an underwriter who in turn markets them publicly (see the following figure).

An underwriter purchases these shares from the mutual fund at net asset value and then sells them to investors at the public offering price. The difference between bid and offering prices represents the underwriter's spread and its only source of remuneration. In this segment of the financial community, an underwriter of mutual fund shares is also often identified as a *sponsor*, or *distributor*, or even as a *wholesaler*. These terms should be thought of synonymously because the underwriter has an exclusive agreement with that fund for sales and distribution purposes.

It is important to note that the NASD Rules of Fair Practice prohibit an underwriter (or any NASD member) from purchasing mutual fund shares for itself unless it is for a bona fide investment account. This means that NASD firms may not act as market-makers in mutual fund shares or even purchase these shares in anticipation of a customer's order. They may act only in response to an actual order initiated by, or accepted from, a customer.

Selling-Group Approach. A substantial percentage of mutual fund underwriters utilize the services of a selling group to gain broader distribution of these shares. The selling group is comprised of broker/dealer members of the NASD who contract with the underwriter to act as its agent. In return, the underwriter compensates these firms with a portion of the sales charge known as a *selling concession* (see the following figure).

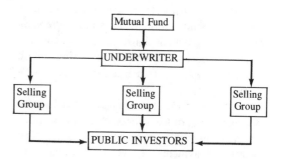

The selling concession may be paid only to fellow members of the NASD after they sign a sales agreement that includes (1) a provision for the amount of concession to be paid for the service rendered; (2) a promise binding the members to sell the shares only at the public offering price, determined as set forth in the offering prospectus (in fact, NASD rules prohibit members who are not subject to a sales agreement from offering mutual fund shares at another price if that fund has an effective underwriting agreement with any NASD member); (3) a requirement to refund to the underwriter the entire concession if those shares are redeemed within seven business days after purchase; (4) prohibitions for withholding entry of customer orders to purchase or redeem, so as to profit from such action; and (5) a stipulation barring repurchase of those shares from a customer when acting as principal, unless such purchase is made at the next established bid price quoted by that fund. Although the NASD member normally earns money only when a customer buys mutual fund shares, the firm can charge the customer a commission for a redemption if it acts as agent; that is, as an intermediary between the customer and the mutual fund. (A commission redemption charge, if applicable, is separate and distinct from a redemption fee that may be levied by the fund itself.) The customer can avoid such commission expense by redeeming those shares directly to the mutual fund or its designated representative.

Plan-Company Approach. When an underwriter offers mutual fund shares under the various periodic payment plans, still another entity is often interposed between the investing public and the underwriter. That organization is called a *plan company*.

Officially, the plan company acts as a sales manager or coordinator for offerings of extended contracts involving purchase of mutual fund shares. As payments are received, the plan company subscribes from the underwriter for the ap-

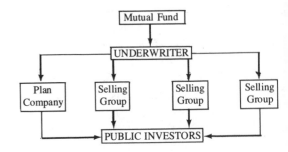

propriate amount and ensures proper credit to each planholder's account for valuable units of accumulation in the plan company itself. For this reason, plan companies must register with the SEC under federal law as unit investment trusts, although in reality they are merely middlemen accommodating indirect public participation in a mutual fund. Because these contractual payment arrangements use the maximum permissible load calculated under federal laws, at 9% of the total money invested, there is sufficient compensation available for all parties involved in the offering and distribution process.

Note that whether the mutual fund shares are sold loaded or no-load, the fund itself receives only the net asset value of those shares for investment purposes. The sales load is retained by the underwriter and any other sales organizations it employs for the marketing functions.

In summary, the offering and placement of mutual fund shares may be accomplished by mutual fund to (1) investing public; or (2) underwriter to investing public; or (3) underwriter to selling group to investing public; or (4) underwriter to plan company to investing public.

In the last case, the plan company generally uses its own sales force, bypassing the members of the selling group completely.

Purchase Plans. Mutual fund purchases may be arranged in several ways as an accommodation to the investor. Despite this fact, the underlying relationships between management company and sales organizations remain basically unchanged in each instance.

The least complicated of all procedures is the single payment. This payment is an outright purchase of shares, either directly from the fund itself or indirectly from its underwriter or participating selling-group member, as the individual cases may be. When customers enter purchase orders, they specify either (1) the number of full shares they want to acquire; or (2) the dollar amount they want to invest in full shares. (It may actually work out to be slightly above or slightly below that dollar figure if the instructions state "to the nearest full share.")

In either event, at the time of entry the customers do not know the actual execution price per share. The purchase price is always determined after receipt of the order by the mutual fund or its underwriter, as the circumstances may be, using a formula described in the offering prospectus. This practice, known as *forward pricing*, has been in effect since 1969. (The forward-pricing technique is equally applicable for redemption requests.

Example: If, at 2:00 P.M. eastern time, a mutual fund's underwriter receives an order to buy 100 shares of that fund, it will be arranged based on the offering price to be determined at 4:00 P.M. that day (New York Stock Exchange closing time). If the order is received after 4:00 P.M. eastern time, the investor's purchase price is the offering price in the mutual fund's next determined quotation the following day. When a purchase is effected, a bona fide confirmation is prepared and sent to the customer describing the exact details of the transaction.

Regulation T of the Federal Reserve Board requires full payment for these shares on the fifth business day (no later than the seventh business day after trade date in any event). Brokers and dealers are forbidden to extend any credit to customers on purchases of mutual fund shares in a margin account because they are considered new issues and, as such, are not marginable. Nor may they help to arrange a loan elsewhere to enable a customer to pay for such a transaction. Purch-

ases not fully paid for in the time provided must be liquidated immediately.

For customer purchases transmitted by a selling-group member, the NASD requires full payment to the underwriter promptly (no later than the tenth business day after trade date). Payment not made by this time necessitates immediate liquidation of the shares and can subject that member to disciplinary action under the NASD Rules of Fair Practice.

When fully paid for, the mutual fund certificates are registered in the purchaser's name and address and delivered to that party. The customer has become a stockholder in this management company with full rights and privileges in just about the same respects that prevail for stock ownership in any publicly held corporation.

The other two purchase plans available are somewhat more unusual because their characteristics relate to continuing purchase programs (*see* Contractual Periodic-Payment Plan; Voluntary-Accumulation Plan).

The Investment Advisor. Most open-end investment companies do not have in-house ability or facilities for deciding which securities should be bought or sold. They must rely on the counsel of professionals to make these determinations for them (*see* Management Group).

The Custodian. As required by the Investment Company Act of 1940, monies and securities are held in the custody of a custodian (in nearly all cases, a commercial bank or trust company). In addition to custody arrangements for the investment company itself, the bank also provides safekeeping of monies and securities for investors engaged in available accumulation programs. The shareholder pays a nominal annual fee for such service. This is, of course, supplemental to the transaction processing fee of $.50 to $1 charged on accumulation-plan purchases (*see* Voluntary-Accumulation Plan).

Other services provided by these commercial banks include (1) bookkeeping responsibilities for the mutual fund; (2) maintenance of the underwriter's sales records; (3) functioning as transfer agent, performing changes of ownership as directed; (4) functioning as registrar for the investment company, providing it with current stockholder information and ensuring against overissuance of certificates; and (5) functioning as disbursement agent for the investment company, with responsibility for distributing dividends and/or capital gains when authorized by the fund's directors or trustees.

Note that in none of these circumstances does the custodian bank play any part in determining which securities are to be bought or sold by the investment company. Nor does it have any role in arranging such purchases or sales through, or to, a broker/dealer organization. Thus, it is important for the investor to realize that the size and reputation of the custodian bank has no bearing on the investment company's ability to achieve its objective. The use of a particular bank as custodian can be no assurance against loss of capital or decline in value of the shares of any investment company.

See also Investment Company; Investment Company Act of 1940 and 1970 Amendments; Management Company.

NASD Regulations. NASD rules specifically prohibit members from the following activities with regard to investment companies: (1) purchasing mutual fund shares from an underwriter at a discount from the public offering price unless the underwriter is also a member of the NASD; (2) selling mutual fund shares at a discount from the public offering price to another broker/dealer if the NASD member is acting as an underwriter unless that broker/dealer is also an NASD member and unless a valid selling agreement has been signed by that member and is effective (The selling agreement must also provide that if the fund shares sold are tendered for redemption within seven business days after confirmation of the transaction, both the under-

writer and selling group member involved must give their remuneration on that sale to the mutual fund itself as a form of penalty.); (3) offering mutual fund shares to nonmember broker/dealers or to the public except at the public offering price determined in accordance with procedures set forth in the offering prospectus; (4) withholding placing customer orders with the underwriter in order to profit as a result of that action; (5) purchasing mutual fund shares for personal or firm accounts unless it is for bona fide investment purposes (This means that NASD members may purchase shares only in response to customer orders already received and not in anticipation of such orders or for trading purposes); (6) participating as a principal underwriter for mutual fund shares if the fund redeems its shares at a price above net asset value; (7) purchasing mutual fund shares from a stockholder of record at a price below the next established bid quoted by that fund if they are party to a selling group agreement with the underwriter of those shares (Note, however, than an NASD member can act as the shareholder's agent, tender the shares to the mutual fund or its underwriter at the next established bid, and charge the customer a fair and reasonable commission for its services.); (8) favoring or disfavoring the distribution of mutual fund shares on the basis of brokerage commission received or expected to be received from that fund's activities or from its advisor. (The intent of this rule is to prevent reciprocal business demands from interfering with a member's responsibility to the mutual fund and its own customer's investment requirements. Member firms should seek orders for execution on the basis of value and the quality of its own brokerage services and not on the basis of its sales of a particular investment company's shares.)

Section 26 further emphasizes a need for mutual fund sales charges to be "fair and reasonable" even though a member's markup is exempted from provisions of the 5% guideline. The exemption is granted because it is a continuing new issue offered under terms of an accompanying prospectus. However, the NASD Board of Governors has ruled that a sales charge exceeding 8.5% of the offering price is excessive.

That maximum charge must be further reduced, perhaps scaled down to 6% of the offering price, unless one or more of the following privileges is extended to investors: (1) dividend reinvestment at net asset value; (2) rights of accumulation (cumulative quantity discounts); (3) regular quantity discounts, beginning from the $10,000 level at 7.75% or from the $15,000 level at 7.5%.

See also Breakpoint Sales; Sales Load; Dividends (Selling Dividends).

Investment Company Act of 1940 and 1970 Amendments. The purpose of this Act, along with the 1970 amendments, is to protect the investor against unfair and improper activities by the investment company, its management group advisors, underwriters, and other promoters.

This law prescribes: (1) registration with the SEC for investment companies doing business in the United States; (2) a declaration of and adherence to diversified or nondiversified status; (3) approval of investment objectives by the shareholders, prohibiting changes in this goal without consent of majority vote of those shareholders; (4) formalized contracts between the investment company and its advisors and underwriters (These contracts may be effective for two-year periods but must be approved annually by the board of directors or by majority vote of the investment company's shareholders.); (5) restrictions on the composition of an investment company's board of directors, limiting the number or percentage of advisors, underwriters, brokers, and bankers serving in this capacity (Activity with, or on behalf of, investment companies by these interested persons is also closely supervised and curtailed.); and (6) a maximum sales charge of 9% for contractual investment

programs, offering an opportunity to investors for recovery of all or a substantial portion of any sales charge levied if early cancellation is requested.

The scope of the Act and its amendments is comprehensive and provides considerable investor protection.

Example: To ensure viability of operation, a registered investment company must have a net worth of at least $100,000 either prior to, or as a result of, an intended public offering of its securities. If it does not have a net worth of $100,000 prior to the offering, the law requires that no more than 25 responsible persons agree to purchase for indefinite investment enough shares to qualify under this provision.

Issuance of Debt Securities and Preferred Stock. Issuance of debt instruments is permitted under the Act, although the practice is severely restricted by the SEC in the interest of the shareholders.

Example: Face-amount certificate companies are limited to issuance of privately placed promissory notes in minimal amounts. Closed-end management companies are allowed publicly to offer senior securities, such as bonds or preferred stock. But these securities must have provisions for voting privileges, restrictive distributions, and continuous asset coverage included as a condition of the offering. A closed-end management company issuing bonds must ensure net asset coverage of this debt by at least 300% after the offering has been completed. The formula for net asset coverage of bonds is:

$$\frac{\text{total assets} - \text{total liabilities (excluding bonds)}}{\text{aggregate amount of debt securities}} = \frac{3 \text{ or more}}{1}$$

If coverage subsequently declines below 100%, the bondholders of a closed-end company have the right to elect a majority of the board of directors until their protection exceeds 110% of net asset value again. No cash distributions may be paid to any stockholders unless the bond holders would have at least 300% asset coverage after the payment.

A preferred stock offering by a closed-end company necessitates net asset coverage of at least 200% immediately after completion of the offering. The formula for net asset coverage of preferred stock is:

$$\frac{\text{total assets} - \text{total liabilities (excluding bonds)}}{\text{aggregate amount of bonds} + \text{liquidation right of preferred stock}}$$

$$= \frac{2 \text{ or more}}{1}$$

Voting privileges are extended to the preferred stockholders to elect two directors at all times and a majority of the board if dividends are in arrears for a total of two years' payments. No cash distributions are allowed for the common stockholder unless the preferred holder enjoys at least 200% asset coverage after such a distribution is completed.

In the case of open-end management companies (mutual funds), no bond or preferred stock offerings are allowed under the law. The only class of securities permitted to be issued by mutual funds is common stock. However, these companies can hold any issuer's bonds and preferred stocks in their investment portfolios. In addition they are permitted to contract long-term debt by borrowing from any regulated bank, provided that total borrowings are protected continuously by at least 300% net asset coverage. Should the coverage shrink below 300%, the mutual fund must reduce its borrowings and increase the ratio to the 300% level within three business days thereafter.

Distribution of Dividends. The Investment Company Act of 1940 requires dividend distributions to be paid solely from *net investment income,* which means from dividends and interest received from securities in the portfolio after deductions for expenses. Investment income does not mean profits or losses realized on the sale of securities or other properties. Such distributions, if declared by the directors, represent capital gains distributions. Capital gains distributions may not be made more often than once every twelve months, although investment income may be disbursed more frequently.

All distributions, whether they be dividends or capital gains, must be accompanied by a statement disclosing the nature or source(s) of such payment because of tax ramifications for the investor.

Prohibited Activities. The SEC was given considerable latitude for deciding which activities an investment company may participate in are appropriate to the public interest, although they may sometimes appear to be in contravention of the law.

Example: Unless specific consent is given by the SEC, the Investment Company Act of 1940 prohibits an investment company from (1) purchasing any security in a margin account; (2) participating in a joint trading account, except for an underwriting in which they are a member of the group; (3) selling a security short, except in connection with an underwriting participation; (4) acquiring securities issued by another investment company if they would then own more than 3% of the voting stock in that company, securities issued by that company valued at more than 5% of their own total assets, or securities issued by all investment companies in their portfolio with an aggregate value of more than 10% of their own total assets (An exemption from this particular prohibition, however, is generally granted to investment companies that acquire less than 3% of the outstanding stock of other investment companies and offer their own shares for sale at a public offering price that includes a sales load of not more than 1.5%. Furthermore, no mutual fund is obligated to redeem shares tendered to them by another investment company if the amount offered to them by any one company within a thirty-day period exceeds 1% of their total outstanding securities.); (5) acquiring any security or interest in a broker/dealer, underwriter, or investment advisor, unless such an entity is a corporation whose outstanding securities will be owned by one or more other registered investment companies and the gross income of such an entity is principally derived from the usual and related activities of broker/dealers, underwriters, and investment advisors; or (6) acquiring more than 10% of the voting stock of an insurance company unless the investment company already owns at least 25% of that stock at the time of such acquisition. (Thus, a provisional hedge is created that enables an investment company to buoy the financial condition or improve the capitalization of an insurance concern previously authorized as a permissible speculation. Still another loophole is established when this prohibition is deemed not to apply to the acquisition or promotion of a new insurance company.)

Disclosure of Records. The keynote of investor protection built into the Investment Company Act of 1940 revolves around disclosure. Every investment company is required to keep the stockholders informed at periodic intervals about the relevant activities and details pertaining to the company. At least semiannually, the company must transmit to its stockholders (1) a balance sheet accompanied by a statement of the aggregate value of investments as of the balance sheet date; (2) a list of the quantity and value of each security in the portfolio as of the balance sheet date; (3) a statement of income for the period itemized with respect to each revenue and expenditure representing more than 5% of total income or expense; (4) a statement of surplus for the period itemized with respect to each aggregate remuneration paid by the company during this period debit or credit account representing more than 5% of total charges or credits; and (5) a statement of the to all officers, all directors and members of any advisory board as regular compensation, each director and advisory board

member as special compensation, and each entity of whom any officer or director of the company is an affiliated person; and (6) a statement of the aggregate dollar amounts of purchases and sales of investment securities, excluding U.S. government securities, during the period covered by the report.

To reinforce the integrity of these documents, the law requires an annual examination of the investment company's books and records by an independent accountant. Thus, one of the semiannual transmissions to the stockholders will reflect the result of this audit and will be accompanied by a statement from the accountant certifying all findings and expressing an opinion as the the state of the company's records. Selection of the independent accountant is accomplished by a majority of the board of directors who are "disinterested" (unaffiliated) persons of that investment company. Their choice is then subject to ratification by the stockholders at the next annual meeting.

Custodian. In addition to discouraging conflicts of interest, the Investment Company Act of 1940 affords protection to the shareholders of investment companies in the safekeeping of monies and securities owned by the company. With few exceptions, all money and securities must be in the custody of a commercial bank or trust company that (1) has shareholders' equity of at least $500,000; (2) publishes a report of its financial condition for public consumption at least once each year; and (3) is chartered by federal or state authorities and is subject to examination by their regulators.

Although the law does provide for other custody arrangements under circumstances requiring approval from the SEC, for all practical purposes the responsibility is enjoyed exclusively by banking institutions.

See also Investment Company; Mutual Fund; Registration Statement; SEC Statement of Policy.

Investment Letter. *See* Private Placement.

Involuntary Underwriter. *See* Underwriter.

Issued Date. *See* Municipal Security (Organization of the Syndicate).

Issued-and-Outstanding Stocks. That portion of authorized stock distributed among investors by a corporation.

See also Common Stock.

Issuer. An *issuer* of a security is a corporation, trust, or association engaged in a distribution of its securities. Public offerings of its certificates may be attempted if a registration statement on file with the SEC has become effective, pursuant to the Securities Act of 1933.

J

Joint and Survivor Annuity. *See* Annuity Contract.

Joint Customers. This category of joint customers covers two or more people pooling their resources to conduct securities business collectively.

Cash Account. The following documents are required for cash accounts of joint customers: (1) new account report form; (2) joint account agreement form (*see* the following figure).

Margin Account. The following documents are required for margin accounts of joint customers: (1) new account report form; (2) joint account agreement form (*see* following figure); (3) customer's agreement; (4) loan-consent agreement; and (5) a signed credit agreement.

Two Types of Joint Account. The joint account agreement requires the participants to state above their signatures whether the account will be maintained as a tenancy in common (Ten in Com) or with rights of survivorship (W/R/O/S).

Joint tenants in common. This means that a fractional interest in the assets is ascribable to each of the participants, and in the event of death, the estate of the decedent inherits that percentage share.

Example: Assume that three partners maintained a joint account as tenants in common and one of them had a 40% interest in the account. If that partner unexpectedly died (1) the decedent's estate would inherit 40% of the asset value in the account; and (2) the entire account may be enjoined from further activity until the estate is settled and disposition of the decedent's assets is accomplished. This form of registration normally delays transfer or sale of securities under those circumstances until satisfactory documentation regarding distribution is furnished to the corporation's transfer agent. If securities are held by the broker in street name, they may be sold on instruction of the other partners. However, no disbursement of money or securities may be made until proper legal documents are received from the decedent's executor or administrator.

Joint tenants with rights of survivorship. This type of account makes no percentage assignment of assets. On the death of a tenant, the other parties automatically inherit the decedent's share. In the foregoing example, if the account was maintained with rights of survivorship (W/R/O/S), the surviving partners would automatically gain title and possession of the account assets and could immediately transfer and/or dispose of the securities. In some states, for technical reasons, this format is also sometimes called *tenants by entireties.* However, in those states, such registration can be used only for tenancies between husband and wife.

See also Credit Agreement; Customer's Agreement; Loan-Consent Agreement; New Account Report Form.

Jurisdiction of Offenses and Lawsuits. *See* Securities Exchange Act of 1934 (Section 27).

JOINT ACCOUNT AGREEMENT

Gentlemen:

In consideration of your carrying a joint account for the undersigned, the undersigned jointly and severally agree that each of them shall have authority on behalf of the joint account to buy, sell (including short sales) and otherwise deal in, through you as brokers, stocks, bonds and other securities and commodities, on margin or otherwise; to receive on behalf of the joint account demands, notices, confirmations, reports, statements of account and communications of every kind; to receive on behalf of the joint account money, securities and property of every kind and to dispose of same; to make on behalf of the joint account agreements relating to any of the foregoing matters and to terminate or modify same or waive any of the provisions thereof; and generally to deal with you on behalf of the joint account as fully and completely as if he alone were interested in said account, all without notice to the other or others interested in said account. You are authorized to follow the instructions of any of the undersigned in every respect concerning the said joint account with you and to make deliveries to any of the undersigned, or upon his instructions, of any or all securities in the said joint account, and to make payments to any of the undersigned, or upon his order, of any or all monies at any time or from time to time in the said joint account as he may order and direct, even if such deliveries and/or payments shall be made to him personally, and not for the joint account of the undersigned. In the event of any such deliveries of securities or payments of monies to any of the undersigned as aforesaid, you shall be under no duty or obligation to inquire into the purpose or propriety of any such demand for delivery of securities or payment of monies, and you shall not be bound to see to the application or disposition of the said securities and/or monies so delivered or paid to any of the undersigned or upon his order. The authority hereby conferred shall remain in force until written notice of the revocation addressed to you is delivered at your main office.

The liability of the undersigned with respect to said account shall be joint and several. The undersigned further agrees jointly and severally that all property you may at any time be holding or carrying for any one or more of the undersigned shall be subject to a lien in your favor for the discharge of the obligations of the joint account to you, such lien to be in addition to and not in substitution of the rights and remedies you otherwise would have.

It is further agreed that in the event of the death of either or any of the undersigned, the survivor or survivors shall immediately give you written notice thereof, and you may, before or after receiving such notice, take such proceeding, require such papers and inheritance or estate tax waivers, retain such portion of and/or restrict transactions in the account as you may deem advisable to protect you against any tax, liability, penalty or loss under any present or future laws or otherwise. The estate of any of the undersigned who shall have died shall be liable and each survivor shall continue liable jointly and severally, to you for any net debit balance or loss in said account in any way resulting from the completion of transactions initiated prior to the receipt by you of the written notice of the death of the decedent or incurred in the liquidation of the account or the adjustment of the interests of the respective parties.

* (a) It is the express intention of the undersigned to create an estate or account as joint tenants with rights of survivorship and not as tenants in common. In the event of the death of either of the undersigned, the entire interest in the joint account shall be vested in the survivor or survivors on the same terms and conditions as theretofore held, without in any manner releasing the decedent's estate from the liability provided for in the next preceding paragraph.

*(b) In the event of the death of either or any of the undersigned the interests in the account as of the close of business on the date of the death of the decedent (or on the next following business day if the date of death is not a business day), shall be as follows:

....or his or her estate..%
Name of Participant

....or his or her estate..%
Name of Participant

....or his or her estate..%
Name of Participant

but any taxes, costs, expenses or other charges becoming a lien against or being payable out of the account as the result of the death of the decedent, or through the exercise by his or her estate or representatives of any rights in the account shall, so far as possible, be deducted from the interest of the estate of such decedent. This provision shall not release the decedent's estate from the liability provided for in the paragraph next preceding "(a)" above.

The undersigned request you to open the joint account under the following designation:

....

Subject to the provisions hereof, all notices or communications for the undersigned in respect of the joint account are to be directed to

Name...

Address..

City...Zone (if any)...............State...........................

Each of the undersigned has signed the Customer's Agreement and Consent to Loan of Securities which are intended to cover, in addition to the provisions hereof, the terms upon which the joint account is to be carried.

Dated, ... Very truly yours,

....
(City)   (State)

                                    ....

                                    ....

                                    ....

*Strike out paragraph (a) or (b) whichever is inapplicable, and if paragraph (b) is retained, fill in the names and percentage amounts of the interests of the respective parties.

L

Last Trading Day. The final day under an exchange's rules during which trading may take place in a particular futures or options contract. Contracts outstanding at the end of the last trading day must be settled by delivery of underlying physical commodities or financial instruments, or by agreement for monetary settlement if the former is impossible.

Legals. *See* Prudent Man.

Lending at a Premium. When a security is lending at a premium, the short seller is obliged to pay lenders a fee for the use of their certificates. This fee is paid in addition to the cash collateral deposited with the lender and is calculated on a basis of per 100 shares (or $1,000 bond) for each business day the certificate is borrowed. It might be expressed as a $1 premium, or $2, or $3, and so on, depending on the forces of supply and demand.

In calculating this expense, premiums do not count for weekends or holidays. They begin on the day the security is borrowed and accrue up to, but not including, the day it is returned. Thus, if a certificate is borrowed on Monday, June 7 and returned on Thursday, June 24, there are thirteen days of premium money involved. (June 12, 13, 19, and 20 do not count because they are nonbusiness-day Saturdays and Sundays.)

The very mention of a premium is usually sufficient to bring a deluge of certificates into the market, which in turn eliminates the premium entirely. Obviously, then, requests for pre-miums are infrequent and are encountered only in the case of (1) closely held companies; (2) companies with relatively small capitalizations of stock; (3) issues with a substantial short interest; or (4) issues for which professional arbitrageurs seek assurance their stock loan will not be recalled for an extended period of time.

June

S	M	T	W	T	F	S
		1	2	3	4	5
6	7	8	9	10	11	12
13	14	15	16	17	18	19
20	21	22	23	24	25	26
27	28	29	30			

See also Borrowing Stock Certificates; Lending at a Rate.

Lending at a Rate. When a security is lending at a rate, the lender of the certificate pays interest to the borrower (the short seller) for the money received as collateral. The interest due is calculated on a daily basis, weekends and holidays included, until the borrowing arrangement ceases.

Under the circumstances, the lender organization doesn't often object to payment of the interest. It still represents one of the most inexpensive forms of financing its own and its customers' activities. It receives unrestricted use of cash equal to 100% of the security value loaned to the short seller. Even if the firm pays the short seller 3 to 4% for the use of this money, it is still ahead financially. If it attempts to borrow the same amount of money at a commercial bank, it must (1) deposit more in collateral value than the loan amount; and (2) pay interest to the bank at a rate somewhere between 2 to 4% higher than the rate between brokers, depending on prevailing money market conditions.

See also Borrowing Stock Certificates; Lending at a Premium.

Letter of Intent. *See* Sales Load.

Letter Security (Stock or Bond). *See* Private Placement.

Level Debt Service. *See* Municipal Security (Assessing Debt).

Leverage. This financial condition is evidenced by a high percentage of debt in relation to equity in a corporation's capital structure. This type of capitalization is highly speculative because a company's profits and its ability to honor obligations are extremely sensitive even to minor changes in sales and income.

Leveraged Company. *See* Dual Purpose Investment Company.

Life Annuity. *See* Annuity Contract.

Limitation of Functions of Exchange Members. *See* Securities Exchange Act of 1934 (Section 11).

Limited Access to Books and Records. A shareholder's right to inspect financial information that a corporation makes public in accordance with federal, state, exchange, and NASD regulations.

See also Common Stock.

Limited Financial Liability. *See* Corporation.

Limited Partner. *See* Limited Partnership.

Limited Partnership. A partnership may include among the principals some limited partners who are not liable to the same degree as the general partners. A limited partner, however, is only a silent partner, represented by capital, but with no voice in the management of the business.

Example: Jane Doe and you, as general partners, take Sam Smith into your business as a limited partner. In recognition of his dollar contribution, you general partners pay him a return on his investment depending on the income or profits of the business. He has limited personal financial liability should dissolution become necessary because of failure or litigation. Ordinarily, he may be held liable only to the extent of his investment in your partnership.

Unfortunately, a partnership cannot be composed of limited partners alone. In most states, a majority of the capital must be contributed by general partners. Partnership interests, both general and limited, are not readily transferable either; to do so requires approval from the general partners even if a new investor can be found. Thus the assets of the participants remain relatively frozen in the affairs of the business.

See also Partnership.

Limit Order. This order is one in which customers set a maximum price they are willing to pay, as a buyer, or a minimum price they are willing to accept, as a seller. Under no circumstances may a member violate these instructions by paying more or selling for less than this price.

However, although the words may not necessarily appear on the order ticket, it is always understood that a price limitation includes an *or better* instruction.

Therefore, if a member can purchase the stock below the stated limit, or sell it for more than the specified price, as the case may be, the member must do so immediately! Failure to consummate an order that can be executed in accordance with the customer's terms and conditions holds an exchange member financially responsible for missing the market. There is liability for missing the market just as there is liability for neglecting to obey instructions on receipt of a market order.

See also Alternative Order; At-the-Opening Order; Buy Minus; Choosing Types of Stock Orders; Fractional Discretion; Good-til-Cancelled Order; Market Order; Scale Orders; Sell Plus; Stop-Limit Order; Stop Order; Switch Order.

Odd-Lot. In defining a limit order, the customer sets the maximum price to be paid as a buyer or the minimum price to be accepted as a seller. (Remember, for odd-lot limit orders, the stated prices must include the differential.) A broker attempting to execute a limit order must do so within the framework of this restriction. Although the specialist certainly tries to "do better" (improve on the limit price), no member of the NYSE can execute a limit order at a less favorable price than dictated in the instructions.

Therefore, in the case of an odd-lot limit order to

1. *buy*, the effective sale is the first round-lot transaction below the limit. When the differential is then added to that round-lot price, the execution terms do not exceed the customer's maximum designation.

2. *sell long*, the effective sale is the first round-lot transaction above the limit. When the differential is then subtracted from that round-lot price, the execution terms do not violate the customer's minimum designated price.

3. *sell short*, the effective sale is the first round-lot transaction that is both (a) higher in value than the last different price; and (b) above the limit.

Odd-lot limit orders have an advantage over round-lot limit orders in that they must all be executed on the first possible transaction. That is, because odd lots are never represented in the NYSE's auction market quotations, they do not have to wait their turn for execution and actively compete with each other as do round-lot orders. Their contra party is always the specialist who is obliged to satisfy all odd-lot orders at the first opportunity to do so. The following table lists some sample odd-lot limit order executions.

Bear in mind that because of the customer's restrictive price and the unknown variable of market fluctuation, it is possible that a customer's limit order will not be executed. If a round lot never trades low enough (for a buy order) or high enough (for a sell order) after entry, the odd-lot limit order cannot be executed. This is why many odd-lot orders are also entered with GTC time stipulations. Day or good-til-cancelled designations are acceptable adjuncts to odd-lot orders, just as they are for round-lot orders.

Open buy-limit and sell-stop orders are also reduced in value for forthcoming distributions, on the ex-dividend date, in a manner identical to that for round lots. However, there is no semiannual reconfirmation of orders between member organizations and specialists as is required with round-lot orders.

See also Differential; Odd-Lot Stock Execution; Stop-Limit order (Odd-Lot); Short-Stop and Short-Stop-Limit Orders.

Liquidation. Any transaction that offsets or closes out a long (or short) position.

Liquidity. A market is liquid when it has a high level of trading activity, allowing buying and selling with minimum price disturbance.

Listed Options Quotations. *See* figure on pp. 232-233.

Living (Intervivos) Trust. This legal instrument appoints some person or institution to perform a specific function with a designated sum of

Previous Round-Lot Transaction	Terms	Subsequent Round-Lot Transactions*	Execution Price
Not pertinent	Buy at 10½	10¾, 10⅝, 10½, |10⅜|	10½ (10⅜ + ⅛)
" "Buy at 21¾		|21½,| 21⅝,	
			21⅝ (21½ + ⅛)
		21¾, 21⅞	
" "	Buy at 34⅜	34⅜, 34½, |34¼,| 34	34⅜ (34¼ + ⅛)
" "	Buy at 79	79, 80, 79, |78|	78⅛ (78 + ⅛)
" "	Sell long at 86¼	86¼, |86½,| 86¾, 87	86⅜ (86½ – ⅛)
" "	Sell long at 5⅝	5½, |5¾,| 5⅝, 5⅞	5⅝ (5¾ – ⅛)
" "	Sell long at 38	|38¼,| 38½, 38, 37¾	38⅛ (38¼ – ⅛)
" "	Sell long at 93⅞	93⅞, 93⅝, |94| 94¼	93⅞ (94 – ⅛)
138	Sell short at 137½	137¾, |138,| 138¼, 137⅞	137⅞ (138 – ⅛)
55	Sell short at 55⅛	55⅛, 55, |55¼,| 55⅜	55⅛ (55¼ – ⅛)
49⅞	Sell short at 49¾	|50,| 50⅛, 49⅞ 49¾	49⅞ (50 – ⅛)
69	Sell short at 69	68¾, 69, |69¼,| 69½	69⅛ (69¼ – ⅛)

*The effective sale (boxed in this table) is always the first possible round-lot transaction capable of satisfying the customer's instruction.

money. The terms of this incumbency become effective during its creator's lifetime.

See also Fiduciary Accounts.

Load. *See* Sales Load.

Loan-Consent Agreement. This agreement is the specific permission from margin-account customers allowing the brokerage firm to lend the customer's securities to itself or to someone else. Although this agreement is not mandatory for maintenance of margin accounts, most firms require it as a good business practice because of its importance in facilitating short-sale transactions. It usually appears as a separate statement requiring a separate signature on the customer's agreement form (see the figure on 234).

See also Credit Agreement; Customer's Agreement.

Loan Value Percentage of Securities. *See* Margin Account (Long Account).

Long. One who has bought a contract(s) to establish a market position and who has not yet closed out this position through an offsetting sale; the opposite of Short.

Long Market Value. *See* Margin Account Long Account).

MOST ACTIVE OPTIONS

Chicago

	Sales	Last	Chg.	N.Y. Close
CALLS				
SP100 Mar220	73012	1⅝	+ 1-16	214.79
SP100 Mar215	60377	3⅝	+ ⅜	214.79
SP100 Mar210	26724	6⅞	+ ⅝	214.79
SP100 Mar225	20760	½	— 1-16	214.79
SP100 Apr220	17243	4	+ ⅛	214.79
PUTS				
SP100 Mar210	59105	1 1-16	— ¼	214.79
SP100 Mar215	47491	2 15-16	— 7-16	214.79
SP100 Mar205	25188	5-16	— 1-16	214.79
SP100 Mar200	13863	⅛	....	214.79
SP100 Mar220	10011	5⅞	— ⅞	214.79

American

	Sales	Last	Chg.	N.Y. Close
CALLS				
MMIdx Mar320	13066	1¼	— 1-16	7.72
MMIdx Mar315	10414	2⅝	+ ⅛	7.72
MMIdx Mar305	7012	7¾	+ ⅜	7.72
MMIdx Mar310	6401	4¾	+ ⅜	7.72
Texaco Apr30	4280	1 1-16	+ 1-16	29⅛
PUTS				
MMIdx Mar305	5443	2⅜	— ⅞	7.72
MMIdx Mar310	4825	4⅛	— 1⅛	7.72
MMIdx Mar300	3494	1 1-16	—11-16	7.72
MMIdx Mar295	2675	½	— 3-16	7.72
MMIdx Apr270	1236	1-16	....	7.72

Philadelph

	Sales	Last
CALLS		
AnheusB Mar45	2748	2⅛
AldSig Jun50	2518	2¾
VL Idx Mar230	1759	2½
McDIn May17½	1757	1⅛
AnheusB Jun45	1629	4
PUTS		
F N M Jun30	1449	1¾
VL Idx Mar225	1203	1 5-16
Waste May40	892	⅞
McDIn May15	813	⅞
PhibroS Apr40	740	1-16

Option & NY Close	Strike Price	Calls-Last Mar	Calls-Last Jun	Calls-Last Sep	Puts-Last Mar	Puts-Last Jun	Puts-Last Sep
RalPur	45	10	r	r	r	r	r
55¼	50	5⅝	r	7½	1/16	r	r
55¼	55	1	3¼	4¾	1	2⅜	r
55¼	60	r	1¼	2¾	r	r	r
Sears	35	9¼	10	r	r	r	r
44⅜	40	4⅜	5⅜	5¾	1/16	11/16	1¼
44⅜	45	13/16	2¼	3¼	1¼	2½	3
44⅜	50	s	15/16	1⅝	s	r	5½
SwAir	20	2½	r	r	⅛	r	r
22¾	22½	⅞	2⅜	r	r	1⅜	r
22¾	25	⅛	1¼	2	2⅝	3⅜	r
Syntex	30	20¾	r	s	r	r	s
51½	37½	r	16	s	r	r	s
51½	42½	9	r	s	1/16	r	s
51½	45	6⅜	8⅜	8½	1/16	¾	2
51½	50	2½	4⅞	6½	¾	1¾	r
51½	55	5/16	2½	3½	3½	4¾	r
Tektrn	45	15½	r	s	r	r	s
60¾	50	r	12	r	r	r	r
60¾	55	6½	r	r	r	r	r
60¾	60	1½	r	r	¾	r	r
60¾	65	r	2½	r	r	r	r
Toys	30	r	r	r	1/16	r	r
37⅞	35	3	4½	6	⅛	1⅛	1⅝
37⅞	40	⅜	1⅞	r	2¼	3⅝	r
37⅞	45	r	⅝	s	r	r	s
Viacom	50	7¼	r	r	r	r	r
57⅜	55	3	5¼	r	½	2½	r
57⅜	60	⅞	3⅜	5	r	r	r
57⅜	65	3/16	r	s	r	r	s
57⅜	70	⅛	r	s	r	r	s
WalMrt	25	10¼	r	11¾	r	r	r
36⅛	27½	7⅛	r	s	r	r	s
36⅛	30	6	6⅞	6⅞	1/16	½	⅞
36⅛	35	1 9/16	3⅛	4	11/16	1⅝	2

Option & NY Close	Strike Price	Calls-Last Apr	Calls-Last Jul	Calls-Last Oct	Puts-Last Apr	Puts-Last Jul	Puts-Last Oct
Alcoa	35	r	r	r	1/16	r	r
42⅞	40	3⅝	4¼	r	7/16	r	r
42⅞	45	1	1⅞	3	r	r	r
42⅞	50	r	⅞	r	r	r	r
AmGenl	40	1½	2¾	r	r	r	r
AGreet	35	1¾	r	r	r	r	r
AT&T	20	2⅜	2¾	3⅛	⅛	⅜	r
22⅜	22½	¾	1¼	1¾	⅞	1¼	1⅝
22⅜	25	3/16	9/16	¾	2¾	3⅛	3¼
22⅜	30	r	⅛	s	r	r	s
Apple	25	1½	2½	r	r	r	r
Avon	20	11	s	s	r	s	s
31	25	6	r	r	r	r	½
31	30	2	2 9/16	2⅞	½	r	r
31	35	¼	¾	1½	r	r	r
Beth S	15	r	5½	r	r	r	r
19¾	17½	r	3½	4	r	½	r
19¾	20	15/16	1 13/16	2⅜	⅞	1⅜	r
19¾	22½	⅜	⅞	1⅜	r	r	r
Burl N	70	7¼	9¼	r	⅜	r	r
77¼	75	3¾	6	r	r	r	r
77¼	80	1⅜	3	r	r	r	r
C N W	20	9¼	9½	s	r	r	s
29⅝	22½	7	r	r	r	r	r
29⅝	25	4⅝	5¾	r	¼	r	r
29⅝	30	1⅛	2½	3¾	1⅞	r	r
CIGNA	50	18	s	s	r	s	s
68¼	60	7⅝	9⅛	10	r	1¼	r
68¼	65	3⅞	6¼	r	1¼	r	r
68¼	70	1½	3¼	4¾	4	r	r

Option & NY Close	Strike Price	Calls-Last May	Calls-Last Aug	Calls-Last Nov	Puts-Last May	Puts-Last Aug	Puts-Last Nov
67¼	60	8	9¾	s	⅝	r	s
67¼	65	5¼	7¼	r	2	3	3¾
67¼	70	2⅝	r	r	r	r	r
67¼	75	1⅜	2¾	3½	r	r	r
Diebld	35	r	7	s	r	⅞	s
41¾	40	2⅞	r	r	1⅛	2⅜	r
41¾	45	1⅛	r	r	r	r	r
Edwrds	35	8	r	r	⅜	r	r
42⅝	40	4	5⅛	r	1	r	r
42⅝	45	2	2⅝	r	r	r	r
FptMc	15	r	1¾	r	⅝	1	r
15½	17½	⅜	¾	r	r	[illegible]	r
15½	20	1/16	¼	s	r	r	s
Gn Dyn	65	r	r	s	r	13/16	s
78¼	70	r	12	r	r	r	r
78¼	75	6	8¼	r	2	r	r
78¼	80	3¼	r	7	r	r	r
78¼	85	2	s	s	r	s	s
Harris	25	5¼	r	r	¼	r	r
29¾	30	1⅞	2⅝	r	2	r	2⅜
29¾	35	7/16	15/16	1¾	r	r	r
Hewlet	35	7	8	s	¼	1	s
41¼	40	3⅛	4⅜	6	1 7/16	2¼	3
41¼	45	1⅛	2⅜	3⅝	4⅝	4¾	r
41¼	50	5/16	1¼	1⅞	½	r	r
H Inns	50	14	r	s	r	r	s
64¼	60	5½	7	r	⅞	r	2¼
64¼	65	2¾	5	5	2¾	r	r
64¼	70	1¼	2½	r	r	r	r
Honwll	60	r	r	s	1/16	r	s
73⅞	65	10¼	r	s	½	r	s
73⅞	70	6¾	9½	s	1½	3	s
73⅞	75	3¾	6½	8½	3½	r	r
73⅞	80	2	3½	5½	6⅝	r	8
73⅞	85	1	r	r	r	r	r
73⅞	90	½	1⅞	s	r	r	s
Humana	25	r	7	s	3/16	r	s
31½	30	2½	r	r	1	1⅝	r
31½	35	9/16	15/16	2 1/16	4⅛	4¼	r
In Flv	35	r	4¾	r	r	r	r
38¼	40	13/16	1⅝	r	r	r	r
Limitd	20	15⅜	s	s	r	s	s
35¾	22½	13¼	s	s	r	s	s
35¾	25	r	r	s	3/16	r	s
35¾	30	5⅞	6⅞	7⅝	5/16	r	r
35¾	35	2¼	4	r	1¼	2¼	r
35¾	40	1⅛	2⅜	r	r	5¼	r
Medtrn	50	7¼	r	r	r	1¾	r
56¼	55	4⅛	6	r	2½	r	r
56¼	60	r	3½	5½	r	r	r
Mobil	25	3⅞	4⅛	4½	5/16	⅝	⅞
28½	30	⅝	1¼	1½	2¼	2¾	3
28½	35	⅛	5/16	½	r	r	r
N B I	10	r	r	r	r	9/16	r
N Semi	12½	1¾	2⅛	2⅞	5/16	11/16	15/16
13½	15	11/16	1 1/16	1⅝	2	r	r
13½	17½	¼	½	r	r	r	r
Nthrop	40	8½	9½	r	⅜	¾	r
47¾	45	4½	5¾	r	1¼	2¼	3¼
47¾	50	2 1/16	3⅝	r	r	r	r
47¾	55	⅞	s	s	r	s	s
Occi	22½	3	r	r	¼	⅝	¾
25⅛	25	1⅜	2	2¾	15/16	1½	1 13/16
25⅛	30	¼	9/16	1⅛	4⅞	5	5¼
25⅛	35	1/16	¼	s	9⅝	r	s
25⅛	40	1/16	r	s	r	r	s
Ow Ill	60	5⅛	6	r	r	r	r
64	65	3	4⅛	r	4	r	r
64	70	1	2	r	r	r	r

Understanding Options Quotations

On the facing page is an excerpt from the options section of the financial news. Let's look at the elements.

Underlying Stock. The first column lists the underlying stocks in alphabetical order. Below the name of each company is the day's closing price on the exchange on which the stock is traded. The closing price is repeated for each option series traded on the stock.

Strike Price. The second column lists the strike prices. Notice how they occur in multiples of 5—and, in some cases, in multiples of 2½. Notice also how the strike prices approximate the closing price of the underlying stock. (For underlying stock whose price is over $200, option strike prices occur in multiples of $10.)

Calls and Puts. The next six columns reflect the current expiration cycles for calls and puts. The figures under these column headings are the premiums as of the close of business for the day. In most cases, they reflect a dollar value that has to be multiplied by 100 (shares) to arrive at the dollar cost of the option.

Example: The Alcoa Jul 25 call closed at 4¼, or $4.25. To get the dollar total of the premium, multiply by 100: $4.25 times 100 shares equals $425 for the total cost of the call. The letter symbols in the price columns are explained at the bottom of the newspaper page:

- "r" means "not traded."
- "s" means "no option offered."
- "o" means "old."

Example: Look at a few of the entries in quotations.

- The Alcoa Apr 40 call has an intrinsic value of 2⅞ (stock price of 42⅞ less the strike price of 40). Yet its last trade was at 3⅝. The ¾ point is time value.

- The AT&T Jul 22½ put is ⅛-point in the money (strike price of 22½ less stock price of 22⅜). Its premium of 1¼-point is almost pure time value. The AT&T Jul 30 put is not traded (r), and the October is not even offered (s).

Volume and Open Interest. At the bottom of all the listings for each exchange are tabulations of volume and open interest for puts and calls.

- *Volume* represents the total number of contracts, puts or calls, trading on the exchange for the day.

- *Open interest* is the total number of open positions at the close of trading, which have not been closed either by exercise or covering purchases.

233

CUSTOMER'S LOAN CONSENT

Until you receive written notice of revocation from the undersigned, you are hereby authorized to lend, to yourselves or to others, any securities held by you on margin for the account of, or under the control of, the undersigned.

Dated, ...

....
(Signature)

....
(City)　　　　　　(State)

....

Witness...

....

Long Sale. To comply with SEC Rule 10a-1 and 10a-2 (*see* Plus-Tick and Zero-Plus-Tick Rules), each sell order entered for stock traded on a national securities exchange must be marked "long" or "short," as the case may be, to indicate the status of the customer's title to the security in question. It must also indicate this person's willingness and ability to settle the contract in accordance with the customs of that exchange.

If the order is marked "long," it means the customer owns that security and is prepared to make delivery of the certificate on the usual settlement date. A customer is deemed to own a security if that person or that person's agent (1) has title to it; (2) has entered into an unconditional contract to purchase it but has not yet received the certificate; (3) owns another security immediately convertible or exchangeable for the one to be sold, *and* has tendered this security for conversion or exchange; (4) has an option to purchase or acquire that security *and* has exercised that option; or (5) has rights or warrants to subscribe to that security *and* has exercised that privilege.

See also Rules of Fair Practice (Section 1); Short Sale.

Lowest Net Interest Cost NIC). *See* Competitive Bid.

Lump-Sum Distribution. *See* Annuity Contract.

M

M. (1) Abbreviation of 1,000. For example,"5M" means 5,000; "25M" means 25,000). The symbol is usually used to denote the face value of a bond.

(2) Preceding the name of a stock in the National Quotation Bureau's daily pink sheet, an "M" indicates the security can be margined.

M1. The nation's money supply, defined as total currency in circulation plus all demand deposits in commercial banks is designated *M-1*.

M2. M-1 plus savings and time deposits of less than $100,000 in commercial banks, some overnight borrowings in the domestic and Eurodollar market, repurchase agreements, and money market mutual funds are designated *M-2*.

Main Room. *See* Trading Floor (NYSE).

Maintenance Call. A maintenance call is a demand issued to the customer to deposit money or securities with the broker when market fluctuations decrease the equity in a margin account to a point below the broker's minimum maintenance requirement.

See also Long Account (Exchange and Broker Requirements); Mixed Account; Short Account.

Maintenance Margin. A sum, usually smaller than — but part of — the original margin, which must be maintained on deposit at all times. If a customer's equity in any futures position drops to, or under, the maintenance margin level, The broker must issue a "Margin Call" for the amount of money required to restore the customer's equity in the account to the original margin level.

Maloney Act. In 1938, Congress legislated an amendment to the Securities Exchange Act of 1934 providing the legal means by which broker/dealers not subject to stock exchange authority could offer investors an equal degree of ethical and proprietary responsibility in securities transactions. This amendment (Section 15A) is commonly known as the *Maloney Act*, named after its sponsor, the late Senator Francis T. Maloney of Connecticut.

The Maloney Act requires any national securities association to register with the Securities and Exchange Commission. Based on the terms of its petition a securities association is empowered to establish operating standards designed to promote just and equitable principles of trade and to require adherence to high standards of commercial honor and integrity. Only two securities associations have ever registered under this Act, the National Association of Securities Dealers (NASD) in 1939 and the Municipal Securities Rulemaking Board (MSRB) in 1975.

See also Municipal Securities Rulemaking Board; National Association of Securities Dealers.

Management Company. Any investment company conducting its business in a manner other than as a face-amount certificate company or unit investment trust company is identified as a *management company.* An overwhelming majority of investment companies registered with the SEC are classified as management companies. These institutions employ the corporate approach to organization and, for the most part, have obtained their charters from the secretary of state of one of the fifty states in the United States.

The assets of management companies may be diversified or nondiversified (*see* Diversified Company; Nondiversified Company.)

Closed-End Versus Open-End Company. Management companies are popularly subclassified as closed-end or open-end companies, with three characteristics of operation serving to differentiate between them. These characteristics refer to their means and methods for (1) capitalization; (2) determining current market prices for their shares; and (3) redeeming shares previously issued.

Capitalization. A closed-end company obtains substantially all its capital through a one-time public offering of its shares. Although it is not precluded from occasional future offerings, such offerings are not general practice and certainly cannot compare with the capitalization activities of the open-end companies.

An open-end company acquires capital from an initial public offering similar to that made by a closed-end company but then proceeds to offer additional shares continuously and perpetually. It may issue as many shares as necessary to meet current demand (subject to the registration requirements of the Securities Act of 1933). An open-end company does have the ability to restrict its size by terminating its offering for a specific or indefinite period. If it does so, it must amend its registration statement, thus making full disclosure of this fact. If the restriction is to be permanent, it may then be reclassified as a closed-end company.

Thus, a closed-end company more or less has a fixed capitalization, whereas the open-end company's capitalization is constantly changing.

Current market prices. After the initial offering has been completed at a fixed price, the shares of a closed-end company will fluctuate in value, reflecting the aggressiveness of the forces of supply and demand. Trading activity may take place in the over-the-counter market and/or on a stock exchange, if the company's shares are accepted and listed there.

The current market price of an open-end company is not determined in this manner, however. The very nature of its capitalization process reveals its unlimited supply ability, and so price structures founded on competitive forces are impractical. Instead, the current market price of an open-end company is dependent on, and determined by, its net asset value per share. (*Net asset value per share* is another name for shareholders' equity. It is derived by adding the valuation of the securities in the portfolio to all other assets, subtracting total liabilities and dividing the difference by the number of shares outstanding at the moment.) The net asset value per share is calculated daily and is then employed as the bid price in the quotation for that company. The offering price is usually net asset value *plus* a predetermined sales charge called the sales load. *See* Net Asset Value; Sales Load.

Redemption characteristics. Once the initial offering has been completed, the closed-end company does not redeem shares held by its owners. Persons interested in liquidating their holdings must go into the marketplace, find a buyer, and negotiate a price acceptable to both parties.

Infrequently, it may develop that a closed-end company decides to repurchase some of its own shares for treasury or retirement purposes. Before it can repurchase shares it must (1) give each stockholder of record six months' notice of its intent to make such a purchase in the marketplace; or (2) give all stockholders an opportunity to tender their shares pursuant to a formal offer filed with the SEC.

An open-end company always stands ready, willing, and able to redeem its shares within terms and conditions described in the offering prospectus. The government has reasoned that if the company is willing to offer as many shares as necessary to meet demand, it must also be prepared continuously to meet supply by repurchasing those shares from stockholders anxious to sell.

Most open-end companies' distributors redeem those shares from the stockholder at net asset value without further expense. They operate on the theory that the initial sales charge covers all such services. A few distributors do levy a 0.5% fee on redemption, but those organizations also charge less on the initial load. As a result, the overall expense for the investor is about the same. In all instances, an open-end company is obliged to honor these requests promptly, using a determination of net asset value as the basis for redemption. The company is obliged to make payment for those shares within seven business days thereafter.

Example: Let us assume that you tendered for redemption 1,000 shares of an open-end investment company. If its quotation at the next calculation became $6.77–$7.30, you may expect to receive $6,770 ($6.77 net asset value × 1,000 shares) within seven business days. If there was also a 0.5% redemption fee in effect, the $6,770 proceeds would be reduced by $33.85 ($6,770 × .005 and your check would amount to $6,736.15

It should be obvious that shares of a closed-end company can trade at any price levels in the marketplace, without respect to net asset value

per share. The shares of most closed-end companies do, in fact, sell at significant discounts from net asset value because they have been historically less popular than shares of open-end companies. The per-share net asset values of closed-end companies often have no bearing on the share's market prices. A closed-end company's net asset value per share would be an important consideration only if that company decided to go out of business and liquidate its assets.

On the other hand, the offering price of an open-end company's shares can be no lower than its net asset value and may be higher than net asset value only by the amount of any sales charge.

See also Diversified Company; Investment Company; Net Asset Value per Share; Nondiversified Company; Sales Load.

Management Group. Most open-end investment companies rely on the counsel of professionals to decide which securities should be bought or sold. They enter into a contractual arrangement with an investment advisory organization, frequently referred to as a management group. The similarity between the names *management company* (mutual fund) and *management group* (investment advisor) is often understandably confusing to the novice. Close examination of the circumstances reveals that the officers and directors of the investment company are usually the same persons who serve as the executives of the investment advisor and the underwriter organizations, too! The plan company, when used, is also included in this maze of interrelationships. The plan company is, after all, merely a marketing arm of the fund's underwriter specializing in promotion and sales of contractual plans. In a majority of situations, the only real distinction is a legal one, with each organization founded under separate charters or trust agreements.

Preventing Conflicts of Interest. The potential for conflicts of interest and other associated inequities has been recognized by the federal government. The following preventive rules have been adopted within the Investment Company Act of 1940 and its amendments of 1970.

1. Before any management group or principal underwriter may act for or serve a management company, a contract must be written and approved by a majority of the outstanding voting stock of the company. The contract (a) must describe precisely all compensation to be paid thereunder; b) may be terminated without penalty on no more than sixty days' written notice by the board of directors or by a majority of the voting stock of the company; (c) must be approved annually by the board of directors or by majority of the outstanding voting stock; and (d) will automatically terminate in the event it is assigned to someone else.

2. At least 40% of the board of directors of each investment company must consist of persons who are not the regular brokers, investment advisors, principal underwriters, investment bankers, commercial bankers, or any employees thereof for that investment company. Furthermore, the company cannot use the services provided by those persons or their affiliates, unless at least a majority of the board members are not persons serving in each of those respective categories.

3. Notwithstanding this requirement, an investment company will still be allowed to have a board of directors composed solely of interested persons of its investment advisor, plus one "outsider," if (a) it is a no-load, open-end management company; (b) it has only one class of securities outstanding, with each share having equal voting privileges; (c) any fees levied above net asset value on the offering or discount from net asset value on redemption does not in the

aggregate exceed 2%; (d) all promotion expenses, executive salaries, and office rentals are borne by the investment advisor, and (3) the advisor is the only such group employed, receiving an annual fee of not more than 1% of the investment company's average annual assets.

4. Unless prior approval is obtained from the SEC, no affiliated person or principal underwriter of the investment company may normally (a) act as principal in the purchase or sale of securities or property with that investment company; (b) borrow money or other property from that investment company; or (c) act as joint participant in a transaction with that investment company.

5. No affiliated person or principal underwriter of the investment company may act as agent in the purchase or sale of any securities or property for that investment company in order to receive compensation (a) from any other source, unless it conforms to that person's usual business as underwriter or broker; (b) that exceeds a reasonable commission on exchange transactions, 2% on secondary distributions, or 1% on all other transactions, unless a larger commission is specifically approved by the SEC.

Services Performed. The actual terms and conditions of service by management groups varies according to size and prevailing relationships. However, in broad terms, we can state that such groups always (1) analyze economic conditions in the country in general and the marketplace in particular; (2) provide research information on industries and companies in which investments are contemplated; and (3) provide advisory counsel on specific securities to be bought or sold.

In many instances the management advisory group will also (1) arrange purchase and sales transactions for the investment company; (2) pay for legal fees and contingent expenses incurred by the investment company; (3) absorb employee and director expenses of the investment company; (4) provide clerical services to conduct business in behalf of the investment company; and (5) act as public relations agent for the investment company, promoting proper images through various forms of advertisement.

The advertising responsibility is usually accorded to the principal underwriter but occasionally may be delegated to the advisory group. When practiced by the underwriter, who is a member of the NASD, the material must be sent to the Washington, D.C., office of the NASD for its approval within ten days after publication or use. (That assumes this member has been subjected to NASD review of its advertising practices for at least one year. Otherwise, the filing requirement would call for advance submissions to the Association). Advertising materials prepared by the management advisory group, which is not an NASD member, must be approved by the SEC prior to use.

Advisement Fee. In return for these services, the management group accepts a fee from the investment company as specified in their contract. Most fees are predicated on the investment company's average net assets, determined annually, scaled down from 1% for organizations with minimal assets to 0.25% for the larger, more substantial mutual funds. The standard fee approximates 0.50% of the average annual net assets, payable to the management group in monthly installments. This figure is an important component and the largest liability in the formula used to calculate net asset value per share each day.

$$\text{Net asset value} = \begin{array}{c} \text{Security values plus} \\ \text{other items of worth} \\ \hline \text{total assets} \end{array} - \begin{array}{c} \text{Management group fee} \\ \text{plus other obligations} \\ \hline \text{total liabilities} \end{array}$$

Some analysts of investment company operations attempted to gauge the efficiency of a particular fund by examining its expense ratio and comparing it to other funds with similar objectives. The expense ratio formula is:

$$\text{Expense ratio} = \frac{\begin{array}{c}\text{annual operating expenses}\\ \text{(including management fee)}\end{array}}{\text{average annual net assets}}$$

Be aware, however, that for this analysis to be truly significant the comparison must be drawn between funds that are of similar size and that have a similar objective. Because the ratio is a function of the assets of the company, the larger funds normally carry smaller ratios. Operating expenses do not increase in direct proportion to the size of assets. As a form of assurance to investors, some advisory groups will refund a portion of their fee if the expense ratio exceeds a predetermined percentage of the fund's assets.

Some mutual fund management groups have even begun contracting to tie their fee to the performance of the fund instead of, or in addition to, a percentage of the annual assets. The fee is then related to the performance of a well-known index or average over an annual period. The models most frequently used in these comparisons are the Dow Jones Average, Standard & Poor's Composite Index, or even the New York Stock Exchange Index. The SEC insists that if this means of compensation is employed for management advisory groups as a reward for superior service, then a penalty clause in the contract must also be included, using a like formula, for underperformance.

See also Investment Company; Investment Company Act of 1940 and 1970 Amendments.

Managing Underwriter. *See* Syndicate.

M and W Formations. *See* Double Tops and Bottoms.

Manipulation of Security Prices and Deceptive Devices. With respect to securities registered on a national exchange, Section 9 of the Securities Exchange Act of 1934 specifically prohibits:

1. Wash sales (purchase and sale of the same security at the same time and price, by the same customer, through the facilities of the same brokerage firm). Do not confuse this with the term "wash sale" in the IRS tax rules.

2. Matched orders (purchase and sale of the same security, at the same time and price, by the same customer, through the facilities of different brokerage firms).

Both of these activities are considered improper because there is no change of beneficial ownership as a result of either transaction. This prohibition not only applies to individuals who engage in such practices in order to raise prices fraudulently, but also includes restrictions against any group of people acting together, "who participate in any undue activity intent upon defrauding the public." The statute does not inhibit the transactions of aggressive traders in the marketplace so long as they deal with someone other than themselves or with people who are not working together with them to induce unnecessary activity by others.

3. Dissemination of false or misleading statements; in this vein the SEC considers it a form of fraud, and thus a violation of this section of the law, for anyone to (a) distort or exaggerate information about a publicly owned company for the purpose of inducing someone to purchase or sell that company's stock; (b) knowingly and willfully circulate untrue information about a publicly owned company to deceive someone into purchasing or selling that company's stock; or (c) make promises or forecasts about the performance of a publicly owned company's stock in the marketplace without a substantive basis for that belief.

4. Use of tip sheets or touts to promote the purchase or sale of securities in which the writer or sponsor has a personal interest.

5. Pegging or fixing prices of securities (stabilization procedures to facilitate a bona fide distribution of securities is the lone exception to this restriction).

6. Purchasing, selling, or endorsing any securities option contract in contravention of rules specifically prescribed by the SEC as necessary and appropriate in the public interest.

Section 10 of the 1934 Act prohibits the following deceptive practices:

1. Churning (overtrading) in discretionary accounts.

2. Repurchase agreements used to manipulate securities prices (daisy chains and matched orders are typical).

3. Converting a customer's securities and monies for a broker's personal use without the customer's specific written consent.

4. Confirmations of transactions for customers without proper disclosure of essential facts. Each broker/dealer must disclose to its customer the capacity in which it has acted. It must also reveal any personal interest the firm or its principals may have in a security when it acts as a dealer in a transaction in that security with a customer. When acting as agent, and only on request, the broker/dealer must furnish its customer with the time of execution of the order and the name of the party on the contra side of the transaction. Under certain conditions it may also be obliged to notify the customer of the amount of commission charged to the other party in that transaction.

5. Concealment of essential information in promoting purchases or sales of any security. All material information considered to be relevant for an intelligent investment decision must be disclosed to a customer under terms of this rule. The minimum penalty for failure in this regard is the voiding of the transaction.

6. Boiler room sales (the use of high pressure sales tactics to promote activity in registered or unregistered securities).

7. Secret transactions in fictitious accounts.

8. The use of nonpublic material information by an insider for personal financial gain in securities transactions. The term insider has

been broadly interpreted to include anyone who possesses material information not available to the public. The public courts have held the tipper financially liable as well as the tippee.

9. Solicitation of purchases on a stock exchange to facilitate a distribution of securities. Under terms of this rule, it is illegal for a participant in a primary or secondary distribution to purchase personally or to pay someone to purchase or solicit purchases of any security of the same issuer on a national securities exchange. An important exception allows a broker/dealer to pay ordinary salary to its own sales force in performance of its regular duties. But they cannot be paid specifically to induce a customer to transact business on an exchange in a security of the same issuer during the period of distribution.

10. People engaged in making tender offers or offers of exchange from purchasing or acquiring the same security in the marketplace until the offering period has expired.

11. Tendering securities not owned in response to a public offer (short-tendering), anticipating that the price of the security will decline when the tenderor announces the pro-rata amount of that issue which will be accepted and paid for.

12. Purchases or bids for a security subject to a public distribution by any party with a financial interest in that offering. This includes the issuer or selling stockholders in whose behalf the offering is conducted as well as its underwriters and selling group members. However, there are several important exemptions regarding application of this prohibition. It does not pertain to (a) over-the-counter transactions; (b) privately negotiated transactions in substantial quantity without involvement of a broker/dealer; (c) purchases by the issuer more than forty days after the distribution begins, in order to satisfy a sinking fund or similar commitment; (d) transactions by a registered odd-lot dealer on a national securities exchange; (e) unsolicited agency transactions by a broker/dealer; (f) the exercise of a right or conversion privilege to acquire the security in distribution; (g) stabilizing transactions in accord with provisions of SEC rules; (h) standby underwritings of a rights offering in accord with provisions of SEC rules; (i) purchases or bids by a participating broker/dealer ten or more business days prior to the effective date of the registration statement (five or more business days in cases of unsolicited purchases); or (j) distributions of securities by an issuer with employees under stock-option plans or savings, investment, or payroll deduction plans.

13. Stabilizing transactions contrary to specific procedures set forth in SEC Rule 10b-7.

14. Extensions of credit unless the borrower is furnished with a written explanation of the terms and conditions at the time the arrangement is agreed to. As an adjunct to the "truth-in-lending" law passed by Congress in 1970, the SEC rule directs the broker/dealer also to include applicable maintenance-margin procedures, which are appropriate under certain conditions. At least 30 days' written notice must be given to change any terms and conditions thereafter.

15. An issuer of publicly owned securities from failing to inform promptly the stock exchanges where its securities are traded (or the NASD if they are traded over the counter) about its cash dividends, stock splits and other stock distributions, rights, or other subscription offerings. "Promptly" is deemed to be at least ten days prior to the record date, or if that is impractical, on or before the record date.

See also Churning; Daisy Chains; Matched Orders; Repurchase Agreement; Rules of Fair Practice (NASD); SEC Rule 10b-7; Securities Exchange Act of 1934; Stabilization; Wash Sale.

Margin. An amount of funds that must be deposited with the broker for each contract as a guarantee of fulfillment of the contract. Also called Security Deposit.

Margin Account. The margin account exists

under Regulation T for the purpose of executing margin purchases in listed equity securities (such as common stocks, preferred stocks, warrants) and a select number of over-the-counter equity securities. Nonconvertible bonds (corporate, government, and municipal) and securities options are also tradable in the margin account; however, they are subject to different requirements.

A customer must also use the margin account for the purpose of executing short sales. A customer may sell short in this account any type of debt or equity security, whether it be a listed or unlisted security. Long sales of existing long positions and cover shorts of existing short positions are also permitted. The Federal Reserve Board determines which over-the-counter stocks can be purchased on margin in the account. In general, it makes this determination based on a set of criteria which includes the degree of national investor interest, the depth and breadth of the market, the availability of information respecting the stock as well as the character and permanence of the company. Any OTC stock made eligible for margin is referred to as an *OTC Margin Stock*. There is no limitation of margin transactions imposed on listed equity securities. So long as the security is tradable on a national securities exchange it may be purchased on margin in the margin account.

Required Documentation. The following documents are required for margin accounts of individual customers: (1) new account report form; (2) customer's agreement; (3) loan-consent agreement; and (4) a signed credit agreement.

When instructions are to be given by someone other than the customer personally, a trading authorization form, limited or full, must be signed by that customer and filed with the firm before the agent's instructions can be accepted.

A joint account agreement form is also required for margin accounts of joint customers.

See also Corporate Accounts; Fiduciary Accounts; Joint Customers; New Account Report Form; Trading Authorization; Unincorporated Associations.

Long Account. In a long margin account, a customer owns the specific securities purchased or sold and these securities are held in the account for the customer.

Federal requirements. The Federal Reserve Board establishes requirements for a customer who purchases securities in a margin account. The following are the important terms to remember with respect to long margin accounts: (a) *Long positions* are the securities held in an account for the customer (securities owned by the customer); (b) *Initial margin requirement* is the percentage of the purchase which a customer must deposit when a transaction is made; (c) *Margin* is the amount of money and/or value of securities (that is, equity) that is required to be deposited with the broker in order to secure the loan made to the customer; (d) *Reg T call* is the demand for cash and/or securities that is issued to a customer under federal margin regulations because a transaction is initiated in a margin account. Federal margin calls, or Reg T calls, must be paid "promptly," which means on the fifth business day (settlement date) and no later that the seventh business day following the trade date. When a customer cannot comply within the time limit due to exceptional circumstances, an extension of time may be requested of a national securities exchange or the NASD. Any unsatisfied portion of such a call must be liquidated if not collected by the end of any time extension.

1. *Calculating Reg T excess.* Once a margin account is opened and a long position is established, the market value in the account will normally fluctuate. When market appreciation occurs, Reg T excess will be generated. This excess represents additional funds available to the customer for withdrawal or for additional transactions. To determine the amount of Reg T excess that exists in the account we use the Margin Required method. In this method we compare

the actual equity in the account with the amount of equity currently required to be in that account according to Regulation T. (*Equity* is the net worth in a customer's margin account. In a long account, equity equals the current market value of the securities less the debit balance.)

Example: Let us calculate Reg T excess for customer Joe Smith's account using the Margin Required method:

Long Position

100 shares Stock A @ 80 =	$ 8,000
100 shares Stock B @ 70 =	7,000
100 shares Stock C @ 50 =	5,000
Market value	$20,000
Debit balance	$ 7,000

Current Reg T initial requirement is 60%.

Calculations:

Step 1: Calculate the equity with the formula:
Equity = long market value* − debit balance

or:

Equity = LMV − Dr
= $20,000 − $7,000
= $13,000

*We refer to market value for long positions as "long market value" to distinguish it from the value of securities held in a short position.

Step 2: Calculate the margin required for this account:

Margin
required = initial margin requirement × LMV
= 60% × $20,000
= $12,000

Step 3: Calculate Reg T excess by comparing:

Reg T excess = equity − margin required
= $13,000 − $12,000
= $1,000

Therefore, in customer Joe Smith's account there is a Reg T excess of $1,000. This excess is available simply because the actual equity in his account is more than the amount necessary to margin his account properly at 60%, the current requirement.

Remember that (1) *long market value* is the total value of the long positions in a particular account calculated for the current prices of the securities held (the abbreviation for long market value is LMV); (2)*equity* is the net worth in a customer's account. Equity in a long margin account equals the long market value minus the Debit Balance; or Equity equals LMV minus Dr.

2. *Withdrawing Reg T excess.*

Example: As stated earlier, customer Joe Smith may either withdraw the $1,000 excess from his account or apply it toward a new purchase on margin. Let us consider the first alternative for Joe Smith. Joe's account at present looks like this:

LMV	Equity	Balance	Reg T Excess
$20,000	$13,000	$7,000 Dr	$1,000

After he withdraws $1,000, his account looks like this:

LMV	Equity	Balance	Reg T Excess
$20,000	$12,000	$8,000 Dr	0

Notice that when Joe Smith withdraws $1,000 cash, his debit balance therefore increases to $8,000. Then, the Reg T excess decreases to 0 and the equity also decreases to $12,000 because equity = LMV − Dr.

3. *Purchasing additional securities with Reg T excess.*

Example: Joe Smith's other alternative is to use $1,000 to meet all or part of the initial requirement on additional purchases. Let us consider this possibility and see what happens to customer Smith's account. To do this, we must use the formula:

Reg T call = (initial requirement × cost) – Reg T excess

Example: Joe Smith buys 100 shares of Stock D at 80, and the initial margin requirement is still 60%.

Calculations:

Step 1: Calculate the cost of stock:

Cost = 100 × $80 = $8,000

Step 2: Calculate the Reg T call:

Reg T call = initial requirement × cost) – Reg T excess
= (60% × $8,000) –$1,000
= $4,800 – $1,000
= $3,800

As can be seen, the 60% initial requirement on the purchase, or $4,800, was reduced by the $1,000 Reg T excess. Federal regulations permit the trade to be calculated in this manner because prior to the purchase the account had $1,000 more equity than needed to margin it properly at 60%. After applying the trade to the account, the account totals are:

Reg T Call	LMV	Equity	Balance	Reg T Excess
$3,800	$28,000	$13,000	$15,000 Dr	0

Note that the debit balance has increased by $8,000, the cost of the additional purchase; the Reg T excess had decreased to $0; there is a Reg T call for $3,800; the LMV has increased $8,000, the value of the new purchase; and the equity remains the same because both LMV and Dr have increased equally. This is shown by Equity = LMV – Dr.

As soon as the customer deposits the $3,800, the Reg T call will be eliminated. The debit balance will be reduced by the amount of the deposit and the equity will be increased by the same amount. After depositing $3,800 into the account, the totals are:

Reg T Call	LMV	Equity	Balance	Reg T Excess
0	$28,000	$16,800	$11,200 Dr	0

These totals are confirmed by applying our basic formula:

Equity = LMV – Dr
= $28,000 – $11,200
= $16,800

4. *Depositing securities to meet a Reg T call.* Occasionally, a customer will desire to use eligible, fully-paid-for securities to meet a Reg T call. This is permissible under Regulation T. If a customer does deposit securities, their value may be applied against the Reg T call. On the other hand, should the customer wish to sell other securities held long in his/her account to meet the margin requirement, the sale should be made the same day as the purchase. Sales made after the purchase date are considered liquidations. A practice of meeting margin calls by liquidation is prohibited.

Let us consider how much stock Joe Smith must deposit in his account to meet his Reg T call of $3,800, which came as a result of his additional purchase of Stock D. Joe Smith cannot simply deposit stock currently worth $3,800 in to market. According to regulations, only a percentage of the market value of securities is allowable for loan purposes. That is, if the loan value percentage is 40%, then the loan value of $5,000 worth of stock is $2,000. The loan value percentage is the complement of the initial margin requirement percentage. That is, if the current initial requirement is 60%, then the current loan value percentage is 40% because together th initial requirement and the loan value percentage must add up to 100%. Therefore, the loan value will vary as the initial margin requirement varies.

If Joe Smith deposited stock worth $3,800, then he could not meet his Reg T call of $3,800 because the loan value of $3,800 worth of stock is only $1,520 ($3,800 × 40% = $1,520). To determine how much stock Joe Smith must deposit to meet his Reg T call we use the following formula:

$$\text{Dollar amount of stock to meet Reg T call} = \frac{\text{Reg T call}}{\text{Loan value \%}}$$

Example: Current initial margin requirement is 60%; current loan value is 40%; outstanding Reg T call is $3,800.

Calculations:

$$\begin{aligned}
\text{Dollar amount of stock to meet Reg T call} &= \frac{\text{Reg T call}}{\text{Loan value \%}} \\
&= \frac{\$3,800}{40\%} \\
&= \$9,500
\end{aligned}$$

This means that Joe Smith must deposit $9,500 worth of eligible securities to meet the Reg T call of $3,800. In essence, the broker is lending him 40% (the loan value) on the $9,500 security deposit. Keep in mind the following points: (a) *Loan value percentage* is the complement of the Reg T initial margin requirement percentage (100% – initial margin requirement percentage); (b) Loan value of securities = loan value percentage × long market value of securities (LMV).

5. *Liquidating securities to meet a Reg T call.* Stock exchange and NASD regulations prohibit a customer from making a practice of meeting margin calls by liquidation. The broker/dealer, however, is not limited to a choice of securities to be sold in the general account if the customer fails to honor a commitment. The security purchased should be liquidated plus any additional securities if necessary to cover any loss.

These rules do not preclude the customer from selling another security on the same day as his purchase in order to use the proceeds of the sale to pay for the purchase. Such permissible activity is identified by the Federal Reserve Board as a *margin substitution.* If a series of such transactions on the same day happen to increase the customer's debit balance by no more than $500, the firm is permitted to waive the call for more margin without liability for a rule violation.

6. *Calculating buying power of Reg T excess. Buying power* is a term to indicate the amount of securities a customer can purchase using existing Reg T excess in the account. To calculate buying power, we use the following formula:

$$\text{Buying power} = \frac{\text{Reg T excess}}{\text{initial margin requirement}}$$

Example: Let us apply this to customer Joe Smith's account. How much in securities can Smith purchase without depositing additional margin if the Reg T excess is $1,000 and the initial requirement is 60%?

Calculations:

$$\begin{aligned}
\text{Buying power} &= \frac{\text{Reg T excess}}{60\%} \\
&= \frac{\$1,000}{60\%} \\
&= \$1,666.67
\end{aligned}$$

A variation of this formula is to add a zero (0) to the excess and divide by 6: 1,000 excess, add 0

$$10,000 \div 6 = 1,666.67$$

This means that Joe Smith can purchase, at most, $1,666.67 worth of securities with his $1,000 Reg T excess without depositing additional funds. If he actually made a $1,666.67 purchase, the calculations would be:

$$\begin{array}{rl}
\$1,666.67 & \text{purchase cost} \\
\times \quad .60 & \text{initial requirement percentage} \\
\hline
\$1,000.00 & \text{initial margin required} \\
-1,000.00 & \text{Reg T excess} \\
\hline
0 & \text{Reg T call}
\end{array}$$

Summary. Federal margin requirements for purchases may be summarized as follows: (1) The initial requirement on a margin account is established by the Federal Reserve Board under Regulation T. (2) Federal margin calls must be met promptly and in any event within seven business days of the trade date. Extensions of time are permissible but only under unusual circumstances. (3) Reg T excess may be withdrawn from the account as cash or used to meet the initial requirement on additional purchases. (4) The loan value on stock deposited into the account may be applied to meet outstanding Reg T calls. (5) Buying power represents the maximum amount of securities a customer can purchase without depositing additional margin.

Key formulas may be summarized as follows:

1. Equity $= LMV - Dr$

2. Margin required $=$ initial margin requirement $\times$ LMV

3. Reg T excess $=$ equity $-$ margin required

4. Reg T call $=$ (initial requirement $\times$ cost) $-$ Reg T excess

5. Loan value percentage $= 100\% -$ initial requirement percentage

6. Loan value $= LMV \times$ loan value percentage

7. Deposit of securities to meet Reg T call $= \dfrac{\text{Reg T call}}{\text{initial requirement percentage}}$

8. Buying power $= \dfrac{\text{Reg T execess}}{\text{initial requirement percentage}}$

Exchange and broker requirements:

1. *Initial and maintenance margin requirements.* For the protection of the member organizations as well as a means of establishing minimum fair practice rules, the New York Stock Exchange, other major exchanges, and the NASD have established both initial and maintenance margin requirements. Using these rules as a minimum and a model, brokers carrying margin accounts have developed their own policies and rules that either equal or exceed the requirements of these regulatory bodies. These requirements are to supplement the Federal Reserve Board's initial requirement, which applies only at the time a transaction is made. Once met, the FRB initial requirement never applies to that trade again even if the percentage is later increased.

For illustrative purposes, the explanations and examples that follow are based on the minimum requirements of the NYSE. Remember that brokers may, and often do, set higher requirements as their own house rules and policies.

2. *$2,000 NYSE minimum initial equity requirement.* Rule 431 of the New York Stock Exchange Constitution and Rules sets forth the basic margin requirements for NYSE member firms. One of its most important requirements is that which requires a margin customer to establish an initial equity of at least $2,000 when making a margin transaction. Like the Reg T initial requirement, this rule is an initial requirement. Once it is met on a particular transaction, it does not apply again until another transaction is made. This means that during the interim the equity can fall below $2,000 as a result of market fluctuation; no additional margin will be required unless the equity also falls below the broker's or the NYSE's maintenance requirements.

Example: Assume that a customer opens a margin account and purchases 150 shares of KIM stock 20 (cost $3,000). With a Reg T initial requirement of 60%, this customer will incur a Reg T call of $1,800. However, because of the NYSE minimum equity rule, the customer will have to deposit a total of $2,000.

That is, the customer must deposit enough funds to meet the larger of the two requirements, either the Reg T initial requirement or the NYSE

$2,000 minimum equity requirement.

If however, the net purchase cost in a transaction is less than $2,000, this minimum amount does not apply. Under no circumstances do NYSE minimum rules require the customer to deposit funds greater than the net purchase cost. The customer must deposit funds at least equal to the net cost when that cost is below $2,000, so as to satisfy the NYSE minimum equity rule.

Example: Assume that Sandra Young opens a General Margin Account and makes a purchase of 100 shares of SKH stock 18 (net cost $1,800). With a Reg T initial requirement of 60%, this trade is subject to a $1,080 (60% × $1,800) Reg T call. It is also subject to an $1,800 requirement to satisfy the NYSE minimum equity rule. In this case, the $2,000 minimum equity rule does not apply because the actual net cost of the purchase is less than $2,000. Once again, customer Young must deposit funds to meet the larger of the two requirements, which in this case is the NYSE requirement, $1,800.

3. *NYSE minimum maintenance requirement.* So far we discussed two types of initial margin requirements: (1) the Federal Reserve Board initial Reg T requirement and (2) the NYSE initial $2,000 equity requirement. The combination of these two requirements effectively serves to ensure that sufficient margin is deposited initially when a margin transaction is made. However, what happens once these two requirements are met and no longer apply? Obviously some sort of requirement must be established to make certain that sufficient margin is maintained in the account as prices of the margined securities fluctuate. The NYSE minimum maintenance requirement is designed to accomplish this purpose.

The NYSE minimum maintenance rule requires customers to maintain an equity in their account equal to at least 25% of the current market value of their long positions. Therefore, if customer Joe Smith has a General Margin Account with a long market value of $10,000, he will be required to maintain an equity of at least $2,500 (25% of $10,000). Most NYSE member firms establish their own house maintenance requirement at a higher percentage than the NYSE 25% minimum. These firms are perfectly free to do this; however, they may not set lower requirements.

In the event that declining market prices or some other actions cause the equity in an account to fall below the 25% minimum, the customer will incur a maintenance call. This is a call for additional margin to raise the equity back to at least the 25% level. Once a maintenance call is incurred, the NYSE rules require that it be "met promptly and in any event within a reasonable period of time."

Example: Let us illustrate this idea of maintenance call with the following figures and graph. When customer Joe Smith purchased 100 shares of SKH stock @ 100, it cost him $10,000. He deposited $6,000 to meet the initial Reg T call of 60%, and his broker lent him $4,000. At that point in October the 25% minimum maintenance requirement was $2,500, which Smith obviously met. As the long market value of SKH stock decreased over the next three months to $5,000, the equity declined to $1,000 because the debit balance remained constant at $4,000 (Equity equals LMV minus Dr). Thus, Smith's equity eventually declined, at $1,000, to only 20% of LMV. (Smith actually received a maintenance call before the LMV plunged to $5,000.) Smith now had a maintenance call of $250 because the NYSE minimum maintenance rule requires an equity level of at least 25%, or $1,250.

In the following graph, the equity, after decreasing in dollar value from $6,000 to $1,000, finally goes below the 25% maintenance level. The decline in LMV of SKH stock appears across the top of the graph as you read from October to January. When the equity graphically goes below the 25% line, customer Smith receives a maintenance call.

4. *Four ways of meeting maintenance calls.* A maintenance call can be met by four methods:

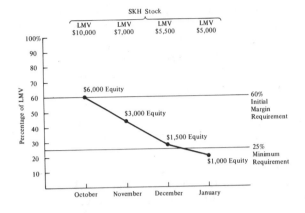

The $4,000 maintenance requirement represents the minimum equity that this account may have without incurring a maintenance call. Because the equity in the account is only $3,000, the account then is on call for $1,000. We calculate this by using the following formula:

Maintenance call = maintenance
requirement − equity

Calculations:

Maintenance call = (25% × LMV) − $3,000
= (25% × $16,000) − $3,000
= $4,000 − $3,000
= $1,000

The following four sections discuss in detail the four ways in which this particular maintenance call may be met.

5. *Meeting a maintenance call with a cash deposit.* To meet the $1,000 call by deposit of cash, the customer must deposit $1,000 (the exact amount of the call). This deposit will reduce the debit balance by $1,000 and increase the equity by the same amount, bringing it in line with the maintenance requirement. Note that the LMV will not change.

Assume that the customer deposits $1,000. The new status of the account will be as follows:

25% Maintenance Requirement	LMV	Balance	Equity
$4,000	$16,000	−$12,000 Dr	= $4,000

6. *Meeting a maintenance call with a securities deposit.* A securities deposit to meet this $1,000 maintenance call requires a deposit of approximately $1,334 of securities. We use the formula for a 25% maintenance requirement:

Securities deposit
to meet
maintenance call = 4/3 maintenance call

Securities deposit = 4/3 × $1,000
= $1,334

A deposit of $1,334 worth of securities will increase both the long market value and the

(a) deposit of cash; (b) deposit of securities; (c) liquidation (selling) of securities in the account; or (d) market appreciation.

A cash deposit requires only that the customer deposit the exact amount of the call. With a 25% maintenance requirement, a securities deposit requires a deposit in value equal to 4/3 times the call. With the same 25% maintenance level, a liquidation of securities requires a sale of securities equal to four times the call. Note that these two formulas for securities deposits and liquidations are based on a minimum maintenance requirement of 25%. (The formulas vary as the maintenance requirement varies.

Example: A 30% maintenance requirement necessitates a deposit of securities equal to 10/7 times the call and the sale of securities equal to 10/3 times the call. The derivation of these four formulas goes beyond the purpose of this presentation.

Example: Assume a customer has an established margin account which reflects the following status:

Long positions

300 shares of GGG stock @ 40 = $12,000
50 shares of HHH stock @ 80 = $ 4,000

25% Maintenance Requirement	LMV	Balance	Equity
$4,000	$16,000	−$13,000 Dr	= $3,000

equity by that amount. The minimum maintenance requirement will also increase by $334 (25% of $1,334).

Assume that the customer deposits stock worth $1,334. The new status of the account will be as follows:

25% Maintenance Requirement	LMV	Balance	Equity
$4,334	$17,334	–$13,000 Dr	= $4,334

7. *Meeting a maintenance call by liquidating securities.* The sale of securities in the account to meet a 25% maintenance call requires that securities with a value of four times the call be liquidated. Therefore, to meet the $1,000 maintenance call, the customer must sell stock worth $4,000. We use the formula for a 25% maintenance call:

Liquidation
to meet a
maintenance call $= 4 \times$ maintenance call

Liquidation $= 4 \times \$1,000$
$= \$4,000$

Assume that the customer sells 100 shares of GGG stock @ 40 (proceeds $4,000) in the account. The new status of the account will be as follows:

25% Maintenance Requirement	LMV	Balance	Equity
$3,000	$12,000	–$9,000 Dr	= $3,000

Note in these figures of the account that the sale has reduced the LMV and the debit balance each by $4,000 ($16,000 to $12,000 LMV and $13,000 to $9,000 Dr). The equity thus has remained the same, $3,000. The equity now equals the 25% maintenance requirement of $3,000 (25% of $12,000). The maintenance requirement decreased by 25% ($4,000 to

$3,000), which reflects the 25% decrease in LMV.

8. *Meeting a maintenance call by market appreciation.* Many times, particularly when the maintenance call is low (as in the example cited, $1,000), the market will rise so that the call, while it was valid when originally issued, would not require such a request for funds on a current calculation.

Should the market value of the account increase to $18,000 after the $1,000 maintenance call was issued, the account would now show:

25% Maintenance Requirement	LMV	Balance	Equity
$4,500	$18,000	–$13,000 DA	= $5,000

Note that the equity is now more than sufficient to meet the maintenance requirement ($5,000 vs. $4,500 so no call is necessary.

It should be kept in mind that the waiving of such a call is at the policy of the broker. Often, the broker will insist that the original call still be answered.

9. *Calculating the point below which a long account will incur a maintenance call.* Often it is helpful and necessary to know ahead of time just when a margin account will incur a maintenance call. To calculate the point below which a long account incurs a 25% minimum call we use the following formula:

LMV incurs maintenance call $= 4/3 \times$ debit balance

Let us apply this formula to an account whose status is as follows:

25% Maintenance Requirement	LMV	Equity	Balance
$5,000	$20,000	$8,000	$12,000 Dr

To determine the point at which this account will incur a 25% maintenance call, use the formula just given:

LMV incurs maintenance call $= 4/3 \times$ debit balance
$$= 4/3 \times \$12,000$$
$$= \$16,000$$

This means that when the LMV falls below $16,000, this account will incur a maintenance call.

Now let us reexamine the data in the figure on page 248. In that figure, the long market value of SKH stock incurs a minimum maintenance call when the LMV drops to $5,000. However, as the graph shows, the equity actually dips below the 25% level before LMV decreases to $5,000. With this new formula let us calculate precisely when the account incurs a maintenance call.

LMV incurs maintenance call $= 4/3 \times$ debit balance
$$= 4/3 \times \$4,000$$
$$= \$5,333$$

Inspection of the graph shows this to be correct.

Summary of exchange and broker requirements.

1. The New York Stock Exchange requires that a $2,000 minimum equity be established each time a purchase in a margin account is made. Between purchases, the equity may fall below the $2,000 level and no call will be incurred unless the equity also falls below the minimum maintenance requirement. This $2,000 minimum does not apply for initial transactions with a net cost below $2,000. With such transactions the customer must pay the full net cost.

2. The NYSE also requires that equity equal to 25% of the current long market value be maintained in the account. This is known as the 25% maintenance requirement.

3. Brokers may and often do set higher requirements than the minimum guidelines of the NYSE.

4. A maintenance call is incurred when the equity in an account falls below the minimum maintenance requirement.

5. NYSE maintenance calls must be collected 15 business days from the date on which the account went on call.

Key formulas may be summarized as follows:

1. Minimum maintenance requirement $= 25\% \times$ LMV
2. Maintenance call $=$ minimum maintenance requirement $-$ equity
3. Meeting maintenance calls by
   a. Deposit of cash $=$ exact amount of call
   b. Deposit of securities $= 4/3 \times$ maintenance call
   c. Sale of securities $= 4 \times$ maintenance call
   d. Market appreciation. Price of security rises to where the equity equals or exceeds the 25% requirement before the maintenance call is due.
4. Point below which security value in account incurs maintenance call $= 4/3 \times$ debit balance.

Short Account. A short position is the number of shares of stock or bonds sold out of an account but not owned. A short sale is the sale of a security which the customer does not own.

Once a short position is established it may be kept open as long as the minimum maintenance requirement is met and borrowed stock can be held. The short seller is liable for any interest or dividends declared and paid on the securities short in the account. In such cases the amount of the interest or dividend value is charged to credit balance with no reduction of SMA.

Regulation T prescribes the same initial requirement for short sales that it does for long purchases. A customer making a short sale and incurring a Reg T call is required to meet such call promptly but no later than within seven business days; extensions of time with good reason are permitted. Reg T excess can be generated on a short position and such excess will be credited to the SMA. Short sales are also subject to NYSE minimum equity and maintenance requirements. In brief, essentially the same type of rules apply to short sales that apply to long purchases, with a few exceptions.

Initial requirements for short sales. Assume that customer Joe Smith opens a general margin account and executes a short sale of 100 shares of RSU stock @ 80 (proceeds $8,000). With a Reg T initial requirement of 75%, Smith incurs a Reg T call of $6,000.

$$\begin{aligned} \text{Reg T call} \ &= \text{initial requirement} \times \text{proceeds} \\ &= 75\% \times \$8,000 \\ &= \$6,000 \end{aligned}$$

When customer Joe Smith deposits $6,000 cash within the required seven-business-day period, he eliminates the Reg T call. Customer Smith's account now looks like this:

Short Market Value	Equity	Balance
$8,000	$6,000	$14,000 Cr

Here we note three distinct differences from a long account:

1. Market value is referred to as short market value (SMV) so as to easily distinguish it from long market value (LMV).

2. The balance in the account is now a credit balance. In a short account the credit balance reflects the money held in the customer's account as collateral against the short position. It will be used at some future date to cover the cost of purchasing the stock to close out the short position. The credit balance reflects the money held in the customer's account after all commitments have been paid in full. The abbreviation for credit balance is Cr.

3. Equity in a short account is now calculated as credit balance less short market value:

$$\text{Equity} = \text{Cr} - \text{SMV}$$

This formula is in complete agreement with the formula used in long accounts. In a customer's account, long market value (LMV) and credit balance (Cr) are the assets while short market value (SMV) and debit balance (Dr) are the liabilities.

Because we are concerned here only with a short account, our simple formula is:

$$\text{Equity} = \text{Cr} - \text{SMV}$$

Let us use this formula to calculate Customer Joe Smith's equity:

$$\begin{aligned} \text{Equity} \ &= \$14,000 - \$8,000 \\ &= \$6,000 \end{aligned}$$

When a short sale is executed in an account with an SMA, such SMA can be used to meet all or part of the Reg T requirements. In this calculation, we use the following formula:

$$\text{Reg T call} = (\text{initial requirement} \times \text{proceeds}) - \text{SMA}$$

Example: The initial requirement is 60%, the SMA equals $1,000, and there are short sale proceeds of $10,000 (100 shares of SKH stock @ 100).

Calculations:

$$\begin{aligned} \text{Reg T call} \ &= (\text{initial requirement} \times \text{proceeds}) - \text{SMA} \\ &= (60\% \times \$10,000 - \$1,000 \\ &= \$6,000 - \$1,000 \\ &= \$5,000 \end{aligned}$$

The New York Stock Exchange also applies a $2,000 minimum equity requirement on all short sales. However, unlike that for purchases, this requirement must be met under all conditions even if the short sale is less than $2,000. If customer Joe Smith were to open a margin account and execute a short sale for $500, he would still have to deposit $2,000 to satisfy this requirement. In most cases margin customers sell short for amounts much larger than $2,000 and by meeting the resulting Reg T call, the customers also meet the $2,000 equity requirement. The minimum equity rule requires that a $2,000 equity be established in the account each time a short sale is made.

Summary: (1) Short market value (SMV) is the total value of the short positions in a particular account calculated for the current prices of the securities held; (2) Credit balance (Cr) in a short account is the money held as collateral against the short position; (3) Equity is the net worth in a customer's account. Equity in a short margin account equals the credit balance minus the short market value; or Equity = Cr – SMV.

Reg T excess. Reg T excess is generated in a short account when the actual equity becomes larger than that required to margin the account at the current Reg T initial requirement. Such excess is created whenever the value of the short positions declines, thus increasing the account's equity. The formula for computing Reg T excess in the short account is the same as for the long account:

Reg T excess = equity – margin required (that is, initial requirement × SMV)

Example: Let us illustrate how Reg T excess is generated by examining the following account:

The initial requirement is 80% and customer Jane Doe's account is as follows:

Short Position
100 shares of MHN stock @ 60 = $6,000
100 shares of CNK stock @ 40 = $4,000

SMV	Equity	Balance
$10,000	$8,000	$18,000 Cr

Note that this account is properly margined at 80% because the equity ($8,000) is 80% of SMV

($10,000). Assume now that the SMV declines to $9,000. Following this decline the account is now as follows:

SMV	Equity	Balance
$9,000	$9,000	$18,000 Cr

Equity = Cr – SMV
= $18,000 – $9,000
= $9,000

While the equity has increased to $9,000, the amount needed to properly margin the account, 80% of SMV, has decreased to $7,200. We calculate the Reg T excess as follows:

Reg T excess = equity – margin required
= $9,000 – (initial requirement × SMV)
= $9,000 – (80% × $9,000)
= $9,000 – $7,200
= $1,800

This means that customer Jane Doe's account has generated $1,800 Reg T excess.

At most firms, Reg T excess is credited automatically to the SMA where it is protected in the event the short market value goes back up at a later date. Once Reg T excess is credited to the SMA it may always be withdrawn in cash provided such withdrawal does not (1) reduce the equity below $2,000 or (2) place the account on a maintenance call (*see* Special Memorandum Account).

Maintenance requirements. The NYSE minimum maintenance requirements for short positions vary depending on the price of the security. The NYSE minimum maintenance requirement for a long position is 25%, regardless of the price. The following is a breakdown of the minimum maintenance short requirements:

Price of Short Security	NYSE Minimum Maintenance Requirement
16¾-higher	30% of market value
5-16⅝	$5 per share
2½-5	100% of market value
Less than 2½	$2.50 per share

Because of the varied short requirements, it is necessary to compute each individual short position separately to determine the total minimum maintenance requirement for the account.

Example: Let us illustrate these minimum maintenance requirements.

Short account
100 shares of ROP stock @ 60 = $6,000
500 shares of DBY stock @ 10 = $5,000
300 shares of FTZ stock @ 4 = $1,200

SMV	Equity	Balance
$12,200	$6,600	$18,800 Cr

Calculations:

Security	Minimum Maintenance Requirement
100 shares ROP	$1,800 (30% × $6,000)
500 shares DBY	$2,500 ($5 × 500 shares)
300 shares FTZ	$1,200 (100% × $1,200)
Total	$5,500

Remember that the maintenance requirement represents the minimum amount of equity that an account may have without incurring a maintenance call. In the illustration above, the account has maintenance excess of $1,100. (An equity of $6,600 minus the maintenance requirement of $5,500.) In the event that the equity falls below the minimum maintenance requirement, the account will incur a maintenance call. This call must be met by a deposit of additional margin or liquidation of all or a portion of the short positions.

Calculating the point above which a short account will incur a maintenance call. Often it is helpful and necessary to know ahead of time just when a short account will incur a maintenance call. To calculate the point above which a short account incurs a 30% minimum maintenance call we use the following formula:

SMV incurs maintenance call = 10/13 × Credit Balance

This formula is appropriate for short positions where securities are 16¾ or higher, thus requiring at least 30% of market value. These are generally the securities which are sold short.

Example: Let us apply this formula to an account whose status is as follows:

30% Maintenance Requirement	SMV	Equity	Initial Balance	Requirement
$6,000	$20,000	$10,000	$30,000 Cr	50%

Above what point will this account incur a 30% maintenance call?

Calculations:

SMV incurs maintenance call = 10/13 × Credit Balance
= 10/13 × $30,000
= $23,077.

This means that when the SMV rises above $23,077, this account will incur a maintenance call. When SMV rises to $23,077, the equity falls to $6,923 ($30,000 Cr – $23,077 SMV). At the same SMV, or $23,077, the 30% maintenance requirement is $6,923. If the SMV rises any further, causing the equity to fall, the minimum maintenance required will be greater than the equity. This will set off a maintenance call on the short account.

You can see this graphically in the example shown in the following figure. As the SMV climbs from January to April, equity falls because the credit balance remains constant (Equity = Cr – SMV). In March, when SMV hits $23,077 equity of $6,923 meets the 30% line. A further rise in SMV plunges equity below the 30% minimum maintenance requirement line. This brings forth a maintenance call for the short account.

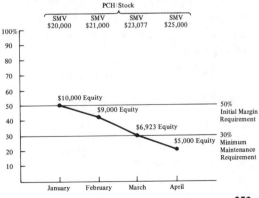

Cover short transactions. A customer executing a short sale is normally doing so with the hope of buying in the same security at some future date at a lower price and thereby realizing a profit. The act of buying in a short position is commonly referred to as a *cover short transaction.* When a cover short transaction is made, the customer uses part of the credit balance in the account to offset the purchase cost.

Because a cover short transaction serves to close out a position, there will be an overall reduction in the requirements on the account. At times, this reduction will be such that Reg T excess will be generated. To determine whether any Reg T excess is available after a cover short transaction, the standard Reg T excess formula may be used. That release is the same amount as the margin required on the short position. In other words, if the margin required is 50%, you release 50% on the cover. If 65% is required, you release 65%, and so on.

Reg T excess = equity – margin required
(that is, initial requirement × SMV)

This formula is applied to the account after the cover short transaction is executed and the status of the account is updated. It is important to keep in mind that you always release the greatest amount to the SMA whether the excess or the permissible release.

Maintenance requirements. The total main tenance requirement for a moxed account is calculated by combining the requirements for the long positions with those for the short positions. The individual requirements are the same as covered previously:

NYSE Minimum Maintenance Requirements

Long Positions	Short Positions
25% of LMV	16¾-higher = 30% of SMV
	5-16⅝ = $5 per share
	2½-5 = 100% of SMV
	Less than 2½ = $2.50 per share

Example: Let us apply these figures to a mixed account with the following long and short positions:

Long Positions

300 shares of UUU stock @ 40 = $12,000
100 shares of VVV stock @ 20 = $ 2,000

Short Positions

500 shares of WWW stock @ 30 = $15,000
200 shares of XXX stock @ 12 = $ 2,400

Calculations:

Long Positions	Maintenance Requirement
UUU stock	= $3,000 (25% of $12,000)
VVV stock	= 500 (25% of $ 2,000)

$3,500 maintenance requirement, long account

Short Positions	Maintenance Requirement
Stock WWW	= $4,500 (30% of $15,000)
Stock XXX	= 1,000 ($5 × 200)

$5,500 maintenance requirement, short account
$9,000 ($3,500 + 5,500) maintenance requirement, mixed account

Mixed account transactions. Trades in a mixed account are handled the same as for the respective long and short accounts. Purchases and short sales are individually subject to the Reg T initial requirement as well as the NYSE $2,000 minimum equity. Long sales and the covering of short sales release 50% or more to the SMA, depending on the status of the account. Below are some illustrations of transactions in a mixed account where we can apply the various appropriate formulas.

Example: In the mixed account of Fred Kraft, the initial requirement is 50% and the accounts are as follows:

Long Positions

100 shares of AAA stock @ 80 = $8,000
100 shares of BBB stock @ 70 = $7,000
100 shares of CCC stock @ 50 = $5,000

Short Positions

200 shares of DDD stock @ 30 = $6,000
100 shares of EEE stock @ 10 = $1,000
500 shares of FFF stock @ 4 = $2,000
LMV = $20,000
Long balance = $4,000 Dr
SMV = $9,000
Short balance = $9,000 Cr
Equity = $16,000
SMA = $1,500

Long Account				Short Account	
LMV	*Equity*	*SMA*	*Balance*	*SMV*	*Balance*
$20,000	$16,000	$1,500	$4,000 Dr	$9,000	$9,000 Cr

Note that this account is margined properly in that equity of $16,000 exceeds margin required of $14,500 [50% × ($20,000 + 9,000)] by $1,500. Therefore, Reg T excess is equal to the SMA.

Question 1: Customer Fred Kraft purchases 100 shares of stock GGG @ 60 (cost $6,000). How much cash must he deposit?

Calculations:

$$\begin{aligned} \text{Reg T call} &= (50\% \times \text{cost}) - \text{SMA} \\ &= (50\% \times \$6,000) - \$1,500 \\ &= \$3,000 - \$1,500 \\ &= \$1,500 \end{aligned}$$

Question 2: (Disregard Question 1) Customer Fred Kraft sells 100 shares of AAA stock @ 80 (proceeds $8,000). What is the new SMA?

Calculations:
either

$$\begin{aligned} \text{New SMA} &= (50\% \times \text{proceeds}) + \text{prior SMA} \\ &= (50\% \times \$8,000) + \$1,500 \\ &= \$4,000 + \$1,500 \\ &= \$5,500 \end{aligned}$$

or

$$\begin{aligned} \text{New SMA} &= \text{equity} - \text{margin required} \\ &= \text{equity} - [\text{initial requirement} \times \\ &\quad (\text{LMV} + \text{SMV})] \\ &= \$16,000 - [50\% \times (\$12,000 + \$9,000)] \\ &= [\$16,000] - [50\% \times \$21,000] \\ &= \$16,000 - \$10,500 \\ &= \$5,500 \end{aligned}$$

Customer Kraft has a new SMA of $5,500.

Question 3: (Disregard Questions 1 and 2) Customer Fred Kraft covers the 500 shares of FFF stock @ 4 (cost $2,000). What is the new SMA?

Calculations:

In a cover short transaction we recalculate for Reg T excess after the transaction.

$$\begin{aligned} \text{Reg T excess} &= \text{equity} - \text{margin required} \\ &= \$16,000 - [50\% \times (\$20,000 + \$7,000)] \\ &= \$16,000 - (50\% \times \$27,000) \\ &= \$16,000 - \$13,500 \\ &= \$2,500 \end{aligned}$$

The alternative way of computing this account would be to release 50% of the cost of the covering short (50% × $2,000 = $1,000). At this point, recalculate the account and credit any additional excess to the SMA (New SMA, $2,500 = $1,000 + $1,500).

Since $2,500 is the same as the current SMA ($2,500), no additional credit to the SMA may be made.

Summary of mixed accounts. (1) A mixed account is one which contains both long and short positions. (2) The formulas for calculating the mixed account are essentially the same as the long and short account formulas.

The key formulas are:

1. Equity   = LMV + Cr – Dr – SMV

2. Margin required   = initial requirement × (LMV + SMV)

3. Reg T excess   = equity – margin required

4. Maintenance
   required   = the amount for long maintenance
   requirement + the amount for short-
   tenance requirement

5. Reg T call
   on a long
   purchase   = (initial requirement × cost) – SMA

6. Reg T call
   on a short
   sale   = (initial re-
   quirement × proceeds) – SMA

7. New SMA
   after a
   long sale   = either (50% × proceeds) +
   prior SMA or equity – margin
   required whichever is greater

8. New SMA
   after a cover
   short transaction = (50% of the cost of cover) +
   prior SMA or equity – margin
   required, whichever is
   greater.

See also Arbitrage Account; Cash Account; Exempt Security (Margin Trading); Initial Margin Requirement; Maintenance Call; Margin Substitution; Reg T Excess; Short Sale; Special Memorandum Account.

Long Options. Long options are not marginable and have no loan value. Even though the purchase of an option is not marginable, the transaction may take place either in the cash or margin account. If it does take place in the margin account, the investor still has to pay in full for the option. The value of the option contract cannot be considered for any calculation of a client's equity in the account. Under Reg T payment is due in seven business days.

The initial Regulation T and maintenance requirements for naked puts and calls issued by a registered clearing agency is 100% of the current option premium plus a fixed percentage of the value of the underlying instrument, minus any gain, with a minimum requirement of 100% of the current option premium plus another fixed percentage of the value of the underlying instrument. (The value to be used for the underlying instrument is the current market value of the underlying instrument for all options other than those on U.S. Treasury securities. For U.S. Treasury securities, the value to be used is the principal amount.)

The following is a summary of the fixed percentage requirements and underlying value to be used for each type of option:

Security or Index	Initial and/or Maintenance Margin Required*	Minimum Margin Required	Underlying Component Value
1. Stock	15%	5%	The equivalent number of shares at current market prices
2. Industry index stock group	15%	5%	The product of the current index group value and the applicable index multiplier
3. Broad index stock group	5%	2%	The product of the current index group value and the applicable index multiplier
4. U.S. Treasury bills—95 days or less to maturity	.35%	1/20%	The underlying principal amount
5. U.S Treasury notes	3%	1/2%	The underlying principal amount
6. Foreign currencies	4%	3/4%	The product of units per foreign currency contract and the closing spot price.

*Based on premium value plus in-the-money or less out-of- the-money of underlying stock.

Covered call position. If one sells a call option versus a long stock position or versus a convertible security exchangeable for an equivalent number of shares, there are no margin requirements for the option.

If the underlying stock is paid in full, the covered call may be sold in a Special Cash Account. If an appropriate amount of money is held in the account, a put option may be sold in a special cash account. This amount must be sufficient to fully pay for the underlying stock if the option is exercised (that is, the amount must equal the aggregate exercise price of the put option written). Federal regulation permits uncovered call writing positions, short straddles, short combinations, and spreads to be executed only in a margin account.

There is no margin required on exercise of a call option and sale of the underlying stock on the same day or on purchase of the underlying stock and exercise of a put option on the same day. However, the client is required to pay any debit arising from a difference between the cost of the stock purchase and the proceeds from the stock sold.

Uncovered short option margin requirement. In all cases, the minimum equity per position may not be less than the premium plus 5% of the current share price.

Example:

Premium	$ 350
15% of $4,800	720
	1,070
Less: Out-of-money	– 200
Total requirement	$ 870

The option premium is added to the 15% of the current value of the underlying shares. If the option is out of the money, that amount may be subtracted but the minimum amount may never be less than the premium plus 15% of the current shares.

After this initial margin requirement has been met, the position is marked to the market based on fluctuations of the stock price.

Margin requirements for strategies.

Calculations:

Market value of 100 shares of IBM	$ 6,700
15% requirement of market value	× .15
	$1,005
Plus premium	+ 400
	$1,405
Number of put contracts	× 5
Total requirement	$ 7,025
Premium received	– 2,000
Margin call	$ 9,550

If IBM stock declines to 62 one month later, what is the maintenance margin requirement and what maintenance margin call will be issued?

Calculations:

Market value of 100 shares of IBM	$ 6,200
15% requirement of market value	× .15
	$ 930
Plus premium	+ 400
Minimum maintenance margin requirement	$ 1,330
Number of put contracts	× 5
Maintenance margin requirement for put position	$ 6,650

Example: An investor writes uncovered 1 RCA July 30 call at ½ when RCA is trading at $24 (Assume $2,000 initial equity is already in the account.)

Calculations:

Market value of 100 shares of stock	$2,400
15% requirement of market value	× .15
	360
Amount the call option is out-of-the-money	– 600
Since the $120 does not equal the $250 minimum, $250 must be used.	(240)

The minimum would be:

Premium	$ 400
Plus 5% of market value	120
Minimum requirement	$ 520

Margining straddles. An investor writes one straddle (an uncovered put option and an uncovered call option with the same exercise price and expiration date for the same underlying security), necessitating a margin requirement equal to the larger of the put or call requirement figured separately.

Example: A client writes 1 Avon April 40 put at 2⅛ and 1 Avon April 40 call at 8¼ when Avon is trading at $46. (Assume $2,000 initial equity is already in the margin account).

The margin requirement is the greater of either:

1. *Put Computation:*

Market value of 100 shares of stock	$4,600.00
15% requirement of market value	× .15
	$ 690
Plus premium	212.50
	$ 902.50
Less out-of-the-money	600
	$ 302.50

However, the requirement may never be less than 5% of market value and the premium:

Market value	$4,600.00
5% requirement of market value	× .05
	230.00
Plus premium	212.50
Initial margin requirement	$ 442.50

2. *Call Computation:*

Market value of 100 shares of stock	$4,600
15% requirement of market value	× .15
	$ 690
Amount the call option is in-the-money	+ 825
Initial margin requirement for one call option	$1,515

This is the actual requirement. Margin is only required on the greater side of a straddle. The call risk is $1,515 versus the put of $442.50. Consequently, the call side of $1,515 is the requirement.

Because the margin requirement for the call side ($1,515) is the greater of the two computations, the $1,515 is the initial margin requirement.

Example: A client writes 1 Honeywell June 70 put at 9 and writes 1 June 60 call at 5½ when Honeywell is trading at 63.

1. *Put Computation:*

Market value of 100 shares of stock	$6,300
15% requirement of market value	× .15
	$ 945

Margining combinations. The margin requirement is the greater of that for the put side or call side as figured separately plus the premium.

Plus premium	+ 900
Initial margin requirement for one put contract	$1,845

Since $1,845 is higher, that is the requirement.

2. *Call Computation:*

Market value of 100 shares of stock	$6,300
15% requirement of market value	× .15
	$ 945
Premium on the call	+ 550
Initial margin requirement	$1,495

Margining spreads A spread involves buying and writing (selling) options of the same type—puts or calls. Any risk with the position must be margined. If the spread is *qualified,* unique margin requirements may be applied to the spread position. For a spread to be qualified, the short option must expire at the same time as (or before) the long option. If the spread is unqualified, then both options are margined as separate contracts rather than as one position; in other words, the long option must be paid for in full and the short option must be margined as an uncovered option. The following examples pertain to qualified spreads only.

Example: A calendar call spread:

Short 1 April 50 call at 2½	(+ 250)
Long 1 July 50 call at 4	(− 400)
	− 150 spread debit

The first step is to pay for the long call, $400. The premium of $250 received from the short call may be applied toward the payment of the long call. The investor must therefore pay the $150 difference, which in this case is the spread debit. The next step is to determine the risk of being short the call option. By writing the April 50 call, the writer is obligated to deliver 100 shares of stock at 50 if exercised. If the writer is assigned, the writer may exercise the long call and buy 100 shares of stock at 50 to deliver against the assignment notice. Since there is no risk associated with being exercised, because the writer may acquire stock at the same price as for delivery, the margin requirement for the short option is zero.

The margin requirement for calendar put spreads would be determined in the same manner.

Example: A bullish vertical (perpendicular) call spread:

Short 1 May 70 call at 3	(+ 300)
Long 1 May 60 call at 7	(− 700)
	− 400 spread debit

Once again, the long call must be paid for in full, $700. The premium of $300 received from the short call may be applied toward the payment of the long call. So the investor must pay the $400 difference, which in this case is the spread debit.

The next step is to determine the risk of being short the call option. By writing the May 70 call, the writer is obligated to deliver 100 shares of stock at 70 if exercised. If the writer is assigned, the writer may exercise the long call and buy the stock at 60 to deliver against the assignment notice. Since there is no risk associated with being exercised, because the writer may acquire stock at a better price than for delivery, the margin requirement for the short option is zero.

The margin requirement for a bearish vertical (perpendicular) put spread would be determined in the same manner.

Example: A bearish vertical (perpendicular) call spread:

Short 1 June 60 call at 4½	(+ 450)
Long 1 June 65 call at 1½	(− 150)
	+ 300 spread credit

The long call must be paid for in full, $150. The premium of $450 received from the short call may be applied toward the payment of the long call. The investor therefore does not have to pay for the long call from cash out of pocket and has a $300 credit to be used to meet the margin requirements for the short option.

By writing the June 60 call, the writer is obligated to deliver 100 shares of stock at 60 if exercised. If the writer is assigned, the writer may exercise the long call and buy stock at 65 to deliver against the assignment notice. Since the writer buys stock at 65 and delivers (sells) at 60, a $500 loss is generated. The $500 difference between the long aggregate exercise price and the short aggregate exercise price is the risk associated with this spread position, thus creating a margin requirement of $500. The $300 credit may be applied toward the $500 margin requirement. So the margin call is $200.

The margin requirements for a bullish vertical (perpendicular) put spread would be determined in the same manner.

As a general rule, whenever an investor establishes a qualified spread with a debit, the margin requirement is the amount of the debit. Whenever an investor establishes a qualified spread with a credit, the margin requirement is the difference between a long aggregate exercise price and the short aggregate exercise price. Of course, the credit amount may be applied toward meeting the margin requirement of a credit spread.

The above margin requirements pertain to spread positions. The NASD and the NYSE require a minimum equity of $2,000 in the account in order to transact spreads. All spreads must be done in a general (margin) account.

See also Option; Regulation T; Uncovered Option.

Margin Agreement. *See* Customer's Agreement.

Margin Call. A demand for additional funds because of adverse price movement.

Margin Debt Securities. *See* Convertible Bonds (Margin Trading).

Margin Department. *See* Broker/Dealer Organization.

Margin of Profit Ratio. The complement of the expense ratio, this ratio shows the percentage of the sales dollar not eaten up by operating costs. It is derived by dividing operating income by net sales.

$$\text{Margin of profit ratio} = \frac{\text{Operating income}}{\text{Net sales}}$$

Example:

$$\text{Margin of profit ratio} = \frac{\$\,200,000}{2,000,000} = 0.10 \text{ or } 10\%$$

Note that the margin of profit ratio plus the operting ratio equals 100%.

See also Income Statement.

Margin Substitution. Margin customers frequently desire to switch positions in their accounts by selling one security and buying another. The short seller frequently wishes to cover one security and to sell another short. A *margin substitution* is the liquidation of one security in an account to cover the requirement for a commitment of another security on the same trade date. That is, in a substitution any commitment (a trade that establishes a position) can be substituted against any liquidation (any trade which closes out a position.)

Commitment	Liquidation
Purchase	Long sale
Short sale	Cover short

This means that a purchase (commitment) can be substituted against a long sale or a cover short (liquidations). Similarly, a short sale (commitment) can be substituted against a long sale or a cover short (liquidations). In short, anything on the left can be paired with anything on the right and vice versa . But something on the left or on the right cannot be paired with something on the same side.

Equal and Unequal Substitutions

1. *Equal Substitutions*. In an equal substitution the customer pairs a commitment with a liquidation of the same value. With an equal substitution the status of the customer's account remains the same.

Example: Let us illustrate this point. Assume that the status of customer Joe Smith's account is as follows:

LMV	Equity	Balance
$40,000	$20,000	$20,000 Dr

On the same day customer Smith buys $10,000

of AAA stock and sells $10,000 of BBB stock, with a 50% initial requirement. After the two transactions, the account totals are the same (excluding commissions, taxes, and any other fees).

LMV	Equity	Balance
$40,000	$20,000	$20,000 Dr

2. *Unequal substitutions.* In an unequal substitution, the customer pairs a commitment with a liquidation of different value.

Example: A customer may purchase stock of $10,000 value and pair it with a long sale of $5,000. In such a substitution the difference between the two amounts is treated as a net commitment or net liquidation, whichever trade is the larger.

Example: Let us illustrate this point and calculate such a difference. The initial requirement is 50% and customer Joe Smith on the same day sold short $15,000 and covered $10,000 of another short position. What is the Reg T call?

Calculations:
We can offset these two trades because the short sale is a commitment and the cover short is a liquidation.

$ 15,000 short sale
$–10,000 cover short
———————————————
$– 5,000 net commitment

Reg T call = (initial requirement × proceeds) – SMA
= 50% × $5,000 – 0
= $2,500

In the following four examples, use a 50% initial requirement for your calculations; consider all accounts as restricted with no SMA.

Example:

Purchase $10,000 cost
Long sale $ 5,000 proceeds

What is the Reg T call?

Calculation:
Treat as an unequal substitution; treat as a $5,000 purchase (commitment)

Reg T call = 50% × $5,000
= $2,500

Example:

Short sale $18,000 proceeds
Long sale $24,000 proceeds

What is the Reg T excess released to SMA?

Calculation:
Treat as an unreal substitution; treat as a $6,000 long sale (liquidation). This is a restricted account that remains restricted after the sale.

New SMA = (50% × $6,000) + 0
= $3,000

Example:

Purchase $6,000
Cover short $8,000

Account remains restricted after substitution trades.
What is the Reg T excess released to SMA?

Calculations:
Treat as an unequal substitution; the $2,000 not used for substitution is calculated for release ($2,000 × 50% = $1,000), which may be place in the customer's SMA.

Example:

Purchase $ 8,000
Long sale $10,000
Short sale $ 6,000

What is the Reg T call?

Calculations:

Treat as an unequal substitution; treat as either $4,000 purchase or $4,000 short sale ($8,000 + $6,000 − $10,000); requirements are the same.

$$\text{Reg T call} = 50\% \times \$4,000$$
$$= \$2,000$$

See also Margin Account; Short Sale.

Margin Transaction. When customers purchase securities on margin, they in effect establish collateralized loans. The customers agree to leave their securities on deposit with the broker to be held as collateral against funds that they borrow from the broker to make the purchase. The broker holds the securities in street name (that is, in the broker's name) and charges the customers interest on their loans. Specifically a *margin transaction* is one in which the broker renders financial assistance to a customer by extending credit or performing a special financial service such as obtaining a stock loan.

The Federal Reserve Board under Regulation T has established different requirements for various types of margin transactions. The major types of margin transactions are as follows: (1) exchange-listed and OTC margin stocks; (2) U.S. government and municipal bonds; (3) nonconvertible corporate bonds; and (4) arbitrage.

The credit accounts in which these transactions are done are in addition to the most common type of securities account, the cash account. (In the cash account customers are not permitted to borrow funds and must pay for all their purchases in full. Neither are they permitted to execute short sales or to make other types of specialized margin transactions reserved for certain of the margin activities listed above.)

Generally speaking, customers trade on margin for the purpose of utilizing the leverage principle and enhancing their ability to gain a greater return on their investments. Leverage in margin accounts permits customers to buy more shares of a security because they are borrowing funds from the broker. Therefore, if a customer's investment appreciates in value, the rate of return on his or her own capital will be greater. A customer will also trade on margin for the purpose of making specialized types of transactions, such as short sales.

See also Arbitrage Account; Debit Balance; Exempt Security (Margin Trading); Margin Account.

Marketable Securities. This part of a corporation's current assets consists of U.S. government securities. Cash that the company does not need immediately it puts to work by investing it, usually in short-term instruments such as Treasury bills. The value of such investments is shown on the balance sheet at the lower of their cost or their market value; in the vast majority of cases the market value of the securities is higher than their cost, so cost usually appears on the balance sheet. An indication elsewhere, possibly in a footnote, cites the current market value of the securities.

See also Balance Sheet (Assets).

The category of marketable securities includes Treasury bills, Treasury certificates of indebtedness, Treasury notes, and Treasury bonds. These securities are classified as "marketable" because there are continuous bids and offerings for them in the marketplace, and they are freely traded there. Each of these government obligations has at least one unique feature to distinguish it from the others. Their yields are computed in the same way as corporate bond yields.

1. *Treasury bills* are issued with three-month, six-month, and one-year (maximum) maturities. They are issued and traded at a discount from face value. Denominations vary.

2. *Certificates of indebtedness* carry maturities ranging up to one year and are issued in denominations of $1,000 to $500 million. Unlike Treasury bills, they have a fixed rate of interest.

3. *Treasury notes* are available in bearer or registered form, in denominations of $1,000 to $500 million, with maturities of one to ten years, and with a fixed rate of interest.

4. *Treasury bonds*, registered or bearer form, have maturities from 5 to 35 years in duration. Carrying a fixed interest rate on face values of $500 to $1 million, they trade at a percentage of face value.

See also Bearer Bond Certificates; Certificates of Indebtedness, Registered Bond; U.S. Treasury Bills; U.S. Treasury Bonds; U.S. Treasury Notes.

Market Index (NYSE). *See New York Times* Market Indicators.

Market-Maker. This options exchange member trades for his or her own account and risk. The member is charged with the responsibility of trading so as to maintain a fair, orderly, and competitive market. He or she may not act as agent. The term may also refer to a firm actively making bids and offers in the OTC market.

Market-Maker in the Pink Sheets. The ability to proclaim oneself a market-maker in the NQB pink sheets is not restricted to NASD members. Any subscriber may advertise his or her willingness to trade in specific stocks. To avoid the possibility of fraudulent representation and manipulation of price, especially for shares of small "shell" corporations that are virtually assetless, the SEC implemented Rule 15c2—11 in 1971. (The SEC acted because it, rather than the NASD, has power over these corporations.) This rule requires anyone submitting bid or offering prices to any quotation medium, or indicating a willingness to be a market-maker in a particular security, insure that one of the following circumstances prevails:

1. The issuer has in existence a registration statement effective within the previous ninety days (forty days for statements filed under Regulation A) that is not the subject of an SEC stop order, and the broker/dealer has on file a copy of the prospectus (or offering circular under Regulation A).

2. The corporation files periodic reports with SEC, the broker/dealer has a reasonable basis for believing that the corporation is current in its filing, and the broker/dealer has in its files a copy of the corporation's most recent annual report required to be filed with the SEC (as distinguished from the annual report sent to stockholders).

3. The broker/dealer firm has the following information on file concerning the corporation and makes it available to any person interested in a proposed transaction. It must also furnish this information to the quotation medium at least two days before the quotation is to be published: (a) the exact name of the issuer and its predecessor; (b) the address of its principal executive offices; (c) the state of incorporation, if it is a corporation; (d) the exact title and class of the security; (e) the par or stated value of the security; (f) the number of shares or total amount of the securities outstanding as of the end of the issuer's most recent fiscal year; (g) the name and address of the transfer agent; (h) the nature of the products or services offered by the issuer; (j) the nature and extent of the issuer's facilities; (k) the name of the chief executive officer and members of the board of directors; (l) the issuer's most recent balance sheet, profit-and-loss, and retained earnings statements; (m) similar financial information for whatever portion of the two preceding fiscal years the issuer or its predecessor has been

in existence; (n) whether the broker/dealer or associated person is affiliated directly or indirectly with the issuer; (o) whether the quotation is being published or submitted on behalf of any other broker/dealer, and if so, the name of such broker/dealer; and (p) whether the quotation is being submitted or published on behalf of the issuer, or any director, officer, or any person who is the beneficial owner of more than 10% of the outstanding units or shares of any equity security of the issuer. (If so, the name of such person, and the basis for any exemption under federal securities laws for any sales of such securities on behalf of such person, must be stated.)

However, the provisions of this important rule do not apply to (1) quotations of any security traded on a national securities exchange that same day or on the business day before submission to the quotation system; (2) quotations of foreign securities and ADRs exempt from compliance with the Securities Exchange Act of 1934, Rule 12(g); or (3) quotations of any security already reflected in an interdealer system at specified prices on at least twelve days within the previous thirty calendar days and having no more than a four-business-day gap without a two-sided quotation.

Market-Maker Under NASDAQ. To qualify as a registered market-maker under NASDAQ rules, broker/dealers must do the following:

1. They must continuously maintain net capital of $50,000 or $5,000 for each security in which they will provide quotations, whichever is the lower amount.

2. They must honor their quotations for at least the normal unit of trading (usually 100 shares or 10 bonds, as the case may be). Failure to do so is a violation of the NASD Rules of Fair Practice and is called *backing away.*

3. They must maintain trading hours of at least 10:00 A.M.- 4:00 P.M. eastern time.

4. They must agree to file daily and monthly reports of trading activities, as required by the NASD Board of Governors.

5. They must apply to NASDAQ for permission to participate as a market-maker in each security desired. Dealers may enter their own quotations at the start of business on the second business day following submission of their applications.

See also National Association of Securities Dealers Automated Quotations; National Quotation Bureau Inc; Specialist.

Market Order. This order is one in which the customer requests execution immediately at the best available price. Thus, a market order to buy stock requires purchase at the lowest offering price available at the time of entry. A market order to sell stock requires disposition at the highest bid price available at the time of entry.

If a member fails to honor such instructions due to negligence, the member is guilty of *missing the market.* This oversight requires that the member promptly reimburse the customer for any loss resulting from this mistake. Missing the market certainly does not occur often, but it can happen if a member accidentally misplaces the order after receiving it from the telephone clerk or if the member foolishly accepts too many market orders in different securities at the same time. In the latter situation, if the member is executing an order at one end of the trading room, it is possible to miss the market in another order at the opposite end of the floor.

See also At-the-Opening Order; Buy Minus; Choosing Types of Stock Orders; Limit Order; Sell Plus; Stop Order; Switch Order.

Market Order (Odd-Lot).

1. *To Buy or to Sell Long.* Just as round-lot market orders require execution at the best available price, so, too, do odd-lot market orders, but with one modification. Because odd-lot orders have no standing in the trading crowd (that is, they may not be bid, offered, or used to initiate

transactions), these orders must wait until a round-lot execution occurs. The *first* round-lot transaction after receipt by the specialist serves as the effective sale for all odd-lot market orders to buy or sell stock long (see the following table).

Sample Odd-Lot Market Order Executions

Order	Next Round-Lot Transaction	Execution Price
Buy at market	12	12⅛ (12 + ⅛)
Buy at market	37¼	37⅜ (37¼ + ⅛)
Buy at market	87⅝	83¾ (87⅝ + ⅛)
Sell long at market	21⅞	21¾ (21⅞ − ⅛)
Sell long at market	46	45⅞ (46 − ⅛)
Sell long at market	101½	101⅜ (101½ − ⅛)

2. *To Sell Short.* Odd-lot market orders to sell short impose one additional requirement to execute such orders in compliance with federal and exchange regulations. Specifically, in an odd-lot short sale, the effective sale must be higher in value than the last round-lot transaction at a different price.

Example: Assume the sequence of round-lot transactions shown on the following ticker tape:

40⅛, 40, 40⅛, 40⅛, 40⅛
(1)   (2)   (3)   (4)   (5)

Trade 2 is lower in value than 40⅛ and cannot qualify as an effective sale for an odd-lot short seller. Trade 3 is higher in value than the previous transaction at 40 and can qualify as an effective sale for an odd-lot short seller. Trades 4 and 5 are also higher in value than 40 (which was the last different-price transaction), and can, therefore, also qualify as an effective sale for an odd-lot short seller. This requirement prevents an odd-lot short seller from being instrumental in depressing the price of the security. The following table lists some sample odd-lot market executions to sell short.

Sample Odd-Lot Market Order Executions to Sell Short

Previous Round-Lot Transaction	Terms	Subsequent Round-Lot Transactions*	Execution Price
16¼	Sell short at market	16⅜, 16¼, 16⅛	16¼ (16⅜ − ⅛)
37⅝	Sell short at market	37½, 37⅜, 37½	37⅜ (37½ − ⅛)
74	Sell short at market	73⅞, 74, 74⅛	73⅞ (74 − ⅛)
126¼	Sell short at market	126, 125½, 126½	126⅜ (126½ − ⅛)

*Boxed price is the effective sale because exchange rules require execution of an odd-lot order based on the first possible round-lot price.

See also Differential; Odd-Lot Stock Execution.

Market Value (Price). (1) The last reported sale price for an exchange-traded security.

(2) For over-the-counter securities, a consensus among marketmakers.

See also Par Value.

Mark to Market. The daily adjustment of an account to reflect profits and losses. The UPC provides the membership with protection from the hazard of volatile prices by permitting the unsecured member to *mark to the market*. A *mark to the market* is a written demand by a broker/dealer who is unsecured on an open or pending contract to furnish collateral equal to the difference between the original contract value and the current market value of that security. The broker satisfies this request by depositing sufficient funds with that member firm or in a mutually agreed-upon depository. This arrangement is also used for securities loans between broker/dealers. Deposits and/or refunds can continually be adjusted while the agreement is pending. To ensure the safety of funds deposited with a broker/dealer, the Uniform Practice Committee requires that they be segregated on the books of the firm.

For example, if the value of a borrowed security appreciates, the certificate lender demands more money as collateral; if it declines, the certificate borrower demands a partial refund of its money. This continuous adjustment process is called marking to the market. A mark may be exchanged between borrowing and lending firms as often as necessary to maintain these loans equitably. Sometimes they are even exchanged when the security fluctuates as little as one or two points from the last valuation.

See also Buy-In Procedures; Borrowing Stock Certificates.

Markup and Markdown. When a firm acts as principal in a transaction (that is, it acts directly with the customer as a trader on the opposite side of the order, the difference between this firm's lower cost price and its sale price to the customer is known as its *markup.*

Example: A firm might report the following transaction to its customer, "As principal, we are selling to you for your account and risk 100 shares of Connecticut General Insurance Company at 65¾ net." The dealer has a markup of one point because it bought the shares at 64¾ and sold them to the customer at 65¾. Under NASD remuneration rules, markups must be fair and reasonable. Conversely, if the customer is a seller and the firm buys as principal, the difference between the lower price paid to the customer and the sale price to the market-maker is called a *markdown,* and it too must be fair and reasonable.

Example: If the dealer buys "Conn Gen" shares at 64¼ from Sam Smith and sells them to a market-maker at 64¾, then the firm has a half point markdown.

The customer's report of execution does not *always* reveal the markup or markdown, and, therefore, in the public interest, interpretation of the phrase "fair and reasonable" becomes a matter of ethics. Fair and reasonable also applies to agency transactions, but the required disclosure of commission in these cases ordinarily does not lend itself to the potential inequities of principal transactions.

The 5% Guideline Policy. The markup and markdown issue was thoroughly investigated by the NASD Board of Governors in 1943, at which time the association formulated its basic policy on the subject. This policy, subsequently interpreted and reaffirmed in several disciplinary proceedings, is not a rule or regulation because the Board of Governors realized that it is virtually impossible to define the term *fair* in a random trading situation.

Instead, the board implemented a 5% guideline, which requires consideration of all relevant factors on each transaction. The policy does not mean that a member will be in violation of the guideline if its markup/markdown exceeds 5%. (The markup is calculated based on the prevailing offering price by market-makers; the markdown is calculated on the prevailing bid price by market-makers.) On the other hand, it does not mean that a member firm will be safe from prosecution if it stays below 5%, either. Rather, it requires the member to consider all of the Board's suggestions as an overall package and then allow its judgment and the association's code of ethics to guide its decision. The firm must be prepared to defend that decision if a complaint is lodged against it.

The 5% guideline does not apply to transactions that require delivery of a prospectus or offering circular, after which the securities are sold at the specific public offering price stated therein. Those transactions include SEC- registered public offerings of corporate securities and open- end investment company shares. (mutual funds). Otherwise, it is effective for all securities transactions in the over-the- counter marketplace, including oil and gas leases, royalties, listed securities in the third market, and others. It also encompasses consideration of a wide variety of related activities in the over-the-counter market such as proceeds sales and simultaneous transactions.

Considerations in Applying the 5% Policy.

1. *Type of security involved.* Most stocks customarily involve a greater degree of market risk for a dealer with an inventory than for one who positions a similar amount of value in bonds. Therefore, other factors notwithstanding, stock transactions employ higher percentage markups and markdowns than do bond transactions.

2. *Availability of the security in the market.* Closely held or inactively traded securities, which often necessitate unusual effort or cost for purchase or sale, may permit higher than usual percentage markups and markdowns.

3. *Price of the security.* Arithmetically speaking, lower- priced securities usually carry higher percentage markups and markdowns, while higher-priced securities entail lower percentage profits on similar transactions.

Example:

⅛-point ($.125) markup on a $ 1 stock = 12.5% profit +

⅛-point ($.125) markup on a $50 stock = 0.25% profit

Yet the ⅛-point markup is allowed for the $1 stock in order to make it worthwhile for a dealer to execute transactions in such a low-priced security. For this reason a dealer may have the same ⅛-point markup on a $1 stock as on a $50 stock. Each brings the firm only a $.125 profit though the percentages are quite different.

4. *Amount of money involved in a transaction.* Following similar logic, minimal amounts of money carry higher percentage markups and markdowns to cover the cost of processing such activity. Orders involving substantial sums, conversely, carry smaller percentage profits.

5. *Disclosure.* Revealing the amount of markup or even commission prior to a transaction is a factor to consider. However, this in itself is not sufficient cause for justifying unfair prices or excessive charges because most unsophisticated investors have no basis or knowledge for comparison.

6. *Pattern of markups and markdowns.* The history of a dealer organization's pricing policies is an important factor, too, although this will not condone a member's practice of gouging unsuspecting customers. What is pertinent here is an examination of a member firm's economic relationship with its customers to see that it is according them fair and equal treatment on transactions.

7. *Nature of a member's business.* Owing to the wide variety of services offered by some members, the 5% guideline policy has enough flexibility to permit these organizations to pass along the expense of maintaining continuous customer conveniences. However, the NASD does not excuse the use of excessive or improper charges for services or facilities that are necessary to the performance of a member's business.

The NASD member must be prepared to defend any markup or commission charge in relation to these factors considered collectively in order to highlight extenuating circumstances peculiar to the transaction.

See also Interpositioning; Principal Transaction; Proceeds Sale; Simultaneous Transaction.

Matched Orders. These sales and purchases by the same beneficial owner of the same security at the same time and price give the impression of extensive trading in that security. This is a violation of the Securities Exchange Act of 1934.

See also Manipulation of Security Prices and Deceptive Devices.

Maximum Price Fluctuation. The maximum amount the contract price can change, up or down, during one trading session, as fixed by Exchange rules.

Member Firm. This term is used to describe a company that has an officer or partner a member of the New York Stock Exchange, another organized exchange, or clearing corporation.

See also New York Stock Exchange, Inc.

Member's Orders. *See* Municipal Security (Priority of Orders).

Message Switching. *See* Broker/Dealer Organization (Order Department).

Microfilm Records. *See* Reporting Requirements of the SEC (Brokers and Dealers).

Minimum Capital. *See* Financial Protection Requirements (NYSE).

Minimum Maintenance Requirement NYSE). *See* Margin Account (Long Account).

Minumum Price Fluctuation. Smallest increment of price movement possible in trading a given contract. Also called tick or point.

Missing the Market. The failure by a member of the exchange to execute an order due to his or her negligence is called *missing the market*. The member is obliged to promptly reimburse the customer for any losses due to the mistake.

See also Limit Order; Market Order.

Money. Mention the word "money" to most people, and they probably think in terms of the paper bills and coins they use to pay for many goods and services. This is technically known as *currency in circulation*, and it represents only a small fraction of what is actually used to support the American economy. The term *money* means much more to an economist or a banker. Both realize that money is primarily credit, and credit is a "product" manufactured or withheld by the banking institutions in the United States. Real economic growth is predicated on the willingness and ability of (1) a borrower to obtain credit and (2) a bank to extend credit. Without either of these essential factors, industrial/agricultural production may increase near-term, but ultimately it declines—with accelerating velocity. The long-term consequences are unemployment and a lower standard of living—that is, either a business recession or depression, depending on the severity of the decline.

The Federal Reserve defines a couple of types of money supply. *M-1* is currency in circulation, plus all kinds of checking accounts (interest-paying or not). *M-2* is equal to M-1 plus savings deposits under $100,000, some overnight bank borrowings in the domestic and Eurodollar market, repurchase agreements between banks and individuals, plus most money market mutual funds.

Money Market Company. Historically unique financial conditions prevailing in the late 1970s and early 1980s led to the popularity, development, and growth of money market investment companies. Stated simply, this was because financial debt instruments with short-term maturities were yielding investors significantly higher rates of return than intermediate or long-term obligations of governmental or corporate issuers. This is a situation known as a negative yield curve. Coupled with that was the fact that thrift institutions (savings banks, savings and loan associations, and others) were paying interest to savings depositors at 5-6% when money market instruments were yielding 15-16%. The situation was ripe for an investment vehicle that could provide the public with these higher rates of return at nominal risk—an investment with immediate liquidity in times of financial need. Money market investment companies were organized to satisfy these demands.

Structured as Massachusetts business trusts

or as corporate entities, these investment companies offer subscribers a fractional interest in a portfolio of short-term debt securities. The average maturity of issues in that constantly changing portfolio is generally less than ninety days. The holdings, which vary from company to company, differ in proportion as to U.S. Treasury, government agency, bank certificates of time deposit (CD), bankers' acceptance, repurchase agreements, and commercial paper debt instruments. This diversity of assets provides investors with more protection of principal in the event of a default than if holdings were concentrated in just a few issues. The fact that subscribers' monies are pooled in these investment companies enables management to buy and sell in large quantities. It gives management an opportunity to negotiate better transaction prices (thus increasing yield) in a marketplace where less than a few million dollars is considered an "odd lot."

Money market investment companies are open-ended. That is, they offer an unlimited number of participations to subscribers and, by the same token, stand ready to redeem any specified amount of a holder's interest in that fund. Share or unit purchases may be made directly from the investment company or through an authorized agent, such as a broker/dealer or custodial bank. There is no sales charge levied on purchases or sales. All transactions are arranged at net asset value of the securities then held in the company's portfolio. Payment is required in the form of federal funds (FF) because of the nature of securities settlement procedures in this money instrument marketplace. Therefore, a subscriber's deposit of an ordinary check drawn on a personal account is not actually invested until the second day after receipt by the investment company. It normally takes that long to convert clearing house funds (CH) into federal funds. Redemption requests may be handled in a variety of ways.

1. *By telephone.* Holders may authorize the same-day liquidation of a specified amount of asset value by calling a certain phone number and providing appropriate identification. The company honors the request based on value determined at the close of business that day (normally 4:00 P.M. eastern time) and, at the holder's preference, either (a) sends its CH check for those proceeds or (b) wires FF proceeds to a designated bank account the following business day.

2. *By mail.* Holders may authorize the liquidation of a specified amount of asset value by sending written instructions to a designated address. Redemption requests must be in proper form with signatures guaranteed by a domestic bank or recognized broker/dealer organization. On acceptance, the company honors the request at the close of business that day and sends its check for the proceeds as soon as possible thereafter.

3. *By check writing privilege.* Holders may issue checks payable to any third party drawn on the asset value in their money market account. The free draft privileges offered by these funds provide investors with several obvious advantages. First, dividends continue to accrue for the benefit of the fund holder until the check is presented for payment and the assets are actually liquidated (redeemed). Second, while some money market investment companies have set minimum dollar amounts for the writing of checks against holdings (that is, $500 or $250), most do not, enabling subscribers to use this privilege in lieu of unproductive ordinary checking accounts at commercial banks. Monthly statements are provided for reconciliation purposes. Complete liquidations of account cannot be completed by this method. Below some preset balance, varying from fund to fund, holders must use the telephone or mail method for redemption.

The most unique feature of money market investment companies is that they calculate, declare, and pay dividends daily to their holders.

Those dividends are reinvested and distributed monthly in the form of additional shares or units, at net asset value, to all entitled holders. Monthly statements serve as official notification for these distributions although investors liquidating their accounts before month end are paid their dividends through the day of redemption. Dividends for these investment companies are comprised of and defined as: (1) interest payments receivable from the obligors whose securities are held in portfolio; (2) interest payments receivable from repurchase agreements arranged with broker/dealers or banks; (3) net premiums receivable for securities loaned to qualified institutions and broker/dealers; (4) the discounted amount, accreted daily, for securities bought below face value and redeemable at par at maturity; (5) the appreciation in market value of securities in portifolio, calculated daily, including amounts over and above the acreted discount for certain issues.

From those positive factors the following negative corrections are also undertaken to arrive at the daily dividend figure: (1) the premium amount, amortized daily, for securities bought above face value and redeemable at par at maturity; (2) the decline in market value of securities in portfolio, calculated daily, including amounts over and above the amortized premium for certain issues; and (3) the estimated expenses of the fund including custodial, management, and SEC share registration fees.

Note that while these investment instruments have short maturities, their market values fluctuate to reflect changes in short-term interest rates. As rates rise, the prices of these instruments decline. The inverse relationship is also true. These value changes, prompted by interest rate volatility, are recognized each day and serve to increase or decrease the amount of dividend payable to money market fund holders. Although interest and premiums receivable usually well exceed subtractions for downward price adjustments, on a day when interest rates rise shar-

ply, the fund could have a negative dividend calculation! This means redemptions must be effected to give back previously paid dividends which had been reinvested in additional shares or units. Recognize that, while income is derived from interest, premiums, and trading profits, it is distributed to holders as nonqualifying dividends—that is, as dividends not entitled to the individual's $100 exclusion or the corporation's 85% exclusion from federal tax liability.

Another interesting and unique feature of money market investment companies is the fact that because they pay out all dividends each day, they can and do maintain their net asset value at a simple $1 per share/unit. Purchase and redemption calculations are thus greatly facilitated for investors. There are no additional charges.

Dividend distribution is an important function for determining yield, the lure for most investing in a money market investment company. The specific method may vary somewhat among interest distributed for a specified period by the average net asset value for the same period. Unrealized gains and losses are not taken into account when making this calculation. The result is then annualized on a 365-day basis.

Example: Most companies calculate yield on a continuing base period of seven calendar days. Every day they add the day's figures and remove the earliest numbers for the preceding seven days, projecting that result out over 365 days to arrive at a rolling average yield. Refer to the following figure for a comparison of average yields and maturities of securities in portfolios of most publicly available money market funds.

The individual subscriber's yield may differ somewhat from that which is published by virtue of a service charge levied by the custodian of the account. That charge, $25-$50 annually, impacts accounts differently because of their variance in size and the way this fee is charged to the subscriber. Some custodians deduct it once each year and others prorate the amount and deduct it monthly.

Other expenses to be considered are those borne by the fund itself. They are already taken into consideration in the calculation of its net asset value. The largest is a management fee paid to the fund's advisors for portfolio and administrative services. The fee is charged to the fund on the basis of its average daily net assets and ranges from an annualized rate of ¼-½% depending on the size of those assets. The larger net assets incur the smaller percentage rates. A second expense is a fee charged by the fund's agent bank for custody and processing services relating to securities in the funds portfolio. It is work-related and the aggregate dollars expended depend on the size of the portfolio and the fund's trading activity. The last recognizable expense is the cost of registering new shares or units with the SEC. As publicly offered securities, participations in the money market investment companies must be SEC registered prior to sale. As the fund grows, more shares or units must be registered for sale thus incurring filing expenses in behalf of the fund. Any other costs, such as advertising or sales promotion are borne by the management group from its advisory fee.

See also Diversified Company; Investment Company; Management Company; Net Asset Value Per Share.

Money Market Instruments. As contrasted with capital notes, bonds, or debentures, money market instruments are debt securities that are issued and will mature in a relatively short period of time—usually within one year. Bankers' acceptances, certificates of deposit, and commercial paper are some securities that fall into this classification.

See also Bankers' Acceptance; Certificate of Deposit; Commercial Paper.

Money Settlement. *See* Stock Clearing Corporation.

Moral Suasion. An expression used to denote the Federal Reserve Board's ability to influence member bank financial policies by threatening to employ drastic powers in order to gain compliance with its own preferences.

See also Federal Reserve System.

Mortgage Bond. These bonds are the most prevalent form of secured obligation in this country today. The investor's protection rests on the pledge of the real assets of the corporation, such as real estate. At the time of the offering, the property is valued for more than the amount of money borrowed so that the bondholder has significant protection. If the borrowing agreement has an *open-end* provision, the corporation can use that same property as collateral for future borrowing. Those future creditors will have an equal claim to that property in the event of default.

On the other hand, if the agreement is drawn with a *closed-end* provision, any future borrowing using the same property as collateral will be junior to the claims of the previous bondholders. Several heavily indebted corporations have thus issued first, second, and third mortgage bonds, all secured by the same piece of property. The first mortgage bondholder has a senior claim on this real estate if the company defaults on payment of interest or repayment of principal.

See also Collateral Trust Bond; Debenture; Equipment Trust Bond; Prior Lien Bond.

Mortgage REIT. *See* Real Estate Investment Trust.

Multiplier Effect of Credit Power. Despite Federal Reserve requirements, the credit power of commercial banks is impressive, far exceeding the amount of money held as a reserve. This is due to the *multiplier effect*, which is the concept that banks' loan power expands or shrinks with decreases or increases in reserve requirements.

Example: The following uses an assumed requirement of 18%, applicable to demand deposits of Reserve City Banks. The table assumes that the credit balance created in a checking account via loan or actual deposit of money will circulate exclusively within the banking system as depositors draw on it to pay their creditors for the goods and services they purchase. That is, the money loaned by Bank 1 is deposited in Bank 2, the money loaned by Bank 2 is deposited in Bank 3, and so forth.

Observe how $100 in currency actually supports more than five times that amount in credit availability. On the basis of $100, Bank 1 loans $82 while setting aside $18 as reserves. When the $82 is deposited in Bank 2, that bank now loans $67.24 to someone while setting aside $14.76 as reserves. This multiplier effect, carried through 20 banks, allows the original $100 deposit in Bank 1 to support over $545 in checking-deposit balances.

If the Federal Reserve Board of Governors

The Multiplier Effect on Bank Deposits

Member Banks	Checking Account Deposit Balances*	Money Loaned*	Money Set Aside as Reserves*
Bank 1	$100.00	$82.00	$18.00
Bank 2	82.00	67.24	14.76
Bank 3	67.24	55.14	12.10
Bank 4	55.14	45.21	9.93
Bank 5	45.21	37.07	8.14
Bank 6	37.07	30.40	6.67
Bank 7	30.40	24.93	5.47
Bank 8	24.93	20.44	4.49
Bank 9	20.44	16.76	3.68
Bank 10	16.76	13.74	3.02
Bank 11	13.74	11.27	2.47
Bank 12	11.27	9.24	2.03
Bank 13	9.24	7.58	1.66
Bank 14	7.58	6.22	1.36
Bank 15	6.22	5.10	1.12
Bank 16	5.10	4.18	.92
Bank 17	4.18	3.43	.75
Bank 18	3.43	2.81	.62
Bank 19	2.81	2.30	.51
Bank 20	2.30	1.89	.41
Total for 20 Banks	$545.06	$446.95	$98.11
Additional Banks	+ 10.50	+ 8.61	+ 1.89
Total for All Banks*	$555.56	$455.56	$100.00

*Some figures have been rounded off.

raises the reserve requirement for demand deposits to its legal limit of 22% from 18%, $100 in currency can support only $454.55 in credit. Thus an increase of 4% in the reserve requirement creates an 18% decline in deposit balances. The multiplier effect works effectively in both directions.

Actual credit statistics are never so precisely accurate as they appear in theory. All currency is not deposited in banks for use as their bases of reserves. The public retains and circulates some funds for everyday money transactions. Currency in circulation is therefore an adverse credit factor for the banking community because it prevents banks from expanding loan accounts to the maximum levels possible. At various times of the year, when demand for credit is strong and currency in circulation is at an unusually high level, commercial banks may become strapped for cash reserves. The Federal Reserve Board takes this currency factor into consideration when determining current monetary policy for the banking system. However, it is not the sole consideration. It is merely a component of an overall analysis of the nation's money supply. M-1 is currency in circulation plus all kinds of checking accounts, whether they pay interest or not.

M-2 consists of M-1 plus savings deposits under $100,000, certain overnight bank borrowings in the domestic and Eurodollar market, repurchase agreements between banks and individuals, plus most money market mutual funds.

See also Federal Reserve System; Velocity.

Municipal Bonds/Notes. *See* Municipal Security.

Municipal Securities Rulemaking Board MSRB). The 1975 amendments to the 1934 Securities Exchange Act mandated the SEC to appoint a Municipal Securities Rulemaking Board (MSRB). The purpose of the MSRB is to formulate entry standards, operating rules, and procedures appropriate for municipal securities concerns that are obliged to register with the SEC under the 1934 Act.

The MSRB is composed of 15 persons; 5 from the banking industry, 5 from the brokerage industry, and 5 who are not affiliated with the municipal securities industry and who represent the interests of the general public. The MSRB's rules thus far parallel those of the NASD. Accordingly, the MSRB has designated the NASD to enforce comnpliance with MSRB rules, although only in the case of the large majority of municipal securities concerns that also happen to be NASD members. Supervision of the banking industry's municipal broker/dealers remains the responsibility of various bank regulators.

Prior to 1975, firms that dealt exclusively with municipal securities (or government issues) were not required to register with the SEC and were for the most part unregulated. While the great majority of such dealers were highly ethical, a significant number of fraudulent trading practices came to light and caused extensive losses for many investors. Technically any fraudulent activity in securities was covered by the Securities Exchange Act of 1934. Yet there was no effective means of policing exempt transactions by firms that belonged neither to an exchange nor to the National Association of Securities Dealers.

On September 5, 1975, the Municipal Securities Rulemaking Board (MSRB) was established pursuant to the enactment of the Securities Acts Amendment of 1975. The MSRB was designed to function as an independent, self-regulatory organization charged with the primary rulemaking authority for the municipal industry. Thus the creation of the MSRB established rules of fair trade practice, uniform practice procedures, and registration of municipal securities brokers/dealers with the MSRB.

Organization. The MSRB consists of fifteen members, five representatives from each of the following three categories: banks, brokers/dealers, and the public. Of the public representatives, one must be a representative of *investors* of municipal securities and one must be a representative of *issuers* of municipal securities.

Funding. The MSRB is funded by three methods: (1) An *initial* fee of $100 from each municipal securities broker/dealer registered with the Securities and Exchange Commission. (2) An assessment of $0.01 per $1,000 of face amount of new municipal securities purchased through an issuer of such securities with maturities of two years or more. (3) An annual fee of $100 from each municipal securities broker/dealer.

Registration. There are three registration categories under the MSRB: (1) municipal securities representative, (2) municipal securities principal, and (3) financial and operations principal. Persons associated with a municipal securities broker/dealer are considered *municipal securities representatives* if their activities include underwriting, trading, or sales of municipal securities; giving financial advice to issuers of municipal securities; or giving research or investment advice with respect to municipal securities. Persons associated with a municipal securities broker/dealer are considered *municipal securities principals* if their activities include the management or supervision of a municipal securities representative; the processing or safekeeping of municipal securities; or the training of municipal securities principals or representatives. Persons associated with a municipal securities broker/dealer are considered *financial and operations principal* if their functions include the preparation of, or the supervision or the preparation of, the financial reports required to be submitted to the SEC; or the supervision of the individuals who are involved in the processing and safekeeping of the municipal securities.

Thus all sales personnel must be registered with the MSRB and, unless exempted due to extensive prior experience, must pass a qualifying examination. Successful completion of this examination permits the representative to solicit *only* municipal securities or U.S. government and agency securities. It *does not* qualify the representative to solicit any corporate securities, including the popular municipal bond unit investment trusts. These, as well as municipal bond mutual funds, are registered investment companies, and any solicitation for their purchase would require an NASD registration. In fact, during the first ninety days of employment, new candidates for MSRB registration may not make any solicitation for customer business *at all* and may not advise customers in any way involving securities. The only persons the candidate may discuss municipal securities with are those also employed in the municipal securities industry.

Enforcement. Unlike either the NYSE or the NASD, the MSRB itself does not *enforce* the rules it promulgates. The actual enforcement belongs to the NASD if the firm involved is a nonbank dealer. If, on the other hand, the firm involved is a bank dealer, supervision and discipline stem from one of the following (depending on the bank's charter): (1) the Federal Deposit Insurance Corporation (FDIC), (2) the Federal Reserve Board (FRB) or, (3) the Comptroller of the Currency.

Note that the U.S. Treasury itself is *not* involved in the enforcement of MSRB rules. Also, while the MSRB rules apply to dealers and underwriters of municipal securities, the issuers are not so regulated. The Glass-Steagall Act of 1933 prohibits commercial banks from underwriting revenue bonds.

Another important distinction to be made is how the MSRB rules define *customer* as "any person other than a broker, dealer, or municipal securities dealer acting in its capacity as such or an issuer in transactions involving the sale by the issuer of a new issue of its securities." Therefore, a dealer bank or broker/dealer trading for its own portfolio is not a customer; and issuers are customers except when dealing in their own issues.

Record Keeping. The MSRB also requires strict adherence to its rules regarding the preservation of certain records. Every municipal securities firm must preserve for at least six years: (1) records of purchases and sales of securities, receipts and deliveries of securities, cash receipts and disbursements; (2) clients' account records; (3) securities records; (4) syndicate transactions records;(5) customer complaint records; and (6) general ledgers.

Every municipal securities firm must preserve for at least three years: (1) records of securities in transfer, borrowed, loaned or to be validated (known as subsidiary records); (2) records of agency and principal transactions; (3) copies of confirmations; (4) cancelled checks and bank statements; (5) bills receivable and payable; (6) all written communications received and sent; (7) all powers of attorney; (8) customer account information; and (9) all records relating to fingerprinting.

All articles of incorporation or partnership, charter, minute books, and stock certificate books must be preserved for the life of the enterprise.

Ethical Practices. Some regulations involving business ethics have been established by the MSRB. There is no rule quite like the NASD's "5%" markup/markdown policy regarding principal transactions. There is, however, a requirement. There is, however, a requirement that all members give and abide by fair quotations that reflect current market prices. The prices at which securities are purchased from and sold to customers should be "fair and reasonable," taking into consideration all relevant factors. Members are prohibited from publishing quotations that are not bona fide: They must be actual bids and

offers to trade at the quoted prices. One exception involves "nominal" (information) quotes that may be published if clearly identified as such.

To help prevent undue influence leading to preferential treatment of some clients, employees of MSRB members are prohibited from receiving or giving gratuities in excess of $100 per year. An occasional ticket to the theater or a sporting event would not violate this policy.

Similar to the NYSE and the NASD, the MSRB has established uniform practice procedures among the members. Most of the procedures address provisions for delivering and receiving municipal securities certificates.

Good Delivery. The Board has stated the *good delivery* requirements for municipal securities. Like stocks, municipal securities settle regular way in five business days. Cash trades settle on the trade date itself. "When-, as-, and if-issued" trades may settle anywhere from six business days to the time stated in the final confirmation. A delayed delivery is any date agreed on by both the buyer and seller.

Because of the complexity and number of laws surrounding municipal finance, it is imperative the buyer be assured that the issue is in conformity with all such laws. For this reason, the issuer retains a recognized law firm specializing in municipal securities to give a *legal opinion* in which the attorneys declare that the bond is indeed a legally binding obligation of the issuer and that the interest payments are exempt from current federal income taxes. So important is this opinion that municipal bonds are not a good delivery if this opinion is lacking. The problem is largely solved by printing this opinion on the face of the bond certificate. (Some older issues may have the legal opinion on a separate document.) Occasionally such bonds are offered for sale *ex-legal* (missing the legal opinion). Provided the buyer agrees to accept delivery ex-legal before the trade is made, the ex-legal delivery is permissible. Otherwise, ex-legal deliveries are not acceptable. The expenses connected with obtaining a legal opinion are generally borne by the issuer.

At times the bearer certificate is mutilated and may not be in good delivery form. If any of the following items cannot be ascertained properly, the certificate may be deemed mutilated: (1) name of issuer, (2) par value, (3) signature, (4) coupon rate, (5) maturity date, (6) seal of the issuer, and (7) bond or note number.

If a certificate is mutilated, then the broker/dealer must have the certificate validated by the trustee, registrar, transfer agent, paying agent, or issuer of the securities or by an authorized agent or official of the issuer. Also, for a bond to be good delivery, all unpaid coupons must be attached to the bond. One exception is that, if delivery is due within thirty calendar days prior to an interest payment date, the seller may deliver a check to the purchaser payable on the delivery date in the amount of the interest due in lieu of the coupon. A coupon may be considered mutilated if the name of the issuer, bond or note number, coupon number, payment date, or signature cannot be properly identified.

Upon delivery of municipal securities to the buying broker/dealer by the selling broker/dealer, the buyer has the right of rejection. The *right of rejection* is the refusal of the securities by the buyer due to the certificate not being in good delivery form.

If the securities have been delivered and then either the buying broker/dealer or selling broker/dealer realizes the certificate does not constitute a good delivery, either party has the right of reclamation. *Reclamation* is the returning of securities by the buyer to the seller; or the demanding of the return of the securities from the buyer by the seller. The key difference between rejection and reclamation is that rejection takes place before acceptance of delivery, whereas reclamation takes place after acceptance of delivery

A *don't know (DK)* is the refusal of delivery of securities or payment of funds due to the lack of knowledge of the trade.

The purchaser does not have to accept partial (less than the amount traded) delivery. All municipal securities trades are assumed to be bearer securities unless otherwise stated.

The seller of municipal securities pays the costs of shipment of securities, which include postage, insurance, drafts, and collection charges.

The MSRB also has determined that the confirmation regarding a municipal security must be delivered to the contra broker/dealer the next business day showing the following information: (1) confirming party's name, address, and telephone number, (2) "contra party" identification, (3) designation of buy or sell, (4) par value of securities, (5) CUSIP number, if any, (6) trade date, (7) settlement date, (8) yield-to-maturity or dollar price of transaction, (9) amount of concession, (10) amount of accrued interest, (11) amount of principal, (12) instruction for delivery or receipt of securities, (13) any other pertinent information which may be deemed necessary, such as "dated date," registered securities and prerefunded securities, or ex-legal.

As can be seen, municipal securities offer the investor a wide range of debt obligations that may be suitable for various investment objectives. Buyers of these securities may be individuals who have tax problems, commercial banks, corporations and other institutions. With the increasing demand for municipal securities, the marketplace has met the challenge to become more efficient, informed, and regulated. The Municipal Securities Rulemaking Board's role will assist the municipal securities industry to meet the present and future needs of the investing public.

Municipal Security. Once referred to as "tax-exempt securities," *municipal securities* are debt obligations issued by a state, a city, a township, a county, a political subdivision of a state, or a U.S. Territory. Municipal *bonds* are long-term debt instruments that bear interest semiannually. Municipal *notes* are issued on a short-term, discounted basis. Interest received by a bondholder is exempted from federal income taxes; the reason is a long-standing precedent based on Supreme Court decisions that federal and local governments may not tax each other. This privilege, however, does *not* apply to *profits* established via the purchase and sale of these securities. Naturally, the tax-free interest feature has substantial appeal, and this appeal increases as the individual's tax bracket increases.

Bond Type. Of the numerous types of municipal bonds, most fall into two broad categories: general obligation and revenue bonds. *General obligation bonds (GOs)*, sometimes known as *full faith and credit bonds*, are backed by the general taxing ability of the issuing municipality: the greater the taxing ability, the more secure the bond. *Revenue bonds* are secured by the revenue from a facility— such as a toll road or power plant—that is constructed by proceeds of the bond issue.

See also General Obligation Bond; Revenue Bond.

Types of Indenture. Municipal bonds, like corporation obligations, may be issued under two types of indenture: the open-end and the closed-end. The *open-end indenture* permits the issuance of subsequent parity (that is, "equal safety") financing under the same indenture. The *closed-end provision* permits no subsequent parity financing, except where necessary to complete a facility or project. Additional bonds may be issued, but they must be junior to the previously issued bonds.

The indenture contains other protective covenants to be adhered to by the issuer to assure bondholder security. These covenants pertain to items such as maintenance of adequate rates,

proper project maintenance, books, records, insurance, and flow of funds provision. The *rate covenant* sets the fee schedule high enough to cover all aspects of debt service, as well as to insure the facility and keep it in good repair. The *flow of funds* provision prescribes the priority of application of gross revenues to properly secure the bond issue. Typically, the schedule of application is: (1) operation and maintenance fund, (2) debt service and/or sinking fund, (3) debt service reserve fund, (4) reserve maintenance fund, (5) renewal and replacement fund, and (6) surplus fund.

The Primary Market. General obligation bonds are usually issued in serial format, while revenue bonds are most frequently issued as term bonds. *Serial bonds* are obligations of the same issuer offered at the same time but with various interest rates and maturities arranged over a period of years. *Term bonds* are obligations of the same issuer offered with a single interest rate and a single maturity date. A *split offering* is a combination of serial and term bonds. Regardless of type, municipals are almost always callable prior to maturity. Therefore, each issue normally has a sinking fund schedule. Generally, term bonds have ten-year minimum call protection. Serial bonds are generally called by inverse order of maturity—the longest first. Within a given maturity, the bond numbers selected for redemption are chosen at random.

Secondary Market. Once the offering has been completed, the bonds are free to trade in the secondary market. For municipals, this market is *entirely* over-the-counter and largely on a principal (dealer) basis. The spread between the bid and asked prices is a function of quality, issuer, length to maturity, supply and demand, and other general market characteristics. Municipal bonds may have a spread anywhere from one to three points, whereas municipal notes may range from ⅛ to ½ point. Likewise, the dealer markup or markdown is based on primarily the same characteristics as the spread. Typically a markup or markdown for municipal bonds is ½ to 1½ points. Dealers are not required to disclose the amount to the client.

Unit of Trading. The most commonly accepted trading unit (a round lot) is for *100 bonds* ($100,000 principal amount), and orders for at least this many bonds bring better prices than those for fewer. The typical unit of trading starts at a minimum of $5,000 and involves multiples of $5,000. A few outstanding issues may be in $1,000 minimum denominations. Normally "M" designates one thousand.

Example: "$10M" represents $10,000 principal amount of bonds.

Traders generally quote serial bonds on a *yield-to-maturity* basis. Thus the State of Florida GOs 6.00% of '96 might be offered on a 6.45% *basis*, indicating a discount to par value, because the yield-to-maturity exceeds the coupon, or nominal, rate. Some longer-maturity term bonds are quoted in dollars and are thus referred to as *dollar bonds*. In either case, all quotations are presumed to be for bearer bonds unless specifically indicated otherwise.

Regulation. Trading in municipal securities is regulated by the Municipal Securities Rulemaking Board (MSRB). This board was established pursuant to the Securities Act Amendment of 1975.

See also Municipal Securities Rulemaking Board (MSRB).

Information on Bonds. The primary source of information on municipal offerings in the secondary market is the *Blue List*. The total number of listings in this list gives an indication of the size and liquidity of the market, and it is referred to as the *floating supply*. Another source is the *Daily Bond Buyer*, which contains news and statistics.

Retirement. In some cases, a municipality may, in effect, retire a bond issue without actually paying off the debt. The issuer sells a new bond offering and, with the proceeds, buys U.S. government securities. The Treasury securities, having the same principals and maturities as the old bond issue, are reserved for the sole purpose of paying off the debt.

See also Advance Refunding.

Tax Treatment of Interest Income. The main appeal of municipal bonds lies in the federal tax-exempt status of their interest payments. Interest paid on bank deposits, corporate debt, and even federal debt is all subject to federal income tax. Therefore the tax-exempt status for municipal securities is naturally appealing; it is most attractive to higher-bracket investors.

Example: An investor in the 40% tax bracket needs to receive a 17.5% yield on a corporate bond to receive the same in-pocket, after-tax income that a 10.5% municipal bond (at par) provides. That municipal bond, bought by an investor in the very highest bracket (50%), yields nontaxable interest that is equivalent to a taxable return of 21.0% on a taxable bond. Such high rates of return as 21.0% are possible only in high-risk situations with none of the safety features offered by municipal bonds, especially GOs.

To compute the equivalent taxable yield, *subtract* the investor's tax bracket from 100% and *divide* the result of the subtraction into the municipal yield.

Example: An investor in the 45% tax bracket is contemplating the purchase of a municipal bond yielding 9.8%. What rate of return must a *taxable* bond afford before the investor earns the same after-tax return? To calculate the *taxable* yield necessary to equal a tax-free yield, divide the tax-free yield by the decimalized equivalent of the investor's tax bracket subtracted from 100%.

$$\frac{\text{Tax-free yield}}{100\% - \text{tax bracket}} = \text{taxable yield}$$

$$\frac{9.80\%}{100\% - 45\%} = \frac{9.80\%}{55\%} = \frac{9.80\%}{.55} = 17.82\%$$

Therefore, for this investor to earn as much income, after-tax , from investing in a corporate (taxable) bond as from a municipal bond yielding 9.80%, the investor must seek a return of 17.82% on the corporate security.

Also the interest on municipal securities is frequently (although not always) exempt from state and local taxes when the security is held by one who resides in the same state as the issuer. Further increasing the appeal of municipals, this triple exemption (from federal, state, and local taxes) is always present in particular issuers—the Commonwealth of Puerto Rico, the Virgin Islands, the Mariana Islands, and Washington, D.C.

Treatment of Gains. Municipal bonds, of course, are capital assets, and their purchase and resale can produce a long- or short-term capital gain or loss.

In rather infrequent instances, underwriters may purchase an entire issue from the issuing municipality at significantly less than par and reoffer the entire issue at a substantial discount to the public. The buyer of an *original-issue discount* offering pays no tax on the difference between purchase price and par value if the bond is held to maturity.

Example: A bond is purchased on the offering for $4,600 and redeemed at par—$5,000—ten years later. The $400 difference is regarded as tax-exempt income. One must *accrete* the original issue discount to determine the gain or loss if the security is sold *before* maturity date. *Accretion* is the adjustment of the tax cost basis in equal annual amounts over the life of the bond.

Example: An investor purchases a $5,000, ten-year bond with an original issue discount of 98 on the offering. Six years later, the investor sells the bond for 99½. The total amount of the discount, $100, must be accreted (added) in equal amounts over the ten year period until the bond matures—$10 each year must be added to the bond's original cost to determine the holder's

"new" cost basis. Therefore, in the sixth year the new tax cost basis is $4,960 (the original cost of $4,900 plus $10 for each of the six years the bond was held). The investor thus establishes a $15 long- term capital gain.

Initial purchase:	$5,000 @ 98	= $4,900
Adjusted tax cost basis—six years later:	5,000 @ 99.2 =	4,960
Sale of bond:	5,000 @ 99.5 =	4,975
Long-term capital gain:		$15

$$(4,975 - 4,960)$$

As can be seen, the cost basis increases each year by 20 basis points. Therefore, in the sixth year the new tax cost basis is $4,960 (98 plus 1.2).

Note that this feature does not apply either to (1) bonds purchased at a discount in the secondary market or (2) the offering of a part of a new serial bond at a discount. Frequently, the longer maturities of a new serial bond are discounted to make the purchase price more attractive. Though actually purchased at a discount, these bonds are not considered to be original issue discount.

When bonds are purchased at a premium and held to maturity, the holder does not create a capital loss for tax purposes. Rather, the holder must amortize the premium over the remaining life of the bond, reducing the cost basis accordingly.

Example: A bond is purchased for $1,100 with exactly ten years left to maturity. The investor holds the bond for seven years and sells it for $1,040. The $100 premium is amortized equally over the ten years from purchase date to maturity. The cost basis is thus reduced by $70 ($100 premium divided by 10 years = $10 annually × 7 years held = $70). Instead of incurring an apparent $60 long-term loss, the investor reports a $10 long-term gain, purchased at an adjusted price (after seven years) of $1,030 and sold for $1,040.

While accrued interest raises the cash outlay to the buyer of a municipal bond and increases the amount received by the seller, it is still interest and hence tax-exempt.

Example: A bond is acquired for $10,500 ($10,000 principal amount plus $500 of accrued interest) and sold for proceeds of $10,900 ($10,800 plus $100 accrued interest). The taxable gain is $800. This figure is based on the principal amounts of the transaction only; that is, the bond is bought for $10,000 and sold at $10,800.

Municipal Notes. Other short-term municipal debt obligations are tax anticipation notes, revenue anticipation notes, and bond anticipation notes. Normally, municipal notes are sold on a discounted basis (municipal bonds bear interest semiannually). *Tax anticipation notes (TANs)* are issued to raise monies secured by the proceeds of a forthcoming tax collection. *Revenue anticipation notes (RANs)* are issued to raise monies secured by the proceeds of future revenues. *Bond anticipation notes (BANs)* are issued as interim financing until a forthcoming bond issue is offered; the proceeds of the bond issue then become security for the BANs.

Taxation of Municipal Notes. The taxation of short-term municipal notes is different from municipal bonds. In anticipation of receiving more permanent revenues, municipalities may sell discounted money-market instruments generally referred to as *TANs, RANs,* and *BANs (tax, revenue,* and *bond anticipation notes).* These are typically sold at a discount and redeemed at par, bearing no stated rate of return. As with a Treasury bill, the yield is simply the difference between acquisition cost and redemption (or sale) proceeds. There is very little secondary market activity in municipal notes, and buyers are expected to hold the notes to maturity. However, as such items are not considered capital assets, their ultimate redemption does not result in a capital gain or loss. Again, like a Treasury bill, the difference between cost and redemption (or sale proceeds) is ordinary income. Since

municipal interest is tax-free income, however, there are no tax consequences to the individual buyer of a TAN, RAN, or BAN.

Assessing Debt. A municipality's *funded debt* is the total amount of debt obligations maturing *after* five years. The municipality's *floating debt* is the total amount of debt obligations maturing *within* five years.

When analyzing the ability of an issuer to take on additional debt, an important ratio is that of *overall debt to actual market value of real estate.* Since real estate is frequently assessed at unrealistically low levels (compared to actual market values), using current values gives a better idea of the potential revenues that might be derived from such property in the event of a reassessment. Generally speaking, overall debt should not exceed 10% of the actual market value of taxable property.

Another useful ratio is *per capita debt,* which is simply total debt divided by the population of the municipality. When analyzing revenue bonds, the analyst should require a feasibility study by a reputable engineering firm.

Most municipalities prefer spreading out their general obligation debt in fairly predictable annual amounts rather than making large, lump-sum "balloon" payments. For this reason serial obligations are arranged so as to require *level debt service*; that is, each annual payment of principal and interest is roughly equal.

Example: Combined annual interest and principal payments might be fixed at about $5,000,000. In the early years of an issue's life, most of each year's payments would be interest, and very little would represent principal. Midway through the life-span, payments are about 50/50, and near maturity they are largely repayment of principal and very little interest.

Underwriting. Municipal bonds are brought to market either through a negotiated sale or by competitive bidding. In a *negotiated offering,* the issuer arranges for the offering with one underwriting group, setting the interest rates and other terms through negotiation. In a *competitive bid*, the issuer distributes an official notice of sale, and underwriting groups (or syndicates) submit competitive bids for the offering. The group offering the lowest interest cost wins the bid.

See also Competitive Bid; Negotiated Offering.

Organization of the Syndicate. Once the bid is accepted by the issuer, an underwriting agreement is signed by both parties stating the final terms and prices of the new bond issue. The managing underwriter then sends a *release letter* to the syndicate members, notifying them of the purchase of the bonds from the issuer by the syndicate. This notice, also called the *syndicate account letter*, designates the syndicate account manager, along with the priority of allocation and participation by each member. The syndicate manager keeps the books and records for the syndicate account.

All municipal bonds are "dated" as of the first or fifteenth of the month of issuance. The offering date, decided by the underwriters, is the date the bonds are sold to the public. Due to possible delays for printing the bonds and other legal procedures, the bonds are offered on a *when, as, and if issued basis.* Normally the bonds are delivered about thirty days after the offering date. Interest accrues from the *dated date (issued date)* up to but not including the settlement date.

Priority of Orders. Although the normal municipal syndicate is organized to last thirty days, an earlier completion of the sale is highly desirable. The following sequence shows the usual sequence in allocating orders (the priority of orders) by the winning syndicate's manager: (1) *Presale orders*—orders received prior to the actual award of the issue to the winning syndicate. (2) *Group account orders*—orders for the syndicate as a whole reflecting each member's proportionate participation. (3) *Designated orders*—orders from customers specifying which syndicate member is to fill it. (4) *Member's orders*—orders received by each member subsequent to the successful bid and award of the bonds.

Spread. The syndicate purchases the bonds from the municipality at a discount from the public offering price. The difference between the two prices is the *spread*, or the profit to the group.

See also Spread.

Credit Analysis. When evaluating the credit standing of an issuer of municipal bonds, the independent rating services are likely to be concerned with such items as: population trends (growth and decline), past debt collection records, industry, property value, constitutional or statutory limitations. As a general rule, a community's debt service should not exceed 25% of its annual budget. Analysts also like to examine *overlapping debt*, that is, debt not directly issued by the municipality itself but for which its residents are at least partially responsible.

Example: The residents of the city of Chicago are also residents of Cook County, which provides many publicly financed facilities like hospitals and jails.

Another general rule is that the rates charged by a financed facility should be expected to generate enough income to cover debt service, operations, and maintenance with at least a 20% "cushion."

Mutual Fund. *See* Investment Company.

N

Naked (Uncovered) Option. A *naked option* is written without any corresponding security or option position as protection in the seller's account.

NASDAQ Committee. *See* Rules of Fair Practice (Section 5).

NASDAQ Option. This is a standardized put or call option whose underlying stock is not listed on a securities exchange but rather traded OTC via the NASDAQ system.

See also Listed Option; National Association of Securities Dealers Automated Quotations Over-the-Counter Price Index; Option.

NASDAQ-OTC Price Index. In May, 1971, a significant addition to stock market indexes was made with the announcement by the NASD of the NASDAQ-OTC Price Index (National Association of Securities Dealers Automated Quotations—Over-the-Counter Price Index). Made possible by developments that permit securities dealers to program over- the-counter stock prices into a central computer, this index gives a broad-based indication of activity in the unlisted securities market. It is updated every five minutes.

All domestic common stocks listed on NASDAQ have been divided into seven categories: (1) composite (all issues); (2) industrials; (3) banks; (4) insurance; (5) other finance; (6) transportation; (7) utilities. As new stocks are added to the system, they too are included. The system adjusts daily for capitalization changes, such as splits, rights to subscribe, new listings, and delistings, in order to prevent these changes from affecting the index value.

Each index was assigned a base value derived from the prevailing market prices on February 5, 1971. The total number of shares outstanding for each was multiplied by its median closing-bid price on that day. The total value for all stocks in each index was then arithmetically equated to a base of 100.

See also American Stock Exchange Market Value Index; Averages and Indexes; Dow Jones Averages; New York Stock Exchange Index; Standard & Poor's Index.

National Association of Securities Dealers Automated Quotations Over-the-Counter Price Index (NASDAQ System). This index is a computer-oriented, broad-based indicator of activity in the unlisted securities market, updated every five minutes.

See also Listed Option; NASDAQ Option; Option.

National Association of Securities Dealers (NASD). *Membership.* Most broker/dealer organizations registered with the SEC in the United States have joined the NASD. It is not mandatory for them to do so. They have joined because they find it convenient and advantageous to participate in the NASD. Admission requirements and qualifications for NASD membership are reasonable and broad enough to include most individuals or organizations willing to comply with the association's rules and regulations. Any broker or dealer transacting investment banking or securities business under the laws of any state and/or the United States is eligible for new or continuing membership in the NASD, unless (1) that broker or dealer has had its registration suspended or revoked by the SEC; (2) that broker or dealer has been suspended or expelled from a registered securities exchange or association; (3) that broker or dealer has associated with any person who was a cause of suspension or expulsion from SEC registration; (4) that broker or dealer knowingly or willingly filed, or caused to be filed, an application, statement, or report with the NASD that was false, misleading or incomplete with respect to a material fact; (5) that broker or dealer has been convicted of a felony or misdemeanor involving a securities transaction or misappropriation of money or securities within ten years prior to application for membership or at any time thereafter; (6) that broker or dealer is enjoined by court order from acting as an investment advisor, underwriter, broker, dealer, or employee of an investment company, bank, or insurance company; or (7) that broker or dealer does not have proper or sufficient personnel qualified with the NASD as principal, financial principal, and representative.

Firms that do not belong to the NASD are generally small, regionally oriented in their business, or highly specialized in their securities activities.

Example: Many specialist concerns on the registered stock exchanges are not NASD members. There is no reason for them to join if they do not trade securities over the counter as a matter of practice. NASD nonmembers who are also not members of registered stock exchanges nevertheless do not escape the scrutiny or supervision of regulatory authorities. They may still be subject to qualification and compliance with SEC, state, and/or local government regulations, depending on the securities activities in which they engage.

A nonmember must be treated by members in the same way members treat their public customers. Members of the association are prohibited from granting discounts, selling concessions, rebates, or special allowances of any kind when transacting business with, or in behalf of, nonmembers.

Organization. The National Association of Securities Dealers was incorporated as a non-stock-issuing, nonprofit, membership organization under the laws of Delaware in 1936 and registered with the SEC in 1939. Excerpts from the association's charter highlight its purposes and reflect compliance with the Maloney Act. These purposes and objectives are to (1) promote the investment banking and securities business; (2) standardize its principles and practices; (3) promote high standards of commercial honor and to promote among members observance of federal and state securities laws; (4) provide a medium through which the membership may consult with governmental and other agencies; (5) cooperate with governmental authority in the solution of problems affecting this business and investors; (6) adopt and enforce rules of fair practice; (7) promote just and equitable principles of trade for the protection of investors; (8) promote self-discipline among members; (9) investigate and adjust grievances between members and between the public and members.

Board of Governors. The terms and conditions of everyday operation as well as the classification, qualification, and responsibilities of members in this corporation are spelled out precisely in the NASD bylaws. The task of making, altering, or repealing these bylaws is assigned to a 31-member Board of Governors, most of whom are elected by the general membership of the association. The remainder are elected by the board itself.

The Board of Governors is aided in its deliberations and policy formulations by an Advisory Council and 27 standing committees. Each of these committees is expert in a technical area of business activity in which member organizations frequently participate (see the following figure). The job of directly supervising these policies for a nationwide membership of approximately 4,600 is herculean. Thus, for purposes of delegating administrative authority, the bylaws provide for partitioning the United States into thirteen securities districts. The membership in each district, therefore, elects (1) a specified number of representatives to serve on the association's Board of Governors and (2) several participants to serve on a District Committee in order to achieve a maximum degree of local administration.

District Committee. The chairman of each district serves on the Advisory Council to the Board of Governors but does not vote on matters of policy. Each District Committee, in turn, then appoints at least three subcommittees to accomplish its specialized goal.

1. The *District Uniform Practice Committee* disseminates information and interpretations handed down by the Board of Governors regarding the *Uniform Practice Code*. This code relates to the mechanics of executing and completing securities transactions between member firms of the NASD. (This code does not regulate the procedural relationships that prevail between a member firm and its customers.) In this respect, the committee may be called on by members in its district to interpret or rule on technical questions concerning trade contracts or the proper deliverability of certificates. It is also empowered to formulate local practice codes dealing specifically with the peculiarities of transactions within its district. These rules, of course, are subject to comment by the local membership and approval by the Board of Governors. They may not conflict with the national board's Uniform Practice Code for the entire association. Disputes arising between members from the same district concerning this code are resolved by this subcom-

mittee. Controversies between members from different districts are mediated and resolved by the Standing National Uniform Practice Committee.

The *District Business Conduct Committee* is responsible for supervising the board's Rules of Fair Practice, which concern primarily the ethics employed by members in the conduct of their business. With this objective, the committee carefully examines members' activities on a continuing basis and administers the Code of Procedure, if necessary. That code, designed to handle trade practice complaints, is a set of rules under which disciplinary proceedings are conducted.

The District Business Conduct Committee is, in reality, the elected officials of the District Committee themselves. However, owing to varying workloads in each district, it is not uncommon to find several local business conduct subcommittees appointed to process much of the necessary hearings and accompanying paperwork.

3. The *District Surveillance Committee* is responsible for deciding whether remedial sanctions need be imposed on members in that locality who may be experiencing financial or operating difficulties. Based on information furnished it from members, customers of that firm, periodic reports filed with regulatory agencies, and on-premises examination by NASD officials, this Committee determines if, and what, penalties need be employed in accordance with Section 38 of the Association's Rules of Fair Practice. These judgments to limit a member's business may be appealed in the form of an official committee hearing and subsequent review by the Board of Governors. However, the facts in such matters are usually self-evident and attempts at correcting the situation are routinely prescribed in the NASD regulation.

The District Surveillance Committee is comprised of two current or former District Business Conduct Committee members, two members of the Board of Governors National Surveillance Committee, and one former member of the Board of Governors.

Code of Procedure. The *Code of Procedure* is prescribed by the Board of Governors for administration of disciplinary proceedings stemming from infractions of the Rules of Fair Practice. All trade practice complaints are heard and passed on initially by the District Business Conduct Committee of the district in which (1) the respondent's main office is located or (2) the action on which the complaint is based took place.

All complaints, whether prompted by another member of the NASD or by the District Committee itself, must be in written form and must cite the rule or interpretation allegedly violated. The respondent is allowed ten business days in which to answer or refute these accusations, also in written form, before the District Business Conduct Committee will sit in judgment. Either party to this allegation has the right to request a formal hearing of the complaint, at which time both may be represented by legal counsel. Otherwise, the committee will determine what form of discipline, if any, will be instituted. It has the power to censure, fine, suspend, or even expel members from the association for serious violations. If, in the opinion of the District Business Conduct Committee, the facts of the complaint are not in dispute and the infraction is a relatively minor one, the committee may offer the accused member *summary-complaint proceedings* instead of the more formalized regular complaint procedure. If accepted, the member agrees to (1) admit guilt; (2) waive formal hearings; (3) accept a penalty of censure and/or fine of up to $2,500; and (4) waive all right of appeal to the Board of Governors.

More serious violations are adjudicated by the District Business Conduct Committee via the regular complaint procedure, which involves formal hearings and a trial. These judgments are subject to review by the Board of Governors on appeal by any participant in this dispute or on the Board's own initiative. The board has authority to uphold, increase, decrease, or modify any penalties after careful consideration.

People aggrieved by the board's decision can then appeal to the Securities and Exchange Commission for satisfaction. If they are unable to find it there, court the public court system is always available to them. Rarely does a complaint proceeding go that far, not only because of the time and expense involved, but also because of the impartiality of judgement at the intervening levels of review.

Code of Arbitration. As any large organization concerned with money matters must, the NASD has developed an arbitration facility for resolution of controversies arising out of, and relating exclusively to, securities transactions. NASD-sponsored arbitration under the Code of Arbitration is available for intramember or customer-member disputes involving securities activities. Only U.S. government securities that are exempted securities, as defined in the Exchange Act of 1934, are excluded from the association's jurisdiction.

Presenting controversies to a Board of-Arbitration is strictly voluntary for the parties concerned. Nevertheless, when parties agree to arbitration, they are bound to adhere to the arbitrator's decision without right of appeal. Arbitrators are appointed by an Arbitration Director, who is himself appointed by the NASD Board of Governors to perform all the administrative functions of this important process. The number and occupations of the arbitrators depend on the parties involved in the dispute. Intramember controversies are resolved by three to five arbitrators, all of whom are employed within the securities industry. Disputes involving public customers, however are resolved by five arbitrators, at least three of whom are not employed in the securities industry. Majority vote rules in all cases. The principal benefits of this process are:

(1) *Impartiality*. Judgment is rendered by the disputant's peers, or disinterested parties, as the case may be. (2) *Ease and speed of operation*. A minimum of paperwork is involved, with cases heard and settled out of court, in most instances, within a few months. (3) *Reasonable cost*. Each party knows in advance the expense he or she must bear to support arbitration proceedings. The fee schedule is fixed by the National Arbitration Committee of the NASD and ranges from $25 per matter to $120 per hearing, depending on the sum of money at question in the dispute.

Registration. As a way of monitoring NASD members, the Board of Governors has established criteria whereby various persons associated with a member organization must qualify and register with the association as principal, financial principal, or representative. The differences between these roles are based on the type of work performed, the degree of responsibility enjoyed, and the type of securities sold.

Registration as principal. Principal registration is the highest form of registration recognized by the NASD. A registered principal may legally participate in most areas of a member's business, including all phases of supervision, solicitation, and training. Registration as principal is required for the following persons who are actively engaged in the management of a member organization's investment banking and securities business other than in the area of accounting and net capital compliance: (1) sole proprietors; (2) officers (titled executives with bona fide administrative responsibilities, such as vice-president, secretary, treasurer); (3) general partners of a broker/dealer partnership active in the business; (4) directors of a broker/dealer corporation active in the business; (5) managers of Offices of Supervisory Jurisdiction.

Employees of member organizations responsible for training principals must themselves qualify as registered principals.

Registration as financial principal. The facet of the securities business denied to the typical principal is preparation or approval of the firm's financial statements and net capital computations. To be involved in these areas of the securities business, a registered principal must also be registered as a financial principal with the NASD. Every member organization is obliged to staff on a continuing basis at least one registered principal who can serve as a financial principal after passing a special qualifying examination. Thus, a financial principal must be a registered principal, but most registered principals are not financial principals. If a registered principal does not work in the department of the organization responsible for the firm's financial statements and calculation of net capital, he or she need not sit for this highly technical examination.

Registration as representative. This type of registration is required as a minimum qualification for the following persons: (1) solicitors of investment banking or securities business, including securities sales people, marketers of variable annuity contracts, research analysts and corporate finance department employees who communicate with customers and prospective clients of the member organization; (2) traders (the employees who make decisions to buy and sell securities for the member firm's account and risk in a dealer capacity); (3) assistant officers— employees who assist principals in their supervisory, administrative, or sales responsibilities and are usually identified by such titles as assistant vice-president, assistant secretary, assistant treasurer (including any employee who merely supervises a function or department related to the solicitation or conduct of the firm's investment banking or securities business); and An application to serve as a foreign associate must be filed with the National Association of Securities Dealers. (4) also included are training directors and assistants (employees responsible for training solicitors, traders, and assistant officers, but who do not train principals).

Exemptions from registration. From the

foregoing commentary it may appear that all employees in a member organization are required to qualify for one registration or the other, but this is not so. The NASD recognizes the impracticality of that approach. Therefore, the following persons are specifically exempted from these registration requirements:

1. Nominal officials, such as limited partners, nonvoting stockholders, or even some employees with officerial titles if those persons have no active voice in the management of their firm and if their functions are related exclusively to that firm's need for capital or coordination of operation.

2. Persons whose functions are related solely and exclusively to the following activities: (a) transactions on a national securities exchange by persons registered with that exchange, such as specialists and commission house brokers, (b) transactions in exempted securities, such as U.S. government obligations, (c) transactions in commodities, (d) clerical or ministerial activities in the firm, such as those performed by secretaries, order clerks, margin clerks, and statisticians.

3. Foreign associates (employees who are not citizens, nationals, or residents of the United States, its territories or possessions, and who conduct their securities activities only with noncitizens and nonresidents of the United States outside U.S. jurisdiction). (An application to serve as a foreign associate must be filed with the National Association of Securities Dealers.)

Committee on Corporate Financing. The areas of NASD responsibility and jurisdiction are not confined to the aftermarket (the over-the-counter trading market created for a security when an initial public offering of that issue begins). The NASD acts just as aggressively prior to, and in the process of, offering securities publicly, to insure that members' actions are consistent with high standards of commercial honor and just and equitable principles of trade.

A national Committee on Corporate Financing must examine all appropriate documents that set forth the terms and conditions of an issue to be distributed. This must be done far enough in advance of the offering so that modifications can be made if the arrangements are deemed to be unfair or unreasonable.

Appropriate documents include copies of the registration statement, preliminary prospectus, underwriting agreement, and eventually, the final prospectus. The committee may also require copies of agreements among underwriters, purchase agreements, consulting agreements, and letters of intent.

Some issues are not subject to the committee's scrutiny, however. Among those excluded from scrutiny are (1) exempt securities, such as U.S. government obligations; (2) investment company securities (except closed-end management company shares, which do require filing with the NASD); (3) variable annuity contracts; and (4) straight debt issues (nonconvertible bonds) rated B or higher by a recognized rating service such as Standard & Poor's, Moody's, or Fitch.

No member of the NASD may participate or assist in the public offering or distribution of any other securities as underwriter, selling group member, or otherwise, unless the Committee on Corporate Financing has reviewed and approved the terms and conditions of all arrangements. The committee does not evaluate the merits of any issue or pass on the fairness of its price. It is concerned only with the reasonableness of the offering arrangements. For this reason, the committee looks at such factors as (1) the expected public offering price and underwriter's compensation; (2) the total amount allocated to persons situated favorably to the issuer or underwriter (This amount should not be disproportionate to genuine public subscriptions. The NASD uses 10% of a member's participation in an offering as a guideline in determining the meaning of "disproportionate." However, an allocation of 100 shares or five bonds will not be considered a violation even if such an amount exceeds the percentage limitation.); (3) securities or options of that issuer acquired by the underwriter and related persons within the previous twelve months, including purchase prices and dates of acquisition; (4) any private placements of that issuer's securities in the previous eighteen months, detailing the identity and employment of the purchasers as well as their relationship or affiliation with the issuer and proposed distribution of this offering.

See also Hot Issue; Interpositioning; Maloney Act; Markup and Markdown; National Association of Securities Dealers Automated Quotations; National Quotation Bureau, Inc.; Over the Counter; SECO Member.

National Association of Securities Dealers Automated Quotations (NASDAQ). NASDAQ is an electronic data terminal device that furnishes subscribers with instant identification of market-makers and their current quotations. It differs from the pink sheets of the National Quotation Bureau in the following ways: (1) Only members of the NASD may have their quotations reflected as market-makers. In this capacity they act as dealers (principals) standing ready, willing, and able to trade for their firm's proprietary account and risk. (2) Canvassing dealers to solicit their markets is obviated because bids and offers from each market-maker registered with the NASD are continuously updated. (3) Security qualifications and market-maker capital requirements are stringently controlled. (4) While there is capacity for approximately 20,000 issues, only about 3,700 equity-type (stocks, warrants, convertible bonds) securities are presently in the system. (5) Only firm markets may be represented in this device. (6) Each participating market-maker must report daily trading volume to the NASDAQ computer center. NASDAQ sets its own qualifications for market-makers (*see* Market-Maker). (7) The service is much more expensive than the National

Quotation Bureau's daily sheets (*see* National Quotation Bureau, Inc.).

NASDAQ service is available at three subscription levels, dependent on the applicant's preferences and requirements.

Level 1 service provides the best quotation for each security on which market-makers are entering quotations that day. Those prices are the highest bid and lowest offering levels of those securities in effect at the time; this is also known as the *inside market*. They are the interdealer quotations released to, and printed in, the newspapers each day.

Level 2 service provides access to the actual prices of all registered market-makers entering quotations on a given day. Each market-maker's bid and offering price is individually identified alongside the name of the firm itself.

Level 3 service is identical to level 2 service with the added feature of enabling a qualified market-maker firm to enter, alter, or delete its own quotations into or from the system. This service is available only to NASD members, but levels 1 and 2 can be provided to nonmembers under certain conditions.

NASDAQ Security Inclusion Requirements. For a security to be authorized for inclusion in the NASDAQ system, it must meet certain initial and maintenance qualifications imposed on it by the Board of Governors of the NASD.

Domestic securities. Eligible domestic securities include the following: (1) stocks, warrants, rights, and convertible debt registered with the SEC under the Exchange Act of 1934; (2) bank securities registered with the Federal Reserve Board, Federal Deposit Insurance Corporation, or Comptroller of the Currency of the United States; (3) insurance company and closed-end investment company securities; and (4) foreign securities and ADRs, when the issuer is registered with the SEC under Section 12(g) of the Exchange Act of 1934.

The initial and maintenance requirements are most easily understood in the following tabular presentation.

Qualifications	Initial Requirement	Maintenance Requirement
Corporate Assets	$ 2,000,000	$ 750,000
Persons owning security	300	300
Total capital and surplus	$ 1,000,000	$ 375,000
Shares publicly owned*	100,000	100,000
Convertible debt publicly owned*	$10,000,000	$5,000,000
Number of market-makers	2 or more	1 or more

*Doe not include officer, directors, and holders of 10% or more of that class of security.

Foreign securities and American Depositary Receipts (Where the issuer is not registered under Section 12(g) of the Exchange Act of 1934, but does file certain financial information and reports with the SEC at designated intervals). The standards for authorization in these securities are the same as for domestic securities, except that (1) there must be at least three market-makers reflecting their bids and offering prices; and (2) the average daily volume in the first ninety calendar days after authorization must not be less than 500 shares.

The NASDAQ system expedites executions by enabling a dealer with a buy or sell order to tell at a glance the market-maker with the best prices and to contact him or her directly. The standard dialogue to consummate the transaction is the same as that described under the NQB system. There is less price negotiation with NASDAQ securities, however, because the constant disclosure of competitors' quotations tends to narrow the spread between the bids and offerings. With its advanced computerization, NASDAQ is developing over the counter from a negotiated marketplace into an electronic auction marketplace similar to the national securities exchanges.

See also National Association of Securities Dealers; Over the Counter.

National Clearing Corporation. *See* Comparison Procedures.

National Futures Asociation (NFA). The futures industry self-regulatory organization established in 1982.

National Market Advisory Board. Mandated by the Securities Act of 1975, the board is responsible for advising the SEC regarding the operations and regulations of the nation's security markets. The board is comprised of fifteen members, serving terms of between two and five years, with a majority coming from the securities industry.

National Quotation Bureau Inc. (NQB). The NQB is a subsidiary of Commerce Clearing House, Inc., a well-known private publisher of financial information and manuals. The NQB distributes to subscribers a list of broker/dealers making bids and/or offerings of securities traded over the counter. In fact, the NQB publishes and distributes several lists of such market-makers each day. The list most widely employed is comprised of broker/dealers making markets in securities of nation-wide interest (see the following figure). It is more popularly referred to as the *pink sheets* for stocks because of the color of the paper it is printed on. Another list, known as the *yellow sheets*, shows market-makers for corporate debt securities. The NQB also publishes a monthly service featuring quotations and market-makers for inactively traded securities. The purpose of that booklet is to provide valuations for portfolio managers, administrators, fiduciaries, and so on, and to help potential buyers and sellers of such securities locate each other.

Examination of the pink sheets on any

given day reveals almost 9,000 issues with an average of five market-makers for each listing. Alongside their names may appear a quotation, but those bids and offerings are not representative of current prices. The information for the pink sheets is collected the previous day, and so the prices that appear therein are history by the time of publication. Dealers must be contacted personally to determine their current prices and even to verify that their organization is still a market- maker in that issue. Broker/dealers are privileged to stop their activities in a particular security at any time.

Some dealers don't even bother to show their prices in the pink sheets, claiming that it is pointless to show figures for a volatile or infrequently traded stock. They merely invite contact by interested parties willing to negotiate by listing their names next to the pertinent issues each day. Still other broker/dealers do not choose to trade on both sides of the market, and so they appear in the sheets as *BW (bid wanted)* or *OW (offer wanted)*. The BW dealer is trying to sell stock and is seeking a buyer; the OW dealer is a buyer seeking sellers.

Market-makers in the pink sheets are not required to be NASD members, but they must conform to the requirements of SEC Rule 15c2-11 (*see* Market-Maker).

Negotiating a Price Through NQB. Before consummating a transaction with any market-maker, a member organization of the NASD normally canvasses competing firms to determine a basis for price negotiation. The firm tries to communicate with at least two or three market-makers to insure that it will trade at fair and equitable prices. The language employed in "shopping the street" in this manner is most important in order to avoid misunderstandings between the two parties without actually revealing the terms and conditions of an order until the participants are ready to act.

Example: If a broker/dealer firm contacts a market-maker asking for a "quotation" or for a "price" rather than for its market, it is subtly telling the market-maker that it wants only an evaluation, an approximation, and will not require that firm to trade with it at those prices. It is signaling that it wants information only and does not want to place an order.

Example: To illustrate this maneuvering, let us suppose that an NASD member wants to buy 100 shares of Connecticut General Insurance Co., Inc., an actively traded over-the-counter stock, in response to a customer's order. The pink sheets show twelve market-makers for that stock on a typical day, and so the NASD member's trading department has a wide selection to choose from.

The firm calls market-maker Fred Foster and asks for his market for "Conn Gen." After the firm has properly identified itself as a fellow NASD member, market-maker Foster reveals his *trading market*, the wholesale prices available only to NASD members as prescribed in the Rules of Fair Practice. He might say, "64½ to 65," or, "I'll trade 64½ to 65," meaning he will buy stock at 64½ from a seller or sell stock at 65 to a buyer. He is unaware of whether the caller is a buyer or seller, or even if he has an order, but he is making a *firm market*. He stands ready to trade immediately at these prices in the usual minimum quantity for activity in that stock. The normal trading unit for over-the-counter stocks is 100 shares, whereas for over-the-counter debt issues it is ten ($1,000 face value) bonds. If that market-maker Foster is unwilling to trade in these quantities, he must disclose this fact at the time he reveals his market. He might say, "64½ to 65, odd lots," or, "It's a 50-share bid," or, "10-share offering," to indicate his position.

The trading department might try to negotiate a price between 64½ and 65. More likely, it will contact, for example, market-maker Suzanne Spire to see if she has a more favorable bid or offering price. Market-maker Spire might say, "64⅜ to 67⅞, subject." A *sub-*

ject market is one in which the market-maker is unwilling to trade immediately at those prices.

In response to the inquiry, she is advising that she must first authenticate her quotation with the party whose market she represents, whether that be a correspondent broker/dealer or another trader in her own firm. Such prices are literally subject to verification. It doesn't take too long to firm up a subject market. A quick phone call to the correspondent or to competing market-makers can confirm that those prices are abreast of current conditions. Subject quotations are generally encountered only if the market-maker is temporarily out of touch in a sensitive or volatile market climate. Sometimes these quotations are refined to such an extent that only the bid or only the offering is subject while the other side is firm.

Some issues trade very infrequently in the over-the-counter market, and, as a result, it is difficult to discover any market-makers willing to provide continuing bids and offerings. A broker/dealer is fortunate to find more than one market-maker listed in the pink sheets for such issues. Furthermore, when queried, the market-maker firm would probably then qualify its prices as a *workout market*. This means that it is unaware of an actual market for the security, but it believes it can execute an order for you in a reasonable period of time. Its quotation may be something like "58 to 68, workout." It invites you to leave your order and allow it to try to work out a price somewhere within that spread (between bid and asked) in whatever time period you specify.

NASD member firms may contact any number of market-makers trying to negotiate the best terms and prices for themselves or their customers. You can contact one, two, or all twelve of those firms in an effort to buy 100 shares of Connecticut General Insurance at the lowest price. If one of those market-makers offers stock firm at 64¾ and this is the lowest offering at the time, a trade can be consummated immediately

if you as purchaser announce such intentions by stating "I'll take 100 at 64¾." The market-maker then replies, "Sold to you," to avoid confusion about which firm was the buyer and which the seller on this transaction. If you as the initiating firm are a seller instead of a buyer, you accept the bid and consummate the transaction by saying, "Sold 100 to you at 64½," and the market-maker replies, "I buy." On a busy day, when verbal misunderstandings are likely, costly errors can be averted in this simple manner.

See also Market-Maker; National Association of Securities Dealers; National Association of Securities Dealers Automated Quotations; Over the Counter.

Nearby. The nearest active trading month on a commodity futures market.

Negative Yield Curve. *See* Money Market Company.

Negotiability. *See* Good Delivery of Securities.

Negotiated Marketplace. *See* Over the Counter.

Negotiated Offering. Negotiated offerings, similar to most corporate underwritings, are normally seen in revenue bond offerings. Since municipals are exempt securities, there is no filing requirement or cooling-off period under the 1933 Act. Rather than a prospectus, each buyer receives a copy of the *official statement*. While not mandated by law, the receipt of an official statement does provide the buyer of a new issue with information similar in nature to what a buyer of a new corporate issue could expect from a prospectus.

See also Competitive Bid, Official Statement.

Net Asset Value per Share. This phrase, though peculiar to the investment company industry, is not unique when its meaning is carefully examined. Net asset value is merely another name for shareholders' equity. It is derived by adding the valuation of securities in the portfolio (using a method described in the offering prospectus) to all other assets, subtracting total liabilities from this sum, and then dividing the difference by the number of shares outstanding at that moment. Or, to restate this formula arithmetically:

$$\text{Net asset value per share} = \frac{\begin{array}{c}\text{security} \\ \text{market value}\end{array} + \begin{array}{c}\text{all other} \\ \text{assets}\end{array} - \begin{array}{c}\text{total} \\ \text{liabilities}\end{array}}{\text{number of shares outstanding}}$$

Federal law requires each open-end management company to calculate its net asset value per share at least once daily. This is done at the close of trading on the New York Stock Exchange on days when the exchange has been open for business. Some companies make this calculation twice each day—at 1:00 P.M. New York City time and at the close of the exchange's daily trading activities. The net asset value per share is then employed as the bid price in the quotation for that company.

See also Management Company; Sales Load.

Net Capital Requirements for Broker/Dealers. *See* Financial Protection Requirements (NYSE).

Net Current Assets. *See* Working Capital.

Net Interest Cost (NIC). *See* Competitive Bidding.

Net Profit. *See* Income Statement Net Income.

Net Profit Margin (After-Tax). *See* Digest of Earnings Reports; Standard & Poor's Stock Reports.

Net Working Capital. *See* Working Capital.

New Account Report Form. Registered representatives must make note of essential facts relative to their customers and their activities on a new account report form furnished by their firm (see the following figure). Registered representatives must then sign this form to signify awareness of these facts and attest to their willingness to assume responsibility for their accuracy. Contingent investigation is conducted on a continuing basis, and if these facts or circumstances change, the representative must update the information promptly and implement any new procedures that may be called for. The firm's records of such inquiries must be dated each time there is a modification in previously furnished information.

The following information is essential for compliance with investment industry rules. It should be compiled on the new account report form.

Essential Information.

1. *Account name.* The complete customer name and any titles must be included. Initials alone do not suffice. At least one given name as well as the family name should appear on this form. For institutional customers, the full legal title is mandatory. Commonly recognized abbreviations may be used only if the title designation is extensive. Stock exchange regulations prohibit carrying accounts in the name of a person other than the customer (third-party accounts), and so care must be exercised in verifying identities.

Example: A broker should not open or maintain an account in the name of a person or institution without that party's authorization to do so. The broker should also be able to vouch for the character and integrity of any customer and of any person permitted to give instructions for that account.

New Account Report Form (Front)

(FULL NAME OF CUSTOMER)

MR.
MRS.
MISS

(ACCOUNT NUMBER)

SOCIAL SECURITY NUMBER OR
TAXPAYER IDENTIFYING NUMBER

CITIZEN OF

HOME ADDRESS

HOME TELEPHONE

BUSINESS ADDRESS

BUSINESS TELEPHONE

OCCUPATION AND EMPLOYER

POSITION

HOW WAS ACCOUNT ACQUIRED?

HOW LONG HAVE YOU KNOWN CUSTOMER?
☐ REGULAR

BANK REFERENCES

TYPE OF CHECKING ACCOUNT ☐ SPECIAL

OTHER REFERENCES

CUSTOMER'S AGE, IF UNDER 25

OTHER BROKERS (IF ANY)

HAVE YOU PERSONALLY MET CUSTOMER?

IS CUSTOMER A MARRIED WOMAN?

IF SO, WHAT IS HUSBAND'S NAME?

SPOUSES OCCUPATION AND EMPLOYER

POSITION

IS CUSTOMER A CORPORATION OR PARTNERSHIP?

HAVE PROPER DOCUMENTS BEEN FILED?

IS ACCOUNT BEING OPERATED BY ANOTHER PERSON THAN THE OWNER?

NAME OF PERSON OPERATING ACCOUNT

EMPLOYER

HAS PROPER POWER OF ATTORNEY BEEN EXECUTED AND FILED IN MAIN OFFICE?

TYPE OF ACCOUNT   ☐ CASH   ☐ STOCK
                 ☐ MARGIN ☐ COMMODITY

TYPE OF POWER ☐ GENERAL
              ☐ LIMITED

(CUSTOMER'S FULL SIGNATURE FOR IDENTIFICATION PURPOSES)

SIA-FORM 111

NEW ACCOUNT REPORT

293

New Account Report Form (Back)

INITIAL TRANSACTION _____ DEPOSIT RECEIVED ☐ YES $ _____ ☐ NO

MARGIN DEPOSITED _____ IF SECURITIES, ARE THEY IN GOOD FORM?

CUSTOMER'S AGREEMENT EXECUTED AND GIVEN TO _____

SIGNATURE CARD GIVEN TO _____ STOCK LOAN CARD GIVEN TO _____

IF STOCK IS TO BE TRANSFERRED, PRINT PROPER INSCRIPTION AND FORWARDING ADDRESS

_____

(USE UNIFORM ABBREVIATIONS WHERE POSSIBLE)

SPECIAL MAILING INSTRUCTIONS, IF ANY _____

IS REGISTERED REPRESENTATIVE REGISTERED IN STATE OF MAILING ADDRESS? ☐ YES ☐ NO

ADDITIONAL INFORMATION

_____

_____

_____

APPROVED _____

DATE _____ _____ (DATE)

(CITY) (STATE) SIGNATURE OF BRANCH OFFICE MANAGER

SIGNATURE OF REGISTERED REPRESENTATIVES.

_____

SIGNATURE OF PARTNER OR OFFICER

It is permissible to maintain an account under a code name, number, or symbol, provided that the new account report form shows the customer's true identity. Written authorization must be received from the customer attesting to underlying ownership of the account and the request must be approved by a person delegated with supervisory authority and responsibility by the firm (*see* Numbered Account).

2. *Address.* The form must show an authenticated residence address with zip code. A post office box is not a valid address; although it can be used for mailing purposes, it is good business practice to obtain a more permanent location from the customer for official notifications or subpoenas.

3. *Telephone number.* A business and/or residence telephone number is helpful for prompt communication.

4. *Social security or taxpayer identification number* U.S. Treasury, Internal Revenue Service, and some transfer agent requirements make this item necessary for proper business practices. Federal law now mandates that no brokerage account may be opened for a customer domiciled in the United States unless this number is furnished or a bona fide attempt is made to obtain it for the new account report form. Using this number, broker/dealers are further obliged to report annually to the Internal Revenue Service total dividends paid to customers on stocks held for them in street name (registered in the name of a brokerage organization but held in behalf of a customer for reasons of convenience). Furthermore, some transfer agents will not reregister stock certificates in customer name until they are furnished with the customer's social security or taxpayer identification number.

5. *Citizenship.* The customer's nationality must be ascertained for several reasons: (a) Some industries and certain corporations restrict the extent of foreign ownership of their shares. Shipping, communications, and various other industries adhere to this policy. Its applicability in a given situation must be verified before purchase of such issuer's stocks or convertible bonds. (b) Some issues of foreign securities that have not met the registration requirements of the SEC may not be offered to U.S. citizens.

6. *Age.* For other than institutional customers, verification of legal age is essential. Unless emancipated by court decree, minors normally do not have proper authority to transact personal securities business for themselves or others. Trades effected on a minor's instructions can be rescinded in the future, leaving the firm with sizable losses. The age of majority for securities transaction purposes varies from state to state. It is always a good practice to consult with the brokerage firm's legal or compliance department when first confronted with a situation where a prospective customer is less than 21 years old. Firm policy should prohibit accounts and transactions for minors except in the following cases: (a) The transaction is accomplished under the terms of the appropriate state's Uniform Gifts to Minors Act (UGMA) (*see* Uniform Gifts to Minors Act). (b) The minor is merely a beneficiary under a trust agreement, valid will, or court-established guardianship. In these instances, a properly authorized trustee or fiduciary is appointed, and all instructions relating to these accounts must be given by the person. (c) The minor is recognized in a court order with majority status as a head of household. The legal term for this is emancipation.

Overseeing purchases and sales in behalf of a minor is a serious responsibility, and one that all registered representatives should be aware of. A person serving in this fiduciary capacity must act according to prudent man guidelines that generally prevail. (*See* Prudent Man.)

7. *Occupation, employer, type of business.* To counsel and service an account wisely, the registered representative must be aware of the customer's financial circumstances and investment objectives. Improper recommenda-

tions can lead to disciplinary action by regulatory authorities, as well as expensive litigation. Suitability is not confined to individual accounts for the general public. Knowledge of an institutional customer's business and investment requirements is equally important for providing proper service to such an account.

Example: It would be foolish and irregular to recommend investments in distilled beverage companies to institutions allied with temperance activities.

Furthermore, banking and insurance companies, as well as certain pension plans and trust funds, are restricted in their investments to purchase of securities selected from a legal list, as mentioned in the previous paragraph.

Employment information obtained for this section of the form is also important to ensure compliance with special rules of conduct set forth by the NASD and the New York Stock Exchange (NYSE) and American Stock Exchange (AMEX) for people associated with the financial community.

a. Employees of the NYSE and the AMEX or their affiliated companies must provide the member firm with written permission from the secretary of the exchange in order to open or maintain any securities or commodities accounts.

b. Employees, partners, and officers of stock exchanges or NASD member organizations must furnish written consent from their employers or co-partners to open and maintain any accounts (cash or margin, securities, or commodities accounts) at other member organizations. Duplicate copies of all confirmations and statements must also be sent promptly to the employer or co-partner, as the case may be.

c. Employees of banks, trust companies, insurance companies, or financial institutions doing business as agents or principals in securities-related activities must furnish written permission from their employers to open and maintain margin accounts. (This restriction does not apply to cash accounts for people in this category.) Important persons designated as officers of these concerns and independent insurance agents are not employees, and so it is not necessary for them to obtain a superior's written permission to open margin accounts.

d. An account for the spouse of any person in the foregoing categories is treated as if it belongs to the restricted person unless a legal separation order exists; or the restricted person gives written certification to the firm that the assets in the account belong exclusively to the spouse and that the restricted person maintains no financial interest therein.

8. *Bank and brokerage references.* Verification of these references is a simple but essential prerequisite for getting to know the customer. They are important indicators of a customer's ability to pay and willingness to abide by the customs and procedures for securities transactions in the financial community.

9. *How the account was acquired.* This information helps to determine the depth of investigation necessary to validate other data furnished by the prospective customer and the references supplied to you. Obviously, an account established via "cold call" prospecting needs a more searching inquiry than one established on a personal recommendation from a close friend or business associate who has had years of satisfactory financial experience with the prospective customer.

10. *Name and occupation of person(s) with authority to create activity in this account.* For good business practice and compliance with industry regulations, this information must be determined before accepting instructions from someone other than the customer. In instances where orders are given by an intermediary, a trading authorization form (power of attorney) must be signed by the customer prior to purchase or sale of any security (*see* Trading Authorization).

11. *Payment/delivery and/or duplicate*

iling instructions. Completion of this infor-
tion is important from several standpoints.
st, it is used to provide customers with effi-
it service with minimum effort and expense
he firm. Second, it avoids potentially embar-
;ing experiences related to the enforcement of
leral Reserve Board regulations. It is best for
1 customer and brokerage firm to discuss and
iblish these arrangements prior to any activ-
afterward may be too late to avoid liquidat-
the transaction at a loss in order to comply
1 credit rules.

When furnishing instructions for this section of the form, the registered representative
should also remember that the firm must send
confirmations, statements, and other communications directly to customers at their designated
address. Customers may make the following alternate arrangements with approval from a
member or allied member: (a) They can give
written instruction to send such material instead
to a person holding their power of attorney; verbal instructions are acceptable only if the customer is also receiving a copy of the materials;
(b) They can give written instruction to hold all
mail for up to two months if they are going on va-
cation or traveling domestically or three months
if they are traveling abroad.

12. *Signatures and acceptances.* Each new
account report form must be signed by a member
or allied member as well as by the registered representative who introduces the account to the
firm. Although the member organization may
permit approval by the manager of a branch office in the absence of a member or allied
member, the form still requires the signature of a
principal as soon as practicable. Authority to accept new accounts under NASD regulations is
reserved exclusively for NASD members and
principals. Their signatures are mandatory to ensure that they have supervised the investigation
and are willing to accept responsibility for its reliability.

Supplementary Documentation. Although

completion of a new account report form evidences a thorough inquiry into the essential
facts, it is often necessary to furnish the firm
with additional documents for mutual legal protection. In most member organizations, it is usually the registered representatives' responsibility
to secure these documents. In a few instances,
such as for discretionary accounts, documentation must be in hand and approved prior to the
transaction.

See also Corporate Account; Credit Agree-
ment; Customer's Agreement; Discretionary
Account; Fiduciary Account; Joint Customers;
Loan-Consent Agreement; Prudent Man; Regis-
tered Representative (Responsibilities); Trading
Authorization; Uniform Gifts to Minors Act
(UGMA); Unincorporated Associations.

New York Stock Exchange, Inc. (NYSE).
New York City is the center of the financial
world in the United States and the New York
Stock Exchange, Inc. (NYSE) is its focal point.
The NYSE is the leading securities marketplace
of Wall Street because of its influence, size, and
functions in the U.S. and international
economies. It is impossible to work in the securities industry and not be involved in some way
with activities of the NYSE. Indeed, the
nickname of the exchange, the "Big Board,"
tells the story by itself.

The New York Stock Exchange, Inc., is a
central marketplace where purchases and sales
of securities issued by select corporations can be
arranged at fair prices determined through in-
teraction of the forces of supply and demand.
These transactions, physically carried out on the
premises of the exchange itself, must be accomplished only by people qualified by the exchange to act in that capacity. Such an individual
is identified as a *member,* and the business organization that person represents in performing
this responsibility is called a *member organization,* whether it conducts its affairs as a partnership or as a corporation.

The NYSE is not the oldest institution of its kind in the world. It is not even the oldest in the United States, having been preceded by the Philadelphia Stock Exchange.

Functions of the NYSE. In terms of trading volume, the NYSE isn't the busiest securities exchange in the world, either; that distinction belongs to the Tokyo Stock Exchange. However, there are few people who will refute the claim that the NYSE is the most significant, centralized, international marketplace. It offers investors (1) outstanding marketability; (2) ease of operation; (3) prompt and accurate trade publicity; (4) timely release of corporate information from issuers whose securities are traded on its premises; (5) continuous opportunity for participation in a wide variety of business ventures; (6) the greatest number of listed companies having sound financial structures, impressive tangible assets, and substantial capital; and (7) equitable facilities for enlightened speculation.

A substantial corporation meeting the NYSE's discriminating standards can apply for the privilege of having its securities traded on the exchange. Henceforth, the corporation is known as a *listed company* of the NYSE. Its securities, consequently, are called *listed securities*. While the NYSE is not directly involved in arranging for financing by listed corporations, it does indirectly facilitate such offerings by providing liquidity for equity or debt issues. (*Liquidity* refers to the easy ability of investors to convert their securities holdings into cash, and vice versa.)

As a central marketplace, the NYSE provides the facilities for supply and demand factors to arrive at equitable prices for all parties concerned. The exchange itself does not interfere or influence these price determinations. It merely allows the value levels and fluctuations to be established via the mechanics of an open auction market. Buyers and sellers are permitted to compete with each other accordingly, and actual transactions frequently result in compromise

valuations somewhere between the highest bid and lowest offering price. The only role played by the exchange in these mechanisms is to monitor activity in an effort to prevent any unfair and inequitable manipulation through fraudulent practices.

Brief History of the NYSE. The NYSE was founded by 24 brokers in 1792 as an outdoor marketplace under a buttonwood tree in front of what was 60 Wall Street in New York City. It was organized and continued to do business for 179 years as a voluntary association. *Voluntary associations* originated in medieval England. They combined some features of partnerships with the corporate form of business organization. Voluntary associations provide continuity of existence but include unlimited financial liability for their memberships.

Although the number of exchange members grew steadily, unlimited financial liability did not prove to be a burden until the late 1960s. At that time, several member organizations failed, resulting in sizable losses for their customers and creditors. Although it was not obligated to do so, the exchange nevertheless committed a special trust fund for the purpose of making restitution to the customers of those firms. By 1971, the Customer Assistance Program had raised a total of $140 million in cash and other commitments through assessments levied against the entire membership. (The problem was not confined to the New York Stock Exchange community. As a result, the Securities Investors Protection Act of 1970 came into being.)

In February 1971, the NYSE membership voted to incorporate the exchange to forestall potential liabilities for its individual members in matters relating to community problems and thus ensure its own continuous existence.

As a *not-for-profit* corporation, under New York state laws, the NYSE does not issue shares of stock to represent participation therein. Instead, ownership is jointly held by the entire membership of the exchange, presently numbering 1,366. Although this number is fixed under the bylaws, it has varied markedly during the lifetime of the exchange. A membership is traditionally referred to as a *seat* on the exchange; over the years the terms have become synonymous. Ownership of a seat may be transferred or sold to an applicant subject to approval of the governing body of the exchange. Typically, it is sold at a price determined in accordance with the forces of supply and demand, although occasionally it is transferred to someone for a nominal consideration independent of this auction process. Authorities of the NYSE do not influence the prices of securities traded on its premises, nor do they set the values at which memberships may be transferred. The officials of the exchange merely supervise activities to ensure an orderly transaction of such business.

Organization of the NYSE. The governing body of the NYSE consists of a twenty person Board of Directors elected by the general membership for a two-year term of office plus a Chairperson of the Board, who is chosen and elected by the same directors for a variable term of office. The Chairperson is the chief executive officer of the exchange, and by regulation (1) cannot be a member of the exchange; (2) cannot be affiliated with a broker/dealer organization; (3) cannot engage in any other business while serving in this capacity; and (4) may appoint a president, several vice-presidents, and other officers deemed necessary for efficient management and operation of the exchange.

Of the other twenty people serving on the NYSE Board of Directors (1) ten are representatives of the public having no affiliation with brokers or dealers in securities; and (2) ten are members of the NYSE or are principal partners or senior executive officers of member organizations.

By majority vote of the Directors then in office, the Board may (1) adopt, repeal, amend, or interpret rules and regulations of the exchange; and (2) prescribe and impose any penalties for

neglect of, or refusal to obey, any rules and regulations.

Membership on the NYSE is restricted to persons who are at least the minimum age of majority. There are no bans regarding race, nationality, religion, or sex.

Applying for membership. An applicant for membership must make arrangements for purchase or transfer of a seat on the exchange through the Office of the Secretary. The applicant is required to complete a comprehensive application form that includes (1) the details of that person's complete business history; (2) letters of recommendation from three responsible persons; and (3) evidence of sponsorship by two persons who have been members or allied members of the exchange for at least one year. (An allied member is, in a partnership, a general partner who is not a member of the exchange. In a corporation, an allied member is a voting stockholder employee who is not a member of the exchange, but owns 5% or more of the voting stock or is a director on its board or has been designated by that organization as a principal executive officer.)

The NYSE Constitution provides that final approval for admission as a member must be granted by two-thirds of the Directors present at a meeting of the exchange's board. Before final approval by the board, however, the secretary of the exchange must post notice of the proposed transfer in the *Weekly Bulletin* and on an information board on the floor of the exchange at least ten days prior to submission of the application to the board. The applicant and all sponsors must also appear before a committee of the board during this time.

Obligations of membership. On election to the exchange by the board of directors, a member is obliged to (1) complete payment for the purchase price of the seat to the seller; (2) pay an initiation fee to the NYSE; (3) make a contribution to the NYSE Gratuity Fund (This is a fund created to provide death benefits to the next of kin of each deceased member by means of voluntary contributions. Coverage is limited to NYSE members exclusively and varies from $20,000 to $100,000, depending on the member's seniority at the exchange.); (4) sign the NYSE Constitution, pledging to abide by it and be subject to jurisdiction of the exchange's board of directors; and (5) pass a written qualification exam within one year. (Members who intend to work in their offices rather than on the floor of the exchange must sit for an allied member examination instead of the usual floor examination.)

Financing membership. The purchase of a membership in the NYSE may be financed in whole or in part by (1) the applicant's own means; (2) a gift to the applicant; (3) funds obtained from a subordinated loan; or (4) funds advanced by a member organization under terms of an ABC Agreement.

If the seat is purchased with the applicant's personal funds, the member must certify that no future agreement will be entered into regarding that membership unless specific approval is first gained from the exchange.

If any part of the purchase price of a seat has been advanced as a gift, the applicant must furnish the exchange with a general release from the donor proving that no payment is expected from the new member. A similar release is filed when a membership is transferred for a consideration.

If funds are borrowed to purchase a seat, the applicant must obtain such financing under a subordination agreement approved by the exchange. In this document, which matures in not less than one year, the lender agrees not to lay claim to the seat if the member defaults. No one can become a member of the NYSE through default in a loan agreement.

Because memberships in the NYSE are expensive and must be owned only by individuals rather than by firms, seats are frequently purchased under a special contract with funds advanced by a partnership or corporation (*see* ABC Agreement).

Classification of Members. New York Stock Exchange members are often classified and identified by the activities in which they engage on the trading floor. However, they are not restricted to specific functions, and we frequently find many members participating in several different activities during a typical working day.

See also Bond Broker; Commission House Broker; Competitive Market-Maker; Competitive Trader; Specialist; Two-Dollar Broker.

Types of Membership Organization. New York Stock Exchange rules permit members of the exchange to conduct their activities under any of the three forms of business organization: (1) individual proprietorship; (2) partnership; and (3) corporation.

Individual proprietorships. The affairs of an individual proprietorship are limited by the member's own physical and capital capabilities. Moreover, individual members are prohibited by regulation from dealing with the public or from carrying customer accounts. Active individual proprietor members confine their activity to (1) executions of orders in behalf of other members; and/or (2) trading securities for their own account and risk.

Partnerships and corporations. Most NYSE members have formed partnerships or corporations to enable them to make use of larger pools of capital and the increased talent resources of these multiprincipal business organizations. With prior approval from the exchange, partnerships and corporations may carry customer accounts and have dealings directly with the public. Their financial organizational structures frequently appear as follows:

Partnership	Corporation
Member of the NYSE	Member of the NYSE
General partners	Voting stockholders
Limited partners	Nonvoting stockholders
Subordinated lenders	Subordinated debentures

Note that in either business structure, there must be at least one general partner or one voting stockholder, as the case may be, who owns a seat on the NYSE and thus makes it possible for that business entity to identify itself as a member organization. Should that member die, the exchange's Board of Directors allows the firm a reasonable period of time to replace the deceased member with another general partner (voting stockholder) acceptable to the board, to maintain its status as a member organization. Of course, this presents no problem if the firm is rep- resented by two or more seats on the exchange, or if its *franchise* is vested to them under an ABC Agreement, with its provisions for easy transferability of ownership.

The Departmental System of the NYSE. For an institution to perform both as an operating agency and a regulatory authority, a delegation of specific responsibility must be implemented. The NYSE is no exception to that rule, as illustrated in the following summarized chart of organization.

Organization of the NYSE

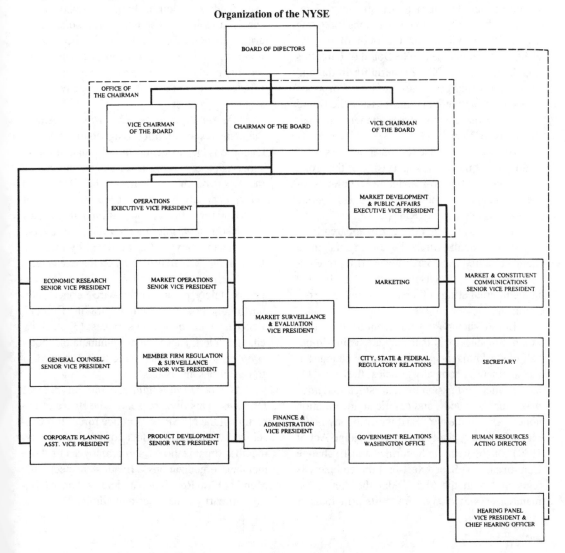

Every one of the departments and sub-departments plays an important role in the general scheme of activity in the exchange community. However, from a practical point of view, it is unlikely that the typical member, allied member, or registered representative will ever have personal contact with most of these offices. The following discussion outlines the responsibility of those departments as it affects the day-to-day activity of the sales, trading, and operations personnel within a member organization.

Corporate Services Department. The Corporate Services Department investigates and determines the eligibility of corporations for listing and trading privileges on the floor of the exchange. Although the NYSE Board of Directors establishes the qualifying criteria for initial and continued listing privileges, it is the Corporate Services Department that must assure the Board that those requirements have been met (*see* Qualifications for Listing).

Another important responsibility assigned to this department is its supervision of the proxy and representation-to-management policies of the exchange in the interest of all public shareholders (*see* Proxy Rules).

These days, when dissent is apparently in vogue, it is neither unlikely nor unusual for a member, allied member, registered representative, or even the firm itself to become embroiled in the internal affairs of a publicly traded corporation.

Before such parties represent to the corporation's management that they are acting in behalf of stockholders in petitioning for changes in management or company policies, they must (1) have written permission from the stockholders to make such demands; and (2) file an information notice (a) with the NYSE (if the company is not registered under the Securities Exchange Act of 1934); or (b) with the Securities and Exchange Commission on Schedule 14b if the company is registered with the SEC under the Act. (If a member organization or any of its principals or representatives even volunteers voting advice to a customer without prior request from that customer, it may have to file as a participant with the SEC under the proxy rules of the Commission.)

Specifically, when an unregistered company is the subject of such actions, the NYSE's notification is necessary if a party employed by, or affiliated with, a member organization (1) requests more than ten security holders to sign a proxy or to vote for or against or abstain from voting on any proposal; (2) requests another security holder to join in calling a meeting of security holders, to join in litigation against an issuer, or to join or assist in the formation of a securities holders' committee; (3) becomes a nominee for director; (4) becomes a member of a security holders' committee or group; or (5) contributes funds for the cost of a prospective or present proxy contest.

Market Operations Department. Among the many responsibilities assigned to the Market Operations Department is the administration and supervision of trading rules and regulations on the floor of the exchange. The Department serves in an advisory capacity to members relating to interpretation or application of those rules. It is also responsible for providing and overseeing the ancillary services utilized by members to facilitate their transactions on the exchange.

Such ancillary services include: (1) telephone, teletype, and other wire services connecting member firms with the trading floor; (2) ticker tape and quotation services; (3) stock exchange clerk/pages and annunciator board privileges; and (4) pneumatic tube communication facilities and others.

Member Firm Regulation and Surveillance Division. This division serves the Board of Directors of the NYSE as its police force. It is concerned with the conduct of the members, member organizations, and employees of those member organizations. In this respect, the Member Firm Regulation and Surveillance Division primarily supervises and administers those regulations, policies, and interpretations of the board that relate to the conduct and operation of member organizations, including (1) internal, legal, and financial structures; (2) registration requirements for members, allied members, branch office managers, representatives, and supervisory analysts; (3) monitoring trading activities of firms and customers; and (4) extensions of credit to customers on securities transactions.

Among the specific duties of the Member Firm Regulation and Surveillance Division are the oversight of (1) qualifications and conduct of all registered persons; (2) protection of customers' financial interests; and (3) sales literature. *(See* Advertising; Financial Protection Requirements ; Registration of Personnel).

Surveillance Coordination Department. To insure the integrity of a member organization's net capital position the board of directors of the NYSE requires each firm to subject itself to an annual audit and several examinations of operating condition during the course of a year. An annual audit requirement is applicable to all broker/dealers under SEC Rule 17a-5, and the NYSE's required audit, satisfying the federal regulation, is a comprehensive verification of firm records. The member organization employs an independent public accountant of its own choice and makes arrangements for that person to conduct a formal audit of the firm's books and financial activities. The accountant communicates and cooperates with the Surveillance Coordination Department to ensure that the audit conforms to the standards of scope and detail necessary for compliance with exchange regulations.

Supplementing the annual audit is a mandated series of internal examinations performed by the member firm itself. Its results are reportable to the exchange and to various other supervisory bodies.

See also Financial and Operational Combined Uniform Single Report (FOCUS).

In keeping with the NYSE policy of financial disclosure to customers and in accord with SEC Rule 17a-5, member organizations must send customers an annual statement of the firm's financial condition determined at the time of the formal audit. The statement must include (1) an unconsolidated balance sheet; (2) a notice of required net capital as well as present net capital, as defined by the exchange, with an explanation showing how it is calculated; and (3) any material inadequacies in firm controls if such inadequacies are found to exist.

Furthermore, within forty days after each calendar (or fiscal) semiannual period, the firm must also send its customers (1) an uncertified balance sheet; and (2) a statement of the firm's current net capital and required net capital, computed in accordance with NYSE Rule 325 and SEC Rule 15c3-1. Thus, customers of member organizations are assured of at least two financial statements annually; one as the result of a formal audit and another one as of a date six months later.

See also Arbitration; Depository Trust Company; Securities Industry Automation Corporation (SIAC); Securities Investor Protection Corporation (SIPC); Stock Clearing Corporation (SCC).

New York Stock Exchange Index. The New York Stock Exchange publishes a composite index of all its listed common stocks (NYSE Composite Index). This index is further broken down into four groups—(1) industrial; (2) transportation; (3) utilities; (4) finance—and is printed on the tape every half-hour. This composite index is identified as the "market."

Example:

The five New York Stock Exchange indexes reflect the combined market-value changes in the component issues. Each index is weighted; this means that the price of each stock is multiplied by the number of listed shares in making the calculations. Wide price fluctuations in cyclical issues with a small number of shares will not distort the true value of the index, because both price and total value are used as determinants. Movements in the composite index (the "market") are shown in dollars and cents because most public investors find this form easier to understand. The group indexes are shown only in terms of point movements up or down from their previous values.

All five indexes were originally set at 50.00 as of the close of the market on December 31, 1965, because this was the approximate average price of listed shares at that time. If necessary, base market values are adjusted daily to allow for changes in capitalization, new listings, or delistings.

Example: If an issue is delisted, the base market value is decreased so that the level of the index will not be affected. The formula for computing the current index is:

$$\text{Composite index} = \frac{\text{current market value}}{\text{base market value}} \times 50$$

Example: If the base market value is $800 billion and the curent market value is $700 billion, the current index will be 43.75.

$$\frac{700}{800} \times 50 = \frac{35,000}{800} = 43.75$$

A net money change in the average price of NYSE shares is derived from the net change in the NYSE Composite Index as follows:

$$\text{Change in average price} = \frac{\begin{array}{c}\text{average price}\\ \text{of shares listed}\end{array}}{\begin{array}{c}\text{composite}\\ \text{index value*}\end{array}} \times \text{change in index}$$

Example: Assume that the composite index value is 43.75, up .05 from 43.70 and that the average price of shares listed is 35.00. The ticker tape will show this as "Market up 4 cents."

$$\frac{35.00}{43.70*} \times .05 = .04, \text{ or 4 cents up}$$

*Use the changed composite index and reflect the change we use in the formula.

See also American Stock Exchange Market Value Index; Averages and Indexes; Dow Jones Averages; NASDAQ-OTC Price Index; Standard & Poor's Index.

Next-Day Contract. As an accommodation to investors, principally for tax reasons, the NYSE also permits next-day contracts in corporate and municipal securities traded on its premises toward the latter days of a calendar year. *Next-day contracts* call for settlement between purchasing and selling firm on the next business day after trade date. If the seller's settlement date falls within a calendar year, any profit on that transaction is taxed as a capital gain for that year.

This type of contract has little appeal for a seller establishing a capital loss, however. In calculating an annual loss, it is the *trade date* that counts. Therefore, losses can be taken through the last business day of the year under any contract settlement terms.

Contract settlement terms are summarized in the following table.

Type	Settlement Date
Regular Way (RW)	
Corporate and municipal securities	= Fifth business day after trade date
U.S. government obligations	= Next business day after trade date
Seller's Option (S-?)	
Corporate and municipal securities	= 6 business to 60 calendar days after trade date
U.S. government obligations	= 2 business days to 60 calendar days after trade date
Cash	= Same day as trade date
When-Issued (WI)/When-Distributed (WD)	= On a date in the future to be determined
Next-Day (ND)	= On the business day following trade date

See also Cash Contract; Corporate Bond Transaction; Regular-Way Contract; Seller's-Option Contract; When- Issued/When Distributed Contract.

Nine-Bond Rule. Unless prior consent of the NYSE can be obtained, all orders handled by member firms for nine or fewer listed bonds must be sent to the floor of the exchange for a diligent attempt at execution.

Orders for ten or more bonds are not subject to these restrictive conditions. Nor are orders for less than ten bonds that (1) mature within twelve months; (2) have been called prior to maturity and will be redeemed within twelve months; (3) are obligations of the United States, Puerto Rico, or the Philippine Islands, or any state, territory, or municipality therein; (4) will be executed as an *agency transaction* and the customer specifically directs the order to be executed elsewhere than on the exchange (Members may not solicit such instructions before attempting diligent execution on the floor.); (5) is part of a primary distribution or part of a secondary distribution that was effected off the floor of the exchange; (6) are unrelated to the current market price if the intent of such order is to correct an error or make a gift; (7) are unregistered, as defined in the Securities Act of 1933; (8) are less than a normal unit of trading (that is, baby bonds, those bonds whose face value is less than $1,000); (9) are executed for persons situated outside the United States and before or after trading hours on the New York Stock Exchange. Another permissible exception to the nine-bond rule allows execution of an order with a nonmember market-maker over the counter. The member organization is required to act only in an agency capacity in such transactions.

See also Corporate Bond Transaction.

No-Load Mutual Funds. *See* Investment Companies.

Nominal Price. Price quotations on futures for a period in which no actual trading took place.

Nominal Quotations. *See* Rules of Fair Practice (Section 5).

Nominal Yield (Coupon Rate). This is the annual interest rate percentage payable, specified in the indenture and printed on the face of the bond certificate. It enables purchasers to determine their yearly flow of dollar income. Nominal yield is not related to market value.

For bonds that are issued in denominations of $1,000 and whose annual interest rate is expressed as a percentage of that amount, the number of interest dollars received annually by the investor is calculated by converting that percentage rate into a decimal and multiplying by $1,000.

Example:

A 4% nominal yield = $1,000 × .04, or $40
A 5⅝% nominal yield = $1,000 × .05625, or $56.25
A 7¾% nominal yield = $1,000 × .0775, or $77.50

To reduce administrative effort, many corporations issue bonds in minimum denominations of $5,000, and a few have even issued them in $10,000 pieces. The only effect this has on calculation of interest dollars is to require multiplication of the nominal yield by $5,000 or $10,000, as the case may be, instead of by $1,000.

Example: A 6 ¼% nominal yield for a bond with a $5,000 face value would return $312.50 annually ($5,000 x .0625).

The nominal yield is a yearly rate that is usually paid in equal installments, semiannually. Thus a 4% nominal yield would require distribution of $20 in interest on the first or fifteenth day of January and July, or March and September, or any other calendar dates designated in the indenture, as long as the payments are separated by six-month intervals.

Examples:
January and July
February and August
March and September
April and October
May and November
June and December
 See also Bond (Quotations); Current Yield; Yield-to-Maturity.

Nonconvertible Bond. *See* Exempt Security (Margin Trading).

Noncumulative Preferred Stock. Preferred stock on which omitted dividends do not accrue and the shareholders have no claim to them in the future.
 See also Cumulative Preferred Stock.

Nondiversified Company. This type of management company is one that declares itself not subject to the limitations on concentration of assets that apply to diversified companies. Such a statement is filed at the time of registration with the SEC and is usually preferred by venture capital companies and holding companies. Venture capital companies specialize by investing solely in new corporations and/or fledgling industries. *Holding companies* concentrate sizable investments in a few firms hoping to gain control of those concerns or a significant voice in their management. The typical investment company is diversified and does not try to influence management decisions of companies whose shares it acquires. The comparatively few nondiversified companies so registered have great flexibility for concentration of investments. As a result, their asset value may prove to be extremely volatile. They have great appeal for speculators who wish to express confidence in management's ability to perform wisely. There are also special tax considerations influencing the decision to register as diversified or nondiversified.

See also Diversified Company; Management Company.

Nonequity Options. The term, *standardized options*, includes stock (equity) options as well as options on other underlying interests including stock indexes, government debt securities and foreign currencies. The basics are the same: puts, calls, and strategies in general—but there are differences in pricing, units of trading, settlement, expiration dates, margin, taxation and other areas.

As with stock options these other standardized options may be used to hedge positions or for purely speculative purposes.

Index Options. Stock indexes are figured and reported by several institutions including securities exchanges. Such indexes may be representative of overall market movement (broad-based index) or a particular industry (narrow-based index). The S&P 100 Index (CBOE) is the most actively traded broad-based index and the Airline Index (AMEX) is representative of a narrow-based index.

When an index option is exercised, there is no transfer of securities—no purchase or sale is required. Instead, a cash settlement is made for the dollar difference between the strike price and the closing index price on the day of the exercise.

The various index prices are reported regularly, and puts and calls may be traded at strike prices near the current index price levels.

The following table shows the currently traded index options. While each market reserves the right to establish the particular "multiplier" for each index option that they trade, the usual such multiplier is 100. Just as with stock options (assuming a multiplier of 100), a premium of 3½ represents total premium cost of $350—a 1⅝ premium totals $162.50, and so forth.

INDEX OPTIONS

Monday, January 27, 1986

Chicago Board

S&P 100 INDEX

Strike	Calls–Last			Puts–Last		
Price	Feb	Mar	Apr	Feb	Mar	Apr
180	....	20¾	....	1/16	3/16	....
185	16	....	17	⅛	⅜	1
190	11⅛	11½	13	7/16	1 1/16	1¾
195	6¾	8¼	9⅜	1¼	2⅜	3¼
200	3⅜	5	6⅜	3⅛	4⅜	5⅛
205	1⅜	2 15/16	4¼	6⅛	7⅜	8
210	7/16	1 9/16	2⅜	10¼	11½	11¼
215	⅛	11/16	1⅜	14⅞	14⅞	....
220	1/16	⅜	⅞	....	....	20¼

Total call volume 182,691. Total call open int. 558,150.
Total put volume 114,982. Total put open int. 471,157.
The index: High 201.48; Low 199.93; Close 201.00, +1.07

S&P 500 INDEX

Strike	Calls–Last			Puts–Last		
Price	Feb	Mar	Apr	Feb	Mar	Apr
190	....	....	....	....	3/16	....
210	....	3¾	....	....	....	....

Total call volume 11. Total call open int. 219.
Total put volume 5. Total put open int. 275.
The index: High 207.69; Low 206.43; Close 207.39, +0.96.

S&P OTC 250 INDEX

Strike	Calls–Last			Puts–Last		
Price	Feb	Mar	Apr	Feb	Mar	Apr
170	....	....	....	⅜	....	....
185	....	....	....	1	....	....

Total call volume 0. Total call open int. 93.
Total put volume 12. Total put open int. 35
The index: High 193.35; Low 192.35; Close 193.31, +0.95.

American Exchange

MAJOR MARKET INDEX

Strike	Calls–Last			Puts–Last		
Price	Feb	Mar	Apr	Feb	Mar	Apr
260	....	....	....	1/16	....	....
265	....	....	....	3/16	¾	....
270	15½	15¾	....	½	1⅜	2 1/16
275	10½	12½	....	1⅛	2½	....
280	7⅛	9⅛	.	2½	4	5⅜
285	4⅛	6½	8	4⅜	6⅜	....
290	2¼	4⅛	6⅛	7¾	....	10½
295	1 1/16	2½		11¼	13½	....
300	⅜	1 9/16	2 15/16	16	....	....
305	1⅛	1	1¾	....	....	....
310	1/16	1½	....	....	....	....
315	1/16	¼	....	....	....	....

Total call volume 18,349 Total call open int. 49,907
Total put volume 13,315 Total put open int. 46,045
The index: High 285.74; Low 283.79; Close 284.83, +1.04

COMPUTER TECHNOLOGY INDEX

Strike	Calls–Last			Puts–Last		
Price	Feb	Mar	Apr	Feb	Mar	Apr
105	....	....	....	....	½	....
110	4¾	....	....	1¼	....	....
115	2½	4⅛	.	....	4	....
120	11/16	1¾	3	....	....	....

Total call volume 45 Total call open int. 155
Total put volume 105 Total put open int. 252
The index: High 114.93; Low 113.43; Close 114.19, +0.38

OIL INDEX

Strike	Calls Last			Puts–Last		
Price	Feb	Mar	Apr	Feb	Mar	Apr
120	4⅞			1 5/16	2½	3
125	1⅞	3⅜	....	3½	4⅜	....
130	⅝	1⅜	....	....	....	....
135	1/16	...	....	....	....	....
140	....	....	½	....	....	....

Total call volume 259 Total call open int. 828
Total put volume 83 Total put open int. 412
The index: High 125.03; Low 123.33; Close 123.86, –1.17

AIRLINE INDEX

Strike	Calls Last			Puts–Last		
Price	Feb	Mar	Apr	Feb	Mar	Apr
105	11½	....	13½	⅜	....	
110	6⅛	....	....	....	2¼	....
115	2¾	5⅞	....	3	....	....

Total call volume 128 Total call open int. 401
Total put volume 92 Total put open int. 193
The index: High 116.94; Low 114.06; Close 114.19, –0.75

Philadelphia Exchange

GOLD/SILVER INDEX

Strike	Calls–Last			Puts–Last		
Price	Feb	Mar	Apr	Feb	Mar	Apr
75	....	....	....	....	¼	....
80	....	13⅛	....	....	....	....
85	....	....	....	¾	1⅝	....
90	3⅞	6½	....	2¼	3½	....
95	1⅝	3¼	5	4¾	....	....
100	11/16	1¾	3⅜	....	....	....
105	15/16	....	....	....	....	....
110	....	....	....	....	....	....

Total call volume 311 Total call open int. 1,833
Total put volume 103 Total put open int. 1,118
The index: High 93.14; Low 90.93; Close 91.61, –0.50

VALUE LINE INDEX OPTIONS

Strike	Calls–Last			Puts–Last		
Price	Feb	Mar	Apr	Feb	Mar	Apr
195	....	....	....	1/16	....	....
200	....	15¾	....	....	....	....
205	9⅞	....	....	9/16	1¼	....
210	5½	7⅜	8½	1 9/16	2¾	....
215	2 9/16	4⅜	....	4¼	5⅛	....
220	15/16	2¼	....	7	8¾	....
225	¼	1⅛	2¼	....	....	....
230	⅛	½	....	....	....	....

Total call volume 5,096 Total call open int. 1,072
Total put volume 1,453 Total put open int. 18,482
The index: High 214.70; Low 213.90; Close 214.44, +0.59

NATIONAL O-T-C INDEX

Strike	Calls–Last			Puts–Last		
Price	Feb	Mar	Apr	Feb	Mar	Apr
190	....	....	....	....	2⅞	....
200	....	2⅛	....	....	....	....

Total call volume 2 Total call open int. 630
Total put volume 1 Total put open int. 726
The index: High 192.15; Low 190.72; Close 192.01, +1.07

Pacific Exchange

TECHNOLOGY INDEX

Strike	Calls–Last			Puts–Last		
Price	Feb	Mar	Apr	Feb	Mar	Apr
100	11½	....	....	....	....	....
105	....	....	....	¼	....	1⅛
110	3¼	5	....	1¾	4¾	....
115	1	....	....	....	....	....
120	....	1 1/16	....	....	....	....

Total call volume 338 Total call open int. 3,118
Total put volume 43 Total put open int. 701
The index: High 111.22; Low 110.43; Close 110.61, +0.14

N.Y. Stock Exchange

NYSE OPTIONS INDEX

Strike	Calls–Last			Puts–Last		
Price	Feb	Mar	Apr	Feb	Mar	Apr
110	....	....	....	1/16	3/16	....
115	4⅞	6¼	....	⅜	13/16	1⅛
120	1 11/16	2 9/16	3⅜	1 13/16	2 9/16	3⅛
125	¼	⅞	1½	5⅜	....	....
130	....	¼	½	....	....	....

Total call volume 4,551. Total call open int. 18,944
Total put volume 2,994. Total put open int. 40,780
The index: High 120.04; Low 119.29; Close 119.87, +0.55.

NYSE DOUBLE INDEX

Strike	Calls–Last			Puts–Last		
Price	Feb	Mar	Apr	Feb	Mar	Apr
220	1/16	....	....	1/16	5/16	....
225	....	....	....	3/16	¾	....
230	....	....	....	11/16	1⅜	....
235	6⅜	....	....	1 13/16	3	4
240	3¼	5⅛	....	3⅜	....	6⅛
245	1½	3½	....	7⅜	....	....
250	9/16	1¾	2⅜	....	....	13¼
255	⅛	⅞	1⅜	....	....	....
260	1/16	⅜	....	....	....	....

Total call volume 2,023. Total call open int. 13,855.
Total put volume 1,912. Total put open int. 13,609
The index: High 240.08; Low 238.58; Close 239.74, +1.10

NASD

NASDAQ 100 INDEX

Strike	Calls–Last			Puts–Last		
Price	Feb	Mar	Apr	Feb	Mar	Apr
250	12⅞	....	....	9/16	....	....
255	....	....	....	1⅜	....	....
260	5 9/16	8½	....	3⅜	....	....
265	3	5⅞	....	6⅛	7¼	....
270	1½	....	6	9⅜	....	....

Total call volume 188. Total call open int. 633.
Total put volume 76. Total put open int. 741.
The index: High 262.10; Low 259.56; Close 261.59, +1.19.

An index responds only to price movements in the stocks on which it is based. Strike prices are set at five-point intervals. Index options can never be completely covered—they can mitigate risk, but can never be considered a true hedge.

Example:

Chicago Board
S & P 100 Index

Strike Price	Calls Feb	Mar	Puts Apr	Feb	Mar	Apr
200	3⅜	5	6⅝	3⅛	4⅜	5⅛
205	1¼	2⅞	4¼	6⅛	7½	8

Close 201.00 + 1.07

Refer to the foregoing illustration. With an index "price" of 201.00, the 200 calls are in-the-money and the 200 puts are out-of-the-money. The time value of the March 200 calls is 4 (intrinsic value is 1). There is no intrinsic value to the February 200 puts.

With a multiplier of 100, the 205 strike price options have a dollar value of $20,500 (100 × 205). Had a speculator exercised a 205 put during the trading day, he or she would have received the difference, in cash, between the strike price and the index closing price.

$20,500	−$20,100	= $400
Strike Price	Closing Price	Exerciser Receives

Had the index level risen dramatically after the client had given the exercise instruction, it is possible that he or she would have been required to pay money to the assigned writer. The index level may have approximated 201 at the time the exercise instruction was given, but if the closing value had been 208, the put holder would have to pay $300.

$20,500	−$20,800	= ($300)
Strike Price	Closing Price	Exerciser Pays

Hedge Ratio. Portfolio managers very often utilize index options to minimize market risk. It is necessary to determine the hedge ratio required to protect a given portfolio; the number of options that must be purchased. The hedge ratio takes into consideration the dollar value of the portfolio as well as its beta. This *beta* expresses the anticipated volatility of the portfolio versus the volatility of the index used to hedge the portfolio.

Example: If a given portfolio is expected to be 40% more volatile than the S&P 100 Index, it is said to have a beta of 1.4. Presuming a portfolio valued at $25,000,000 having a 1.4 beta, the number of put contracts (S&P 100 Index—strike price 190) necessary would be:

$$\text{Number of Contracts} = \frac{\text{Beta} \times \text{Portfolio Value}}{\text{Index Value}}$$

$$= \frac{1.4 \times \$25,000,000}{\$19,000}$$

$$= 1842$$

Thus, at least in theory, 1842 S&P 100 Index puts would protect the portfolio against any downside risk.

The margin required on a short index option position is the amount of the premium plus 5% of the index value. Out-of-the-money options may be reduced, but no lower than the premium plus 2% of the index value.

Example: What is the required margin on a short S&P 100 Index February 200 call? The premium is 3¾ and the index price is 201.00

Premium	$ 375.00	
5% of index price	+ 1,005.00	(5% + $20,100)
Margin requirement	$1,380.00	

Since the option is in-the-money, no reduction is permitted.

Gains and losses on broad-based index options are treated as 40% short term and 60% long term, regardless of holding periods. Narrow-based index options, taxwise, are treated in the same manner as stock options.

Debt Options. Puts and calls are also traded on certain U.S. government securities—such options are called debt options. While in the future, underlying debt securities may include Treasury bills, notes, and other instruments, at this writing only one type of debt option is actively traded: the thirty-year, 9⅞% U.S. Treasury Bonds maturing in 2015 (9⅞ of 2015). We shall confine our remarks and limit our questions to this one product. Refer to the following table.

INTEREST RATE OPTIONS

Monday, January 27, 1986
For Notes and Bonds, decimals in closing prices represent 32nds; .1.1 means 1 1/32. For Bills, decimals in closing prices represent basis points; $25 per .01.

Chicago Board Options Exchange

U.S. TREASURY BOND—$100,000 principal value

Underlying Issue	Strike Price	Calls Last Mar	Jun	Sep	Puts—Last Mar	Jun	Sep
11¼%	110	6.22	....	....	....	....	....
		....	....	....	1		
9⅞%	102	....	....	....	....	2.02	
due 11/2015	104	1.15	....	2.26	1.11	2.29	
	106	0.22	....	....	2.19	....	

Total call vol. 38 Call open int. 16,585
Total put vol. 240 Put open int. 15,802
3 p.m. prices of underlying issues supplied by Merrill Lynch: 11¼% 118 29/32; 11¼% 116 23/32; 10⅜% 110 21/32; 9⅞%(b) 105 5/32; 9⅞%(n)104 9/32; 9⅜% 103 12/32; 9⅛% 101 31/32

Am Exp	40	r	r	s	r	⅛	s
55½	... 45	10½	11½	s	⅛	¾	s
55½	... 50	6¾	7¾	8⅛	11-16	1¼	1⅝
55½	... 55	3	4⅛	5½	2⅛	2⅞	r
Am Hom	60	5	r	r	0.1⅛		

Example: The contract size is $100,000; each option represents the right to buy or sell $100,000 face amount of the underlying debt security. Strike prices and premiums are expressed in points and 32nds. A strike price of 104 represents 104% of $100,000 or $104,000—a premium of 2.26 = 2 and 26/32nds% of $100,000 or $2,812.50 (2 26/32% × $100,000).

With the underlying security trading at 105.5 (105 5/32nds), 104 calls would be in-the-money; 104 puts would be out-of-the-money. A 104 call option trading at a price of 1.5 would be at-the-money; the strike price and the premium,

added together, would exactly equal the price of the underlying security (104 + 1.5 = 105.5).

The value of a debt option is dependent on the price of the underlying debt instrument. As interest rates rise, bond prices fall. Under this condition, call prices would fall and put prices would increase.

For uncovered short debt options, the required margin is the premium plus $3,000 for Treasury note options and $3,500 for Treasury bond options. Margin can be reduced by whatever amount an option may be out-of-the-money, but in no event can the required margin on either notes or bonds be less than the premium plus $500.

Example: A client writes an uncovered T-bond 102 call. The premium is 1.8 and the bonds are then trading at 103.2. The required margin is:

Premium	$1,250	(1 8/32 × $100,000)
	+ 3,500	
	$4,750	

Since the option is in-the-money, no reduction on the margin requirement is permitted.

Foreign Currency Options. There are currently (mid-1987) eight different foreign currencies on which options are traded.

Their values fluctuate with the relative values of the currencies versus U.S. dollars. Prices (premiums) of foreign currency options may vary with changes in the value of either the foreign currency and/or the U.S. dollar.

Settlement of foreign currency option exercises must occur within the country issuing that currency. These options expire on the Saturday before the third Wednesday of the expiration month.

The value of the underlying currency, the strike prices and the premiums are expressed not in dollars, but in either cents, tenths of cents, or hundredths of cents. The unit pricing is in cents

309

for British pounds, Canadian dollars, West German marks, and Swiss francs—tenths of cents for French francs—hundredths of cents for Japanese yen.

Example: A strike price of 135 for British pounds means 135 cents. Expressed in dollars it is equal to $1.35. Similarly, a strike price of 52 for Canadian dollars, West German marks, or Swiss francs means 52 cents, or $0.52. When working with these currencies you can easily convert underlying values, strike prices, and premiums to dollars and cents simply by moving the decimal point two places to the left:

British pounds	0.31	= $.0031
Canadian dollars	2.25	= $.0225
West German marks	34.75	= $.3475
Swiss francs	145.60	= $1.456

When working with French francs, where the unit price is a tenth of a cent, convert by moving the decimal point three places to the left:

	.135	= $.000135
French francs	2.40	= $.0024
	135.51	= $.13551

For Japanese yen—priced in hundredths of a cent—move the decimal four places to the left:

	0.14	= $.000014
Japanese yen	1.92	= $.000192
	51.10	= $.00511

In contrast with equity options (where the unit of trading is normally 100), there are several different units of trading. These range from 12,500 British pounds to 6,250,000 Japanese yen. All foreign currency options are currently traded on the Philadelphia exchange.

The following exhibit shows unit pricing and the unit of trading for each of the foreign currency options.

Currency	Pricing Per Unit	Philadelphia Exchange
British pounds	cents	12,500
Canadian dollars	cents	50,000
West German marks	cents	62,500
Swiss francs	cents	62,500
French francs	tenths of cents	125,000
Japanese yen	hundredths of cents	6,250,000
Australian dollars	cents	50,000
ECU (European Currency Unit)	cents	62,500

If the value of a foreign currency decreases relative to the U.S. dollar, it is expected that put premiums will increase and call premiums will decrease. Conversely, should foreign currency values increase relative to the U.S. dollar, call premiums will increase and put premiums will decrease.

Different foreign currencies utilize different pricing units and each exchange utilizes different trading units.

Philadelphia Exchange

Option and Underlying	Strike Price	Calls– Last			Puts– Last	
		Feb	Mar	Jun	Feb	Mar
62,500 West German marks—Cents Per Unit						
D mark	41	0.87	1.13	1.82	0.15	0.30
41.69	42	0.30	0.55	1.29	0.60	0.78

To calculate the dollar value of the underlying foreign currency, multiply the value in the left-hand column (This figure is analogous to the closing price of the foreign currency.) by the unit of trading. The figures on the left (as well as the premiums themselves) are shown in cents.

Underlying 41.69 cents = $.4169 (move decimal two places to the left) $.4169 × 62,500 = $26,056.25

FOREIGN CURRENCY OPTIONS

Monday, January 27, 1986

Philadelphia Exchange

Option & Underlying	Strike Price	Calls—Last			Puts—Last		
		Feb	Mar	Jun	Feb	Mar	Jun
12,500 British Pounds-cents per unit.							
BPound	115	s	23.70	s	s	r	s
139.40	125	s	r	r	s	r	1.30
139.40	130	r	r	r	r	0.70	2.25
139.40	135	r	r	r	0.70	1.55	4.40
139.40	140	1.50	2.10	r	3.00	4.00	6.90
139.40	145	0.25	0.80	2.00	r	7.05	9.60
139.40	150	r	0.30	1.05	r	r	r
50,000 Canadian Dollars-cents per unit.							
CDollr	70	r	r	r	r	0.50	1.00
70.76	71	0.18	0.35	0.80	0.56	1.00	r
70.76	72	r	0.19	0.37	r	1.72	2.35
70.76	73	r	r	0.20	r	2.40	r
62,500 West German Marks-cents per unit.							
DMark	34	s	r	7.92	s	0.01	r
41.69	35	s	6.70	r	s	r	r
41.69	36	r	5.76	r	r	0.01	r
41.69	37	r	4.85	r	0.01	0.01	0.06
41.69	38	r	3.81	4.20	0.01	0.01	0.13
41.69	39	r	2.84	3.31	0.01	0.05	0.22
41.69	40	r	1.90	2.55	0.03	0.13	0.45
41.69	41	0.87	1.13	1.82	0.15	0.30	0.70
41.69	42	0.30	0.55	1.29	0.60	0.78	s
41.69	43	0.08	0.26	0.88	r	r	1.74
41.69	44	r	r	0.57	r	r	r
125,000 French Francs-10ths of a cent per unit.							
FFranc	125	r	r	r	r	r	1.25
135.51	130	r	r	r	0.15	r	r
135.51	135	r	2.40	r	r	2.20	r
6,250,000 Japanese Yen-100ths of a cent per unit.							
JYen	40	s	r	10.98	s	r	r
51.10	42	s	r	9.03	s	r	r
51.10	48	r	3.06	r	r	0.02	0.14
51.10	49	2.08	2.20	2.54	0.03	r	0.26
51.10	50	1.26	1.36	1.92	0.10	0.20	0.48
51.10	51	0.48	s	1.26	0.37	0.60	s
51.10	52	0.13	0.33	0.79	r	r	r
62,500 Swiss Francs-cents per unit.							
SFranc	44	r	5.32	r	r	r	r
49.19	45	r	4.30	r	r	0.01	r
49.19	46	r	3.36	r	r	r	r
49.19	47	r	2.45	r	r	r	r
49.19	48	1.40	1.56	r	0.13	0.28	0.70
49.19	49	0.62	0.93	r	0.40	r	r
49.19	50	0.22	0.48	1.40	r	r	r

Total call vol. 8,376   Call open int. 195,474
Total put vol. 8,609   Put open int. 176,849
r—Not traded. s—No option offered.
Last is premium (purchase price).

Chicago Board Options Exchange

Option & Underlying	Strike Price	Calls—Last			Puts—Last		
		Feb	Mar	Jun	Feb	Mar	Jun
25,000 British Pounds-cents per unit.							
BPound	130	s	r	r	s	0.70	r
139.39	140	r	r	r	2.40	3.80	7.05
139.39	145	r	r	r	r	8.00	r
139.39	150	r	0.30	r	r	r	r
100,000 Canadian Dollars-cents per unit.							
CDollar	71	r	r	r	r	0.94	r
125,000 West German Marks-cents per unit.							
DMark	37	s	r	r	s	r	0.06
41.69	38	r	3.75	r	r	r	r
41.69	39	r	2.88	r	r	r	r
41.69	43	r	0.27	r	r	r	r
250,000 French Francs-10ths of a cent per unit.							
FFranc	125	r	r	r	r	r	1.25
12,500,000 Japanese Yen-100ths of a cent per unit.							
JYen	47	r	4.10	r	r	r	0.06
51.12	48	r	3.12	r	r	0.04	r
51.12	49	r	2.20	2.54	0.03	r	r
51.12	50	1.22	1.42	r	r	0.22	r
51.12	51	0.46	0.70	1.28	r	0.56	r
51.12	52	r	0.30	0.78	r	r	r
125,000 Swiss Francs-cents per unit.							
SFranc	49	r	r	r	0.38	r	r

Total call volume 888.   Total call open int. 17,458.
Total put volume 1,277.   Total put open int. 12,329.
r — Not traded. s—No option offered.
Last is premium (purchase price).

To calculate the cost of purchasing an option (excluding commission), multiply the premium by the unit of trading. Again, keep in mind that the option premiums are expressed in cents.

The cost of a March 42 put would be:

Premium 0.78 cents   = \$.0078 (move decimal two
                             places to the left) \$.0078
                             $\times$ 62,500
                             = \$487.50

To calculate the aggregate exercise price, multiply the strike price by the unit of trading. The aggregate exercise price of a June 41 call would be:

Strike Price 41 cents   = \$.41 (move decimal two
                             places to the left) \$.41
                             $\times$ 62,500
                             = \$25,625

To calculate time value, subtract the in-the-money amount from the total premium. The in-the-money amount of the February 42 put is .31 cents (compare the strike price, 42, with the underlying value, 41.69—a put holder can, at least in theory, buy the underlying foreign currency at 41.69 cents and put it at 42, making a "profit" of .31 cents. The total premium is 0.60. Subtracting the in-the-money amount (intrinsic value) leaves a time value of .29 cents. 0.60 (premium) −.31 in-the-money equals .29 cents.

Time Value .29 cents   = \$0.0029 \$.0029
                             $\times$ 62,500 (unit of trading)
                             = \$181.25

Nonmarketable Security. Savings bonds are considered "nonmarketable" because they are offered publicly through an agent of the Treasury Department and redeemed directly by an agent of the Treasury Department. They do not trade freely in the open market. There are two types of nonmarketable securities: Series EE and Series HH bonds.

See also Marketable Securities; Series EE Bond; Series HH Bond.

No-Par Value. Stock with no dollar value assigned on the issuance of certificates but with an arbitrary equity interest assigned for use in preparing financial statements.

Normal Scale. *See* Scale.

Normal Trading Unit. *See* Rules of Fair Practice (Section 6).

Not Held (NH). This instruction, when specifically stated by a customer, permits a member to use personal judgment in determining when to execute that order. Ordinarily, stock exchange members are prohibited from exercising any discretionary authority in a customer transaction. However, under these specific circumstances some leeway is allowed, and the member may decide on (1) the price of execution, and/or (2) the time of execution, without violating the spirit or purpose of the regulation. In submitting this instruction with the order, a customer literally agrees not to hold the exchange member financially responsible for missing the market if his or her judgment proves to be faulty. Under no circumstances may a specialist ever accept such instructions from a customer. The specialist's vantage point in the marketplace makes this form of discretion prone to claims of partiality by competitors or other public investors.

See also Participate but Do Not Initiate (PNI).

Notice Day. A day on which notices of intent to deliver pertaining to a specified delivery month may be issued.

Numbered Account. It is permissible to maintain a brokerage account under a code name, number, or symbol, provided that the new account report form shows the customer's true identity and provided that written authorization is received from the customer attesting to underlying ownership of the account. The request for a numbered account must also be approved by a person delegated with supervisory authority and responsibility by the firm (see the following figure).

See also New Account Report Form.

O

Odd-Lot Limit Order. *See* Limit Order.

Odd-Lot Stock Execution. An odd lot is any number of shares less than a normal trading unit. Because most stocks on the New York Stock Exchange trade in multiples of 100 shares, an odd lot in those securities is less than 100 shares. For issues assigned trading privileges in units (multiples) of ten shares, an odd lot is less than ten shares.

Most odd-lot orders on the NYSE are processed via computerized facilities owned by the exchange. But the orders are actually executed on behalf of the specialist's personal trading account. The specialist accommodates odd-lot customers in addition to maintaining an orderly round-lot market, which is a primary responsibility.

Role of the Specialist. Some member organizations execute their own customer's odd-lot orders by dealing directly from proprietary (firm trading) accounts. The technique they employ varies somewhat from firm to firm. For the most part these firms are geared to handle only market orders. All other orders are forwarded to the NYSE for execution. Therefore, this discussion deals only with the rules and procedures employed for odd-lot executions by the specialist on the exchange.

Specialist firms are principals on all odd-lot purchases or sales transacted on the exchange. That is, they always act as *dealer* in odd-lot transactions whether they are (1) accommodating customers in buying or selling their odd lots;

or (2) adjusting inventory positions by buying or selling round lots.

With reference to accommodating "customers," bear in mind that specialists normally do not do business directly with the public. Primarily, their customers are the other member firms of the NYSE who transmit the public's odd-lot order to them for execution. Therefore, the other member firms are agents (brokers) on these transactions, whereas the specialists maintain their status as principals.

In exception to regulations that preclude charging a commission on principal transactions, the NYSE permits the specialist to levy a special charge for service on each transaction (*see* Differential).

The following table provides a summary of odd-lot orders.

The following definitions apply specifically to odd-lot transactions.

At-the-Close. An odd-lot order to be executed on the final quotation of the day.

Basis Price. An artificial round-lot transaction created somewhere between the final bid and offer prices if a stock did not trade that day and had a spread in the closing quotation of at least two points.

Bunching. Combining two or more odd-lot orders for entry and execution as a round-lot transaction.

Differential. A fee charged by the specialist for execution of a customer's order. The fee is added to the effective sale on purchase transactions and subtracted from the effective sale on

Summary of Odd-Lot Orders

	Market Order	Limit Order	Stop Order	Stop-Limit Order
Buy	Customer pays the price of the first round-lot transaction plus the differential.	Customer pays the price of the first round-lot transaction that is *below*, the limit, plus the differential.	*After the electing sale*, the customer pays the price of the first round-lot transaction, plus the differential.	*After the electing sale*, the customer pays the price of the first round-lot transaction *below* the limit, plus the differential.
Sell Long	Customer receives the price of the first round-lot transaction minus the differential.	Customer receives the price of the first round-lot transaction that is *above* the limit, minus the differential.	*After the electing sale*, the customer receives the price of the first round-lot transaction, minus the differential.	*After the electing sale*, the customer receives the price of the first round-lot transaction *above* the limit, minus the differential.
Sell Short	Customer receives the price of the first round-lot transaction higher than the last different price, minus the differential.	Customer receives the price of the first transaction higher than the last different price that is *above* the limit, minus the differential.	*After the electing sale*, the customer receives the price of the first round-lot transaction higher than the last sale, minus the differential.	*After the electing sale*, the customer receives the price of the first round-lot transaction that is higher than the last sale and *above* the limit, minus the differential.

sale transactions. On the New York Stock Exchange, if the effective sale is above 5/32, the odd-lot differential is 1/8 point.

Effective Sale. A round-lot transaction on which a customer's odd-lot order is executed.

Electing Sale. A round-lot transaction that activates (triggers) a stop order.

On-the-Quotation. An odd-lot market order to be executed at the prevailing offering or bid price rather than at the price of a round-lot transaction.

See also At-the-Close Odd-Lot Order; Basis Price Odd-Lot Order; Bunching; Differential; Limit Order (Odd-Lot); Market Order (Odd-Lot); On-the-Quotation; Short-Stop and Short-Stop Limit Order; Specialist; Stop-Limit Order (Odd-Lot); Stop Order (Odd-Lot).

Odd-Lot Theory. The behavior of the small investor is a focal point of interest for many market forecasters. Some go so far as to say, "The odd-lot customer is always wrong." This is an overstatement, but the investing patterns of the small investor have been refined into a number of interesting theories. The best-known of these was advanced by Garfield A. Drew, who noted that odd-lot customers frequently became heavy buyers as the market neared its top and reduced their buying in a down market prior to a rally. The changes in the odd-lot customer's buying can, therefore, be charted and used as an effective market signal.

Odd-lot purchases normally exceed sales. This results from the fact that clients often purchase an odd lot on a number of occasions until they accumulate a round lot. The subsequent sale will not, therefore, be reflected in the daily odd-lot figures but will become part of the normal round-lot trading volume. Odd lots on the New York Stock Exchange are generally handled directly by the specialist. A customer wishing to purchase fifty shares of General Electric buys directly from the specialist, not from another client with a similar amount to sell. Total purchases and sales of odd lots, therefore, directly reflect the attitude of small investors and can easily be studied for changing trends. Working from the normal imbalance of purchases versus sales, we watch the behavior pattern of the odd-lot purchaser. When it indicates a significant change of direction, an adherent to this theory makes a commitment—in the opposite direction.

The following tables illustrate the way odd-lot statistics are released to the public, both on a daily and weekly basis. The daily figures are not as relevant for the followers of this theory. The daily release can be misleading because of a single unusual event that may have occurred on that day. In any event, it is incomplete. It does not include the odd-lot orders executed by Merrill Lynch, Pierce, Fenner & Smith, Inc., which undoubtedly constitute a considerable amount because of that firm's usually high volume of activity. Their figures, however, are included in the weekly statistics, which are also reported to the SEC. Based on the weekly analysis depicted in the table, twice as many odd-lot sellers than buyers indicate that the sophisticated round-lot investor should be buying stock.

Odd Lot Trading

NEW YORK–The New York Stock Exchange specialists reported the following odd-lot transactions (in shares):

	Customer Purchases	Short Sales	Other Sales	Total Sales
July 31, 1987	319,502	1,849	534,738	536,587

See also Advance-Decline Theory; Confidence Theory; Dow Theory; Short Interest Theory; Technical Analysis.

Off-Board. This expression may refer to transactions over the counter in unlisted securities or to transactions involving listed shares that were not executed on a national securities exchange.

See also Secondary Distribution.

0ffering (Asked) Price. This price is the lowest available for a round lot.

See also Order Execution (NYSE).

Offering Date. *See* Municipal Security (Organization of the Syndicate).

Offer Wanted (OW). *See* National Quotation Bureau, Inc.

Office of Supervisory Jurisdiction (OSJ). *See* Rules of Fair Practice (Section 27).

Officer. This designation includes the president, vice-president, secretary, treasurer, controller, or any other person who performs functions corresponding to those performed by the foregoing. Normally, an assistant to any of these people is not classified as an officer unless the assistant has access to confidential information that could derive personal benefit from market transactions.

See also Reporting Requirements of the SEC (Reports of Officers, Directors and Principal Stockholders).

Office Ticket. *See* Order Ticket.

Official Statement. The figure shows the cover of an *official statement* announcing a new issue of municipal securities. Significant information regarding this issue is summarized on its title page. The following text explains the information to which the circled numbers in the figure on the next page refer:

1. The *issuer* of the securities is "Salt River Project Agriculture Improvement and Power District, Arizona."

2. The *type* of bond is *revenue* and does not constitute an obligation of the state of Arizona or any of its municipalities. Payment of interest and principal depends

wholly on revenues paid by users of electric power generated by the Salt River Project Electric System.

3. The *total borrowing* amounts to $110,000,000.

4. The issue contains $30,950,000 in *serial* bonds maturing annually from 1983 to 2004.

5. The issue also contains two *term* bonds in amounts of $22,800,000 and $56,250,000 maturing in 2010 and 2019, respectively.

6. The issue is a *split offering* because it is comprised of both serial and term bonds.

7. This is the *dated date* showing the *issue date* as of March 1, 1979.

8. The *maturity date* for each maturity year is January 1.

9. The *interest payment dates* of each bond are January 1 and July 1 until redeemed.

10. The *paying agents* for the bond's interest and principal are First National Bank of Arizona, Continental Illinois Bank, Trust Company of Chicago, and Citibank.

11. The *type of ownership* of the bonds is coupon form in the minimum denomination of $5,000, registrable as to principal only and exchangeable for fully registered bonds in any integral multiple of $5,000.

12. The *trustee*, the custodian of monies, and official representative of the bondholders is First National Bank, Phoenix, Arizona.

13. This statement describes the *sinking fund* provision of the term bonds and permits the redemption of the bonds at par beginning in 2005 for the 2010 bonds, and in 2011 for the 2019 bonds.

14. This statement describes the *call provision* of the serial bonds and permits the redemption of the bonds any time after January 1, 1989. Holders of bonds retired at that date

NEW ISSUE

(18) **Ratings — Moody's: Aa**
Standard & Poor's: A+

$110,000,000 (3)

(1) # Salt River Project Agricultural Improvement and Power District, Arizona

Salt River Project Electric System Revenue Bonds, (2)
1979 Series A

(7)

(8)

To be dated March 1, 1979 (9)

To mature January 1, as shown below

Principal and interest (July 1, 1979 and January 1 and July 1 thereafter) payable at the principal offices of First National Bank of Arizona, Phoenix, Arizona, or Continental Illinois National Bank and Trust Company of Chicago, Chicago, Illinois, or (10) Citibank, N.A., New York, New York, at the option of the holder. Coupon Bonds in the denomination of $5,000 registrable as to principal only and exchangeable for fully registered Bonds in any integral (11) multiple of $5,000. First National Bank of Arizona, Phoenix, Arizona, is the Trustee. (12)

(13) The 1979 Series A Bonds maturing on January 1, 2010 and January 1, 2019 are subject to redemption on any interest payment date on and after January 1, 2005 and January 1, 2011, respectively, from amounts accumulated in the Debt Service Fund with respect to Sinking Fund Installments at the principal amount thereof plus accrued interest to the redemption date. The 1979 Series A Bonds may be redeemed as a whole, or in part, in inverse order of maturities, at any time on or after (14) January 1, 1989 at prices ranging from 102% for the period January 1, 1989 to and including December 31, 1990, to 100% on and after January 1, 1997, plus accrued interest to the date of redemption, as further described herein.

(15) **Interest is exempt, in the opinion of Bond Counsel, from Federal income taxes under existing laws, and from income taxes within the State of Arizona.**

(16) The 1979 Series A Bonds are being issued for the purpose of financing improvements to the District's Electric System. Proceeds of the 1979 Series A Bonds will also be used to make a deposit in the Debt Reserve Account and to pay financing costs (including bond discount). The 1979 Series A Bonds and the presently outstanding Revenue Bonds are payable solely (17) from and secured by a pledge of and lien on the Net Revenues of the District's Electric System, subject to the prior lien of the Prior Lien Bonds, and from certain reserve funds, all as defined and more particularly described in this Official Statement. As of January 2, 1979, there were $257,086,438 Prior Lien Bonds and $1,402,905,000 Revenue Bonds outstanding.

(4) ## AMOUNTS, MATURITIES, COUPON RATES AND PRICES OR YIELDS
$30,950,000 Serial Bonds

Amount	Maturity	Coupon Rate	Price or Yield	Amount	Maturity	Coupon Rate	Price or Yield
$ 500,000	1983	5.40%	100%	$1,300,000	1994	5.90%	100%
550,000	1984	5.40	100	1,400,000	1995	6.00	100
600,000	1985	5.40	100	1,500,000	1996	6.10	100
650,000	1986	5.45	100	1,650,000	1997	6.15	100
750,000	1987	5.45	100	1,800,000	1998	6.20	100
800,000	1988	5.50	100	1,950,000	1999	6.25	100
850,000	1989	5.50	100	2,100,000	2000	6.30	100
950,000	1990	5.60	100	2,250,000	2001	6.35	100
1,000,000	1991	5.70	100	2,450,000	2002	6.40	100
1,100,000	1992	5.75	100	2,700,000	2003	6.45	100
1,200,000	1993	5.80	100	2,900,000	2004	6.50	100

(23)

(6)

(5) **$22,800,000   6⅝% Term Bonds Due January 1, 2010**
Price 100%

$56,250,000   6.80% Term Bonds Due January 1, 2019 (24)
Price 99½%

(Accrued interest to be added)

(19)

The 1979 Series A Bonds are offered when, as and if issued and accepted by the Underwriters, and subject to the approval of legality by Messrs. Mudge Rose Guthrie & Alexander, New York, New York, Bond Counsel. Certain legal matters will be passed upon for the Underwriters by Messrs. Sullivan & Cromwell, New York, New York. It is expected that the 1979 Series A Bonds in definitive form will be available for delivery in New York, New York, on or about March 8, 1979.

(20)

Salomon Brothers (21)

February 26, 1979 (22)

will receive a 2.0% premium over face value to compensate them for the inconvenience of surrendering their bonds prior to maturity. The percentage of premium is scaled down thereafter until January 1, 1997, at which time holders of called bonds will be repaid only face value plus accrued interest to the call redemption date.

15. Designation that the interest received by the bondholder is exempt from federal income tax.

16. A brief description of the *purpose and use* of the bond proceeds.

17. A brief explanation of the *security* behind the payment of interest and principal for the bond issue.

18. Description of the bond *ratings* by Moody's and Standard & Poor's.

19. This section identifies the general counsel retained by the issuer who will give the *legal opinion*.

20. The approximate *settlement date* for the bonds is March 8, 1979.

21. The principal *underwriter* offering this issue is Salomon Brothers. The contents of the official statement, not just the title page, must be examined for the names of other participating underwriters, if any.

22. The *offering date* is February 26, 1979, although the settlement date is approximately March 8, 1979. Therefore, interest accrues from issue date up to but not including the settlement date.

23. The *scale* of the serial bonds gives a lower

yield on the shorter-term bonds than on the longer-term bonds ("normal scale").

24. The term bonds of 2019 are priced at a discount to give a higher *basis* (yield to maturity) than the nominal yield of 6.80%.

See also Municipal Security.

Offset. Elimination of a current long or short position by making an opposite transaction.

On-the-Quotation. It is not mandatory to base an odd-lot price on an actual round-lot transaction, although that method overwhelmingly predominates. It is possible to use a quotation rather than a transaction as a basis for price determination. Odd-lot customers too impatient to wait for a round-lot transaction can enter their orders to buy or sell immediately at a price related to the existing round-lot quotation on the floor of the exchange. The customer can buy at the prevailing offering price plus the differential, or sell long at the prevailing bid price minus the differential. (Odd-lot customers are prohibited from selling short on a bid price. They require a bona fide round-lot sale above the last different price in order to qualify.)

This is no imposition on the specialist because (1) the specialist alone acts as the accommodating principal on all odd-lot trades; and (2) the worst round-lot price that might occur is a transaction at the prevailing bid or offering, which would require the specialist to deal with the odd-lot customer at that time, anyway.

Besides, if that arrangement inconveniences the specialist's preference for a security position, there is nothing to prevent the specialist from buying a round lot from the offeror (or selling to the bidder) in that quotation to make adjustments thereto. In fact, quite often, in the act of adjusting inventory, the specialist creates the effective sale for a customer's order. In this way the specialist performs an important service for the customer. The SEC and the NYSE both recognize the value of this public service. To facilitate the specialist's flexibility of operation, they permit the specialist to sell short from inventory at a price below the last different price, if (1) the result of that sale does not create a short position of 100 shares or more; or (2) if forced into a short position by virtue of customers' orders. In the latter event, there is no limitation on the number of shares sold short because the specialist does not act as the aggressor.

Example: Assume that the specialist's position is even (that is, neither long nor short). Then the specialist receives orders from four customers, each of whom wants to buy fifty shares of that issue at the market. But before the specialist can purchase two round lots for reallocation to those customers as odd lots, two brokers trade a round lot of that issue on the exchange at a price below the previous sale. This transaction now (1) serves as the effective sale for each of those odd-lot orders; (2) requires the specialist to sell stock to those customers from an inventory that does not exist; and (3) leads to a short position in the specialist's account at a depressed value from the last transaction at a different price.

The specialist's transaction is permissible even though the specialist sells short and sells at a depressed value. This is so because the specialist acted because of the customers' orders.

See also Differential; Odd-Lot Stock Executions.

Omnibus Account. An account carried by one Futures Commission Merchant with another Futures Commission Merchant in which the transactions of two or more persons are combined and carried in the name of the originating broker, rather than designated separately.

Open Box. *See* Active Box.

Open Contracts. Contracts which have been bought or sold without the tansaction having been completed by subsequent sale or purchase, or by making or taking actual delivery of the financial instrument or physical commodity.

Open-End Investment Company. *See* Investment Companies; Management Company.

Opening, The. The period at the beginning of the trading session officially designated by the Exchange during which all transactions are considered made "at the opening."

Opening Price (or Range). The range of prices at which the first bids and offers were made or first tansactions were completed.

Opening Transaction. This term refers to any transaction that increases an investor's position. In an *opening purchase transaction*, an investor becomes the holder of an option, that is, establishes a long option position. In an opening sale transaction, an investor becomes the writer of an option, that is, establishes a short option position.

See also Closing Transaction; Option.

Open Interest. This statistic represents total number of outstanding option or commodity contracts issued by the responsible clearing corporations.

See also Newspaper Financial Tables.

Open Market Operations. The activity of the Federal Open Market Committee, in behalf of the Federal Reserve Banking System, to arrange outright purchases and sales of government and agency securities, matched sale/purchase agreements, and repurchase agreements in order to promote the monetary policy of the Federal Reserve Board.

See also Federal Reserve System.

Open-Market Purchase. This is the retirement of a debt issue through its purchase by the issuer in the open market. Open-market purchase is attempted by a corporation only if the bonds are trading below par value and only if the corporation's directors are willing to accept partial retirement. It is unlikely that a corporation would ever be able to buy back all of its debt, especially at prices below redemption value.

Open Order. *See* Good-Til-Canceled Order.

Open Outcry. The continuous auction process in which bids and offers on trading floor are mode out loud. (on some exhanges, hand signals predominate.)

Operating Ratio. *See* Expense Ratio.

Operating Revenues. *See* Net Sales.

Option. An option contract gives the holder the right to buy (in the case of a call option) or to sell (in the case of a put option) a specified quantity of a security (called the *underlying security*) at a specified price (called the *exercise price* or *striking price*). Conversely, the writer of the option contract is obligated to sell (in the case of a call option) or to buy (in the case of a put option) that quantity of the security at the exercise price. The *unit of trading* is typically one hundred shares of stock, although under certain circumstances it may be more than this amount.

The buyer of the option pays a *premium* to the seller to secure the rights of buying or selling the underlying security at the exercise price. This premium is the market price of the option. The holder of the option may choose to exercise the right to buy or sell at any time during the life of the option; if he or she does not choose to do

so, the option expires worthless after the *expiration date*.

Listed options are standardized puts or calls traded on a national securities exchange or in the over-the-counter market via the NASDAQ system (NASDAQ is a computer-oriented, broad-based indicator of activity in the unlisted securities market, updated every five minutes). The Options Clearing Corporation (OCC) is issuer and guarantor of exchange-traded and NASDAQ put and call options. It also serves as the clearing agency for options transactions. Other over-the-counter options are traded directly between buyer and seller, and have no secondary market and no standardization of striking prices and expiration dates.

The exchanges have generally uniform standards governing the selection and maintenance of underlying securities for options trading.

With two exceptions, options are traded during the same hours in which the underlying securities are traded in their primary markets. Options trading continues for ten minutes after the close of each day's stock trading (that is, 4:10 P.M. eastern time). On the business day prior to the expiration date, all options cease trading at 4:00 P.M. eastern time.

See also Exercise Price; Expiration Date; NASDAQ Option; Option; Underlying Security.

Background. In 1971 the Chicago Board of Trade (CBT), the major U.S. futures contracts exchange, began research and development of an exchange-traded (listed) options market. Two years later, the Chicago Board Options Exchange (CBOE) opened with trading in call options on sixteen underlying stocks. The growth of the listed options market was so great that many new stocks were added to the list. In June, 1976 the American Stock Exchange also began trading listed options. The success and growth of both options marketplaces brought about the opening of three other exchanges to such trading: the Pacific Stock Exchange, the Philadelphia Stock Exchange and, in

1984, the New York Stock Exchange. In addition, trading in NASDAQ options commenced in 1985. Currently there are options on approximately three hundred fifty securities on the various exchanges in the NASDAQ system. Exchange-traded, NASDAQ, and over-the-counter stock options are compared in the following table.

Comparison of Exchange-Traded and Over-the-Counter Options

Category	Exchange-Traded and NASDAQ Stock Options	Over-the-Counter Traded Stock Options
Prospectus requirement	Yes	No
Obligor Guarantor	Options Clearing Corporation (OCC)	NYSE member firm
Expiration date	Standardized by exchanges	Negotiated between buyer and writer
Cash dividends	No adjustment exercise price	Reduce exercise price by amount of dividend
Margin requirement	For uncovered options: 30% times market value of stock plus amount that the option is in-the-money or minus amount that the option is out-of-the-money	For uncovered options: 50% times market value of stock plus amount that the option is in-the-money or minus amount that the option is out-of-the-money
Easily marketable	Yes	Limited marketability
Reporting of trades	Yes	No
Publication of closing prices	yes	No

The securities on which options are available are determined from time to time by the respective exchanges on which the options are traded. The exchanges have agreed that all securities selected as underlying securities for options will be registered and listed on a national securities exchange. Contrary to the listing of shares of the nation's principal stock exchanges, corporate issuers neither apply for, nor participate in, the decision to approve their stocks for option transactions on an exchange.

See also Nonequity Options.

Transactions in Options. Options, like other types of securities, may be purchased or sold (written) by placing an order with a broker. Orders should contain certain specifics: whether the order is for puts or calls; the underlying security; expiration month and exercise price; the number of contracts to be purchased or written; whether the purchase or sale is an opening or closing transaction. Since one option contract typically represents 100 shares of the underlying security, ten contracts represent 1,000 shares. The price (premium) of an option, which is paid by the purchaser and received by the writer (seller) of the option, is determined in the exchange's auction market. When an option holder exercises an option, both the seller of the stock and buyer of the stock customarily pay a commission. For the examples following, all commissions have been omitted for both option and stock transactions; in actual trading, however, commissions need to be carefully calculated because they may be significant and can affect, or even eliminate, the profitability of a strategy which theoretically appears attractive.

Buyer-Writer Relationships. The relationships between buyers and writers in both call and put options are summarized in the following table:

Comparison of Option Buyer to Option Writer

Synonymous Terms	Call	Put
Buyer Holder Long	Right to purchase 100 shares of stock	Right to sell 100 shares of stock
Seller Writer Short	Obligation to deliver (sell) 100 shares of stock	Obligation to purchase 100 shares of stock

Buying a Call Option.

Example: Let's assume XYZ stock is trading on the New York Stock Exchange at $18 per share. An option contract that expires in January with an exercise price of $20 is trading for $3. The investor who feels the stock will increase in value to above $20 between now and the end of January purchases one XYZ January 20 call option contract for $300 (100 shares times $3). After the purchase is made, the stock rises to $27 a share. At this time the buyer of the call option decides to exercise the contract by purchasing the stock at $20 a share, thus paying $2,000 to the writer. Now the investor is long 100 shares which may be immediately liquidated at $27 for a profit of $700. Since $300 was paid for the option contract, the net profit is $400. The return on this investment is approximate 133% ($400 divided by $300.

Let's consider this strategy for another investor who buys the stock at $18 and holds it for the same period of time until the stock reaches $27, and then liquidates the stock position. The investor makes a $900 profit in a month's time, for a 50% return. Clearly, the buyer of the option had a larger percentage return given the same movement of the stock.

Buying a Put Option.

Example: CBA is selling at $21 per share. The investor, bearish on the stock, decides to buy a put with an exercise price of $20 for $300. The stock declines to $15, and the buyer exercises the put. At this time the investor buys the stock in the market for $15 a share and simultaneously delivers the stock via exercise at $20 a share, thus making $500 on the stock transaction. The option buyer's net profit is $200 ($500 less the put's cost of $300).

Now we should look at the other side of the market because, as we know, for every buyer there must be a seller. The sellers are called writers. An investor owns 100 XYZ purchased at $28 per share. He decides to write (sell) an XYZ,

July 30 call covered by the long stock position. The investor writes the call option for $3½ and receives the $350 premium. By writing the call option, the writer is obligated to deliver 100 shares of stock between now and July at $30 per share on exercise by the buyer. If the stock rises above 30, the writer will be exercised at $30 a share. Therefore, the writer's profit will be $550 ($350 of premium plus $200 profit on the stock, from $28 to $30 per share). The sum of $550 gives a return of approximately 20% based on an original investment of $2,800.

Conversely, if the stock stays below $30 until expiration in July, the call will not be exercised. Therefore, the investor will remain the owner of the stock and will keep the $350 premium.

Example: This illustration demonstrates the basic purpose of writing (selling) put options. An investor wants to buy TLX but thinks the present price of $51 is too high. The investor might write (sell) one put expiring in April with an exercise price of 50 for $500.

If the TLX subsequently declines below $50 before the April expiration date, the writer will be exercised. The investor will be put the stock at $50 per share, but the effective cost is actually $45 per share ($5,000 minus $500 premium received). The investor is now long 100 shares of TLX purchased at 45—a better price than $51.

On the other hand, had TLX subsequently risen above $50 by the April expiration date, the writer would not have been exercised. Thus the put writer would have pocketed the $500 premium and would not have become an owner of the stock.

See also Listed Option; Margin; Options Clearing Corporation; Regulation of Options Trading; Tax Effects of Options Trading; Trading Policies.

Option Strategies. The following lists five basic option strategies and three more sophisticated option strategies. The basic strategies are: (1) buying call options; (2) buying put options; (3) writing covered call options; (4) writing uncovered call options; and (5) writing put options.

The more sophisticated strategies are: (1) buying straddles; (2) selling combinations; and (3) establishing spreads.

See Call Options; Combinations; Put Options; Spreads; Straddles.

Regulation.

Position limits. In order to regulate trading activity and to limit speculation, the exchanges and the NASD have promulgated certain trading restrictions. They have determined that unless subject to qualifications set forth below, no one individual, or individuals acting in concert with others, shall either own or write more than 3,000, 5,500 or 8,000 contracts on the same side of the market for the same underlying security depending upon conditions cited below. *The same side of the market* refers to one benefiting from either a rising market or a falling market. An individual who buys calls or writes puts benefits from a rising market. Likewise, anyone who buys puts and writes calls benefits from a falling market. Therefore, the 3,000 position limit applies to any combination of long calls and short puts, or short calls and long puts on the underlying security.

Example: In the case of a 3,000-contract limitation, an investor may purchase 2,000 January 50 Exxon calls and write 1,000 April 50 Exxon puts. The month and expiration dates are not taken into consideration. On the bearish side of the market, an investor may buy 3,000 GM puts and thus not be able to write any calls on the same underlying stock; or the investor may buy 2,200 IBM puts and write 800 IBM calls and thus reach the 3,000-contract limitations.

Underlying stocks with large capitalizations and significant trading volume are allowed larger position limits for their listed options. Those limitation criteria are as follows and make

for a triple-tier option regulation whose components are subject to change every six months:

I. *8,000 Option Contract Position Limit*
   A. At least 120 million outstanding underlying shares and at least 30 million shares traded in latest six months.

OR

   B. At least 40 million shares traded in latest six months.

II. *5,500 Option Contract Position Limit*
   A. At least 40 million outstanding underlying shares and at least 15 million shares traded in latest six months.

OR

   B. At least 20 million shares traded in latest six months.

III. *3,000 Contract Limitations Apply to All Other Options*

Exercise Limits. The exchanges have also established exercise limits. The rule states that, subject to the same numerical limits and exceptions cited for position limits, no individual, or individuals acting in concert with others, may exercise more than 3,000 contracts (equal to 300,000 shares of stock) or 5,500 contracts, or 8,000 contracts of the same class during any five consecutive business days. Since Kodak puts are one class and Kodak calls a different class, one might exercise as many as 3,000 Eastman Kodak calls as well as 3,000 Eastman Kodak puts during the same five consecutive business days.

Acting in concert. Includes anyone having a beneficial interest in an account. Moreover, the term "in concert" refers to situations where one or more persons arrange or control options transactions for more than one customer account. Examples of in-concert relationships include: (1) an individual who trades for a personal account as well as for a trust or corporation; (2) an investment advisor who executes transactions for clients using his service; (3) a registered representative with discretionary power over customer accounts who buys and sells options in their behalf; and (4) two or more customers who have an agreement or understanding to coordinate transactions or divide responsibility for options activities between them.

Reportable position. In order to keep abreast of the position limits, the exchanges established a reportable position requirement. A reportable position is one which requires a brokerage house to report daily to the exchange the name of any client who is long or short 200 or more contracts in the same security on the same side of the market. The position limits and exercise limits pertain to all clients regardless of how many accounts they may have at various brokerage firms.

Although the Options Clearing Corporation is the issuer and obligor for listed option contracts, it does not own underlying stock to deliver pursuant to exercise of a call, nor will it pay money if an investor exercises a put option. It is only an intermediary for buyers and sellers of listed options contracts.

An exercise notice submitted to the Clearing Corporation by a Clearing Member (brokerage firm that is also a member of the OCC) will be assigned by the Corporation to a randomly-selected Clearing Member account which is short an option of the same series as the option being exercised. The Clearing Member may then allocate the exercise notice to one of its customers. The method may be on a random selection basis or by a "first-in, first-out" basis.

Experience has shown that options may be exercised even at times when they are only marginally in-the-money. It should be noted that some holders of options, such as exchange members and other brokers and dealers, may have lower transaction costs than the typical public customer and may find it advantageous to exer-

cise an option at a time when it would not be profitable for a public customer to do so. The writer of an option must, therefore, assume that he or she may be assigned an exercise notice at any time during the life of that option.

See also Margin Account (Option); Options Clearing Corporation.

Trading Policies. The nature of options and their associated risks demand that the registered representative know each client's financial background, needs, resources, and investment objectives prior to executing any options orders or even opening an options account. Critical standards of suitability for option purchasing, writing, or spreading programs by certain client categories have not been determined by any regulatory agency. The burden of responsibility in such matters must fall on the shoulders of each member organization, its officials, and its registered representatives on a case-by-case basis. Each member firm should specifically define its own criteria for suitability and adequate net worth. These are the criteria with which it feels most comfortable operating in terms of customer needs and requirements.

Example: Several firms have adopted policies excluding option accounts for clients with a net worth below $15,000; others have set $25,000 or even higher minimums. A few firms prohibit uncovered (naked) writing transactions, and most firms will not sanction more than 15-20% (an exchange recommendation) of a client's investment assets for purchase of call or put options. Investment assets normally include cash, stocks, bonds, negotiable instruments, and other assets and investments designed to produce income or capital appreciation.

Obtaining Information about the Client. In approving accounts for options transactions, the Registered Options Principal (ROP) (that member of a firm that manages its options business) has an obligation to use due diligence to learn the essential facts regarding each client.

Such facts should pertain to (1) the client's ability to understand and evaluate the risks and obligations that accompany the purchase and writing of option contracts, and (2) the client's detailed financial situation.

Example: The inquiry should establish whether the client has had any prior experience in trading options; whether the client has an active options account at another brokerage firm, and if so, the extent of the options positions at such firm. In addition, information regarding the client's marital status, number of dependents, occupation, age, residence, amount and sources of income and net worth is essential to a proper determination of his or her financial ability to assume the associated risks.

The following checklist illustrates the type and amount of client information recommended to judge an individual's sophistication and capability for activity in the listed options market.

Should a client decline during the inquiry to provide any or all of the information requested, the registered representative should so note; he or she may also want to obtain a statement from the client evidencing refusal to provide this information.

The Registered Options Principal is under an obligation to make a judgment, based on information obtained from the client or elsewhere, about the advisability of accepting the client for listed options transactions.

Once a client's account has been approved for options trading, the registered representative has a continuing responsibility to keep current the personal data on the client. In the event the registered representative learns of a material change in the client's financial situation, he or she is obligated to note this on the client's account card. This development should be brought immediately to the attention of the branch manager or Registered Options Principal who originally approved the account.

Restrictions on Options Accounts. It is consistent with suitability rules for a client to be given approval to engage in certain kinds of option transactions, but not others (covered writing, but not uncovered writing, for example). Special care must, therefore, be taken by the registered representative to ascertain whether any conditions have been placed on the types of option transactions the customer can initiate. If any restrictions have been placed on the client's account, the registered representative may neither accept nor recommend a transaction that is inconsistent with the terms of the account.

Disclosure Statement Requirements. All options issued by the Options Clearing Corporation are registered under the Securities Act of 1933. Therefore, its disclosure requirements are fully applicable to the offer of listed options to clients. Because options information is unique, all regulatory bodies require delivery of an OCC prepared Disclosure Statement (with appropriate supplements) to all clients who plan to engage in option transactions whether as buyers or writers (sellers) of option contracts. Moreover, the current Disclosure Statement must be furnished to each option client at or prior to the time the client's account is initially approved for options trading. If a new Statement or supplement is issued subsequent to that approval, it must be supplied to each approved options client no later than with confirmation of the client's next options transaction.

The burden of establishing delivery of a Disclosure Statement lies with the member organization and its Registered Options Principals. Thereafter the responsibility is delegated to the registered representative who ordinarily maintains personal and continuing contact with the options clients. It is he or she who must, therefore, maintain adequate records for the rim to rely on as evidence of that delivery. A number of firms have instituted procedures requiring the registered representative to obtain a dated written receipt from each options-approved client acknowledging acceptance of the Disclosure

Statement, both initially and subsequently, as necessary.

Written Agreement. Within fifteen days after approving an account for listed options transactions, the member organization must obtain a signed pledge from the client in which, at the very least, the client promises: (1) to be bound by rules of the exchanges, the NASD, and the Options Clearing Corporation that apply to the trading of listed options. It is recommended that the names of the New York Stock Exchange, the American Stock Exchange, the Philadelphia Stock Exchange, the Pacific Stock Exchange, the Chicago Board Options Exchange, the NAS-DAQ, and the Options Clearing Corporation be noted specifically to avoid jurisdictional misunderstanding; and (2) not to violate, either alone or in concert with others, the position and exercise limits established by the exchanges.

The agreement should also note that these restrictive limits apply to options contracts of the same class in the client's accounts at all brokerage firms at one time, and not just to one particular firm. Positions held by a client in options of the same class, listed on more than one exchange or in the NASDAQ marketplace, are taken cumulatively and may not exceed the limits of any one regulatory body.

This document, which is mandatory for firm records, is known as an *Options Agreement* in the CBOE, PHLX, PSE, NYSE, and NASD rules and as an *Account Statement* under AMEX rules. The information required by all is identical. In addition, some members have found it useful to include provisions in their agreement specifying the obligations incurred by clients writing and buying options, such as underlying security delivery, payments for options, and margin requirements for options. Some have even provided for limited discretion by the firm in closing open contracts on the last trading day before expiration of the option. The firm may also choose to structure its agreement form to ob-

lige clients to advise the firm of any significant changes that take place in their investment objectives, financial situation, or needs. This provision, however, if included, still does not relieve the firm, and particularly the registered representative, of the obligation to keep current with the client's financial position.

In the event this statement is not received within the fifteen-day prescribed period, the registered representative should refuse to accept from the client any opening orders to buy or sell listed options.

Many option clients seek advice from the registered representative and the member firm regarding listed options investment strategies. Under the exchange suitability rules, every ROP or registered representative who recommends an option transaction to a client must have reasonable grounds to believe that the recommended transaction is not unsuitable for the client. A current reasonable inquiry as to the client's investment objectives, financial situation, and needs must precede any such recommendation.

The need to gain a customer's confidence to provide worthwhile purchase and sale advice cannot be overstressed. Gaining confidence is the best way to make the client feel comfortable about revealing his or her personal financial situation and investment objectives. These key factors are instrumental in making investment recommendations and decisions. The risks involved in the purchase of put and call options which must be considered also depend on such factors as the relationship between the option's exercise price and the market price of the underlying stock, the time period remaining until the option expires, price volatility, and other characteristics of the underlying stock. Where appropriate, they should be brought to the client's attention.

It is recognized that some clients decline to give all the information necessary for comprehensive analysis and advice. With one important exception (see the following), an option transaction may still be recommended to them, but only if the member firm, ROP, or registered representative has other information indicating it is not unsuitable for the client. Under these circumstances, all order tickets should be marked "Unsolicited" or "Solicited" or "Recommended" or "Not Recommended," as the cases may be, depending on firm terminology.

Uncovered Writing. The one exception concerns uncovered (naked) writing transactions. Before making any such recommendation, the ROP or registered representative must be satisfied that it is not unsuitable for the client. He or she must also be satisfied the client is capable of evaluating the risks of an uncovered writing transaction and has the financial capacity to carry such a position. Clients who write uncovered options must meet higher suitability requirements. Under exchange rules, these requirements apply to both solicited and unsolicited uncovered writing transactions, including the uncovering of a previously covered position. If the client does not furnish sufficient information to provide a reasonable basis for such belief, uncovered writing transactions may not be recommended.

In considering suitability of recommended options transactions, ROPs and registered representatives will ordinarily begin with information obtained at the time the client's account was originally approved. for options transactions. However, in order that recommendations be based on reasonably current information, the client account record should be updated. This is especially needed if it is believed that changed circumstances have rendered the information inaccurate or insufficient.

Client Confirmations and Statements. Every member organization is obliged to furnish each client promptly with a written confirmation of that person's transactions in option contracts. Minimally, the confirmation must show the number of contracts, the underlying security, the expiration date, and settlement date.

Options account clients are also assured of a statement of account each month, provided there has been an entry in the account that month. An SEC rule and most stock exchanges require presentation of statements to clients at least quarterly. This practice applies to regular securities account clients, but most firms send a customer a statement in any month where an entry has been made. Likewise all options accounts, whether on a cash account or margin account basis, must record any purchase, sale, or exercise of a listed option contract or any debit or credit, entry of money or securities in such accounts and must send a statement to the client that month.

All advertisements, market letters, and sales literature which are issued by a member firm or its registered representatives pertaining to options must be approved in advance of their distribution or use by: (1) a general partner or officer of the firm who is a Registered Options Principal; and (2) The American Stock Exchange, the NASD, or Chicago Board Options Exchange. Copies of the material showing the names of the author and approving ROP, as well as the source of any recommendations contained therein, must be retained by the firm for three years.

The Securities Act of 1933 prohibits use of any written material or television advertisements (or other material constituting a prospectus as defined in the Act) relating to a registered security unless certain conditions are met:

1. Market letters and sales literature pertaining to listed options may not be sent to anyone unless a current prospectus of the Options Clearing Corporation is also sent to that person, either beforehand or with the letters or literature.

2. Advertisements may be used (and copies of the advertisements may be sent to people who have not received a prospectus of the Options Clearing Corporation) if the material meets the requirements of Rule 134 under the Securities Act of 1933. Under Rule 134, adver-

tisements must be limited to general descriptions of the security being offered and of its issuer. In the case of listed options, an advertisement must have the following characteristics: (a) It should state the name and address of the person from whom a current Disclosure Statement of the Options Clearing Corporation may be obtained; (b) The text may contain a brief description of options, including a statement that the issuer of every such option is the Options Clearing Corporation. The text may also contain a brief description of the general attributes and method of operation of the exchange or exchanges on which such options are traded. It may include a discussion of how the price of a listed option is determined; (c) It may include any statement or legend required by any state law or administrative authority; (d) Advertising designs and devices, including borders, scrolls, arrows, pointers, multiple and combined logos, and unusual typefaces and lettering, as well as attention-getting headlines, photographs, and other graphics may be used, provided that such material is not misleading.

There are special risks attendant to options transactions, some of which involve complex investment strategies. These factors should be reflected in any communication that includes a discussion of the uses or advantages of listed options:

1. Any statement referring to the opportunities or advantages presented by listed options should be balanced by a statement of the corresponding risks. The risk statement should reflect the same degree of specificity as the statement of opportunities. Broad generalities should be avoided. Thus, a statement such as "With options, an investor has an opportunity to earn profits while limiting risk of loss" should be balanced by a statement such as "Of course, an options investor may lose the entire amount committed to options in a relatively short period of time."

2. It should not be suggested that options are suitable for most investors or for small investors. In point of fact, it is strongly suggested that all literature discussing the uses of listed options should include a warning that options are not for everybody.

3. The mechanism for trading listed options in the context of an exchange auction market is relatively new. Adequate experience with such trading under varying market conditions is presently lacking. Accordingly, statements suggesting the certain availability of a secondary market for listed options should be avoided. Instead, references to the secondary market should be expressed in such terms as, "The secondary markets and exchanges and the NASDAQ marketplace for listed options are intended to provide a means for the liquidation of positions in such options," or, "If the price of the underlying stock goes down, the holder of a listed call option may not be able to realize any remaining value of the option by selling it in the secondary market on an exchange where that option is listed."

See also Conduct of Broker/Dealers; Registered Options Principal; Reporting Requirements of SEC; SEC Rule 134; Securities Act of 1933.

Evaluating Options. Several criteria determine the value of an option. Most important is the volatility of the underlying stock. Generally speaking, a volatile stock commands a higher premium than a nonvolatile stock. A volatile growth-type issue would normally command a higher premium than a utility given the same exercise price and expiration date for both.

Another important factor is the time remaining in the life of the option contract. The longer the time remaining, the higher the option price.

Over the life of an option contract, certain decisions by corporate management may affect the stock price: cash dividends, stock dividends, stock splits, or any other change of capitalization such as mergers, acquisitions, and so forth. To eliminate any unfair advantage, the exchanges have standardized certain adjustments in the terms of option contracts made necessary by changes in the capitalization in the underlying securities.

See Dividends; Stock Splits.

Options Agreement. *See* (Trading Policies).

Options Clearing Corporation (OCC). The Options Clearing Corporation (OCC) acts as a middleman between buyers and sellers of listed options. In effect, the Options Clearing Corporation is a seller to all buyers and a buyer to all sellers.

The OCC becomes holder and obligor of each option contract on behalf of the parties to that transaction. It is also the issuer of listed and NASDAQ options, in response to transactions executed on the trading floors of the participating exchanges and in the marketplace subject to NASD options jurisdiction.

Consequently, as an issuer of publicly traded securities, the OCC registers those options with the SEC under terms of the Securities Act of 1933 and provides a Disclosure Statement covering these options.

Due to marketability provided by the options exchanges and OTC market-makers, buyers and sellers may trade their respective positions to other investors, and, therefore, compete against the marketplace rather than against the original buyer/seller of that option.

In order to permit a viable secondary market in which an existing position (either long or short) may be liquidated by an offsetting closing transaction, options issued by the Clearing Corporation have standardized terms which include the expiration date and exercise price for each series of options, leaving only the premium as a variable.

No certificates are issued by the Options Clearing Corporation to evidence issuance of options. Rather the OCC maintains a daily record of options issued in each of the accounts of its clearing members (those members of an exchange who are also members of the OCC). Each clearing member in turn is required to maintain a continuous record of customer positions in options. Ownership of options is evidenced by confirmations and periodic statements which customers receive from their brokers and which show, for each put or call long or short, the underlying security, the number of shares subject to the option, the exercise price, and the expiration month.

See also Exercise Price; Expiration Date; Listed Option; Premium; Regulation of Options; Trading (Reportable Position); Secondary Market; Securities Act of 1933.

Option (on Bond Price). In the municipal secondary market, a broker/dealer may want to hold (reserve) bonds for a specified price until checking with the client to determine if the client wants to purchase them. This privilege, granted by the trader, "guarantees" the quoted price for a limited period of time. Such a practice of agreeing to hold a price "firm" is known as an *option*. The usual time period for the option is one hour. A *broker's broker* is an agent who locates municipal bonds for other municipal bond traders.

See also Municipal Security.

Order Department (Room). *See* Broker/Dealer Organization.

Orders. You ordinarily are a prospective *buyer* of a stock if you (1) believe that issue has potential for near-term or long-term growth in value; or (2) think an investment in that stock provides an attractive rate of return in the form of dividend income; or (3) have previously sold it without owning it (a short sale) and are now inclined to cover (or eliminate) that liability by acquiring that stock in the marketplace.

If you are anxious to buy this stock at present price levels, enter a market order. The stock will be purchased immediately at the best offering price available from a seller of that issue.

If you are interested in buying the stock, but only at a price below the level at which the issue is now trading, enter a limit order. Specify the maximum price you want to pay if values ever decline far enough. If ever your bid becomes the highest bid, you will buy the stock from a seller anxious to dispose of it at that level.

On the other hand, you may already have a position in that stock, albeit a short position. Now you want to (1) protect yourself against an unlimited loss if the price should rise above the level at which the short sale was executed; or (2) realize a profit if the value of the stock begins to rise after declining below your short sale price.

As a person with a short position, you may enter a stop order to buy at a price above the current market level. Although it is true that you can buy stock now at a cheaper price, that is not your present intention. You believe the stock will decline below the current level, and you simply want to use the stop order as insurance in case you are wrong. If you are wrong and the price moves up to, or through, the memorandum price specified in the stop order, the stock will be purchased at that time as if it were a market order. This purchase will eliminate your short position.

Of course, if you are fearful of market orders in a rising market, you could sacrifice your protection somewhat by entering a stop-limit order to buy. Once the stop portion of the order is

elected, your instruction becomes a limit order to buy that stock. You must then take your chances that an anxious seller will appear and satisfy your bid before the price continues moving higher in its upward trend. If the latter situation occurs, your limit order to buy might never be executed.

You ordinarily are a prospective *seller* of a stock if you own it and (1) believe the issue has exhausted its potential for near-term or long-term growth in value; or (2) think an investment in that stock no longer provides an attractive rate of return in terms of dividend income (in comparison with other investments); or (3) need the money for other investments or for a financial emergency; or (4) realize that your inability to follow the daily price fluctuations of that stock could be costly (if the stock declined below a predetermined level). You are also a prospective seller if you believe that the price of the stock will decline, even if you do not own the stock. You can act on your expectation about the stock's price by becoming a short seller—that is, you sell something you do not own.

If you are anxious to sell stock you own at present price levels and do not want to risk missing the market, enter a market order. Your stock will then be sold immediately to the party with the highest prevailing bid price.

If you are interested in selling the stock, but only at a price above the level at which the issue is now trading, enter a limit order. Specify the minimum price acceptable to you if values ever rise high enough. If ever your offering becomes the lowest prevailing offering, you will sell your stock to a buyer anxious to acquire it at that price level.

On the other hand, you may own that stock and recognize that should it decline below a certain level, contrary to your expectations, it could (1) sharply reduce or even eliminate a paper profit you have patiently accumulated; or (2) expose your capital to the potential of greater loss than that represented at this lower-than-cost-price plateau. If so, enter a sell-stop order at a price below the current market. Although it is true that you can sell your stock now at a better price, that is not your present intention. You sincerely believe the stock will rise above this level, not decline. You simply are using the stop order as insurance in case you are wrong. If you are wrong and the price does fall to, or through, the memorandum price specified in the stop order, your stock will be sold at that time as if it were a market order.

If you are a person fearful of market orders in a falling stock market, you could sacrifice your protection somewhat by entering a stop-limit order to sell. Once the stop portion of the order is elected, your instruction becomes a limit order to sell that stock. You must then take your chances that a buyer will appear and satisfy your offering before the price continues moving lower in its downward trend. If these conditions are not fulfilled, of course, your limit order to sell will not be executed.

As a short seller, playing a role as speculator or opportunist, you can also enter market, limit, or stop orders to accommodate your belief in the imminent decline of a particular stock's price. The only difference in treatment for your short orders (as compared with your long orders) is that short orders are prohibited from depressing the price of the stock in the execution process. The self-serving benefit realized in forcing the price to decline with your own short sale is unfair and is considered manipulative by the SEC.

Each of the three types of orders may be supplemented with instructions that can affect tactics and/or time of execution of that order.

See also All or None (AON); Alternative Order (Either/Or); At-the-Close Order; At-the-Opening Order; Buy Minus; Buy-Stop Order; Cancellation; Day Order; Fill or Kill (FOK); Good-til- Cancelled Order; Immediate or Cancel (IOC); Limit Order; Market Order; Not Held (NH); Participate but Do Not Initiate (PNI); Scale Order; Sell Plus; Sell-Stop Order; Stop-Limit Order; Stop Order; Switch Order.

Order Ticket. Federal and NYSE regulations prescribe creation of an order ticket for each execution instruction entered on the trading floor of the exchange. In fact, there is an order ticket prepared in the member firm's office by a salesperson as well as one with the same instructions prepared for the floor of the exchange. Understandably, the information required for an order ticket written in the office of a member firm is more detailed than that prepared for execution purposes on the trading floor.

Office Tickets. Rule 17a—3 of the SEC requires noting on each order ticket (1) the date of receipt and effective lifetime (the time period during which the order instruction should be valid); (2) the time of entry (either transmitted to the floor or received from a customer); (3) the type of transaction, whether buy or sell (It is also necessary that sell orders be marked long or short. It cannot be assumed that a sale is long merely because most sales are of this nature. "Long" denotes that the seller owns that security and will deliver it promptly to complete the sale. "Short" indicates that the seller does not own that security or, if it is owned, will not deliver it to complete that transaction. In all cases of short sales, the certificate must be borrowed from someone to satisfy the requirement of that sale contract.); (4) the quantity of shares (or bonds); (5) the name or ticker symbol of the security; (6) the terms and conditions (type of order, description, tactics to be employed, and so forth); (7) the account number or name of the customer (NYSE Rules 123 and 410 prohibit changing a customer account name after entry unless written approval is granted by a member, allied member, or authorized employee on the order ticket itself.); (8) any modification or cancellation of quantity, terms, or conditions; (9) the price(s) of execution; and (10) the time of execution or cancellation (to the extent feasible).

Floor Tickets. The NYSE requires members to preserve for at least twelve months each floor ticket, which must contain: (1) the date, time of receipt, and effective lifetime of the order; (2) the type of transaction (buy or sell; if sell, long or short); (3) the quantity of shares (or bonds); (4) the name or ticker symbol of the security; (5) the terms and conditions—order type, tactics to be employed (An order entered on the floor of the Exchange without any terms or conditions is treated as a normal market order.); (6) the price(s) of execution (*see* Trading Variations); (7) the name(s) of contra broker/dealer(s); and (8) the name of the member organization initiating this customer's order. (Under certain circumstances, when the order is for an account in which the member or member organization has an interest, this must be noted on the ticket.)

Basically, only three types of orders are permissible for entry on the floor of the New York Stock Exchange: (1) market orders; (2) limit orders; and (3) stop orders. These orders are sometimes qualified by additional instructions, but merely to adjust the tactics employed for execution. If such supplementary information is removed, what remains is a basic market, limit, or stop order, as the case may be.

See also Cancellation; Choosing Types of Stock Orders; Order Transmission; Super DOT System.

Order Transmission (NYSE). When an order is transmitted to the floor of the exchange, a telephone clerk examines it to see if it (1) is in the proper format prescribed by the exchange; and (2) contains all the essential information.

The clerk must then give this order to a member of the stock exchange for execution. Ordinarily, the telephone clerk gives orders that can be executed immediately (such as market orders or limit orders at current prices) to the firm's commission house broker to save unnecessary floor brokerage expense. If the commission house broker is unavailable, orders are given instead to an available two-dollar broker. These members can be anywhere on the trading floor at the time an order is received. To attract the attention of the appropriate party, the clerk presses one of several levers on a panel situated in the booth nbear the teletype lmachine or telephone. This activates a radio-controlled paging device. Brokers rent a pocket-sized receiver from the exchange that can be activated by the telephone clerks of as many as four different firms; the receiver uses different colored lights for each signal. A lowpowered transmitter operates effectively in each of the trading rooms on the floor of the exchange. This efficient system directs the member to the proper booth to determine the reason for that summons.

Of course, if an order cannot be executed immediately (such as limit or stop orders obviously away from current prices), the telephone clerk won't bother to locate the commission house broker or a two-dollar broker merely to deliver it to a specialist at a particular trading post. Instead, the clerk uses the Exchange's pneumatic tube system, built under the trading floor to connect the telephone booths with the trading posts. Messages, orders, and even execution reports are often placed into a plastic carrier called a widget and quickly transported to their proper destination.

See also Bid and Offer; Super DOT.

Original-Issue Discount. *See* Municipal Security (Treatment of Gains).

Out-of-the-Money. *See* In-, At-, and Out-of-the-Money.

Overall Debt to Actual Market Value of Real Estate (Ratio). *See* Municipal Security (Assessing Debt).

Overlapping Debt. *See* Municipal Security (Credit Analysis).

Over the Counter (OTC). When properly qualified with the NASD as a member organization, a broker/dealer may commence trading activities for itself and/or for customers in the over-the-counter marketplace. Over the counter is not located in a centralized area as is typical of the registered securities exchanges. In fact, over the counter is anywhere other than on a registered exchange. Over the counter is a marketplace where buyers seek out sellers (and vice versa) and then attempt to arrange terms and conditions acceptable to both parties. It is a *negotiated marketplace* that exists anywhere and everywhere as opposed to the *auction marketplace* represented by activity on the securities exchanges. All that is essential for an over-the-counter market to function is a buyer and a seller of a security.

The concept of the over-the-counter market is broad enough to include private transactions by public investors as well as the more frequent trading activities of professional brokers and dealers. Therefore, it is virtually impossible to pinpoint exact total trading volume in any given security. At best, figures for any given day are an estimate based on the number of existing issues related to stock exchange volume in listed securities on that day. Without a doubt, there is a greater number and variety of issues traded over the counter than on the securities exchanges. (About 50,000 stocks and bonds trade over the counter versus approximately 4,000 stocks and bonds on all securities exchanges collectively.)

Types of OTC Securities. The types of securities traded over the counter are as follows:

1. Almost all transactions in U.S. government, state, municipal, and foreign country obligations are effected over the counter.
2. The overwhelming majority of industrial, rail, and utility debt issues are traded over the counter.
3. The equity issues of smaller, regional, or closely held corporations are traded over the counter primarily because they cannot or will not meet the stock exchanges' listing requirements.
4. Most banks and insurance companies fall into this category, although with recent popular trends toward mergers, holding companies, full disclosure, and overall projection of public image, many of these companies have obtained listing privileges on the major securities exchanges.
5. All open-end investment company shares (mutual funds) are also found over the counter.
6. Primary distributions of corporations offering their shares publicly trade in this market too, often even if the company can qualify for a listing on the New York Stock Exchange or the American Stock Exchange. At the determination of the exchange at least thirty days may elapse between filing a listing application with the exchange, a certification statement with the SEC, and the time when such documents become effective. This consideration usually works in the best interest of the exchange, because in the interim, activity in the over-the-counter market can wring out speculative excesses frequently associated with the popular public offerings of securities.
7. Even some listed stock is traded over the counter in what is often referred to as the third market. The term *third market* alludes to over-the-counter transactions in listed stocks, warrants, and closed-end investment company shares by nonmember broker/dealers of that exchange. The *first*, or *primary market*, represents transactions on registered stock exchanges by members of those exchanges. The *second market* consists of over-the-counter transactions in unlisted securities by broker/dealers registered with the SEC. The *fourth market* consists of over-the-counter transactions in either listed or unlisted securities between institutional investors, without benefit of a participating broker/dealer.
8. Also traded over the counter are receipts

evidencing the shares of a foreign corporation on deposit or under the control of a U.S. banking institution (*see* American Depositary Receipts ADR).

How Trading Is Conducted Over The Counter. A typical over-the-counter transaction is often initiated by a customer seeking to buy or sell a security. The instruction is accepted by a registered representative who, in turn, writes it down on an order ticket and presents it to an over-the-counter trader in the firm for execution. The entire buy or sell order can be consolidated on one ticket because it is handled by a single trader in that firm. This contrasts with the way a stock exchange order is often processed. With stock exchange orders, two tickets are generally required when the quantity involved is less than 100 shares (an odd lot) as well as 100 shares (a round lot) or multiples of 100 shares. An over-the-counter transaction may also be initiated by a broker/dealer desiring to take or eliminate a position in a security for its own account.

The first problem is to locate someone who is willing and able to negotiate terms on the contra side of the transaction. This normally means communicating with a broker/dealer who stands ready to provide continuing bids and offerings for that security or, in other words, to act as a *market-maker.*

There are various means by which experienced dealers locate market-makers or anybody interested in trading with them. Two of the most popular sources of such information are represented by the National Quotation Bureau, Inc.

(NQB), and the National Association of Securities Dealers Automated Quotation system (NASDAQ).

NASD members are not required to deal personally or exclusively with a market-maker in a security. There are times when a firm may find it advantageous to deal with a market-maker indirectly or to avoid the market-maker entirely if an offsetting order execution can be arranged with another member organization or within the firm itself (*see* Interpositioning).

See also Market-Maker; National Association of Securities Dealers (NASD); National Association of Securities Dealers Automated Quotations (NASDAQ); National Quotation Bureau, Inc. (NQB).

Overtrading. An NASD member firm encountering difficulty in distributing a commitment of securities that have a sizable markup may be tempted to pay an inflated price for another issue in a customer's portfolio. This then provides the customer with funds to purchase the member's security at the public offering price. Although the member would lose money in disposing of the customer's issue at prevailing market prices, the markup on the public offering is sufficient to establish an overall profit. Because the customer receives an artificial price for the security, the practice violates NASD principles; it is often referred to simply as overtrading.

See also Rules of Fair Practice (Section 8).

OW. *See* National Quotation Bureau, Inc.

P

Paid-In Capital (Capital Surplus). This item in the liabilities section of the balance sheet shows the amount of money that the company received from the sale of shares of common stock to the public *in addition* to the par value.

Example: Roxbury Manufacturing starts in business by selling 20,000 shares of stock at their original par value of $10 each. After this initial offering, the common stock section of the balance sheet shows $200,000. At this time, there is *no* paid-in capital. If, at a later date, the company issues another 10,000 shares at $20 each, the "extra" monies received—the amount *over* the par value—are indicated in the paid-in capital section of the balance sheet. The *basic* amount received ($10 par value) is added to the common stock account. The overage (the $10 that *exceeded* par value) goes into the paid-in capital account.

Common stock	$300,000
$10 par	
Authorized, issued and outstanding	
30,000 shares	
Paid-in capital (capital surplus)	100,000

This entry indicates that the founders of the business invested a total of $400,000 in common stock, of which $100,000 exceeded the total par value of $300,000. Generally, therefore, the *total* of these two accounts (common stock and paid-in capital) indicates the amount of money the company has received through the sale of its common stock to investors.

See also Balance Sheet Liabilities); Common Stock (Balance Sheet).

Paper Loss/Profit. An unrealized loss or profit on a security still held is called a *paper* loss or profit. The loss or profit becomes actual when a security position is closed out by a purchase or sale.

Parity. This is the relationship between convertible preferred and common stocks at which neither a profit nor a loss is realized by: (1) purchase of the convertible issue, (2) exchanging it for common shares, and (3) immediate sale of the common shares in the marketplace.

The formula for calculating parity is:

$$\frac{\text{par value of the convertible}}{\text{conversion price}} = \frac{\text{market price of the convertible}}{\text{market price of the common}}$$

Example 1: A $100 par convertible preferred stock with a $25 conversion price is selling at $78. If it is selling at parity with the common, where must the common stock be trading?

$$\frac{\$100 \text{ par value}}{\$25 \text{ conversion price}} = \frac{\$78}{x}$$

$$100x = \$78 \times \$25$$
$$100x = \$1,950$$
$$x = \$19.50$$

This problem is relatively easy because, with a $25 conversion price, we recognize the conversion ratio to be a simple four shares. Then, logically, if four shares are equal to a $78 package, each share is worth one-fourth of that, or $19.50.

Example 2: What is the parity price of the underlying common stock if the $100 par convertible preferred has a $36.20 conversion price and is trading at 91¼?

$$\frac{\$100 \text{ par value}}{\$36.20 \text{ conversion price}} = \frac{\$91.25}{x}$$

$$100x = \$91.25 \times \$26.20$$
$$100x = \$3,303.25$$
$$x = \$33.03$$

Example 3: If a common stock is selling at 15¾, what is the parity price of the $25 par value convertible preferred stock with a conversion price of $21.40?

$$\frac{\$25 \text{ par value}}{\$21.40 \text{ conversion price}} = \frac{x}{\$15.75}$$

$$\$21.40x = \$25 \times \$15.75$$
$$\$21.40x = \$393.75$$
$$x = \$18.40$$

Example 4: When a $50 par value preferred stock is convertible into 2.4 shares of common stock and the preferred is trading at $56, what is parity for the common? Because the formula depends on the conversion price and not on the conversion ratio, first translate the ratio into the conversion price. Calculate the conversion price by dividing the preferred stock's par value by the conversion ratio:

$$\frac{\$50 \text{ par value}}{2.4 \text{ shares}} = \$20.83 \text{ conversion price}$$

Then,
$$\frac{\$50 \text{ par value}}{\$20.83 \text{ conversion price}} = \frac{\$56}{x}$$

$$50x = \$56 \times \$20.83$$
$$50x = \$1,166.48$$
$$x = \$23.33$$

See also Convertible Preferred; Conversion Price; Conversion Ratio; Intrinsic Value.

Partial Delivery of Securities. *See* Good Delivery of Securities.

Participate but Do Not Initiate (PNI). This instruction can be given by customers who want to enter substantial orders but who do not want to become aggressive and upset existing price equilibrium in the marketplace. It is therefore recognized as a variation of the not-held qualification with an added requirement for the executing member to avoid causing volatility. The member may buy or sell (as the case may be) so long as such activity does not (1) create a new price; or (2) satisfy available quantities to such an extent that a minimal order from another broker would set a new price.

The customer must realize that a few transactions may be missed in the process, but the *overall* average execution price on completion of the order will be favorable.

See also Not Held (NH).

Participating Annuity Agreement. *See* Fixed Annuity.

Participating Preferred Stock. This type of preferred stock offers the privilege of receiving extra dividends, if declared by the directors of the corporation. After all preferred stockholders (including participating stockholders) receive their usual fixed dividend and the common stockholders have been paid their previously determined normal dividend, additional distributions must include the participating preferred stockholders equally with the common stockholders. Understandably, a corporation in need of capital is reluctant to include this feature in a preferred issue except as a last resort because it infringes on a most attractive feature for becoming a common stockholder.

See also Callable Preferred; Convertible Preferred; Cumulative Preferred; Prior Preferred.

Participating Trust. This is a legal entity that issues shares reflecting an interest in another investment company, an institution generally organized as a management company. It is the trust's only investment security. As money comes into the trust through a continuous offering of these shares of beneficial interest, it is immediately invested in more shares of the management company. Thus, purchasers of trust units acquire an indirect interest in the diversified portfolio of the management company. Their personal investment is limited to a single holding, a share in the participating trust itself. As the value of the underlying portfolio fluctuates, the value of the trust unit is similarly adjusted for purchase and redemption purposes. Most contractual purchase-plan arrangements for mutual funds are organized in this fashion, with a participating trust serving as the investment intermediary for the fund.

See also Fixed Trust; Investment Company; Unit Investment Trust Company.

Partnership. There are three principal types of business organization in the United States today: corporation, proprietorship, and partnership. The partnership is only a slight improvement over the proprietorship (*see Individual Proprietorship*). *A partnership* is composed of two or more proprietors who band together to establish and conduct a business. You may wish to form a partnership with Jane Doe. You pool your monies and your talents and, together, strive for success. Although a partnership is usually founded on larger sums of capital and a greater diversity of abilities than a proprietorship, as partners you still share the legal and physical shortcomings of the individual proprietorship. As partners, you may also have difficulty in arranging long-term financing. You are hindered by the possibility of the incapacitation or death of your partner, whose participation is essential to the continuation of the business. Furthermore, as partners, Jane Doe and you are financially responsible for each other's actions. You both, in fact, incur personal, unlimited liability on the failure of your joint venture.

See also Corporation; Individual Proprietorship; Limited Partnership.

Par Value. For bookkeeping reasons, the incorporators and accountants of any fledgling corporation assign each share of stock a monetary value representative of the capital with which it has been founded. This valuation, known as the *par value*, is imprinted on the face of each certificate.

Example: 100,000 shares at $2.50 par equals $250,000 value.

Common Stock. In a few instances, where no such assignment has been made, the certificates are inscribed as *no par value*. The accountants must nevertheless maintain such equity interest at a stated value in preparing financial statements for the concern. The stated value is an arbitrary one that may reflect the market value or the money received by the corporation on the original offering of that security. In any event, a par value, or lack of one, has little significance for the common stockholder in the company. As the underlying owner of the corporation, the common stockholder has the most junior claim upon the dividends or assets in the event of liquidation proceedings anyway.

Preferred Stock. Par value for preferred stock is very important to the preferred stockholder for the following reasons:

1. The fixed annual dividend is often expressed as a percentage of the par value.

Example: A 5% dividend on a $100 par equals $5 per share annually, while a 5% dividend on a $10 par equals $.50 per share each year.

2. The preferred holder's claim on the assets of a corporation in dissolution is frequently represented by that par value, plus: (a) any dividends in arrears, per share, and (b) dividends accruable from the last payment date.

See also Market Value (Price).

Payment Date. On this date a corporation or its disbursement agent makes payment of a distribution to its previously determined holders of record.

See also Distribution Dates.

Payout Ratio. Most corporations pay out at least a part of their net earnings to common shareholders through cash dividends. The percentage of earnings so distributed is known as the *payout ratio*. As a rough guideline, growth companies may be expected to have low payout ratio (10%), compared with a typical manufacturing company payout of approximately 50%. This ratio is derived by dividing the total common dividends paid by the total net earnings, which is net income minus preferred dividends.

$$\text{Payout ratio} = \frac{\text{common stock dividends}}{\text{net income} - \text{preferred dividends}}$$

Example: A corporation with $1,000,000 in net income pays $50,000 in preferred dividends and $375,000 in common stock dividends. Its payout ratio is:

$$\text{Payout ratio} = \frac{\$375,000}{1,000,000 - 50,000} = 0.394 \text{ or } 39.4\%$$

See also Income.

Penalties for Violation of SEC Regulations. *See* Securities Exchange Act of 1934 (Section 32).

Penalty Plans. *See* Contractual Periodic-Payment Plan.

Per Capita Debt. *See* Municipal Security (Assessing Debt).

Permanent Mortgage REIT. *See* Real Estate Investment Trust.

Philadelphia Plan. The typical equipment trust bond offering is arranged under what is known as the *Philadelphia Plan*. Its terms provide for an equity downpayment by the issuer of bonds (who is also the user of the equipment) equal to 20% of the total cost needed to buy the equipment. The issuing corporation also appoints an independent trustee (usually a large commercial bank) to: (1) take title to the equipment purchased (the corporation only leases it until the entire debt is retired); (2) supervise the insuring and maintenance of the equipment; (3) disburse interest payments to the bondholders from the lease payments made by the corporation; and (4) repay principal at maturity or, if redeemed earlier, by accelerated payments from the corporation.

See also Equipment Trust Bond.

Pink Sheets. *See* National Quotation Bureau Inc.

Pipeline Theory. *See* Subchapter M (Internal Revenue Code).

Plan Company. *See* Investment Company.

Plus-Tick and Zero-Plus-Tick Rules.

SEC Short-Sale Restrictions. To correct inequities that occurred on stock exchanges prior to 1934, the SEC implemented Rules 10a-1 and 10a-2 relating to the mechanical processes for executing short sales. It was not unusual in those days to discover groups of speculators pooling their capital and selling short for the sole purpose of driving down the price of a particular security to a level where the stockholders would panic and unload their fully owned shares. This, in turn, caused even greater declines in value. When prices had dropped low enough, the original *bear-raiders* covered their short positions at bargain prices and pocketed a pretty penny of profit.

But that is now history. With the advent of those SEC rules, it is a violation of the Securities Exchange Act of 1934 for anyone to sell a stock exchange security short if, in the execution of the sale, that party depresses the last different price of that security appearing on the consolidated ticker tape.

In day-to-day terms, this means that in order to comply with federal requirements a person selling short (1) must use the last sale appearing on the consolidated ticker tape as a point of reference (Instead, the SEC permits each exchange to establish as a point of reference the last sale only on its own premises. The New York and American stock exchanges are now using this privilege as their official policy.); (2) must ensure that the order is executed at a price that constitutes a plus tick or a zero plus tick; and (3) cannot sell at a minus tick or at a zero minus tick.

The prospective short seller need not wait for someone else to create a plus tick or zero plus tick first. The seller can offer stock at a price that, if accepted by a purchaser, is identifiable as a plus or zero plus transaction. Often, this means that the short seller must play a passive role while the purchaser acts as the aggressor.

Example: Minus tick. The last sale is at 68⅝, which is a *minus tick* from 68¾.

Quotation, 68⅝ to 68⅞

The short seller can offer stock at 68¾ or at 68⅞. If a purchaser accepts, the short sale is a *plus tick*. This transaction complies with the restrictions imposed under SEC rules.

Example: Plus tick. The last sale is at 53½, which is a *plus tick* from 53⅜.

Quotation, 53⅜ to 53⅝

The short seller can offer stock at 53½ (zero plus tick) or 53⅝ (plus tick). If a purchaser accepts, the short sale is either a zero plus tick or a plus tick. In either case, this transaction complies with the restrictions imposed under SEC rules.

In neither example above, can the short seller "hit" the bid prices shown. In the first instance, to do so would constitute a zero minus tick (65⅝), and in the latter instance, an ordinary minus tick (53⅜).

Initial Transaction of a Stock Exchange. The initial transaction for a security after listing on the stock exchange is arbitrarily decreed to represent a plus tick. It can, in fact, be a short sale. Every subsequent transaction is identified as zero plus, plus, minus, or zero minus, as the case may be. These designations continue daily, with identification of each day's first transaction dependent on the previous day's closing price. Thus, if a stock closed at 25 on the NYSE on Monday and it was a minus tick, an opening sale on Tuesday below 25 is a minus tick; at 25, it is a zero minus tick; above 25, it is a plus tick.

Ex Dividends and Ex Distributions. A reduction in price on the day a security begins trading ex dividend, ex rights, or ex any distribution necessitates a readjustment of the previous day's closing price by the value of that distribution. However, the identifying designation of that transaction is maintained, although on a lower plateau.

Thus, with a distribution of 25¢ per share (¼), if the previous close was at 37½ (plus tick) and if the first transaction on the ex date was at (1) 37¼, the transaction constitutes a *zero plus tick* because the difference is equal to the reduction in price ($37\frac{1}{2} - 37\frac{1}{4} = \frac{1}{4}$); (2) 37⅜ or above, the transaction constitutes a *plus tick* because the difference is less than the reduction in price ($37\frac{1}{2} - 37\frac{3}{8} = \frac{1}{8}$); (3) 37⅛ or below, the transaction constitutes a *minus tick* because the difference is more than the reduction in price ($37\frac{1}{2} - 37\frac{1}{8} = \frac{3}{8}$).

Recall that for cash distributions not equal to the multiple of the minimum trading variation (⅛ point in most instances), the market price of that security is reduced by the *next highest* ⅛ *point*. Thus, if the distribution is set at 26¢ per share, the reduction for dividend is ⅜ of a point. Accordingly, if the previous close was 37½ (plus tick), and if the first transaction on the ex date is at (1) 37⅛, the transaction now represents a zero plus tick; (2) 37¼ or above, the transaction now represents a plus tick; (3) 37 or below, the transaction now represents a minus tick.

See also Securities Exchange Act of 1934 (Section 10); Short Sale; Tick.

Pneumatic Tube System. *See* Order Transmission (NYSE).

Point and Figure Chart. *See* Technical Analysis.

Position Limit. The maximum amount of put or call contracts placed on the same side of the market being held by any one account or group of related accounts. Short puts and long calls are placed on the same side of the market; short calls and long puts are also placed together.

Pot. *See* Group Sales.

Power of Attorney. *See* Trading Authorization.

Preemptive Right. *See* Subscription Privilege.

Preferred Dividend Coverage. To find out how well the preferred dividends are covered by earnings, simply divide the net income by the preferred dividend requirements.

$$\text{Preferred dividend coverage} = \frac{\text{net income}}{\text{preferred dividends}}$$

Example:

$$\text{Preferred dividend coverage} = \frac{\$105,525}{\$\ 4,500} = 23.2 \text{ times}$$

The calculation shows that the earnings cover the preferred dividends 23.2 times over.

See also Income Statement.

Preferred Stock. A corporate charter can authorize two distinct forms of capital stock: common and preferred. Although common stock is *always* found in the capital structure of a corporation, the same is not true of preferred stock. Preferred stock may be likened to a silent partner in a partnership (*see* Partnership; Limited Partnership).

Preferred stockholders carry no voice in the management of the concern. Consequently, the circumstances and conditions under which such shares can be sold to investors are not applicable to all corporations or suitable for all purchasers.

The "preference" associated with these shares relates generally to the: (1) ability to command a fixed dividend payment before common shareholders receive dividends; and (2) prior claim (to common shareholders only) to the corporation's assets in the event of its dissolution and liquidation.

As a way of attracting investors to become owners of a corporation, the directors may decide to offer preferred stock, which has certain attractions over common stock. Preferred stock represents equity in the corporation, but to a limited degree. The preferred stockholders have little or no voice in the management of the company. In return for their money, they must be paid a fixed dividend before any payment is made to the common stockholders. In liquidation proceedings, the preferred stockholder's claim to the corporation's assets enjoys a priority over the common stockholder's claims.

Types. Admittedly, the characteristics of preferred stock are relatively unattractive to today's investors who, for the same money, can enjoy a comparable return through ownership of a bond and have senior status as creditors of the company. A corporation intent on a successful offering of preferred stock must be prepared to make further concessions to attract the investing public. These special privileges enable us to classify preferred stock into five distinct types:

1. *Cumulative preferred* assures shareholders that missed dividend payments "accumulate," that is, the issuing corporation must make them up before making any distributions to common stockholders.
2. *Participating preferred* permits holders to receive additional dividends, if issued.
3. *Convertible preferred* may be converted into a predetermined number of common shares at a certain market price

See also Conversion Price; Conversion Ratio; Parity)
4. *Prior preferred* gives holders seniority over other preferred stockholders of the corporation.
5. *Callable preferred* permits the issuer to retire the stock at its option.

Not to be overlooked is the possibility of incorporating any or all of these features into the same issue. It is possible for a corporation to offer a cumulative, participating, convertible, callable, prior preferred stock if it becomes desperate for capital and cannot obtain it another way.

Five Types of Preferred Stock

Type of Stock	Characteristics
Cumulative	Claims previously deferred dividends before common stock can share in profits
Participating	Can receive extra dividends beyond fixed amount
Convertible	Can exchange shares for common stock
Prior	Claims seniority over other preferred stocks in payment of dividends or in distribution of assets if the corporation goes out of business
Callable	Gets premium price if stock is redeemed soon after issuance, otherwise, only par value if company retires it

See also Common Stock; Dividends; Par Value.

Balance Sheet. Preferred stock, like common stock, is an equity security. Holders of such stock are considered to be owners of the corporation, in contrast to bondholders who are considered creditors. Fittingly, preferred stock, which is ordinarily senior to common stock with respect to dividends and liquidation rights, is listed first in the stockholders' (shareholders') equity section of the balance sheet.

Such stock is "carried" not at its market value, but at its total par value, which in most instances is approximately equal to the amount the company received when the stock was first sold to the public. This listed figure usually approximates the amount that the preferred shareholders are entitled to receive if the company is dissolved. Most balance sheets detail information about any preferred stock listed, such as par value, convertibility (if any), dividend rate, and the number of shares authorized, issued, or outstanding.

Example:

Preferred stock	$75,000

6% Cumulative—$100 par
authorized, issued, and outstanding
750 shares

All 750 authorized shares of preferred stock are issued and outstanding.

750 shares $\times$ $100 par = $75,000 Book value
(Total par value)

Each share of $100 par preferred stock is entitled to a dividend at 6% of the par value each year. In other words, 6% of $100 equals a $6-per-share annual dividend. The balance sheet entry indicates that such dividends are cumulative. In the event that any preferred dividends are "skipped," the company may not pay dividends on the common stock until all back dividends on the preferred stock (arrearages) have been paid.

See also Balance Sheet (Liabilities).

Preferred Stock Ratio. *See* Balance Sheet (Capitalization Ratios).

Preliminary Prospectus. In compliance with SEC rules governing purchases of primary issues before the effective date, it is often necessary to send customers a preliminary prospectus to solicit their indications or even to accept unsolicited indications within the provisions of state or federal securities laws. This statement is often called a *red herring* because of a red-lettered caveat in the border of the front page. SEC regulations require the following commentary to appear in red print in the border of every preliminary prospectus: "A registration statement relating to these securities has been filed with the Securities and Exchange Commission, but has not yet become effective. Information contained herein is subject to completion or amendment. These securities may not be sold nor may offers to buy be accepted prior to the time the registration statement becomes effective. This prospectus shall not constitute an offer to sell or the solicitation of an offer to buy nor shall there be any sale of these securities in any state in which such offer, solicitation, or sale would be unlawful prior to registration or qualification under the securities laws of any such state."

The preliminary prospectus, or red herring, is a summary of pertinent details from the registration statement. It contains most facts known about the offering to that moment. Admittedly, it

is incomplete because it lacks a final price and other pertinent information; it may even contain some unintentional inaccuracies. This is why it must never be used as a means of soliciting orders, even in this preliminary stage of negotiation. The SEC may also request inclusion of a "maximum" offering price in the red herring to give the reader an idea of value for this issue, even though the final price is generally set below this ceiling.

Solicitation of orders, or even acceptance of unsolicited orders prior to the effective date, is a violation of the Securities Act of 1933. The red herring is the only form of written communication permissible between a participating investment banker and a potential purchaser while the registration statement for that security is pending at the SEC.

The process of soliciting and accepting indications of interest enables investment bankers to gauge the extent of consideration their customers may have for investment purposes at this time. If they find too many customers are disinterested, they can cancel their participation in the underwriting group without financial loss or penalty.

See also Final Prospectus; Indication of Interest; Registration Statement.

Premium. This amount of money is paid by the buyer of an option to the seller to secure the rights of buying or selling the underlying security (the market price of the option). The premium is the sum of the intrinsic value of the option and the time value.

See also Evaluating Options; In-and Out-of-the-Money; Intrinsic Value; Time Value.

Prepaid-Charge Plan. *See* Contractual Periodic-Payment Plan.

Presale Orders. *See* Municipal Securities (Priority of Orders).

Price-Earnings Ratio. The *price-earnings (P/E) ratio* is one of the most significant measurements. It relates a corporation's profitability to the market price of its common shares, thus affording a measure of the relative "expensiveness" of the common stock. Typically, growth stocks have high P/E ratios; companies with poorer prospects sell at lower earnings multiples. To obtain this ratio, divide the market price of the company's common stock by the earnings per share:

$$\text{Price earnings ratio} = \frac{\text{current market price of the common stock}}{\text{common stock earnings per share}}$$

Example: Company A earned $1.04 per share. Its common stock is selling in the open market at 23¼.

$$\text{Price earnings (P/E) ratio} = \frac{\$23.25}{\$1.04} = 22.4$$

Each share of common stock is selling for about 22 times the amount of earnings generated by each share.

See also Digest of Earnings Reports; Quotations.

Primary Distribution. This offering is the original sale of a company's securities. The sale of authorized but unissued shares of stock is a primary sale, while the resale of treasury shares is a secondary sale.

See also Securities Exchange Act of 1934 (Section 11).

Primary Earnings per Share. This ratio is probably the most widely used measure of a company's fortunes. As a result, it is also the most widely advertised measure—the so called "bottom line." This most important measurement is determined by dividing the net earnings (which is equal to net income minus preferred dividends) by the number of common shares outstanding.

$$\text{Primary earnings per share} = \frac{\text{net earnings (from income statement)}}{\text{number of shares of common stock outstanding}}$$

Example:

$$\text{Primary earnings per share} = \frac{\$105,525}{30,000} = \$3.52$$

The expression "earnings per share" has practically been replaced by the more modern expression *primary earnings per share*. The newer term reflects earnings as they would be if all "common stock equivalents" were issued and outstanding as common stock, thus diluting "ordinary" earnings per share by 3% or more. Common stock equivalents include warrants, stock options, and certain convertible bonds and convertible preferred shares. Common stock equivalents, if they exist, are clearly labeled. Corporations now report primary earnings per share so that the investing public does not have to refigure the "ordinary" earnings per share. Nor does the public have to determine which convertible items are considered common stock equivalents. When earnings are figured to include all possible additional shares of common stock, whether common stock equivalents or not, then such earnings are reported as *fully diluted*.

See also Fully Diluted Earnings per Share.

Primary Market. *See* Over the Counter.

Primary Movement. *See* Dow Theory.

Primary/Secondary Distribution. If the security in an offering is authorized but previously unissued stock or bonds, it is identified as a *primary distribution*. If the offering represents securities held by stockholders or bondholders or securities held by the corporation itself in its treasury, it is called *secondary distribution*. The issuer is therefore capable of making both primary and secondary distributions whereas a stockholder or bondholder can only make a secondary distribution. Some offerings of securities called *split offerings,* are comprised of both types of distributions.

See also Investment Banker; Private Placement; Public Offering.

Prime Rate. The key economic factor influencing a bank to borrow federal funds and re-lend them to its customers is the difference between the prevailing percentage rate paid for the federal funds and the bank rate charged to customers. The interest rate charged to the bank's best customers, called the *prime rate*, is a preferential rate and is supposed to be the lowest percentage at which that bank can realize a profit from borrowers. The actual prime rate may vary from bank to bank but is generally about 1.5% above the average federal funds rate at major banks in large cities.

See also Federal Reserve System.

Principal Transaction. As *principal*, the securities firm reports to the customer that it executed this order in the capacity of a dealer. That is, it acted directly with the customer as a trader on the opposite side of the order. After purchasing the stock from the market-maker, the firm places it into its newly created inventory and then sells it to the customer from this position, but at a higher price. It might report to the customer, "As principal, we are selling to you for your account and risk 100 shares of Connecticut General Insurance Company at 65¾ net." The price thus established is a net price that includes the firm's remuneration for this transaction. No further charges are added to the price quoted to the customer when the firm acts as principal. The

firm may not change the execution price and then add a commission, because then it is acting as broker and dealer on the same transaction, a relationship prohibited by regulation.

See also Agency Transaction; Interpositioning; Markup and Markdown.

Prior Lien Bond. Sometimes, when a company's financial condition deteriorates to such an extent that money becomes critical for continuing operation or even existence, the mortgage bondholders may be requested to forego their status in favor of a new class of creditors willing to lend capital. With approval, the corporation issues a new bond whose purchasers assume the seniority of the first mortgage bondholders. Accordingly, this debt instrument is a *prior lien bond.*

Prior Preferred Stock. Also known as *preference stock*, this somewhat ambiguous designation is applied to some preferred stock issues. It generally refers to a seniority of one preferred stock over another with respect to (1) receipt of dividends or (2) a claim on the assets of the corporation in the event of dissolution.

The extent of the issue's superiority is not readily discernible from the title alone. Making such a determination necessitates a careful examination of: (1) the offering prospectus when the issue was initially distributed or (2) a manual of corporate information published by Moody's, Standard & Poor's, or some other statistical services publication.

See also Callable Preferred; Convertible Preferred; Cumulative Preferred; Participating Preferredk.

Private Placement. A *private placement* is the distribution of securities to a "limited number" of purchasers made without the filing of a registration statement. Such a purchaser customarily certifies to the issuer, in a written agreement known as an *investment letter*, that the purchase is for investment purposes, without immediate intention to reoffer the securities publicly. If the purchaser's financial circumstances change in a relatively short period of time thereafter, he or she may transfer title to this so-called "letter" security to another investor, but only in another private placement. In such secondary private placements, the seller should obtain an investment letter from the new purchaser. Otherwise, if the new buyer reneges on the promise to hold for investment and attempts a public sale soon after, the seller can be defined as a statutory underwriter and be liable for penalty under the Securities Act of 1933. The procurement of an investment letter may not always enable the seller to avoid a penalty, but it can surely mitigate it. Moreover, it allows the seller to sue the buyer and gain legal and financial satisfaction as a result.

Securities placed privately may be represented by either equity or debt instruments. Although *letter stock* usually gets most of the publicity in the press and various trade journals, substantial quantities of *letter bonds* are also subject to the SEC rules, too.

Each certificate is imprinted with a legend that warns the holder of the prevailing distribution restrictions under the law. However, the absence of such a legend is no assurance of the certificate's legal transferability.

See also Public Offering.

Proceeds Sales. *These sales,* more commonly referred to in the financial community as *swap transactions,* are orders from customers to sell their securities and use the proceeds of the sale to purchase other securities for them. The member organization, therefore, receives two orders from the same customer at the same time. However, whether it decides to act as principal or agent, it must treat the transaction as a single order for the purpose of establishing total profit/commission.

See also Markup and Markdown; Switch Order (Contingent or Swap Order).

Profit Zone. This is the area in which a position makes a profit. The term usually refers to strategies that have two break-even points—an upside and a downside break-even. The range between the two points is the profit zone (range).

See also Break-even Point.

Profit and Loss (P&L) Statement. *See* Income Statement.

Prompt Receipt and Delivery of Securities. *See* Rules of Fair Practice.

Proprietorship. *See* Individual Proprietorship.

Prospectus. *See* Registration Statement.

Proxy. Corporations distribute to stockholders an advisory and voting solicitation, generally at least once each year. It gives the stockholder a right to elect directors and decide on other important matters brought before an annual or special meeting of the company. Beneficial owners cannot cast their votes directly because the corporation recognizes only the brokerage firm as its stockholder from its street name registration of certificates. The Proxy Department of the brokerage firm sends a request form to each of the beneficial owners, soliciting instructions regarding casting of this ballot. The form is called a *proxy.* By definition, a proxy is simply an authorization or power to act for someone else.

Prior to a shareholders' meeting, stockholders receive a proxy from the company. The proxy is a power of attorney appointing a third party (usually a company representative) to vote for the stockholder if he or she cannot attend the meeting. Shareholders receiving a proxy may vote as they decide or may give this proxy to parties of their choice, permitting them to vote as they see fit. (The term "proxy" may also apply to the person to whom the vote is given.) Practices vary among corporations as to how such proxies are applied in the voting process. Some companies employ statutory voting rules; others use cumulative voting procedures.

See also Beneficial Owner; Broker/Dealer Organization (Proxy Department); Common Stock; Cumulative Voting; Statutory Voting.

Proxy Contest. In this situation a person or group of people other than a company's management attempts to solicit shareholders' proxies, usually to change the management of the company.

See also Borrowing Stock Certificates; Specialist.

Proxy Materials. In the interest of commercial honor and equitable trade principles, when NASD members hold shares registered in their name (street name) in behalf of other beneficial owners, members are expected to transmit all legally required information furnished by the issuing corporation for dissemination to the stockholders. Such information includes proxy materials, annual reports, and financial statements.

NASD member firms assume the obligation of complying with this procedure, but the corporation must furnish the firm with (1) sufficient copies of the material for the beneficial owners; and (2) satisfactory reimbursement for out-of-pocket expenses, including reasonable clerical costs.

The same services should be provided for any person soliciting proxies from the stockholder if that person has filed with the Securities and Exchange Commission under Section 14a-4 of the Securities Exchange Act of 1934 and furnishes sufficient copies of the materials and satisfactory reimbursement of expenses, too.

Beneficial owners who reside outside the United States are not included in these provisions or statutes, although NASD members may accommodate them on a voluntary basis, and many certainly do.

See also Rules of Fair Practice.

Proxy Rules (NYSE). It is a well-known fact that many publicly owned corporations are unable to solicit proxies directly from the beneficial owners of their shares because of their inability to identify those parties. Many beneficial owners prefer to have their shares registered in the name of a nominee, such as a bank or trusteeship, established for this specific purpose. Still others maintain their holdings registered in the name of their brokerage firm (street name).

Although the exchange's board of directors does not have jurisdiction over the banking community, it does have authority in the affairs of the member organizations. Thus, if a corporation (or any dissident party, for that matter) desires to solicit proxies from the beneficial owners of specific shares, and they agree to furnish the member organization with (1) copies of all soliciting materials and (2) reimbursement for out-of-pocket expenses, the member organization must then transmit this material and proxy request to the beneficial owners. They must still transmit the materials even though the beneficial owners may instruct them not to do so. The only allowable exception, at the discretion of the member organization, is with respect to beneficial owners located outside the United States.

Under these circumstances, unless the meeting or the matter on the agenda is of unusual interest, many of these beneficial owners never respond to the brokerage firm's request for voting instructions. In general, if the beneficial owner does not convey voting instructions to the firm by the tenth day prior to the meeting date, the member organization has permission to vote that stock as it sees fit. However, if the matter to be determined at this meeting is of substantive interest (including such issues as a fight for control changing the purpose or powers of the corporation, altering the capitalization, authorizing the expenditure of capital funds, and so on) to the stockholders of the company, a member organization of the NYSE may not vote this stock without specific authorization to do so. (Written authorization is preferable, although verbal instructions are acceptable if the firm makes and retains a written record of the verbal communication.)

See also New York Stock Exchange, Inc. (Corporate Services Department).

Proxy Department. *See* Broker/Dealer Organization.

Proxy Statement. This material information is required by the SEC to be given to a corporation's stockholders as a prerequisite to solicitation of votes. It is required for any issuer subject to the provisions of the Securities Exchange Act of 1934.

Prudent Man. A person who oversees purchases and sales on behalf of a minor must act according to *prudent man* guidelines that generally prevail. Liberally interpreted, this means that all transactions in behalf of a minor should be in accord with conservative management of one's own assets. In states without clearly defined guidelines, it is safest to invest or trade only in U.S. government securities or in issues that appear on lists published and approved by that state's banking or insurance commissioners. They are already recognized as appropriate investments for financial institutions in that state, and the securities are usually identified simply by the term "legals," that is, legal investments or legalist securities. Representatives who condone and assist in obviously improper activity in these accounts subject themselves and their firms to financial liability.

See also Fiduciary Accounts; Uniform Gifts to Minors Acts.

P&S. *See* Broker/Dealer Organization.

Public Housing Authority (PHA). A unique type of revenue bond is the *public housing authority (PHA)* issue. Congress, in order to assist in the construction of low-income housing, authorized government backing for certain locally issued project bonds. The revenues (rents) of the project are expected to pay the debt service, but, if they are not sufficient, the full faith and credit of the United States government provides the ultimate security through the Housing and Urban Development Department. Thus, the investor gets tax-exempt income (as the issue is a municipal bond) but also receives a government guarantee, a most attractive combination. Municipal notes maturing in one year or less issued under this arrangement for the purpose of financing short-term projects are called project notes (PNs).

See also Municipal Security.

Purchase and Sale (P&S) Department. *See* Broker/Dealer Organization.

Put Options.

Buying. An investor generally buys puts for two reasons: (1) to participate in any price decline in the underlying security or, (2) to hedge a long stock position against a price decline.

Participating in price decline. The bearish put buyer seeks to benefit from a decline in the market price of the underlying security. This strategy gives the put buyer the ability to speculate with a limited amount of capital because the premium of the put is often considerably less than the cost of selling short the underlying security. By leveraging the funds, the purchaser of puts has an opportunity to benefit more from any significant decrease in the price of the security than if the security itself had been sold short. Since the put buyer is in a leveraged position, the buyer may lose the entire investment should the stock increase in market value.

Example: A speculator purchases 1 XYZ December 40 put when the market price of XYZ is $41¼ and pays a premium of $200.

If XYZ is trading at $35 at the option expiration date, the put holder (buyer) has the choice of either exercising the put or liquidating the option on the exchange. Assuming XYZ is trading at its intrinsic value of $5, the put holder may realize a $300 profit ($500 – $200) by closing out (that is, selling) the long put position. By trading the put, the speculator has earned a 150% return ($300 ÷ 200), whereas the stock declined by only 15%. Of course, the return would have been greater had the put option been sold for more than intrinsic value.

If XYZ is above $40 at the option's expiration date, the put option will expire worthless. The option holder loses the entire $200. However, this is the maximum loss no matter how high the stock rises. The break-even point for the put buyer is the exercise price minus the premium paid for the put. In the foregoing example, the break-even point is $38 ($40 –$2).

Protecting long stock position. The second reason to purchase a put is to hedge a long stock position against a price decline. Puts may be purchased to protect profits in an existing long position in an underlying stock, or to protect a newly acquired position in an underlying stock against a substantial decline in its market value. In either case, the protection is provided only during the life of the put. The holder of the put is able to sell the underlying security at the put exercise price regardless of decline in the underlying security's market price.

Example: An investor who owns 100 shares of XYZ (purchased at $18) which is currently trading at $30 per share buys 1 XYZ November 30 put for a premium of $225. The investor has locked in a sale price of $30 until the expiration date. Should the stock continue to increase through November, the put option will expire worthless, thus causing the investor to lose $225 but also allowing him or her to participate in the stock's price appreciation.

Should the stock decline subsequent to the put purchase, the investor may exercise the put and deliver 100 shares of stock at $30, thus creating a $1,200 ($3,000 – $1,800) profit from the stock transaction. However, the $1,200 profit is reduced to $975 by the $225 premium cost for the put.

In summary, a person purchases a put for high-percentage profit potential, for the limitation of loss, for leverage, or for the protection of a long stock position.

Writing Uncovered Put Options. An investor generally writes puts for two basic reasons: (1) to realize option premium income; or (2) to acquire the underlying security at a net cost which is less than the current market price at the time the option is written.

Depending on the movement of the underlying stock, one of the two objectives will be accomplished.

Example: An investor writes a ZYX September 50 put when the market price of ZYX is $50 and receives a premium of $400.

If ZYX is above $50 at the option's expiration date, the writer will not be assigned an exercise notice. Since the option expires worthless, the investor keeps the $400 premium as his or her profit.

If ZYX is below $50 at expiration date, the option writer will be assigned an exercise notice and has the obligation to purchase 100 shares of stock at $50 per share. Since the writer received a premium of $400, the net cost of the stock is $4,600 ($5,000 – $400). However, such net cost may be substantially above the actual market price prevailing at the time the put is exercised.

The break-even point in this example is $46 per share (exercise price – option premium). If the stock is selling at $43 when the put is exercised, the investor has a $300 paper loss and must wait for the stock to rise above $46 to earn a profit.

Of course, the put writer may close out the position prior to exercise and realize either a profit or loss depending on the price paid to buy back the option.

See also Call Option; Option.

Q

Qualifications for Listing (NYSE). The minimum qualifications for stock listing have been upgraded frequently in recent years. At the present time, these qualifications are as shown in the following table.

Criterion

1. Earning power	$2.5 million pretax and $2 million for the preceding two years *or* $6.5 million over the last three years and $4.5 million in the most recent year, and all three years must have been profitable
2. Net tangible assets	$18 million
3. Aggregate market value of common stock publicly held	$18 million
4. Publicly held shares	1.1 million
5. Number of share-holders	2,000 round-lot stockholders *or* 2,200 stockholders and an average trading volume of 100,000 or more in the most recent six-month period

Consideration is also accorded to (1) the degree of national interest in the company; (2) its relative position and stability in the industry; and (3) whether it is engaged in an expanding industry and is expected to maintain its relative position.

See also New York Stock Exchange, Inc. (Corporate Services Department).

Quick Asset. The total current assets that may be quickly converted into cash, should the company deem it necessary, are called *quick assets*. The only item under current assets that is not considered very liquid is inventory. Therefore, to figure quick assets, merely subtract inventory from total current assets.

Example: A company's total current assets are:

Cash	$ 75,000
Marketable securities	150,000
Accounts receivable	375,000
Inventory	400,000
Total current assets	$1,000,000

Subtracting inventory ($400,000) from the total ($1,000,000), we arrive at a figure of $600,000 for quick assets. Of course, the same amount may be derived by adding together cash, marketable securities, and accounts receivable—if these figures are all you have to work with. The formulas are as follows:

Quick assets = total current assets − inventory

Quick assets = cash + marketable securities + accounts receivable

See also Balance Sheet (Assets).

Quick Asset Ratio. An even more stringent test of a company's ability to meet its current obligations is the *quick asset ratio*, also called the *liquidity ratio* or *acid test ratio.* This ratio indicates the relationship between quick assets (that is, total current assets less inventory) and current liabilities:

$$\text{Quick asset ratio} = \frac{\text{quick assets}}{\text{current liabilities}}$$

Example: Using these figures for our corporation:

Quick assets   = total current assets − inventory

Quick assets   = \$1,000,000 − \$400,000
                  = \$600,000

$$\text{Quick asset ratio} = \frac{\text{quick assets}}{\text{total current liabilities}}$$

$$\text{Quick asset ratio} = \frac{\$600,000}{\$400,000} = 1.5$$

The quick asset ratio of 1.5 indicates that our corporation has one and one half times the total of its short-term liabilities in quick assets alone. A "safe" quick asset ratio for the average manufacturing concern is 1 to 1. In other words, the corporation should have enough quick assets to pay off all the current liabilities.

See also Quick Asset.

Quotations. Most investors are unable to scan the ticker tape to keep informed about market activity and price trends in their favorite issues. In many instances, it is physically impossible to do so simply because some kinds of securities transactions are not publicized on a ticker tape system. Such transactions include over-the-counter executions (except for Instinet and some "third market" transactions), especially transactions in U.S. government, federal agency, municipal, and numerous corporate issues not traded on a securities exchange. Investors interested in these as well as exchange-traded securities rely primarily on the daily newspapers for relatively

current market information about their favorite stocks and bonds. The newspapers provide a synopsis of the previous day's financial activity; information obtained from the various stock exchanges, the NASD, OTC market-makers, and government securities dealers. Due to space limitations, some newspapers provide less detailed and less comprehensive coverage of financial information than others. On a national level, *The Wall Street Journal,* a daily publication of Dow Jones & Company, Inc., is well known and respected for the depth and accuracy of its coverage; its presentation is, therefore, utilized in this section. However, at least one newspaper in each major city in the United States devotes some space to quality financial reporting, too. The prime difference among them is the extent of coverage devoted to local issues of interest to each paper's readers.

The Listed Stock Tables. The style and statistical information tables used for stocks listed on the New York and American Stock exchanges are provided by the Associated Press, a major news wire service. The format is, therefore, uniform throughout the country. Issues that have traded each day are recorded in alphabetical order and appear as shown in the following table.

This segment of the page makes it possible to determine: (1) the stock exchange whose activity is highlighted; (2) the date of such activity; (3) top volume in equity issues broken down by share and warrant quantities and by marketplace; 4) cumulative and historical comparison of trading volume; and (5) the ten most active stocks that day, showing each one's trading and volume statistics.

Let us isolate the Cabot Corporation (abbreviated Cabot C) to explain their meaning (*see* the figure on page 353):

1		2	3	4	5	6	7	8	9	10
52 Weeks					P.E.	Sales				Net
High	Low	Stocks	Div.	Yld	Ratio	100s	High	Low	Close	Chg.
64¾	34	Cabot Corp.	2	3.1	8	x190	u65½	62¾	65¼	+ 2¾

1. The first columns indicate both the highest and lowest prices at which this issue traded in the past year. Past year encompasses a span of 52 weeks preceding the current week. This practice avoids hundreds of meaningless daily announcements of "new" highs and lows at the beginning of each year until a reasonable amount of price fluctuation has established itself.

2. This column briefly identifies the issue, citing its full name or abbreviated title. If it is one of several preferred stocks issued by that company, some means of distinguishing this item from the others also appears. It may be a designation of *a*, *b*, or *c* preferred or, if the issues carry different dividend rates, that associated rate may be used instead.

3. If the company habitually makes a dividend distribution to its stockholders, or has made an unexpected one thus far this year, that information appears next to the corporation title or abbreviation. Thus, Cabot Corp. has established a policy of paying a $2.-per-share dividend annually. Because of the unique character of some distributions, they appear with a footnote designation. The meaning of the footnote is recorded at the end of the stock tables in a box labeled "Explanatory Notes."

Example: If the dividend amount is followed by the letter *e*, a glance at those notes reveals that this sum was paid in the preceding 12 months but is not indicative of a fixed or habitual rate. Although it was not the case with Cabot Corporation, stock splits or stock dividends of 25% or more paid in the past 52 weeks are also identified in these stock tables. Between the name and the cash dividend amount per share would be a small *s*. That identifier is shown for

Dover Corporation which is listed in the column next to Cabot Corporation.

4. Yield is the percentage rate of return for someone purchasing this stock at the current price. It is calculated by dividing the annual cash dividend per share by the last sale price ($2 dividend by 65¼).

5. The P.E. ratio, meaning price-earnings ratio, is an equation used by some investors to gauge the relative value of a particular security. It compares the current market price of an issue to the latest twelve-month earnings announcement on a per-share basis. Thus, because the number 8 appears in this column and the stock is selling at about $64, simple arithmetic advises that twelve-month earnings are approximately $8 per share (64 ÷ 8). No figure appears in this column if the issue is preferred stock or if the company has no earnings or deficit income to report. Negative P.E. ratios are meaningless.

6. Daily quantity figures are recorded only in terms of the number of round lots traded. Because the typical trading unit is 100 shares, the actual share volume is derived by adding two zeros to the number of round lots shown. Thus, a figure of 190 actually means 19,000 shares changed hands today. One important exception to this statement concerns ten-share trading unit stocks. The quantity figure for these issues is always stated in full and is recognizable by the letter *z* preceding the volume. Sales indicated as "z100" mean, in fact, that a total of 100 shares traded today. The *x* preceding the volume figure signifies that this issue began trading ex-dividend today.

7. *High* refers to the highest-priced transaction for that issue this day.

52 Weeks High	Low	Stock	Div.	Yld %	P-E Ratio	Sales 100s	High	low	Close	Net Chg.
45½	36	Benef	pf4.30	12.	..	3	35½	d35¼	35¼	− ¾
26½	20	Benef	pf2.50	13.	..	z70	20	20	20	.....
19⅜	2⅞	BengtB		..	36	1231	12⅛	11½	11½	− ⅝
7¼	3	BerkeyP		..	14	134	5⅛	4⅞	5	.....
29⅛	18¾	BestPd	.24	1.3	6	500	19½	d18½	19	− ⅞
25⅞	19½	BethStl	1.60	6.3	4	1471	25¾	24½	25⅜	+ ⅞
47¾	32⅜	BigThr	.88	1.8	15	160	47¾	47	47¾	+ 1
33⅜	14⅝	Binney	.92	4.2	10	56	22⅞	22⅛	22⅛	− ⅜
29¼	16⅞	BisFSL	s.80	3.9	6	43	20¾	20¼	20⅝	− ⅞
25¼	18½	BlackDr	.76	3.4	9	578	22¼	21⅝	22¼	+ ¼
24½	18½	BlairJn	s 1	5.3	6	64	19¼	18¾	18¾	− ⅜
25½	15⅝	BlissL	1.10	5.5	6	45	20	19¾	20	+ ⅛
27¼	21¼	BlckHR	1.60	6.2	10	245	26⅜	25½	26	+ ⅜
37⅝	22⅝	BlueB	1.80	4.8	7	243	37⅜	36⅜	37⅛	+ ⅞
5¾	3⅝	BobbieBr		..	5	137	4	3¾	3⅞	+ ⅛
68⅞	37¼	Boeing	s1.80	2.8	8	4346	64⅜	62¾	63¼	− 1
42½	29¾	BoiseC	1.50	3.7	6	675	41⅞	40¾	40⅞	− ⅞
27⅞	23	Borden	1.82	7.9	5	322	23¾	23	23	− ⅝
40⅞	27⅛	BorgW	2.30	5.4	6	1095	u42⅞	40⅞	42⅝	+ 2
8⅜	4⅛	Bormns	.20e	4.4	8	23	4⅝	4½	4½	.....
24¼	19⅞	BosEd	2.72	13.	6	46	21¼	21	21	+ ⅛
84¾	69	BosE	pf8.88	13.	..	z460	70	69	70	.....
11⅛	9	BosE	pr1.17	13.	..	11	9⅛	9⅛	9⅛	− ⅛
14	11	BosE	pr1.46	13.	..	22	11⅛	11	11⅛	+ ⅛
13¾	6¾	Braniff	.20	2.2	..	447	9⅜	9⅛	9¼	.....
29⅞	23⅜	BrigSt	1.20a	5.0	7	68	24⅛	23¾	24	.....
39¼	31	BristM	1.44	4.2	10	1673	35⅜	34¼	34½	− ⅝
44¼	35½	BristM	pf 2	5.1	..	4	39½	39	39½	+ 1⅛
37⅞	19	BritPet	1.02e	2.7	8	987	u38½	37⅝	38¼	+ 1⅛
19½	12½	BrkwGl	1.08	7.3	7	263	15⅛	14⅝	14⅞	− ¼
25	18¾	BkyUG	2.22	11.	6	41	20⅜	20	20	− ¼
30⅛	16¾	BwnSh	1	3.5	6	94	28⅞	28⅜	28⅞	+ ¼
30	9⅝	Brown	.30	1.1	8	133	28¼	28	28¼	+ ¼
28¾	22½	BwnGp	2	7.8	4	20	26	25⅝	25⅝	− ⅛
17⅞	11⅝	BwnFer	.70	4.1	10	355	17⅝	17	17	.....
15⅜	10⅞	Brnswk	.90	6.2	6	428	15	14½	14⅝	− ⅜
30	24⅝	Brnsk	pf2.40	8.1	..	55	30	29½	29½	− ⅜
33½	17½	BrushW	s 1	3.2	10	148	31½	30⅞	31	+ ⅝
25	16½	BucyEr	.88	4.2	8	1000	21½	20½	21	+ ¾
19½	15⅞	BufFor	s 1	6.3	8	26	16⅝	16	16	− 1
16⅜	9¼	Bundy	1	9.2	7	23	10⅞	10⅝	10⅞	+ ¼
19½	15⅛	BunkrH	1.96	13.	..	21	15⅝	15⅛	15¼	+ ⅛
32⅜	19	BunkR	1.20	4.0	8	161	30⅜	29⅜	29¾	.....
32	22⅞	BnkR	pf1.50	5.1	..	13	30	29⅝	29⅝	− ⅜
20	15	BurlInd	1.40	7.8	7	784	18⅛	17⅞	17⅞	− ⅛
80¾	38	BurlNo	2.10	2.8	6	1182	76⅞	73⅛	74⅛	− 1⅜
7½	5⅝	BrlNo	pf .55	11.	..	7	5⅞	d 5	5	− ⅞
71½	37½	BrlNo	pf2.85	4.3	..	103	67½	65¾	65¾	− 1¼
35½	21¼	Burndy	1	2.8	10	37	35⅜	35⅛	35⅜	+ ⅛
8⅞	3	BrnsRL		..	23	1022	8½	7⅞	8⅛	− ¼
87½	64⅜	Burrgh	2.60	3.3	10	851	79⅞	76¾	77¾	− 1
30¼	14	ButlrIn	s.80	2.9	7	34	28⅜	27¾	28	.....
18	8⅜	Buttes		..	97	462	u18¼	17⅜	17⅜	+ ⅛
		— C–C–C —								
43⅞	27	CBI Ind	s1a	2.4	15	x109	42¼	41⅝	42	+ ¾
56¾	44⅛	CBS	2.80	5.3	8	666	53¼	52⅝	52⅝	+ ½
37½	30½	CBS pf	1	2.8	..	2	35⅞	35⅞	35⅞	+ ⅞
11¼	6	CCI		..	6	303	10⅝	9¾	10	.....
12⅞	6⅞	CLC		..	37	82	10¾	10	10⅜	− ¼
18¾	10⅛	CNA Fn		..	4	775	17¾	17⅜	17¾	+ ⅝
22¾	15¼	CNA pf	1.10	5.1	..	14	21½	21½	21½	+ ½
11⅞	9⅛	CNAI	1.14a	12.	..	34	9¾	9⅝	9⅝	− ⅛
71	48⅛	CPC	3	4.5	9	666	68¼	67	67¼	− ½
16¾	14⅛	CP Nat	1.88	12.	9	14	15⅛	14¾	15⅛	+ ¼
28½	16¼	CTS	.80	3.8	9	157	21⅜	20¼	20⅞	− ⅛
64¾	34	CabotC	2	3.1	8	x190	u65½	62¾	65¼	+ 2¾
21⅝	9⅝	Cadence		..	6	22	16¾	16⅜	16⅜	− ⅛
36⅛	13¼	Caesars s		..	24	1198	16⅞	16¼	16¼	− ⅝

NYSE-Composite Transactions

Wednesday, February 13

Quotations include trades on the American, Midwest, Pacific, Philadelphia, Boston and Cincinnati stock exchanges and reported by the National Association of Securities Dealers and Instinet

52 Weeks High	Low	Stock	Div.	Yld %	P-E Ratio	Sales 100s	High	low	Close	Net Chg.
20	13⅝	DanRiv	1.12	6.0	5	121	18⅞	18⅝	18⅝	.....
30¼	22⅞	DanaCp	1.56	5.9	5	139	26⅝	26¼	26½	.....
28⅞	16⅜	Daniel	.30	1.1	13	58	28⅜	27⅞	27⅞	− ⅜
49⅝	37¼	DartInd	2	4.7	6	262	43¼	42¾	42⅞	.....
49¼	37	Dart pf	2	4.8	..	5	42½	42	42	− ¼
74½	46	DataGen		..	14	704	66¼	65⅛	65⅝	+ 1⅝
48⅛	27⅝	DataTer	.30	1.0	9	275	30⅛	28½	28⅝	− 1⅛
119	67¾	Datapnt		..	19	65	u120	118	118⅛	− ⅞
18½	13½	Dayco	.56b	4.1	3	30	13¾	13½	13¾	+ ⅛
49¼	36½	DaytHd	1.80	3.8	7	x495	48⅝	47⅞	47⅞	− ⅜
17¼	13¾	DaytPL	1.74	13.	7	141	13⅞	d13⅝	13¾	.....
76	57⅜	DPL pf	7.37	12.	..	z100	60	60	60	− 1
41½	33¼	Deere	1.80	5.4	7	1358	36⅛	35⅜	35¾	+ ¼
14	11½	DelmP	1.48	13.	6	97	11¾	11½	11¾	.....
47⅜	36	DeltaA	1.20	3.3	7	827	36½	36⅛	36¼	− ¼
8¾	5⅜	Deltec	2.50c	..	..	21	8	8	8	+ ¼
17	8⅝	Deltona		..	5	329	16¼	15½	15¾	+ ¼
21¾	16⅛	DenMf	s1.16	5.8	7	78	20½	20	20	.....
23⅜	13⅜	Dennys	.88	6.0	6	197	14⅞	14½	14¾	− ⅛
20	14⅝	Dentsply	.88	5.0	10	124	17½	17	17½	+ ½
14	10	DeSoto	1	6.9	8	95	u14⅝	14	14½	+ ½
15⅞	12¼	DetEd	1.60	13.	7	941	12⅝	12¼	12⅝	+ ⅛
68½	56¼	DetE	pf5.50	9.6	..	1	57¼	57¼	57¼	+ ¼
76¾	58¼	DetE	pf7.68	13.	..	z100	59½	59½	59½	− 1½
25¾	21	DE	pfF 2.75	13.	..	5	21⅜	21⅜	21⅜	− ⅛
25⅞	20⅞	DE	pfB 2.75	13.	..	4	21¼	21⅛	21⅛	+ ¼
21¾	16½	DetE	pr2.28	14.	..	5	16¾	16½	16⅝	.....
25⅝	19¾	Dexter	1	4.2	9	12	23¾	23¾	23¾	+ ¼
15⅛	8⅛	DiGior	.56	4.7	7	141	12⅜	11¾	12	− ¼
25	14	DiGior	pf.88	4.6	..	z30	19¼	19¼	19¼	− 1¾
27	20⅝	DiGior	pf2.25	9.2	..	18	24⅝	24¼	24⅜	+ ⅛
26½	16⅝	DialCp	1.20	6.6	5	30	18⅜	17⅝	18⅛	+ ¼
47½	32½	DiaInt	2.20b	5.0	10	85	44¼	42¾	44¼	+ 1¼
21¼	16⅛	DiaInt	pf1.20	6.0	..	8	20	20	20	.....
36¾	19⅛	DiamS	1.60	4.6	10	x916	35¾	34¾	35	− ¾
38⅝	18¾	Diebold	.70	1.9	12	97	37¾	36¾	37¼	+ ½
77⅞	48⅝	DigitalEq		..	17	1392	u79⅝	77⅞	78⅝	+ ¾
15⅜	8½	Dillingm	.60	4.3	7	268	14⅜	13¾	14	− ¼
27¾	22	Dillngm	pf2	7.5	..	1	26½	26½	26½	.....
23¼	15½	Dillon	s 1.08	6.5	9	51	16½	16¼	16½	− ⅜
48⅛	33	Disney	.72	1.5	12	854	47⅛	46⅜	46½	+ 1½
8¾	2⅝	Divrsfdln		..	11	185	7⅝	7⅜	7⅜	.....
6⅞	3⅜	DivrsMtg		..	..	137	4⅝	4⅜	4⅝	+ ⅛
19¼	10	DrPeppr	.68	4.6	13	555	15	14⅝	14⅞	+ ⅛
27	12⅝	Documat		..	17	45	13⅝	13⅜	13½	+ ¼
73¾	34⅜	Dome g	s.50	.7	..	109	72⅞	71¾	71¾	− ¼
24	18¾	Donald	n.60	2.8	8	6	21¼	21	21⅛	+ ⅛
6½	3¼	DonLJ	.14	2.2	15	625	6⅜	6⅛	6¼	− ⅛
31	25½	Donnly	1.14	3.7	9	87	30¾	30⅜	30½	− ¼
20	12⅛	Dorsey	.75	5.2	5	67	14½	14⅜	14½	.....
40⅝	27¾	Dover s	.86	2.2	12	24	39⅛	38¼	38¼	− ¾
39	24⅜	DowCh	1.60	4.2	9	6415	u39¼	38	38	− ½
49½	32½	DowJn	1.60	3.7	13	29	43¾	43⅛	43½	.....
38⅜	23⅞	Dravo	1.36	3.6	11	213	u38¾	38	38⅛	+ ⅜
62¾	36¼	Dressr	1.10	1.7	11	1220	u63½	61½	63	+ 2¼
17¼	14¼	DrexB	1.72	12.	..	11	14⅝	14⅝	14⅝	.....

52 Weeks High	Low	Stock	Div.	Yld %	P-E Ratio	Sales 100s	High	low	Close	Net Chg.
5¾	3⅜	Genesco		..	100	100	4⅛	4	4	− ⅛
28⅝	17¼	Genst	g s1.60	..	..	168	28¼	27½	27⅝	− ¼
26⅞	21	GenuPt	s.88	3.8	10	165	23¾	23¼	23¼	− ¼
33⅞	23½	GaPac	1.20	3.6	11	2851	u34⅞	33	33½	− ⅜
36	30	GaPac	pf2.24	6.2	..	60	u36⅜	35¾	36	+ ¾
34¾	30	GaPac	pfB	6.2	..	37	u36	34⅞	36	+ 1¼
24⅝	19⅝	GaPw	pf2.56	13.	..	21	19¾	d19½	19½	− ⅜
25	18⅝	GaPw	pf2.52	13.	..	7	19⅝	19½	19½	.....
27¼	22	GaPw	pf2.75	12.	..	4	23⅛	23	23	− ⅜
77¼	58	GaPw	pf7.72	13.	..	z20	58¼	58¼	58¼	− ¾
66½	27¾	Geosrc	.80	1.2	16	104	65¼	64¼	64¼	− ¾
30⅞	23	GerbPd	1.62	6.8	7	93	24¼	23⅝	24	+ ⅜
97¾	36	Getty	1.50e	1.6	13	705	94⅜	92½	92½	− 1
18¼	14¾	Getty	pf1.20	7.9	..	1	15¼	15¼	15¼	.....
11⅞	6¼	GiantPC		..	14	66	6¾	6½	6¾	+ ¼
16⅝	10	GibrFn	.60	5.9	5	213	10⅛	d 9¾	10⅛	+ ⅛
37	14	GidLew	1	3.1	6	343	33⅜	31¾	32¾	− ¼
19½	12	GiffHill	.92	5.1	5	226	18⅛	18	18⅛	− ⅛
28	23⅜	Gillette	1.72	7.2	6	2153	24⅜	23½	23¾	− ¾
13¼	6⅞	GinosInc	.40	3.2	..	87	12⅝	12¼	12½	+ ⅛
25¾	16	GleasW	.80	3.1	7	32	25¾	25½	25½	− ¼
53⅞	14⅞	GlobMar	.20	.4	13	187	u55⅜	54¼	54¾	+ 1⅛
17	10⅝	GldWFn	.54	4.1	5	396	13⅛	13	13⅛	+ ⅛
24	17½	Gdrich	1.44	7.2	4	75	20¼	19⅞	19⅞	− ⅛
92⅜	79⅛	Gdrich	pf7.85	9.9	..	z50	79⅛	79⅛	79⅛	.....
18⅛	11⅞	Goodyr	1.30	10.	6	1588	13	12¾	13	+ ⅛
29	16⅞	GordJw	.72	2.6	5	37	27½	27¼	27¼	+ ¼
29¼	22	Gould	1.72	7.1	6	263	24¼	23¾	24⅛	− ¼

Wednesday's Volume
72,185,250 Shares; 372,300 Warrants

TRADING BY MARKETS

	Shares	Warrants
New York Exchange	65,230,000	372,200
American Exchange	....	....
Midwest Exchange	2,904,200	....
Pacific Exchange	1,702,100	....
Nat'l Assoc. of Securities Dealers	901,450	100
Philadelphia Exchange	964,900	....
Boston Exchange	237,700	....
Cincinnati Exchange	227,300	....
Instinet System	17,600	....

NYSE – Composite

Volume since Jan. 1:	1980	1979	1978
Total shares	1,837,261,110	957,966,682	704,758,240
Total warrants	10,475,200	4,093,049	3,288,000

New York Stock Exchange

Volume since Jan. 1:	1980	1979	1978
Total shares	1,629,566,840	844,175,032	615,205,130
Total warrants	10,474,900	3,963,900	3,287,900

MOST ACTIVE STOCKS

	Open	High	Low	Close	Chg.	Volume
Colg Palm	13½	13¾	12⅞	13¼	− ⅛	1,356,400
Capit Hold	20	20⅛	19	19¼	− ¾	1,036,700
IBM s	70	70½	69¼	69⅜	+ ½	807,000
GulfWstn	22	22⅛	21⅛	21⅜	− ⅛	667,100
DowChem	39⅛	39¼	38	38	− ½	641,500
Texaco Inc	39½	39⅝	37¾	38	− 1¼	640,600
Baxt Travnl	43⅛	43¼	40¼	40⅝	− 2½	504,700
Tesoro Pet	27¾	27⅞	26⅝	26¾	− ⅜	502,600
Gulf Oil	47½	47⅞	46⅜	46½	− ½	480,100
Int T&T	28⅜	29¼	28⅜	29¼	+ 1⅛	478,600
ValeroEnr n	23	23⅛	21⅛	21¼	− 1	473,200
SearsRoeb	17⅝	17⅝	17¼	17⅜	.....	449,500
Boeing s	64⅜	64⅜	62¾	63¼	− 1	434,600
Exxon	67⅜	67½	64⅛	66⅞	+ ⅜	403,500
ScovillInc	18⅛	18⅛	17¼	17½	− ⅜	401,300

EXPLANATORY NOTES

(For New York and American Exchange listed issues)

Sales figures are unofficial.

The 52-Week High and Low columns show the highest and the lowest price of the stock in consolidated trading during the preceding 52 weeks plus the current week, but not the current trading day.

u–Indicates a new 52-week high. d–Indicates a new 52-week low.

s–Split or stock dividend of 25 per cent or more in the past 52 weeks. The high-low range and dividend begin with the date of split or stock dividend, and do not cover the entire 52-week period.

n–New issue in the past 52 weeks. The high-low range begins with the start of trading in the new issue and does not cover the entire 52-week period.

g–Dividend or earnings in Canadian money. Stock trades in U.S. dollars. No yield or PE shown unless stated in U.S. money.

Unless otherwise noted, rates of dividends in the foregoing table are annual disbursements based on the last quarterly or semi-annual declaration. Special or extra dividends or payments not designated as regular are identified in the following footnotes.

a–Also extra or extras. b–Annual rate plus stock dividend. c–Liquidating dividend. e–Declared or paid in preceding 12 months. i–Declared or paid after stock dividend or split up. j-Paid this year, dividend omitted, deferred or no action taken at last dividend meeting. k–Declared or paid this year, an accumulative issue with dividends in arrears. r–Declared or paid in preceding 12 months plus stock dividend. t–Paid in stock in preceding 12 months, estimated cash value on ex-dividend or ex-distribution date.

x–Ex-dividend or ex-rights. y–Ex-dividend and sales in full. z–Sales in full.

wd–When distributed. wi–When issued. ww–With warrants. xw–Without warrants.

vj–In bankruptcy or receivership or being reorganized under the Bankruptcy Act, or securities assumed by such companies.

8. *Low* refers to the lowest-priced transaction for that issue this day. Both these columns are included for the benefit of readers interested in determining the extent of the security's daily fluctuation. Note: the letter *u* next to 65½ signifies that this price is a new high for the year. If the stock had traded at a yearly low price, the letter *d* would appear next to that price in the column labeled low.

9. *Close* is the final sale price of that security on the exchange today. In the interest of conserving newsprint, some papers omit the high and low prices, but all of them publish the closing price because of its importance. It is the basis on which collateral value is determined for loans arranged under Federal Reserve Board Regulations T, U, G, and other financing procedures. It is the item most investors refer to when discussing a security's current price.

10. Net change (*Net Chg.*) is the difference between yesterday's closing price and today's closing price. It is an indicator of daily price trend, and it enables you to determine a monetary result of activity on an issue you particularly favor. Sometimes, the numerical difference between the two closing prices appears illogical. Some investors may wonder why a stock closing at 28 yesterday and 26¾ today shows a net change of only "—¾" instead of an apparently obvious "—1¼." The answer lies in the fact that this issue is trading ex dividend one-half point today. A price reduction resulting from a corporate distribution is not calculated in the net change column. Net change is designed to consider trading factors only, not to reflect internal corporate affairs.

The Over-the-Counter Stock Tables. Over-the-counter stock information is furnished to the major newspapers by United Press International (UPI). It is limited to NASDAQ issues and is further categorized into the most active and less active lists. The most active list is identified as *Over-the-Counter Markets* (see the following table). It is composed of about 1,400 issues that have the highest dollar value of average weekly volume.

Let us examine the statistical detail published for Alaska International Corp., a NASDAQ issue framed in the stock table for purposes of easy identification.

			2			4
Stock & Div.		1	Sales 100s	Bid	3 Asked	Net Chg.
Alaska Intl.	.24		92	6	7	+ ¼

1. This is the name of the issuer and the annual dividend rate per share established by the board of directors of the company. The dividend is ordinarily paid in quarterly installments (that is 6¢ per share every three months). If the company has no fixed yearly rate, this amount is followed by a letter code whose meaning can be found in the "Explanatory Notes" at the bottom of the tables.

2. This figure is yesterday's sales volume for the issue in terms of the number of 100-share units traded by registered NASDAQ market-makers. Thus, the figure 92 equals 9,200 shares of stock. Trades between customers and NASD members who are not NASDAQ market-makers in this issue are reported weekly to the NASD in Washington, D.C. Those figures do not appear in the newspapers.

3. Due to the nature of OTC activity and the lack of a central marketplace, specific high-, low-, and last-sale trade information is superseded in the list by a closing quotation. These prices are representative of bids and offers submitted by registered NASDAQ market-makers in this issue.

4. In this table, net change is related to the closing bid prices on a day-to-day basis because the bid is the most meaningful indicator of value in a quotation. Thus, a change of + ¼ next to the quotation of 6-7 indicates that yesterday's closing bid was 5¾.

An additional OTC-NASDAQ securities

Over-the-Counter Markets

4:00 p.m. Eastern Time Prices, Thursday, December 30

All over the counter prices printed on this page are representative quotations supplied by the National Association of Securities Dealers through NASDAQ, its automated system for reporting quotes. Prices don't include retail markup, markdown or commission. Volume represents shares that changed ownership during the day. Figures include only those transactions effected by NASDAQ market makers but may include some duplication where NASDAQ market makers traded with each other.

Volume, All Issues, 9,729,900

SINCE JANUARY 1

	1976	1975	1974
Total sales	1,675,010,581	1,390,411,700	1,179,708,948

MARKET DIARY

	Thur	Wed	Tues	Mon	Thur
Issues traded	2,557	2,556	2,557	2,556	2,555
Advances	682	487	607	617	496
Declines	226	339	303	273	302
Unchanged	1,649	1,730	1,647	1,666	1,757
xNew highs	104	93	121	96	83
xNew lows	7	5	7	8	10

x-Based on 4 p.m. Eastern time bid quote.

ACTIVE STOCKS

	Volume	4:00 Bid	Chg.
Amer Express Co	231,300	40¼	+ ¾
Anheuser Busch Inc	153,900	22⅜	+ ¾
Tosco Corp	153,000	4½	+ ¼
De Beers Consol ADR	128,000	2⅜	+3-16
Govt Employee Ins	127,300	7⅛	+ ⅛
Penn Offshore Gas B	122,600	14⅜	+ ¼
Rank Organisation ADR	121,600	2⅛	+ ⅛
Energy Reserves Grp	91,900	1⅞	+1-16
Amer Pacific Intl	89,100	5¼	+ ⅛
St Paul Companies	87,600	35¾	+ ¼

Stock & Div.	Sales 100s	Bid	Asked	Net Chg.
--A A--				
AaronBro .10d	2	7¼	8	...
AccelratnC .80	32	14¼	15	...
Accelrators In	42	2¼	2⅝	+ ⅛
AcetoChm 5.5i	8	15½	16¼	+ ¼
ACMAT Corp	3	1⅛	1⅝	...
AcmeElc .40g	4	12⅝	13⅛	+ ⅜
AddWesley .40	17	6¾	7¼	+ ⅛
Advance Ross	52	3¾	4⅛	+ ⅛
Advan MicroD	137	25¼	26	+ ⅜
AeroSystem 5i	65	1	1⅜	...
Aerosonc .06d	6	2⅛	2½	...
Aerotron Incp	14	2½	2⅞	...
Advent Corp	40	10⅛	10⅝	+ ¼
Affil Bnksh .84	13	16½	17½	...
AgMet Incorp	93	10⅛	10⅝	+ ⅛
Agnico Eagle	91	3¾	4	+ ⅛
AlaBncp 1.32g	38	25¾	26¾	...
Alanthus C .25	2	3½	4	...
Alaska Gold	9	3¼	4	+ ⅛
Alaska Intl .24	92	6	7	+ ¼
Alberts Inc .20	8	7½	8¼	...
AlexandA 1.06	42	38⅛	38⅝	− ⅛
Alex Bald 1.20	51	14½	15	+ ⅛
Alicolncp .17d	163	9¾	10¼	...
Allegheny Bv	35	3¾	4⅛	...
Allergn Ph .10	10	24	24¾	...
AlliedBncs .84	69	29⅜	29⅞	− ¼
Allied Leisure	19	3½	4¼	...
Allied Tele .56	50	13	13½	+ ⅛
AlliedVnLin B	1	3¾	4½	...

Stock & Div.	Sales 100s	Bid	Asked	Net Chg.
Charles Rv .20	x1	16½	17½	+ ⅛
CharmSh .10d	2	12¾	13¾	...
Chart Hous .72	60	26⅞	27⅜	+ ⅜
ChathamM .80	33	11⅜	11⅞	− ⅛
Chef Pierre In	9	16¼	17	...
ChmLeaTk .80	10	10¾	11¾	...
ChemedCorp 1	36	24½	25½	+ 1
Chemineer .20	11	11¾	12¼	...
ChiBridge 1.40	86	54½	56½	− ½
Ch NW Trans	12	4½	4¾	...
Chilton Cp .20	18	6¼	6¾	− ⅛
ChrisSec 5.58	2	123	127	...
Christensn .40	33	18½	19	+ ⅛
ChubbCrp 1.48	116	39⅝	40⅛	+ ⅜
Cinevideo Intl	10	3	3¾	...
Cinn FclC .64g	2	19¾	20¼	...
Circl Seal .40d	1	16⅞	17⅝	...
Circle In 1.24d	12	15⅝	16⅛	...
CitzSthnCp .96	16	17¼	18¼	...
CitSoNBGa .52	369	7⅞	8¼	− ⅛
CitizenFid 1.44	5	32	33	...
CitznUtils B 2	13	31⅜	31⅞	...
CitzUtil A 3.5i	8	33⅜	33⅞	...
City Natl Cp 1	5	17½	19	...
Clabir Cp .06d	22	1⅞	2¼	...
ClarkJL Mf 1a	54	31¾	32¾	+ 1
ClevTrust Rlt	22	2⅜	2⅞	...
Clevetrust 2.60	18	51¼	52¼	...
Clow Corp .40	2	6½	7	...
CoastlStCp .28	27	4⅝	5	− ¼
Cobe Labrator	7	22¼	23	+ ½

Stock & Div.	Sales 100s	Bid	Asked	Net Chg.
Fidelity Co Va	98	2¾	3	...
FidelityUnLf 1	41	24⅜	24⅞	+ ⅛
5th 3rd Bc 1.80	z50	30	30¾	...
Fingerhut Cp	266	6½	6⅞	+ ¼
Finnigan Corp	29	10½	11¼	...
1stAla Bcsh 1g	27	20¾	21¾	...
FirstAmFn .32	20	13¼	14¼	...
1st Amtenn .40	35	9	9½	...
1stBcgAla .65d	z95	13¼	14	...
1stBGOh 1.20g	12	25¾	26¾	− ¼
1st Bncshr Fla	35	5¾	6¼	...
1stBks SC 1.10	15	22½	23½	...
1stBnkSys 1.52	81	44¼	45	− ¼
1st Boston 2	20	23½	24¼	...
1st Colony .48	15	12⅜	12⅞	+ ⅛
1stComRI .47b	12	4¼	5¼	− ¼
1stCmlBkInc 1	17	13¼	13¾	− ⅛
FstCnnBc 1.80	5	22½	24	...
1stCtlRIE .70d	21	8	8½	

Stock & Div.	Sales 100s	Bid	Asked	Net Chg.
K C Lflns 1.40	5	35¾	36¾	− ¼
Kar Prodct .24	17	17	17¾	− ¼
Kayot Incorp	14	4¼	5	− ¼
K D I Corptn	190	¾	15-16	...
KearnyNat .48	12	6	6½	...
KearneyTr .40	96	9¼	9⅝	...
KeithClark .50	1	9	10	...
Kelly Serv .80	5	24	24¾	...
Kemper C 1.20	89	31½	32¼	...
Kenai Drilling	174	3⅜	3¾	+ ¼
Kenington Ltd	21	5	5¾	+ ¼
Ky CenLife .20	21	7⅝	8	...
Keuffl & E .80	6	13	14	+ ¼
Key Pharmcal	29	4¾	5¼	+ ⅛
Keyes Fibr .72	25	16⅜	16¾	...
KeystCus FdA	21	7¼	7¾	...
Keystn Foods	48	7¾	8¼	+ ⅛
Keyst Intl .50a	30	19	19¾	+ ¼
Keystone OTC	27	6⅝	7⅛	...
Keystn PCmt	2	10½	11¼	...
Kimball Intl B	24	10	10½	...
KnapeVogt .90	9	17¾	18¾	...
KnudsenC .60g	3	10⅞	11⅜	− ⅛
KogerPrp .10d	56	10	10¾	− ¼
KossCorp .20a	23	4⅝	5⅛	+ ¼
KRM Petrolm	206	4⅛	4½	+ ⅛
Krueger W .60	27	13	14	...
Kuhlman .50a	39	10⅞	11¼	...
--L L--				
LacledeSteel 1	6	15¼	16	...
LakeSDisPw 1	10	11¼	11¾	...
LncstrCol .56a	49	16⅝	17⅛	...
Lance Inc .88a	8	22¼	23	...
Lanchart Ind	8	3⅝	3⅞	...
LandmBFI .36	82	5¼	5¾	+ ⅛
LaneComp .60	7	19¾	20¾	+ ¼
Lawrys Fd .24	201	24	25	...
Lawson Pr .24	3	13	14½	...
La ZBoyCh .56	25	20¼	21	...
LearPetrol 10i	22	9⅜	9⅞	+ ⅛
Leggett Plt .40	42	12⅜	12¾	...
LeonarSil .10d	10	9⅝	10⅛	+ ⅜
Lexitron Corp	69	4⅛	4⅝	+ ⅛
LewisPalm .12	3	8¾	9¼	...
Liberty Home	32	2¾	3⅛	...
LibNatLife .80	119	25¼	25¾	+ ¼
Life InvInc .10	112	6⅝	7⅛	+ ⅜
Lil ChFd .20e	8	5⅜	5⅞	...
Ltd Stores .08	62	23¼	24	+ ¼
Lin Broadcast	38	17⅜	17¾	...
Lin 1st Bk 1.88	23	23¾	24½	+ ½
LinFstBpf 1.05	9	12¼	13	...
LincTel&Tel 2	4	28¼	29¼	...
Lindberg .80a	6	12¾	13¼	+ ⅜
Lion Cntry Saf	107	⅝	1	+ ⅛
LiqAirNA 1.40	9	32¾	33½	+ ½

EXPLANATORY NOTES

z-Sales in full.

a-Annual rate plus cash extra or extras. b-Paid last year. c-Declared or paid since stock dividend or split, no regular rate. d-Paid this year, no regular rate. e-Declared or paid in 1975 plus stock. f-Declared or paid in 1976 plus stock. g-Annual rate plus stock dividend. h-Paid this year, latest dividend omitted. i-Paid in stock in 1976. k-Percent paid in stock in 1975. r-Ex-rights. x-Ex-dividend. y-Ex-distribution. (z)-No representative quote.

Name	Bid	Asked
ACS Enterprise	3/8	9-16
Admar Grp Inc	5/8	11-16
AdvDisplay Tec	2 3-32	2 3-16
AdvMedic Imag	1 1/8	1 1/4
AdvMedical Pr	1-16	1/8
Adv Monitoring	11-16	1/2
AdvnNMR Syst	5 1/8	5 1/2
AdvNMRSyst ut	31	35
AdvNMRSys wt	5	5 1/4
AdvProdcts Tc	7 1/4	8
Advantage Cos	3 1/2	4
Advisors Captl	17-32	5/8
Aerosonic Corp	1 11-16	1 3/4
AFN Inc	7/8	1 1/8
AFP Imaging	1 1/2	1 5/8
Agouron Pharm	9 1/2	10
AirTrans Hld	1/2	3/4
AirshipIntl Ltd	13-16	15-16
AJ Ross Logist	5/8	11-16
Alaska Apollo	15-16	1/2
Alcide Corp	4 1/4	4 3/8
Alcide Corp wt	1 3/8	1 3/4
AllAm Semicon	2 1/8	2 3/8
Allied Security	32	34
Allstar Video	3-16	5-16
Allure Cosmtcs	11-16	23-32
AllureCosm ut	7/8	29-32
Alpha Solarco	9-16	5/8
Alpine Intl Cp	1/2	5/8
AlterntvHlth ut	4 1/2	5
Alternlv Hlth	1 1-16	1 1/8
Alyx Medical	2 7/8	3 1/8
Alyx Med ut	3 1/4	3 5/8
Amarco Resrc	3/8	15-32
Amer Bionetics	2 1/8	2 3/8
AmerEco Envir	3-32	1/8
Am Business	15-16	1 1-16
AmCell Netwrk	11 3/4	12 1/2
AmClaims Eval	4 3/4	5 1/4
Am Comm Tel	3-32	5-32
AmConsultg Cp	8 3/4	9 1/4
Am Dynamics	1-32	3-32
Am Equine Prd	1/4	1/2
AmFiber Optics	3-16	5-16
AmGuarn Fnc	7/8	31-32
AmHome Indus	5-32	7-32
Amer Kefir Cp	1 1/8	1 5-16
Am Med Alert	3/4	1 1-16
Am Medical El	2 3/4	3 5/8
Am Medical Tc	2 1/4	2 11-32
AmMobile Syst	3 5/8	4
AmMobile Sys	1 1/8	1 3/8
AmSafety Closr	7/8	1 1/4
Am Screen Co	1 1/4	1 5/8
AmSolar King	3 3/8	3 1/2
Amer Telecom	2	2 1/8
AmVideo Telcn	3/8	1/2
AmVision Cntrs	1 3/8	1 7-16
Amtech ut	2 3/4	3 1/2
Analytical Surv	1 5/8	1 7/8
AnCon Genetics	1 5/8	2
Angio-Medic ut	8 1/4	8 3/4
Annandale Corp	3/8	5/8
APA Optics Inc	5 3/4	6 1/2
Apogee Robotc	1	1 1/8
ApogeeRobot ut	1 1/2	1 5/8
Appld DNA Sys	2 1/8	2 1/4
Appld Microbio	3 1/8	3 5/8
AppliedMic ut	8 1/4	9 1/2
Aquanautics Cp	1/2	17-32
Aridtech Inc	23-32	27-32
AristaInvst ut	5 3/4	6 1/2
ARNOX Corp	6 1/4	6 3/4
ARNOX Cp ut	8 1/4	9
ARNOX Cp wt	2 1/8	2 3/4
Arrays Inc	19-32	5/8
Artech RecvSys	2 1-16	2 7-16
ASA Intl Ltd	5-32	7-32
ASARCO wt	12 1/4	12 5/8
ASDAR Corp	9-16	21-32
Aspen Explortn	7-16	1/2
Aspen Leaf	3/4	15-16
Audec Corp	3/4	7/8
Austin McDanl	1 1/2	2
Automedix Sci	1/2	11-16

Name	Bid	Asked
Brainerd Intl R	1 1/4	1 3/4
Brilund Ltd	13-16	1
Bristol Gaming	1 3-32	1 3-16
Brokers Secur	2 1/2	2 7/8
BSD Medical	2 1/8	2 3/8
BullRun GldMn	3 13-16	4
BurkeMills Inc	2 3/8	2 5/8
Business Card	9-16	5/8
BusComputr Sol	3-16	11-32
Byers Inc	1/4	9-32
Cable Advertis	3-16	1/4
Cableguard	1 7/8	2 1/4
Cadema Corp	1 5/8	1 3/4
CademaCorp pf	4 1/2	4 3/4
Cal-Star Fncl	1/2	7/8
Cmbrdg Analyt	3 1/8	3 3/4
Cambridge Med	2 1/8	2 3/8
Cam-Net Comm	6 1/8	6 1/4
Camera Platfm	7 3/4	8
Camille St.Mor	7/8	1 1-16
Candela Laser	6	6 3/4
Candlewood Bk	9 1/2	10
Canton Indust	3/4	27-32
Canterbury ut	2 3/8	2 1/2
Canyon Resourc	2 1-16	2 1/4
Capital TelSys	1/4	3/8
Caprock Corp	4 1/8	4 3/8
Cardinal Indus	1	1 1-16
Card Tel	3 1/2	3 7/8
Card Tel wt	2 1/8	2 3/8
Care America	1	1 1/4
CareAmerica ut	1 3-16	1 1/2
CareAmer wt	1	1 1/8
Caribbean Selct	1 1/4	1 3/8
Carolina Mntn	8	8 3/4
Carolyn Bean	2 1/2	2 3/4
CAS MedicalSys	3/4	7/8
CatchA RisStr	1	1 3/4
CatchARis wt	1/4	11-16
CCR VideoCorp	7/8	1 3-16
Celcor Inc	7/8	1 3/8
Cellcom Corp	1/2	9-16
Celltronics	1 5-32	1 3/8
Cellular Amer	1	1 1/8
Cellular Inc	8 1/2	9 3/4
Cellular Prodct	3 3/8	3 7/8
Central Corp	5 5/8	5 7/8
Centurion Min	5 3/4	6
Century Enrgy	5-16	1/2
Century Medicp	1 3/8	1 5/8
Century MediC	1 1/2	2
Century PrkPic	5-32	7-32
Certron Corp	2	2 3/8
Chantal Pharm	4 1/8	4 3/8
CheckRobot	6 1/2	7 1/4
Celerity Cmp	7-32	9-32
Celerity wt	1-16	3-32
Cherne Industr	4 5/8	5
Chief ConsMin	7 1/4	7 1/2
Choice Drug	4 7/8	5 1/4
ChoiceDrug ut	5 3/4	6 1/2
Chopp Computr	3/4	7/8
Circuit Systm	3	3 7/8
Ciro Inc	7/8	1 1/4
Cistron Biotech	1	1 1/8
Citadel Gold	3 1/8	3 3/8
CistronBio wt	5/8	3/4
Cleopatra Kohl	3/4	1
Cliff Engle	12 1/8	12 3/4
CliffEngle wt	12 1/2	14
Clinitherm Corp	1 3/8	1 5/8
Coachman ut	2 1/8	2 1/2
CMS Advertisg	6 5/8	7
CMS Advrts wt	4 5/8	4 3/4
CNS Inc	.2 3/4	3 1/4
Codercard	9-32	5-16
Cognitive Syst	1 3/4	2 1/2
Coin Phones	1 7/8	2 1-16
Colonial Comcl	1/2	9-16
ColoVent Captl	1	1 1-32
Colorocs Cp	5 1/4	5 3/4
Colorocx wt88	1 7/8	2 1/8
Computr Comm	15-16	1 1/2
Comptr Compnt	1	1 1/4
Cmptr Comp ut	3 1/8	3 3/4

Name	Bid	Asked
CXR Telcom /Cp	7-32	9-32
Cyanotech Cp	1	1 1-16
Cybermedic Inc	5-32	3-16
CytRx Corp	2 3/8	2 5/8
CytRx Corp ut	14	15
CytRx Corp wt	2 1/4	2 3/8
Dallas OilMin	7-16	1/2
Daltex Medical	1 7/8	2 1-16
Daltex MdSci ut	8	8 3/4
Daltex Med wt	13-16	1
DASA Corp	13-32	1/2
Dart Drug St	1 3/8	1 3/4
Dasibi Environ	1 7/8	2 1/4
Datakey Inc	5 1/4	6 1/4
Dataline Inc	7	7 3/4
Datamag Inc	13 1/4	14
DataMd Clinic	15-16	1 1/2
Davidson Tisdl	1	1 1/2
Decision Syst	3 1/2	4
Del E Webb wi	1 3/4	2 1/4
DenningMobil R	1 5/8	1 3/4
Denpac Corp	3-32	5-32
DermaLock Md	1 1/2	1 11-16
Desk Top Fncl	1	1 3/8
Dews Laborator	5/8	3/4
Dexon Inc	2 1/2	2 7/8
Diagnon Corp	1/2	27-32
Diagnostic Sci	7-16	11-16
Diagnostic Ven	1 1/4	1 1/2
Diagnostic ut	3	3 3/4
DigitlDiag ut	1 1/2	2 1/8
Digitl Metcom	3/4	7 1/2
Digital Optr	4 1/2	5
Digital Prodcts	1 1-32	1 3-16
Digital Solutn	3 3/8	3 7-16
Digital Trans A	1	1 1/8
DigtlTransm ut	1	1 1/8
Digitext Inc	1 3/4	2 1/2
Dimensn Med	1 3/8	1 3/4
Direct Pharm	2	2 1/4
Discovery Assc	1	1 1/8
Disc Technol	3-32	1/8
Disc Tech wt	1-32	1/8
Discus Corp	1 3/8	.1 5/8
Disease Detect	1-16	1/8
DiseaseDet wt	1 3/2	3-32
Divrsifd Hlth	4 3/4	4 7/8
Diversifd Tech	5 1/8	5 1/2
DMI Furniture	1 3/4	2
DNA Plant	1	1 3/8
Douglas Cmptr	7/8	1 1-16
Duratek Corp	4	4 1/8
DustyMac Mine	15-16	1
Dynamic Sci	3-16	1/4
DynatecIntl Inc	7-32	1/4
Dynatroncs Lsr	13-16	15-16
Earth Sciences		1 1/8
Earthworm Inc	1 1/2	1 9-16
EAS Tech Inc	3-32	5-32
Eastek Corp	2 1/2	2 7/8
Eateries Inc	2	2 1/4
EFI Corp	1 5-16	1 1/2
ElectrncCn ut	7/8	1
El-De Electro	1/4	3/8
Electro Kin A	7-16	1/2
Elecromedc wi	1 7/8	2 1/4
Eli Scientfc	1 3/4	1 7/8
El Missiles Cm	3/4	1
Endotronics	3/8	1/2
Energy Assets	1/2	9-16
English Greenh	1/2	9-16
EnglishGrn ut	9-16	5/8
Environ Diagns	5/8	3/4
Envirosure M	3-16	1/4
Enzon Inc ut	33	37
Epitope Inc	5 1/2	6
EquitableRs wt	4	4 3/8
Ethigen Corp	3 1/4	3 3/8
EthigenCp wt	3	3 1/2
Eurocapital	1	1 1/8
Executv Tlcm	5-16	7-16
Exploration Co	9-32	5-16
EyeCareCtr ut	4 1/4	4 5/8
Eye Technolgy	7-32	11-32
Fairfield FBT	8 3/8	8 7/8

Name	Bid	Asked
Franchiselt	7/8	29-32
Frankln ConMn	21-32	23-32
Franklin Tel	1/8	3-16
Fresh Juice	5 3/4	6
Galagraph Ltd	1 5/8	2 1/8
Gascard Club	3 1/4	3 3/4
Gascard Cl ut	3 1/2	3 3/4
GBI Intl Ind	2 17-32	2 3/4
GBI IntlInd wt		
	1 1-32	1 11-32
Gemini Technol	2 1/4	2 1/2
Geodome Resrc	2 7/8	2 15-16
Geotel Inc	1 1/4	1 1/2
GoldExpress Cp	3/8	13-32
GoldKing Consl	3/8	1/2
GoldenCycle G	7 1/4	8 1/4
Goldenbell Res	3 3/8	3 1/2
GoldnQuail Res	7-16	9-16
GoldenNo Resr	4 1/4	4 1/2
Golden Triangl	3	7-16
Gold Reserve	3 7/8	4 1/8
Gray Com .30	153	172 1/2
Grease Monkey	21-32	11-16
GrtAmer Bancp	1 3/4	2 1/4
Grt Australia	1 3/8	1/4
GrtWestern Sys	3-16	5-16
Grow Ventures	1	1 3/8
Gynex Inc ut	3	3 1/2
Gyrodyne CAm	34	39
Hadron Inc	1	1 1/8
Halsey Drug Co	1 7/8	2 1/8
Hart Indus Inc	5-32	3-16
Hawkeye Entrt	5-32	7-32
Hlth Conc ut	1 3/4	2 1/2
Health EduTec	1 1/8	1 3/8
HemaCare Corp	1 1/8	1 3/8
Hemisphr Devel	7-16	1/2
Hemodynamcs	6 1/4	6 3/4
HE VenturesInc	7/8	1
High Resolutn	5	5 3/4
High Resolutn	(z)	(z)
Highwood Resr	3	3 1/4
Hitech Enginr	1 1/4	5-16
HOH Water ut	2 5/8	3 1/2
Hometown Bcp	5 1/4	5 3/4
HookerEnt Inc	1	1 3-16
Horizon Gold	2 1-16	2 3-16
Hornbeck Offsh	7 1/4	8 1/2
Howtek Inc	15 1/2	16 1/2
HughKeith Entr	2 3-16	2 1/2
Hycor Biomed	1	1 1-16
ICN Pharm wt	3 1/2	4 1/4
Identix Inc	2 7/8	3 1/8
IFEX Inc	7/8	1 1/4
IGENE Biotech	3 3/4	4 1/4
Imagn Films	3 3/4	4 1/4
Imagn Film ut	4	4 3/4
ImageMgm Sys	1 1/4	1 1/2
ImmuCell Corp	3-32	5-32
ImmuCell wt	1-32	1-16
ImmunoTher	4	4 1/4
Imre Corp	3 7/8	4 1/8
IMT Incorp	1 3/8	1 1/2
IMT Incorp wt	1/4	25-32
Inamed Corp	2 7/8	3
INCOMNET	1 3/8	1 1/2
Indp Air Hldg	3-32	5-32
Indepth Data	1 5/8	1 3/4
IndTech Corp	11-16	1
InferGene ut	1 3/8	1 3/4
Infrasonics	1 15-16	2 1/8
InlandGold Sil	2 1/2	2 9-16
Inmedica Devlp	7-16	9-16
Insta Cool NA	7/8	3 1/4
Insta Cool ut	2	2 1/8
InstaCool wt	7-32	1/4
INTEK Divrsfd	1 3/8	1 1/2
InterCareInc ut	11-16	1 1/2
Interdyne Co	11-16	7/8
Interferon Scien	3 1/2	4
Interfund Corp	1 3/8	1 1/2
Interleukin 2	1 1/2	1 19-32
Intrmk Gaming	3 1/4	3 1/2
IntermkGm ut	4 1/4	4 1/2

list composed of approximately 950 less active issues is published daily, too (see the following table). These tables are in abbreviated form, however; they lack dividend information, trading volume, and net-change disclosures. Quotations are represented as of 2:00 P.M. (New York time), as opposed to the active list, whose prices are shown as of 4:00 P.M. (New York time), the usual market closing time.

About every six months, the National NASDAQ Committee of the NASD meets to determine what revisions are necessary in each of these listings. Some stocks are downgraded due to lack of trading volume, whereas others are promoted to the higher- prestige category. Any issue deleted from the NASDAQ system at any time is immediately dropped from its appropriate listing.

Corporate bonds. The format for the tables of bonds listed on the New York and American stock exchanges differs from the listed stock tables in that (1) instead of dividend information, the corporate description reveals interest rate and maturation year; (2) instead of price-earnings information, there is a column to represent the issue's current yield (with the exception of convertible bonds, for which this detail is of little significance to an investor); (3) instead of volume represented in terms of the number of 100-share round lots, it is shown in terms of $1,000 par value bonds traded that day; and (4) bond prices are shown as a percentage figure of $1,000, par value, whereas stock prices are listed in actual dollars and fractions thereof.

Example: A bond price shown as 106 means 106% of $1,000, or $1,060 per bond. A stock listed at 106 means $106 per share.

To practice reading these tables, examine a Mobil Corporation debenture listed on the New York Stock Exchange, framed in the following segment of the bond tables.

1	2	3	4	5	6	7
Bonds	Cur Yld	Vol	High	Low	Close	Net Chg.
Mobil 8½ 01	8.0	166	106¼	106	106⅛	+ ¼

1. The bond description sets forth the abbreviated name of the issuer, the interest rate, and the year of maturity. In this illustration the issuer of the bond is the Mobil Corporation, the interest rate is 8½% of the bond's $1,000 face value, and the bond must be redeemed in the year 2001. The specific month and day of maturation cannot be determined from these tables. Interested investors must refer to the bond's indenture or to a research service that provides such information.

2. The current yield is a function of the investor's annual interest dollars and the latest value of the bond. The analytical formula is the annual interest divided by the current market value shown in column 6. Therefore, the current yield for this debenture is:

$$\frac{\$85 \quad (8\tfrac{1}{2}\% \text{ of } \$1,000)}{\$1,061.25 \,(106\tfrac{1}{8}\% \text{ of } \$1,000)} = .08, \text{ or } 8\%$$

The current yield of a convertible bond is not calculated in this bond table. It is identified by the letters *cv* appearing in this column. Investors do not normally buy convertible bonds for their yield. They look for a movement in the underlying stock to provide them with capital gains. Interest income is of secondary importance.

3. Volume figures are expressed in the number of $1,000 face value bonds traded today. Simply add three zeros to the number in this column to find that $166,000 worth of face value Mobil bonds changed hands on the NYSE.

4. *High* indicates the highest value at which these bonds traded today (106¼% of $1,000 = $1,062.52). It cannot be determined from this information how many bonds traded at that price. It could have been a single bond, 100 bonds, or maybe even more.

New York Exchange Bonds

Thursday, December 30

Total Volume, $30,640,000

SALES SINCE JANUARY 1

1976	1975	1974
$5,239,215,900	$5,178,337,500	$4,052,123,400

	Domestic Thurs	Domestic Wed	All Issues Thurs	All Issues Wed
Issues traded	847	841	866	855
Advances	437	391	451	398
Declines	196	217	196	223
Unchanged	214	233	219	234
New highs, 1976	190	162	198	166
New lows, 1976	0	0	0	1

Dow Jones Bond Averages

1974 High	1974 Low	1975 High	1975 Low	1976 High	1976 Low		THURSDAY 1976		THURSDAY 1976		THURSDAY 1975	
....	....	....	....	93.07	85.68	20 Bonds	93.07	+ .48	....	....	....	....
91.70	78.52	88.05	81.03	98.58	87.46	10 Utilities	98.58	+ .70	close		81.03	+ .23
80.82	70.81	79.05	74.51	87.57	78.58	10 Industrial	87.57	+ .26	close		74.68	+ .05

CORPORATION BONDS

Volume, $30,080,000

Bonds	Cur Yld	Vol	High	Low	Close	Net Chg
AMF 10s85	9.4	4	106½	106¼	106¼	−1⅜
ATO 4⅜s87	cv	2	67	66	67	+1
AddM 9⅜95	9.5	10	98¼	98	98¼	+ ⅞
AetnCr 9¾86	9.3	5	104¾	104¾	104¾	+1¼
AirRe 3⅞87	cv	1	95¾	95¾	95¾	.....
AlaB 9½s84	9.0	3	106⅛	106⅛	106⅛	+ ⅛
AlaP 9s2000	8.9	43	101	100¾	101	+ ¼
AlaP 8½s01	8.6	42	98½	97½	98½	+1¼
AlaP 8⅞s03	8.8	41	100⅞	100⅜	100¾	+ ⅜
AlaP 8¼s03	8.7	15	95	95	95	− ½
AlaP 10⅞05	9.8	5	110⅝	110⅝	110⅝	−1⅜
Alaska 6s96	cv	26	76⅜	75¾	76¼	.....
Alexn 5½96	cv	114	60	59¾	60	.....
AldSu 5¾87	cv	2	53	53	53	+1
Alcoa 4¼s82	4.8	25	89¼	89¼	89¼	+ ¼
Alcoa 5¼s91	cv	34	108⅞	107⅞	108⅞	+1⅜
Alcoa 6s92	6.7	19	89	88½	89	+1
AluCa 9½95	9.2	5	103½	103½	103½	+ ⅜
AMAX 8s86	7.8	69	102	101¾	102	+ ⅛
AHes 6¾96	7.8	10	86	85½	86	+1
AForP 5s30	7.8	10	63¾	63¾	63¾	.....
AAirl 4¼s92	cv	12	58¾	58⅝	58⅝	− ⅛
AAirln 11s88	10.	13	109	108¼	108¼	− ¾
AAirl 10⅞88	10.	17	108¼	107¾	108¼	+ ½
AAirln 10s89	9.6	3	104¼	104	104¼	.....
ABrnd 5⅞92	6.9	5	85	85	85	.....
ABrnd 8⅛85	7.7	9	104⅞	104⅞	104⅞	− ⅜
ACan 3¾s88	5.0	2	75	75	75	+2½
ACeM 6¾91	cv	5	55	55	55	.....
AExC 8½s85	8.0	10	106	106	106	+ ½
AHoist 4¾92	cv	1	112	112	112	− ½
AHoist 5½93	cv	14	91⅞	91½	91⅞	.....
AMedcp 5s97	cv	20	63⅝	63	63⅝	+ ⅝
AMed 9½98	9.9	3	96	96	96	+ ⅜
AmMot 6s88	cv	61	60	59½	59½	− ½
ASug 5.3s93	7.3	3	72⅝	72⅝	72⅝	.....
ASu 5.3s93r	..	2	72¼	72¼	72¼	+2½
ATT 2¾s80	3.0	7	90¾	90¾	90¾	+ ½
ATT 2¾s82	3.2	10	85	85	85	− ½
ATT 3¼s84	4.0	10	80¾	80¾	80¾	.....
ATT 4⅜s85	5.1	219	86	85⅝	86	+ ⅝
ATT 2⅝s86	3.7	10	70⅝	70⅝	70⅝	.....
ATT 2⅞s87	4.0	1	72	72	72	.....
ATT 8¾2000	8.2	229	107¼	107	107¼	+ ⅜
ATT 8.7s02	8.1	109	107	106¾	107	+ ⅛
ATT 7s01	7.3	127	95⅞	95½	95½	+ ⅝
ATT 6½s79	6.4	34	101½	101⅛	101⅛	− ⅜
ATT 7⅛s03	7.4	134	96¾	96½	96¾	+ ¼
ATT 8.80s05	8.0	246	109¾	108⅜	109¾	+1
ATT 7¾s82	7.3	120	106	105¾	105¾	+ ⅛
ATT 8⅝s07	7.9	40	109⅜	108¾	109⅜	+ ¾
Ames 10s95	10.	25	96½	96½	96½	+ ⅜
Amfac 5¼94	cv	29	63⅝	62	62	− ⅜
Ampx 5½94	cv	119	66¼	65	65	− ½
Anhr 7.95s99	7.7	20	103¼	103¼	103¼	+ ¾
ApcoO 5s88	cv	5	119	119	119	+3¾
AppP 11⅛83	10.	7	110⅛	110⅛	110⅛	.....
Arco 8.70s81	8.1	11	107¾	107¾	107¾	+1¼
Arco 8s82	7.6	26	105⅝	104½	105⅝	.....
Arco 8⅜s83	7.9	10	106	106	106	− ⅝
Arco 7½82	7.2	25	104⅝	104⅜	104⅝	+ ⅛
Arco 7¾86	7.5	5	103⅞	103⅞	103⅞	− ⅝
Aristr 9½89	10.	21	93½	93⅜	93⅜	.....
ArizP 9½s82	8.9	11	107	106½	107	− ⅛
ArizP 9.8s80	9.2	6	107	107	107	+ ⅛
ArizP 10⅝00	9.5	7	112	112	112	+ ½
Armco 8½01	8.1	25	104½	104½	104½	+1
Armr 4½83	cv	5	96½	96½	96½	+3⅜
ArRub 4½87	cv	2	70⅛	70⅛	70⅛	.....
AsCp 8½77	8.5	3	100⅜	100⅜	100⅜	− ⅛
AsInv 4½83	5.5	5	82½	82½	82½	+1¾
Atico 6¾82	13.	30	54	53½	54	+ ½
AtRch 7¾03	7.7	24	101	101	101	+ ¾
AvcoC 5½93	cv	22	60½	60⅜	60½	− ½
AvcoC 7½93	9.7	12	77⅝	77⅝	77⅝	+ ⅛
AvcoC 9⅝01	cv	33	108¾	108	108¼	− ¾
AvcoF 11s90	9.9	11	110⅞	110	110⅞	+ ⅞
AvcoF 8½s84	8.3	55	102	102	102	+1½
B&O 4s80	4.6	5	87½	87⅜	87½	+1⅜
B&O 4¼s95	7.6	8	56½	56¼	56¼	− ¼
B&O 4½s10f	cv	50	60	58⅝	60	+3⅞
B&O 11s77	11.	10	102 3-16	102 3-16	102 3-16	
BalGE 10s82	9.1	8	109¾	109	109¾	.....
BalGE 9⅞05	8.9	10	111½	110¾	110¾	+ ¼

Bonds	Cur Yld	Vol	High	Low	Close	Net Chg
DetE 12½79	11.	28	111¼	111⅛	111⅛	.....
DetE 12¾82	11.	5	114¼	114⅛	114⅛	.....
DetE 11⅞00	10.	2	115	115	115	− ⅜
DetE 10⅝06	9.8	8	108	107½	108	.....
DialF 8¼s89	8.5	10	96½	96½	96½	+ ¼
Dilling 5½94	cv	15	67½	67½	67½	.....
Dilling 9¾99	cv	1	109⅞	109⅞	109⅞	+ ⅞
Divers 5⅞93	cv	36	55	54½	55	+ ⅛
Divers 9⅞91	13.	20	73¾	73⅜	73¾	+ ½
Dow 6.70s98	7.3	1	92	92	92	.....
Dow 7.75s99	7.7	2	100¾	100¾	100¾	+ ⅛
duPont 8s81	7.5	6	106	106	106	.....
DukeP 7¾02	8.1	25	96	95½	95¾	+ ¾
DukeP 9¾04	8.8	4	111	111	111	.....
DukeP 13s79	11.	16	113½	113¼	113½	− ½
DuqL 3¾88	5.6	1	67	67	67	−1½
Duq 8¾2000	8.4	15	104¾	104¾	104¾	+ ¾
ESys 4½s92	cv	23	89½	89	89½	+ ¼
EasAir 5s92	cv	32	53	52½	52½	−1
EaAir 4¾93	cv	25	53½	52½	53	+ ½
EqtLf 6¾90	cv	1	95	95	95	.....
Evans 6¼94	cv	9	83½	83	83	−1
Exxon 6s97	6.8	2	87⅝	87½	87⅝	+ ½
Exxon 6½98	7.1	21	92½	91¾	91¾	− ¾
ExP 7.65s83	7.3	12	105⅜	105	105⅜	+ ⅜
Fairch 4⅜92	cv	33	59½	59	59½	+ ¼
Famly 5s81	6.6	1	75½	75½	75½	− ½
Famly 4¾90	8.9	80	53⅝	53⅝	5-⅝	− ⅛
Farah 5s94	cv	10	53¾	53¾	53¾	.....
Feddrs 5s96	cv	21	55½	55½	55½	+ ½
Feddr 8⅞94	10.	10	88	86	88	+2
FedN 4⅜s96	cv	61	86	85¾	85¾	+ ¼
Fiber 4¾93	cv	1	55	55	55	.....
Fiber 6¾s98	cv	78	76	75¼	75¼	− ¾
Finan 10¼90	9.9	25	104	104	104	+1
FstChi 6¼78	6.3	2	100	100	100	.....
FstChi 7¾86	7.5	10	103⅜	103⅜	103⅜	.....
FstCm 7¾02	9.0	5	86	86	86	+2⅝
FstIntl 9¾99	8.9	5	109⅛	109⅛	109⅛	+3⅛
FstNBAtl 9s84	8.7	9	104	104	104	+1
FNBo 7.6s81	7.4	5	102⅜	102⅜	102⅜	+ ⅛
FsPenn 7s93	cv	25	70	70	70	.....
FstSec 7s79	7.1	10	99¼	99¼	99¼	+ ⅝
FtUnRl 7s91	cv	20	91½	91½	91½	+1
FisbM 4¾97	cv	9	71	71	71	.....
FishF 6½94	cv	32	79	78½	79	+ ½
FlexiV 4¾97	cv	26	65	65	65	.....
FlaPL 8⅛80	7.8	10	104½	104½	104½	+ ½
FlPLt 10¾81	9.8	13	109½	109½	109½	+ ⅜
FlaPL 9⅛84	8.4	10	108	108	108	.....
FoodF 4s79	4.5	11	89½	88	89	− ½
Ford 8⅛90	7.8	10	104	104	104	.....
Ford 7.40s30	7.2	5	102⅝	102½	102½	− ⅛

Bonds	Cur Yld	Vol	High	Low	Close	Net Chg
MPac 4¼05	7.6	1	55¾	55¾	55¾	− ⅛
MPac 4¾20f	..	3	56	56	56	+1¾
MoPac 5s45f	..	33	54⅜	53⅞	53⅞	+ ¼
MoAl 8.45s05	8.0	23	106¼	105½	105½	.....
Mobil 8½01	8.0	166	106¼	106	106⅛	+ ¼
MobO 7⅜01	7.5	42	98	97⅞	98	+ ⅞
MohD 5½94	cv	4	54	53	53	.....
MohD 12s89	cv	43	109	105½	107	+ ⅛
Monsan 9⅛s	8.6	25	107½	106½	106½	−1
Monsan 8s85	7.5	50	106⅜	106⅜	106⅜	+ ⅞
MonW 4⅞90	6.2	2	78	78	78	+1
MntW 4⅞80	5.2	10	93¾	93¾	93¾	+ ¾
MntW 7⅜88	7.5	80	98	95½	98	+2½
MontW 9s89	8.7	1	104	104	104	.....
MntW 8⅝86	8.3	30	104	104	104	+ ⅞
Morgn 4¾98	cv	11	87	86¼	86¼	− ¼
MtSTl 7⅜11	7.6	1	96½	96½	96½	+2⅜
MtSTl 7¾13	7.8	56	100	99	100	+1⅛
MtSTl 9¾12	8.7	5	112⅝	112⅝	112⅝	+ ⅛
MtSTl 9⅝15	8.6	15	112	112	112	+ ½
NBisc 4¾87	6.0	10	79	79	79	+ ½
NCan 7s01	cv	21	100¼	99¾	100¼	− ¼
NCash 4⅜87	5.6	17	77⅝	77⅝	77⅝	+1⅛
NCash 6s95	cv	42	88	87⅛	87⅛	− ⅞
NDist 4½92	cv	7	98⅝	98	98⅝	−1⅜
NHom 4¾96	cv	75	46½	46	46	.....
NInd 5¾88	cv	6	65	65	65	− ¼
NInd 10s99	10.	14	97½	96½	97½	+1½
NMdE 6¾96	cv	14	80⅛	78¼	80⅛	+1⅞
NTea 3½80	4.9	5	71½	71½	71½	+1½
NEMtl 7⅜97	8.4	5	88	88	88	.....
NEnTT 3s82	3.6	13	83⅞	83⅞	83⅞	+2⅜
NEnT 8⅝09	8.2	33	105½	104⅝	104⅞	+ ½
NEnT 8.2s04	8.0	55	102½	102	102½	+ ½
NEnT 6½79	6.5	20	100¼	100¼	100¼	+ ¼
NEnT 7⅜07	7.7	25	95½	95⅜	95½	+ ½

EXPLANATORY NOTES

(For New York and American Bonds)

Yield is current yield. cv–Convertible bond.

ct–Certificates. f–Dealt in flat. m–Matured bonds, negotiability impaired by maturity. st – Stamped. ww – With warrants. x–Ex-interest. xw–Without warrants.

vj–In bankruptcy or receivership or being reorganized under the Bankruptcy Act, or securities assumed by such companies.

Year's high and low range does not include changes in latest day's trading.

5. *Low* is the minimum value at which the Mobil bonds traded today on the NYSE. It is not apparent here, either, how many of these debentures changed hands at this price.

6. The *Close* is the last price at which a transaction took place today in the Mobil 8½% bonds on the NYSE. One or more bonds may have been involved in that transaction, which took place sometime between 10:00 P.M. and 4:00 P.M. eastern time on this date. Just because a sale is the last transaction of the day does not mean it must occur at or close to the end of the trading day on the exchange.

7. *Net Chg.*, representing net change in value between day-to-day closing prices, is expressed as a percentage of a bond's $1,000 typical face value. Thus, a change of + ¼ means an increase in value of ¼% of $1,000 ($2.50 per bond) over the previous closing price of that issue. The Mobil debentures due 2001 obviously closed yesterday at 105⅞ (106⅛ – ¼).

Government bonds. A portion of the business section in the daily newspaper is often used to present price information for most U.S. government, government agency, and quasi-government debt securities (see the following table). Some local papers may publish such information weekly only, although the major ones print daily quotations solicited from market-makers in those issues. The listings are categorized by issuer. In the case of U.S. government securities, they are categorized by type (such as bills, notes, bonds) and arranged in order of maturity. The earliest maturation dates are first, without regard to interest rate or yield. As with securities traded over the counter, only bid and asked prices are shown, defined in increments as small as ¹⁄₃₂% of the issue's par value. (Treasury bills, of course, are traditionally presented in terms of an annualized percentage discount from par value; hence the peculiarity of their numerically higher bid than asking price.) The figure in the column labeled "Yield" is a yield-to-maturity, not a current yield. Yield-to-maturity gives a more relev-

ant number for institutional investors for whom the securities have greatest appeal.

In analyzing the table, focus on the 4½s of May 1975-85 outlined in the section headed "Treasury Bonds and Notes."

1	2	3	4	5	6
				Bid	
Rate	Mat. Date	Bid	Asked	Chg.	Yld.
4¼s	1975-85 May	86.4	87.4	+ .12	6.25

1. These bonds pay 4¼% interest. The small letter *s* following the interest rate is the traditional way these securities are identified; that is, in the plural form. It means that there is more than one debt instrument outstanding in this series to represent the obligation characterized by this issue. The absence of an *n* after the maturation month informs us that this is a bond and not a government note. That is, its maturation date was set for more than ten years after the date

2. What appears to be a double maturation date (1975-85) is, in reality, how the reader is advised that this issue is a term bond. The earlier year signifies that any time after May 1975 until the time the bond must be redeemed in May 1985, the government can retire it at par by exercising its option to call this issue pursuant to such privilege stated in the indenture. In 1977, it seems unlikely to do so because it cannot borrow medium-term funds at better than the 4¼% it is paying on this bond now. This is also why the Treasury Department did not call the bond in 1975 or 1976 either.

3. A holder anxious to sell this bond must accept the bid price of 86.4 which is 86 ⁴⁄₃₂% of $1,000, or $861.25 per bond.

4. An investor interested in buying the bond must pay the offering price of 87.4 which is 87 ⁴⁄₃₂% of $1,000, or $871.25 per bond.

5. This issue was up .12 or ¹²⁄₃₂% of $1,000 ($3.75) from yesterday's bid. Net changes are always measured from day to based on the bid

Government, Agency and Miscellaneous Securities

Thursday, December 30, 1976

Over-the-Counter Quotations: Source on request. Decimals in bid-and-asked and bid changes represent 32nds 101.1 means 101 1-32. a-Plus 1-64. b-Yield to call date. d-Minus 1-64.

Treasury Bonds and Notes

Rate	Mat.	Date	Bid	Asked	Bid Chg.	Yld.
8s,	1977	Feb n	100.12	100.14	.....	4.11
6s,	1977	Feb n	100.5	100.9	.....	4.08
6½s,	1977	Mar n	100.14	100.18	+ .1	4.06
7⅜s,	1977	Apr n	100.26	100.30	− .2	4.37
6⅞s,	1977	May n	100.25	100.29	.....	4.31
9s,	1977	May n	101.14	101.18	− .2	4.58
6¾s,	1977	May n	100.28	101	+ .2	4.23
6½s,	1977	Jun n	100.27	100.31	.....	4.48
7½s,	1977	Jul n	101.18	101.22	.....	4.50
7¾s,	1977	Aug n	101.27	101.31	.....	4.48
8¼s,	1977	Aug n	102.7	102.11	.....	4.58
8⅜s,	1977	Sep n	102.17	102.21	.....	4.69
7½s,	1977	Oct n	102.3	102.7	.....	4.72
7¾s,	1977	Nov n	102.12	102.16	.....	4.77
6⅝s,	1977	Nov n	101.16	101.20	.....	4.77
7¼s,	1977	Dec n	102.8	102.12	+ .2	4.77
6⅜s,	1978	Jan n	101.13	101.17	+ .1	4.90
6¼s,	1978	Feb n	101.9	101.13	+ .1	4.95
8s,	1978	Feb n	103.8	103.12	.....	4.98
6¾s,	1978	Mar n	101.29	102.1	+ .1	5.09
6½s,	1978	Apr n	101.22	101.26	− 1	5.07
7⅛s,	1978	May n	102.17	102.21	+ .1	5.09
7⅛s,	1978	May n	102.18	102.22	+ .1	5.12
7⅞s,	1978	May n	103.17	103.21	+ .1	5.07
6⅞s,	1978	Jun n	102.11	102.15	+ .1	5.14
6⅞s,	1978	Jul n	102.12	102.16	+ .1	5.20
6⅝s,	1978	Aug n	102.1	102.5	+ .1	5.25
7⅝s,	1978	Aug n	103.16	103.20	+ .1	5.28
8¾s,	1978	Aug n	105.7	105.11	+ .1	5.26
6¼s,	1978	Sep n	101.16	101.20	+ .3	5.26
5⅞s,	1978	Oct n	100.29	101.1	+ .2	5.27
5¾s,	1978	Nov n	100.23	100.25	+ .2	5.31
6s,	1978	Nov n	101.4	101.8	+ .2	5.29
8⅛s,	1978	Dec n	105.1	105.5	.....	5.36
5¼s,	1978	Dec n	99.26	99.28	+ .2	5.32
7s,	1979	Feb n	103.1	103.9	+ .1	5.34
7⅞s,	1979	May n	105.1	105.9	+ .2	5.47
7¾s,	1979	Jun n	104.30	105.6	+ .1	5.49
6¼s,	1979	Aug n	101.11	101.19	+ .4	5.59
6⅞s,	1979	Aug n	102.27	103.3	.....	5.59
8½s,	1979	Sep n	107	107.8	+ .2	5.61
6¼s,	1979	Nov n	101.20	101.24	+ .3	5.58
6⅝s,	1979	Nov n	102.16	102.24	+ .3	5.58
7s,	1979	Nov n	103.12	103.20	+ .1	5.61
7½s,	1979	Dec n	104.23	104.31	+ .1	5.67
4s,	1980	Feb	95	95.16	+ .4	5.59
7½s,	1980	Mar n	104.26	105.2	+ .4	5.77
6⅞s,	1980	May n	103.1	103.9	+ .1	5.79
7⅝s,	1980	Jun n	105.11	105.19	+ .3	5.83
9s,	1980	Aug n	109.17	109.25	+ .3	5.95
6⅞s,	1980	Sep n	103.6	103.14	+ .5	5.84
3½s,	1980	Nov	100.3	100.7	+8.3	5.81
5⅞s,	1980	Dec n	99.30	100.2	.....	5.86
7s,	1981	Feb n	103.16	103.24	+ .4	5.96
7⅜s,	1981	Feb n	104.25	105.1	+ .5	5.97
7⅜s,	1981	May n	104.24	105	+ .5	6.06
7⅝s,	1981	Aug n	105.25	106.1	+ .6	6.11
7s,	1981	Aug	104.2	105.2	+ .4	5.74
7s,	1981	Nov n	103.22	103.30	+ .6	6.05
7¾s,	1981	Nov n	106.14	106.22	+ .6	6.14
6⅜s,	1982	Feb	100.30	101.14	+1.7	6.04
8s,	1982	May n	107.18	107.26	+ .8	6.26
8⅛s,	1982	Aug n	108.4	108.12	+ .6	6.33
7⅞s,	1982	Nov n	107.4	107.12	+ .6	6.35
8s,	1983	Feb n	107.30	108.6	+ .8	6.36
3¼s,	1978-83	Jun	85.2	86.2	+ .8	5.88
7s,	1983	Nov n	103.13	103.17	+ .3	6.36
6⅜s,	1984	Aug	99.26	100.26	+ .6	6.24
3¼s,	1985	May	83.20	84.20	+ .4	5.57
4¼s,	1975-85	May	86.4	87.4	+ .12	6.25
7⅞s,	1986	May n	107.20	107.23	+ .11	6.72
8s,	1986	Aug n	108.20	108.24	+ .10	6.75
6⅛s,	1986	Nov	98.8	99.8	+ .16	6.23
3½s,	1990	Feb	83.22	84.22	+ .14	5.11
9¼s,	1990	May	111.4	111.20	+ .26	6.93
4¼s,	1987-92	Au[illegible]	84.26	85.26	+ .8	5.63
[illegible]	[illegible]	[illegible]	[illegible]24	85.24	+ .2	[illegible]

U.S. Treas. Bills

Mat	Bid Discount	Ask Discount	Mat	Bid Discount	Ask Discount
12-30	4.31	4.13	4-21	4.45	4.39
1- 6	4.32	4.10	4-28	4.47	4.39
1-11	4.30	4.10	5- 3	4.50	4.42
1-13	4.28	4.10	5- 5	4.50	4.42
1-20	4.25	4.09	5-12-	4.50	4.42
1-27	4.25	4.11	5-19-	4.50	4.44
2- 3	4.27	4.17	5-26	4.51	4.43
2- 8	4.28	4.18	5-31	4.51	4.43
2-10	4.32	4.22	6- 2	4.52	4.44
2-17	4.33	4.23	6- 9	4.52	4.44
2-24	4.33	4.23	6-16	4.52	4.44
3- 3	4.33	4.25	6-23	4.52	4.46
3- 8	4.35	4.25	6-28	4.50	4.42
3-10	4.35	4.27	6-30	4.50	4.46
3-17	4.35	4.27	7-26	4.58	4.48
3-24	4.36	4.30	8-23	4.60	4.52
3-31	4.34	4.30	9-20	4.63	4.55
4- 5	4.40	4.32	10-18	4.64	4.56
4- 7	4.40	4.32	11-15	4.64	4.56
4-14	4.43	4.35	12-13	4.60	4.56

Fed. Home Loan Bank

Rate	Mat	Bid	Asked	Yld
7.20	2-77	100.10	100.14	4.05
3.05	2-77	100.14	100.18	4.02
5.95	5-77	100.22	100.30	4.50
3.70	5-77	101.12	101.20	4.47
7.15	8-77	101.10	101.18	4.65
3.80	8-77	102.10	102.18	4.70
5.75	11-77	101.8	101.24	4.72
7.45	11-77	101.28	102.12	4.70
9.15	11-77	103.12	103.28	4.67
7.25	2-78	102	102.16	4.98
9.38	2-78	104.12	104.28	4.95
7.60	5-78	102.24	103.8	5.15
9.10	11-78	106.8	106.24	5.31
3.65	2-79	105.20	106.4	5.58
9.45	2-79	107.8	107.24	5.58
3.65	5-79	106.4	106.20	5.65
3.75	5-79	106.8	106.24	5.69
9.50	8-79	108.20	109.4	5.75
7.50	11-79	104	104.16	5.79
8.15	11-79	105.24	106.8	5.77
7.05	2-80	102.20	103.4	5.94
7.75	2-80	104.16	105.16	5.81
7.30	8-80	103.16	104	6.06
7.80	10-80	104.24	105.24	6.07
6.70	11-80	102.2	102.10	6.02
7.75	11-80	105.4	105.20	6.10
7.60	2-81	104.16	105	6.21
8.65	11-81	109.8	109.24	6.30
6.60	11-81	101	102	6.12
8.63	2-82	108.16	109.16	6.42
7.30	5-83	103.4	104.4	6.50
7.38	11-83	103.24	104.8	6.60
8.75	5-84	110.12	111.12	6.77
7.75	5-84	104.28	105.12	6.81
7.85	8-84	105.20	106.4	6.81
7.38	11-84	103.4	103.12	6.61
8.10	11-85	106.28	107.12	6.97
7.38	11-93	99.20	100.20	7.28

World Bank Bonds

Rate	Mat	Bid	Asked	Yld
6.38	1-77	100	100.4	2.22
6.40	3-77	100.4	100.16	3.77
8.40	9-77	102	102.16	4.70
7.00	3-78	101.4	101.20	5.57
4.25	5-78	97.28	98.12	5.53
6.88	9-78	101.12	101.28	5.69
4.25	1-79	96.24	97.8	5.70
8.00	1-80	104.8	104.24	6.24
8.30	7-80	105.8	105.24	6.45
4.75	11-80	94.28	95.12	6.12
8.35	12-80	105.24	106.8	6.53
8.00	7-81	104.12	104.28	6.72
3.25	10-81	95.24	96.24	4.01
4.50	2-82	90.4	90.20	6.71
8.15	1-85	104	104.16	7.39
5.00	2-85	86.28	87.12	7.07
8.60	7-85	106.4	106.20	7.53
8.85	12-85	107.24	108.8	7.56
8.38	7-86	105.16	106	7.48
7.80	12-86	102.4	102.16	7.44
4.50	2-90	75.16	76	7.39
5.38	7-91	80.12	80.28	7.57
5.38	4-92	79.16	80	7.61
5.88	9-93	83	83.24	7.61
6.50	3-94	87.20	88.4	7.76
6.38	10-94	86.16	87	7.73
8.63	8-95	104	104.16	8.15
8.13	8-96	100.16	101	8.02
9.35	12-00	108.24	109.16	8.42
8.85	7-01	105.24	106.8	8.25
8.38	12-01	102.24	103.8	8.07

Bank [illegible]ops

[illegible]ked Yld

FNMA Issues

Rate	Mat	Bid	Asked	Yld
4.50	2-77	99.24	100.4	3.22
6.30	3-77	100.4	100.12	4.19
7.05	3-77	100.8	100.16	4.25
8.30	3-77	100.16	100.24	4.13
6.38	6-77	100.16	100.24	4.60
6.50	6-77	100.18	100.26	4.58
7.20	6-77	100.28	101.4	4.55
6.83	9-77	101.4	101.16	4.63
7.38	9-77	101.16	101.28	4.57
7.85	9-77	101.24	102.4	4.68
7.25	12-77	101.24	102.8	4.77
7.55	12-77	102	102.16	4.89
8.45	3-78	103.12	103.28	5.03
6.70	3-78	101.12	101.28	5.04
7.15	6-78	102.4	102.20	5.23
7.45	6-78	102.20	103.4	5.17
7.15	9-78	102.16	103	5.26
7.45	9-78	103	103.16	5.25
6.75	12-78	102.12	102.28	5.17
8.95	12-78	106.4	106.20	5.31
7.25	3-79	103	103.16	5.53
7.85	6-79	104.16	105	5.63
9.80	6-79	108.16	109.16	5.58
6.40	9-79	101.12	101.28	5.63
7.80	9-79	104.16	105	5.78
8.50	10-79	106.12	106.28	5.77
6.55	12-79	101.24	102.8	5.70
7.75	12-79	104.24	105.8	5.78
6.88	3-80	101.24	102.24	5.91
7.25	3-80	103.4	103.20	5.98
7.38	4-80	103.16	104	6.00
8.50	6-80	107.4	107.20	6.01
7.50	9-80	103.16	104.16	6.11
8.75	9-80	108.4	108.20	6.10
6.60	12-80	101	102	6.02
8.00	12-80	105.28	106.12	6.15
7.05	3-81	102.8	103.8	6.15
7.35	3-81	103.20	104.4	6.21
7.25	6-81	103.4	104.4	6.17
7.95	6-81	106	106.16	6.25
7.25	9-81	103.8	104.8	6.19
9.70	9-81	112.20	113.20	6.29
6.45	12-81	100.24	101	6.21
7.30	12-81	103.12	104.12	6.25
8.88	3-82	109.28	110.28	6.38
6.65	6-82	100.12	101.12	6.35
6.80	9-82	100.28	101.28	6.40
8.60	10-82	109.4	109.20	6.57
7.35	12-82	103	104	6.52
7.75	3-83	105.4	105.20	6.62
6.75	6-83	100.12	101.12	6.48
7.30	6-83	102.24	103.24	6.57
8.10	6-83	106.24	107.8	6.69
6.75	9-83	100.12	101.12	6.49
8.00	12-83	106.20	107.20	6.61
8.40	12-83	108.8	109.8	6.71
6.25	6-84	97.12	98.12	6.53
8.20	7-84	106.2	107.20	6.88
7.95	9-84	105.20	106.20	6.82
6.90	12-84	100	101	6.73
7.65	3-85	103.8	104.8	6.86
7.90	10-85	105.12	105.28	6.99
7.95	7-86	105.12	105.28	7.05
7.90	9-86	105.4	105.20	7.08
7.30	12-86	101.30	102.6	6.99
7.80	10-91	103.24	104.8	7.32
7.00	3-92	97.8	98.8	7.14
7.05	6-92	97.24	98.24	7.18
7.10	12-97	96.16	97.16	7.33

Federal Land Bank

Rate	Mat	Bid	Asked	Yld
7.45	1-77	100	100.4	4.64
8.25	4-77	100.28	101.4	4.34
6.25	7-77	100.20	100.28	4.61
7.50	7-77	101.10	101.18	4.57
6.35	10-77	100.28	101.12	4.56
6.60	10-77	101.8	101.16	4.65
6.70	10-77	101.10	101.18	4.67
6.10	1-78	101.2	101.10	4.81
8.70	1-78	103.16	104	4.76
4.13	2-78-73	98.8	99.8	4.81
5.13	4-78	99.8	100.8	4.92
7.60	4-78	102.16	103	5.17
6.40	7-78	100.28	101.28	5.12
9.15	7-78	105.8	105.24	5.23
7.35	10-78	102.24	103.8	5.42
5.00	1-79	98.28	99.12	5.32
7.10	1-79	102.20	103.4	5.47
6.85	4-79	101.28	102.28	5.50
8.55	4-79	105.28	106.12	5.56
7.15	7-79	103.4	103.20	5.61
6.80	10-79	102	103	5.63
6.70	1-80	101.20	102.20	5.75
7.35	4-80	103.20	104.4	5.95
7.50	7-80	103.28	104.28	5.95
8.70	10-80	107.28	108.12	6.19
7.10	[illegible]	[illegible]	103.12	6.14
[illegible]	[illegible]	[illegible]	[illegible]	[illegible]

price. Therefore, yesterday's bid was 85.24 (86⁴⁄₃₂ — ¹²⁄₃₂), equal to $857.50 per bond.

6. The $871.25 offering price per bond is equivalent to a yield to maturity of 6.25% when one takes into account the guaranteed appreciation if held until 1985, plus the interest coupon of $42.50 ($1,000 × 4¼%) per year.

With the exception of the U.S. Treasury bills, identical analysis can be accorded to all of the other debt instruments listed in this table. Treasury bills, which range in duration up to one year from date of issuance, are listed in order of maturity month and day. There is no column for yield because bill prices are already discounted and expressed in terms of that security's yield-to-maturity. Hence, the bid price is always numerically higher than its offering price. The higher percentage discount from par value always means a lower dollar price.

Example: Look at the January 20 bill noted in the tables. Its remaining lifetime is just 21 days from December 30, 1976. This bill is offered at a dollar value, discounted from its face amount. If purchased on December 30, 1976, the average rate of return for that investor, on an annualized basis, would be 4.09%. Because it is purchased for less than face amount and redeemed at maturity for its face amount, the difference in dollars, based on the money actually invested, equals 4.09%.

Tables for Investment Companies (Mutual Funds). The *Wall Street Journal*'s financial stock and bond tables additionally include market statistics for the most popular investment companies. Information about the larger mutual funds is published daily, whereas figures for the smaller funds, closed-end companies, specialty funds, and dual-purpose funds appear weekly in the Monday edition of the newspaper. Funds are arranged in alphabetical order and by management group (the entity that controls several funds, each fund with different investment ob-

jectives. Because of these centralized control relationships, they are referred to in the industry as "families of funds"), also in alphabetical order.

The bid price in the quotation of a mutual fund is identified as its net asset value (NAV). As is the case with any OTC security, the holder of these shares can, in most instances, dispose of them at the bid price, albeit via redemption rather than to another investor or to a market-maker. The offering price is a fixed price dependent on the bid. It is inclusive of the maximum sales charge employed to sell those shares to the investing public. This price is subject to sales-charge discounts made available to quantity purchasers (breakpoint transactions). Many offerings are without a number, just the letters *N. L.* "N. L." means "no load" and indicates that (1) there is no sales charge for this fund; and (2) the offering price is the same as the bid price.

Let us briefly analyze the quotation for the Audax Fund. It is shown as $7.93 bid and offered at $8.67, up $.04 from yesterday's closing bid price. Change in NAV is figured on the basis of closing-to-closing prices. The difference between current bid and offer prices is a sales charge of $.74 ($8.67 − $7.93). If that charge is then divided by the offering price itself, the result is the percentage of sales load levied. This percentage equals 8½%, the maximum amount permitted under current NASD rules.

$$\frac{\$\,74}{\$8.67} = .085, \text{ or } 8\tfrac{1}{2}\%$$

The funds represented in the top two weekly listings in the table are closed-end investment companies. Those listed in the bottom table are open-end funds. The most unique feature about the closed-end funds is that their market prices are not tied directly to their net asset values. This point is brought forth dramatically in these tables when both the NAV and open-market price of each fund's stock are presented side by side. The right-hand column shows the per-

Mutual Funds

Thursday, December 30

Price ranges for investment companies, as quoted by the National Association of Securities Dealers. NAV stands for net asset value per share; the offering includes net asset value plus maximum sales charge, if any.

	NAV	Offer Price	NAV Chg.
Acorn Fnd	13.94	N.L.	+ .11
Adv Invest	11.18	N.L.	+ .06
Aetna Fnd	7.95	8.69	+ .01
Aetna InSh	13.26	14.49	+ .05
Afuture Fd	9.62	N.L.	+ .07
AGE Fund	5.40	5.51	+ .11
Allstate	9.55	10.27	+ .04
Alpha Fnd	11.43	(z)	+ .04
Am Birthrt	9.75	10.66	+ .05
Am Equity	5.36	5.87	+ .03
American Funds Group:			
Am Bal	8.32	9.09	+ .03
Amcap F	5.67	6.20	+ .05
Am Mutl	10.11	11.05	+ .05
Bnd FdA	15.21	16.62	...
Cap FdA	6.70	7.32	+ .04
Gth FdA	4.66	5.09	+ .04
IncF Am	16.85	18.42	+ .06
I C A	14.60	15.96	+ .08
Nw Prsp	16.49	18.02	+ .09
Wash Mt	7.21	7.88	+ .03
American General Group:			
A GenBd	8.99	9.83	+ .01
A GC Gr	4.35	4.75	+ .01
A Gn Inc	6.73	7.36	+ .01
A GnVen	11.20	12.24	+ .13
Eqty Gth	7.01	7.66	+ .04
Fd Amer	6.89	7.53	+ .03
Prov Inc	3.93	4.24	+ .01
Am Grwth	5.39	5.81	+ .04
Am Ins Ind	4.98	5.44	+ .03
Am Invest	5.44	N.L.	+ .07
AmNat Gw	2.79	3.05	+ .01
Anchor Group:			
Daily Inc	1.00	N.L.	...
Growth	7.29	7.86	+ .03
Income	7.71	8.31	+ .03
Reserv	10.22	N.L.	+ .01
Spectm	5.01	5.40	+ .02
Fund Inv	7.38	7.96	+ .03
Wa Natl	10.68	11.51	+ .06
Audax Fnd	7.93	8.67	+ .04
Axe-Houghton:			
Fund B	8.06	8.76	+ .04
Income	5.02	5.46	+ .01
Stock Fd	6.38	6.97	+ .01
BLC Gwth	10.87	11.88	+ .01
Babsn Inc	1.82	N.L.	...
Babsn Inv	9.99	N.L.	+ .05
Beacon Hll	8.75	N.L.	+ .03
Beacon Inv	9.77	N.L.	+ .05
Berger Group Funds:			
100 Fund	7.45	N.L.	+ .06
101 Fund	9.31	N.L.	+ .03
Brksh Cap	8.43	9.21	+ .07
Bondsk Cp	5.03	5.50	+ .03
Bos Found	9.67	10.57	+ .02
Brown Fnd	3.57	3.85	+ .03
Calvin Bullock Funds:			
Bullock	13.45	14.70	+ .07
Canadn	7.85	8.58	+ .03
Div Shrs	3.26	3.57	+ .02
Income	15.04	16.44	+ .04
Ntwide	10.34	11.30	+ .05
NY Vent	11.52	12.59	+ .05
C G Fund	10.48	11.33	+ .04
CG Inc Fd	8.73	9.44	+ .03
Cap Presv	1.00	N.L.	...
Century Sh	11.98	12.92	+ .10
Chalng Inv	10.41	11.38	+ .03
Charter Fd	13.92	15.21	+ .09
Growth	8.66	9.46	+ .05
Income	10.73	11.73	+ .02
Resrch	16.06	17.55	+ .03
Lifelns Inv	7.40	8.09	− .25
Lincoln National Funds:			
Selct Am	7.34	N.L.	+ .03
Selct Spl	13.69	N.L.	+ .06
Loomis Sayles Funds:			
Cap Dev	10.94	N.L.	+ .07
Mutual	13.89	N.L.	+ .08
Lord Abbett:			
Affilatd	8.44	9.10	+ .05
Bond Deb	11.48	12.55	+ .03
Income	3.55	3.83	+ .02
Lutheran Brotherhd Fds:			
Broth Fd	10.92	11.93	+ .02
Broh Inc	9.45	10.33	− .07
Bro MBd	10.08	11.02	+ .01
Broth US	10.07	11.01	...
Mass. Company:			
Freedm	8.25	9.02	+ .03
Indep Fd	7.60	8.31	+ .03
Mass Fd	10.97	11.99	+ .05
Mass Financial Svcs:			
MIT	11.41	12.30	+ .07
MIG	9.21	9.93	+ .03
MID	15.07	16.25	+ .07
MFD	12.40	13.37	+ .04
MCD	13.22	14.25	+ .06
MFB	16.08	17.34	+ .04
Mather Fd	13.24	N.L.	+ .08
ML CapFd	14.07	15.05	+ .04
ML RdyAs	1.00	N.L.	...
Mid Amer	5.32	5.81	+ .04
Money Mkt	1.00	N.L.	...
MONY Fd	9.91	10.83	+ .06
MSB Fund	15.24	N.L.	+ .03
Mutl BnFd	9.64	10.54	+ .04
M I F Fd	9.02	9.75	+ .04
M I F Gro	4.02	4.35	+ .01
Mutual of Omaha Funds:			
Amer	11.96	12.14	+ .02
Growth	4.41	4.79	+ .02
Income	9.65	10.49	+ .04
Mutl Shars	29.34	N.L.	+ .23
Natl Indust	11.29	N.L.	+ .01
National Securities Funds:			
Balanc	9.89	10.66	+ .03
Bond	4.67	5.04	+ .01
Dividnd	4.17	4.50	+ .02
Preferd	7.54	8.13	+ .02
Income	5.53	5.96	+ .03
Stock	8.48	9.14	+ .04
Grwth	5.94	6.40	+ .01
New Eng Life Fds:			
Equity	17.85	19.40	+ .11
Grwth	9.14	9.93	+ .05
Income	14.36	15.61	+ .04
Side	14.35	15.60	+ .07

z-Quote not available. NL No load. x-Ex-dividend. r Ex-rights. d Ex-distribution a-funds redemption price.

Closed-End Funds

Thursday, December 23

Following is a weekly listing of unaudited net asset values of closed-end investment fund shares, reported by the companies as of Friday's close. Also shown is the closing listed market price or a dealer-to-dealer asked price of each fund's shares, with the percentage of difference.

	N.A. Value	Stk Price	Diff
Diversified Common Stock Funds			
AdmExp	15.68	12¾	−18.7
BakerFen	56.21	35	−37.7
Carriers	17.87	14⅜	−19.6
CentSec	8.69	5⅞	−32.3
GenAInv	13.85	11¾	−15.2
Lehman	14.72	12¼	−16.8
Madison	16.93	12⅝	−25.4
NiagaraSh	13.88	12⅜	−10.8
OseasSec	4.57	3⅞	−15.2
Tri-Contl	27.00	21⅝	−19.9
United	11.57	10⅜	−10.3
US&For	z	z	z
Specialized Equity and Convertible Funds			
AmUtilS	14.90	11½	−22.8
bASA	z	z	z
BancrftCv	22.38	17	−24.0
Castle	23.29	17¾	−23.8
ChaseCvB	z	z	z
CLIC	(−7.92	....	....
Diebold	9.07	6⅛	−32.5
Japan	12.48	9	−27.9
KeysnOTC	10.03	7⅛	−29.0
NatlAvia	23.49	15⅝	−33.5
NewAmFd	16.80	12	−28.6
PetroCp	26.76	27½	+ 2.8
RETIncC	z	z	z
S-GSecInc	1.59	1¼	−21.4
Source	16.99	13¼	−22.0
StdSh	38.59	24¾	−35.9
ValueLn	z	z	z

a-Ex-Dividend. z-Not Available. b-as of Thursdays close.

Dual-Purpose Funds

Thursday, December 23

Following is a weekly listing of the unaudited net asset values of dual-purpose, closed-end investment funds' capital shares as reported by the companies as of Friday's close. Also shown is the closing listed market price or the dealer-to-dealer asked price of each fund's capital shares, with the percentage of difference.

	Cap. Shs. Price	N.A. Val Cap. Shs.	% Diff.
Am DualVest	7¾	9.44	−17.9
Gemini	18¼	24.63	−25.9
Hemisphere		1.66	− 2.1
Income and Cap	7⅛	10.59	−32.7
Leverage	12⅛	17.00	−28.7
Pegasus Inco&Cap	8¾	9.56	− 8.5
Putnam Duo Fund	7⅜	10.27	− 8.2
Scudder Duo-Vest	7⅝	10.44	−26.9
Scudder D-V Exch	20	31.16	−35.8

Lipper Analytical Distributors.

Weekly Mutual Funds

AmFd Govt Sec	25.53	25.98
Am Gen Growth	(z)	(z)
BLC Income Fd	11.87	12.97
Capital ExchFd	30.60	(z)
Congress Str Fd	31.80	(z)
Constitution Fd	x46.55	N.L.
Daily IncomeFd	(z)	(z)
Deposit FndBos	22.78	(z)
Devnshire St Fd	11.83	N.L.
Divesifcatn Fd	36.22	(z)
Exchang FdBos	42.38	(z)
Exeter Fund	41.67	(z)
Federal StFund	(z)	(z)
Fiduciary ExFd	24.32	(z)
Josten GrwthFd	(z)	(z)
Lincoln Nat Inc	(z)	(z)
LordAbt Dev Gr	10.55	11.53
MassFund Incm	15.67	17.13
MoneyMkt Oplv	17.36	18.42
Nassau Fund	12.63	N.L.
Ocean TechnFd	(z)	(z)
Safeco IncomeF	(z)	(z)
Scudder Dev Fd	47.62	48.59
2nd Fiduciary	30.59	(z)
SecurtyBond Fd	10.10	10.39
Sentinel Trustes	10.70	11.63
S & P Liq Asset	(z)	(z)
Sun Growth Fd	9.40	10.05
Vance Sandr Fd	52.13	(z)

centage premium (+) or discount (–) at which the stock sells in comparison to that fund's net asset value. In all but one instance, the closed-end companies are selling at discounts from net asset values. Some funds are selling by as much as 35-37% below what each share would be worth if the company liquidated itself. Histori-cally, that situation is typical for most closed-end investment company shares.

Stock Option Tables. *See* page 232.

Quotation and Size. *See* Bid and Offer.

Quotations and Transactions (Published). *See* Rules of Fair Practice (Section 5).

R

Radio-Controlled Paging Devices. *See* Order Ticket [Order Transmission (NYSE)].

Range. The high and low prices, or high and low bids and offers, recorded during a specified time.

    See Bid and Offer.

Rate Covenant. *See* Municipal Security (Type of Indenture).

Ratings. Many corporate bonds are assigned ratings that reflect the issuer's ability to pay. One or more of the three major rating services gauges a corporation's ability to honor an obligation by assigning to its publicly owned debt a letter rating that indicates its investment quality. These advisory services are: (1) Fitch Investors Service, 79 Wall Street, New York City; (2) Moody's Investors Service, 99 Church Street, New York City; and (3) Standard & Poor's Corporation, 345 Hudson Street, New York City.

    Each organization examines the corporation's financial statistics and management policies to determine the quality of the debt and then interprets this information according to its own confidential criteria. As a result, it is not unusual to find the same corporate issue carrying a confusing *split rating* (two unequal grades assigned by different services). Nor is it necessarily an adverse reflection on a corporation for its bonds to have no rating at all. Private placements and bonds of corporations in certain industries are often unrated as a result of the issuing firm's policy.

    In general, an issue's rating hinges on:

1. the corporation's past earnings records;

2. the corporation's current financial position, including: (a) working capital; (b) the amount of debt outstanding, its maturities, sinking fund provisions, and ranking; and (c) the extent of its tangible assets;

3. the nature of the corporation's business, including: (a) the character of the industry; (b) the necessity of its product; and (c) the firm's position in the industry;

4. the continuity and consistency of management policies and controls; and

5. the corporation's labor relations.

    In descending order of quality, each service rates corporate bonds as shown in the following table:

Ratings of Bonds

Investment Bracket	Fitch	Moody's	Standard & Poor's
Top quality	AAA	Aaa	AAA
	AA	Aa	AA
	A	A	A
Medium quality to speculative	BBB	Baa 1-2-3*	BBB
	BB	Ba	BB
	B	B	B
Poor quality	CCC	Caa	CCC
	CC	Ca	CC
	C	C	C
Value is questionable	DDD		DDD
	DD		DD
	D		D

*The number 1 added to these ratings indicates the high end of the category, number 2 the mid-range ranking, and number 3 the low end.

The gradations within each investment bracket are slight compared to the quality gap between the brackets themselves. While market price is not a factor in assigning a rating to an issue, the rating assigned certainly affects the market price of that security. Generally speaking, assuming equal maturity dates, lower quality bonds: (1) carry higher interest coupons than issues found with higher ratings; or (2) trade at lower prices than bonds with higher ratings having identical interest coupons. This economic fact of life provides greater compensation for investors as a reflection of the greater risk involved in owning lower rated bonds.

Real Estate Investment Trusts (REITs). A *real estate investment trust*, or REIT as it is commonly referred to (pronounced "reet"), can be compared to a closed-end type of investment company. Whereas a closed-end company invests in a portfolio of securities, a REIT invests in various ventures, all related to the field of real estate. This includes income-producing properties, such as shopping centers and office buildings, as well as short-term construction loans and long-term mortgages. As a result, purchasers of REIT shares achieve two important goals not usually realized by the average real estate investor: (1) *diversification*—a limited amount of capital acquires a proportionate participation in the trust's package of investments; (2) *liquidity*—the investor's shares in this trust portfolio can be sold easily in the over-the-counter stock market or on an exchange where the REIT may be traded.

Organization and Capitalization. A real estate investment trust is organized according to a legal trust instrument with its business supervised by a self-appointed board of trustees. This contrasts with a closed-end company's birth by means of a charter and the use of the corporate directorship style of command. This difference between the two investment companies is strictly technical in nature. For all practical purposes the two businesses are managed alike. A way to recognize one format from the other is through description of its ownership title. Equity in a trust is called a *certificate of beneficial interest* (CBI) while that of a corporation is vested in a *share of common stock*. Both forms of business obtain a significant percentage of their capital through public offerings of such ownership interest. The similarity in their capitalization process usually ends there.

A REIT often supplements its equity capital with large borrowings from banks and insurance companies as a way of giving it a degree of leverage in its business dealings. (Leverage can be defined as a high percentage of debt in relation to equity capital. It is hoped that the borrowed funds can be employed to earn a greater sum than the interest that must be paid for the use of those monies.) During their peak popularity in the mid-1960s, REITs sometimes borrowed two to five times the amount of their equity capital. The risk involved in this practice of heavy borrowing is that the real estate investment may not generate enough money to pay the interest carrying expenses or to repay the principal amount when it comes due. Bankruptcy and receivership then usually result as the equity capital is quickly dissipated. These investment vehicles are structured for persons capable of bearing capital risk in anticipation of receiving higher current income than that realizable from more conservative media. Because these trusts are not concerns registered under the Investment Company Act of 1940, they are not subject to its restrictive borrowing provisions.

Mortgage and Equity REITs. Real estate investment trusts are usually classified broadly as either mortgage or equity. A REIT's assignment to a particular category depends on its principal investment practices. A *mortgage REIT* acts primarily as a financier for construction of commercial and residential properties. It lends money to builders and developers of real estate projects. It benefits from the difference in rates between its own borrowing expense and the interest received from holdings of these loan and mortgage contracts. An *equity REIT* is primarily a landlord or owner of commercial and residential real estate. It invests in income-producing properties such as shopping centers, office buildings, warehouses, and apartment houses. It is also the more conservative of the two categories because any borrowing it undertakes is nominal compared to its equity capitalization. If an equity REIT wants more investment capital, it is more inclined to issue additional shares of beneficial interest rather than borrow it. Therefore, its income is derived primarily from rent monies paid by the lessees of the properties it owns.

These classifications, as mentioned before, are broad. Often, a REIT is found to be a combination of mortgage and equity investment in order to enjoy the best of both worlds— mortgage for speculative growth opportunity and equity for a solid foundation of continuous current income. Moreover, within the field of mortgage REITs, there is a breakdown between those trusts that invest in short-term loans and those that invest in long-term loans (so-called "permanent" loans). Those trusts specializing in short-term loans finance the construction phase of real estate projects. They are frequently called *construction and development (C&D) REITs.* They provide interim credit until longer-term mortgages can be obtained when the project is completed. The *permanent mortgage REITs* are often sponsored by large life insurance companies. They extend credit on commercial and residential properties, sometimes for as long as forty years.

Taxation Tests for REITs. Real estate investment trusts are permitted the same conduit treatment of income as that allowed for regulated investment companies. They, too, are subject to the terms of Subchapter M of the Internal Revenue Code. Thus, if a trust is able to meet the qualifications prescribed in the Code, it avoids

being taxed as a separate entity. Instead, it passes this liability on to the beneficial owners of its certificates.

In order to qualify for conduit treatment, a REIT must annually satisfy four tests regarding organizational structure, source of income, nature of assets, and distribution of income. The tests are intended to prove that (1) there is a pooling arrangement of funds invested primarily in the real estate field; and (2) income realized from these investments is passive income as opposed to monies generated from the operation of businesses involving real estate. Moreover, substantial amounts of the realized income must be paid out to the certificate holders on a current basis.

Organizational structure. A REIT must be an unincorporated legal entity managed by one or more trustees. It cannot be a personal holding company. Beneficial ownership must be evidenced by transferable securities held by 100 or more persons.

Source of income. At least 75% of a REIT's income must be derived from one or more of the following: (1) real property rentals; (2) interest from real property mortgages; (3) gain from the sale of real property or from mortgages secured by real property; (4) distributions from other REITs; (5) abatements or refunds of taxes paid on real property; and (6) income and gain from foreclosure property. (Foreclosure property is real estate acquired by a REIT through default on a lease or on an indebtedness that such property secured.)

An additional 15% of a REIT's income must also come from those sources or from interest, dividends, or gains from the sale of stock or other securities. Thus, it is permissible for a REIT to have *some* of its capital invested in other than real estate ventures, should management deem it wise to do so. Furthermore, as a deterrent to frequent trading of assets, the Internal Revenue Service has decreed that no more than 30% of a REIT's income can come from sales of real property held less than four years and securities held for one year or less (requirement effective for sales in 1978 and thereafter).

Nature of assets. At the end of each quarter, a REIT must have at least 75% of the value of its assets invested in real estate, government securities, or held in cash. Not more than 5% of its assets can be in securities of any one nongovernment or non-REIT issuer. Those holdings, whatever the amount, may not exceed 10% of the voting securities of that issuer. Moreover, except for foreclosure property, a REIT may not hold real property primarily for resale to customers.

Distribution of income. A REIT is required to distribute each year at least 90% of net investment income to its beneficial owners. Net investment income is defined as rental income and/or interest income, less expenses. But it does not include, nor does the IRS mandate distribution of, capital gains (that is, profits from sale of real property, leases, mortgage instruments, or securities). If the REIT chooses to retain any monies, capital gains, or the minimal percentage of investment income allowable, it must pay taxes on these funds at regular corporate rates. Distributed investment income is taxable for the trust's certificate holders as ordinary income. Capital gains, on the other hand, are treated by REIT investors as long term, regardless of how long a period they have owned an interest in the REIT. This is exactly the same treatment provided for holders of regulated investment companies.

See also Subchapter M (Internal Revenue Code).

Receivers-in-Bankruptcy. *See* Fiduciary Accounts.

Reclamation. *See* Rejections and Reclamations.

Record Date. This date is set by the corporate board of directors for the transfer agent to close the agency's books to further changes in registration of stock and to identify the recipients of a forthcoming distribution.

See also Distribution Dates.

Redemption Call. Most debt and preferred stock issues outstanding have call provisions written into their indentures or agreements, as the category may be. This means that the company may retire the issue at its option by repaying dollars to the owners of these securities. An absolute, or full, call of an issue requires all holders to submit their bonds or shares for redemption. A partial call necessitates only that the holders of specific certificate numbers do so. These certificate numbers are chosen at random by the company, often by electronic means. Frequently they include securities held by a brokerage firm in its own name, but on behalf of customers. If these securities are held in safekeeping or are segregated by owner through individual identification methods, the brokerage simply submits the appropriate certificate to the company and credits that customer with the cash received. However, if the securities are segregated in bulk form, the firm must either (1) maintain on its records the specific certificate numbers of each callable security set aside for each customer account; or (2) adopt an impartial lottery system in which probability of selection is proportional to its holdings of all customers' certificates in that issue.

Partial calls at prices favorable to the holders when compared to current market value may not be allocated to accounts in which that brokerage firm's partners, officers, directors, approved persons, or employees have an interest until all bona fide customers have been satisfied.

The following figure is typical of a partial redemption of an outstanding bond pursuant to call. Holders of both bearer and registered bonds must compare the serial numbers on their certificates to the numbers cited in the Notice of Redemption. If their numbers match any of those in

Notice of Redemption

European Investment Bank

8¾% 15-Year Bonds of 1971 Due January 1, 1986

NOTICE IS HEREBY GIVEN that, pursuant to the provisions of the Paying Agency Agreement dated as of January 1, 1971 by and between the European Investment Bank and The Chase Manhattan Bank (National Association), as American Paying Agent, and Banca Commerciale Italiana S.p.A. and Banque Internationale à Luxembourg S.A., as European Paying Agents, $750,000 in principal amount of the above Bonds will be redeemed and prepaid on January 1, 1977 at the principal amount thereof together with accrued interest thereon to said redemption date.

The serial numbers of the coupon Bonds to be redeemed are as follows:

75	2690	4669	6979	8518	10031	12269	14443	16915	19222	21564	23403	25126	27276	28698
102	2764	4671	7078	8534	10036	12295	14467	16931	19317	21638	23441	25148	27280	28735
131	2806	4681	7108	8637	10056	12365	14488	16952	19353	21656	23454	25280	27321	28739
160	2813	4723	7185	8638	10059	12434	14670	16954	19428	21661	23473	25303	27355	28753
161	2872	4724	7212	8652	10073	12517	14689	16958	19450	21664	23482	25353	27372	28865
224	2950	4738	7223	8716	10100	12528	14761	17012	19512	21732	23720	25429	27493	28894
301	3016	4753	7242	8730	10112	12565	14811	17023	19587	21797	23726	25461	27495	28925
390	3025	4773	7279	8741	10168	12601	14848	17027	19607	21806	23736	25480	27523	28934
444	3030	4800	7295	8825	10171	12609	14908	17062	19619	21812	23762	25514	27582	28965
494	3046	4856	7301	8888	10208	12684	14914	17078	19621	21844	23822	25516	27599	29077
602	3231	4870	7347	8931	10222	12712	15045	17096	19643	21850	23924	25610	27604	29083
648	3445	4886	7356	8942	10254	12814	15163	17111	19919	21919	23954	25656	27610	29093
680	3466	4899	7393	8956	10288	12822	15176	17146	19950	22011	23976	25680	27634	29145
758	3479	4917	7428	8977	10297	12873	15193	17149	19984	22038	23977	25702	27655	29205
763	3484	4955	7485	8987	10298	12905	15240	17164	20014	22046	24018	25758	27659	29247
880	3490	5007	7573	9045	10303	12993	15311	17208	20028	22051	24019	25781	27684	29359
900	3500	5077	7601	9100	10338	13033	15316	17247	20059	22193	24021	25788	27709	29369
937	3501	5093	7603	9130	10382	13078	15372	17314	20334	22271	24057	25845	27766	29378
1254	3518	5299	7606	9146	10384	13115	15392	17452	20344	22279	24147	25873	27797	29413
1268	3543	5303	7629	9153	10396	13181	15405	17463	20371	22338	24320	25982	27835	29481
1401	3594	5458	7645	9210	10455	13213	15457	17473	20378	22372	24322	25995	27842	29498
1418	3624	5468	7673	9241	10460	13222	15477	17528	20428	22389	24352	26008	27914	29502
1422	3644	5534	7793	9288	10465	13243	15484	17543	20441	22402	24388	26031	27967	29524
1489	3690	5571	7877	9299	10471	13269	15558	17570	20451	22404	24408	26104	27971	29561
1763	3717	5667	7880	9317	10568	13272	15623	17832	20474	22513	24417	26193	28032	29576
1770	3756	5726	7884	9332	10577	13298	15718	17861	20551	22591	24444	26201	28073	29585
1777	3758	5800	7963	9383	10586	13303	15757	17880	20564	22620	24452	26235	28074	29588
1779	3774	5837	7975	9425	10692	13386	15779	17893	20578	22637	24453	26374	28080	29600
1808	3776	5842	7976	9446	10819	13390	15819	18121	20652	22697	24467	26383	28100	29637
1835	3820	5881	8013	9491	10830	13454	15892	18125	20657	22709	24507	26454	28144	29740
1991	3888	5924	8020	9512	10901	13477	15893	18183	20686	22711	24518	26473	28169	29855
2081	3905	5952	8024	9570	10927	13495	16006	18186	20704	22723	24571	26493	28172	29888
2083	3985	5990	8028	9629	10932	13583	16008	18268	20727	22769	24662	26522	28179	29893
2161	4015	5991	8029	9636	10937	13799	16210	18386	20772	22826	24666	26619	28197	29932
2162	4056	6056	8086	9672	10950	13828	16253	18399	20861	22977	24717	26732	28288	29947
2187	4178	6183	8187	9727	11038	13850	16260	18412	20990	23001	24761	26875	28315	
2203	4190	6200	8189	9740	11359	13907	16262	18435	21044	23035	24764	26894	28329	
2231	4192	6304	8190	9783	11364	13928	16299	18446	21061	23042	24799	26928	28339	
2245	4257	6317	8224	9803	11389	13959	16303	18823	21114	23046	24815	26960	28354	
2253	4348	6434	8232	9806	11626	13999	16319	18870	21193	23052	24818	27006	28432	
2311	4356	6446	8236	9822	11637	14006	16336	18914	21217	23055	24886	27039	28458	
2424	4369	6616	8247	9832	11757	14019	16398	18919	21218	23110	24889	27045	28522	
2493	4393	6665	8262	9876	11841	14039	16441	18934	21224	23193	24900	27048	28534	
2502	4453	6776	8308	9931	12108	14098	16484	18947	21301	23235	24924	27067	28552	
2531	4519	6785	8311	9952	12146	14116	16493	19021	21355	23278	24947	27073	28573	
2535	4569	6830	8314	9995	12203	14181	16509	19049	21403	23288	24988	27133	28595	
2547	4585	6927	8327	10008	12220	14294	16527	19206	21430	23385	25010	27178	28596	
2665	4629	6967	8511	10010	12227	14322	16907	19220	21546	23392	25121	27221	28642	

The serial numbers of the registered Bonds to be redeemed in part and the principal amounts to be redeemed are as follows:

Serial Number	Principal Amount to be Redeemed	Serial Number	Principal Amount to be Redeemed	Serial Number	Principal Amount to be Redeemed	Serial Number	Principal Amount to be Redeemed
R4	$ 2,000	R6	$ 1,000	R 9	$13,000	R12	$ 3,000
R5	13,000	R7	2,000	R11	9,000		

In case of partial redemption of a fully registered Bond without coupons, the Authenticating Agent will authenticate and deliver Coupon Bonds or fully registered Bonds of authorized denominations in exchange for, and in aggregate principal amount equal to, the unredeemed portion of any fully registered Bond redeemed in part.

Interest on said Bonds shall cease to accrue on the redemption date and on said date the redemption price will become due and payable on each of said Bonds called for redemption.

Payment of Registered Bonds and Coupon Bonds to be redeemed will be made upon presentation and surrender thereof, together with all coupons, if any, appurtenant thereto maturing subsequent to the redemption date, at the principal office of The Chase Manhattan Bank (National Association) in the Borough of Manhattan, City and State of New York, or, at the option of the holder at the principal office of Banca Commerciale Italiana, S.p.A., Milan, Italy and, in the case of Coupon Bonds only, at the principal office of Banque Internationale à Luxembourg S.A., Luxembourg, Grand Duchy of Luxembourg. Such Bonds and coupons should be surrendered at The Chase Manhattan Bank, N.A. (Agency Division), 1 New York Plaza, New York, New York 10015 or, at the option of the holder, at Banca Commerciale Italiana, S.p.A., Sede di Milano, 6 Piazza della Scala, Milano, Italy or Banque Internationale à Luxembourg S.A., 2 Boulevard Royal, Luxembourg, Grand Duchy of Luxembourg.

Coupons which shall mature on, or shall have been matured prior to, said redemption date should be detached and surrendered for payment in the usual manner.

EUROPEAN INVESTMENT BANK
By The Chase Manhattan Bank (National Association),
American Paying Agent

in N. Y.
Dated: December 2, 1976.

FIGURE 9
Notice of Redemption Call

the advertisement, they must present those bonds to the Chase Manhattan Bank, N.A., in New York City or to two other banks situated outside the United States in order to claim the principal amount plus accrued interest to January 1, 1977. Interest will no longer accrue or be paid on the called certificates after January 1, 1977, and so if those bondholders delay redemption of their bonds, their investment funds will be idle after that date.

A company may use a full or partial call in a convertible issue to literally force the holders to exchange their securities for the common stock or else accept only the call price as their reward. Usually, at this time, the call price is significantly lower than the market value of the comparable shares.

Example: Look at a typical redemption notice illustrated in the following figure. Many technical facts are set forth in this advertisement, but the key points have been summarized in the six items positioned on the left side of the illustration. Note how often the bondholder is advised that unless some personal action is initiated before the close of business on December 23, 1976, (1) the conversion privilege will be revoked; (2) accrued interest on the bond will cease; and (3) the holder must accept the redemption price as an only choice between recovery of principal and idling of investment funds.

The corporation has allowed one month for the news to circulate and for the holders of these bonds to make a decision. In the interim, the brokerage must communicate with the beneficial owners of the bonds held in this brokerage firm's custody and solicit instructions from them. During this period, too, Georgia-Pacific has contracted with Blyth Eastman Dillon to stabilize the price of the underlying common stock in the marketplace. This is done to ensure that the stock remains at a price that is continuously more advantageous for the holder to convert than to redeem each bond. Even so, for those holders who choose to sell the bond rather than convert, Blyth

Eastman Dillon is prepared to pay $1,092.50 flat for each $1,000 par value debenture. In turn, it will convert each bond and probably sell the stock for its higher value in the marketplace. The intent of both actions taken by Blyth Eastman Dillon is to enable Georgia-Pacific to exchange its debt security for more outstanding equity with a minimal outlay of cash. The minimal cash requirement is necessary only to redeem any bonds of holders who neglect to act in time. They will be paid $1,059.40 plus $29.86 in accrued interest to December 23, 1976.

See also Beneficial Owner; Broker/Dealer Organization.

Refunding. If the corporation is financially sound yet unable (due to lack of excess capital) to repay bondholders this substantial amount of money at one time, it can retire a given bond obligation through a process called refunding. *Refunding* is the issuance of a new debt security using the proceeds received to: (1) redeem an older bond at maturity; or (2) redeem an outstanding bond prior to maturity via exercise of a call privilege if it was previously issued under less favorable terms.

See also Sinking Fund.

Registered Bond. A "registered" bond certificate signifies that the holder's name and address are inscribed in the issuer's records for the purpose of: (1) sending communications to the appropriate holders; (2) making direct repayment of the principal amount at maturity, or earlier, and/or (3) disbursing periodic payments of interest on this debt.

Bonds can often be issued registered as to principal only or interest only, or they may be fully registered, as determined by the issuer at the time of the initial offering. Bonds registered as to *principal only* have the holder's name inscribed on the certificate, with the interest coupons attached. Bonds registered as to *interest only* are bearer certificates, but the holder's

GEORGIA-PACIFIC CORPORATION

HAS CALLED FOR REDEMPTION ALL OF ITS
6¼% CONVERTIBLE SUBORDINATED DEBENTURES DUE 2000

Conversion right terminates on December 23, 1976.

1. Each Debenture is convertible into Common Stock of Georgia-Pacific Corporation until the conversion right expires at the close of business on December 23, 1976 at a conversion price of $29.80 per share, representing a conversion rate of 33.56 shares per $1,000 principal amount of Debentures.

From January 1, 1976 through November 22, 1976, the sale prices for Georgia-Pacific's Common Stock as reported on the New York Stock Exchange's consolidated transactions reporting system ranged from a high of $38.00 to a low of $27.45 per share. On November 22, 1976, the last reported price was $37.25 per share. As long as the price of the Common Stock is at least $32.625 per share, holders of Debentures will receive upon conversion Common Stock having a market value greater than the amount which would be received either upon redemption or purchase by certain Purchasers as described below.

2. The conversion right expires at the close of business on December 23, 1976. Failure to convert your Debentures by such date could result in a monetary loss to you by virtue of the above described facts.

3. Georgia-Pacific has entered into an agreement with Blyth Eastman Dillon & Co. Incorporated and certain other Purchasers, under which the Purchasers have agreed, on the terms and conditions set forth therein, to purchase Debentures submitted to them any time prior to the close of business on December 23, 1976 at $1,092.50 flat (without accrued interest) per $1,000 principal amount of Debentures. Please note that this price exceeds the price obtainable by surrendering Debentures for redemption by $3.24 for each $1,000 principal amount of Debentures.

4. Debentures not converted or submitted to the Purchasers by the close of business on December 23, 1976 will be redeemed for cash at the redemption price of $1,059.40 for each $1,000 principal amount of Debentures, plus $29.86 accrued interest to December 23, 1976.

GEORGIA-PACIFIC CORPORATION
6¼% CONVERTIBLE SUBORDINATED DEBENTURES DUE MAY 15, 2000
NOTICE OF REDEMPTION

November 23, 1976

Notice is hereby given, that Georgia-Pacific Corporation (G-P) has exercised its right, pursuant to Section 1101 of the Indenture, dated as of May 15, 1975, to redeem all of its 6¼% Convertible Subordinated Debentures due May 15, 2000 (the Debentures) on December 23, 1976, the date fixed for redemption.

TERMS OF REDEMPTION.

Redemption Date. December 23, 1976.

Redemption Price. The redemption price of the Debentures is 105.94% of the principal amount of the Debentures, plus interest accrued from July 1, 1976 to December 23, 1976 in the amount of $29.86 per $1,000 principal amount of Debentures, making a total of $1,089.26 payable on December 23, 1976 for each $1,000 principal amount of Debentures.

Redemption Procedure. Payment of the amount to be received on redemption will be made by G-P at Citibank, N.A., Agent, Receive and Deliver Department, 2nd Floor, 111 Wall Street, New York, New York 10015, forthwith on presentation of the Debentures at any time on or after the Redemption Date.

Cessation of Interest. On and after December 23, 1976 interest on the Debentures will cease to accrue.

CONVERSION RIGHTS.

The principal amount of any Debenture may be converted at the option of the holder thereof, until the conversion right expires at the close of business on December 23, 1976, into shares of Common Stock of G-P at a conversion price of $29.80 per share, representing a conversion rate of 33.56 shares (rounded to the nearest 1/100th of a share) per $1,000 principal amount of Debentures.

Price of Common Stock. The last sale of G-P Common Stock as reported on the New York Stock Exchange's consolidated transactions reporting system on November 22, 1976 was at $37.25 per share. The market value of the shares of G-P Common Stock into which $1,000 principal amount of Debentures is convertible (and cash in lieu of fractional shares) was $1,250.11, based on such last sale price and a conversion rate of 33.56 shares per $1,000 principal amount, but such value is subject to change depending on changes in the market value of G-P's Common Stock. From January 1, 1976 through November 22, 1976, the sale prices for G-P's Common Stock have ranged from a high of $38.00 to a low of $27.45 per share (adjusted for all stock splits and dividends). As long as the price of G-P's Common Stock is at least $32.625 per share to the redemption date, the holders of Debentures will receive upon conversion Common Stock (and cash in lieu of fractional shares) having a market value greater than the amount which would be received either upon surrender of Debentures for redemption or purchase by the Purchasers as described below.

Conversion Procedure. Debentures may be surrendered for conversion during the usual business hours at Citibank, N.A., Agent, Receive and Deliver Department, 2nd Floor, 111 Wall Street, New York, New York 10015, together with a written notice of election to convert such Debentures in the form printed on the reverse side of the Debentures or in the form on the Letter of Transmittal enclosed herewith. Such notice shall state the name or names (with addresses) in which the certificate or certificates for Common Stock issuable on conversion shall be issued. If Common Stock is to be issued to other than the registered holder of a Debenture, such Debenture must be accompanied by proper instruments of transfer and by funds in the amount of any stock transfer tax which may be payable (see Instruction 3 under "Instructions if Debentures Are Surrendered for Conversion" in the Letter of Transmittal).

Effective Date of Conversion. Each conversion of Debentures will be deemed to have been made at the close of business on the date of receipt by such Bank of such Debentures accompanied by such written notice, and at such time the rights of the holders of such Debentures as such holders shall cease, and the person(s) entitled to receive the Common Stock issuable upon conversion will be treated for all purposes as the record holder(s) of such Common Stock on that date.

Adjustments, Fractional Shares, etc. No adjustments in respect

5. You may obtain from Citibank, N.A., Agent, Receive and Deliver Department, 2nd Floor, 111 Wall Street, New York, N.Y. 10015 (tel. 212-558-5010), copies of a Letter of Transmittal which may be used to accompany Debentures surrendered for conversion into Common Stock or for purchase by the Purchasers.

6. You have, as a further alternative, the right to sell Debentures through brokerage facilities. You should consult your own broker as to this procedure.

The conversion right terminates on December 23, 1976.

Debentures remaining unconverted will be redeemed at the redemption price (including accrued interest) of $1,089.26 per $1,000 Debenture.

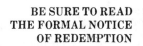

BE SURE TO READ THE FORMAL NOTICE OF REDEMPTION

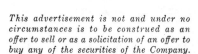

This advertisement is not and under no circumstances is to be construed as an offer to sell or as a solicitation of an offer to buy any of the securities of the Company.

of interest or dividends will be made upon the conversion of any Debenture. No fractional shares or scrip representing fractional shares will be issued upon the conversion of any Debenture. If more than one Debenture is surrendered for conversion at any one time by the same holder, the number of full shares which will be issuable upon conversion thereof will be computed upon the basis of the aggregate principal amount of Debentures so surrendered. If the conversion of any Debenture results in a fractional share interest, G-P will pay a cash adjustment in respect of such fractional interest in an amount equal to the same fraction of the last sales price per share of Common Stock on the New York Stock Exchange on the business day which next precedes the day of conversion.

SALE OF DEBENTURES TO PURCHASERS AT HIGHER THAN REDEMPTION PRICE.

G-P has entered into an agreement with Blyth Eastman Dillon & Co. Incorporated and certain other purchasers (the Purchasers) under which the Purchasers have agreed to purchase all Debentures submitted to them at any time up to the close of business on December 23, 1976 at a price of $1,092.50 flat (without accrued interest) for each $1,000 principal amount thereof. This price is higher than the $1,089.26 for each $1,000 principal amount of Debentures payable upon redemption as described above.

The Purchasers have agreed to convert all Debentures so purchased into Common Stock, and G-P has agreed to pay the Purchasers a commission for their undertaking. G-P's agreement with the Purchasers also provides that if the Purchasers purchase Debentures on the open market, they will convert such Debentures into Common Stock.

G-P has been informed by the Purchasers that the Agreement Among Purchasers provides that, for the purpose of stabilizing the price of G-P's Common Stock or otherwise, the Purchasers may buy and convert Debentures, and may purchase and sell shares of Common Stock and other securities of G-P convertible into Common Stock, in the open market or otherwise, for either long or short account, at such times, in such amounts, on such terms and at such prices as Blyth Eastman Dillon & Co. Incorporated may determine, and may overallot in arranging sales. Any such transactions, if commenced, may be discontinued at any time.

Debentures may be surrendered for sale to Blyth Eastman Dillon & Co. Incorporated, as Representative of the several Purchasers, c/o Citibank, N.A., Agent for the Purchasers, Receive and Deliver Department, 2nd Floor, 111 Wall Street, New York, New York 10015, prior to the close of business on December 23, 1976, using the Letter of Transmittal enclosed herewith.

FEDERAL INCOME TAXES.

Counsel for G-P has advised that, under present law, for Federal income tax purposes:

(1) Conversion of the Debentures into Common Stock will not result in taxable gain or loss, and the tax basis of the Debentures will be allocated to the Common Stock.

(2) Taxable gain, loss or income will be recognized with respect to the receipt of cash for any fractional share interest.

(3) Taxable gain or loss will be recognized with respect to any Debentures sold to the Purchasers or surrendered to G-P for redemption.

G-P suggests that holders of the Debentures consult their own tax advisers regarding the Federal income tax treatment applicable to them resulting from the conversion of the Debentures into Common Stock and the receipt of cash in lieu of fractional shares.

GEORGIA-PACIFIC CORPORATION
By R. B. PAMPLIN
Chairman

The Representative of the Standby Purchasers is:

BLYTH EASTMAN DILLON & CO.
INCORPORATED

---

name and address are registered with the issuer for the purpose of disbursing interest checks. *Fully registered* bonds look like stock certificates. No coupons are attached, and principal and interest payments are made directly to the holder recorded on the issuer's books.

Registered Exchange. The following exchanges are registered with the Securities and Exchange Commission: (1) American Stock Exchange; (2) Boston Stock Exchange; (3) Chicago Board Options Exchange; (4) Cincinnati Stock Exchange; (5) Instinet System (Institutional Trades Via Computer); (6) Midwest Stock Exchange; (7) New York Stock Exchange; (8) Pacific Stock Exchange; (9) Philadelphia Stock Exchange; and (10) Spokane Stock Exchange.

The Honolulu Stock Exchange is specifically exempted from registration with the SEC. Exemption was obtained via a written request to the SEC. Its granting was predicated on the exchange's ability to demonstrate that its activity is minimal.

Registered Options Principal. Options trading policies that are adopted by the member firm must be disseminated to all registered representatives, firmly adhered to, and closely monitored by a Registered Options Principal (ROP). A Registered Options Principal of a member organization is someone designated with authority to manage that firm's options business. Such person must be registered in this capacity and must qualify by a written examination for the responsibility it entails. There is no limitation on the number of ROPs a firm appoints. At least one of them must be an officer or general partner with overall responsibility for supervision of the firm's options business. That person is called a Senior (or designated) ROP. In addition, every firm with retail customers must have a compliance ROP (CROP) charged with implementing compliance procedures. The CROP may have no sales-related function.

See also Options; Trading Policies.

Registered Representative. Registered representatives who work as salespeople are expected to solicit and service customer transactions. The legal and financial ramifications of such actions are crucial to the successful operation of a brokerage organization. Every effort must be made to establish and maintain business relationships on a level that creates good will and deters ill will and/or litigation.

Rules of the National Association of Securities Dealers, the New York Stock Exchange, and the American Stock Exchange that deal with customer accounts impose deep responsibilities on the registered representative and on his or her broker/dealer firm. Rule 405 of the New York Stock Exchange, Rule 411 of the American Stock Exchange, and Sections 2 and 21 of the National Association of Securities Dealers' Rules of Fair Practice require due diligence toward every customer, every order, and every account opened and maintained by member organizations. To comply with these rules, registered representatives must learn the essential facts relative to their customers and their activities. They must make note of this information on a new account report form furnished by their firm. Registered representatives must then sign this form to signify awareness of these facts and attest to their willingness to assume responsibility for their accuracy.

The necessary contingent investigation is conducted on a continuing basis, and if these facts or circumstances change, the representative must update the information promptly and implement any new procedures that may be called for. This is why the firm's records of such inquiries must be dated each time there is a modification in previously furnished information. Even a customer's death, bankruptcy, or insolvency does not exempt the representative from performing these mandatory duties. In all such circumstances, a registered representative must immediately (1) cancel all open orders and instructions from the customer (including buy and sell orders, unsettled contracts, powers of attorney, and so forth); and (2) change the title and the account to reflect both the customer's and the account's changed status.

Example: Estate of John Doe, deceased.

Securities positions in an open account for such persons should not be established or increased unless instructions and authorizing documents are received from a properly accredited source. In most instances, liquidating transactions should not be effected either, unless (1) the securities are held in the name of the brokerage firm, and (2) the firm feels that any credit it has extended to this customer is in jeopardy because of deteriorating market conditions. In any event, no cash or securities disbursements are permitted without legal authorizing documents in hand.

See also Corporate Accounts; Credit Agreement; Customer's Agreement; Discretionary Account; Fiduciary Accounts; Joint Customers; Loan-Consent Agreement; New Account Report Form; Trading Authorization; Unincorporated Associations.

Registered Secondary Distribution. *See* Secondary Distribution.

Registered Security. Any security that is sold in interstate commerce or through the U.S. Postal Service must be registered with the SEC before a public offering or distribution can be made by: (1) its issuer; (2) affiliated persons (persons who can influence management decisions in that corporation. This category may include officers, directors, principal stockholders, and members of their immediate families. Their shares in the company are often described as "control stock."); or (3) people who acquire unregistered securities from an issuer or from an affiliated person with a view to their immediate resale. These people are defined as *statutory underwriters*, even though they may be individuals and even though they may not be fully engaged in the securities business.

See also Affiliated Person; Exempted Security; Issuer; Securities Act of 1933; Involuntary Underwriter.

Registrar. Often a trust company or bank, the registrar maintains a record of all shareholder names and addresses. A registrar is charged with the responsibility of preventing the issuance of more stock than authorized by the company. It insures that the transfer agent issues exactly the same number of shares cancelled with each re-registration of certificates.

See also Broker/Dealer Organization (Cashiering Department); Transfer Agent.

Registration Fees. *See* Securities Exchange Act of 1934 (Section 31).

Registration of Personnel (NYSE). The Member Firm Regulation and Surveillance Division of the NYSE has the task of overseeing qualification and conduct of all registered persons in the financial community—managers, supervisors, and representatives alike.

Backgrounds and capabilities of persons with a sales responsibility are especially subject to screening and examination by this department. Those persons who are in direct and constant communication with the public have greater opportunities to engage in practices detrimental to the exchange, to the member firm employer, and/or to a customer's best interests. Consequently, the Member Firms Surveillance Department must devote more time and effort to monitoring activities of a salesperson than it does to overseeing anyone else. Many potential problems are avoided through careful background investigations and high entry standards for sales candidates.

With approval from the NYSE's Board of Directors, the Member Firms Surveillance Department has set forth the following criteria and procedures for qualification as a registered representative: (1) The applicant must agree to devote a major portion of time to the business of the member organization; (2) The applicant must be at least the age of majority (normally 18-21 years old, depending on the state of domicile); (3) The applicant must have a minimum of four months of on-the-job training and experience in the securities industry, preferably with a member firm or with a general securities-oriented broker/dealer (The NASD, whose registration procedures are similar to those of the NYSE, has no minimum age, working experience, or major-portion-of-time requirement for qualification purposes.); and (4) The applicant must pass a six-hour qualification examination administered under controls set forth by the joint efforts of the NYSE/NASD.

Applications for registration with the NYSE include eleven agreements germane to the conduct of a registered representative in the performance of assigned duties. (The NASD uses the same application form but not the eleven agreements. The industry-wide document is entitled "The Uniform Application for Securities and Commodities Industry Representative and/or Agent," Form U-4, as shown in the following figure. The NYSE addendum appears in the figure on page 379. A synopsis of these agreements follows in order to provide you with an understanding of the exchange's ethical objectives for sales personnel in the industry. A registered representative (1) may not guarantee payment for a debit balance in a customer's account without prior consent of the exchange; (2) may not guarantee any customer against losses; (3) may not share in the profit or losses realized in any customer's account (An important exception allows registered representatives to share in such profits and losses, but only in proportion to the percentage of a registered representative's personal investment at risk in the account. In any event, the member firm employer must give written approval to these arrangements before the relationship can be established.); (4) may not create or maintain a personal securities or commodities transaction account except with a NYSE member firm or with a bank; and prior written approval from the member firm employer, who must receive duplicate copies of all activity; (5) may not rebate or pay out any part of compensation received as a registered representative for a fee, bonus, or other remuneration in connection with business sought or procured; (6) must appear at the request of any NYSE department or committee to give testimony and produce records relative to any inquiry being made by the exchange; (7) must realize that any changes in compensation arrangements in any form may be subject to disap-

proval by the exchange; (8) may not take or accept compensation of any kind from anyone other than the member firm employer in connection with securities, commodities, or insurance activities, unless prior written consent of the NYSE can be obtained; (9) must promptly notify the member firm employer and the exchange if the representative (a) becomes the subject of investigation or proceeding by a regulatory body; (b) is refused registration or has it suspended, revoked, or disciplined by a regulatory body or member organization; (c) is the subject of a major complaint of any customer or broker/dealer in securities; (d) becomes involved in any litigation or arbitration alleging violation of any regulatory body's rules or bylaws or is party defendant to any bankruptcy, contempt proceeding, cease and desist order, injunction, or civil judgment; (e) is arrested, summoned, arraigned, indicted, or convicted for a criminal offense— minor traffic violations are not criminal offenses— (even though all charges may subsequently be dropped or eradicated from the record on appeal); (f) violates any provision of the NYSE Constitution or Rules; (10) must agree that any controversy with any member or member organization (including affiliates or subsidiaries thereof) in connection with personal employment will be settled by the NYSE arbitration at the request of either party to the dispute; (11) must agree to testify, produce records, and accept discipline even after employment has been terminated. However, the registered representative must be given written notice of any inquiry concerning allegations of improper conduct within one year after an official termination notice has been filed with the exchange by the former employer.

It is critical for persons who have successfully qualified with the NASD/NYSE (and are therefore now registered representatives) to realize they are still not yet eligible to deal with public customers. The final and most important step is to register with the securities department

UNIFORM APPLICATION FOR SECURITIES AND
COMMODITIES INDUSTRY REPRESENTATIVE and/or AGENT

Mr.
1. APPLICANT'S NAME Ms. _____

　　　　　　　　　　　　　LAST　　　　　　　　　FIRST　　　　　　　Middle (If None, so specify)

2. [ ][ ]—[ ][ ]—[ ][ ][ ][ ]　　　3. DATE OF EMPLOYMENT _____
SOCIAL SECURITY NUMBER

4. NASD FIRM NUMBER [ ][ ][ ][ ]　　5. FIRM NAME _____

6. FIRM ADDRESS _____

7. OFFICE OF EMPLOYMENT OF APPLICANT _____

8. NASD DISTRICT IN WHICH OFFICE IS LOCATED _____

9. **TO BE REGISTERED WITH THE FOLLOWING:** (Check All Applicable)

SECURITIES AND EXCHANGE COMMISSION ONLY (SECO) ☐

NATIONAL ASSOCIATION OF SECURITIES DEALERS (NASD) ☐

American Stock Exchange ☐	Chicago Mercantile Exchange ☐	New York Stock Exchange ☐	
Boston Stock Exchange ☐	Cincinnati Stock Exchange ☐	Pacific Stock Exchange ☐	
Chicago Board of Trade ☐	Detroit Stock Exchange ☐	PBW Stock Exchange ☐	
Chicago Board Options	Intermountain Stock Exchange ☐	Spokane Stock Exchange ☐	
Exchange ☐	Midwest Stock Exchange ☐	Other (Specify) ☐	

10. **TO BE REGISTERED WITH THE FOLLOWING JURISDICTIONS:** (Check all applicable)

AL ☐	DE ☐	IN ☐	MA ☐	NV ☐	ND ☐	SC ☐	VA ☐
AK ☐	DC ☐	IA ☐	MI ☐	NH ☐	OH ☐	SD ☐	WA ☐
AZ ☐	FL ☐	KS ☐	MN ☐	NJ ☐	OK ☐	TN ☐	WV ☐
AR ☐	GA ☐	KY ☐	MS ☐	NM ☐	OR ☐	TX ☐	WI ☐
CA ☐	HI ☐	LA ☐	MO ☐	NY ☐	PA ☐	UT ☐	WY ☐
CO ☐	ID ☐	ME ☐	MT ☐	NC ☐	RI ☐	VT ☐	PR ☐
CT ☐	IL ☐	MD ☐	NE ☐				

11. **TYPE OF APPROVAL REQUESTED:**

STANDARD REGISTRATION (Registered Representative)

FULL REGISTRATION/GENERAL SECURITIES ☐
LIMITED REGISTRATION ☐
REGISTERED COMMODITY REPRESENTATIVE ☐
AGENT OF ISSUER ☐
INV. CO. & VARIABLE CONTRACTS PRODUCTS ☐
SECURITIES TRADER ☐
REAL ESTATE SECURITIES ☐
DIRECT PARTICIPATION PROGRAMS ☐
OTHER (Specify) _____ ☐
　PART TIME (NASD or SECO) ☐
　FULL TIME (NASD or SECO) ☐

INTERMEDIATE REGISTRATION

BRANCH OFFICE MANAGER ☐
SUPERVISORY ANALYST ☐
OFFICER (Title) _____ ☐
OTHER (Specify) _____ ☐

PRINCIPAL REGISTRATION

Member (Exchange) ☐
　Regular _____ ☐
　Associate ☐
Approved Person (Exchange) _____
　Holder of Voting Stock ☐
　Holder of Non-Voting Stock ☐
　Subordinated Lender ☐
　Holder of Debentures ☐
　Director ☐
　General Partner ☐
　Limited Partner ☐
　Officer (Title) _____ ☐
Allied Member/Gen. Securities Principal ☐
Sole Proprietor ☐
Manager Office of Supv. Jurisdiction ☐
Financial and Operations Principal ☐
Direct Participation Programs ☐
Investment Co. & Variable Contracts Products ☐
Underwriter Principal ☐
Other (Specify) _____ ☐

12. To the best of my knowledge and belief the applicant at the time of approval will be familiar with the statute(s), constitution(s) and rules of the agency, jurisdiction or organization with which this application is being filed, and the rules governing registered persons, and will be fully qualified for the position for which application is being made herein. I agree that notwithstanding the approval of such agency, jurisdiction or organization, which hereby is requested, I will not employ the applicant in the capacity stated herein without first receiving the approval of any authority which may be required by law. This firm has communicated with all the previous employers of the applicant during the past three years, as set forth below:

EMPLOYER	NAME AND POSITION OF PERSON CONTACTED	EMPLOYED FROM/TO	CONTACTED BY PHONE, LETTER OR INTERVIEW

In addition, I have taken appropriate steps to verify the statements contained in this application and to inquire into the past record and reputation of the applicant.

Date _____　Print Name of Appropriate Signatory _____　Signature of Appropriate Signatory _____
　　　　　　　　　　(See Instruction 12)

DO NOT WRITE IN THIS SPACE

Experience _____　　　　　　Clearance _____
Further Training Required _____　Exam Taken: Date _____
Exam Required _____　　　　Grade _____
Issue _____　　　　　　　Date Approved: Cond. _____
Exam Grade OK _____　　　　Final _____

PERSONAL HISTORY

13. Mr. Ms.

Last Name   First   Middle   Maiden (If Applicable)

14. Social Security Number

15. Address

16. City   State   Zip

17. / /   Date of Birth

18. Place of Birth

19. Citizen of US? Yes ☐ No ☐

If no, state country of citizenship_____.

20. Marital Status

21. Alias (If None, Indicate)

22. If Married, Full Name of Spouse & Maiden Name (If Applicable)

23. Mother's Full Maiden Name

24. Father's Full Name

IF MORE SPACE IS NEEDED FOR ANY OF THE FOLLOWING QUESTIONS, ATTACH A SEPARATE SHEET

25. EDUCATION

Educational Institutions Attended: HIGH SCHOOL ☐   COLLEGE ☐   GRADUATE SCHOOL ☐

Specify Highest Year Completed: 9 ☐ 10 ☐ 11 ☐ 12 ☐   1 ☐ 2 ☐ 3 ☐ 4 ☐   1 ☐ 2 ☐ 3 ☐ 4 ☐

NAME AND ADDRESS OF INSTITUTION (STREET, CITY, STATE, ZIP CODE)	FROM MO.	YR.	TO MO.	YR.	COURSE	DAY OR EVENING	DID YOU GRADUATE	DEGREE

26. EMPLOYMENT HISTORY

The following is a complete, consecutive statement of my business history for the past ten years starting with my current position. (All time must be accounted for including self-employment, unemployment, part-time securities, commodities, insurance and real estate industries or related positions and all military service.)

NAME OF EMPLOYER AND COMPLETE ADDRESS (STREET, CITY, STATE, ZIP CODE)	FROM MO.	YR.	TO MO.	YR.	POSITION HELD	REASON FOR LEAVING	FULL OR PART-TIME

27. **RESIDENTIAL HISTORY** (Give all home addresses starting with present address for the past 10 years.)

ADDRESS (Street, City, State, Zip Code)	FROM MO.	YR.	TO MO.	YR.

28. The following is a complete list of all brokers, dealers or banks with which I am carrying accounts in securities or commodities or with which I have carried such during the past ten years. (If "none", so state.)

NAME AND ADDRESS OF FIRM OR BANK	ACCOUNT NUMBER	CASH OR MARGIN	FROM/TO	OPEN OR CLOSED

I authorize and request any and all of my former employers and any other person to furnish to the agency, jurisdiction or organization with which this application is being filed, or any agent acting on its behalf, any information they may have concerning my credit worthiness, character, ability, business activities, educational background, general reputation, together with, in the case of former employers, a history of my employment by them and the reasons for the termination thereof. Moreover, I hereby release each such employer and each such other person from any and all liability of whatever nature by reason of furnishing such information to the agency, jurisdiction or organization or any agent acting on its behalf.

Further, I recognize that I may be the subject of an investigative consumer report ordered by the agency, jurisdiction, or organization with which this application is being filed, and that I have the right to request complete and accurate disclosure by such agency, jurisdiction, or organization of the nature and scope of the investigation requested.

_____
Date

29. _____
Signature of Applicant

U-4 Form, Uniform Application for Registration

THE TEN YEAR LIMIT DOES NOT APPLY TO QUESTIONS 30 THROUGH 54.

30. A. Have you ever taken and passed a qualifying examination for registration in any capacity with the NASD, a national securities or commodities exchange or SECO? If yes, state below the type of examination, the approximate date taken and with what regulatory body application was made. ...... Yes____ No____ [   ]

Type of Exam	Approximate Date Taken	Regulatory Body

B. Have you ever been granted a waiver of qualifying examination with an agency or organization? If yes, state below the type of examination, the approximate date and by what agency or organization. .... Yes____ No____ [   ]

Type of Exam	Approximate Date	Regulatory Body

C. Have you ever taken a qualifying examination for any jurisdiction? If yes, state below the type of examination, the approximate date taken and the name of the jurisdiction administering it. .... Yes____ No____ [   ]

Type of Exam	Approximate Date Taken	Regulatory Body

D. Have you ever been exempted or excluded from taking a qualifying examination by any jurisdiction? If yes, state below the type of examination, the approximate date and the name of the jurisdiction issuing the exemption or exclusion. .... Yes____ No____ [   ]

Type of Exam	Approximate Date	Regulatory Body

IF THE ANSWER TO ANY OF THE FOLLOWING QUESTIONS IS YES, ATTACH COMPLETE DETAILS:

31. Have you ever been registered or licensed by any agency or jurisdiction to sell or to deal in securities or commodities as a principal or employee with any registered broker-dealer or to function as an investment adviser? If yes, specify the name of the broker-dealer or investment adviser, dates registered and agency or jurisdiction with which you were registered. .... Yes____ No____ [   ]

32. Are you currently engaged in any other business either as a proprietor, partner, officer, director, trustee, employee or otherwise? .... Yes____ No____ [   ]

33. Do you or any member of your immediate family have any beneficial interest in any investment partnership or corporation (including hedge funds, investment clubs, etc.) or any other domestic or foreign accounts whose primary function is investing in securities or commodities (excluding companies registered under the Investment Company Act of 1940)? .... Yes____ No____ [   ]

34. Are you now or have you ever been licensed to sell insurance? .... Yes____ No____ [   ]

Type of License(s) and jurisdiction(s) where licensed _____

35. Are you now or have you ever been licensed to sell real estate? .... Yes____ No____ [   ]

Type of License(s) and jurisdiction(s) where licensed _____

36. Are you currently bonded? (If yes, specify insurance company and amount.) .... Yes____ No____ [   ]

37. Have you ever been refused a fidelity bond? .... Yes____ No____ [   ]

38. Has any surety company paid out any funds on your coverage or cancelled your bond? .... Yes____ No____ [   ]

39. Are you now or have you ever been a regular or associate member of any stock exchange or commodity exchange/contract market? .... Yes____ No____ [   ]

40. Have you ever been an officer, director, general partner, owner of ten (10) percentum or more of the voting securities, or controlling person of, or otherwise engaged in any other managerial or supervisory capacity with any broker or dealer for which a trustee has been appointed pursuant to the provisions of the Securities Investor Protection Act of 1970, or that has been liquidated under any other circumstances? .... Yes____ No____ [   ]

41. To your knowledge, are you now or have you ever been the subject of any investigation or proceeding by any securities, commodities or insurance agency, jurisdiction or organization? .... Yes____ No____ [   ]

42. Are you now or have you ever been a defendant in any litigation alleging the violation of any agreement with or provision of a securities or commodities industry self-regulatory organization's constitution, by-laws or rules, or any securities, commodities or insurance law or regulation? .... Yes____ No____ [   ]

43. Are you now or have you ever been a director, controlling stockholder, partner, officer, sole proprietor, or associated person with a broker-dealer or insurer which during the time of such association was suspended, expelled, or had its registration denied or revoked by any agency, jurisdiction or organization? .... Yes____ No____ [   ]

44. Are you now or have you ever been subject to an order of the NASD, a securities or commodities exchange, an agency or any jurisdiction which revokes, suspends or denies membership or registration? .... Yes____ No____ [   ]

45. Has any permanent or temporary injunction ever been entered against you or any broker-dealer, insurer, investment adviser or commodities firm with which you were associated in any capacity at the time such injunction was entered? .... Yes____ No____ [   ]

46. Are you now or have you ever been (whether or not publicly disclosed) suspended, expelled, fined, barred, censured or otherwise disciplined, or found to have violated any securities or commodities law or rule by any securities or commodities agency, jurisdiction or organization; or been refused membership therein or withdrawn your application for such membership; or been refused a license to sell insurance or had one suspended or revoked for cause by any jurisdiction or agency? .... Yes____ No____ [   ]

47. Are you now or have you ever been named as an aider, abettor, or a co-conspirator in, or cause of, any action mentioned in questions 40, 41, 42, 43, 44, 45 and 46, taken with respect to a broker-dealer or insurer? .... Yes____ No____ [   ]

_____   _____
Date   Signature of Applicant

377

48. Are you now or have you ever been suspended, expelled, fined, barred, censured or otherwise disciplined by an employer in the securities, commodities or insurance industry? .... Yes____ No____ [

49. Have you ever had denied, suspended or revoked a license, permit, certificate, registration or membership required to engage in securities, commodities, insurance or other business or profession? .... Yes____ No____ [

50. In your previous business connections or employment, have you ever been:
    a. a subject of a major complaint or legal proceeding? .... Yes____ No____ [
    or,
    b. discharged or requested to resign by an employer because of dishonest or unethical acts alleged to have been committed by you? .... Yes____ No____ [

51. Have you or any firm, corporation or association of which you have been a principal or officer ever failed in business, made a compromise with creditors or ever filed or been declared bankrupt under any bankruptcy acts? .... Yes____ No____ [

52. Have you ever been:
    a. Arrested or indicted for any felony or misdemeanor involving the purchase, sale, or delivery of any security, or arising out of the conduct of the business of a broker, dealer, fiduciary, investment company, investment adviser, underwriter, bank, trust company, insurance company or other financial institution, or involving any crime in which violence or threats of violence against any person, dishonesty, the wrongful taking of any property, or any manner of fraud was a factor, or involving conspiracy to commit any of the foregoing? .... Yes____ No____ [
    or,
    b. Convicted of, or pleaded *nolo contendere* to, any felony or any misdemeanor, except minor traffic offenses? .... Yes____ No____ [

53. Have you ever been a principal or employee of any firm, corporation or association which, while you were associated with it, was convicted of, or pleaded *nolo contendere* to, any felony or misdemeanor? .... Yes____ No____ [

54. Are you currently the subject of an unsatisfied judgement or lien? .... Yes____ No____ [

THE FOLLOWING SHOULD BE READ VERY CAREFULLY BY THE APPLICANT

1. I hereby certify that I have read and understand the foregoing statements and that my responses are true and complete to the best of my knowledge.

2. To induce the agency, jurisdiction or organization with or to which I am filing or submitting this application to receive and consider it:
    A. I agree that any decision of the agency, jurisdiction or organization as to the results of any examination(s) that I may be required to pass will be accepted by me as final;
    B. (1) I understand that I am not authorized to sell, or offer for sale, any securities until I have received my license or registration certificate or an official notification of its effective date;
        (2) I understand that I am to sell only those securities authorized by my employer.
    C. I agree to abide by the Statute(s), Constitution(s), Rules and By-Laws as any of the foregoing are amended from time to time of the agency, jurisdiction or organization with or to which I am filing or submitting this application;
    D. If I shall violate or be charged with the violation or possible violation of any Statute, Rule, Constitution or By-Law of any agency, jurisdiction or organization with or to which I am filing or submitting this application, I agree to be subject to and abide by the penalties of the Statute(s), Constitution(s), Rules and By-Laws of such agency, jurisdiction or organization.

3. Further, and in consideration of the securities or commodities self-regulatory organization receiving and considering this application, I submit myself to the jurisdiction of such organization(s).

4. I, _____, the undersigned applicant do solemnly swear that the answers to the above questions and the statements herein made are true, and that I have not herein made any statement which is at this time and in the light of the circumstances under which it is made, false or misleading in any material respect.

5. I, the undersigned, for the purpose of complying with the laws of the State of _____ relating to either the registration or sale of securities or commodities, hereby irrevocably appoint the administrator, or such other person designated by law, and the successors in such office, my attorney in said State upon whom may be served any notice, process or pleading in any action or proceeding against me arising out of or in connection with the offer or sale of securities or commodities, or out of the violation or alleged violation of the aforesaid laws of said State; and I do hereby consent that any such action or proceeding against me may be commenced in any court of competent jurisdiction and proper venue within said State by service of process upon said appointee with the same effect as if I was a resident in said State and had lawfully been served with process in said State. It is requested that a copy of any notice, process or pleading served hereunder be mailed to me at my residence.

Date _____   Signature of Applicant _____

Date _____   Signature of Witness _____

(Witness must be either a partner of the firm, officer of the corporation, branch office manager, or authorized employee. Please indicate which).

(NOTARIZATION OF APPLICANT'S SIGNATURE)

STATE OF _____ \
                                    } ss:
County _____ /

Subscribed and sworn before me this _____ day of _____ A.D., 19____

_____ Notary Public

My commission expires _____ County of _____ State of _____

378

FORM U-4
AD-G-1

NEW YORK STOCK EXCHANGE, INC.

AGREEMENT

MUST BE COMPLETED BY ALL REGISTERED REPRESENTATIVES, BRANCH OFFICE MANAGERS AND OFFICERS

hereby certify that I have read and understand the foregoing statements and that each of my responses thereto is true and complete, and that the responses in any and all prior applications filed with the New York Stock Exchange, Inc. were true and complete. In consideration of the New York Stock Exchange, Inc.'s receiving and considering my application:

(a) I authorize and request any and all of my former employers and any other person to furnish to the Exchange, *or any agent acting on its behalf,* any information they may have concerning my credit worthiness, character, ability, business activities, *general reputation, mode of living and personal characteristics,* together with, in the case of former employers, a history of my employment by them and the reasons for the termination thereof. *Moreover,* I hereby release each such employer and each such other person from any and all liability of whatsoever nature by reason of furnishing such information to the Exchange *or any agent acting on its behalf.*

Further, I recognize that I will be the subject of an investigative consumer report ordered by the Exchange, and that I have the right to request complete and accurate disclosure by the Exchange of the nature and scope of the investigation requested.

(b) I authorize the New York Stock Exchange, Inc. to make available to any prospective employer, or to any Federal, State or Municipal agency, any information it may have concerning me, and I hereby release the New York Stock Exchange, Inc. from any and all liability of whatsoever nature by reason of furnishing such information.

(c) I agree that the decision of the New York Stock Exchange, Inc. as to the results of any examinations it may require me to take will be accepted by me as final, *and that I shall be subject to the penalties provided for under Rule 345 (d) of the Board of Directors, as from time to time amended,* if, in the opinion of the Exchange, I have

1) violated any provision of the Constitution or of any rule adopted by the Board of Directors;
2) violated any of my agreements with the Exchange;
3) made any misstatements to the Exchange; or
4) been guilty of (i) conduct inconsistent with just and equitable principles of trade, (ii) acts detrimental to the interest or welfare of the Exchange, or (iii) conduct contrary to an established practice of the Exchange.

(d) I have read the Constitution and Rules of the Board of Directors of the New York Stock Exchange, Inc. and, if approved, I hereby pledge myself to abide by the Constitution and Rules of the Board of Directors of the New York Stock Exchange, Inc. as the same have been or shall be from time to time amended, and by all rules and regulations adopted pursuant to the Constitution, and by all practices of the Exchange.

Further, and in consideration of the New York Stock Exchange, Inc.'s approving my application, I submit myself to the jurisdiction of such Exchange, and I agree as follows:

(a) That I will not guarantee to my employer or to any other creditor carrying a customer's account, the payment of the debit balance in such account, without the prior written consent of the Exchange.

(b) That I will not guarantee any customer against loss in her/his account or in any way represent to any customer that I or my employer will guarantee the customer against such losses.

(c) That I will not take or receive, directly or indirectly, a share in the profits of any customer's account, or share in any losses sustained in any such account.

(d) That I will not make a cash or margin transaction or maintain a cash or margin account in securities or commodities, or have any direct or indirect financial interest in such a transaction or account, except with a member organization or with a bank. I understand and agree that no such transaction may be effected and no such account may be maintained without the prior consent of my employer, and that except for Monthly Investment Plan transactions such employer must receive promptly, directly from the carrying member organization or bank, duplicate copies of all confirmations and statements relating to such transactions or account. I further understand and agree that I shall receive no compensation for commissions or profits earned on any transaction or account in which I have a direct or indirect financial interest, except with the approval of my employer and in accordance with the rules of the Exchange.

(e) That I will not rebate, directly or indirectly, to any person, firm or corporation any part of the compensation I receive as a registered employee, and I will not pay such compensation, or any part thereof, directly or indirectly, to any person, firm or corporation, as a bonus, commission, fee or other consideration, for business sought or procured for me or for any member or member organization of the Exchange.

(f) That at any time, upon the request of Regulation and Surveillance, or of any Committee or Department of the New York Stock Exchange, Inc., I will appear before such Committee or Department and give evidence upon any subject under investigation by such Committee or Department, and that I will produce, upon request of the Exchange, all of my records or documents relative to any inquiry being made by the Exchange.

(g) I understand that any changes in compensation in any form, or additional compensation in any form, may be subject to disapproval by the New York Stock Exchange, Inc., and that I may not be compensated for business done by or through my employer after the termination of my employment, except as may be permitted by the Exchange.

(h) I agree that I will not take, accept or receive, directly or indirectly, from any person, firm, corporation or association, other than my employer, compensation of any nature, as a bonus, commission, fee, gratuity or other consideration, in connection with any securities or commodities transaction or transactions, except with the prior written consent of the Exchange.

(i) I will notify my member organization and Regulation and Surveillance promptly if, during the tenure of my employment I become the subject of: any investigation or proceeding by any governmental or securities industry self-regulatory body; a refusal of registration, injunction, censure, suspension, expulsion or other disciplinary action by any governmental or securities industry self-regulatory body; a major complaint by a customer of a member organization or by a broker-dealer in securities; a disciplinary action by a member organization; any litigation or arbitration alleging my violation of any agreement with or provision of any securities industry self-regulatory body's, constitution, by-laws, or rules or any securities law or regulation; or any bankruptcy or contempt proceeding, cease and desist order, injunction or civil judgment as party defendant; or any arrest, summons, arraignment, indictment, or conviction for a criminal offense (other than minor traffic violations); or any material allegation that I have conducted myself in a way which may be inconsistent with just and equitable principles of trade, or detrimental to the interest and welfare of the Exchange, or contrary to an established practice of the Exchange; or if I violate any provision of the Exchange Constitution or of any rule adopted by the Board of Directors or of any securities law or regulation or of any agreement with the Exchange.

(j) I agree that any controversy between me and any member or member organization or affiliate or subsidiary thereof arising out of my employment or the termination of my employment shall be settled by arbitration at the instance of any such party in accordance with the arbitration procedure prescribed in the Constitution and Rules then obtaining of the New York Stock Exchange, Inc.

(k) If the Exchange, during the period of one year immediately following receipt by the Exchange of written notice of the termination of my employment gives me written notice that the Exchange is making inquiry into any specified matter or matters occurring prior to termination of such employment, I agree that I will thereafter, comply with any request of the Exchange for me to appear and testify, submit records, respond to written requests, attend hearings, and accept disciplinary charges or penalties with respect to the matter or matters specified in such notice in every respect in conformance with the Constitution, Rules and practices of the *Exchange in the same manner* and to the same extent as required to do if I had remained an employee. If I refuse to accept such written notice or, having been given such notice, refuse or fail to comply with any such request of the Exchange, I agree that such refusal or failure may, in the discretion of the Exchange, act as a bar to future Exchange approval of my employment until such time as the Exchange has completed investigation into the matter or matters specified in such notice; has determined a penalty, if any, to be imposed against me; and until the penalty, if any, has been carried out.

_____   _____

(Date)   (Signature of Candidate)

Witness _____

(Witness must be either a partner of the firm, officer of the corporation, branch office manager, or authorized employee. Please indicate which.)

of the state in which those persons are employed as well as with each state of domicile for customers whose business will be solicited. Some of those states also require an examination designed to test the applicant on that state's securities laws.

See also New York Stock Exchange, Inc.

Registration Requirement for Securities. *See* Securities Exchange Act of 1934 (Section 12).

Registration Statement. Unless grounds for exempting the security can be established, an offering of securities to the public requires the filing of a registration statement with the SEC before the offering commences. The registration statement includes all pertinent information and documents relative to the affairs of the issuing company and to the offering in particular. The SEC examines the registration statement for at least twenty days, trying to determine whether there are obvious omissions or misrepresentations of the material facts.

The Securities Act of 1933 attempts to protect the public against issuance of fraudulent securities by requiring issuers or distributors of securities to furnish potential purchasers with pertinent and accurate information regarding the underlying company. Accordingly, purchasers are then able to make informed decisions on whether to invest their money.

This law is, therefore, applicable to investment companies of all three classifications and broaches a unique problem for mutual funds in particular. Prior to the issuance of face-amount certificates, unit investment trust certificates, or management company shares, a registration statement must be filed with the Securities and Exchange Commission. This statement remains with the commission for at least twenty days while it investigates the essential facts. No offering may commence until the SEC allows the registration statement to become effective. Of course, effectiveness of a registration statement

does *not* signify SEC approval of the issue, nor does it even guarantee adequacy or accuracy of the information in that document. Investors who lose money as a result of a purchase and sale transaction must seek satisfaction and restitution through litigation. SEC rules, however, insist that purchasers be furnished with a prospectus (a condensation of the registration statement prior to solicitation of an order or at worst no later than with confirmation of purchase. If the latter event prevails, the investor has a reasonable period of time to consider the information in the prospectus and to cancel the transaction at no personal loss. A mutual fund, despite all its unique sales and distribution characteristics, still must comply with federal law. But a mutual fund does require a special approach as a result of its continuous offering and unlimited capitalization.

Although its capitalization may be virtually unlimited, the fund's effective registration statement permits an offering of only a specified number of shares. Thus, when the maximum amount is approached, a new registration statement must be issued and distributed. It is not inconceivable for a fund to postpone offering its shares when its registration is delayed at the SEC. Even while operating under an effective statement, the fund is obliged to update the essential information in its statement and prospectus *at least* once every sixteen months. If material changes occur in the interim, an amended statement must be filed at that time. If a statement is not filed promptly, the fund risks exposing itself and its underwriter to liability for recovery of losses sustained by investors who used the inadequate or inaccurate prospectus to decide on their commitment.

See also Deficiency Letter; Effective Date; Securities Act of 1933.

Reg T Call. *See* Initial Margin Requirement.

Reg T Excess. If the value of the collateral in a customer's margin account appreciates above current federal requirements, under certain conditions the broker can extend the customer additional credit. This credit is commonly referred to as *Reg T excess*. The customer may either withdraw the excess from the account as cash or use it to meet the requirements on additional purchases. In addition to being subject to the rules and requirements of Regulation T, a customer's margin account is also subject to those of the various securities exchanges as well as the NASD and the broker's own house policies and requirements. For the most part, stock exchange and NASD requirements are designed for the protection of the broker who has extended the credit.

See also Exempt Security (Margin Trading); Margin Account; Regulation T; Special Memorandum Account.

Regular-Way Contract (Sale). The contract most frequently used in the industry is known as a *regular-way contract*. Its settlement date provisions include the following:

1. On transactions involving corporate, state, municipal securities, and most federal agency issues, delivery of the certificates to the purchaser's office is due on the fifth business day after the date of the trade. A customer must wait until settlement date to withdraw the proceeds. (Although trade details for exempted securities are not specifically prescribed in the Uniform Practice Code, custom within the industry has established the settlement dates for these contracts as the fifth business day after the day of the trade.)

2. On transactions involving U.S. government obligations, delivery of the certificates to the purchaser's office is due on the first business day after the date of the trade. (Delivery dates vary considerably between dealers in odd lots of U.S. government securities, with settlements called for anywhere from the first to the fifth business day after the date of the trade. An odd lot is generally considered to be less than $100,000 face value of certificates.)

An overwhelming number of stock exchange bond contracts are executed regular way. But "regular way" has a different meaning for corporate or municipal bonds and U.S. government obligations.

Corporate and municipal transactions executed regular way require settlement between participating firms on the fifth business day after trade date. (Without benefit of an intervening holiday, this is the same as the seventh calendar date after the trade date; that is, Monday to Monday, Tuesday to Tuesday, Wednesday to Wednesday, and so forth. The presence of an exchange-recognized holiday extends settlement date by the holiday period itself.) Regular way for U.S. government bonds calls for settlement on the next business day after the trade date.

See also Cash Contract; Corporate Bond Transaction; Delivery Dates; Delivery-Option Contract; Next-Day Contract; Rules of Fair Practice (Section 1); Seller's-Option Contract; When-Issued/When-Distributed Contract.

Regulation A Security. *See* Exempted Security.

Regulation D Security. *See* Exempted Security.

Regulation G. This federal margin regulation applies to all lenders other than broker/dealers and banks.

See also Regulation T.

Regulation T. The amount a customer must deposit in a margin account and, conversely, the amount the broker may lend is prescribed by the Board of Governors of the Federal Reserve Board by authority of the Securities Exchange Act of 1934 under Regulation T. Regulation T applies to all broker/dealers and contains the major federal margin regulations governs the extending of credit. (Regulations U is the margin regulation that applies to banks. Regulation G applies to all lenders other than broker/dealers and banks. Regulation X places the burden of responsibility regarding credit for securities on the borrower as well as the lender.)

See also Initial Margin Requirement; Margin Account; Reg T Excess.

Regulation U. This federal margin regulation applies to banks.

See also Regulation T.

Regulation X. This federal margin regulation places the burden of responsibility regarding credit for securities on the borrower as well as the lender.

Rehypothecation. A broker's practice of pledging customer securities from a margin account to serve as collateral at a bank in order to finance the customer's debit balance in this account is called rehypothecation.

See also Hypothecation of Customer Securities; Segregation.

Rejections and Reclamations. If a selling broker/dealer attempts to deliver an unnegotiable security, or one in the wrong denomination, the purchasing firm can reject delivery and refuse to make payment without prejudice to its rights in the transaction. The securities must be returned to the seller with an NASD Rejection Form explaining the reason for denial. If the securities have already been accepted and paid for when an irregularity is discovered, the Uniform Practice Code permits either party to the transaction to reclaim (recover) its certificates or money, as the case may be. That is, the selling firm may reclaim its certificates and return the money, or the buyer can return the certificates and reclaim its money.

There are definite time limits within which such claims must be made. Minor irregularities, such as those that affect only the money value of

the security or the contract, require reclamation to be made within fifteen days from the day of delivery. But major irregularities, such as in transactions involving wrong, duplicate, or stolen securities or overdeliveries of securities as well as refusal of transfer by the company's agent, allow reclamation to be made as long as thirty months after the day of original delivery.

See also Good Delivery of Securities; Close-Out Procedures.

Related Persons. *See* Rules of Fair Practice (Section 36).

Release Letter. *See* Municipal Securities (Organization of the Syndicate).

Reorganization Department. *See* Broker/Dealer Organization.

Repo (Repurchase Agreement). (1) A Federal Open Market Committee arranges with a dealer in which it contracts to purchase a government or agency security at a fixed price, with provision for its resale at the same price at a rate of interest determined competitively. It is used by dealers in government and municipal securities to reduce carrying costs. This transaction is not legal for nonexempt securities.

See also Federal Reserve System; Manipulation of Security Prices and Deceptive Devices.

(2) A method of financing inventory positions by sale to a nonbank institution with the agreement to buy the position back.

Reportable Position. *See* Regulation of Options Trading.

Reporting Requirements of the SEC.

Periodical and Other Reports. Corporations registered with the SEC under Section 12 of the Securities and Exchange Act of 1934 must file with the commission notice of change in financial information at set intervals, as well as from time to time when material events occur. These reports then become readily available for public inspection. Some of these documents and their SEC form numbers are: (1) Form 6K: a report of information by private foreign corporations after public announcement abroad; (2) Form 8K: a report of current information, filed the month following a material event in the corporation's affairs; (3) Form 10K: an important annual report, with certified financial statements attached; (4) Form 10Q: a quarterly report required of most registered companies; and (5) Form NIR: an annual report of management investment companies in lieu of filing Form 10K.

Furthermore, anyone who acquires 5% or more of any class of equity security (including common stock, preferred stock, warrants, rights to subscribe to common stock, and convertible bonds) including those issued by insurance or investment companies, must promptly notify (1) the issuing corporation, (2) the stock exchanges where, and if, listed, and (3) the SEC of (1) the title of the security and its issuer; (2) the identity and background of the beneficial owner; (3) the source and amount of funds used for the purchase of the security; (4) the purpose of the transaction and the total investment interest, including options, held by the beneficial owner; (5) the terms of any contract, arrangement, or understanding with respect to those securities, by the beneficial owner; and (6) the names of, and the amount of compensation paid to, those people who solicit stockholders in behalf of the beneficial owner. Material changes in any of these facts must also be reported to the SEC and the other aforementioned regulatory bodies.

This section of the Act now also carries SEC reporting requirements for institutional investment managers who have discretion in accounts holding $100 million of aggregate market value in equity securities on the last day of the month in any of the preceding twelve months.

The report, which when filed with the SEC becomes public information, includes quantity, description, CUSIP number and market value of each equity issue in the account. (CUSIP is an acronym for Committee on Uniform Security Identification Procedures. The CUSIP number is an exclusive identification number for virtually all publicly owned stock and bond certificates.) If any transaction, or series of transactions in the same issue, during the reporting period has a market value of at least $500,000, the notification must also cite (1) trade and settlement date(s) for the transaction(s); (2) whether the transaction was a purchase or sale; and (3) the price(s) and quantity per share at which each transaction was effected.

Reports of Officers, Directors, and Principal Stockholders. All officers, directors, and people who hold 10% of an equity security of an issuer registered under Section 12 of the Securities Exchange Act of 1934 must file a statement of beneficial ownership of those securities with (1) the SEC (Form 3); and (2) a national securities exchange, if it is registered there.

Equity securities subject to the rules of this section include any class of stock, warrant, right, convertible bond, or option to acquire an issue (as owner or writer of this privilege). Subsequent changes in beneficial ownership must be reported to the aforementioned authorities within ten days after the month in which the change occurs (Form 4).

With few exceptions, officers, directors, and holders of 10% or more of a given class of equity security may not retain a profit realized through purchase and sale or sale and repurchase within a six-month time period.

Example:

| Bought 100 XYZ at | 40 | on | April 4, 1980 |
| Sold long 100 XYZ at | 50 | on | September 10, 1980 |

10-point "profit" 5 months and 6 days

or

Sold long 100 XYZ at 50 on March 13, 1980   (versus
                                         stock
                                    acquired
                                      years
                                      ago)

(Repurchased
100 XYZ at 45) on April 25, 1980
          5-point "profit" 1 month and 12 days

An issuer can recover any profits insiders may have realized through such short-term maneuvers. In these cases, either the corporation itself or any of its stockholders can initiate a lawsuit. Legal grounds are founded on the supposition that the insider benefited from nonpublic knowledge of corporate affairs because of his or her important relationship to the company.

In a similar vein, Section 16 of the 1934 Act also prohibits any officer, director, or principal stockholder of an equity security from (1) selling shares in this issue short; or (2) selling shares long, unless the certificates are delivered to satisfy the sale within twenty calendar days after the trade.

Books, Records, and Reports of Brokers and Dealers. An important disclosure on the need for each broker/dealer to maintain and preserve specific books, records, correspondence, and memoranda appears in Section 17 of the Securities Exchange Act of 1934 and its rules. Original copies of information may be microfilmed immediately if proper facilities are available for enlargement and facsimile reproduction. Such material must be indexed to permit easy location of a particular document. For security reasons, microfilm duplicates must be stored in a location different than that of the original.

1. Every broker/dealer must preserve for the life of the enterprise all partnership articles and agreements. An incorporated concern must preserve its charter, bylaws, minute books, stock certificates books, and corporate resolutions for the same length of time.

2. Every broker/dealer must preserve for at least six years after closing a customer account all records and documents relating to the terms and conditions for maintaining that account.

3. The following records must be preserved for at least six years, the first two years in an easily accessible place:

a. Daily trade blotters, showing (1) purchases and sales of securities; (2) receipt and deliveries of securities (including certificate numbers); and (3) receipts and disbursements of money.

b. Ledger records, showing the firm's (1) assets and liabilities; (2) income and expenses; (3) capital accounts.

c. Ledger accounts, showing (1) each cash and margin account of customers, principals of the firm, and of the firm itself; and (2) all trading and monetary activity related to these accounts.

d. Securities records, showing (1) long and short positions by security, reflecting account designations and titles; and (2) the physical location of all such security positions.

4. The following detail records must be preserved for at least three years, the first two years in an easily accessible place:

a. A record reflecting (1) securities failed to receive and failed to deliver; (2) securities in the process of name or denomination transfer; (3) securities borrowed and securities loaned; (4) dividends and interest receivable and dividends and interest payable; and (5) monies borrowed and monies loaned.

b. A memorandum of each customer order given or received, whether executed or unexecuted. Such records must contain (1) the terms and conditions and any special instructions pertaining to the order; and (2) times of entry, execution, and/or cancellation. Similar information is required for principal orders and executions on registered stock exchanges in the United States.

c. A separate record showing all purchases and sales in the brokerage firm's own account.

d. Copies of confirmations and notices of debits and credits for customers and officials of the firm.

e. An individual record of cash and margin accounts showing the name and address of the beneficial owner. For margin accounts, the customer's signature on a hypothecation agreement must also be kept on file.

f. A record of all securities options owned by, or guaranteed by, that broker/dealer organization.

g. All checkbooks, bank statements, cancelled checks, and cash reconciliations.

h. Copies of all bills payable and bills receivable relating to the business of the broker/dealer.

i. Originals of all communications received and copies of all communications sent, including interoffice and intraoffice memoranda relating to the brokerage business.

j. All internal audit working papers, trial balances, computations of net capital, aggregate indebtedness, financial statements, and branch office reconciliations.

k. All guarantees of accounts, powers of attorney, and corporate resolutions for customer accounts.

l. Copies of all written agreements relating to the broker/dealer's business.

5. Each broker/dealer must preserve for at least three years after termination of employment of any principal or other employee an application or questionnaire completed when originally hired. The form must include the following information: (a) name, address, social security number, and starting date of employment; (b) date of birth; (c) educational institutions attended and whether graduated therefrom; (d) a complete statement of business connections within the preceding ten years, including reasons for termination and whether the position was on a part-time or full-time basis; (e) a record of disciplinary actions imposed by regulatory agencies or national securities exchanges or associations, and the reasons for such actions; (f) a record of denials, sanctions, expulsion, or revocation of registration while the applicant was employed by a broker/dealer organization in any capacity; (g) a record of temporary or permanent injunctions issued against the applicant or against any broker/dealer organization with whom he or she was employed at the time; (h) a detailed statement of arrests, indictments, or convictions for felonies or misdemeanors (other than minor traffic offenses); (i) disclosure of other names by which the applicant has been known or has used in his or her lifetime.

6. The principals of a broker/dealer organization that has terminated its business are still responsible for retention of the aforementioned records and documents for the stipulated time period.

Section 17 is also oriented toward submission of periodic reports to the SEC by brokers and dealers. In this respect, prompt notification is required when stabilization occurs to facilitate a distribution of securities. Whether these transactions are made by the manager of a group (syndicate) or by an authorized representative, the details of "pegging" (fixing of securities prices) must be brought to the attention of the SEC.

Once every calendar year, each registered broker/dealer is obliged to file with the SEC a certified statement of its financial condition prepared by an independent public accountant. Each securities concern must also:

1. Report its income and expenses for the preceding calendar year. NASD and most ex-

change members are exempted from the SEC requirement because they report such information to the association or exchange instead.

2. Report its financial status with Securities Investors Protection Corporation (SIPC) in terms of meeting its annual assessment obligation.

3. Report its net capital and aggregate indebtedness as defined by Rule 15c3-1.

4. Report noncompliance with the capital rules to which it is subject. This communication to the SEC is a telegraphic notice of deficiency, which must be followed by a detailed, hard-copy report within 24 hours.

5. Report over-the-counter market-making activities in securities registered on a national securities exchange. Participants in this third market report to the SEC quarterly. However, if it intends to use special credit privileges to finance these activities, the firm must also file a notice with the SEC five days prior to applying for such credit.

6. Report its active status and withdrawal as a market-maker in over-the-counter securities deemed eligible for margin from a list published periodically by the Federal Reserve Board. However, no report is necessary unless the firm intends to use special financing privileges available for registered market-makers.

7. Report its use of special credit privileges available for financing dealer transactions of significant size. A broker/dealer registered with the SEC as a *block positioner* (a securities firm registered with the SEC that has net capital of at least $1 million and occasionally acts as principal in facilitating customer transactions) may obtain unrestricted securities credit on a block transaction in which it acted as principal for as long as twenty business days. This rule was instituted to accommodate a customer's sale of an issue with a current market value of at least $200,000 in one transaction or in a series of transactions at about the same time.

8. Report to its customers semiannually about its own financial condition and its position with respect to its net capital requirement. Specifically the firm must send (a) an unconsolidated balance sheet with appropriate footnotes including the nature, amount, and maturities of subordinated capital in the firm; (b) a statement of its net capital and required net capital, including a ratio of capital to aggregate indebtedness and its required ratio of capital to aggregate indebtedness; and (c) a statement of material inadequacies discovered by the firm's independent accountants regarding internal record-keeping controls or securities safekeeping procedures.

National securities exchanges and associations have not been absolved from SEC reporting requirements. These institutions must file notices of proposed rule changes with the commission, usually at least three weeks prior to their intended adoption. The commission has authority to impose, supplement, alter, suspend, or revoke any rule or change in rules if such action is deemed to be in the public's best interest. The power is officially extended to the SEC under Section 19 of the Securities Exchange Act of 1934.

By amendment to this section of the Act in 1975, Congress determined that a national and uniform system of clearance and settlement of securities transactions would be in the economic interest of investors. Accordingly, it required securities clearing agencies and transfer agents to register with the SEC, thus subjecting them to the SEC's jurisdiction, operating procedures, and reporting requirements. One of the first procedures adopted pursuant to this amendment was security oriented: With very few exceptions every officer, director, partner, or employee of a national securities exchange, broker/dealer, clearing agency, or transfer agent must be fingerprinted. The fingerprints are then submitted to the Attorney General's office in Washington, D.C., for processing and identification purposes. In this manner certain criminal elements may be recognized and weeded out of the industry before they can compromise the public's financial assets.

This law also directs the SEC to use its authority to end the physical movement of securities certificates in connection with settlement of transactions between brokers and dealers. In this regard, the SEC has commenced an active role in coordinating development of securities depositories situated throughout the United States. Such institutions serve to immobilize stock and bond certificates. When connected with each other via computer, they debit or credit securities positions automatically on the centralized ledger record of each participant in a transaction, regardless of which depository actually holds the certificates in behalf of its delivering member.

Reports of the SEC and the Federal Reserve Board. Section 23 of the Securities Exchange Act of 1934 requires both the SEC and the Federal Reserve Board to submit an annual report to Congress summarizing their oversight activities of the previous year. The SEC, in particular, must also report on (1) its progress and recommendations for achieving the goal of a national market system for trading securities; (2) the developmental progress of a national system for clearance and settlement of securities transactions, including the eventual elimination of securities certificates; (3) a summary of the SEC's activities with respect to municipal securities dealers; (4) the realized cumulative effect on competition as well as on fair and orderly market-making on exchanges since fixed commissions were abolished in May 1975; (5) the effects of SEC rulemaking on (a) the viability of small brokers and dealers, (b) its attempts to reduce unnecessary reporting burdens imposed on them, and (c) the extent of its efforts to assure their ·continued participation in U.S. securities markets.

Reregistering Securities. *See* Registrar; Transfer.

Reserve City Bank. This is a large commercial bank whose head office is in a city where there is a Federal Reserve Bank or branch *and* whose net demand deposits exceed $400 million. Banks with demand deposits lower than $400 million have slightly lower requirements, even when headquartered in a Federal Reserve city.

See also Federal Reserve System.

Reserve Requirements. *See* Federal Reserve System.

Resistance. *See* Support and Resistance Levels.

Restricted Account. A restricted account is one in which the equity is less than the current Federal Reserve Board's initial requirement.

Example: Let us illustrate this point with the following account:

LMV = $4,500
Debit balance = $1,800
60% initial requirement

From these figures we calculate the equity to be $2,700 (LMV − Dr). This account is properly margined since the equity of $2,700 equals the Federal Reserve Board's initial requirement of $2,700 (60% × $4,500). If the LMV drops to $4,400, then this account will be restricted. This is so because the new equity of $2,600 ($4,400 − $1,800) is less than the current initial requirement of $2,640 (60% × $4,400) for this new LMV.

Calculating SMA After a Sale in a Restricted Account. According to Regulation T when a sale is made in a restricted margin account, whatever the required margin is on purchases, that is the amount released on the sale.

Example: Current requirements are 50% on purchases; therefore, sales in a restricted margin account will release 50% to the SMA. Amounts larger than 50% will be released only when it is determined that the account is properly margined.

New SMA after a sale =

    either: (1) 50% of proceeds + prior SMA

      or: (2) Equity – margin required

    whichever of the two amounts is larger

The amount released to the SMA may be withdrawn from the account by the customer on trade date. If not withdrawn, it will normally be credited automatically to the customer's SMA.

Normally, no funds may be withdrawn from a restricted account other than the percentage of proceeds resulting from sales transactions as described above. However an important exception is extended to dividend and interest credits paid by corporations on securities held in that account. Regulation T permits the withdrawal by the client of dividends and interest paid by corporations on securities held in a margin account, provided this withdrawal is accomplished within 35 days after the dividend or interest credit is entered in the account in question and provided it was not used in the meantime as margin on a new commitment. Once beyond the 35-day period, Regulation T excess must exist sufficient to cover the withdrawal.

Illustration of a Sale in a Restricted Account. Assume that there is a 60% initial requirement and that customer Richard Johnson's account is as follows:

Long Position

100 shares JCH stock @ 80	= $8,000
100 shares ERH stock @ 70	= $7,000
100 shares RAH stock @ 50	= $5,000

LMV	Equity	SMA	Balance
$20,000	$8,000	$250	$12,000 Dr

Note that customer Johnson's account is now restricted because the equity of $8,000 is less than the current initial margin required of $12,000 (60% × $20,000). Note, too, that there is an SMA of $250. Johnson still can withdraw the $250 SMA from his account even though it is restricted because withdrawal will not reduce the equity below the $2,000 minimum level and will not place his account on a maintenance call.

Let us assume that customer Richard Johnson sells his 100 shares of RAH stock at 50 for proceeds of $5,000. We use the formula for new SMA to arrive at the status of Johnson's account after the sale:

LMV	Equity	SMA	Balance
$15,000	$8,000	$3,250	$7,000 Dr

either

new SMA = (60% × proceeds) + prior SMA
        = (60% × $5,000) + $250
        = $3,000 + $250
        = $3,250

or

new SMA = equity – margin required
        = $8,000 – (60% × $15,000)
        = $8,000 – $9,000
        = –$1,000 (this negative figure indicates that the account is still restricted because equity is less than margin required)

In this calculation the 60% release resulted in a higher SMA ($3,250) than the regular Reg T excess figure (—$1,000). Therefore, we use the $3,250 figure for the new SMA.

Sale in a Restricted Account to Meet a Previous Reg T Call.

Example: Let us illustrate what it takes to meet a Reg T call by selling securities from a restricted long account. The current account of Benjamin Kersh is as follows:

LMV =	$50,000
Balance =	28,000 Dr
Equity =	22,000
SMA =	0

Kersh decides to buy 100 shares of stock "SKY" at $70 each ($7,000) with an initial margin requirement of 60%.

Question: How much in securities must Benjamin Kersh sell to get cash equal to the amount of the Reg T call on stock SKY?

Regulation T requirement is $4,200 (60% x 7,000). Since the sale of a security in a restricted margin account releases what is required, the sale of $7,000 of securities will cover the call. It should be kept in mind that this sale should be made the same day as the purchase.

Withdrawing Stock from a Restricted Account. A customer may withdraw stock from a restricted account provided that cash or other marginable stock is deposited in its place. The customer may deposit cash equal to 50% (which is the current margin requirement) of current market value of the withdrawn stock.

Example: Let us assume that Sherry Shay wishes to withdraw $6,000 worth of stock from her account which is:

$$LMV = \$35,000$$
$$\text{Long balance} = \$20,000 \, Dr$$
$$\text{Equity} = \$15,000$$

Sherry Shay must deposit $3,000 in cash. Let us show the calculation based on the formula:

Cash to be deposited $=$ 50% of stock value withdrawn

Cash to be deposited $=$ 50% $\times$ $6,000
Cash to be deposited $=$ $3,000

Or, the customer may deposit other marginable stock whose loan value equals 50% of the current market value of the withdrawn stock.

Example: Assume that in the foregoing case Sherry Shay wishes to deposit stock rather than cash to replace the $6,000 worth of withdrawn stock. She must deposit other marginable stock worth $6,000.

Therefore, in the event the margin requirements were 70%, and a customer wished to withdraw $6,000 of marginable securities from a restricted margin account, which is:

LMV	$35,000
DR	–$20,000
EQ	= $15,000

The customer must deposit $1,800 or 30% of the market value or the current loan value. If the margin requirements were 80%, the required deposit would be $1,200; at 90%, only $600.

See also Margin Account; Special Memorandum Account.

Retained Earnings (Earned Surplus). This entry in the liabilities section of the balance sheet shows the amount of profit that the company retains in the business after paying any dividends on the common stock. In a sense, retained earnings represent profits that have not yet been paid out to the common stockholders in the form of dividends.

Example: A company is formed by selling a share of common stock at $100 per share to ten different people. The total amount collected is used to purchase goods at wholesale—for subsequent resale. An early balance sheet is as follows:

Assets		*Liabilities*	
Inventory	$1,000		0
		Stockholders' Equity	
		Common stock $100 par	$1,000

At this point, total assets ($1,000 in inventory) equal total liabilities (zero) and stockholders' equity ($1,000). The company then sells the inventory for a total of $2,000 and uses all the cash to purchase still more inventory. The situation is now:

Assets		Liabilities	
Inventory	$2,000		0

Stockholders' Equity

Common stock $100 par	$1,000
Retained Earnings	$1,000

The $1,000 earned profit, over and above its initial investment, appears in the retained earnings account.

The total of $2,000 under stockholders' equity, however, does not mean that the shareholders will receive $20 back for their $10 investments.

Retained earnings are not cash: The profit has already been reinvested in additional inventory. Since the average balance sheet lists many items at other than their liquidation values, the chances of the shareholders' receiving cash equal to the net worth (shareholders' equity) portion of the balance sheet are small. Remember that shareholders' equity represents the amount that the stockholders would receive, if all assets were sold at the values at which they are carried on the balance sheet (book value) and if all liabilities were paid off at their balance sheet figures.

Example: A company is formed through the sale of 1,000 shares of preferred stock at $100 per share and 500,000 shares of common stock at $1 per share. It uses some of the cash received to purchase machinery and raw materials, but it does not pay for all the items in full. Our balance sheet looks like this:

At this early period of the company's development, it has no profits and therefore no retained earnings. But it operates successfully over time and increases its assets by $200,000 through sales and its liabilities by only $50,000. The difference between the value of the newly acquired items and the additional debt—$150,000—represents a "gain" for the company's owners. At least in theory, the stockholders are "worth" $150,000 more, a profit shown as retained earnings. Keep in mind that the $150,000 thus "earned" is spread out among various assets. To realize this sum in cash, the company would have to liquidate some assets.

See also Balance Sheet (Liabilities).

Retiring Debt.

At a Discount. If the corporation's bonds are trading in the open market at a discount, the management may possibly elect to buy them back. Thus they can retire the obligation at a bargain rate rather than pay the holders full par value at maturity.

The Doktabessie Corporation buys $50,000 of its own bonds in the open market for a total of $40,000. The balance sheet changes as follows:

(1) Cash decreases by $40,000. (2) Total current assets also decrease by the same amount. (3) Working capital, quick assets, current ratio, and acid-test (quick asset) ratio all decline because current assets are reduced while current liabilities remain unchanged. (4) Bonds are reduced by $50,000. (5) Stockholders' equity increases by $10,000 because we have reduced as-

Assets		Liabilities	
Cash	$160,000	Accounts payable	$ 50,000
Inventory	+ 85,000		
Total current		*Stockholders' Equity*	
assets	$245,000	Preferred stock $100 par	100,000
Property, plant, and equipment	+ 405,00	Common stock	
Total assets	$650,000	$1 par	+ 500,000
		Total liabilities and stockholders' equity	$ 650,000

sets (cash) by $40,000 and liabilities by $50,000. Thus we gain $10,000, which is reflected in increased net worth. Since the company has paid off a $50,000 debt at a cost of only $40,000, the stockholders have gained!

While the cash picture is not as good as it was and although some ratios have declined, the overall effect is good in that the stockholders' equity increases.

At a Premium. The Doktabessie Corporation elects to retire some of its bonds through the exercise of a call provision. Since the call price is usually above par, the corporation is paying a premium price for the early retirement of part of its debt. Calling $100,000 par value of bonds at a price of 102 ($1,020 per bond) costs the corporation $102,000. The management is eliminating a $100,000 debt (liabilities), but the cost is $102,000 in cash (assets). It pays the extra $2,000 from retained earnings.

Note the effects on the corporation's balance sheet. Cash decreases from $165,000 to $63,000. Current assets, of course, now total only $796,000 and total assets, $1,617,000. On the liabilities side of the balance sheet, the bonds go down from $500,000 to $400,000 and total liabilities from $971,000 to $871,000. Retained earnings reflect the $2,000 "loss" the company suffered and decreases from $290,000 to $288,000. The new balance sheet shows:

Total assets = total liabilities + net worth
(stockholders' equity)
$1,617,000 = 871,000 + 746,000

The cash spent also adversely affects working capital, current ratio, quick assets, and the liquidity (quick asset) ratio.

Return on Equity. An informative measure of management's efficiency is the *return on equity*, derived by dividing net income by shareholders' equity; (shareholders' equity is the sum of preferred stock, common stock, paid-in capital, and retained earnings.)

$$\text{Return on equity} = \frac{\text{net income}}{\text{shareholders' equity}}$$

Example: With net income of $83,750 (income statement) and shareholders' equity of $735,000 (balance sheet), a corporation's return on equity is calculated as follows:

$$\text{Return on equity} = \frac{\$83,750}{\$735,000} = 0.114 \text{ or } 11.4\%$$

See also Income Statement.

Return on Invested Capital. A measure of how well the company is utilizing its entire capitalization is the return on invested capital. [For a review on how the total capitalization figure is derived, *see* Balance Sheet (Capitalization Ratios). The formula is:

$$\text{Return on invested capital} = \frac{\text{net income} + \text{interest on debt}}{\text{total capitalization (invested capital)}}$$

Example: Given a total capitalization figure of $1,235,000 and the information in Roxbury's income statement, you can calculate the interest on bonds ($40,000) by multiplying the coupon rate, 8%, by the total par value, $500,000. After that, simply fill in the formula:

$$\text{Return on invested capital} = \frac{\$83,750 + \$40,000}{\$1,235,000} = 10.0\%$$

See also Income Statement.

Revenue Bonds. This category of bonds has numerous variations. The typical issuer of a revenue bond is an agency, district, or authority created by legislation, and normally not a state. A facility is constructed with the proceeds of the bond issue, and fees, taxes, or tolls are charged for its use. Some examples of revenue bond projects are: toll bridges and turnpikes, hospitals, university dormitories, water, sewer, and electric districts, and ports.

Since the issuer is an agency and not the municipality itself, the failure of the agency, district, or authority to pay the debt service is normally not a legal obligation of the city or county where the facility is located. This feature may make revenue bonds riskier than general obligation bonds and usually necessitates a correspondingly higher coupon rate. Defaults, while not frequent, may occur more often than with GOs. In some cases, especially with respect to sewer and electric system revenue bonds, the underlying municipality or state assumes the liability for the debt service if the revenues of the project prove to be insufficient. Such issues are thus more like general obligation bonds than revenue bonds, and they are referred to as *double-barrelled* issues.

These are usually issued as *term bonds*.

Industrial development bonds (also called industrial revenue bonds) enjoyed a vogue in the 1960s, but their further issuance has been drastically curtailed by legislation. An authority created by a municipality would issue a tax-exempt bond, construct a factory with the proceeds of the bond issue, and then enter into a long-term lease agreement with an industrial corporation. The leasehold payments ("rent") would then be passed through the authority to the bondholders as tax-exempt income. In effect, the corporation constructed a new plant at municipal borrowing rates, which are lower than corporate borrowing rates due to the tax-free nature of the interest income. Smaller issues (below $10,000,000) may still be offered, and those already outstanding in the secondary market are not affected. However, new issues are essentially restricted to those that improve civic services, such as airports, harbors, or mass transit. Pollution control facilities for corporations may also be constructed through the issuance of industrial development bonds. The security behind any industrial revenue or development bond is the *net lease* entered into by the corporation and the issuer.

See also Municipal Securities.

Right of Accumulation. This privilege, offered by some investment companies, allows the investor to include the total market value of shares already owned in calculating sales charges when a new investment is made in additional shares.

See also Sales Load.

Riskless Transaction. *See* Simultaneous Transactions.

Round Lot. The unit of trading in most stock, rights, or warrants traded on the NYSE is set at 100 shares by the Floor Department of the exchange. This unit is known as a *round lot*. Because of their relative inactivity, some stock issues have been assigned trading units in lots of ten shares. In these particular securities, this unit is considered a round lot. Orders for less than round lots (1-99 shares, rights, or warrants, or 1-9 shares, as the cases may be) are called *odd lots*. Because of differences in the way round lots are executed as compared with odd lots, an order for, say 225 shares, must be written on two separate instruction tickets, one for 200 shares and one for 25 shares.

The unit of trading in most bonds is $1,000 face value, although some debt securities are issued and traded in minimum denominations of $5,000.

Rule 144. *See* SEC Rule 144.

Rules of Fair Practice (NASD). The Rules of Fair Practice were adopted by the National Association of Securities Dealers (NASD to prescribe a code of ethics by which its members are obliged to conduct their business. These rules are relevant to all NASD members and to people associated with members, who are accordingly deemed to have the same duties and obligations as the members themselves. They are not applicable to transactions in certain exempted securities however, as defined in Section 3a (12) of the Securities Exchange Act of 1934.

Section 1: Business Conduct of Members. Section 1 of the rules presents a broad directive to members to "observe high standards of commercial honor and just and equitable principles of trade." Its very ambiguity has enabled the board to comment on and interpret virtually every facet of members' business dealings and hold them subject to compliance with this rule. For instance, under Section 1, the NASD Board of Governors has expressed its viewpoint in behalf of the NASD on the following subjects: (1) application for membership to the NASD; (2) registration of personnel with the NASD; (3) NASD markup policies; (4) free-riding and withholding; (5) special deals; (6) selling dividends; (7) breakpoint sales; (8) interpositioning; (9) reviewing corporate financing and underwriting activities; and (10) backing away.

The Board also uses this section to comment on advertising practices. Sales literature, market letters, and recruiting materials are included in this category, with the exception of (1) intrafirm materials; (2) nondescript tombstone-type advertisements; and (3) personal recommendations to clients tailored to their specific requirements (*see* Advertising). Requirements for prompt receipt and delivery of securities as well as for the distribution of proxy materials (*see* Proxy Materials), are also spelled out in Section 1.

Purchases. No buy order may be accepted from a customer for a special cash account unless the customer (1) agrees to make full payment for that purchase on the fifth business day after the transaction, although in any event no later than the seventh business day after the trade date; or (2) establishes a C.O.D. relationship and accepts securities against full payment equal to any execution even though such an execution may be only a portion of a large order. (A partial delivery equal to the amount stated in the confirma-tion must be accepted and paid for by the customer or agent of the customer.)

Long sales. No sell order may be accepted from a customer unless assurance is received that either (1) the security is held by the selling organization in negotiable form, or by another registered broker/dealer or recognized securities depository in deliverable form, with instructions to forward the certificates to the executing firm versus this sale; or (2) the customer agrees to deliver the certificates in negotiable condition within five business days after execution of the order. (Delivery is required within seven business days if the securities are part of an offering distribution by an underwriter.)

In both instances, the registered representative is obliged to note on the order ticket the location of these securities at the time of sale and the customer's willingness and ability to deliver the certificates in proper form within the specific number of business days after execution of the order.

Short sales. No order to sell short may be accepted from a customer unless the member organization is assured of an ability to borrow or "locate" the appropriate certificate prior to execution of the order.

In the event a C.O.D. (cash on delivery) or R.V.P. (receive versus payment) relationship is requested for purchase/sale transactions, that customer must first provide the member with its agent bank or broker's name and address as well as its own account number there. In exchange for a receipt of a trade confirmation on the next business day, the customer must promptly instruct its agent to accept and settle all deliveries, even partial ones in relation to the entire order. Furthermore, if the agent is a member of an SEC-registered securities depository, such as Depository Trust Co. (DTC), with few exceptions these particular transactions must be confirmed, acknowledged, and settled via book entry record keeping through that depository.

All of the major stock exchanges in the

United States, as well as the Municipal Securities Rulemaking Board (MSRB), have adopted similar rules in order to reduce the number of delayed settlement contracts and unnecessary shuffling of securities paper between members.

Section 2: Recommendations to Customers. Section 2 presents the NASD rule regarding (1) the importance of knowing your customer; and (2) the necessity for obtaining and inscribing the essential facts about a customer on a new account report form for firm records.

Implicit in all business relationships is a member's responsibility for determining the customer's financial circumstances and investment objectives in order to provide the customer with fair treatment and intelligent counsel. *Fair treatment* does not include (1) promoting purchases beyond a customer's capabilities; (2) recommending unsuitable, speculative, or low-priced securities; (3) stimulating overtrading (churning) in customer accounts; (4) short-term trading in mutual fund shares (they are considered long-term investment vehicles); (5) using unauthorized and/or improper discretion in customer accounts; (6) establishing fictitious or third-party accounts; (7) making unauthorized use of customer securities or funds; or (8) making private transactions contrary to the member firm's interests or in violation of laws or NASD regulations.

Section 3: Charges for Services Performed. Any fees levied for accommodating customer's related securities activities must be reasonable and not unfairly discriminatory between customers. Such fees may include charges for collecting dividend or interest payments, tendering securities, reregistering certificates, subscriptions for new securities offered via rights or warrants, and so on.

Section 4: Fair Prices and Commissions. In over-the-counter securities transactions, members are directed to establish "fair and reasona-

ble" markups, markdowns, or commissions, as the case may be. This section contains the Board of Governors' interpretation of the 5% guideline policy (*see* Markup and Markdown).

Section 5: Publication of Transactions and Quotations. No member shall publish or circulate any communication about transactions or quotations unless the member is confident that such prices are bona fide for such securities. *Nominal* quotations (subject or nonbinding), if used, must be identified as such. These prices or quotations are generally called appraisals, valuations, approximations, and so on as a means of identification.

In accord with this directive, the NASDAQ Committee has adopted the following policy regarding minimum standards for publication of quotations furnished to newspapers, radio, or television. No security shall be quoted by members in these media unless (1) the market price is at least $1.00 bid; (2) there is sufficient investor interest in the issue in that geographic area; (3) there are enough market-makers to ensure realistic prices; (4) the issuer files notices of dividend declarations with the NASD at least ten days prior to the record date for payment; (5) the issuer promptly discloses significant corporate developments through public media and furnishes its shareholders and the NASD with annual financial statements; and (6) all stock and bond certificates of the corporation are imprinted with CUSIP identification numbers.

Furthermore, only interdealer quotations (the inside market) may be published; these, of course do not include retail markups, markdowns, or commissions. Nominal quotations or quotations without bid prices may not be published for public information under any circumstances.

Section 6: Offers at Stated Prices. A dealer who makes a firm quotation for a security must be prepared to transact business at that price in the normal trading unit for that security. Reneging, or *backing away* from a firm quotation, violates principles of fair practice in the association. The normal trading unit for most issues generally means 100 shares for stock and $5,000 to $10,000 for debt securities ($10,000 for debt securities listed in NASDAQ).

Section 7: Disclosure of Price in Selling Agreements. Underwriting syndicate and selling group agreements must disclose (1) the public offering price; and (2) to whom and under what circumstances any price concessions may be allowed.

Section 8: Securities Taken in Trade. To prevent the practice of overtrading, the NASD requires that a member offering securities through an underwriting syndicate or selling group in which that member participates may purchase other securities in trade (swap) from customers only (1) at fair market prices prevailing at that time; or (2) if the member acts as agent in the transaction (*see* Overtrading).

Section 9: Information Obtained as a Fiduciary. Anyone serving in the capacity of transfer agent, disbursement agent, trustee, and so on cannot make use of information possessed about the ownership of securities in order to induce purchases, sales, or exchanges in those issues, unless requested to do so by the issuing corporation.

Section 10: Influencing or Rewarding Employees of Other Firms. No member or employee or a member organization may give anything of value in excess of $50 per person, per year (cash or merchandise) to someone representing, or associated with, a customer, if that payment or gratuity is related to business accepted from the recipient or the recipient's employer. Bona fide employment contracts for services rendered are not subject to this limitation if (1) a written agreement is established specifying the nature of the employment and the compensation to be paid; and (2) written consent is obtained from the recipient's principal employer.

The member organization must make and retain a separate record of all payments, gratuities, and compensation paid to such persons, as specified under SEC Rule 17a-4.

The payment of continuing commissions to formerly employed registered representatives or to their beneficiaries is not necessarily deemed improper by the Board of Governors of the NASD (*see* Continuing Commissions).

Section 11: Payment Designed to Influence Market Prices. Except for obviously legitimate paid advertising practices, members are prohibited from giving anything of value to someone in order to influence or reward comment in a public medium that may affect the market price of a security.

Section 12: Disclosures on Confirmations. At or before completion of a customer transaction, the NASD member must furnish that customer with a confirmation that states the following facts:

1. Whether the member acted (a) as principal; (b) as the customer's agent; (c) as agent for another person; or (d) as agent for the customer and another person.

2. On principal transactions, whether the NASD member is a bona fide market-maker in that issue. If not, and the member acted as principal in an equity security valued at less than $200,000 in a "riskless" or contemporaneous transaction, the customer's confirmation must disclose the amount of the member's markup or markdown on that transaction.

3. On agency transactions, indication must be made concerning (a) the name of the party on the other side of the trade or the fact that this information will be disclosed on request; and (b) the source and amount of all commissions received or to be received on that transaction by the member organization.

Members who execute orders in listed securities in the third market and act as brokers in such transactions are frequently charged a one-eighth point fee over the going price on the exchange by the market-maker. If that member intends to pay that fee out of the commission to be charged on the transaction, the member must specifically notify the customer of this fact in a legend on the confirmation.

See also Comparison.

Section 13: Disclosure of Control. Broker/dealers who control, or are controlled by or with, the issuer of a particular security must make written disclosure to the customer of this fact before completion of any transaction in that issue.

Section 14: Disclosure of Participation in Primary or Secondary Distributions. A broker/dealer who participates, or has a financial interest, in the primary or secondary distribution of any security offering must give any customer considering purchase of that issue written notification of this fact before completion of the transaction.

Section 15: Discretionary Accounts. Section 15 spells out the restrictions on and authorizations required for the use of discretion in customer accounts (*see* Discretionary Accounts).

Section 16: Offerings at the Market. A member who participates, or has a financial interest, in the primary or secondary distribution of a security *not* trading on a national securities exchange cannot represent that offering as a *market offering* or an offering *at the market* if that member is the only market-maker for that issue. Those "market" terms imply competitive forces of supply and demand, and this is obviously not true if there is only one market-maker.

Section 17: Solicitation of Purchases on an Exchange to Facilitate a Distribution of Securities. A broker/dealer participating, or having a financial interest, in any distribution of a security may not (1) pay compensation in any form to someone for soliciting purchases of any se-

curity of the same issuer on a national securities exchange; (2) offer, sell, or induce a buy order for a security in the process of distribution if that broker/dealer has agreed to compensate someone for soliciting purchases of any security of the same issuer on a national securities exchange; or (3) cause a purchase or a sale of any security of the same issuer on a national securities exchange by paying someone to solicit purchasers for the security.

Ordinary salaries paid to registered employees for their regular duties are not subject to this rule provided that no special inducements are included for performance of the actions listed above.

Section 18: Use of Fraudulent Devices. Manipulative, deceptive, or other fraudulent contrivances (such as boiler room operations and bucket shops) in a securities transaction are contrary to just and equitable principles of trade in the NASD (*see* Manipulation of Prices and Deceptive Devices).

Section 19: Customers, Securities, and Funds. NASD members and employees are forbidden to make improper use of a customer's securities or monies. This directive includes the following prohibitions:

1. A firm may not pledge or lend a customer's securities (a) without written authorizaticn to do so (debit balance with the firm); (b) that are fully paid for, without specific written permission designating the amounts and names of securities to be hypothecated or loaned.

2. It is prohibited to hold fully paid securities in cash accounts or excess collateral securities in margin accounts, unless the securities are (a) identified to show the interest of the customer in each case; and (b) segregated—held in safekeeping, physically separated from securities available for use by the firm in the conduct of its own business (*see* Segregation).

3. No member firm may guarantee any

customer against loss in any securities transaction.

4. No member firm may share in the profits or losses in any customer account, unless (a) prior written approval is granted by a registered principal of the firm; and (b) the sharing is proportionate to the financial contribution of the participant. Accounts maintained for the immediate family of a member or employee of the firm are not subject to this proportionate interest interpretation. (Immediate family means spouse, parents, parents-in-law, children, siblings, or any relative to whose support the member or employee contributes directly or indirectly.)

Section 20: Installment or Partial Payment Sales. Customer transactions in which payments for purchases are to be made in installments or over a period of time are not permitted unless (1) the provisions of Regulation T of the Federal Reserve Board are satisfied; and (2) the member organization has possession or control of the securities while this obligation is outstanding.

Section 21: Books and Records. Each member is charged with the responsibility for keeping and preserving books, records, accounts, memoranda, and correspondence in conformity with all applicable laws, rules, and regulations. The NASD specifically applies this rule to maintenance of the following: (1) account information, including name, address, age, signature of registered representative and registered principal accepting the account for the firm (Discretionary account records must also include customer occupation and the signatures of the persons exercising authority in that account.); (2) a complaint file to include all written statements from, or in behalf of, a customer alleging a grievance involving the activities of the firm or its employees in connection with solicitation, execution, or disposition of the customer's securities or funds. The file should contain all correspondence relating to the complaint as well as to its ultimate resolution.

See also Recordkeeping Requirements of the SEC.

Section 22: Disclosure of Financial Condition. In accordance with SEC Rule 17a-5, broker/dealers are obliged to send their customers (defined as any person for whom, or with whom, the firm (1) has executed a transaction; or (2) holds or owes monies or securities for that month or the month following which the report is to be sent) the following documents at the same time they file the annual Form X-17A-5 with the SEC: (1) an unconsolidated balance sheet including pertinent information about the firm's subordinated loans; (2) a statement showing required net capital and actual net capital as defined by the SEC and with an explanation thereof; (3) a statement of material deficiencies, if the firm's auditors find evidence of inadequate controls; and (4) a statement indicating that part 1 of the latest Form X-17A-5 is available for examination and copying at the firm's main office and at the SEC in Washington, D.C.

Furthermore, every six months the firm must also send its customers the following documents: (1) an uncertified balance sheet; and (2) a statement of the firm's net capital and required net capital computed in accordance with SEC capital rules.

Section 23: Net Prices to Persons Not in the Investment Banking or Securities Business. NASD members may not buy from, nor sell to, a person not in the investment banking or securities business any security at a price that reflects a discount, concession, or other allowance. Members must therefore deal with non-NASD members on a net dollar or net basis price.

Section 24: Selling Concessions. Selling concessions, discounts, or other price allowances are permitted only for services rendered in the distribution of securities and may be granted only to broker/dealers actually engaged in the investment banking or securities business.

Section 25: Dealing with Nonmembers. NASD members must deal with nonmember broker/dealers at the same prices, commissions, fees, terms, and conditions that are accorded to the general public. Ordinarily, this means that members cannot (1) grant special allowances to nonmember broker/dealers that are not available to the general public; or (2) sell any security to nonmember broker/dealer at a price other than that made available at the time to the general public.

However, the provisions of this rule do not apply to (1) foreign broker/dealers, so long as the member secures an agreement from them to abide by this rule if they subsequently reoffer the securities to purchasers in the United States; (2) transactions in certain exempted securities (U.S. government, and so on, as defined in Section 3(a)(12) of the Securities Exchange Act of 1934. (It is important to note that this exception does not extend to municipal securities. That is, no special consideration or price discounts may be given to nonmember broker/dealers in municipal securities transactions. Be aware, however, that banks and municipal securities departments of banks are not defined as "broker/dealers." Consequently, they can and often do get favorable treatment from NASD members in municipal securities activities); and (3) transactions on a national securities exchange with members of that exchange.

Section 26: Investment Companies. Section 26, an extensive and important section, is concerned with members' activities in the offering and distribution of open-end management company shares (mutual funds). Unique relationships often prevail in this area of the securities industry and provide reasons for the admonitions contained in this Rule of Fair Practice (*See* Mutual Fund).

Section 27: Supervision. Members must establish, maintain, and enforce written procedures to enable themselves to supervise the ac-

tivities of registered representatives and other employees properly, thus ensuring compliance with securities laws, regulations, and policies adopted by the NASD. At least one office in the organization must be responsible for reviewing the firm's activities in this respect. That office, called an Office of Supervisory Jurisdiction (OSJ), must be managed by a registered principal. A review of activities must include, but is not limited to, the following: (1) investigation of the qualifications and character of persons applying to the NASD for registration as principal, financial principal, and registered representative; (2) written approval of all transactions effected by and through the member organization (In conjunction with this review is a requirement for a registered principal to be made aware of and approve all private securities transactions of employees. That is, an investment in, or sale of shares in, corporations not publicly owned is subject to review and approval by a member firm principal before any employee may participate in that activity.); (3) initialed approval of all sales-related correspondence leaving the firm each day.

Obviously, comprehensive supervision cannot be effective through only one OSJ in any large, or even medium-sized, firm. These organizations must establish several OSJs, strategically located to conform to the pattern of that firm's activities. To evidence their authority, member organizations must (1) provide written procedures for the OSJ to follow to achieve compliance with the regulations; and (2) accomplish a thorough inspection of each OSJ by a senior registered principal at least once each year.

Section 28: Transactions for Personnel of Another Member. Prior to acceptance of the first order for an employee or principal of another NASD organization, the executing firm must secure written approval to open and maintain an account for that individual from this person's employer or fellow principal. This approval may require (1) prior notice for each transaction or duplicate confirmation of each transaction after the fact; and (2) duplicate monthly statements and advices reflecting all activities in that account.

The employer may waive the right to receive duplicate confirmation and/or statements, but must give written approval for the other firm to establish and maintain the account relationship.

Section 29: Variable Contracts of an Insurance Company. Section 29 presents guidelines for members who market investments in variable contracts. The guidelines are parallel to the NASD's rules for mutual fund activities (*see* Mutual Fund). Variable contracts are defined as investment programs providing values or benefits that may vary according to the performance of securities transactions consummated in a separate account maintained by an insurance company. These programs are sold by the broker/dealer affiliate of an insurance company (or any broker/dealer with a valid license to sell insurance) and are subject to federal securities laws. This broker/dealer, who is also a member of the NASD, is prohibited under this rule of fair practice from levying a sales charge for these contracts that is excessive. This means that the sales charge may not be larger than 8.5% of the investor's total payments into the contract. Or, if the contract provides for a single payment instead of a series of payments, the sales charge may not be greater than that shown in the following scale:

First $25,000 — 8.5% of purchase payment
Next $25,000 — 7.5% of purchase payment
Over $50,000 — 6.5% of purchase payment

Section 30: Margin Accounts. The NASD Board of Governors is empowered to establish minimum initial and maintenance deposits of money required from customers doing business on a cash or margin account basis. These requirements do not conflict with the Federal Reserve Board's Regulation T, but may, in fact, be more stringent if deemed necessary by the NASD Board of Governors. Members of the principal stock exchanges in the United States who are also members of the NASD are exempted from provisions of this rule.

(*See also* Margin Account).

Section 31: Failed-to-Deliver Contracts. No NASD member or registered representative thereof may (1) sell a nonexempted security for a proprietary or personal account (a proprietary account is one in which a broker/dealer or one of its principals has a financial interest); or (2) buy a nonexempted security as a broker for a customer if this member organization has a fail to deliver in that security sixty days old or older if it is a domestic issue, or ninety days old or older if it is a foreign issue. American Depositary Receipts (ADRs) and Canadian securities are classified as domestic issues.

Special consideration by the District Director of the NASD district in which the delinquent member's principal office is situated may be applied for when good cause and exceptional circumstances warrant such an appeal.

Section 32: Blanket Fidelity Bonds. The NASD requires member firms to purchase and maintain fidelity bond insurance to protect the firm against financial loss (*see* Blanket Fidelity Bonds).

Section 33: Securities Options. The term "option" means any put, call, straddle, or other privilege of buying or selling a security without being bound to do so. It does not include any tender offer, registered warrant, subscription right, convertible security, or any other privilege in which the writer is the issuer of the security that may be purchased or sold on the exercise of the option. The NASD Board of Governors is authorized to adopt, alter, amend, supplement, or modify rules relating to transactions in over-the-counter options (conventional options that are not traded on a registered stock exchange) as well as those standardized options displayed on the NASDAQ system.

Section 34: Direct Participation Programs. Intent on curbing abuses in the distribution of programs designed to avoid tax liability on current income, the NASD has formulated this rule. The "programs" refer to investments in (1) oil and gas drilling ventures; (2) real estate syndicates (except REITs, that is, real estate investment trusts); (3) citrus grove development; (4) cattle breeding programs; and (5) other items of similar nature and intent, individually or in combination.

This section creates standards by which these programs must abide to ensure adherence to NASD principles of fairness and reasonableness (*see* Direct Participation Programs).

Section 35: Communications with the Public. In this context, "communications" refers to any advertisement or sales literature written, published, or displayed for customer or public consumption. All such communications must be approved by a registered principal (or his designee) of that member organization prior to use and retained for at least three years. Additional requirements are spelled out for communications pertaining to investment companies and options. The NASD subjects all other advertising and sales literature to routine spot checks (*see* Advertising).

Section 36: Transactions with Related Persons. To codify portions of the Association's "free-riding and withholding" interpretation, this section forbids members engaged in fixed-price corporate securities offerings from allocating those securities to "related persons." A *related person* is defined as a person or account which directly or indirectly owns, is owned by, or is under common ownership with the NASD member.

However, this prohibition will not apply after the offering has terminated if the member had made a bona fide offering to unrelated persons as the fixed price.

Section 37: Operating Rules for ITS/CAES. This section gives the NASD's Board of Governors sufficient authority to adopt rules, regulations, and procedures required for the operation of the Association's Computer Assisted Execution System (CAES). It also provides for that facility's ultimate linkage with the New York Stock Exchange's counterpart, the Intermarket Trading System (ITS).

Section 38: Regulating Member Financial/Operating Difficulties. A member organization is considered to be having financial or operating difficulties if one or more of these parameters exist: (1) excess net capital drops 25% in the preceding two months or 30% or more in the last three months; (2) books and records are not current or maintained in accord with SEC rules; (3) there is noncompliance with SEC capital requirements or with the SEC customer protection rule (15c3-3); (4) transactions are not cleared and settled promptly; and/or (5) if it is a Futures Commission Merchant (FCM), net capital is less than 7% of the funds required to be segregated under the Commodity Exchange Act.

Accordingly, selected measures are prescribed to restrict firm growth, reduce liabilities, and deliver out customer free credit balances and fully paid securities.

Even before those situations develop, remedial action must be undertaken if the following conditions exist for fifteen consecutive business days:

Shall Not Expand Business	Must Reduce Business
1. Net capital is less than 150% of SEC requirement.	Net capital is less than 125% of SEC requirement.
2. Aggregate indebtedness (AI) is more than 1,000% of net capital.	Aggregate indebtedness (AI) is more than 1,200% of net capital.

3. Under the SEC Alternative Capital Rule, net capital is less than 5% of the aggregate debits in Rule 15c3-3.

4. Capital withdrawals scheduled in the next 6 months would create one of the above situations.

Under the SEC Alternative Capital Rule, net capital is less than 4% of the aggregate debits in Rule 15c3-3.

Capital withdrawals scheduled in the next 6 months would create one of the above situations.

Run on a Bank. In this situation, a substantial number of depositors, fearing for the safety of their funds, seek withdrawal of their balances in currency.

S

Safekeeping. This protected condition is maintained as a service by a brokerage firm for its customers' fully paid securities registered in the customers' own names. The practice entails use of vault space to store those certificates until they are withdrawn or sold.

Sale and Lease-Back of Fixed Assets. The Doktabessie Corporation decides to raise cash by selling and leasing back some of its expensive machinery. The corporation sells machinery carried on its balance sheet at $30,000. This sale reduces the property, plant, and equipment from $617,000 to $587,000. At the same time it increases current assets from $898,000 to $928,000 because cash goes up to $195,000.

The effects on the balance sheet depend on whether the sale is made at a price greater or lower than the value at which the assets are carried on the balance sheet. If the sale is made for more than the book value of the asset, the corporation makes a "profit." For sales of assets at prices below their book value, the corporation sustains a "loss." In essence, the company is exchanging a fixed asset (machinery) for a current asset (cash). This shift increases current assets at the expense of fixed assets and thus improves working capital and the current ratio. Since current assets increase while the current liabilities remain the same, the corporation's working capital increases (current assets less current liabilities). Also, the current ratio (current assets divided by current liabilities) also improves.

In short (1) If the asset is sold at a profit, total assets increase, and the increase is also reflected in the retained earnings account. (2) If the asset is sold at a loss, total assets decrease (by the difference between the book value and the sale price of the asset sold). The decrease also lowers the retained earnings account by the same amount.

Sales Literature. *See* SEC Statement of Policy.

Sales Load. The offering price for shares of an open-end management company is usually net asset value per share plus a predetermined sales charge, known in the industry as a *sales load*. The difference between bid and offering prices of an open-end company is thus the dollar amount of sales charge levied in the distribution of those shares.

Example:

$21.25 offering price − $20.00 bid price
= $1.25 sales charge

As practiced by the securities industry, the sales charge is traditionally expressed as a percentage of the offering price; that is, it is a percentage of the price that already includes the sales charge.

Example:

$$\frac{\$\,1.25}{\$21.25} = 5.88\% \text{ (percentage of the offering price)}$$

The sales load may also be shown as a percentage of the bid price, that is, the net asset value. However, this method is not popular in the securities industry. Its numerically higher percentage rate makes it a difficult selling point to use with prospective purchasers. Therefore, when it is used, it is shown side by side with the traditional method of disclosure and is identified as a percentage of the money actually invested in the fund.

Example:

$$\frac{\$\,1.25}{\$20.00} = 6.25\% \text{ (percentage of the bid price)}$$

In any event, the prospectus of the investment company always shows the *maximum charge* that is levied before allowance for certain discounts that are generally available.

To determine the offering price under the traditional approach (sales charge as a percentage of the offering price) is not difficult. Start with knowledge of the percentage sales charge and an ability to determine the net asset value per share. Subtract the decimal equivalent of the sales charge from the decimal equivalent of 100% (1.00). Then divide the result into net asset value per share.

The formula is:

$$\text{Offering price} = \frac{\text{net asset value}}{1.00 - \text{sales charge}}$$

Example: The offering price of the XYZ Fund with net asset value of $20 and with a load of 5.88% is calculated as:

$$\frac{\$20.00}{(1.0000 - .0588)} = \frac{\$20.00}{.9412} = \$21.25 \text{ offering price}$$

Although the sales charge is expressed at the maximum rate, every distributor will reduce this percentage charge for quantity dollar subscribers. The dollar level necessary to qualify for this discount is called a *breakpoint*. In fact, a typical offering schedule provides for several breakpoints to entice substantial deposits. The precise dollar value of these breakpoints varies from company to company, but the first such discount

is generally offered at the $10,000 level. The following table shows a typical graduated schedule of sales charges.

Graduated Schedule of Sales Charges for a Typical Investment Company

Amount Deposited	Bid Price	Percentage of Offering Price
Less than $10,000	9.00%	8.5%
$10,000 but less than $25,000	8.70%	8.0%
$25,000 but less than $50,000	8.10%	7.5%
$50,000 but less than $100,000	6.95%	6.5%
$100,000 but less than $200,000	5.25%	5.0%
$200,000 but less than $400,000	4.15%	4.0%
$400,000 but less than $750,000	2.05%	2.0%
$750,000 but less than $1,000,000	1.00%	1.0%
$1 million or above	0.75%	0.75%

Thus, for a deposit up to $10,000 according to that schedule an investor must pay a sales charge equal to 8.5% of the prevailing offering price. However, if the deposit is $10,000 or more but less than $25,000, the sales charge is levied at the rate of 8% of the current offering price. The greater the number of dollars invested, the smaller the percentage sales charge.

Many people cannot or will not make a single, substantial, lump sum investment to qualify for a discount. However, that does not necessarily prevent them from utilizing these breakpoints advantageously. They can furnish the distributor with a *letter of intent* stating their desire to invest a sufficient sum of money within the next thirteen months and thus be privileged to enjoy the economy of a lower sales charge. That letter of intent is binding only on the distributor of these shares and not on the investor. Even if the charges are increased during that period, the distributor's obligation to honor the original commitment continues. On the other hand, if the charges are reduced or total deposits are more than declared in the letter, the subscribers are granted the benefit of a smaller load.

There is no penalty imposed on investors who fail to live up to the terms of that promise.

They are merely charged the load they would normally have paid based on the money they did invest. Furthermore, if a person's financial circumstances change during this period, making it necessary to convert assets into cash, shares already owned may be sold (redeemed) immediately without penalty.

As a further attraction, the letter of intent may be predated by as much as ninety days to enable the investor to take advantage of a recent large deposit and incorporate it with future deposits. So long as the total time encompassed in the letter does not exceed thirteen months, neither the SEC nor the NASD has any objections. Precedent for the practice of back-dating was established by the life insurance industry and stands to benefit the participant in such an arrangement.

As a means of obtaining lower sales charges, use of a letter of intent is restricted to (1) an individual; (2) an individual collectively with spouse or children under 21 years of age; or (3) a trustee or other fiduciary purchasing securities for a single trust, estate, or fiduciary-type account (including pension plan, profit-sharing plan, and so on, qualified under Section 401 of the Internal Revenue Code).

This limitation was imposed to prevent groups of people from pooling their funds in order to avoid proper payment of the legally established sales fees.

The average investor is most likely to use these breakpoints advantageously when the investment company offers its holders a *right of accumulation*.; With a right of accumulation, consideration is given to the total value of the shares already owned when a new investment is made in additional shares. If the market value of presently held securities is sufficient to qualify under their breakpoint schedule, the distributor allows each new purchase, regardless of amount, to be made under the reduced sales charge. For competitive reasons, this practice is now common. For the exact details relative to

any given investment company, a copy of the offering prospectus should be consulted.

See also Management Company; Net Asset Value per Share.

Excessive Sales Charges. It is improper for an NASD member to participate in a public offering of investment company shares if the public offering price includes a sales charge that is excessive. Although the Investment Company Act of 1940 set a maximum sales charge requirement of 9%, this maximum pertains only to periodic-payment (contractual) plans. It has no bearing on single-payment or voluntary-accumulation plans. Nor does the Statement of Policy address itself to this potential inequity either. It simply requires charts, tables, and sales literature in general to express any sales charge at the highest effective rate. The Statement of Policy assumes that if investors are apprised of the highest current charge, competition among mutual funds will keep that sales load to a minimum.

The NASD, through its Rules of Fair Practice, does not leave the subject open to chance or competition. It fixes a maximum sales charge on any single-payment, voluntary-accumulation, or contractual-plan mutual fund transaction at 8.50% of the offering price. Moreover, that maximum load may be employed by NASD members only if the fund offers its investors all three of the following benefits: (1) dividend reinvestment privileges at net asset value; (2) quantity discounts at breakpoints set forth in Section 26 of the Rules of Fair Practice; (3) rights of accumulation (cumulative quantity discounts) for at least ten years from the date of the shareholder's first purchase.

If one or more of these benefits is denied to investors, the maximum sales charge must be scaled down from 8.50% to as little as 6.25% of the offering price to avoid being deemed excessive. The actual scale depends on which of those benefits, if any, are made available.

See also Contractual Periodic-Payment Plan; Investment Companies; Management Company; SEC Statement of Policy; Voluntary-Accumulation Plan.

Savings Bonds. *See* Nonmarketable Securities; Series EE Bonds; Series HH Bonds.

Savings Deposits. This variation of time deposit is also used by commercial banks as a device for acquiring funds. This popular account has widespread appeal because it usually sets no minimum dollar requirements, and the money can be withdrawn without prior approval from the bank. (Most banks reserve the right to deny withdrawal for up to thirty days, but the right has not been universally exercised since depression days of the 1930s.) Because of this accessibility feature, the rate of interest the bank pays is lower than that paid for an ordinary time deposit. Corporations, associations, business partnerships, or other organizations created for profit-making purposes may not maintain a savings deposit at a commercial bank with a balance greater than $150,000. No balance restriction is imposed on individuals or on religious, educational, fraternal, or eleemosynary (charitable) institutions.

See also Certificate of Deposit; Demand Deposit; Time Deposit.

Scale. When a municipal bond issue comes to the marketplace, the managing underwriter writes a *scale* listing the dollar amount maturing in each year with the appropriate offering price stated as a percentage of par or as a basis price (yield-to-maturity), as the case may be. If the issue's shorter-term yields are higher than its longer-term yields, it is known as an *inverted scale*. If the yields are lower in the shorter-term than in the longer-term maturities, it is known as a *normal scale*.

Scale Orders. Because of uncertainty caused by fluctuation in some volatile issues, customers in-

tent on accumulating (or distributing) a security in volume may enter a series of limit orders at prices *scaled* (1) *down* from the value at which the initial *purchase is contemplated;* or (2) *up* from the value at which the initial *sale is contemplated.*

Example: A customer places a scale order to buy 100 XX at 49, scaled down one point for a total of 400 shares. This means that 100 shares are to be bought at 49, 100 at 48, 100 at 47, and 100 at 46.

Example: A customer places a scale order to sell 100 at 37½, scaled up ¼ point for a total of 600 shares. This means that 100 shares are to be sold at 37½, 100 at 37¾, 100 at 38, 100 at 38¼, 100 at 38½, and 100 at 38¾. (With entry of any limit order it is assumed that the price is *or better*, and thus the execution price could be more favorable than the specified limit.)

The principal advantage of these orders is the creation of an average transaction price that may prove more favorable than a single execution. The principal disadvantage is that the entire order may never be executed unless the stock fluctuates in a wide enough price range.

Scalp. To trade for small gains. It normally involves establishing and liquidating a position quickly, usually within the same day.

Secondary Distribution. This type of distribution is a public offering of stock to stockholders. If listed on the NYSE, a member firm may be employed to facilitate such an offering in an over-the-counter net transaction for a purchase, with prior approval of the exchange. Both member and nonmember broker/dealers can participate in this distribution.

This type of distribution involves an amount of stock so very large that because of its overwhelming size (1) it cannot be absorbed in the regular auction market in a reasonable time at reasonable prices; and (2) a special offering or exchange distribution is not feasible.

It is usually an offering of a security by NYSE and NASD member organizations collectively, acting either as principal or agent over the counter (*off-board*).

Two descriptions and procedures apply to secondary distributions in the securities industry.

1. *Registered secondary distributions* are offerings of stock that require an effective registration statement on file with the SEC before the sale is attempted.

2. *Spot secondary distributions* are offerings of stock that do not require SEC registration statements because they are sales by holders not affiliated with the issuing company. These offerings may literally be attempted on the spot, without delay.

Because a member organization of the NYSE is managing or participating in the distribution of a listed stock over the counter, approval must first be obtained from the Market Surveillance Division of the exchange and from a floor official. The exchange's concern centers on whether the offering can be accomplished successfully on the floor instead of off-board. It considers such factors as (1) the price range and volume for the stock on the trading floor in the preceding thirty days; (2) the current quotation and condition of the specialist's records; and (3) the size of the offering and the degree of interest for that security exhibited in the regular auction market.

When approved, the intended offering is announced over the ticker tape, citing (1) the terms and conditions of the distribution; and (2) whether stabilization or overallotment procedures will be employed. Contingent with approval is a requirement to satisfy all bids on the floor of the exchange that are equal to, or higher than, the secondary offering price. Moreover, if the distribution commences after the NYSE market closes (which is usually the case), the dis-

tributor must make that privilege available for at least thirty minutes afterward.

The ticker tape is also used to announce the completion of this distribution or its continuance from day to day if it cannot be completed on the first day offered. The exchange ticker tape does not show the actual execution of these transactions occurring over the counter because secondary distributions are exempted from the Consolidated Tape System's reporting requirement.

The price of a secondary distribution is a *fixed price*, not higher than the last security transaction on the exchange at the time the offering commences. The purchaser's incentive is that no commission expense is incurred because it is indirectly borne by the seller, unless (1) the offering broker/dealer took a risk position in this issue prior to the distribution; or (2) competitive bids for the stock are required by law, in which cases buyers may be charged a commission.

See also Bid and Offer; Primary Distribution.

Secondary Market. (1) A term referring to the trading of securities not listed on an organized exchange.

(2) A term used to describe the trading of securities other than a new issue.

Secondary Movement. *See* Dow Theory.

Second Market. *See* Over the Counter.

SEC Rule 10b-6. Once an investment banker accepts an invitation from the syndicate manager to participate in an underwriting group (syndicate), it becomes bound by law to comply with SEC Rule 10b-6. Rule 10b-6 is a segment of the SEC's interpretation of Section 10 of the Securities Exchange Act of 1934. The rule decrees it unfair and improper for any issuer, broker, dealer, or underwriter—having agreed to participate in a public offering of securities prior to the effective date of that offering to— (1) bid for that security or a similar security of the same issuer or purchase it for an account in which it has a beneficial interest; or (2) induce anyone to purchase that security or a similar security of the same issuer. (This restriction also applies to any security for the same class or series and to any right or warrant to purchase that security during this time.)

Because there are exceptions to this interesting rule and because some consideration has been given to bona fide broker/dealers in the normal conduct of their business, the following table summarizes acceptable practices. The activities encompass those of the firm as well as its employees and affiliates from the time a public offering is agreed on until the distribution is completed.

Guidelines for Distribution of Securities in Compliance with SEC Rule 10b–6

	Stock Exchange Transactions	Over-the-Counter Transactions
Purchases as principal		
a. until 2 days prior to effective date	Yes	Yes
b. within 2-day period	No	No
Sales as principal		
a. until 2 days prior to effective date	Yes	Yes
b. within 2-day period	No	No
Purchases as agent		
a. buy order is solicited	No	No
b. buy order not solicited	Yes	Yes
Sales as agent (sell order is solicited)		
a. contra buy order is solicited	No	No
b. contra buy order not solicited	Yes	Yes
Sales as agent (sell order not solicited)		
a. contra buy order is solicited	No	No
b. contra buy order is not solicited	Yes	Yes
Publish quotations in the pink sheets or in NASDAQ communication facilities		
a. until 2 days prior to effective date	No	Yes
b. within 2-day period	No	No
Circulate research information or literature	No	No

SEC Rule 15c2-11. This SEC rule regulates submission and representation of quotations of little-known securities whose asset value is questionable.

SEC Rule 15c3-1. This SEC rule (called the "net capital" rule) governs the liquid capital that a broker/dealer must maintain in terms of aggregate indebtedness to customers.

SEC Rule 15c3-3. *See* Bulk Identification/ Segregation.

SEC Rule 144. This Securities and Exchange Commission rule permits sales of restricted securities that are currently subject to terms of an investment letter by affiliated and nonaffiliated persons in modest amounts and in an occasional transaction without first registering them with the SEC. Issuers or underwriters (generally broker/dealers) cannot make use of this privilege; it may be used only by: (1) affiliated and nonaffiliated persons who are not broker/ dealers and who acquired these securities in a private transaction; and by (2) affiliated persons who acquired their securities in the public marketplace.

To qualify for the exemption, the seller and

the issuer must scrupulously abide by the following conditions and guidelines:

1. If the issuing corporation is subject to the reporting requirements of Sections 14 or 15(b) of the Securities Exchange Act of 1934, it must have filed with the SEC all necessary reports due within the past ninety days, as well as its most recent annual report. That this requirement has been met must be verified prior to sale of the securities.

2. If the issuing corporation is not subject to these reporting requirements, it must make publicly available: (a) its exact name and predecessor company, if any; (b) the address of its principal executive offices; (c) the state of incorporation; (d) the title, class, and par or stated value of its securities; (e) the total amount of securities outstanding; (f) the name and address of the transfer agent; (g) the nature of the product, services, facilities, and business of the corporation; (h) the name of the corporation's chief executive officer and the directors on the board; (i) complete financial statements for the most recent period and the two immediately preceding years; and (j) the names of broker/dealers or associated persons affiliated directly or indirectly with the corporation.

3. Securities to be sold under this rule must be fully paid for and owned for at least two years prior to the intended transaction. (There is no holding period for nonrestricted securities owned by affiliated persons, but they too must be fully paid for and fully owned securities.)

4. If securities to be sold under this rule: (a) exceed 500 shares, or (b) aggregate more than $10,000 in value, then a notice of sale must be filed with the SEC at the same time the order is entered. If the security is listed on one or more stock exchanges, it is also necessary to file a concurrent report with the principal exchange where it is traded. Securities not completely distributed within ninety days thereafter require submission of amended notices at the time of further sale.

5. To avoid being classified as a public distribution, thus negating the exemption offered under this rule, the amount of any stock sold by the customer, including sales for persons in concert with that customer within the preceding three months, must not exceed: (a) 1% of the shares outstanding (for over-the-counter securities); or (b) if traded on registered stock exchanges, the greater of (1) 1% of the shares outstanding; or (2) the average weekly volume of that security on all exchanges in the four weeks prior to receipt of this order.

Nonaffiliated persons do not have a volume limitation to contend with. They may sell their entire holdings within the ninety-day effective period for a Form 144 filing without regard to the number of shares outstanding or activity on the stock exchanges. Affiliated persons must, however, abide by these volume requirements for their unregistered shares.

If the order is executed on an exchange, there is no need to advise the buyer that this is unregistered stock. It will automatically become registered after the transaction. But if it is traded over the counter, the market-maker should be advised of the status of the stock because there is a possibility the firm may become a statutory underwriter as a result of this transaction. That possibility may be realized if the market-maker acts as a principal for its own account instead of as an agent for a customer.

6. There must be no solicitation of buy orders in anticipation of this sale. (A dealer firm having made a written bid or offer in the pink sheets or NASDAQ communication system within the past sixty days may be queried as to possible interest. So, too, may customers who indicated a bona fide unsolicited interest in that issue within ten business days prior to receipt of the Rule 144 order.) If the registered representative's employer is a market-maker in that security, the firm may continue its activity in that issue during the distribution only if it published its quotations in an interdealer system on at least twelve of the preceding thirty days, with a gap of

FORM 144

SEC 1147 (4-72)

WASHINGTON, D.C. 20549

NOTICE OF PROPOSED SALE OF SECURITIES
Pursuant to Rule 144 under the Securities Act of 1933

ATTENTION: Transmit for filing 3 copies of this form concurrently with placing an order to execute sale.

1(a) NAME OF ISSUER		(b) IRS IDENT. NO.	(c) S.E.C. FILE NO.	

1(d) ADDRESS OF ISSUER				(e) TELEPHONE NO.
STREET	CITY	STATE	ZIP CODE	AREA CODE / NUMBER

2(a) NAME OF PERSON FOR WHOSE ACCOUNT THE SECURITIES ARE TO BE SOLD	(b) SOCIAL SECURITY NO. OR IRS IDENT. NO.	(c) RELATIONSHIP TO ISSUER	(d) ADDRESS	
			STREET	CITY / STATE / ZIP CODE

INSTRUCTION: The person filing this notice should contact the issuer to obtain the I.R.S. Identification Number and the S.E.C. File Number.

3(a) Title of the Class of Securities To Be Sold	(b) Name and Address of Each Broker Through Whom the Securities Are To Be Offered	SEC USE ONLY Broker-Dealer File Number	(c) Number of Shares or Other Units To Be Sold *(See instr. 3(c))*	(d) Aggregate Market Value *(See instr. 3(d))*	(e) Number of Shares or Other Units Outstanding *(See instr. 3(e))*	(f) Approximate Date of Sale *(See instr. 3(f)) (MO. DAY YR.)*	(g) Name of Each Securities Exchange *(See instr. 3(g))*

INSTRUCTIONS:

1. (a) Name of issuer
   (b) Issuer's I.R.S. Identification Number
   (c) Issuer's S.E.C. file number, if any
   (d) Issuer's address, including zip code
   (e) Issuer's telephone number, including area code

2. (a) Name of person for whose account the securities are to be sold
   (b) Such person's Social Security or I.R.S. identification number
   (c) Such person's relationship to the issuer (e.g., officer, director, 10% stockholder, or member of immediate family of any of the foregoing)
   (d) Such person's address, including zip code

3. (a) Title of the class of securities to be sold
   (b) Name and address of each broker through whom the securities are intended to be sold
   (c) Number of shares or other units to be sold (if debt securities, give the aggregate face amount)
   (d) Aggregate market value of the securities to be sold as of a specified date within 10 days prior to the filing of this notice
   (e) Number of shares or other units of the class outstanding, or if debt securities the face amount thereof outstanding, as shown by the most recent report or statement published by the issuer
   (f) Approximate date on which the securities are to be sold
   (g) Name of each securities exchange, if any, on which the securities are intended to be sold

TABLE I - SECURITIES TO BE SOLD

Furnish the following information with respect to the acquisition of the securities to be sold and with respect to the payment of all or any part of the purchase price or other consideration therefor:

Title of the Class	Date Acquired	Nature of Acquisition Transaction	Name of Person from Whom Acquired	Amount of Securities Acquired	Date of Payment	Nature of Payment

INSTRUCTIONS

1. If the securities were purchased and full payment therefore was not made in cash at the time of purchase, explain in the table or in a note thereto the nature of the consideration given. If the consideration consisted of any note or other obligation, or if payment was made in installments describe the arrangement and state when the note or other obligation was discharged in full or the last installment paid.

2. If within two years after the acquisition of the securities the person for whose account they are to be sold had any short positions, put or other option to dispose of securities referred to in paragraph (d)(3) of Rule 144, furnish full information with respect thereto.

TABLE II - SECURITIES SOLD DURING THE PAST 6 MONTHS

Furnish the following information as to all securities of the issuer sold during the past 6 months by the person for whose account the securities are to be sold.

Name and Address of Seller	Title of Securities Sold	Date of Sale	Amount of Securities Sold	Gross Proceeds

REMARKS:

INSTRUCTIONS:

See the definition of "person" in paragraph (a) of Rule 144. Information is to be given not only as to the person for whose account the securities are to be sold but also as to all other persons included in that definition. In addition, information shall be given as to sales by all persons whose sales are required by paragraph (e) of Rule 144 to be aggregated with sales for the account of the person filing this notice.

ATTENTION:
The Person for whose account the securities to which this notice relates are to be sold hereby represents by signing this notice that he does not know any material adverse information in regard to the current and prospective operations of the Issuer of the securities to be sold which has not been publicly disclosed.

_____
(SIGNATURE)

DATE OF NOTICE

The notice shall be signed by the person for whose account the securities are to be sold. At least one copy of the notice shall be manually signed. Any copies not manually signed shall bear typed or printed signatures.

SEC 1147 (4-7:

no more than four business days between publication of such quotations.

7. A broker/dealer organization distributing these securities for its customers may act in an agency capacity, charging only the customary brokerage commmission for the service rendered. That commission must represent the sole expense borne by the customer to promote the sale of this security.

8. The broker/dealer may purchase the securities for its own account only if it is a market maker in that security or if the quantity involved is of "block-size" is defined as 10,000 or more shares or $200,000 or more in value. It may subsequently solicit buy orders from its customers to dispose of these shares.

SEC Rule 144

1. allows the sale of restricted securities (investment letter) or unrestricted but unregistered securities

2. by affiliated and nonaffiliated persons

3. within any 90-day period

4. but the sale is limited to the greater of
   a. 1% of shares outstanding, or
   b. average weekly volume for previous 4 weeks

5. filing and reporting details are inapplicable for non-affiliated persons holding unregistered or restricted stock for 3 or more years.

SEC Rule 147. Intrastate offerings of securities by resident corporations to purchasers located within those same borders are exempted from registration under the Securities Act of 1933. SEC Rule 147 defines and describes the ways and means by which this exemption may be achieved and maintained. To qualify for the exemption, the issuer, if incorporated, must be chartered under the laws of that state and must also be doing business therein. *Doing business* is defined as deriving 80% of gross revenues from sales in that state, having at least 80% of its assets within that state, and applying at least 80% of the offering proceeds to purchase property or facilitate sales within that state. In addition, the issuer must maintain a principal office in that state. Moreover, not only must purchasers be state residents at the time of the offering, but any resales within the following nine months must also be to qualified residents. To prevent contravention of these procedures, thus forfeiting the exemptive privilege, the issuer is obliged to place a restrictive legend on each of the certificates, to block reregistration of those securities on the books of its transfer agent, and to obtain written representation from each purchaser as to residence.

There are several ways in which issuers can avoid the time, expense, and paperwork associated with a registered securities offering to raise capital. All of them are identified as private placements. SEC Rules 504, 505, 506, 144, and 147 set forth qualifications permitting unregistered distributions by eligible issuers.

An issuer's intrastate offering is exempted from SEC registration if the following requirements are met: (1) 80% of the issuer's business must take place within the state. (2) The issuer must have a principal office in the state. (3) The purchasers must be residents of the state. (4) Resales within nine months must be to state residents. (5) The issuer must put a restrictive legend on certificates, block reregistration, and verify residence of purchaser in writing.

See also Exempted Securities.

An issuer's private placement is exempted from registration if the following requirements are met:

	SEC Rule 504	SEC Rule 505	SEC Rule 506
Aggregate offering value within 12 months	$500,000	$5 million	Unlimited
Number of investors	unlimited	35 nonaccredited unlimited for accredited	
Issuer qualifications	no reporting or investment companies	no investment co. or Reg. A ineligible issuer	None
Limitations on resale	Restricted unless registered in states that require delivery of a disclosure document	Restricted Certificates are legended and reregistration blocked	Restricted

See also SEC Rules 504, 505, 506; Securities Act of 1933.

SEC Rule 415. *See* Shelf Distribution.

SEC Rule 504. Issuers who are not investment companies or subject to the public reporting requirements of the 1934 Securities and Exchange Act have limited assets and/or few shareholders. Those small companies can publicly sell to any number of investors unregistered securities valued up to $500,000 during any twelve-month period. There are no information disclosure requirements under this rule.

See also Exempted Security.

SEC Rule 505. Any issuer who is not an investment company or disqualified from selling under Regulation A can publicly offer unregistered securities valued up to $5 million during any twelve-month period. However, in accord with this rule, that distribution may be made to no more than 35 nonaccredited investors. There is no limitation imposed on the number of accredted investors who may subscribe.

As defined in Regulation D, an *accredited investor* is any of the following: (1) financial institutions such as banks, insurance companies and investment companies, or even employee benefit plans; (2) private business development companies; (3) colleges or university endowment funds as well as other nonprofit organizations with assets of $5 million or more; (4) corporate or partnership "insiders"; (5) purchasers of at least $150,000 of the securities being offered, with the total purchase price not exceeding 20% of the purchaser's net worth at time of sale; (6) individuals with a net worth in excess of $1 million; (7) individuals with income in excess of $200,000 in each of the last two years, with a reasonable expectation of having income in excess of $200,000 in the year of purchase; and (8) any entity 100% owned by accredited investors.

See also Exempted Security.

SEC Rule 506. Any issuer, whether or not a reporting company under the 1934 Exchange Act, entitled to make private placements under Section 4(2) of the 1933 Act, can use the registration exemption available in this rule. The rule permits offerings with no value restrictions in any time period to as many as 35 non-accredited persons. The issuer must reasonably believe, prior to making the distribution, these non-accredited persons individually, or with a purchaser representative, understand the merits and risks of the investment. There is no limitation on the number of accredited persons who may subscribe although the offeree's sophistication in such matters is, nevertheless, relevant.

SEC Statement of Policy. Some officials in the financial community have always contended that investment company securities are not bought by investors; rather, they are sold by salespersons. The objective of the Statement of Policy is to provide that these securities are sold in a fair and proper manner.

The Statement of Policy was formulated in 1950 to regulate sales practices with respect to the offering of investment company shares. Because mutual funds especially are engaged in continuous offerings, much of the policy appears directed toward them. However, remember that it is just as applicable for face-amount certificates and unit investment trusts as it is for both varieties of management companies.

On March 8, 1979 the SEC repealed the Statement of Policy and its detailed provisions are no longer enforced by the Commission. However, the SEC did not repudiate the contents of the Statement because it believes many of its principles are still valid. Instead, the SEC now stresses that while the SOP does not have the status of a restrictive rule, investment companies and users of sales literature are nevertheless responsible for ensuring that materials used are not, in fact, misleading. Moreover, it emphasizes that the term "sales literature" continues to include any communication used to induce the purchase of investment company shares. That is, it encompasses the spoken word as well as all written material used in connection with offerings of investment company shares.

Although the Statement of Policy is a product of the SEC, it was formulated with the assistance of the National Association of Securities Dealers. The NASD was also delegated with authority to administer this doctrine for its own membership. The SEC supervised the activities

The SEC supervised the activities of nonmembers. (The nonmembers usually include the mutual fund itself, its advisory group, and the custodian bank, whereas the underwriter, plan company, and selling group participants are subject to NASD jurisdiction.)

With repeal of the Statement of Policy by the SEC, the NASD decided it would no longer enforce its provisions. The NASD has undertaken a study to determine what Association rules should be adopted to preserve and codify the important principles of this useful doctrine. In the meantime, it remains necessary for NASD members to file copies of investment company sales literature for approval with the Association's Advertising Department in Washington, D.C. within ten days after the first use or publication. Members with less than a year of spot-check review by the Association must submit such material prior to use.

The following sets forth essential features of the SEC's Statement of Policy.

Definition and Rules Concerning Sales Literature. The definition of sales literature includes any communication (whether in writing, by radio, or by television) used by an issuer, underwriter, or dealer to induce the purchase of shares of an investment company. Sales literature should always be thought of as supplementary material because federal law still requires that potential investors be provided with a formal prospectus in any event. The Securities Act of 1933 makes presentation of the prospectus mandatory no later than with confirmation of any purchase. Nevertheless, the Statement of Policy will not permit sales literature to be distributed publicly if it is materially misleading, by implication or otherwise, due to (1) a false statement of an important fact; or (2) omission of information that, in light of the circumstances, is construed as deceptive.

This standard is also applicable to sales literature prepared for circulation only among

413

dealers or wholesale representatives. Occasionally, however, this posture is impractical. Therefore, the NASD may relax these principles if the material (1) is not directly contrary to the basic concept of the Statement of Policy; (2) is limited to single copies for each dealer office and is clearly marked "Not for Reproduction"; and (3) is labeled "Not for Use with Members of the Public" and is accompanied by a *caveat* from the underwriter explaining that use of such material with the public would constitute a violation of the Statement of Policy.

Guidelines on Misleading Activities. Under the Statement of Policy it is considered *materially misleading:*

1. To refer to the effectiveness of a registration statement on file with the SEC as representing government approval of the issue. Nor may reference be made to federal or state regulation of any investment company without explaining that this does not involve supervision of management, investment practices, or policies of that company.

2. To represent or imply that shares of an investment company are similar to, or as safe as, government bonds, insurance company annuities, savings accounts, or life insurance; or that they have the fixed income, principal, or any other features of a debt security. Nor may statement or implication be made that the management of an investment company is under the same kinds of investment restrictions, or is operated under limitations similar to, or has fiduciary obligations such as those imposed by government authorities on savings banks and insurance companies.

3. To represent or imply that banking institutions serving as custodians of fund securities, transfer agents, or dividend disbursing agents (a) will provide protection for investors against possible depreciation of assets; or (b) that such institutions maintain any supervisory function over management in such matters as purchase and sale of portfolio securities or declaration of dividends, or provide any trusteeship protection. Any comment beyond "The ABC Bank is custodian" or "The cash and securities are held in custody by the ABC Bank" requires a complete explanation of that bank's limited role in the affairs of the investment company.

4. To represent or imply that investment companies in general are direct sources of *new* capital to industry or that a particular investment company is such a source unless the extent to which such investments are made is disclosed. (Investment companies usually buy and sell securities in the secondary market and do not often engage in corporate financing activities.)

5. To make any extravagant claims regarding management ability or competence.

6. To represent or imply that investment companies are operated as, or are similar to, cooperatives (legal entities formed to provide low-cost services or facilities to a limited number of members).

7. To represent or imply that investment company shares generally have been selected by fiduciaries. (Fiduciaries are persons or institutions to whom property is legally entrusted for the benefit of another. They are not normally buyers of mutual fund shares because state laws generally prohibit them from delegating investment authority to someone else. After all, that is what they would be doing if they invested the trust's assets in a mutual fund.)

8. To represent or imply an assurance that an investor's capital will increase, or that purchase of investment company shares involves a preservation of capital and a protection against loss in value. Unless an explanation of inherent market risks is provided, discussions of the following descriptive features are also considered misleading: (a) accumulation of capital; (b) accumulation of an estate; (c) preservation of capital; (d) protection against loss of purchasing power; (e) diversification of investments; and (f) financial independence or profit possibilities.

9. To state or discuss the redemption features of investment company shares without explaining that the value of the shares on redemption may be more or less than the investor's cost, depending on the market value of the portfolio securities at the time of redemption.

10. To use any comparison of an investment company security with any other security, medium of investment, or any security index or average, without pointing out (a) that the particular security, index, or average and the period involved were especially selected; (b) that the results disclosed should be considered in the light of the company's investment policy and objectives, the characteristics and quality of the company's investments, and the period selected; (c) the material differences or similarities between the subjects of the comparisons; (d) what the comparison is designed to show; and (e) anything else that may be necessary to make the comparison fair.

This last point is particularly relevant because of human temptations to emphasize virtues while ignoring or downgrading the advantages of a competing investment. Unless full disclosure can be accomplished in a manner that is not unfair, sales literature must abstain from comparisons between dissimilar, or even similar, securities and other investment media. Indiscriminate attacks on ordinary life insurance, for example, or to promote cancellation of such policies merely to use their cash surrender values for mutual fund shares is in poor taste and considered unfair under the Statement of Policy.

11. To represent or imply that the performance of any particular company may be measured by, compared with, or related to, the performance of a particular industry, unless the extent and scope of the portfolio of that company is such that its performance will generally approximate that of the industry.

12. To use any chart or table that (a) is inaccurate in factual detail; (b) tends to create a false or misleading impression as to any material aspect of the investment company's past performance or of an assumed investment of anyone in that investment company; or (c) appears to represent the investment company's past performance or imply that investor experience will be repeated in the future. In this regard, it should be borne in mind that any chart or illustration of asset value performance that is not drawn to the same scale throughout, that does not encompass at least that fund's latest ten years' results (if the fund is less than ten years old, the illustration must show its performance for its entire lifetime), or that makes price projections into the future is deceptive and unfair. Preparation of any chart or table not specifically illustrated in a sample format appearing in the Statement of Policy should be cleared by the NASD or the SEC prior to use.

13. To fail to include in any sales literature designed to encourage investors to switch from one investment company to another or from one class of security of an investment company to another class, the substance of the following statement in a scparate paragraph in type as large as that used generally in the body of the piece:

> Switching from the securities of one investment company to another, or from one class of security of an investment company to another, involves a sales charge on each such transaction, for details of which see the prospectus. The prospective purchaser should measure these costs against the claimed advantage of the switch.

The practice of switching is also called "twisting," referring to unscrupulous salespersons glibly talking customers into making frequent sales and purchases of mutual fund shares. Mutual funds are designed to be long-term investment vehicles, and frequent switching does not generally work to the investor's advantage.

14. To fail to include in any sales literature that does not state the amount or rate of the sales commission a clear reference to the prospectus for information concerning the sales commission and other related information.

15. To employ material in whole or in part from published articles or documents descriptive of, or relating to, investment companies unless such material, or the literature including such material, complies with the Statement of Policy. In addition, such material may not be taken out of context in a way that alters its intended meaning.

16. To combine into any one amount, distributions from net investment income and distributions from any other source. It is misleading to include income representing dividends and interest from securities held in portfolio with income generated as a result of purchase and sale transactions. Investment income represents a return on capital invested, while other distributions are indicative of a return of capital employed.

17. To represent or imply an assurance that an investor will receive a "stable," "continuous," "dependable," or "liberal" return, or that the investor will receive any specified rate of return.

18. To represent or imply a percentage return on an investment in the shares of an investment company unless it is based on one of the following formulas:

a. *A historical basis.* Dividends from net investment income paid during the preceding fiscal year are related to the average monthly offering price for that fiscal year:

$$\frac{\text{Net investment income paid for fiscal year}}{\text{average monthly offering price during fiscal year}} = \frac{\text{rate of return}}{\text{(historic basis)}}$$

b. *A current basis.* Dividends paid from net investment income during the latest twelve months are related to the prevailing offering price, adjusted to reflect any capital gains distribution made during this period.

$$\frac{\text{net investment income paid in preceding 12 months}}{\text{(current offering price} + \text{capital gains distributed in that 12-month period)}} = \frac{\text{rate of return}}{\text{(current basis)}}$$

It is important to note that in both instances the use of either approach is predicated on an annual distribution of investment income. Applying these formulas for a lesser or even greater time period is considered misleading. Although investment companies may distribute income as often as they prefer during the year (the usual practice is quarterly), net capital gains may be distributed only once in any twelve-month period.

Every such commentary, whether current or historic in nature, must be accompanied by a statement to the effect that the return is based on dividends paid in the period covered and is not a representation of future results. In the same text material, the asset value per share at the beginning and end of the period or the increase or decrease in asset value (stated in percentage) must also appear. The current method may prove to be more advantageous for sales personnel to use if a fund has recently raised its dividend rate.

Examples: Rates of return applied via formula methods:

Historic Basis

(Income distributions for fiscal 1976)	$ .24	= 5.49% rate of return
(Average monthly offering price for fiscal 1976)*	$4.37	

*Usually determined on the last business day of each of twelve months involved.

Current Basis

Income distributions during preceding 12 calendar months	=	$ .31
Current offering price on 4/30/77	=	$4.90
Capital gains distribution in preceding 12 calendar months	=	$ .61
Adjusted offering price	=	$5.51

Therefore,

$$\frac{\$\ .31}{(\$4.90\ +\ \$\ .61)} = 5.63\%\ \text{rate of return}$$

19. To discuss or portray the principles of dollar cost averaging without making clear (a) that the program will incur a loss if they discontinue their investment plans when the market value of accumulated shares is less than the amount of dollars invested; (b) that the program is investing funds primarily in securities subject to market fluctuations and that the method involves equal dollar investments in such shares at regular intervals continuously, regardless of price levels; (c) that investors must take into account their financial ability to continue the plan through periods of low price levels; (d) that such plans do not protect against loss in value in declining markets; and (e) that any such type of continuous investment plan does not ensure a profit and does not protect against depreciation in declining markets.

20. To use the phrases *dollar averaging* or *averaging the dollar* (although the phrases "dollar cost averaging" or "cost averaging" are not objectionable) in referring to any plan of constant dollar investment in the shares of an investment company periodically regardless of the price level of those shares. Despite these restrictions, the principles illustrated by this continuing deposit program have proved advantageous for most investors who are in for the long-term pull.

Example: To demonstrate this program's effectiveness, assume that monthly investments of $100 are made in shares of a no-load mutual fund in the following manner. (A no-load fund is utilized in this model merely to simplify the explanation for calculating an average cost price. In the majority of instances, of course, a sales charge is already included in the offering price and the deposit does not really purchase full asset value in the loaded shares.)

Dollar Cost Averaging Program

Monthly Deposits	Offering Price at Time of Investment	Number of Shares and/or Fractional Shares Bought
$100	$5.00	20
$100	10.00	10
$100	20.00	5
$100	10.00	10
$100	15.00	6⅔
$500 total investment	$60.00 aggregate offering prices	51⅔ shares owned

$$\text{Average price of investment} = \frac{\text{aggregate offering price of shares}}{\text{number of deposits made}}$$

Therefore,

$$\frac{\$60}{5} = \$12\ \text{average price of investment}$$

$$\text{Average cost per share} = \frac{\text{total money deposited}}{\text{total shares and fractions owned}}$$

Therefore,

$$\frac{\$500}{51⅔} = \$9.68\ \text{average cost per share}$$

Note that the average cost per share is lower than the average price of investment. This arithmetic fact is always true so long as the security has price fluctuation in the purchase program. The investor is able to buy more shares and fractions at the lower price levels with the same amount of money. Thus, the denominator (total shares) in the calculation of average cost increases and results in a lower cost per share. The formula for average price of investment alone does not include this factor in its computation.

If the Statement of Policy does not thus eliminate the potential inequities associated with mutual fund sales, it certainly comes a lot closer to doing so than any other regulatory aspect of investment found in the financial industry.

See also Investment Companies; NASD Supplement to the SEC Statement of Policy.

Securities Act of 1933. The purpose of the Securities Act of 1933 is to protect the public against the issuance and distribution of fraudulent securities. (The term *securities* is broadly defined to include any note, stock, bond, evidence of debt, interest or participation in a profit-sharing agreement, investment contract, voting trust certificate, fractional undivided interest in oil, gas, or other mineral rights, or any warrant to subscribe to, or purchase, any of the foregoing.) The Act does so by requiring the filing of a registration statement with the Securities and Exchange Commission. This statement sets forth, in a public record, all relevant information pertaining to the specific offering. Information prescribed for inclusion in registration statements filed with the Securities and Exchange Commission is as follows:

1. The name of the issuer.
2. The name of the state or sovereign power under which the issuer is organized.
3. The location of the issuer's principal office.
4. The names and addresses of the directors and other senior officials.
5. The names and addresses of the underwriters (if any).
6. The names and addresses of persons owning 10% or more of any class of stock of the issuer.
7. The amount of securities owned by the directors, senior officials, underwriters, and 10% holders.
8. The general character of the issuer's business.
9. A statement of the issuer's capitalization.
10. A statement of securities reserved for options outstanding, with names and addresses of persons allotted 10% or more of these options.
11. The amount of capital stock of each class included in this offer.
12. The issuer's funded debt.
13. The purposes to which the proceeds of this offering will be applied.
14. Remuneration payable to the issuers directly, naming them specifically when annual payments exceed $25,000.

15. The estimated net proceeds to be derived from the offering.
16. The price at which the public offering will be attempted.
17. Commissions, fees, and so on, to be paid to the underwriters.
18. Itemized detail of expenses incurred by the issuer in connection with this offering.
19. The net proceeds derived from any securities sold by the issuer in the preceding two years and the pertinent details of that sale.
20. Any consideration paid to a promoter in the preceding two years.
21. The names and addresses of any vendors of property or goodwill to be acquired with the proceeds of this offering.
22. Full particulars of any dealings between the issuer and its officers, directors, and holders of 10% or more of its stock that transpired in the preceding two years.
23. The names and addresses of counsel passing on the legality of the issue.
24. The dates and details of material contracts created outside the issuer's ordinary course of business within the preceding two years.
25. A certified, detailed balance sheet of the issuer drawn within the preceding ninety days.
26. A certified profit-and-loss statement of the issuer for the latest fiscal year and the preceding two years.
27. Certified financial statements of any issuer or business to be acquired with proceeds of this offering.
28. A copy of the underwriting contract or agreement.
29. A copy of the law firm's written opinion attesting to the legality of the issue.
30. A copy of all material contracts referred to in item 24.
31. A copy of the issuer's charter, bylaws, trust agreement, partnership agreement, and so forth, as the case may be.
32. A copy of the underlying agreement or indentures affecting any security offered or to be offered by the issuer.

This law is sometimes called the "Full Disclosure Act" by persons in the securities industry.

If a securities issuer fails to furnish complete and accurate information, purchasers of that security may sue to recover realized losses.

Example: Someone who subscribes for a security based on incomplete or erroneous facts, at $50, and subsequently sells it at $30, can institute suit for recovery for the amount of the loss ($20). Willful violators of this Act can suffer a $10,000 fine and/or five years in jail.

See also Affiliated Person; Cooling-Off Period; Exempted Security; Exempted Transaction; Indications of Interest; Investment Banker; Issuer; Public Offering; Registered Security; Syndicate; Trust Indenture Act of 1939; Underwriters.

Securities and Exchange Commission. The Securities and Exchange Commission (SEC) was created under provisions in this section, with full authority to interpret, supervise, and enforce the Securities Act of 1933 and the Securities Exchange Act of 1934. The SEC was also given power to oversee all future legislation concerning the securities market.

The executive body of the SEC is composed of five commissioners, including its chairperson, who are appointed by the President of the United States, with consent of the Senate, for five-year terms of office. No more than three commissioners may be members of the same political party, and all must devote their full time to this job during their tenure of office.

See also Securities Exchange Act of 1934.

Securities Depositories. *See* Reporting Requirements of the SEC (Brokers and Dealers).

Securities Exchange Act of 1934. The importance of the Securities Exchange Act of 1934 and its subsequent sets of amendments cannot be denied. The 1934 Act created the Securities and Exchange Commission and established the basic rules for broker/dealers regarding fair prices and protection of the general public. Therefore, it is impossible to work professionally in the securities industry without feeling the effects of this Act and without knowing its key provisions.

The Act is extremely broad in scope; it encompasses acts of omission as well as commission relating to securities activities. Its provisions also created the Securities and Exchange Commission and gave it authority to supervise and enforce the Securities Act of 1933, the Sec-

urities Exchange Act of 1934, and all subsequent laws relating to the securities industry. Exact, detailed information can be obtained only from careful examination of the Act itself. The following paragraphs briefly describe the Act's 35 sections. Its most important provisions are supplemented by current commentary and interpretation rendered by the SEC in its general rules.

Section 1: Title. The official title of this law is the Securities Exchange Act of 1934.

Section 2: Objectives. While the Securities Act of 1933 was designed to protect the public against fraud in the issuance and distribution of securities, the Securities Exchange Act of 1934 was designed principally to protect the public against unfair and inequitable practices in securities transactions and related activities *after issuance.*

Section 2 explains the necessity for regulation and includes as the law's objectives: (1) supervision and control of all securities activities in the United States; (2) reporting and supervision of insiders' transactions; (3) protection of interstate commerce, federal taxing power, the national banking system, and Federal Reserve banking activities; and (4) maintenance of fair and honest securities markets.

Section 3: Exemption. Exempt obligations include those issued by or guaranteed as to payment of principal or interest by (1) the United States; (2) any state or commonwealth in this country; (3) any municipality within a state or commonwealth in this country and securities issued by certain governmental agencies that are exempted by special order of the Secretary of the Treasury.

Exemption from regulation under this Act does not apply in cases of fraud, however, and the SEC has authority to initiate civil and/or criminal proceedings against the guilty parties.

See also Exempted Security.

Section 4: The Securities and Exchange

Commission. The Securities and Exchange Commission (SEC) was created under provisions in this section, with full authority to interpret, supervise, and enforce the Securities Act of 1933 and the Securities Exchange Act of 1934, and to oversee all future legislation concerning the securities market.

See also Securities and Exchange Commission.

Sections 5 and 6: Registration Requirements for Exchanges. It is unlawful for any broker/dealer or exchange to make use of the U.S. Postal Service, or engage in interstate commerce, in order to employ any facility of an exchange, unless that exchange is (1) registered with the SEC; or (2) specifically exempted from registration with the SEC.

See also Registered Exchange.

Section 7: Margin Requirements. The Act grants official authority to the Federal Reserve Board to regulate credit used to purchase, carry, or trade securities, except in the case of exempted securities transactions.

See also Margin; Regulation T; Regulation U; Regulation G; and Regulation X.

Section 8: Borrowing Restrictions. Section 8 of the Securities Exchange Act of 1934 restricts the borrowing activities of broker/dealers. A broker/dealer organization is prohibited from financing its activities using securities registered on a national securities exchange as collateral unless it borrows from: (1) a member bank of the Federal Reserve System; (2) a nonmember bank that has filed an agreement of compliance with this law with the Federal Reserve Board; or (3) broker/dealers and stock exchange members in situations as permitted by the Federal Reserve Board.

All broker/dealer organizations are prohibited from: (1) Hypothecating a customer's securities to commingle them with other customers' securities without that customer's written consent to do so; (2) Hypothecating a customer's

securities to commingle them with securities owned by anyone other than bona fide customers (Consequently, broker/dealers must refrain from using their own securities with those of any customer in the same loan arrangement.); (3) Rehypothecating a customer's securities subject to a lien in excess of the amount necessary to finance the debit balance in the customer's account; (4) Lending a customer's securities to anyone without the customer's written consent to do so.

In all cases, the term customer does not include general or limited partners, directors or officers of the brokerage firm, or any member of a joint group, unit, or syndicate with that broker/dealer organization.

Section 9: Manipulation of Security Prices on Exchanges. With respect to securities registered on a national exchange, this section specifically prohibits: (1) wash sales and matched orders (purchase and sale of the same security at the same time and price, by the same customer, through the facilities of the same or different brokerage firms); (2) dissemination of false or misleading statements; (3) use of tip sheets or touts to promote the purchase or sale of securities in which the writer or sponsor has a personal interest; (5) pegging or fixing prices of securities; (6) purchasing, selling, or endorsing any securities option contract in contravention of SEC rules.

See also Manipulation of Security Prices and Deceptive Devices.

Section 10: Manipulative and Deceptive Devices. This section admonishes against use of misleading and fraudulent contrivances to influence prices on national securities exchanges. Sale of securities not owned or not designated for delivery to settle a contract is prohibited, unless the order is marked "short." All sell orders must be specifically labeled "long" or "short," as the case may be. A short sale in a security listed or admitted to unlisted trading privileges on a national securities exchange, whether it be executed on the exchange or over the counter, must be executed at least one-eighth point higher than the previous different-priced transaction in that issue appearing on the consolidated ticker tape system. This *plus tick rule* effectively prevents anyone selling short from depressing the price of the security in the execution process. (The settlement of all short sales still requires prompt delivery to the purchaser by means of borrowed certificates.)

A number of activities are specifically prohibited by SEC rules that grew out of the basic provisions of Section 10.

See also Manipulation of Security Prices and Deceptive Devices; Plus Tick Rule; Short Sale.

Section 11: Limitation of Functions of Exchange Members. Although each stock exchange has been accorded sufficient authority to formulate its trading rules, the SEC retains overriding jurisdiction to ensure that those rules are in the public's interest. In this regard, the activities of specialists and other members with discretionary authority in the execution of orders on the floor of the exchange (including the trading floor, rooms, lobbies, and adjacent premises, as well as the telephones and other facilities used primarily by exchange members in these areas) are strictly regulated. Specialists, in particular, are singled out as market-makers. They are required to maintain a fair and orderly succession of prices in issues assigned to them or face cancellation of their registration.

Section 11 also prohibits extension of credit by a broker/dealer to a customer on the purchase of a new issue if it has participated in a distribution of that issue within the past thirty days. Thus, an underwriter or a member of a selling group is precluded from purchasing for a customer's margin account, or even from arranging for credit to maintain, a security that was part of a primary distribution within the preceding thirty

days. The limitation does not apply if the firm, acting as creditor, does not buy that security for the customer's account as agent or sell it as principal. Nor is it subject to this restriction if the customer (1) is a broker/dealer or bank; or (2) acquires the new issue through exercise of a right or warrant, having beneficially owned the security giving rise to the subscription at the time the privilege is extended to its holders.

The 1975 amendments to this section of the Securities Exchange Act gave the SEC authority to regulate activities of securities-information processors and mandated that the SEC appoint a National Market Advisory Board (NMAB) to counsel it on the operation and regulation of securities markets in the United States.

See also National Market Advisory Board; Primary Distribution; Securities-Information Processors; Specialist.

Section 12: Securities Registration Requirement. An issue must be registered with the SEC before it may be listed on a national securities exchange. Securities can be admitted to unlisted trading privileges on petition by the exchange's governing body only if the commission deems that the specific admission is appropriate to the public interest. (All stock traded on the NYSE is fully listed. The AMEX does have some issues admitted to unlisted privileges but has not applied for this exemption for an issue since the early 1930s.)

Other corporations whose issues trade exclusively over the counter but nevertheless meet the minimum specifications of 500 stockholders of record and $1 million in total assets must also register with the SEC.

Registration involves submission of an initial application to the SEC citing the same information prescribed for a public offering under the Securities Act of 1933. However, the registration requirement does not pertain to: (1) securities issued by an investment company registered pursuant to the 1940 Investment Company

Act; (2) most securities issued by savings and loan associations, cooperative banks, homestead associations, and the like, supervised by state or federal authorities; (3) securities issued by non-profit religious, educational, fraternal, or charitable institutions; (4) securities issued by an insurance company, if the company is subject to regulation by a state agency and files an annual statement with the commissioner of insurance in its state of jurisdiction; or (5) participation in a collective trust maintained by a bank or by an insurance company in a separate account.

See also Investment Company Act of 1940; Securities Act of 1933.

Section 13: Periodical and Other Reports. Corporations registered with the SEC under Section 12 must file with the commission notice of change in financial information at set intervals, as well as from time to time when material events occur. These reports then become readily available for public inspection. Persons who acquire 5% or more of any class of equity security, as well as institutional investment managers with discretion in accounts holding $100 million of aggregate market value in equity securities are also required to file reports with the SEC.

See also Reporting Requirements of the SEC.

Section 14: Proxies. The policies and procedures for proxy solicitations and offers to tender securities are contained in this section. Section 14 spells out the type and timeliness of information required for presentation to stockholders and makes it unlawful to use misleading or erroneous facts and figures. The dominant feature of this section and its accompanying SEC rule is full and complete disclosure to facilitate an intelligent voting judgment by the shareowner.

Copies of the proxy statement and form of voting authorization itself must be filed with the SEC at least ten days prior to the date it is sent to the security holder. Additional soliciting material must be filed at least two days before submission to the voter

See also Proxy; Proxy Statement.

Section 15: Over-the-Counter Markets. Bond and stock transactions consummated off the trading floor of a national exchange and the conduct of all brokers and dealers participating in securities activities are the subject of this section of the Act. Unless a securities concern (1) is engaged exclusively in intrastate business or (2) deals only in U.S. government and government-guaranteed securities, commercial paper, or bankers' acceptances, it must qualify and register with the SEC as a broker/dealer organization.

Since December 1975, any brokerage firms that deal in municipal securities, including banking institutions engaged in municipal securities activities, have also been obliged to register with the SEC as broker/dealers. (In lieu of filing for the whole bank, it is permissible to register only an identifiable municipal department or division within the bank as a broker/dealer in municipal securities). This registration directive is not confined to the over-the-counter marketplace; it applies equally to stock exchange firms as well. However, because there are significantly more broker/dealers participating in over-the-counter activities than in exchange transactions, the requirement appears in this section of the statute.

See also Conduct of Broker/Dealers.

Section 16: Reports of Officers, Directors, and Principal Stockholders. All officers, directors, and persons who hold 10% of an equity security of an issue registered under Section 12 must file a statement of beneficial ownership of those securities with the SEC and a national securities exchange, if it is registered there. Subsequent changes in beneficial ownership must be reported to the aforementioned authorities within ten days after the month in which the change occurs.

See also Reporting Requirements of the SEC.

Section 17: Records and Reports of Brokers

and Dealers. This section discloses the requirements for each broker/dealer to maintain and preserve specific books, records, correspondence and memoranda, and to submit periodic reports to the SEC (*see* Reporting Requirements of the SEC).

Section 18: Liability for Misleading Statements. Provision for the civil liability of people who file misleading statements, applications, reports, or documents with the SEC is contained in this section of the Act. An unknowing person who acts on erroneous information and loses money as a result can bring suit against the guilty party for recovery both of his or her losses and of the contingent legal expenses incurred in the litigation process. However, suits must be instituted within one year after discovery or within three years after dissemination of the distorted facts, whichever event occurs first.

Section 19 grants the SEC official authority to (1) suspend registration of a national securities exchange; (2) suspend registration of, or trading in, a security listed on an exchange or traded in the over-the-counter marketplace; and (3) suspend or expel any member or officer of a self-regulatory organization for failure to comply with the rules and regulations of the SEC. (Self-regulatory organizations are those registered with the SEC under the Securities Exchange Act and presently include all national securities exchanges, the NASD, and the Municipal Securities Rulemaking Board.)

Section 19: SEC Powers over Self-Regulatory Organizations. The scope of the law allows for a self-regulatory body to represent registered clearing associations and transfer agents, if one should eventually be organized.

All self-regulatory bodies submit their rules and regulations to the SEC for approval; until this is done, the rules are neither effective nor enforceable. The SEC must publish a notice and text of the proposed rule or regulation in the Federal Register, thus enabling all interested persons to submit their views and criticisms. Unless the SEC determines quickly that the rule is contrary to public and industry interest, it may be approved and become effective no sooner than thirty days after publication.

The SEC can also appropriate money from Congress to institute special studies and inquiries into the technical aspects of the securities industry with an eye toward improving its fairness and efficiency.

See also Securities Exchange Act of 1934 (Section 18).

Section 20: Liabilities of Controlling Persons. A party who directly or indirectly controls a person who faces a penalty under this law can be subject to liability to the same extent unless it is proved that the controlling party did not induce the act that constituted the violation.

Section 21: Investigations, Injunctions, and Prosecution of Offenses. The SEC has authority to conduct investigations regarding alleged violations of the Securities Exchange Act. The commission has the right to obtain injunctions enjoining further violations and to prosecute offenders. Even if it simply appears that an action in violation of this Act is about to be committed, the SEC, in its discretion, is empowered to bring court action to enjoin that action or seek a restraining order or injunction against that specified practice.

It is important to note that persons subpoenaed to testify and produce records for an SEC hearing must appear and submit such documents, although they can claim immunity from self-incrimination if compelled to offer damaging evidence.

Section 22: SEC Hearings. The manner and location at which public and private hearings may be held is included in this part of the Act.

Section 23: Rules and Regulations; Annual

Reports. The SEC and Federal Reserve Board are empowered to formulate whatever rules and regulations may be necessary for their respective functioning in the public interest. As long as they act in good faith, both agencies are held free of liability if any of their actions is subsequently invalidated by judicial authority. They are, however, precluded from adopting any rule or regulation that would impose a burden on competition in contravention of the purpose of this Act. Moreover, they are obliged to show that new rules and regulations are in compliance with the spirit and purpose of the Securities Exchange Act.

Both the SEC and the Federal Reserve Board are each required to submit an annual report to Congress summarizing their oversight activities of the previous year. Both are also advised to use their annual reports to Congress as a medium for recommending future legislation on matters within their respective jurisdictions.

See also Reporting Requirements of the SEC.

Section 24: Information Filed with the SEC. Reports and documents submitted to the SEC become public information unless the party who files the material requests confidential treatment for all or part of it. Requests for privacy will be considered on individual merit. But even if the SEC exempts information from public accessibility, the material may still be made available to the Federal Reserve Board to enable it to perform its duties properly.

Photostatic copies of all publicly available information can be obtained from the public reference room of the SEC in Washington, D.C., for a reasonable fee.

Section 25: Court Review of SEC Orders. Anyone who is disciplined by the SEC may obtain a judicial review of the order by filing a petition in a District Court of Appeals of the United States within sixty days after notice is handed down by the SEC.

Section 26: Unlawful Representation. No action, or failure to act, by the SEC or Federal Reserve Board may be represented or construed as approval or guarantee of the quality or accuracy of any registration statement or report filed with either agency.

Section 27: Jurisdiction of Offenses and Lawsuits. The various federal district courts of the United States and of the District of Columbia have exclusive jurisdiction in matters regarding application and penalties imposed under the Securities Exchange Act of 1934.

Section 28: Effects on Existing Law. The rights and remedies of this law are in addition to any other rights and remedies existing under other federal and state laws. However, recovery for financial losses sustained is expressly limited to actual losses suffered.

Two important parts were added to this section of the Securities Exchange Act by the 1975 amendments. First, the law now prohibits any state or local government from levying a tax on transfer of securities ownership if the sole consideration for imposition of that tax was (1) the use of a registered transfer agent within its jurisdiction; or (2) delivery of the security to the purchaser via the facilities of a registered clearing agency within its jurisdiction. The amendment was obviously directed against New York State, the larger of the two U.S. states with any kind of a transfer tax (the other being Florida). Previously, although the transaction and delivery of certificates may have occurred outside New York, the seller became liable for a transfer tax when the securities were reregistered if the issuer's sole transfer agent was situated in New York.

The second addition to this section exempts from liability a fiduciary, or someone with investment discretion over an account, who pays a commission for a brokerage or research service in excess of what another broker/dealer may be charging for a comparable service. In this age of highly competitive rates among firms offering basically the same services, the only consideration for personal liability a fiduciary need undertake is that payment for services purchased be reasonable in relationship to their value.

Section 29: Validity of Contracts. Any contract, arrangement, or agreement that binds someone to waive compliance with, or protection offered under, this law shall be null and void.

Section 30: Foreign Securities Exchanges. This section prohibits use of the mails or any instrumentality of interstate commerce to effect a securities transaction on a foreign exchange that is contrary to the rules prescribed by the SEC, if the issuer of that security (1) is a resident of the United States; (2) is organized under the laws of the United States; or (3) has its principal place of business in the United States.

Section 31: Registration Fees. The annual fee schedule for registration of national securities exchanges is set forth in this section of the Act. It is .03 of 1% of the total value of all equity-type securities sold on the exchange in the preceding calendar year. Transactions in bonds and exempted securities are not included in the calculation process. However, the charge does apply to over-the-counter transactions in equity securities that may be traded on national securities exchanges, whether or not the transaction is actually effected on those exchanges. it is customarily paid by the seller of a security subject to the fee. Important exemptions from liability for the SEC fee include (1) sales of stock offered pursuant to an effective registration statement (spot secondaries and listed options sales nevertheless continue to be subject to the SEC fee); (2) private placements of stocks by the issuing corporation; (3) the purchase or sale of securities pursuant to, and in consummation of, a tender or exchange offer; (4) the purchase or sale of securities on the exercise of a warrant or subscription right or on the conversion of a converti-

ble security; and (5) transactions executed outside the United States and not reported or required to be reported to the Consolidated Tape Association.

Section 32: Penalties. Any person who willfully violates any section of the Securities Exchange Act or accompanying regulations is subject to a $100,000 fine and/or five years' imprisonment. If it can be proved that the party judged guilty had no knowledge of the violated rule or regulation, then that party is subject only to the fine. If a national securities exchange is found in violation, it is subject to a maximum fine of $500,000.

A corporation that fails to file necessary information, documents, or reports can be subjected to a fine of $100 per day for each day the infraction continues. This fine is in lieu of any criminal penalties.

Section 33: Separability of Provisions. If application of any provision of this Act is held to be illegal, it will not affect the validity of any other provisions described therein.

Section 34: Effective Date. Various sections of this Act became effective July 1, 1934, and the remainder became effective on October 1, 1934, June 1, 1975, December 1, 1975, and January 1, 1976.

Section 35: Authorization of Appropriations. Congress appropriated $51 million in fiscal 1976 and $55 million in fiscal 1977 for the SEC to carry out its duties and responsibilities. Appropriations for subsequent years will be determined by Congress each year thereafter.

See also: Conduct of Broker/Dealers; Execpted Security; Manipulation of Security Prices and Deceptive Devices; Reporting Requirements of the SEC; Securities and Exchange Commission.

Securities Industry Automation Corporation (SIAC). The Stock Clearing Corporation (SCC) is aided in achieving its goals by the Securities

Industry Automation Corporation (SIAC). A subsidiary corporation of the NYSE and AMEX, SIAC is organized to provide computerized trade processing services to SCC as well as to the American Stock Exchange's own clearing corporation. Its programs and computers utilize purchase and sales information submitted by participating firms to arrange simplified securities and money settlements for exchange members. It also provides daily record keeping and activity information for the Depository Trust Company (DTC). A member of the Federal Reserve banking system, DTC serves the NYSE and AMEX as well as certain banking and institutional investors as a vehicle for storage and immobilization of their stock and bond certificates.

See also Comparison Procedure; Depository Trust Company; New York Stock Exchange, Inc.; Stock Clearing Corporation.

Securities-Information Processors. The 1975 amendments to Section 11 of the Securities Exchange Act of 1934 give the SEC authority to regulate activities of securities-information processors. These are persons or groups who collect, prepare, distribute, or publish information or material used in connection with quotations or transactions in the national securities market systems. These persons must register with the SEC and conform to its requirements that trade information be prompt, accurate, and reliable.

Securities Investor Protection Corporation (SIPC). Technically, the Securities Investor Protection Corporation, more frequently referred to simply as SIPC (pronounced *sip-ick*), is not part of the administration of the NYSE. Yet, its purpose and activities are germane to the financial protection offered to NYSE customers.

SIPC was established to supplement the forms of financial protection offered by NYSE firms for their customers. In fact, its provisions are so broad as to include all broker/dealers and not just stock exchange members. SIPC was established in 1970 as a government-sponsored private corporation specifically to resolve most of the financial deficiencies in customer accounts resulting from broker/dealer bankruptcies.

In the event that a financial catastrophe occurs too quickly for effective remedial action, dissolution proceedings of the firm must begin. Unfortunately, forced liquidation of assets doesn't always generate premium prices. The financial community has seen instances, particularly during the 1960s, when a firm's liabilities exceeded the proceeds from sale of its assets, thus jeopardizing customer securities and monies.

On notification of a brokerage concern's failing financial condition or bankruptcy petition, SIPC will request a federal court to appoint a trustee to assume management control of that concern. The trustee is empowered to (1) advise customers and creditors of the firm's insolvency, permitting them to make appropriate claims on the firm's assets; (2) liquidate the firm's assets in an orderly and reasonable manner; (3) distribute to customers their identifiable nominal cash balances and fully paid for securities; (4) compensate customers for the net value of their margin accounts or, if there is a shortage of money or securities to make those payments, for the insurable equity in these accounts; and (5) reimburse creditors for valid claims on the firm's assets but only to the extent that there are sufficient assets available.

SIPC insures and guarantees repayment of money and securities in customer accounts valued up to $500,000 per separate customer. (*Separate customer* does not mean separate *accounts* of each customer. Thus, if a person has a cash account, margin account, bond account, and so on, these must be combined to determine the $500,000 responsibility of SIPC. For example, if one person holds one account jointly with spouse, another account jointly with children, and another account jointly with someone else, these three accounts are considered *separate customers*, and each is guaranteed up to the full amount of SIPC insurability.) As much as, but not more than, $100,000 of this insurance may be utilized for repayment of a credit (cash) balance in the account. No other creditors of a brokerage firm have these assurances.

Examples:

to restore customer accounts held by the affected broker/dealers.

See also Financial Protection Requirements (NYSE); New York Stock Exchange, Inc.

Segregation. When a customer maintains his or her fully paid for securities at the brokerage firm, they are registered in the broker's name (street name). These securities, along with any se-

Value of Accounts

	Customer A	Customer B	Customer C	Customer D	Customer E
Credit balance	0	0	$15,000	$150,000	$160,000
+ Equity in security value	$35,000	$520,000	$25,000	$ 15,000	$420,000
= Customer guaranteed by SIPC	$35,000	$500,000	$40,000	$115,000	$500,000

SIPC obtains funds for its guarantees through mandatory annual assessments levied on the gross securities-generated revenues of all broker/dealer organizations registered with the SEC under the Securities Exchange Act of 1934. (Excluded are broker/dealers whose business consists *exclusively* of (1) distribution of open-end investment companies or unit investment trust shares; (2) the sale of variable annuities; (3) the sale of insurance; or (4) rendering advisory services to registered investment companies or insurance company separate accounts.) Customer protection offered by this corporation is therefore not confined to NYSE member organizations and has, in fact, been utilized by the non-member firms much more frequently since inception of SIPC.

Furthermore, if a financial crisis in the investment community were to grow into a calamity, SIPC has officially been granted authority to employ up to $1 billion from the U.S. Treasury

curities representing excess collateral in margin accounts, must be kept physically separate—that is, segregated—from all other securities held by the firm. These securities are said to be held in *segregation*, or *seg*.

The actual owners of the securities are identified by means of (1) a tag on each certificate with the underlying customer's name indicated (*individual identification*); or (2) a list serving as a cover for an envelope containing one or more certificates of the same issue for all customers in the same secure condition. Although each certificate is not individually earmarked, the outside list indicates the quantity set aside for each party with an interest in the securities inside the envelope (*bulk identification*).

The NASD recommends any of the following three procedures for segregation of customer securities: (1) physical separation of securities by name of issue, registered in street name, with a cover sheet reflecting all changes in ownership that occur and an indication of the proportionate interest of the individual customers; (2) physical separation of securities by name of issue, registered in street name or customer name, with a tab affixed to each certificate to reflect the name of its beneficial owner; (3) physical separation of specific certificates clipped together for each customer and maintained in separate folders that identify the customer.

In each of these methods, the firm's records must indicate the dates when the securities were segregated. if the securities were not in actual custody of the member at the time, the records must also show their location and the means used to identify them as customer property.

See also Rules of Fair Practice (NASD).

Securities held with the Depository Trust Company or Free Account Net Settlement may be segregated by specific instructions.

Generally speaking, certificates with a market value equal to the debit balance are released from segregation if financing of a transaction is to be arranged via securities loans to brokers and dealers. When financing is arranged by means of a collateral loan at a bank, securities worth 140% of the customer's debit balance are rehypothecated. All other certificates in those accounts must be segregated.

This variation occurs simply because a bank demands a cushion of protective collateral value for its loan, whereas a broker loan is arranged on a dollar-for-dollar basis and is continuously marked to the market. Consequently, the firm that carries customer margin accounts has no ability to control those securities to its own advantage when conducting business in a dealer capacity. The Margin Department values each customer account in consideration of market price fluctuations and continuously advises the Box Section which securities to segregate and which to place in the active box. In some firms, daily pricing is required by management. In any event, no firm should undertake it less frequently than once a week or when activity occurs

in that particular account, whichever happens first.

See also Active Box; Broker/Dealer Organization (Cashiering Department); Rehypothecation; Safekeeping.

Self-Regulatory Organization. *See* Securities Exchange Act of 1934 (Sections 18 and 19).

Seller's-Option Contract. If a selling broker is aware of the customer's inability to satisfy the delivery terms of a regular-way contract as prescribed, then the broker at the time of the offering must state the number of calendar days needed for completion of that contract. This is known as a *seller's option.* The buyer has a right to refuse acceptance of these unusual terms, but only at the time when the transaction is effected. Consequently, a selling broker under these circumstances generally must make a price concession of ¼ to ½ point to attract a buyer's willing participation.

Examples:

"10 XYZ 4¼s of 1991 at 82½, sellers 15"
"4 PDQ 7½s of 1998 at 94, sellers 28"
"8 CBA 8¼s of 2001 at 97⅝, sellers 39"

Seller's-option contracts in corporate or municipal bonds are allowable under NYSE rules for any period of time running from six business to sixty calendar days; those for U.S. government issues, from two business to sixty calendar days. In other words, such contracts may be created for settlement beginning from the point at which a regular way ceases, but never for any longer than sixty calendar days after trade date.

In the unlikely event that two or more seller's-option bond orders are entered at the same price, the offeror willing to settle soonest after trade date will assume priority for execution purposes.

After execution, the seller has an option of delivering the bonds earlier than the specified settlement date. The purchasing firm must be prepared to pay for them. But the seller must give 24-hour written notice to the purchaser announcing the intention to deliver early. In no event may the seller give this written notice before the regular-way settlement of a contract effected on the day of the original transaction.

In other words, the earliest possible notification date for a corporate or municipal bond seller's-option contract would be on the fifth business day after trade date; the earliest possible physical delivery of securities on the sixth business day. For U.S. government obligations, earliest notification can take place on the next business day after trade date and physical delivery can be arranged for the second business day.

See also Cash Contract; Corporate Bond Transaction; Next-Day Contract; Regular-Way Contract; When-Issued/When-Distributed Contract.

Selling Concession. *See* Selling Group.

Selling Group. To help the underwriters in a syndicate achieve broad distribution of the securities in the registration statement, the syndicate manager (or managing underwriter) may employ the services of a selling group. A *selling group* consists of selected members of the NASD who agree to act as the underwriters' agents and offer some of these securities to their customers under terms presented in the registration and prospectus. They must sign a contract with the managing underwriter that subjects them to the same terms and restrictions of the underwriting agreement. But they do not receive the full underwriter's spread because they assume no personal responsibility or financial liability to the issuing corporation. Their remuneration for services rendered is granted by the syndicate manager in the form of a *selling concession*, a fraction of the underwriter's spread. The selling group concession may range from 25 to 75% of the underwriters' spread, depending on the an-

ticipated degree of difficulty in marketing the issue. The greater the foreseen difficulty, the larger the concession needed to attract selling-dealer efforts. Furthermore, selling groups are not normally allocated a sizable percentage of the issue to distribute; they receive merely a token amount to satisfy some of their customers and possibly develop a continuing interest in the aftermarket.

It is not unusual to find some investment bankers acting both as underwriters and members of the selling group in the same securities distribution. In a popular offering, it is almost impossible to accommodate customer demands from underwriting allocations alone, and many investment bankers, using their influence with the manager, turn to both devices to satisfy their clients.

Even in obviously successful offerings, where there is seldom question about the underwriters' ability to market the securities themselves, most syndicate managers find it expedient to employ a selling group. Members of today's selling group may be tomorrow's managing underwriters in other offerings, and today's manager may well want to participate in their deals to accommodate its customers.

See also Spread; Syndicate.

Sell-Out Procedures. *See* Close-Out Procedures.

Sell Plus. This instruction requests a member to dispose of the security via market or limit order, as the case may be, but at a price higher than the previous different-priced transaction for that stock.

Example:

Previous different price	Sale at this price qualifies
75	75⅛

See also Buy Minus.

Sell-Stop Order. This order is entered with a memorandum price below present market levels because it is intended either to (1) curtail a loss on a present stock holding; (2) preserve a profit for stock previously purchased at lower prices; or (3) dispose of the stated security via a short sale, but only if a transaction at that price creates a technical sell signal.

Example: If investor Andrea Morse buys a stock at 15, anticipating growth in value, she can suffer a loss of capital if the price declines contrary to her expectations. To combat this possibility, investor Morse can enter a sell-stop order at 13 (or at some other price below the present 15). If the price rises or stays above 13, her position is maintained without further action required. But if the price of that security declines to 13 or below (instead of trading exactly at 13, a price gap may occur; penetration will also activate the stop order—that is, 13¼, 13⅛, 12⅞, and so forth), her memorandum becomes a market order and her stock is sold immediately at the best available price. This will (1) liquidate her position; and (2) curtail her loss at about $200 plus commissions and transfer tax expenses ($1,500 purchase cost –$1,300 sale proceeds). The exact loss cannot be determined until the stock has actually been sold at the best available price.

Example: If investor Ben Russet purchases a stock at 54 and watches it appreciate to 65, he will no doubt be elated. As it continues to move higher, he will certainly want to hold that security. But if it begins to decline, the paper profit will soon dissipate. A sharp decline might eventually result in a loss. Many people, unable to follow the intra-day fluctuation of stocks closely, might be inclined to enter a sell-stop order. Investor Russet can enter a sell-stop order at 60 (or some price below the present 65) and attempt to preserve most of his paper profit in case there is a violent price decline. If the price falls to 60 or below (instead of trading exactly at 60, a price gap may occur; such penetration will also

activate the stop order—that is 60⅛, 59⅞ and so forth his memorandum is activated, making it a market order to sell at the best available price. This will (1) liquidate his position; and (2) officially establish his profit at about $600, less commissions and transfer tax expenses ($6,000 sale proceeds $5,400 purchase cost). The exact profit can be determined only when the actual sale is effected.

Example: Suppose that a technician, Bess Rinni, observes that a stock price is experiencing a great deal of difficulty in moving above 50. Apparently there are sufficient sellers available to satisfy all purchase orders. Therefore, she reasons, when buying interest peters out, the path of least resistance will lead downward. To take advantage of this movement if and when it happens, she enters a sell-short-stop order at 48 (or at some price level below the present 50). Should that stock decline to 48 or below (instead of trading exactly at 48, a price gap may occur; such penetration will also activate the stop order—that is, 48⅛, 47⅞, and so forth), her memorandum is activated, directing a short sale at the first practicable opportunity, in accordance with federal regulations governing such sales. If the stock doesn't decline to that price, technician Rinni has lost nothing but time. In fact, she may have saved considerable loss by not selling short at 50 should the stock move up above that level thereafter.

See also Buy-Stop Order; Order; Stop Order.

Separate Account. *See* Variable Annuity.

Serial Bond. Serial bonds are obligations of the same issuer offered at the same time but with various rates of interest and maturities arranged over a period of years. Title to the equipment that is pledged for an equipment trust bond officially passes to the corporation after the entire issue is retired. This type of issue requires repayment of a portion of the borrowing each year by setting a series of maturity dates for the entire debt over consecutive years. This self-liquidating debt arrangement is described as a *serial bond.*

In the debt arrangement of an equipment trust (serial) bond, much less of the principal comes due for redemption in the first few years after issuance than in later years. This permits the corporation to build revenues with the new equipment acquired via the borrowing. This graduated redemption procedure is called a *balloon effect.* This balloon effect offers investors a further degree of protection through constant reduction of the debt, and, as a result, serial bonds are usually well rated. Moreover, because all companies in each of these industries (railroads, truckers, airlines, and oil companies) use basically identical equipment, the collateral can be sold without difficulty if the issuer defaults. This type of bondholder protection makes equipment trust securities quite appealing to most investors.

Serial bonds with ballooning maturities and ballooning interest rates are not used only for equipment trust obligations. The principle of changing rates and/or maturation amounts over the life of an issue is also typical of municipal revenue bonds. General obligation bonds are usually offered in serial format.

See also Split Offering; Term Bonds.

Series EE Savings Bond. Series EE savings bonds are registered securities offered in various denominations (minimum of $50) and at 50% below face value and redeemed at face value by an agent of the Treasury Department after 12 years. (It is therefore a nonmarketable U.S. government security.) The difference between subscription and redemption prices represents *accrued interest* for the investor. The interest itself does not accrue in equal increments over the lifetime of the bond. Instead, a small amount of interest accrues in the early years and much more in the later years, providing the investor with an average rate of return on current issues (Oct.

1987) equal to 6% if held until maturity.

The federal income tax payable by the holder for this interest may be declared and paid annually as it accrues, or at maturity in one lump sum—at the bondholder's choice.

No one owner may acquire more than $15,000 worth of these bonds in one year. However, this limitation applies to the issue price, not to face value. Since Series EE bonds are issued at a 50% discount from face value, the actual limitation is $30,000 in face value. This regulation is designed to prevent the draining of bank deposits when these bonds are favored by the public because of their comparatively high interest rates.

See also Nonmarketable Security; Series HH Bond.

Series HH Bond. Series HH bonds are registered securities offered in various denominations (minimum of $500) and at face value; they are redeemed ten years later also at the face value. They are therefore considered nonmarketable U.S. government securities. Every six months during the lifetime of this kind of bond, the Treasury Department sends each holder a check for the interest due on that obligation. The current rate (Oct. 1987) on Series HH savings bonds is 6%.

An interesting feature of Series HH and Series EE bonds is a U.S. government regulation precluding any one owner from acquiring more than $15,000 of the Series EE bonds and $20,000 of the Series HH bonds in any one calendar year. These dollar limitations are placed on the issue prices, not on the face (par) values of these securities. Thus, for the Series EE savings bond, the ceiling is actually $30,000 in face value annually because it is issued at a 50% discount from face value. The Series HH savings bond has a *true* $20,000 limitation because it is designed to prevent draining of bank deposits when these bonds are favored by the public because of their comparatively higher interest rates.)

See also Nonmarketable Security; Series EE Bond.

Series of Options. Options of the same class that have the same exercise price and expiration date are of the same series.

Example: All IBM January 120 puts.

See also Class of Options; Listed Options.

Settlement Dates. *See* Delivery Dates.

Settlement Price. A figure determined by the closing range which is used to calculate gains and losses in futures market accounts. Settlement prices are used to determine gains, losses, margin calls, and invoice prices for deliveries.

Severally and Jointly. *See* Underwriting Agreement (for Municipal Bonds).

Severally but Not Jointly. *See* Underwriting Agreement (for Corporate Securities).

Shelf Distributions. Generally corporations use registered distributions to raise long-term capital. These situations involve issuers who seek an investment banker's guarantee of payment with a promise to offer those securities immediately at a fixed price.

Sometimes, however, registration statements must be filed and become effective before certain stockholders (that is, affiliated persons intent on offering a sizable amount of securities) may dispose of their securities. Yet those selling stockholders, and even some issuers whose shares must be registered with the SEC, may not be inclined to dispose of their holdings at one time or at one price. When issuers or affiliated persons want to sell securities over a period of time, or at a variety of prices (as compared to the one-time price in a typical underwriting), they can often register those instruments with the SEC and reserve the right to sell within two years following the effective date. These are called

self distributions and are registered and sold under *SEC Rule 415.*

This rule permits the seller to make at-the-market offerings from authorized capital or from a personal portfolio ("shelf") anytime over a two-year period, without further prior notice, as financial needs dictate. Information in the prospectus must be kept current during the distribution period and given to purchasers with their trade confirmations. If material changes do occur in the affairs of that corporation while the seller is still in the process of distribution, an amendment to the registration statement must be filed and included with the offering prospectus. Transactions on a securities exchange are subject to the distribution rules of that exchange. Moreover, because two years are a long time and offer too many possibilities for inadvertent violation of SEC regulations, most broker/dealers request letters of indemnification from sellers before acting on their behalf. after all, SEC Rule 10b-6 applies to a shelf distribution, as well as to any other registered offering, of securities. That rule could theefore impact the further activities of participants during this period.

Shopping the Street. *See* National Quotation Bureau, Inc.

Short. One who has sold a contract to establish a market position and who has not yet closed out this position through an offsetting purchase the oposite of a Long.

Short Against the Box. This expression is used to denote a situation in which a person is both long and short the same quantity of the same serity at the same time. This person has thus established a fully hedged position and cannot benefit or lose from future fluctuations in price. A decline in equity in one position is offset by an increase in equity in the other position.

Example: If you sell short 100 shares of a stock you own at $40 per share and the price of that security (1) rises five points, the long position equity gains five points but the short position suffers by that amount; (2) declines five points, the long position equity loses five points but the short position gains by that amount. To be hedged in such a fashion you must be long and short an equal amount of stock. If the long or short quantity is larger than the contra position, the net difference is subject to market risk.

There are a number of reasons why people sell short against the box, but the most popular one is to defer a liability for payment of a tax on capital gains until some future date, without exposure to market risk.

Example: Assume a customer purchased a security some time ago and had a paper profit in that issue. Unwilling to sell it now and thus become liable immediately for federal tax on the capital gain, this person can do either of two things: (1) he or she can continue to hold the serity at the risk of the market (when ready to sell the customer can hope there will still be a profit on which to pay a tax); (2) he or she can immediately sell that security short versus the certificate currently held by the broker in behalf of the customer. (The customer's statement will then show that security position to be both long and short in the account.)

The second alternative permits this person to lock up (guarantee) the present gain without further risk and postpone tax liability for that profit. A person becomes liable for payment of the capital gains tax only when the long-position certificate is physically delivered to close out the short position. If this action is deferred until the following year, the customer has (1) protected a profit when prices may be most advantageous; (2) avoided paying tax on capital gains in a year when personal income may be abnormally high, thus necessitating payment of higher taxes as a result; and (3) freed some capital at the time of short sale to employ in some other investment.

It must be borne in mind, however, that a person cannot (1) sell short against the box un-less it is done in a margin account; (2) engage in this practice unless someone else's certificate can be borrowed to facilitate delivery by the proper settlement date after sale; or (3) subsequently sell the long position and leave a net short position in that security unless the long sale is executed in the same fashion as a bona fide short sale.

Example: Assume a customer is short against the box an equal number of shares in the same issue.

	Long	Short
XYZ Corporation	500	500

To sell even as few as 100 shares of the long stock position would leave this customer in a net short position (that is, long 400, short 500 = net 100 short). Consequently, such sale must be executed mechanically as if it was a short sale; that is, the sale must be at a price not lower than the previous different-priced transaction in XYZ Corporation. The purpose of this rule is to ensure that the customer does not benefit his or her remaining short position by depressing the market value of that issue.

See also Short Sale.

Short Hedge. The sale of a futures contract(s) to eliminate or lessen the possible decline in value of ownership of an approximately equal amount of the actual financial instrument or physical commodity. A long hedge is the opposite, futures are purchased.

Short Interest Theory (Cushion Theory). A short sale is the sale of a security that one does not own or does not intend to deliver (short against the box). The seller arranges to borrow the security and delivers the borrowed stock to the purchaser. The usual reason for a short sale is an anticipated decline in the market value of the security shorted. The seller hopes to repurchase it at a lower price and realize a profit.

A compilation of the short interest is made as of the fifteenth day of each month by the stock exchanges and reported to the media four business days later. At first glance, one would think that a sharp increase in short sales would presage a decline in the market. But the follower of this theory thinks otherwise. Short sellers at some future point become buyers of stock to cover their positions. This "cushion" of potential buyers will support a declining market and may even accelerate a rising one. Short sellers may repurchase when the market goes up to limit their losses and by doing so, give impetus to the advance.

The short interest theory can be applied to the overall market or to particular issues. The conclusions are based on the size of the short position as related to average daily volume. If the short interest exceeds one day's average volume, the picture begins to look bullish. Should short interest rise above one and a half times daily volume, this theory tells us that the cushion is now large enough to indicate a buy signal. If enough adherents begin to purchase, the stock will rise. The short seller may then be forced to cover, and a further rise will result.

The following table shows a sampling of the monthly short-position statistics released by the New York Stock Exchange in December 1976. Observe that the information includes the current and previous month's figures as well as the average daily volume in each issue. This is designed to help cushion theorists make judgments about near-term price movements in these issues. Note, too, that some issues are marked to advise readers that these securities may be involved in an arbitrage transaction. That is, they have been sold short by traders who own another security and hope to close out that short position with the common stock receivable from the other security. It is a typical technique used in connection with mergers, acquisitions, and redemptions of convertible securities pursuant to call by the issuer. These short interest figures are thus temporarily inflated and are not indicative of potential buying interest by those sellers.

See also Advance-Decline Theory; Confidence Theory; Dow Theory; Odd-Lot Theory; Technical Analysis.

The Short sellers' usefulness is best demonstrated when they are needed most. During periods of falling prices, when there is a scarcity of ordinary demand, the people who are already short represent a built-in buying interest because they must eventually cover (purchase) their short position. This demand serves to cushion the depression of a bear market just as the original sale cushioned the optimism of a bull market. In fact, the cushion theory of investment makes reference to this important supply-demand relationship.

Persons who subscribe to this cushion theory hold that the absence of short sellers in the marketplace is detrimental to liquidity. Followers of this theory eagerly analyze monthly announcements from the New York Stock Exchange and American Stock Exchange (the statistics are published to reflect positions as of the fifteenth day of each month) stating the short interest of individual stocks traded on their premises—that is, the number of shares already sold short which represent latent buying power for that issue (see the following figure). These theorists believe that if an open position totals two or more times the average daily trading volume for that particular security, this situation is a bullish indicator. It forecasts imminent rising prices for that issue. On the other hand, if the short position figure is less than one day's average trading volume, it means that there is little built-in demand for that security. The prospect of an immediate price decline from the current level is, therefore, to be expected.

See also Short Sale.

Short Market Value. *See* Margin Account (Short Account).

New York Exchange Short Interest Registers Record

Short interest on the New York Stock Exchange in the month ended Dec. 15 rose to a record 27,510,879 shares from 24,777,197 shares a month earlier. The previous record was set last Jan. 15, when the short interest was 27,142,204 shares. The shares in the short interest are equal to one-tenth of 1 percent of the total shares listed on the Exchange.

On the American Stock Exchange the short interest increased 49,007 shares to 3,284,454 shares as of Dec. 15. A year ago the short interest was 3,155,234. Short position of 5,000 or more shares existed in 88 of the more than 120 stocks and warrants traded on the Exchange and some short position was shown in 496 issues.

The following figures show some of the important short positions and changes for companies on the New York Stock Exchange.

SHORT INTEREST
NEW YORK STOCK EXCHANGE

	12-15-76	11-15-76	Avg. Daily Volume
Abbott Labs	7,933	20,908	26,025
ASA Ltd	209,255	154,905	57,005
Airco Inc	30,844	17,644	8,055
Aetna Life Casualty	9,750	34,050	56,935
Akzona Inc	34,800	34,800	3,665
Alcan Aluminium Ltd	31,997	29,240	44,850
tAmax Inc	117,548	118,321	10,320
Allied Stores	4,685	19,502	9,910
Aluminum Co America	80,772	43,772	20,580
tAmerada Hess Corp	107,299	38,756	44,985
American Credit Corp	11,459	433	7,290
Amer Broadcasting Cos	38,891	58,562	59,270
Amer Cyanamid Co	63,800	61,706	22,185
Amer Electric Power	18,883	2,083	43,850
Amer General Ins Co	91,300	102,019	20,615
Amer Home Products	32,685	11,132	98,605
Amer Hospital Supply	63,369	118,272	21,070
Amer Motors Corp	71,567	71,267	32,945
American Standard	2,500	17,100	14,805
tAmer Tel & Tel	143,723	88,752	154,890
AMP Inc	247,484	258,174	29,415
Anaconda Co	39,417	32,218	26,365
Apache Corp	20,100	7,500	6,125
Apco Oil Corp	28,802	9,300	5,585
Armstrong Cork Co	43,420	14,820	31,770
tAtlantic Richfield	324,546	336,053	89,570
Auto Data Processing	50,093	24,752	13,150
Avco Corp wts 78	63,900	67,200	3,410
tAvery Intl Corp	111,895	108,195	6,335
Avco Corp	24,155	15,905	23,765
Avnet Inc	8,440	21,365	35,770
Avon Products Inc	73,355	92,405	62,685
Bandag Inc	27,819	20,510	14,305
Braun (C F) Co	33,900	5,400	5,485
Bates Mfg Co	42,358	42,958	1,775
Baker Intl Corp	38,325	41,516	8,515
Beatrice Foods	47,751	32,262	43,035
Beech Aircraft	21,901	16,305	4,805
Baxter Bravenol Lab	27,700	46,191	27,560
Beker Indus Inc	85,999	67,809	8,895
Bethlehem Steel	16,744	44,998	35,005
Black & Decker Mfg	61,809	26,490	51,290
Bally Mfg Corp	52,796	46,200	25,510
Best Products Co	175,075	171,337	20,560
H&R Block Inc	23,388	18,140	37,180
Blue Bell Inc	30,150	29,500	28,715
Boeing Co	75,055	90,633	44,285
Boise Cascade Corp	46,816	41,922	45,200
Braniff Intl Corp	24,202	33,602	39,835
British Pete Amer Sh	207,814	98,950	51,725
tContinental Group	181,728	292,635	22,330
tBrunswick Corp	162,024	19,347	34,885
CBS Inc	23,866	24,384	23,510
Budd Co	97,232	73,585	8,495
Emerson Elec Co	30,327	33,161	25,295
EMI Ltd Am Shs	5,004	38,208	5,330
Engelhard Min & Chem	55,658	69,899	13,720
Esquire Inc	40,200	18,600	6,890
Evans Products	44,191	23,008	81,570
Exxon Corp	43,009	90,208	112,660
Fairchild Cmra & Inst	52,291	79,320	20,825
Farah Mfg Co	32,961	31,461	3,800
Federal Nat Mtg	29,101	92,970	61,930
Federated Dept Stors	97,092	121,833	37,580
First Charter Fin Cp	50,312	49,008	21,575
Florida Power Corp	900	16,000	9,090
Ford Motor Co	48,315	27,730	58,920
tGulf & West Ind wts 78	972,688	831,491	35,010
Golden West Fin Corp	25,896	13,070	6,380
Gardner & Denver	25,020	16,020	26,590
tGeneral	Electric7,140,208		63,470
General Foods	20,440	40,370	32,985
Gneral Host Corp	28,434	30,325	1,610
General Mills	62,200	61,661	17,385
General Motors	206,732	135,873	173,310
Gen Tel & Electronics	70,381	53,536	56,730
tGenuine Parts Co	145,470	119,970	9,265
tGeorgia Pacific Corp	324,413	130,986	64,125
Getty Oil Co	51,173	8,838	5,665
Gibraltar Financial	22,326	12,626	24,910
xFrigitronics Inc	70,200	73,900	6,565
Global Marine Inc	210,950	222,450	6,285
Goodrich (B.F.) Co	31,184	15,221	10,300
Gould Inc	53,353	59,521	18,945
Grace (W.R.) & Co	34,782	35,641	15,860
tGreat Westrn Financl	103,750	35,550	38,665
Guardian Mtg Invest	28,589	24,352	2,590
Greyhound Corp wts 80	20,100	20,000	4,555
Grumman Corp	22,529	12,046	3,280
Gulf Oil Corp	68,738	19,908	99,355
tGulf & Westrn Ind	257,242	159,810	47,600
Hall (Frank B.) & Co	21,300	17,100	4,435
Halliburton Co	123,981	98,075	46,085
Heinz (H.J.) Co	32,545	21,695	16,060
Hercules Inc.	27,200	89,959	31,550
Heublein Inc	50,103	18,037	21,555
Hewlett Packard Co	95,385	173,022	22,750
Holly Sugar	75,828	43,979	5,000
Homestake Mining	69,878	69,794	27,370
Honeywell Inc.	50,345	27,063	41,930
Horizon Corp	10,400	400	3,890
Houston Lighting & Pwr	20,100	36,303	53,690
Howard Johnson Co	46,718	86,548	22,234
House of Fabrics Inc	30,710	20,300	6,205
Hughes Tool Co	46,225	15,100	33,555
tIDS Realty Trust	107,500	107,651	2,850
Illinois Tool Works	None	15,965	1,800
Indianapolis Pwr & Lgt	59,762	200	6,285
Ingersoll Rand Co	65,430	23,426	14,120
Insilco Corp	17,000	500	8,680
Interco Inc	21,593	16,270	6,250
IC Industries Inc	19,401	2,925	6,860
Inter Business Mach	39,034	36,737	71,675
Int Flavors & Fragrnce	83,623	87,451	28,450
Inter Harvester	44,400	20,250	19,060
Inter Minerals & Chem	25,181	49,370	18,075
International Paper	53,880	91,620	46,260
Int Tel & Tel Pr Ser K	38,503	21,511	6,610
tInter Tel & Tel	186,678	161,053	84,210
tInt Tel & Tel Pr Ser N	112,800	500	19,880
IV Intl Corp	50,332	27,152	21,775
Itek Corp	25,588	19,590	4,890
Itel Corp	64,005	28,050	9,110
E. F. Johnson Co	209,587	132,286	8,215
Johns-Manville	37,046	79,500	69,230
Johnson & Johnson	61,791	74,264	27,230
Joy Mfg	30,815	30,715	14,710
tKaiser Alum & Chem	251,003	249,727	7,100
Kaiser Cement & Gypsum	64,585	52,885	7,435
Kaufman & Broad Inc	45,900	44,700	56,190
Kellogg Co	36,832	54,917	22,745
Kentucky Utilities	22,020	17,200	7,325
Kerr-McGee Corp	20,390	54,410	18,765
Kresge (S S)	88,298	107,873	107,410
Lear Siegler Inc	29,227	26,159	13,785
Levi Strauss & Co	27,834	8,690	30,180
LTV Corp	39,204	41,533	18,865
Litton Industries	60,567	55,532	31,435
Loews Corp	36,836	15,643	15,920
Louisiana L & Exp Co	15,418	325	29,225
Lubrizol Corp	62,516	54,316	15,485
Lucky Stores Inc	31,766	40,182	20,710
Melville Shoe Corp	25,375	1,825	36,675
Lykes Corp	32,875	33,925	10,410
Marriott Corp	31,722	23,590	26,640
Martin Marietta Corp	36,317	15,434	13,555
tRevlon Inc	r167,506	s116,539	18,600
tReynolds Metals	101,065	94,790	16,815
Reynolds Ind	7,855	20,555	23,540
Reynolds Ind $2.25	7,800	17,800	3,625
Richardson-Merrell	17,237	5,696	12,265
Rite Aid Corp	13,925	3,333	21,190
Rohm & Haas Co	28,425	36,260	6,145
Royal Dutch Petr Co	88,650	55,067	28,880
Royal Industries	22,027	420	38,885
Ryder System Inc	36,799	38,149	25,095
St Joe Minerals Corp	25,193	23,383	11,080
Santa Fe Intrl	31,335	25,135	24,060
Schlitz (Jos) Brewing	62,620	59,620	18,290
Schlumberger N.V.	88,132	113,252	43,875
Savin Business Mach	62,329	60,900	8,755
Searle (G.D.) & Co	41,500	25,700	53,030
Sears Roebuck	110,829	121,979	60,610
xSambo's Restaurants	34,704	25,699	25,575
Seatrain Lines	35,502	10,046	13,160
Simplicity Pattern	96,565	69,278	45,055
Singer Co	86,224	87,665	13,095
Skyline Corp	25,830	49,030	25,415
SmithKline Corp	35,361	31,339	14,950
Southern Co	103,625	38,400	92,305
Southern Cal Edison	395	57,095	29,640
Southwestern Pub Ser	14,120	1,200	14,805
Sperry Rand Corp	16,048	32,581	27,585
Staley (A.B.) Mfg Co	21,330	32,940	11,005
Standard Oil Calif	61,306	22,626	67,910
Standard Oil (Indiana)	65,570	12,184	51,975
Stauffer Chem Co	25,280	23,237	13,410
Sterling Drug	26,599	650	36,750
Sun Co	48,323	99,683	14,345
Technicare Corp	191,427	146,825	12,510
Swank Inc	15,900	5,300	6,280
Sony Corp Am Sh	111,666	54,015	68,920
tTandy Corp	222,244	88,064	63,155
Tektronix Inc	68,778	71,258	5,450
Teledyne Inc	64,904	58,784	28,525
tTenneco Inc	193,852	163,948	48,190
Texaco Inc	10,277	27,077	143,405
Texas Intl Co	38,900	28,700	42,440
Texas Instruments	125,132	134,059	37,280
Texas Oil & Gas Corp	23,930	22,830	28,115
Tesoro Petroleum	79,219	78,153	23,780
Textron Inc	2,908	61,896	9,800
Thomas & Betts Corp	19,900	9,050	2,320
Tidewater Marine Ser	22,309	21,621	7,515
Timken Co	40,798	15,290	5,055
Transamerica Corp	44,725	34,899	44,010
Trans Union Corp	90,000	90,000	5,340
Trans World Airlines	37,378	51,678	29,425
TRW Corp	64,958	7,445	27,480
UAL Inc	27,122	21,752	45,810
Union Camp Corp	14,803	112,306	20,230
Union Corp	37,800	37,800	6,690
Union Pacific Corp	42,129	23,399	19,550
Untd Energy Res Inc	75,370	58,300	13,640
tUnited Tech Corp	218,225	134,539	43,470
United Tech Ser A pr	10,225	162	3,190
United Nuclear Corp	31,202	27,947	21,915
tUS Steel	184,793	207,679	59,930
United Telecomm Inc	27,887	25,384	28,775
Utah Intl Inc	17,300	38,825	41,540
Upjohn Co	62,255	14,566	27,610
xVard Inc	15,877	27,235	18,100
Valley Ind Inc	66,600	67,200	6,445
Vetco Inc,	161,140	134,440	25,730
Wstn Co of N America	117,969	147,859	4,715
Wisconsin Pwr & Lt	None	10,600	7,305
Wal-Mart Stores Inc	74,025	82,764	12,000
Ward Foods Inc	None	47,460	1,834
Warner Communication	46,602	9,078	83,485
Webb (Del E) Corp	28,871	4,200	20,115
Western Air Lines	27,854	31,704	11,180
Western Union Corp	9,490	33,590	13,725
Westinghouse Elec	32,749	47,478	64,385
Weyerhaeuser Co	87,994	106,174	41,040
Whiting Corp	r21,356	s10,175	1,710
White Cons Ind	61,935	21,431	30,990
Whittaker Corp	80,813	188,174	30,775
Wisconsin El Power	14,700	300	5,470
Winnebago Ind Inc	42,925	38,525	10,910
Woolworth (F W)	32,130	15,060	41,130
tWyly Corp	128,998	108,208	14,880
Xerox Corp	83,673	83,811	68,954
Zapata Corp	14,820	56,145	7,990
Zenith Radio	49,831	73,487	18,700

t-Possibly involved in arbitrage, depending on prices of the securities involved. r-New. s-Old. x-Issue dually traded on New York Stock Exchange and American exchange. Short interest is combined for both exchanges as reported by Big Board.

Short Position. A *short position* is the specific number of shares of stock or bonds sold out of an account in which they are not held.

Short Sale. A short sale is the sale of a security that the customer does not own or that the customer owns but does not intend to deliver. As a general rule, all short sales must be made in a margin account. Regulation T permits a customer to sell short any type of security, regardless of whether it is listed or unlisted or whether it is a debt or equity security. This includes all common stocks, preferred stocks, corporate bonds, and even government securities.

See also Rules of Fair Practice (Section 1).

A short sale usually necessitates a purchase some time in the future to cover the short position. A customer sells short with the expectation that the value of the securities will decline so that when the sale is covered the purchase will be at a price lower than the original sale. Then the customer will realize a profit. At the time the short sale is made the broker borrows securities as a service to the customer to deliver to the purchaser on the settlement.

Obviously, people sell short to make money. They hope that their purchase expense will be lower than their sale proceeds; thus, the difference becomes their profit. If expenses are greater than proceeds, the difference represents their loss. A short sale is really not an unusual investment practice in today's markets. Typically, investors buy a security first and subsequently sell it. What is so strange if they merely reverse this procedure to take advantage of market conditions?

Selling short is sometimes maligned because of its implication of illegality (selling something not owned). However, this is a basic premise of business in the United States, not confined solely to the securities industry. Any time a manufacturer is awarded a contract for merchandise that is not immediately available, to be delivered on a future date at a fixed price,

that concern is selling the merchandise short. It is speculating that it will be able to produce those goods for less money than the contract price of sale.

People selling short in the s rities market are, to be sure, creating an arti   upply. But at the same time, they are a¹   ing an aggressive demand and th   ating the otherwise violent effect :..ᵤ uemand would have on price.

Risk Involved. The practice of selling short should be utilized only by the most sophisticated speculators; that is, only persons who understand and can afford to undertake the many risks involved should sell short. After all, when you purchase and pay for a security, you are assured you cannot lose more than the money you invested. But when you sell short, you create an unlimited financial responsiblity. A rise in price means your cost of purchase to cover that sale will be that much more expensive. How high is up? Infinity!

Because of this potentially limitless financial responsibility, the New York Stock Exchange, the other major exchanges, and the NASD require all short sales to be effected only in margin accounts, where they can be under constant supervision and scrutiny. It is a necessary procedure to ensure compliance with the prescribed equity-maintenance regulations for such transactions.

Indicating the Status of Customer's Ownership. To comply with SEC Rule 10a-1 and 10a-2 (*see* Plus-Tick and Zero-Plus-Tick Rules), each sell order entered for a stock traded on a national securities exchange must be marked "long" or "short," as the case may be, to indicate the status of the customer's title to the security in question. It must also indicate this person's willingness and ability to settle the contract in accordance with the customs of that exchange.

If the order ticket is marked "long," it means the customer owns that security and is prepared to make delivery of the certificate on the usual settlement date (*see* Long Sale).

On the other hand, if the order is marked "short," it means that the customer (1) does not own that security to be sold; or (2) owns the security but does not want to deliver that certificate to satisfy this sale (thus establishing a short-against-the-box position).

In either event, a short designation requires execution on a plus or zero plus tick and necessitates borrowing someone's certificate to complete the sale if it is executed. In fact, the entire process for selling short under any circumstances is predicated on the seller's ability to borrow certificates to make prompt delivery to the purchaser. If you cannot borrow the certificate, you may not sell it short (*see* Borrowing Stock Certificates).

Covering a Short Sale. A short sale is *covered* (that is, the short sale contract is closed) when the short seller purchases the security sold short, thus eliminating the open position.

If short against the box (that is, if the customer is both long and short the same quantity of the security), the customer merely gives instructions to deliver the long position to the lender organization. This pairs off and cancels both positions in the margin account. If the original long position had been held more than six months at the time of the short sale, the resulting profit or loss is taxed as long term. However, if the long position was held six months or less at the time of the short sale, it is always a short-term transaction, regardless of the date when the certificates are actually delivered back to the lender.

If the transaction is a fundamental short sale (that is, a short sale not against the box), the customer must go into the market to purchase the security and deliver it to the lender organization to satisfy the pending obligation. If the purchase expense is greater than the original proceeds, the customer suffers a capital loss, which is treated for tax purposes as short term. If the purchase ex-

pense is less than the original sale proceeds, the customer realizes a short-term capital gain. It is important to note that if a customer purchases a security to cover a short position at a profit, the profit is always taxed at ordinary income rates, regardless of the intervening time period involved in those transactions. Those rates can be as high as 50% of the realized profit. This contrasts with long-term capital gains, which are taxed at much more favorable rates.

Despite this tax disadvantage, a short sale can prove financially rewarding in a hurry, if the sale is timed precisely. Market history has proved that stock prices decline much faster than they rise, even though the longer-term trend of prices for the market, in general, has been bullish for decades.

See also Cushion Theory; Hypothecating Customer Securities; Short Against the Box; Stock Loan.

Short Selling Power. *See* Margin Account (Short Account).

Short-Stop and Short-Stop-Limit Orders. This variety of stop or stop-limit orders is rarely encountered. Some registered representatives have never heard of short-stop and short-stop-limit orders even after many years of servicing customer accounts. The following lists the important aspects of these orders:

1. The stop portion must be activated before there is an order to be executed. Therefore, the price represented applies first to the stop instruction. After this is eliminated, what remains is a simple short-sale order at the market or a short-sale limit order, as the case may be.

2. To determine the execution price once the stop has been activated, do the following: (a) seek the first transaction identified as a plus tick (This is the effective sale for the short-stop order.); (b) compare that price with the limit set by the order. (If that price is higher than the limit price specified in the order, it is also the effective

sale for the short-stop-limit order. If it is not higher, continue searching for the first round-lot transaction that is both a plus tick and above the limit. This is the effective sale for the short-stop-limit order.)

Example: Assume that a customer entered an odd-lot order to sell short at 65¼ stop and that a round-lot sale eventually took place at 65¼ (or below). That trade would activate the stop portion of the order making it a market order to sell short. Now, we must look for the first round-lot sale higher than the electing sale. If the following sale occurred thereafter— 65⅜, 65½, 65⅝—the effective sale would be 65⅜ because it is higher than the electing sale at 65¼. The stock would be sold short at 65¼ after the differential is subtracted.

To illustrate the short-stop-limit order, assume that the customer's odd-lot order had been to sell short at 65⅜ stop limit and had been elected when a round lot traded at 65¼. If the following sales occurred thereafter— 65⅜, 65½, 65⅝—the first sale at 65⅜ is higher than the electing sale but not high enough to satisfy the limit instruction. Therefore, we must continue searching for the round-lot sale capable of satisfying that criterion, too (that is, a round lot at 65½ or above). The effective sale happens to be the following transaction. Therefore, the odd-lot order is sold short at 65⅜, the customer's limit, after the ⅛-point differential is subtracted from the effective sale at 65½. The following table summarizes some sample odd-lot short-stop and short-stop-limit order executions.

See also Differential; Limit Order (Odd-Lot); Odd-Lot Stock Execution; Stop-Limit Order (Odd-Lot); Stop Order (Odd-Lot).

Simultaneous Transaction. A *simultaneous transaction*, also known as a *riskless transaction*, refers to a situation in which the broker/dealer takes a position in a security only after receiving an order from a customer.

Example: A firm might report this transaction to its customer, "As principal, we are selling to you for your account and risk 100 shares of Connecticut General Insurance Company at 65¾ net." If the shares were bought at 64¾ and then sold to the customer at 65¾, the dealer has a markup of one point. This dealer, not a market-maker but still acting as principal, set a price of 65¾ immediately after execution, resulting in a markup of $100 for itself. But it had not established a position in its own account until after the buy order was accepted from the customer. This simultaneous activity is a legal and popular method among NASD members.

See also Markup and Markdown.

Sinking Fund. A corporation can set aside money every year to maturity to meet a maturing obligation if the indenture requires the corporation to establish a sinking fund. A *sinking fund* is an annual reserve of capital set aside out of current earnings so that, over a period of years, enough money becomes available to redeem that bond at maturity. It certainly represents a valuable degree of protection for the investor in the event of default.

Provisions in the indenture for a significant "sinker" exert an influence on a bond's market price. When the corporation is obliged to retire a portion of its debt annually through open market purchases or exercise of a call, it provides a flexible floor in the price of that security. This built-in demand partially offsets the effect of adverse changes in the money market and provides more asset protection for the remaining holders of that issue.

See also Call; Conversion; Open Market Purchase.

SMA *See* Special Memorandum Account.

Sold Last Sale. This ticker tape identification designates a transaction that has fluctuated volatilely between sales. It appears for an issue that has moved one or more points if its previous sale

Sample Odd-lot Short-stop and Short-stop-Limit Order Executions

Previous Round-Lot Transaction	Terms	Subsequent Round-Lot Transactions*	Execution Price
38⅝	Sell short at 38⅝ stop	**38⅝,** 38½, 38⅜, 38¼	Cannot be executed (no higher value sale than 38⅝):
26¼	Sell short at 26 stop	26⅛, **26,** 25⅞, 26̲	25⅞ (26 − ⅛) The first plus tick after the electing sale is the second transaction there-after, also at 26. That sale is the effective sale. The odd-lot short sale is completed at 25⅞.
89⅜	Sell short at 89¼ stop limit	89⅜, **89⅛,** 89̲⅜̲, 89⅝,	89¼ (89⅜ − ⅛)
57⅞	Sell short at 57¾ stop limit	**57¾,** 57⅝, 57¾, 57̲⅞̲	57¾ (57⅞ − ⅛) After the stop order was elected at 57¾, the price declined to 57⅝, an ineligible short-sale price. Although the following sale at 57¾ solved that problem, it was not high enough in value to satisfy the limit requirement of 57¾. The first such sale to satisfy both requirements was the next transaction at 57⅞. Thus, the customer sells short at the limit of 57¾ after the differential is deducted from the effective sale.
143	Sell short at 142½ stop, limit 142	143, **142,** 142̲½̲, 141½	142⅜ (142½ − ⅛)
41⅞	Sell short at 41¾ stop, limit 41½	**41½,** 41⅜, 41̲⅝̲, 41⅞	41½ (41⅝ − ⅛)
18½	Sell short at 18¼ stop, limit 18	18½, 18⅝, 18⅜, **18¼**	Cannot be executed from given information (no sales shown after electing sale at 18¼).

*The electing sale is in boldface type and the effective sale is boxed.

was 1⅞ or below, two or more points if its previous sale was 20 or above

See also Ticker Tape.

Sold Sale (SLD). *SLD* on the ticker tape designates a transaction appearing on the tape out of its proper sequence.

See also Ticker Tape.

Special Bids and Offerings. When it is determined that a sizable order cannot be disposed of in a normal manner, in a reasonable period of time, and at reasonable prices, a *special offering* may be attempted. (Approval from the NYSE is required.)

A special offering is an offering of stock by a member organization from its own portfolio or in behalf of one or more customers at a *fixed price.* The fixed price may not be above the last sale or current offering price in the regular auction market, whichever is lower.

All member firms are invited to transmit their buy orders for any portion of the offering (even odd-lot orders can participate) to the floor of the exchange where they can accept this price in the usual manner. The incentive for the firm and its salespeople to do so is a *special commission* (payable by the seller). Thus, the purchasing customer can trade with the offeror on a net basis (no commission expense), whereas the registered representative receives a higher-than-usual fee from the seller for the service provided.

Important points to remember about this procedure are the following:

1. Prior approval must be granted both by a floor official and the Floor Department of the exchange.

2. The regular market price may decline below the fixed special offering price and defeat the attempted sale unless a limited amount of stabilization is permitted by the exchange. (Generally stabilization practices may involve quantities ranging up to 10% of the amount of stock being offered.)

3. The special offer must remain effective for at least fifteen minutes unless suspended because of a change in market conditions.

4. The party making the offering must be the owner of these shares. Short sales via this procedure are prohibited.

5. Transactions effected in a special offering do not elect stop orders or cause the execution of GTC odd-lot orders.

6. The seller must give written certification to the exchange and the member firm that the shares offered represent all that will be distributed for a reasonable time thereafter.

7. The seller cannot offer additional shares in the regular auction market while the special offering is pending.

The terms of a special offering must be printed on the ticker tape before the offering becomes effective. At that time, too, the member organization must announce whether it has already stabilized, or intends to stabilize, the offering price in the regular auction market. Then, as each transaction is effected pursuant to this offering, an announcement is made of this fact on the ticker tape including the amount of the special commission payable.

Example:

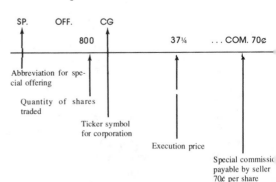

Each customer's confirmation prepared in connection with this unique execution procedure must also detail the terms and conditions of the offering.

The counterpart of a special offering is a *special bid. Special bids* are used for customers who want to buy a sizable amount of stock at a fixed price. The required approvals, written certifications, and mechanical procedures are identical to those used for special offerings. The exception, of course, is that the special bid takes place on the opposite side of the market. Thus, the special bid must be at the price of the last sale or the current prevailing bid, whichever is higher, in the regular NYSE auction market. Special bids are also identified on the ticker tape as they are executed.

Example:

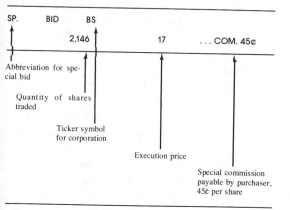

See also Bid and Offer.

Special Cash Account. A customer is required to make full payment in this account on the fifth business day after the trade date, and in no case later than the seventh calendar day or arrange for C.O.D. payment on the fifth business day. The account is defined in Regulation T.

See also Frozen Account.

Special Commission. *See* Exchange Distributions and Acquisitions; Special Bids and Offerings.

Special Deals. According to the NASD Supple-

ment to the SEC Statement of Policy, it is improper for an underwriter to give, or a member organization or registered representative to receive, anything of material value in addition to the cash discounts or concessions set forth in the offering prospectus in connection with the sale or distribution of investment company shares. Any gift valued at more than $50 per person annually, whether in cash or merchandise, is generally considered to be of "material value" and therefore in violation of this rule. However, an occasional cocktail party, dinner, ticket to the theater, sporting event, or the like is considered acceptable if (1) it is extended infrequently; (2) distribution is limited to relatively few persons; and (3) there is no question of propriety about the means or manner of such an action; and (4) it is not conditioned on sales of shares of the investment company.

Specialist. Members appointed by the Board of Directors of the NYSE to maintain an orderly succession of prices in selected stocks are identified as *specialists.* Much of the marketability enjoyed by listed stocks today can be traced to the activities of specialists. Although specialists do not personally participate in every transaction, they do supervise and facilitate executions of orders by all brokers in the trading post area.

The most attractive and important feature of a stock exchange listing is marketability at fair and reasonable prices. Toward this objective, one category of members—the specialists—has been delegated with responsibility for ensuring that each listed stock experiences an "orderly succession of prices." That member is known as the Specialist. Each stock issue traded on the New York Stock Exchange is assigned a specialist to supervise and conduct an equitable market for that security. (The NYSE is but one of the exchanges using the specialist system. We refer to it here as an example of those exchanges that have specialists working in this way.)

The specialist is the lifeblood of activity transacted on the New York Stock Exchange. The specialist's knowledge, ability, skills, and capital are necessary to assure depth and liquidity for the equity securities of corporations responsible for approximately 47% of total assets, 43% of sales, and 94.6% of income of all corporations in the United States. (New York Stock Exchange, Inc., *1985 Fact Book* (New York: New York Stock Exchange, Inc. 1985), p. 78.)

To perform this function, the specialist is obliged to act in a dual capacity—as agent and as principal.

The Specialist as Agent. The specialist in a particular security normally receives orders to buy or sell when a firm's commission house or two-dollar brokers are unable to execute them immediately. Usually, this means that the specialist receives orders away from the current price levels of that issue. Such orders include limit orders to buy and stop orders to sell at prices below the prevailing market level, as well as limit orders to sell and stop orders to buy at prices above the prevailing market level. The specialist then enters them in a book maintained as a constant reminder to satisfy these instructions if and when market conditions favor their execution (see the following figure).

When able to execute an order, the specialist may charge and receive a floor brokerage fee for this service as can any two-dollar broker. (Since May 1, 1975, specialists and other floor brokers are not obligated to charge a minimum rate. Consequently, they can execute some orders without any charge if they so choose.) The brokerage fee is negotiated between the specialist and the firm for whom that order was executed.

Example: When a specialist buys 100 shares of stock at 24 on behalf of a customer of a member firm, the charge may be $3.50 payable from the commission the customer owes to the member organization.

Many specialists in stocks that are popular with the public earn a substantial portion of their income acting in this riskless agency capacity. However, there is no assurance that (1) the customers' instructions can ever be satisfied; (2) these orders will not be cancelled just prior to execution; or (3) sufficient quantities of customers' orders will be given to the specialist for execution. In fact, the specialist's book is often empty of customer orders on the side of the quotation or at the time when they are needed most to maintain depth and price continuity. It is especially important at this time for the specialist to act as a dealer.

The Specialist as Principal. The specialist is encouraged to buy and sell for a personal account and risk in order to maintain marketability and an orderly succession of prices. The specialist is expected to personally bid or offer when the public is reluctant to do so and thus provide continuous two-sided markets in all quotations. (In 1975 the average specialist acted as principal in about 13% of all stock transactions on the exchange.) In addition to maintaining an orderly round-lot market, which is a primary responsibility, the specialist accommodates most odd-lot customers (*see* Odd-Lot Stock Executions).

The exchanges do not expect the specialist to act as a barrier in a rising market or as a support in a falling market. The specialist must merely try to keep these rises and declines *equitable and consistent.* Because of the variable factors influencing supply and demand for individual stocks, a specific formula for an orderly market cannot be defined.

Example: Let us illustrate what a specialist might do in order to keep prices equitable and consistent. Take the hypothetical case of specialist Joe Brown with an absence of public orders at a particular moment. Brown may bid 50 for 100 shares of stock for himself at the same time he is offering 100 shares for sale at 50⅜ from his account. If someone then sells him 100 shares at 50, he may then bid 49¾ for 100 and offer 100 at 50⅛. If someone sells him another

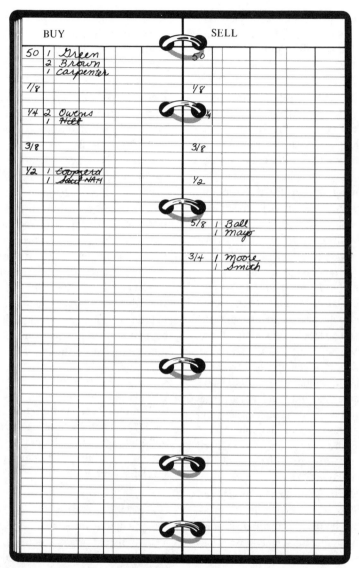

The typical specialist's book is an informal record of orders received from various brokers on the NYSE trading floor. It fits easily into the palm of the specialist's hand; the looseleaf format allows pages to be added or removed easily.

100 at 49¾, he may then drop his quotation to 49½ bid and offer it at 49⅞. In this fashion, he provides liquidity for a security, although it is sometimes at personal expense to himself.

As just described, this can prove to be an expensive public service. If only sell orders prevail, and specialist Brown continually bids for stock, albeit at consecutively lower prices, there is no way for him to deal profitably. However, professional traders, including specialists, realize that prices do not fall continuously, even in bear markets, nor, on the other hand, do they rise continuously in bull markets. Prices of securities do, in fact, fluctuate as speculators, traders, and investors attempt to gain advantage of what they consider to be attractive values. This fluctuation enables specialists to trade out of their positions as they satisfy both supply and demand in a market-making capacity. They do not always have an opportunity to trade profitably. They often incur losses to keep their stock positions at manageable levels and still provide equitable prices for the public.

As a legally recognized market-maker, a specialist enjoys certain financing and tax advantages not available to most investors. The specialist is privileged to maintain both a specialty (trading) account and an investment account for each assigned stock. By keeping these positions physically separate and distinct, the specialist can (1) take advantage of favorable long-term capital gains rates for profits established in an investment account, and (2) arrange financing for securities in the specialty account exempted from the restrictive provisions of the Federal Reserve Board's Regulation U. Generally, this means that the specialist can obtain credit in amounts up to 90% of the market value of the security pledged. A specialist may also repurchase stocks sold at a loss within the past thirty days and still be able to use that loss to offset profits in calculating taxable income. That privilege, known as a wash sale, is denied to most investors under the Internal Revenue Code.

On the other hand, the government does not grant specialists any privileges to provide a tactical advantage over competing brokers in the trading crowd. Specialists must observe the unique rules about executing short sales for themselves or for customers in the same manner as do all other members. This means that when selling short, they too must sell shares short at least ⅛ point above the previous different-priced transaction. Just like everyone else, a specialist cannot depress the price of a stock when selling it short.

The New York Stock Exchange realizes that the specialist's vantage point in the marketplace provides information that could prove personally profitable if the specialist were permitted to use it. Because the contents of the book are generally unavailable to anyone else except NYSE officials, the specialist alone knows how many orders and shares are entered at prices just away from the prevailing quotation— orders that may serve as support or resistance levels. The specialist alone knows of the presence of stop orders and their memorandum price levels—orders that may accentuate price volatility if activated. Consequently, although the NYSE urges specialists to maintain personal trading relative to total volume in each assigned security, it must be done under restrictive regulations to avoid prejudicing the public interest.

Specialist Trading Rules. There are literally dozens of rules pertaining to conduct and activities of specialists in maintaining an orderly market. Five of them are germane to an understanding of specialist trading responsibilities.

When dealing for a personal account, a specialist cannot:

1. *Bid or offer on the same side as any customer's market order held.* (Specialists normally receive market orders when a limit order on the book is cancelled and replaced with a market order.) A specialist is not permitted to buy stock as principal until a customer's market order to buy has been satisfied; nor may the specialist sell stock as principal until a customer's market order to sell has been completed. Note that this restriction does not prevent a specialist from dealing on the opposite side of a customer's market order, provided none of the other rules in the process are violated.

2. *Bid or offer at the same price as any customer's limit order held.* A specialist may not have priority of time over any customer's limit order in the book, even if the specialist was bidding or offering as principal before receipt of the customer's order. The specialist can, of course, combine a personal bid or offering with customer orders at that price if the customer orders are given preference on executions that occur subsequently.

3. *Activate (elect) a customer's stop order on the book.* The specialist may not be a party to any principal transaction if that trade elects a customer's stop order in the book. (In exceptional circumstances, with prior approval from a floor official, specialists may be responsible for activating stop orders. However, they must guarantee that customer an execution at the same price as the transaction that triggered this stop order.) Therefore, the specialist must carefully anticipate the possible result of a personal bid or offering if ultimately accepted by another member in the trading crowd.

4. *Act as broker* and *dealer in the same transaction.* If a specialist wants to buy stock personally from a customer's offering in the book or personally sell stock to a customer's bid in the book, the specialist must summon the broker who entered that order. That broker then executes the customer's transaction and earns the floor brokerage. The procedure is known as a *write-out*, because the specialist sends a notice to the telephone clerk of that firm requesting the appearance of its broker. The broker must reconfirm the details of the order and write an execution report. The specialist is not allowed to deal as principal and act as a customer's agent at the same time because of the inherent conflict of interest.

5. *Stop stock for any member's account.* This restriction means the specialist is not allowed to guarantee any member's *personal account* an execution price and thereby enable that person or firm to avoid market risk. *Stopping*

stock is a specialist's guarantee of price to a customer's broker that enables the broker to try to improve on that price without fear of missing the market.

Ethical Responsibilities of a Specialist. To maintain status as fair and impartial coordinators of market activities, specialists must abide by an ethical code set down by the NYSE. It regulates a specialist's relationship to the company in whose stock this member specializes. (These rules also apply to partners and employees of the specialist's firm.)

Controversies and proxy contests. Specialists may not participate in a proxy contest of the company in whose stock they specialize. As market-makers, specialists are precluded from becoming embroiled in any controversies that may develop between management and dissident groups. However, as investors, specialists are not prohibited from assuming an active role in the affairs of other corporations.

Official capacities. Specialists may not serve as officers or directors in a company if they specialize in its stock. They must not place themselves in a position where they can be privy to nonpublic information. Any inside revelations would surely influence their market activities and legally jeopardize them under penalties provided for by the Securities Exchange Act of 1934. Specialists may hold responsible positions in other, nonbrokerage corporations, provided that to do so does not adversely affect their specialist duties on the floor of the NYSE.

Ownership of securities. Specialists are also prohibited from owning control securities and from becoming principal stockholders in a company in which they specialize. Influential holdings represented by controlling securities would place a specialist in an insider relationship with that company, affecting and restricting any market-making ability. Similarly, as principal stockholders (owners of 10% or more of a class of stock issued by the corporation), their market judgment might be clouded or swayed by the size of their portfolios. Furthermore, by virtue of their substantial holdings, the corporations might also be tempted to accord them preferential treatment.

Remuneration. Specialists may not accept finder's fees or other remuneration from a company in which they act as specialists. The old adage about a person's inability to serve two masters well at the same time is accorded some validity by this denial. The NYSE reasons that if specialists gain employment or compensation from a corporation, they are tempted to act more favorably toward it. This situation prejudices the best interests of both the NYSE and the investing public.

Business transactions. Specialists may not engage in business transactions of any kind with the company in whose stock they specialize. This restriction applies not only to loans, options, contracts, and so forth, but to securities transactions in that issue for or with (1) the company itself; (2) any officer or director of the company; (3) any principal stockholder (owner of 10% or more of a class of stock) of the company; (4) any pension or profit-sharing fund; (5) any financial institution, such as a bank, trust company, insurance company, or investment company. The obvious intent is for specialists to remain independent in their speciality stocks and avoid any conflict of interest or allegations of partiality.

Managing a Specialist's Book.

Example: Green Tiger Oil. When Broker A arrives at the trading post and asks for a quotation in Green Tiger Oil stock, the notations in the specialist's book are as shown in the following figure. The specialist may reflect only the highest-priced bid and lowest-priced offering with the number of shares represented at those prices (size). Other orders at various levels are strictly confidential. Therefore, the specialist announces, "26⅜ to 26½, 500 by 1,200."

If Broker A says, "Take 100," it means that

BUY		SELL
	26	
500 – PERSHING + CO. INC.	**⅛**	
100 – BEAR STEARNS + CO.	**¼**	
100 – LOEWI + CO., INC. 400 – LADENBURG THALMANN	**⅜**	
	½	200 – BACHE HALSEY STUART 1000 – DEAN WITTER + CO. INC.
	⅝	100 – MERRILL LYNCH 600 – FERRIS + COMPANY
	¾	
	⅞	

Green Tiger Oil, symbol GTO. In practice, a specialist usually abbreviates entries recorded in the book, dropping the last two zeros for volume notations and using designated code letters for member firm identification. Thus, the offerings at 26½ would be written: 2-B and 10-DW.

Broker A is accepting 100 shares of the 1,200 offered at 26½, and the specialist gives up the name of Prudential Bache to Broker A. Bache's order was entered on the book before Dean Witter's, and the specialist handles the book on a first-come, first-served basis. The specialist then writes a report to Prudential Bache announcing sale of 100 shares at 26½ to Broker A (or perhaps to another firm given up by Broker A), leaving 100 shares remaining to be sold for Prudential Bache. At the end of the month, the specialist will send Bache a bill for floor brokerage for the execution service just performed as agent.

If, instead, Broker A says "Sold 200," it means that Broker A is accepting 200 shares of the 500 bid for at 26⅜, and the specialist gives up Loewi & Co. and Ladenburg, Thalmann to Broker A, each for 100 shares. The specialist writes execution reports to Loewi and Ladenburg, Thalmann at 26⅜, declares Broker A as the contra broker, and charges those buying firms floor brokerage as agent at month's end. Specialists may charge a floor brokerage fee only for those firms they serve as broker; that is, in an agency capacity.

Example: Ding-a-Ling Toys. Broker B, arriving in the Ding-a-Ling crowd, is informed that the stock is 13⅝ to 13⅞, 400 by 2,000. As shown in the following figure, the presence of Shearson Lehman stop order to sell at 13¾ is not

Specialist's Book for Ding-a-Ling Toys (DALT)

BUY		SELL
	13	
	⅛	
	¼	
	⅜	
100-DREXEL BURNHAM LAMBERT	**½**	
400-GOLDMAN SACHS	**⅝**	
	¾	100 STOP-LOEB RHOADES
	⅞	1000-SHIELDS MODEL ROLAND 1000-THOMPSON McKINNON

revealed because as a memorandum instruction it has no standing in the marketplace. It is a private communication between Shearson Lehman and the specialist.

If Broker B says, "Sold 100" (to Goldman, Sachs on the specialist's book), the price level of that transaction, 13⅝, elects the stop order (at or below 13¾). Now Shearson Lehman's memorandum becomes a market order and must be executed immediately by the specialist, in all likelihood at 13⅝, too. The specialist earns three floor commissions on these transactions, two from Goldman, Sachs and one from Shearson Lehman.

If the specialist does not execute immediately at 13⅝ and attempts to use market judgment by offering Shearson Lehman's stock at 13¾ instead of 13⅝, the specialist risks missing the market. Another broker entering the crowd to sell 300 shares at 13⅝ would completely satisfy Goldman's remaining bid. This would establish the specialist's financial liability to Shearson Lehman at that price, too.

Example: Underground Minerals Unlimited. With the market in UMU represented in the following figure, the specialist accepts an order to sell 100 shares short at the market from Broker Y. Because the previous transaction was at 41⅜ on a plus tick, the specialist can offer Broker Y's stock as low as 41⅜, changing the current offer from 41½ to 41⅜.

If a buyer accepts the offer at 41⅜, it constitutes a zero plus tick (equal in value to the last sale but higher than the last different-priced transaction), and complies with federal laws regarding execution of the short sale (*see* Plus-Tick and Zero-Plus-Tick Rules).

If, instead, Broker C arrives and cleans up the prevailing bid by selling 400 shares to the specialist's book at 41¼ and 200 shares at 41⅛, the specialist can then reduce Broker Y's offering price to 41¼. A subsequent sale at 41¼ would then represent a plus tick and would satisfy the short-sale regulation.

Specialist's Book for Underground Minerals Unlimited (UMU, previous sale 41⅜, plus tick)

BUY		SELL
100 - WHITE WELD & CO.,INC.	**41**	
200 - KUHN LOEB & CO.	**1/8**	
100 - MITCHUM JONES TEMPLETON 300 - TUCKER ANTHONY & R.L. DAY	**1/4**	
	3/8	
	1/2	500 - SALOMON BROTHERS 600 - OPPENHEIMER & CO.
	5/8	
	3/4	
	7/8	

Specialist's Book for Clever Computer Corporation (ccc, previous sale 30⅝, minus tick. Specialist's position = none.)

BUY		SELL
100 - REYNOLDS SECURITIES 200 - PERSHING & COMPANY 400 - ROBINSON - HUMPHREY	**30**	
	1/8	
	1/4	
100 - BLYTH EASTMAN DILLON	**3/8**	
	1/2	300 STOP - MERRILL LYNCH
	5/8	
	3/4	200 - McDONALD & COMPANY 100 - E.F. HUTTON
	7/8	500 - THOMPSON McKINNON 100 - BACHE HALSEY STUART

Example: Clever Computer Corporation. The specialist's brokerage (agency) responsibility is readily identifiable, with the rules firmly fixed. If the specialist merely follows the customer's instructions, personal capital is not exposed to risk. But the specialist's function must often be combined with a dealer's (principal) responsibility to temper minor disparities between supply and demand.

To understand when and where the specialist may bid, offer, buy, or sell for a personal account, it is important to think ahead and project the effect of such transactions on the mar-. ketplace. Observe Clever Computer Corporation in the figure above. The previous sale was at 30⅝, minus tick. The quotation resulting from public orders in the specialist's book is 30⅜ bid for 100 and 30¾ asked for 300 shares in total. With such a wide spread, this should be an ideal time for the specialist, with no position in CCC, personally to bid or offer and narrow the demand/supply gap. The question centers around permissible and appropriate prices at which to participate.

Bids for the specialist's personal account:

1. *Below 30⅜.* These bids are impractical because they do not narrow the spread in the quotation, are not reflected in the marketplace, and do not facilitate marketability.

2. *At 30⅜.* Such bids would violate the

rule about competing with a customer (Paine Webber) at the same price unless the specialist gave Paine Webber priority. Even so, this bid would be dangerous and would accomplish little. It does not narrow the spread in the quotation. Furthermore, if Paine Webber cancelled its order, the specialist would have to cancel, too. If the specialist's bid at 30⅜ was there alone, and a broker then sold stock at that price, the specialist would have participated in a transaction that activated Merrill Lynch's stop order (at 30½ or below). This would violate the specialist's trading restrictions.

3. *At 30½*. Bidding for a personal account at this price would be improper for a similar reason. If a broker sold stock at 30½, the specialist would activate Merrill's stop order, a practice prohibited under the trading rules. (Stop orders to sell become market orders if a trade occurs at or below the memorandum price. Stop orders to buy become market orders if a trade occurs at or above the memorandum price.)

4. *At 30⅝*. This is a valid bid because it narrows the gap between bid and asked prices and would not be instrumental in activating the sell-stop order on the book.

5. *At 30¾*. This is not a "bid" because of the presence of an offering at this price. To *purchase* stock, the specialist can accept an offering at 30¾. This action, however, would be suspect because normally a specialist (a) should not establish or increase a position in a stock on a plus tick (buying on a plus tick is considered a price-manipulative act and could entice public investors into buying the stock as it rises, thus benefiting the specialist's position); and (b) should never purchase more than half the quantity offered at that price (to do so would dominate trading in that issue and deny public investors a reasonable opportunity to share in a subsequent rise in price).

Offers for the specialist's personal account:

1. *Above 30¾*. Such offers are impractical because they do not improve the market. In any event, the specialist cannot compete or have priority over any public customer's order at the same price.

2. *At 30¾*. Action by the specialist at this price does not narrow the spread between demand and supply and accomplishes nothing because all public orders must be accorded priority anyway.

3. *At 30⅝*. This would normally be a valid offer if it weren't for one deterrent. If a broker accepted this offer at 30⅝, the specialist would be selling short on a zero minus tick, an act prohibited by federal regulation.

4. *At 30½*. The spectre of a short sale on a minus tick is also present here and must, therefore, be avoided. Additionally, a sale at this price would trigger the stop order.

5. *At 30⅜*. This is not an offer because of the presence of a bid at that price. However, an acceptance of that bid by the specialist would be illegal anyway, because (a) it would be a short sale on a minus tick; and (b) it would activate the stop order.

This illustration emphasizes the difficulty specialists experience in their market-making activities. Often they are precluded from being too aggressive because of prevailing rules and regulations. As principal in this illustration, the specialist is allowed to bid only at 30⅝ in efforts to improve marketability and also is prevented from offering stock at any price level.

Example: Earthquake Eradicators. When entering the Earthquake Eradicators crowd, Broker D is advised the stock is quoted 57⅜ to 57⅝, 1,800 bid for and 500 offered (see the following figure). The confidential stop order to buy, with no active standing in the crowd, is known only to the specialist. The specialist owns 200 shares long in a personal account.

If Broker D then says "Take it," or "Take 500," the specialist gives up the names of Nesbitt, Thomson for 400 and Wood, Struthers for 100. The specialist then writes execution reports to each of these firms advising them of their sales

Specialist's Book for Earthquake Eradicators (EE, previous sale 57⅜, plus tick. Specialist's position = 200 shares long)

BUY		SELL
100 - KIDDER PEABODY	**57**	
200 - PAINE WEBBER J *C.	**1/8**	
1000 - SALOMON BROTHERS 400 - SHIELDS MODEL ROLAND	**1/4**	
300 - MERRILL LYNCH 1500 - HORNBLOWER WEEKS	**3/8**	
100 STOP - ADVEST & CO.	**1/2**	
	5/8	400 - NESBITT THOMPSON & CO. 100 - WOOD STRUTHERS
	3/4	500 - L.F. ROTHSCHILD 400 - BECKER SECURITIES
	7/8	1000 - STIFEL NICOLAUS & CO. 800 - STERN LAUER & CO.

Specialist's Book for Vigilant Examiners, Inc. (VEI, previous sale 83¼, plus tick. Specialist's position = 100 shares long.)

BUY		SELL
100 - RAUSCHER PIERCE S EC. 200 - LEHMAN BROS.	**83**	
100 - SHEARSON HAYDEN STONE 100 - E.F. HUTTON & CO.	**1/8**	
	1/4	
	3/8	
	1/2	200 - SMITH BARNEY HARRIS UPHAM 300 - REYNOLDS SECURITIES
	5/8	500 - FIRST BOSTON CO.
	3/4	
	7/8	

to Broker D (or the member firm that Broker D discloses). However, as a result of that transaction at 57⅝, the stop order at 57½ has been activated. Now, with respect to that newly created market order, the specialist may (1) buy 100 shares for Advest & Co. immediately from L. F. Rothschild at 57¾, the best available offering; (2) bid 57½ for Advest & Co., using market judgment and hoping the next broker coming into the crowd will be a seller; or (3) sell 100 shares to Advest & Co., from a personal account at 57⅝, allowing Advest & Co.'s broker to write out the execution report.

Example: Vigilant Examiners, Inc. With Vigilant Examiners Inc., in the figure on page 000, quoted 83⅛ to 83½, 200 by 500 shares,

Broker E asks the specialist to be stopped at 83½ on 100 shares. Broker E wants to be guaranteed a price of 83½ to buy 100 shares and have an opportunity to purchase the customer's 100 shares at a cheaper price. (Buyers are stopped at prevailing offerings; sellers at prevailing bid prices.) The previous sale was at 83¼, plus tick. The specialist owns 100 shares long in a personal account.

In undertaking consideration of this request, the specialist realizes that there are two separate orders at 83½ to use as quasi-protection for any guarantee at this price. But the specialist is also aware that either or both of these sell orders may be cancelled or purchased by another broker before Broker E's customer can do better.

Therefore, in granting Broker E's request, the specialist understands that as a last resort 100 shares from the specialist's personal account might have to be sold to Broker E at 83½.

Let us assume that Broker E is stopped at 83½. Broker E gives the order to the specialist for the attempt at improvement. The specialist then bids 83¼ (or 83⅜) in behalf of that customer. This bid narrows the spread in the quotation to ¼ (or ⅛) point.

A variety of circumstances can then occur. A step-by-step analysis reveals how the specialist operates under each of those possible conditions:

1. If either Dean Witter Reynolds or Smith Barney Harris Upham cancels its order to sell, the only action called for would be a reduction in the offering size from 500 in total to 300 or 200, depending on which firm revokes its instructions.

2. If both Dean Witter Reynolds and Smith Barney Harris Upham cancel their sell orders, the specialist notifies Broker E that the stop is off. The specialist allows Broker E to purchase 100 shares from the specialist's account at 83½. The specialist would no longer have Dean Witter Reynolds or Smith Barney Harris Upham stock to accommodate Broker E and therefore must terminate Broker E's opportunity to improve on the price.

3. If a seller arrives at the post, that broker will dispose of stock to Broker E's customer who is making the best bid. In an effort to get a better price than 83½, Broker E's customer who is making the best bid. In an effort to get a better price than 83½, Broker E uses the opportunity to bid 83¼ (or 83⅜, as the case may be), which is the best bid. The specialist, acting as Broker E's agent, writes the execution report and earns the floor brokerage fee.

4. If another buyer arrives instead, that broker can purchase up to the full 500 shares of the offering. This in turn stops out Broker E's customer, causing Broker E to purchase 100 shares from the stock remaining for sale at 83½ by Dean Witter Reynolds or Smith Barney Harris Upham if there is any; in their absence Broker E buys 100 shares from the specialist's own account at 83½. Having been unsuccessful in doing better than 83½, Broker E must buy the stock at the price originally available.

In either of the latter events, the specialist summons Broker E and allows Broker E to write the execution report. Stock that has been stopped out, such as in this instance, is often identified on the ticker tape with the letters *ST* in vertical order after the execution price, as shown.

VEI	83½	S T

Example: Currency Managers and Manipulators. This last illustration involves all the complexities of a real and active trading market with the presence of a stop order and the allowance of stopped stock (see the following figure).

The market in CMM is announced at 65¼ to 65⅝, 400 by 400 shares. The previous sale was at 65½, plus tick. The specialist owns 100 shares long in a personal account. Broker F asks to be stopped at 65¼ on the 100 shares to be sold. (Sellers are stopped at prevailing bids, buyers at prevailing offering prices.) Although most of the prerequisites are there (such as public order, minimum ¼-point spread, and so on), the specialist realizes those bids might be cancelled. If they are cancelled, then the specialist would be obliged to buy Broker F's stock at 65¼. That transaction would be responsible for activating Lehman's stop order. This normally prohibited action may be bypassed only in the public interest. The specialist would need to get approval from a floor official and to guarantee Lehman's sell-stop order, an execution at the same price as the electing sale itself. Under these cir-

Specialist's Book for Currency Managers and Manipulators

BUY		SELL
100- JOHNSON LANE SPACE 100-SHIELDS MODEL ROLAND 200-FAHNESTOCK & COMPANY	**65**	
400- DAIN KALMAN & QUAIL	**1/8**	
200-LAZARD FRERES & CO. 100-EVANS & CO., INC 100- BEAR STEARNS	**1/4**	
	3/8	200 STOP-LEHMAN BROS.
	1/2	
	5/8	300-SHEARSON HAYDEN STONE 100- WOOD GUNDY & CO
	3/4	1000-ALEX BROWN & SONS 500-DONALDSON LUFKIN & J
	7/8	300-FAULKNER DAWKINS & S. 700-NEUBERGER BERMAN & CO

cumstances, it is unlikely the specialist will stop Broker F. Probably, Broker F will sell 100 shares immediately to Lazard on the specialist's book or risk missing the market. That transaction at 65¼ now elects the stop order, and Lehman's newly created market order will be crossed by the specialist at 65¼, pairing it off with 100 shares remaining to be bought by Lazard and 100 for Evans & Co. The specialist will announce in a clear and audible voice, "65¼ for 200, 200 at 65⅜, sold."

On the other hand, if Broker G enters the original crowd instead of Broker F and asks to be stopped for 100 shares to buy at 65⅝, it is likely the specialist will do so. All the permissible fac-

tors are present, along with the added incentive of possible sale of the specialist's own 100 shares at a stabilizing price (65⅝ equals plus tick).

In all likelihood, the specialist would then bid 65½ for 100 shares in behalf of Broker G's customer, trying to do better than 65⅝. Then, the following would happen:

1. If a seller appeared, Broker G's customer, with the best bid, would buy the stock at 65½. The specialist writes the execution report and earns the floor brokerage.

2. If a buyer appeared and bought stock from the lowest offeror at 65⅝, Broker G's customer would be stopped out. That customer would buy stock at 65⅝, either from (a) one of the offerors on the specialist's book; or in their absence, (b) the specialist's account, in fulfillment of the guarantee obligation. In either case, a or b, the specialist would summon Broker G to write out the customer's execution report and thereby earn the floor brokerage. The specialist would do this because Broker G was capable of the same execution when initially entering that crowd.

Specialized Investment Company. These investment companies concentrate their investments in one industry, in a group of related industries, or in a single geographic area of the world. Their principal objective is long-term capital growth with little regard for current income. The number of specialized companies has significantly declined in recent years, and many have diversified to such an extent that they are no longer classified as specialized. Those that still prevail restrict their investments to bank and insurance securities, foreign securities, public utilities, or to companies engaged in advanced scientific endeavors.

See also Investment Company; Nondiversified Company.

Special Memorandum Account.

Purposes of SMA. One of the most important, yet least understood, accounts established by the Federal Reserve Board is the special memorandum account, commonly known as the SMA. The special memorandum account, while being a separate and distinct account under Regulation T, is normally operated in tandem with the margin account. As a matter of fact, most individuals involved in margin trading come to think of the SMA as an integral part of the margin account.

As defined in Regulation T, the SMA is available for a variety of purposes and uses, in addition to those related to the margin account. When used in conjunction with the margin account, the SMA's basic purposes are (1) to preserve and protect Reg T excess against market depreciation and (2) to make such funds available to be withdrawn by customers or to be used by them to meet Regulation T requirements on new margin commitments. An amendment to Regulation T describes how the special memorandum account is to be maintained. The following is the exact text of Section 220.6 of Regulation T special memorandum account.

"§220.6   Special memorandum account.

(a) A special memorandum account (SMA) may be maintained in conjunction with a margin account. A single entry amount may be used to represent both a credit to the SMA and a debit to the margin account. A transfer between the two accounts may be effected by an increase or reduction in the entry. When computing the equity in a margin account, the single entry amount shall be considered as a debit in the margin account. A payment to the customer or on the customer's behalf or a transfer to any of the customer's other accounts from the SMA reduces the single entry amount.

(b) The SMA may contain the following entries: (1) dividend and interest payments; (2) cash not required by this part, including cash deposited to meet a maintenance margin call or to meet any requirement of a self-regulatory organization that is not imposed by this part; (3) proceeds of a sale of securities or cash no longer required on any expired or liquidated security position that may be withdrawn under   §220.4(e) of this part; and (4) margin excess transferred from the margin account under §220.4(e)(2) of this part."

When the market value of securities held long in a margin account increases, the account generates additional credit known as Reg T excess. This happens when the equity in the account increases to a level greater than the current equity required under Regulation T. The increase in the market value is what causes the increase in equity. However, if the market value declines, it follows that the equity also declines. This causes a possible loss of Reg T excess. Without the SMA being used more or less as a depository, additional credit arising from Reg T excess available to customers will be vulnerable to daily downward swings in the market prices of their securities.

Illustration of Use of SMA.

Example: To illustrate how the SMA is used in conjunction with the margin account, let us examine the activity of the following account:

Margin Account of Jane Doe
50% Reg T Initial Requirement

LMV	Equity	SMA	Balance
$10,000	$5,000	0	$5,000 Dr

The following events occur:

1. Long market value in the account increases to $12,000. Following this increase in LMV, the account generates Reg T excess in the amount of $1,000 as calculated by:

Reg T excess = equity − margin required
$$= (LMV - Dr) - (\text{initial requirement} \times LMV)$$
$$= (\$12{,}000 - \$5{,}000) - (50\% \times \$12{,}000)$$
$$= \$7{,}000 - \$6{,}000$$
$$= \$1{,}000$$

This $1,000 Reg T excess can be credited immediately to SMA. The new status of Jane Doe's account is as follows:

LMV	Equity	SMA	Balance
$12,000	$7,000	$1,000	$5,000 Dr

Note that customer Jane Doe's actual debit balance has not changed. However, Doe's "credit line" under the SMA is now $1,000. Furthermore, the broker charges Doe interest only on the debit balance, or the actual amount of the loan, which does not include the SMA.

2. Customer Jane Doe withdraws $500. When Doe withdraws cash, the SMA decreases and the debit balance increases. This situation causes the equity to decrease. The status of Jane Doe's account now is as follows:

LMV	Equity	SMA	Balance
		$1,000	$5,000 Dr
		−500	+ 500
$12,000	$6,500	$ 500	$5,500 Dr

SMA may be applied to meet all or part of a Reg T initial requirement on a margin purchase. From this and previous points about SMA, we can create a modification of a previous formula:

$$\text{Reg T call} = (\text{initial requirement} \times \text{cost}) - SMA$$

Let us assume that Jane Doe now purchases $4,000 worth of securities with the initial requirement at 50%. On this purchase there is an initial margin requirement of $2,000 which can be reduced by the $500 SMA. This results in a Reg T call of $1,500.

Reg T call = (initial requirement × cost) − SMA
$$= (50\% \times \$4{,}000) - \$500$$
$$= \$2{,}000 - \$500$$
$$= \$1{,}500$$

The status of the account is now as follows:

Reg T Call	LMV	Equity	SMA	Balance
	$12,000		$500	$5,500
	+4,000		−500	4,000
$1,500	$16,000	$6,500	0	$9,500 Dr

After customer Doe deposits $1500 in cash to meet the Reg T call, the acccount is as follows:

Reg T Call	LMV	Equity	SMA	Balance
0	$16,000	$8,000	0	$8,000 Dr

Note that the $1,500 deposit of cash reduced the debit balance by $1,500 to $8,000. The LMV remained the same. Therefore, the equity increased by $1,500 to $8,000.

Withdrawal of SMA. Cash may always be withdrawn from SMA in a margin account so long as such withdrawal does not (1) reduce the equity below $2,000 and/or (2) place the account on a maintenance call.

Example: Let us illustrate these two conditions for withdrawal of cash from SMA with the following accounts.

Account 1:
$$LMV = \$20{,}000$$
$$\text{Balance} = 13{,}500\,Dr$$
$$SMA = \$4{,}000$$
$$\text{Equity} = 6{,}500$$
60% initial requirement

How much cash can the customer withdraw from this account?

Calculations:

Step 1: Maintenance requirement = 25% × LMV
$$= 25\% \times 20{,}000$$
$$= \$5{,}000$$

Step 2: $6,500 equity
−5,000 maintenance requirement
$1,500

A withdrawal of more than $1,500 puts the account on a maintenance call.

Account 2:
LMV = $3,200
Balance = $1,000 Dr
Equity = $2,200
SMA = 600
70% initial requirement

How much cash can the customer withdraw from this account?

Calculations:

$2,200 equity
−2,000 minimum level
$ 200

A withdrawal of more than $200 puts this account below the minimum level of $2,000.

Calculating SMA After a Sale in a Properly Margined Account. In a properly margined account, the Reg T excess which is generated is released to SMA. This is true of SMA generated through market appreciation as well as through the sale of securities in that account.

Illustration of a Sale in a Properly Margined Account.

Example: Assume that there is an 80% initial requirement and that customer Morse Wilson's account is as follows:

Long Position
400 shares of SKH stock @ 60 = $24,000
200 shares of RTH stock @ 30 = $ 6,000

LMV	Equity	SMA	Balance
$30,000	$24,200	$200	$5,800 D

Note that his account is properly margined. Equity of $24,200 exceeds the $24,000 margin required (80% × $30,000). The excess amount of $200 is the amount of the SMA.

Let us assume that customer Wilson sells 100 shares of RTH @ 30 for proceeds of $3,000. We use the formula for new SMA to arrive at the status of Wilson's account after the sale:

LMV	Equity	SMA	Balance
$27,000	$24,200	$2,600	$2,800 Dr

either

New SMA = (80% × proceeds) + prior SMA
= (80% × $2,000) + $200
= $2,400 + $200
= $2,600

or

= equity − margin required
= $24,200 − (80% × $27,000)
= $24,200 − $21,600
= $2,600

In this calculation the Reg T excess figure of $2,600 is the same as 80% release of $2,400. Therefore, we use the $2,600 figure for the new SMA. Note that in this latter calculation the $2,600 is not added to the prior SMA. The actual net gain ($2,400) released to the SMA in this case equals 80% of the proceeds from the sale of $3,000. This 80% equals the percentage of the Reg T initial requirement.

New SMA and Prior SMA. One point requires repetition and illsustration. The new SMA is not added on to the prior SMA. The figure for SMA that results from applying the formula to the current account totals becomes the new SMA. SMA is the customer's "credit line" and, like any credit line with a bank or business expense card, and new credit figure is not the sum of the new credit limit plus the old credit limit. Rather, the new line of credit is the new upward limit which is greater than the old limit.

Let us illustrate this point with the following figures of a hypothetical speculative JEC stock, which has a 50% initial requirement:

Date	Initial Margin Requirement	LMV	Equity	SMA	Balance
February	$6,000	$12,000	$7,000	$1,000	$5,000
April	4,500	9,000	4,000	1,000	$5,000
June	5,500	11,000	6,000	1,000	$5,000
August	7,000	14,000	9,000	2,000	$5,000

The fluctuating market price causes the changes in equity, margin required, and SMA. In February with the LMV at $12,000, there is an SMA of $1,000 generated because equity is $1,000 greater than margin required.

Then in April, when LMV drops to $9,000, equity drops to $4,000. At this point, the account is restricted as shown by the fact that the equity dips below the initial margin required. However, equity is not low enough to require a maintenance call. (The 25% minimum maintenance requirement in April is $2,250, and equity is well above that amount.) Even though the account is now restricted, the prior SMA is retained at $1,000.

In June the LMV climbs to $11,000 and causes the equity to rise to $6,000. The account is no longer restricted as shown by the fact that the equity is now above the initial margin required. The difference between equity and margin required is only $500 now. Therefore, the prior SMA of $1,000 remains.

In August the LMV soars to $14,000 and causes the equity to rise to $9,000. Now Reg T excess, the difference by which equity exceeds margin required, is $2,000. Because this is greater than the prior SMA of $1,000 from February, the new SMA is $2,000. Clearly we don't add the $2,000 SMA on to the $1,000 SMA. This Reg T excess is preserved by being automatically transferred to SMA. The net gain from February to August in SMA is therefore $1,000. If the LMV drops in succeeding months, this August SMA of $2,000 nevertheless remains preserved, just as the February SMA of $1,000 remained when LMV and equity dropped in April.

Summary of Special Memorandum Account.

1. SMA serves to protect Reg T excess against a reduction due to market depreciation.

2. At most brokerage firms, Reg T excess is credited automatically to the SMA.

3. An account is not charged interest on the SMA until funds are actually withdrawn from the account and the debit balance increased.

4. SMA may be used to meet all or part of the initial requirement on a margin transaction.

5. Funds may be withdrawn from the SMA so long as the equity is not reduced below $2,000 and/or the minimum maintenance requirement.

6. Cash deposits and additional loan value from securities deposits are applied directly to the SMA, provided there are no outstanding Reg T calls. The key formula is:

Reg T call = (initial margin requirement × cost) − SMA

7. A sale of a long position releases funds to the SMA equal to the current initial Reg T requirement.

8. The exact amount of the release to SMA depends on the amount of equity in the account as well as the prior amount in SMA. New SMA is not added on to prior SMA. A key formula is:

New SMA after a sale =
either:
% of margin required of proceeds + prior SMA
or:
Equity − margin required
whichever of the two amounts is larger.

See also Initial Margin Requirement; Margin Account; Reg T Excess; Restricted Account.

Special Ominbus Account. In a special omnibus account all acivity is carried in a single account established and maintained for the investment advisor's registered broker/dealer affiliate or subsidiary, which, in turn, allocates the transactions among its clientele accordingly. (Under federal regulations, only registered broker/dealers are allowed to maintain special omnibus accounts at other broker/dealer organizations.) Payment and delivery instructions can vary from order to order and may even vary from trade to trade within the same order. An advisor doing business in this manner must furnish the executing firm with a special omnibus account agreement form (see the following figure). The advisor's broker/dealer assumes responsibility for the advisor's clients' compliance with Regulation T of the Federal Reserve Board.

If there is no registered broker/dealer affiliate, or if the firm is unable to complete a special omnibus account agreement form, the investment advisor can still introduce business to a member organization under the broad heading, "A client of (name of investment advisor)," citing an identifying client name or number in the title. In these situations, SEC Rule 17a-3(9) requires the advisor to reveal the full name and address of the beneficial owner of this account to the firm that executes the transaction. If possible, the client's occupation and position should also be determined in order to ensure effective supervision of future allocations of hot issues.

Margin accounts, or for that matter any account other than a special cash account in which deliveries are made to a bank or another brokerage firm versus payment, are very rare under this third-party type of relationship. It is diplomatically difficult to solicit the underlying client (who is a stranger to the executing firm) for a signature on the various supplementary agreement forms. It is suggested, however, that the executing firm have on file a copy of the blanket power-of-attorney form the advisor has obtained from the client.

See also Advisor's Client Account; Third-Party Account.

Special Tax or Assessment Bonds. Municipal securities include special tax and special assessment bonds, both generally regarded as revenue issues. *Special tax bonds* are secured by a specific tax, frequently an excise tax on items such as liquor or tobacco. *Special assessment bonds* are secured by an assessment on those who benefit directly from the completion of the project. Typical of these are curb or sidewalk improvement issues.

See also Municipal Securities; General Obligation Bond; Serial Bond; Term Bond.

Speculator. One who attempts to anticipate price changes and, through buying and selling contracts, aims to make profits; does not use the market in connection with the production, processing, marketing or handlingf of a product.

Split Offering. Bonds issued in a split offering are partly serial and partly term. That is, some have various interest rates and maturities; others have a single interest rate and single maturity date.

See also Serial Bond; Term Bond.

Spot Month. The nearest delivery month on a futures contract.

Spot Price. The current market price of the actual physical commodity. Also called "cash price."

Spot Secondary Distribution. *See* Secondary Distribution.

Spread.

In Bonds. A syndicate group purchases municipal bonds from the issuer at a discount from the public offering price. The difference, called the *spread*, is the gross profit in the underwriting. The manager allocates the bonds to syndicate members at the offering price less the *take-down* , typically around one point ($10 per

BROKER OR DEALER SPECIAL OMNIBUS ACCOUNT AGREEMENT

Gentlemen:

The undersigned broker or dealer requests that you carry a special omnibus account for the undersigned pursuant to Section 220.4 (b) of Regulation T issued by the Board of Governors of the Federal Reserve System under the Securities Exchange Act of 1934.

The undersigned represents that he is a member of a national securities exchange or is registered with the Securities and Exchange Commission under Section 15 of the Securities and Exchange Act of 1934.

The undersigned further represents (i) that the securities and the short sales in such special omnibus account are, within the meaning of Rule 8C-1 and Rule 15C2-1 under the Securities and Exchange Act of 1934, carried by the undersigned for the account of customers of the undersigned (excluding partners, officers and directors of the undersigned and all participants, as such, in any joint, group or syndicate account with the undersigned or any partner, officer or director thereof), and (ii) that such special omnibus account will be used so to carry only securities or short sales for the account of such customers, and (iii) that the hypothecation by the undersigned of the securities in such special omnibus account or of any other securities which the undersigned may carry for the account of customers of the undersigned will not contravene any provision of any law or of any rule or regulation of the Securities and Exchange Commission or of the Board of Governors of the Federal Reserve System. It is understood and agreed that any transaction which the undersigned advises you is made by, or any security which the undersigned advises you is carried for, the undersigned with you for its own account or for the account of anyone other than its aforesaid customers, will be entered in a separate account or accounts with you and will be margined to the full extent that you may from time to time require, and that transactions in such separate account or accounts shall not entitle you to any lien on any of the securities in the aforesaid special omnibus account or on any securities which the undersigned advises you are carried for the account of customers of the undersigned.

It is understood and agreed that, in respect of the transactions in the aforesaid special omnibus account, you are acting as broker for the undersigned and not for any other person, and that the undersigned is liable to you for all commitments incurred and amounts due on transactions in said account.

Very truly yours,

....

Dated ....

....
(City)   (State)

SIA form 119

$1,000 principal amount). Thus, if the take-down is one point and the bonds are reoffered at par, the syndicate member pays $990 to the manager per $1,000 bond and sells it to the public at $1,000, realizing a profit of $10 per bond. In this case the managing underwriter still keeps a half-point if the spread is $15 per $1,000 principal amount.

In some cases, a nonmember of the syndicate has a client order to fill and buys from syndicate members to fill those orders. The non-member's compensation is the *selling concession* and is usually included in the take-down.

Example: The take-down is one point and the selling concession five-eighths of a point. The nonmember makes $6.25 on the sale of each $1,000 principal amount. The member from whom those bonds are purchased makes the other $3.75 ($10 take-down less $6.25 selling concession).

In Options. A *spread* consists of both long and short positions in calls or puts of the same underlying security with different exercise prices and/or different expiration dates.

There are many varieties of put and call spreads. Two we consider are the calendar spread (also known as a horizontal or time spread) and the vertical (also known as a perpendicular or price spread).

The spread is the difference between the amount paid for the long option and the amount received from the short option, this difference representing either a "debit" or "credit" for the investor. Because spread orders require execution of both a purchase and a writing transaction at or about the same time, spread orders are often difficult to execute and there is no certainty such order can be executed within the spread limits designated by the investor.

Option spreading is a strategy used by arbitrageurs and other sophisticated traders attempting to create a predetermined profit while limiting risk to a specified amount.

Once the spread is established, the investor waits until the spread widens (or narrows) and then closes the position to create a profit. Of course, if the spread changes adversely, a loss will be sustained.

Calendar call spread. Example: This type of spread might be established by selling (writing) one January 50 call at $1½ and purchasing one April 50 call at $3¼ for a debit of $1¾ ($175). The investor anticipates that the spread will widen and therefore he or she will profit when the position is closed out. If the January 50 call expires worthless and the April 50 call is selling at 2 in January, the investor will have a net profit of $100. The investor made $150 on the January 50 call (as it expired worthless) and lost $50 on the April 50 call (bought back for 2¾). The spread widened from $1¾ to $2¾, thus creating the $100 profit. This type of spread is most useful when no major price movement in either direction is anticipated.

Vertical (perpendicular) call spread. Example: This type of spread might be established by the purchase of one EK April 45 call at 6¼ and the sale of one EK April 50 at 3¼ for a debit of $3 ($300). See the table below. Here the investor wants the stock to rise so the spread will widen. If the price increases to 54 just prior to expiration date, the investor could close out the the position by liquidating the April 45 at its intrinsic value of $9 and buy back the April 50 at $4. This would create a net profit of $200.

Given: Eastman Kodak (EK) is $48 per Share

	Jan.	Apr.
EAS KD 45	5⅛	6¼
EAS KD 45 p	½	1¼
EAS KD 50	1½	3¼
EAS KD 60 p	2¼	3

The long option creates a $275 gain and the short option a $75 loss. The only dollar amount at risk is the debit, which would be lost should the stock be below $45 at expiration date.

In vertical call spreads, the spread is identified as bullish if the long call option has a lower exercise price than the short option. Conversely, if the long call option has a higher exercise price, the spread is identified as bearish and creates a "credit" for the spread amount.

In the case of vertical put spreads, if the long put option has the higher exercise price, the spread is bearish. Conversely, if the long put option has the lower exercise price, the spread is bullish.

See also Arbitrage; Assignment; Break-Even Point; Downside Protection; Margin; Paper Loss/Profit; Profit Zones; Uncovered Option.

Spread-Load Contractual Plan. *See* Contractual Periodic-Payment Plan.

Stabilizing the Aftermarket. On the effective date in an underwriting, or within a couple of days thereafter, the underwriters begin making their public offering. At about the same time, the security begins trading openly in the marketplace, either on a stock exchange or in the over-the-counter market. This trading activity, which begins on the effective date and is called the *aftermarket*, refers to the market for a security that develops after a public offering begins.

Unless the offering is an immediate sellout, practical problems hindering its success may develop in the aftermarket. The underwriters are bound by the terms of their agreements with the corporation and themselves to offer the security at a fixed price. But the aftermarket price is not so restrictive. It can, and does, fluctuate. Would investors purchase that issue from an underwriter or a member of the selling group at the fixed offering price if they could buy it in the open market for less money? The answer to that is obvious.

So is the solution to this problem. The managing underwriter or its authorized representative is empowered to maintain a bid in the aftermarket at, or perhaps slightly below, the public offering price, on behalf of the syndicate. By pegging the market price to the public offering price, the members of the syndicate and selling group have a reasonable chance of distributing that security successfully. Any losses sustained in this measure are shared among members of the underwriting group. Ordinarily, anyone found manipulating market prices of securities is subject to prosecution by the SEC under terms of the Securities and Exchange Act of 1934. The use of stabilization to facilitate a bona fide distribution of securities is exempted from this otherwise fraudulent practice. However, the actual trading must strictly conform to SEC rules designed to prevent the appearance of misleading market activity. For instance, while the stabilizing party is permitted to initially bid for or buy the security at or below the public offering price (while offering and selling no higher than the syndicate's fixed distribution price), it may not raise its bid or buy above the lowest price at which it purchases that security.

Example: An offering price is set at $26 and the manager decides to stabilize by bidding or buying at $25¾. The syndicate is precluded from subsequently bidding or buying at $25⅞ or above. Prompt notice of stabilizing activities must be filed with the SEC and, if the issue is listed on an exchange, at the appropriate stock exchange.

When stabilizing aftermarket prices, stabilization may also precede the public offering providing notification is given to the SEC and the appropriate stock exchange. The syndicate manager certainly has no intention of repurchasing the entire issue. In fact, the syndicate manager performs this chore reluctantly, often notifying firms participating in the distribution that the stabilizing bid is made with a penalty attached. They are warned in the agreement among underwriters and in the selling group agreement that, if their customers enter the aftermarket and sell this new security at the price of the stabilizing bid, the manager will: (1) deny the member its underwriter's spread or selling group concession on that transaction; (2) penalize it perhaps $.125 per share of $1.25 per bond, as the case may be (penalty syndicate bids are forbidden under NASDAQ rules for issues marketed via that medium); and (3) reconsider that firm's participation in the syndicate or selling group for future offerings.

A *penalty syndicate bid* is written into the agreements between the underwriters and the members of the selling group to ensure that these participants strive to distribute the issue to investment portfolios and not to traders and speculators intent on quick profits.

Although an attempt at public offering at a fixed price is required by terms of the underwriting agreement, the syndicate manager has a prerogative to refrain from stabilization or to withdraw the stabilizing bid without giving advance notice to the members of his group. If the manager sees that the task has turned hopeless, it has authority to release the groups from their obligation to offer only at the established price. When a syndicate agreement is thus broken by the manager, the security is allowed to fluctuate to its true price level, as determined by the forces of supply and demand. The members of the underwriting group who have been unsuccessful in the offering thus far can now sell this security in the aftermarket at whatever prices can be realized. Or they can hold the security, waiting for better days and better prices. In any event, breaking the price restriction does not relieve the underwriters from their financial responsibility to the issuing corporation.

See also Hot Issue; Stabilizing the Aftermarket; Syndicate; Underwriting.

Stabilizing the Market. Generally, during the thirty- to sixty-day life of preemptive rights, the underwriter in a standby underwriting stays right on top of the situation and is quite busy preparing for all eventualities. For instance, if the stock offering is of significant size, the underwriter forms a syndicate with itself as manager. Then, using the standby fee negotiated from the corporation as a cushion of profit protection, the manager will often stabilize the open market price so that the old stock continuously trades above the subscription price of the new stock. That often results in one or more of the following:

1. The rights holders are encouraged to subscribe for the new stock because the subscription price is attractive by comparison with the old stock.

2. Stock acquired via stabilization is "laid off" to the members of the underwriting group. The slang expression lay off is used synonymously for allocation. In this regard, the syndicate manager lays off subscription rights and/or shares of stock on a first-come first-served basis. This encourages them to reoffer it to their customers at a net market price (earning for themselves a lucrative underwriting fee in the process).

3. The syndicate manager purchases rights in the open market below calculated market-value levels. Institutional holders frequently decide not to subscribe to the new stock and may agree to dispose of their valuable rights to the manager at a price just below what they are then worth arithmetically. They elect to do it this way in order to arrange a single transaction at one price for the substantial number of rights they hold.

Example: Assume that: (a) the subscription ratio is six rights for each new share; (b) the subscription price is $15 for each new share; and (c) the price of old stock, ex rights, is $17. The market value of the rights is calculated as follows:

$$\text{Market value} = \frac{\$17 \text{ old stock ex rights} - \$15 \text{ new stock}}{6 \text{ rights for 1 share}}$$

$$= \frac{\$2}{6}$$

$$= \$.333$$

If the manager can buy the rights in the open market below \$.333 per right, it would do so. The manager then lays them off to the members of the syndicate who subscribe at \$15 per share and offer the stock to their customers at a net price just below \$17. For their effort, the underwriters earn the underwriting fee plus the profit on the discounted purchase of rights, subscription, and sale of stock at nearly current market price levels for that issue.

4. The manager acquires subscription rights abandoned by their owners through ignorance or neglect. There are always some rights holders who fail to take appropriate action by the stated expiration date and time. Under terms of the underwriting agreement, the manager claims those rights at no cost, subscribes for the stock, and "lays off" the new shares with members of the group who sell it to their customers at a net market price. This windfall usually results in a profit for the participating underwriters.

See also Ex Rights; Preemptive Right; Stabilizing the Aftermarket; Standby Agreement.

Standard & Poor's 500 Index. The Standard & Poor's 500 index has grown in stature and usage since its inception in 1957. This broad-based index is actually a composite of the four other indexes prepared by the service. Four hundred industrial, twenty transportation, forty financial, and forty public utility common stocks are computed separately and then combined to give the 500 stock figures. This index is a presentation in terms of movement in an overall total of about 300 points. It, like the DJIA, is not expressed as a dollars-and-cents fluctuation of market values.

The serious user of this tool considers it more representative of market activity and direction than the smaller-based averages. Standard & Poor's movements have not, however, shown a marked variation from its greatest competitor, the Dow Jones Industrial Average.

See also American Stock Exchange Market Value Index; Averages and Indexes; Dow Jones Averages; NASDAQ-OTC Price Index.

Standard & Poor's Stock Reports. Market information is published by Standard & Poor's Corporation (S&P). It is subscribed for and referred to extensively by broker/dealers and their registered representatives. In fact, it often serves as a miniature and inexpensive research department for brokers and their customers. The publication is known as *Standard Stock Reports*. Subscription is offered for NYSE, AMEX, and many OTC stocks popular with investors. The NYSE stock reports are printed on yellow paper, the AMEX's on blue paper, and OTC on green paper. Thus, at a glance, you can tell where the principal marketplace is for that issue. The reports are updated frequently, often every three months.

The following figure illustrates the usual stock report presentation and format. It is printed front and back on a 6¼ × 9¼ inch loose-leaf page and is frequently referred to by brokers as a *tear sheet*.

The following discussion confines itself to the specific Standard NYSE Stock Report dealing with General Mills, as shown in the figure on page 463. It is designed to facilitate recognition and analysis of the wealth of information contained in a typical report. Let us analyze this stock report section by section according to the numbering inserted for ease in describing the content as we go along.

1. This is the NYSE ticker symbol for this issue. The footnote cites the other exchanges where the issue is also traded.

2. The number 976 is the page number in the book where this particular report is filed. The NYSE Stock Report service is composed of four volumes with report pages numbered consecutively from Volume 1.

3. This section provides thumbnail statis-

General Mills

GIS[1]   976

Stock—	Price Oct. 29'76	*P-E Ratio	Dividend	Yield
COMMON	30¾	14	[2]$0.76	[2]2.5%

SUMMARY: This leading factor in the packaged food industry has, through acquisition, diversified into a number of unrelated areas, including apparel, crafts, games and toys, furniture, specialty chemicals, and restaurants. Strong established lines, new products, and planned expansion should maintain earnings in an upward course in the years ahead.

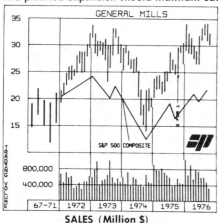

SALES (Million $)

Quarter:	1976-7	1975-6	1974-5	1973-4
Aug.	720	625	544	464
Nov.		763	678	556
Feb.		606	522	498
May		651	564	483

Aided by good growth in volume, sales for the fiscal year ended May 30, 1976 (53 weeks) rose 14.6%, year to year. Despite a $7.0 million plant conversion charge and a $4.0 million loss on the sale of a facility, margins widened. The improvement was attributed to the higher volume and lower raw material costs. Operating income increased 28.7%. Non-operating charges were up less than proportionately, and pretax income rose 37.5%. After taxes at 49.9%, against 48.5%, and adjustments for partially owned companies, net income advanced 31.9%.

Further gains in volume contributed to a 15.2% year-to-year increase in sales for the first quarter of 1976-7. Margins widened in response to cost controls, lower agricultural prices, and the prior elimination of unprofitable and marginal operations. Net income increased 30.9%.

PROSPECTS

Near Term—Sales for the fiscal year ending May 29, 1977, should post a moderate increase from the $2.64 billion of the prior year, with progress expected at both food and non-food operations. Major emphasis on new food products, along with volume gains from established lines and further expansion of the Red Lobster Inns restaurant chain should contribute importantly. In non-food activities, craft, game and toy operations should have another strong year. Fashion and specialty retailing should also do better.

Margins in 1976-7 should be at least maintained on the expected growth in volume, and the absence of plant conversion costs and losses on the sale of a facility. Non-recurring charges during the first quarter and charges to be taken during the second quarter to reflect the devaluation of the Mexican peso will be limiting, but share profits for all of 1976-7 should progress well from the $2.04 of the prior year. Dividends should continue at $0.19 quarterly.

Long Term— Increasing reliance on newer, innovative products offering wider margins, and continued diversification through acquisitions augur well for the future.

RECENT DEVELOPMENTS

Although detailed terms and conditions had yet to be finalized, GIS announced in October 1976 an agreement in principle to acquire York Steak House Systems, an operator of 45 family steak restaurants.

In September, the company reported that it was withdrawing from two ventures involving the production of xanthum gum, and that it had closed the Brown-Saltman furniture production facilities. A $2.1 million net charge was taken in the 1976-7 first quarter to reflect these actions.

DIVIDEND DATA

A dividend reinvestment plan is available. Payments in the past 12 months were:

Amt. of Divd. $	Date Decl.	Ex-divd. Date	Stock of Record	Payment Date
0.17...	Dec. 15	Jan. 5	Jan. 9	Feb. 2'76
0.17...	Mar. 22	Apr. 5	Apr. 9	May 1'76
0.19...	Jun. 28	Jul. 2	Jul. 9	Aug. 2'76
0.19...	Sep. 27	Oct. 4	Oct. 8	Nov. 1'76

[3]COMMON SHARE EARNINGS ($)

Quarter:	1976-7	1975-6	1974-5	1973-4
Aug.	0.65	0.50	0.41	0.40
Nov.		0.70	0.55	0.53
Feb.		0.43	0.31	0.32
May		0.41	0.32	0.34

[1]Listed N.Y.S.E.; also listed Midwest S. E. & traded Boston, Pacific & Philadelphia S.Es. [2]Indicated rate. [3]Based on com. shs. & com. sh. equivalents (stk. options & contingent shs. were applicable); reflects partial adoption of LIFO acctg. aft. 1973–4; adj. for 2-for-1 split in Nov. 1975. *Based on latest 12 mos. earns.

GENERAL MILLS, INCORPORATED

[1]INCOME STATISTICS (Million $) AND PER SHARE ($) DATA

[2]Year Ended May 31	[4]Net Sales	[7]% Oper Inc. of Sales	[7]Oper. Inc.	[8]Depr. & Amort.	Net bef. Taxes	[4] Net Inc.	[6]Common Share ($) Data			[3]Price Range	Price Earns. Ratios HI LO
							[4]Earns.	*Funds Generated	Divs. Paid		
1976--	-----	----	----	-----	------	------	----	----	0.38	34¼ –26⅝	-----
1975--	2,645.0	10.0	264.5	46.71	200.26	100.54	2.04	3.11	0.66	30½ –20⅜	15–10
1974--	2,308.9	8.9	205.5	41.79	145.63	76.21	1.59	2.60	0.58½	30 –14⅛	19– 9
1973--	2,000.1	9.9	198.6	36.35	150.16	75.14	1.59	2.46	0.53	33⅞ –23¼	21–15
1972--	1,662.0	10.8	180.2	34.76	135.19	66.14	1.41	2.39	0.50	32¼ –19⅜	23–14
1971--	1,343.2	11.3	151.3	32.11	108.93	54.67	1.19	2.01	0.48	21 –15½	18–13
1970--	1,120.1	11.0	123.5	27.46	88.67	43.86	0.99	1.72	0.45	19¼ –11⅞	19–12
1969--	1,033.6	11.1	114.3	25.89	86.97	41.62	0.94	1.61	0.44	19⅝ –15	21–16
1968--	922.4	11.3	104.3	22.78	79.94	38.13	0.89	1.47	0.40	21⅞ –17	25–19
1967--	748.9	11.5	86.3	17.98	66.73	32.54	0.84	1.36	0.39½	19 –14⅝	23–18
1966--	628.4	11.7	73.5	12.59	59.32	30.06	0.86	1.39	0.37½	16⅝ –13	19–15

[1]PERTINENT BALANCE SHEET STATISTICS (Million $)

[2]May 31	Gross Prop.	[5]Capital Expend.	Cash Items	Inven- tories	Receiv- ables	Current		Net Workg. Cap.	Cur. Ratio	Long Term DEbt	Share- hldrs. Equity	[6]($) Book Val. Com. Sh.
						Assets	Liabs.					
1975--	739.26	94.44	81.8	353.7	216.0	672.8	377.7	295.1	1.8–1	281.76	640.25	9.88
1974--	685.24	99.83	10.0	345.9	213.6	590.4	313.5	276.8	1.9–1	304.91	560.49	8.43
1973--	593.98	92.24	19.9	353.3	186.5	580.5	312.4	268.1	1.9–1	298.18	483.44	7.41
1972--	529.57	57.49	17.4	242.9	154.9	428.0	248.0	180.0	1.7–1	213.52	426.88	5.48
1971--	502.22	51.28	34.8	179.8	128.3	354.4	204.7	149.7	1.7–1	227.89	377.87	4.31
1970--	470.19	60.40	11.2	153.7	113.4	291.4	150.8	140.5	1.9–1	252.43	332.68	3.32
1969--	419.65	60.39	14.1	129.6	99.6	256.4	119.6	135.1	2.1–1	237.32	307.67	2.81
1968--	378.98	31.01	24.8	112.4	90.8	236.5	112.7	123.7	2.1–1	214.68	294.55	2.10
1967--	349.19	23.05	29.6	88.3	70.4	195.9	97.9	98.0	2.0–1	190.52	227.18	1.53
1966--	278.88	26.70	64.9	58.5	42.7	171.5	75.5	96.0	2.3–1	92.25	119.42	3.02

[1]Data for 1973 & thereafter as originally reported; data for each yr. prior to 1973 as taken from subsequent yr.'s Annual Report; reflects partial adoption of LIFO acctg. aft. 1973. [2]Of the foll. cal. yr. [3]Cal. yrs. [4]Aft. $0.16 a sh. reduction from partial adoption of LIFO acctg. in 1974; bef. spec. cr. of $0.03 a sh. in 1968 & spec. chgs. of $0.15 in 1971 & $0.32 in 1969; sh. earns. based on com. shs. & equivalents (stk. options & contingent shs. where applicable & prior to 1973 conv. pref. stk.). [5]Net expend. prior to 1969. [6]Adj. for 2-for-1 splits in Nov. 1975 & Aug. 1967. [7]Aft. deducting interest expense on grain opers. [8]Depr. only in 1966.

* As computed by Standard & Poor's.

Fundamental Position

In fiscal 1975-6, breakfast and snack items accounted for 26.3% of sales and 38.3% of pretax income (before unallocated expenses); mixes, family flour, seafoods, etc. 25.2% and 18.4%; commercial foods and ingredients 10.3% and 3.1%; restaurants 6.8% and 9.3%; crafts, games and toys 13.1% and 16.3%; fashions, furniture and specialty retailing 14.4% and 11.7%; and specialty chemicals 3.9% and 2.9%. International operations accounted for 16.4% of sales and 14.9% of net income.

The following comprise the company's food operations: Big G ready-to-eat breakfast cerals, headed by Cheerios, Wheaties and Total; Tom's snack items; GoodMark sausage products and beef jerky; Donruss bubblegum; and Mrs. Bumby's potato chips. Others include Betty Crocker prepared cake mixes; Bisquick baking mix; Betty Crocker instant potato products and packaged casseroles; Hamburger Helper and Tuna Helper; Gold Medal flour; Gorton's seafoods; GoodMark breakfast sausages, frankfurters and luncheon meats; imitation bacon chips; frozen pizza; cake decorations; and birthday and party favors. General Mills also operates 185 Red Lobster Inns seafood restaurants, six Betty Crocker Pie Shops, and six Hannahan's restaurants.

The Craft, Games and Toys group consists of the Parker Brothers division, the Kenner Products division, and the Fundimensions division. Fashion operations include David Crystal, Alligator Co., Kimberly Knitwear, Lord Jeff Knitting, Foot-Joy, and Monet Jewelers.

General Interiors produces furniture under the names Pennsylvania House, Shaw, Cushman, Kittinger, Biggs and Dunbar. Specialty retailing is carried out by LeeWards Creative Crafts, Eddie Bauer, David S. Reid, The Talbots, and Olson-Travelworld. The company also makes a variety of specialty chemicals.

Dividends, paid each year since 1898, averaged 34% of earnings in the five years through May 30, 1976.

Employees: 51,778. Shareholders: 29,200.

Finances

In April, 1976, GIS announced a major expansion program for its packaged foods operations. This would include capital spending of about $125 million in 1976-7.

On April 26, 1972 the Federal Trade Commission issued a complaint alleging that GIS and three others shared an illegal monopoly in the dry cereal market. These charges have been formally denied by all of the companies involved, and a period of lengthy litigation, which began April 28, 1976, is expected.

CAPITALIZATION

LONG TERM DEBT: $280,344,000.
MINORITY INTEREST: $5,217,000.
COMMON STOCK: 49,459,808 shs. ($0.75 par).

Incorporated in Del. in 1928. Office—9200 Wayzata Blvd., Minneapolis, Minn. 55440. Tel—(612) 540-2311. Pres—E. R. Kinney. Secy—J. M. Neville. VP-Fin. & Treas—H. H. Porter, Jr. Dirs—J. P. McFarland (Chrmn), H. B. Atwater, Jr., C. H. Bell, T. M. Crosby, K. N. Dayton, J. W. Feighner, P. B. Harris, S. F. Keating, E. R. Kinney, L. W. Menk, J. W. Morrison, G. A. Newkirk, M. Perlmutter, C. F. Phillips, E. S. Reid, W. G. Smith, J. A. Summer, D. F. Swanson, R. L. Terrell. Transfer Agents—Company's Office, Minneapolis; Citibank, NYC. Registrars—Northwestern National Bank, Minneapolis; Citibank, NYC.

tics for this stock using earnings reported in the last twelve months and the company's indicated dividend rate.

4. The "Summary" paragraph contains S&P's general comments about the company and its recommendations for investors.

5. This vertical line chart plots the monthly highs, lows, and closing prices over the last four years. It also shows the annual highs and lows for the five years prior to this time. Technical chart patterns are sometimes easier to recognize over a ten-year period than when the period covered is five years or less. Many investors like to see an issue's market performance over a long period to determine how the stock reacts under different economic conditions and under different managements. Superimposed over the General Mills chart and drawn to the same proportionate scale is the course of S&P's Composite Index for those same years. Investors can compare and determine whether the stock equaled, underperformed, or outperformed the general market during this time. Some technicians believe this comparison is a reflection of management's ability to cope with the changing times.

6. Monthly trading volume is presented for the last five years to enable technicians to relate changes in volume to subsequent market-price movements. It is a way of recognizing advantageous buying and selling opportunities before they become apparent to everybody.

7. Net sales statistics are broken down on a quarterly basis for each fiscal year ending in May. They are then presented in a format designed to facilitate comparison between the same reporting periods for each of the preceding three years.

8. Earnings per common share (E.P.S.) are recorded in the same fashion as net sales, that is, quarterly for comparison purposes. From these last two tables and with the number of outstanding shares (49,459,808) taken from the back side of this report in section 16, we can examine management's efficiency by computing

an after-tax profit margin. First, multiply the shares outstanding by the $.65 E.P.S. to arrive at net income ($32,148,875). Then, divide net income by net sales ($32,148,875 ÷ $720,000,-000) to arrive at an after-tax profit margin of 4.5%

9. This is the date on which this report has been prepared. Updated, future information will be published in the next report, probably three months hence.

10. This is S&P's analysis of the company's business plans. Information is derived from General Mills' news releases and from interviews the S&P analysts have had with the company.

11. Important business and financial news announced by the company since publication of the last Stock Report appears under "Recent Developments."

12. General Mills' dividend information for the preceding twelve months is listed in this table and will also appear in Standard & Poor's Dividend Record book for 1976. This company is one of a growing number of companies that offers stockholders a convenient plan for automatically reinvesting their dividends in additional shares of stock. These additional shares do not come from unissued stock purchased directly from the company. Rather, it is outstanding stock purchased in the open market and allocated to the plan subscribers according to their cash dividend contributions.

13. Relevant details have been culled from the company's balance sheets and income statements over the past ten years and are presented in tabular form to facilitate comparisons. Technical market information such as trading ranges and P/E ratios have been included by S&P for analytical reasons. This information helps investors make value judgments based on the financial statement statistics.

14. "Fundamental Position" is an analysis of the corporation's operating divisions and their percentage contribution to the consolidated sales

and pretax income of General Mills. It also identifies these subsidiaries and affiliated companies by name. This section also sets forth, without further comment, the average dividend payout ratio for the last five years and the number of current employees and stockholders.

15. Any news with potential for having a material effect on the company's capital, current or long term, appears here. This includes such items as business expansion programs, anticipated new financing, debt retirements, and pending litigation or regulatory agency penalties.

16. Capitalization consists of the total par values of outstanding bonds plus the interest of the common shareholder, as shown on the current balance sheet. Note the item labeled "Minority Interest." Like most large concerns, General Mills has significant ownership interests in one or more other corporations, organizations that may provide General Mills with services, raw materials, or finished merchandise for resale. Although General Mills enjoys management control over these companies by virtue of its majority equity holdings, it does not own all the stock outstanding in these corporations. Nevertheless, General Mills has chosen to consolidate their balance sheet items and operating results into its own financial statements. Consequently, it "owes" the minority stockholders in those concerns a proportionate share of benefits although, in fact, it is a liability that will never be paid. Therefore, minority interest is included, like long-term debt, as part of General Mills' total capitalization.

17. This small but important section is often of great interest to analysts and stockholders. It provides (1) the address and phone number of the company's main office; (2) the names of the company's senior officers; (3) the names of the directors serving on its board; and (4) the names and locations of the company's transfer agent(s) and registrar(s). Such information makes it possible to direct inquiries and correspondence, including complaints, to the appropriate parties. For instance, to correct the spelling of a name on a stock certificate, it can be submitted to either the company itself in Minneapolis, Minnesota, or to Citibank (its transfer agent) in New York City. Or, to change an address for dividend and company report purposes, write a letter to either of the registrars, Northwestern National Bank in Minneapolis, Minnesota, or Citibank in New York City.

See also Newspaper Financial Reports; *New York Times* Market Indicators.

Standby Underwriting Agreements. Broker/dealers acting as investment bankers are often asked to ensure success for a public distribution of securities offered directly by the issuing corporation.

A corporation that gives preemptive rights to subscribe to a new issue is uncertain how many holders will actually exercise their privilege. Rather than gamble on the success of this capital project, the corporation contracts with an investment banker to guarantee subscription to any portion not purchased by the holders of those rights. The procedure is known as a *standby underwriting,* because the investment banker does not know what its actual subcription cost will be at the time the agreement is signed. The firm must literally stand by and wait until the rights expire. It may be required to purchase almost all of the issue or perhaps none of it.

If the market price of the old shares fluctuates below the subscription price of the new shares during the effective lifetime of the offering, those rights will be mathematically worthless as long as that condition prevails. Normally, the corporation will not risk the possibility of an unsuccessful rights offering because: (1) it would fail to obtain the needed capital; (2) this obvious lack of investor confidence would damage its reputation; and (3) the directors would be publicly embarrassed before their competitors for exercising such poor judgment. If such a possibility exists, the corporation can employ the services of an investment banker to guarantee purchase of any new shares not subscribed for by the rights holders through subscription for personal account and risk.

Example: A corporation employs Peter Weldon as an investment banker. Weldon does not know his exact commitment at the time of the agreement with the corporation. He must stand by until the expiration date and wait to see the extent of his financial responsibility. He may not need to purchase any of those shares; then again, he may need to purchase all of them. This factor is taken into consideration when the fee for this service is negotiated. The arrangement is known as a *standby underwriting agreement.*

See also Investment Banker; Preemptive Right; Underwriting.

Statement of Account. Under federal law, if there has been any transaction activity, security position, or money balance in a customer's account within the preceding calendar quarter, a statement of account must be prepared and presented to the customer. Many firms comply by sending their customers monthly statements instead of the mandatory quarterly report, particularly in the case of margin account customers. This affords the customers an opportunity to pay the monthly interest charge on their debit balance, and, as a result, they incur only the posted annual rate expense. Otherwise, because that annual rate is calculated daily and posted to the account each month, the interest dollars would compound themselves and cause the customer to pay interest on interest.

Example: The interest charge on a $10,000 debit balance for thirty days at an annual rate of 10% is $83.33.

$$\frac{\$10,000}{1} \times \frac{10}{100} \times \frac{30}{360} = \$83.33$$

Unless the customer pays the $83.33 when posted at the end of the month, that amount is added to the debit balance, increasing the new principal sum for the following month's calculations.

$$\frac{\$10,083.33}{1} \times \frac{10}{100} \times \frac{30}{360} = \$84.03$$

The monthly or quarterly statement is a summary of all that has occurred on the customer's behalf during the period of time under consideration. All purchase expenses are debited to the account, whereas sales proceeds are credited accordingly. However, each purchase and/ or sales transaction is posted on contract settlement date, whereas all other activities are posted on the day those activities occur. For instance, a check received from a customer is credited to the account on the day it is received, and money delivered out of the account is debited on the actual day of disbursement. However, a regular-way sale of a corporate security on June 26 will not be posted until July 3, five business days later. This is often a point of confusion for many customers, especially toward the end of the month when they fail to see that sale posted on the statement. The registered representative must be aware of this sequence of events in order to dispel customer allegations of impropriety in the handling of an account.

Despite the best efforts and intentions of the Controller's Department of the brokerage, occasional mistakes do occur. An issue may not be carried forward in the following month's position listing, or duplicate entries may be processed accidentally and both items posted in the account. Because there are so many opportunities for wrong entries, a typical customer statement often contains a protective hedge in the form of an abbreviated legend, "E & OE," which means, "errors and omissions excepted." This declaration is designed to allow the brokerage firm an opportunity subsequently to correct the mistake without legal liability. A registered representative, therefore, should carefully review a copy of each customer's statements with a view toward prompt discovery and correction of errors before they become a problem that affects the business.

The statement of account may also carry a legend advising customers of financial protection afforded them under SEC Rule 15c3—3. Free credit balances must be maintained in a "special reserve bank account for the exclusive benefit of customers," a rule that denies the brokerage firm the right to use those funds in speculative conduct of its own business. The Controller's Department of the brokerage, employing a formula approved by stock exchange or NASD authority, supervises firm compliance with this rule and ensures that customer money is used only for customer purposes.

See also SEC Rule 15c3—3.

Statutory Underwriter. *See* Underwriter.

Statutory Voting. In this type of voting, you as a stockholder are allocated one vote for each share you hold. You may cast (or refrain from casting) this number for each proposal on the agenda or for a nominee for each directorship on the ballot, as the case may be. Majority holders in the corporation, therefore, support statutory voting because they are thus able to make all decisions. Most corporations use statutory voting.

Example: As the owner of 100 shares, you can cast 100 votes for *each* of five nominees for five directorships to be filled at that election. Any combinations of vote placement are acceptable in statutory voting as long as you do not vote more than 100 shares in favor of any nominee.

Sample Voting Combinations for a Stockholder Owning 100 Shares

	Nominee A	Nominee B	Nominee C	Nominee D	Nominee E
Choice 1	100	0	0	0	0
Choice 2	100	100	100	100	100
Choice 3	0	100	0	100	100
Choice 4	0	100	100	0	0

See also Cumulative Voting; Voting Trust.

Stock Clearing Corporation. The Stock Clearing Corporation (SCC) is a wholly owned subsidiary of the NYSE operated to facilitate delivery and payment for securities contracts effected on the NYSE by member organizations. However, utilization of all services offered by SCC is not restricted to NYSE members alone, although they do constitute the largest number of concerns making use of the available programs. The participants include: (1) clearing members (member organizations of the NYSE); (2) associate members, including (a) members of the AMEX (American Stock Exchange) who are not members of the NYSE, (b) nonmember banks, and (c) management companies registered with the SEC under the Investment Company Act of 1940; (3) affiliate members (clearing corporations of other national stock exchanges), all of whom have signed agreements with the SCC to be bound by the bylaws and rules of that institution and make payments and deliveries as prescribed.

The primary functions of the SCC relate to (1) volume clearance of securities contracts; (2) receipts and deliveries of certificates; and (3) money settlements.

Volume Clearance of Securities Contracts. *Clearance* refers to the pairing off of purchases and sales of each issue traded each day by the same member to arrive at a net balance of securities to receive or deliver.

Example: Suppose a clearing member, acting for various customers in the course of a day, sells 1,000 General Motors shares to several brokers and buys 700 General Motors shares from several other brokers. The commitment to deliver the shares can be satisfied by delivering only 300 shares of that stock to Depository Trust Company (DTC), which will credit a purchasing firm's securities holdings there.

The clearance concept recognizes that for each established contract there must be both a buyer and a seller. Therefore, because transactions occur in a closed community of member organizations, the number of firms participating is limited, and total purchases and sales within that group must always balance out.

The brokerage firm doesn't really care whose certificates they receive to satisfy their buyers or to whom they deliver certificates to accommodate their sellers. But as a result of the matching process accomplished by the automated centralized facilities of SCC, the amount of certificates shuffling to and from each firm is substantially lessened. In the following example, all contracts involve transactions in the same issue of securities on the same day.

Example:

Firm A	Firm B	Firm C
Bought 400	Bought 100	Bought 100
Sold 200	Sold 300	Sold 100
200 to receive	200 to deliver	0 to receive or deliver

Firm B is notified to deliver 200 shares to DTC where it will be credited to Broker A's account. This "netting" process reduces the number of receipts and deliveries among these three firms by 78%.

Volume clearance is used for both stock and bond transactions executed on or off the floor of the exchange as long as the issue is listed on the exchange.

Receipts and Deliveries of Securities Certificates. The delivery of traded certificates is scheduled for the fifth business day after trade date. Thus, the clearance and the notification process must be completed before that date.

On the settlement date, SCC facilities can also be used as the centralized locale where deliveries of certificates ineligible for DTC deposit, or traded elsewhere than on the NYSE, can be accomplished by participating firms. The SCC serves as a central post office for pickups and deliveries of certificates via maintenance of individual locker boxes that each firm uses for this purpose. The SCC not only simplifies the volume clearance of securities but simplifies the physical receipt and delivery process as well.

Money Settlements. The SCC also acts as a central banker for its member firms. Instead of settling financial terms through separate checks with each of the contra broker/dealers, participants satisfy their obligations directly with the SCC, using only one check or draft each day for deposits and withdrawals. The SCC is well aware of the financial details of these contracts because the basic information about quantity and prices is submitted to it in the volume-clearance process and with each delivery effected via its facilities.

This function of the SCC also provides for payment of New York State stock-transfer taxes contingent on a member's activities by debiting the total sum due and including it in the daily settlement sheets. In a similar fashion, floor commissions and monetary collateral demands are processed as requested by the participating firms and also appear on their daily statements.

See also New York Stock Exchange, Inc.; Securities Industry Automation Corporation (SIAC).

Stock Dividends. Classically, stock dividends require the issuance of additional shares, but the par value of the common stock does not change.

Example: Using the same stockholders' equity statement as in the section on splits, let us restate the figures as they appear after the payment of a 30% stock dividend, that is, 90,000 shares (30% of 300,000):

Common stock: at $.40 par value, 600,000 shares authorized, 390,000 shares issued and outstanding	$156,000
Paid-in capital	40,000
Retained earnings	+ 99,000
Total common stockholders' equity	$295,000

Compare the previous figures with these. The total equity does not change. Nevertheless, the common stock account increases by $36,000 (from $120,000 to $156,000), and the retained earnings account decreases by $36,000 (from $135,000 to $99,000). Our common stockholders are no richer or poorer, but the balance sheet changes in that the common stock account increases at the expense of the retained earnings account.

Smaller stock dividends (generally less than 25%) are treated differently. Paid-in capital may also be increased, and the market value of the common stock may be taken into account.

See also Cash Dividends; Stock Splits.

Stock Loan. When a short sale is executed on the floor of the stock exchange or in the over-the-counter market, the selling firm does not tell the purchasing firm that it is a short sale. This item of information is of no concern to the buyer. The buyer is aware that on settlement date, in exchange for the contract money, the firm will receive a certificate. The purchasing firm doesn't really care whose certificate it is receiving.

The customer authorizing a short sale, however, must notify the executing broker that this is to be a short sale *at the time of entry.* To do so ensures compliance with the federal requirement to execute on a plus or zero plus tick. It also alerts the firm to the need to borrow that security *in this customer's* behalf. In most broker/dealer organizations, the task of borrowing certificates is delegated to the Cashiering Department. This department can utilize the period between trade date and settlement date to accomplish this service because delivery of the certificate to the purchasing firm is not made until the fifth business day after the trade date. The following describes some of the methods by which the Cashiering Department may obtain the needed certificates.

Methods of Borrowing.

First choice. The Cashiering Department first turns to securities available from firm-owned inventory and other margin accounts

within its own firm. Margin customers must have already signed blanket hypothecation and loan-consent agreement forms when their accounts were initially established at the firm. If possible and available, it is easier to borrow their certificates than anyone else's.

Securities in a cash account are normally not available for such purposes. If the broker/dealer holds these securities for its customers, they have been fully paid for, and therefore, must be placed in safekeeping. *Safekeeping* involves physical separation and protection in a locked box or vault. Ordinarily, these certificates cannot be used in the conduct of the firm's business.

The only way that securities in a customer's cash account can be loaned or hypothecated is for the customer to give specific written consent per issue to do so. Needless to say, this rarely happens because there is seldom an advantage to be gained by the customer whose certificates are loaned. Securities in a margin account, on the other hand, are not usually fully paid for. When the customer signs the blanket loan-consent form, the certificates serving as collateral are made available for borrowing purposes.

Although the customer has given formal consent, regulatory authorities prohibit a broker/dealer from lending or hypothecating more of the customer's securities than the amount necessary to finance the debit balance with that firm. Thus, although a margin account may contain substantial security value, the amount available for Cashiering Department purposes depends on the customer's debit balance. Security value in a margin account above the amount needed to finance that debit balance must be segregated by the firm. *Segregated* securities represent excess collateral in a margin account. As with securities in cash accounts, they too must be locked in a box or vault to avoid jeopardizing them in the conduct of the firm's business.

Second choice. If the needed certificates are not available within its own firm, the

Cashiering Department must turn to other broker/dealers for help. The cashier contacts other firms known to have many margin accounts or portfolios of many different securities in their proprietary accounts (the firm's own trading accounts or those of its principals that have been pledged to that firm as capital). If at all possible, these firms want to be accommodating. After all, they reason, sometime soon the situation may be reversed. They may become borrowers, and this cashier could be the lender they turn to for help. Besides, there is a valuable monetary reason for wanting to help these borrowers.

It is the custom of the industry to deposit collateral with the lender of certificates as protection for the loan. The collateral required is *cash* equal to the current value of the borrowed security. The lender can and does use this cash in the conduct of the firm's business, free of charge, until the certificate is returned. In addition, the lender can and does use this cash to reduce this firm's own borrowing needs with commercial banks, thus reducing the firm's operating costs.

The request for collateral is no real imposition on the borrower of certificates (the short seller), either. The seller's broker merely uses the money received from the purchasing firm on the short sale and passes it along to the lending firm as the necessary collateral.

The purchasing broker/dealer pays the transaction money and receives a certificate that is then reregistered in the actual buyer's name or in the firm's name (street name) according to instructions. The buyer then steps out of the picture, fully satisfied, unknowingly leaving behind an open contract between the short seller's firm and the lending organization.

This is the most common means of borrowing certificates to accommodate short sellers. The flow of cash and certificates in these activities is shown in the figure below.

Third choice. The cashier, in behalf of the short-selling customer, can approach institutions permitted by law and resolution to lend securities from their portfolios.

The institutions benefit by investing the cash collateral received in short-term instruments, thereby earning additional income.

Desperation. When it becomes apparent that the typical sources of supply cannot furnish enough (or any) of the needed security for the short seller, the cashier may be forced to pay a premium to entice more lenders into the marketplace. The occurrence of requests for premiums is infrequent (*see* Lending at a Premium).

In the rare instance in which one party or group establishes a powerful *corner* in the market, the premiums demanded are outrageous and, often as not, the certificates are unavailable for any fee (*see* Corner).

In recent years, with tighter money conditions prevailing, the industry has seen more instances of a procedure that is the direct opposite of payment of premiums. The cash given to the lender organization as collateral becomes such an attractive commodity that the short seller's

Typical Brokerage Firm Relationship Established with a Short Sale

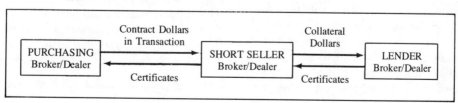

broker, with a choice of numerous available certificates, is able to demand interest from the lending firm (*see* Lending at a Rate).

The Lender's Rights.

Requests certificate return. At any time, for any reason, the lender may ask for the return of its certificates. The certificates may be needed because the customer (1) sold that security and must deliver it to the purchaser; (2) paid off the debit balance in the margin account or reduced it to such an extent that the firm must recall the certificates in order to segregate them and comply with regulations; or (3) has asked to withdraw that security physically from the account and is substituting another issue instead.

The short seller's firm, acting as the borrower, must then return that security within five business days after receiving such notice. This means it must find another lender in the interim period and establish the same relationship if it intends to remain in this short position.

If the short seller's firm cannot find another lender and does not return the certificates, the lender terminates the agreement and holds the firm in default (*see* Buy-in Procedures).

The Lender's Privileges. The lender of the security is entitled to all the privileges of ownership even though it has surrendered physical possession of the certificate. The short-selling customer thus is ultimately responsible for protection of the lender's interests. This point is clearly emphasized when consideration is given to the fact that the lender's certificate has been reregistered into the name of an unknowing third party to the transaction.

To ensure that its customers receive entitled shareholder benefits, the firm lending a stock certificate must maintain an accurate record of all securities loaned. This record is checked daily against various financial information sources subscribed to by all brokerage firms. These sources list, on a continuing basis, all essential amounts and dates relevant to the payment of interest and dividends by publicly owned companies. These sources also provide information about offerings of subscription rights. When according to these periodicals one of the firm's customers (whose certificate was loaned) should get a stockholder privilege, the lending firm creates a receivable on its records. Then the firm claims that item from the borrowing firm as soon as the benefit is distributed by the corporation. Among these privileges are interest, cash dividends, stock dividends and subscription rights.

Interest. If the security in question is an interest-bearing bond, the borrowing firm must send the lending firm a check in the amount of interest so that it can credit or pay its customer. The short seller's margin account is, therefore, debited with that amount.

Cash dividend. If the corporation declares a cash dividend, the borrowing firm must send the lending firm a check for that amount so that it can pay or credit its customer. Thus, a customer whose certificate has been loaned never realizes that the broker/dealer no longer has possession of the security. The short seller's margin account is debited with the actual amount of the dividend or interest on the *record date*, the day the short seller becomes liable for that payment.

Stock dividend. Payment of stock dividends by corporations merely call for a simple bookkeeping entry in the offices of both borrowing and lending firms. If the original loan involves 100 shares and a 2% stock dividend is paid, internal records are adjusted to reflect an outstanding stock loan of 102 shares versus the same amount of money as collateral. The lending customer is credited with these additional shares, whereas the short seller's margin account is adjusted immediately to show a short position of 102 shares as of the record date, the date of established liability. The same technical process is employed for stock split-ups or split-downs.

Subscription rights. When preemptive

rights to subscribe are given to stockholders, the borrowing firm must immediately purchase these rights in the marketplace and deliver them to the lender to permit its customer the privilege of sale or subscription before expiration. The cost of purchasing the rights is immediately debited to the short seller's margin account.

Voting privileges. This is the one privilege of stock ownership the lender's customer may lose. Although the borrower can manufacture all other privileges out of pocket, a short seller cannot create more votes in the corporation's affairs than actually exist. Votes are based on the outstanding stock on the corporation's records. Ordinarily, even this is not much of a problem because so many stockholders do not bother to cast their proxies. If the lending firm's customer insists on casting a proxy, the firm merely allows the use of another, more disinterested, customer's voting right.

In a proxy contest (a fight for control), when every vote is important and stockholders are aggressively solicited by both sides in the controversy, there is a great deal of difficulty in borrowing that stock under any condition. Every cashier who has loaned out that stock certificate immediately recalls it from the borrowers. This is the only way the firm can ensure that its customer will get a proxy and be able to vote. This, of course, places great pressure on the short- selling customer who is literally squeezed into covering the short sale under unfavorable price circumstances. It is not unusual to see a stock skyrocketing in value merely on rumor of a proxy contest, particularly when the stock has a large short interest and speculators have obviously panicked into covering their open positions.

The Borrowing Broker/Dealer's Protection. The borrowing firm, acting on behalf of a short-selling customer, exposes its name and reputation to a degree of risk and financial liability. This fact is recognized by all parties concerned, as well as by the regulatory authorities. The Federal Reserve Board requires short-selling customers to deposit 50% of the net proceeds of such sales with the brokerage firm effecting those transactions. It is from this deposit that all marks to the market, cash dividends, interest obligations, and so on are deducted.

This relationship for a short sale in which the net proceeds amount to $10,000 is shown in the figure below.

Note that the short-selling broker/dealer organization has use of the $5,000 cash deposit from its customer free of charge. It may use this deposit to finance other customers' debit balances in their margin accounts or segregate it in a special bank reserve account. In effect,

Short Sale with Net Proceeds of $10,000

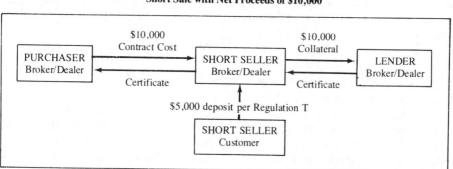

473

whenever any customer sells short, the broker/dealer organization enjoys somewhat of a financial advantage as a result.

The New York Stock Exchange, the NASD, and other major exchanges have also established maintenance requirements for short-sale accounts as an added protection for member organizations. The firm is obliged to request more money as collateral from the customer if the equity shrinks to the minimum levels. If the customer does not deposit the funds, the firm must cover the open contract promptly. Most broker/dealers have instituted their own house rules, which are even stricter than those of the exchanges and the NASD.

Eventually, the short-selling customer will decide to cover the open position.

See also Hypothecating Customer Securities; Segregation; Short Sale.

Stock Market Analysis. Since the latter part of the eighteenth century, when securities were first traded in the United States, investors have sought methods of forecasting movements of stock and bond prices. They have devised averages, indexes, and market theories through the use of technical analysis and complex formulas that comprise fundamental analysis. With these devices, the individual investor and those professionals seeking to advise their clients have attempted to reduce to easily readable terms the innumerable details that affect individual companies and the overall economy. Stock market analysis is an endeavor to read these basic facts in condensed form.

Fundamental analysis is quantitative, based on information in a company's financial statements. It uses arithmetic formulas and ratios as yardsticks to gauge operating strengths and potentials. Fundamentalists believe these statistics will ultimately be reflected or borne out in the market price of the security. Technical analysis, on the other hand, is qualitative. It is based on nonstatistical factors affecting the price of a se-

curity. Such considerations include historic trading patterns plotted on logarithmic (graph) paper, transaction volume, market theories, government policies, management personnel changes, and technological industry developments. By studying a news article, a chart, or an index, investors seek what has happened and can then apply their own interpretations to convert what was to what will be.

See also Fundamental Analysis; Newspaper Financial Tables; Technical Analysis; Ticker Tape.

Stock (or Bond) Power. An owner of stock or (bonds) may use this legal document (either on the back of registered stocks and bonds or attached to them) to assign the interest in the corporation to a third party, allowing that party the right to substitute another name on the company records in place of the original owner's.

See also Good Delivery of Securities.

Stock Record Department. *See* Broker/Dealer Organization.

Stock Splits. When a common stock is split, the number of shares of common stock increases and the par value of the common stock decreases in the same proportion.

Example: A "beginning" common stockholders' equity, before a split, consists of:

Common stock: at $.40 par value, 600,000 shares authorized, 300,000 shares issued and outstanding	$120,000
Paid-in capital	40,000
Retained earnings	+ 135,000
Total common stockholders' equity	$295,000

In a 2-for-1 split, the number of issued and outstanding shares doubles (from 300,000 to 600,000) and the par value is halved (from $.40 to $.20). The new common stockholders' equity looks like this after the split:

Common stock: at \$.20 par value, 600,000 shares authorized, 600,000 shares issued and outstanding	\$120,000
Paid-in capital	40,000
Retained earnings	+ 135,000
Total common stockholders' equity	\$295,000

Because of the 2-for-1 split, the par value changes from \$.40 to \$.20 but the number of outstanding shares doubles. No real change occurs in the balance sheet. The common stock account still comes out to \$120,000:

300,000 shares @ \$.40 par = \$120,000 *and*
600,000 shares @ \$.20 par = \$120,000

Certainly a greater number of shares are outstanding, but at least in theory, the shareholders are no better or worse off than they were before the split. Traditionally a flurry of buying follows a stock split. The market theory is that the stock will sell better at a lower price after the split because it is more "marketable." People tend to favor lower-priced issues even though a lower-priced security bears no more intrinsic value than a higher-priced security. The actual net effect of the split is nil, because the book values on the balance sheet do not change.

See also Cash Dividends; Stock Dividends.

Stop-Limit Order. This is a memorandum that becomes a limit order (as opposed to a market order) immediately after a transaction takes place at or through the indicated stop price.

Example: Suppose a customer gives an instruction to sell long 100 XYZ at 31 stop-limit. If and when a round-lot sale takes place at 31 or below, this memorandum then becomes a limit order to sell long 100 shares at 31 or above (never below 31). The normal stop order would have become a market order and thus would have been executed immediately at the best price available—that is, at 31, higher, lower, or, in other words, at the best existing bid. But, the stop-limit order might never be executed after the stop

portion has been activated because it must wait for someone to accept the minimum offering price stipulated by the customer. The risk associated with entry of any limit order is that it might never be executed. Customers entering them generally play a patient and passive role, awaiting acceptance of their price by a contra party. Market orders, on the other hand, are aggressive and must be satisfied immediately without regard to a specific price.

Although stop orders are acceptable instructions on all stock exchanges in the United States, the American Stock Exchange, in particular, requires round-lot stop orders entered there to be stop-limit exclusively. Fearful of the volatile conditions that can result from concurrent election of many stop orders in thinly capitalized stocks, the AMEX bans entry of this order variety unless it becomes the more passive limit-order type when activated. Moreover, the limit price must be identical to the memorandum price. Thus, a customer may not enter an order such as "buy 100 XYZ at 41 stop, limit 45" as a means of circumventing the AMEX's restriction. A limit price so far removed from the memorandum level is tantamount to a market order which is aggressive. The requirement for stop-limit instructions does not extend to odd-lot orders entered on the AMEX. Customers may enter normal stop orders or stop-limit orders in odd-lot quantities, whichever suits their preference.

See also Choosing Types of Stock Orders; Limit Order; Stop Order.

Odd-Lot. Rather than be exposed to the "best available price" features of a market order once their stop order is elected, some odd-lot customers prefer to enter stop-limit orders instead. Execution of such orders is almost the same as for ordinary stop orders. The difference is that once elected, the stop-limit order is treated as a normal limit instruction and is not necessarily executed based on the value of the following round-lot transaction. If a subsequent round-lot transaction is not at a price at least one-eighth point better than the customer's limit (lower for buy orders; higher for sell orders), the odd-lot order cannot be executed. The risk, of course, is that the order may never be executed if the market continuously moves away from the customer's price. It could thereby defeat the intended purpose for use as a form of insurance. It is also permissible, however, to enter these orders with a limit pricing differing from the stop price and perhaps salvage an execution after all.

Example:

Buy 11 XYZ at 49 stop, limit 49½; or
sell long 31 TDQ at 75¼ stop, limit 75

The following table lists some sample odd-lot stop-limit orders to illustrate different orders, transactions, and execution prices.

See also Limit Order; Odd-Lot Stock Execution; Orders; Short-Stop and Short-Stop-Limit Orders; Stop Order.

Stop Order. The term *stop order* is really a misnomer. In terms of status, a stop order is merely a memorandum that eventually becomes a market order, but only if someone else creates a transaction on the exchange that equals or penetrates the price stated in this memorandum.

Stop orders may be used for a variety of reasons and may be entered as *buy-stop* or *sell-stop*, depending on purpose (*See* Buy-Stop Order; Sell-Stop Order).

Risks Incurred with Stop Orders. On the NYSE, there are several important elements of risk that should not be ignored in considering the use of stop orders. First, there is no assurance

Sample Odd-Lot Stop-Limit Order Executions

Order	Subsequent Round-Lot Transactions*	Execution Price
Buy at 39 stop limit	38½, **39**, 39½, 40	Cannot be executed because the stock never traded below 39 after the stop order was elected.
Buy at 51½ stop limit	51⅜, **51½**, 51½, 51⅜	51½ (51⅜ + ⅛)
Buy at 20¼ stop, limit 21	**20¼**, 20⅜, 20½, 20⅝	20½ (20⅜ + ⅛)
Buy at 63⅞ stop, limit 64	63¾, **64**, 64, 63¾	63⅞ (63¾ + ⅛)
Sell long at 95¼ stop limit	95½, **95**, 95½, 95	95⅜ (95½ − ⅛)
Sell long at 10⅝ stop limit	10¾, **10⅝**, 10½, 10⅜	Cannot be executed because the stock never traded above 10⅝ after the stop order was elected.
Sell long at 47⅛ stop, limit 47	**47**, 46⅞, 47, 47⅛	47 (47⅛ − ⅛)
Sell long at 101 stop, limit 100	102, **101**, 100, 100½	100⅜ (100½ − ⅛)

*The electing sale is in boldface type and the effective sale is boxed.

that the price of execution will resemble the price appearing on the memorandum. As it has happened with issues that fluctuate in a volatile fashion, the best available price following activation of the stop order may be several points away from the memorandum price. Consequently, the original intention to curtail a loss or preserve a profit may be defeated on execution of that order. Such surprises may be avoided if a stop-limit order is entered instead of a normal stop order. The American Stock Exchange requires round-lot stop orders entered there to be stop-limit exclusively (*see* Stop-Limit Order).

The second risk involved with entry of stop orders relates to the responsibilities of stock exchange specialists. The specialist is an individual appointed by an exchange to provide and promote a fair and orderly market in specific stocks. If an unusual concentration of stop orders is observed to be accumulating in those stocks, the specialist may, with approval from an official of the exchange, cancel all existing stop orders and prohibit entry of any new ones. This action is taken because (1) execution of one stop order can start a chain reaction of executions for other stop orders, thereby creating an accelerated violent price movement; or (2) execution of any order at a particular price may suddenly create market orders for many thousands of shares, thereby upsetting supply/demand equilibrium, leading to a disorderly market.

A hazard accompanying these situations exists when customers who have entered stop orders are not aware that the orders were cancelled. (This information is printed on the ticker tape, reported to the major news services, and circulated to each member organization by special notice.) The customers believe that their protection remains effective when, in fact, it does not. Subsequently, if the market price penetrates their memorandum prices, customers often cannot understand why their stop orders were not executed.

Odd-Lot. Remember that a stop order is not an immediate market order but rather a memorandum that becomes a market order when activated. With this in mind, it is easy to handle odd-lot stop orders.

The price appearing on a stop order is not a restrictive instruction. It is only for information purposes and does not include the value of the odd-lot differential. It is simply a notice addressed to the specialist to buy (or sell) this odd lot at the market but only if and when a round-lot transaction occurs at or through the information price appearing on this notice. Thus, in the case of odd-lot stop orders, the round-lot transaction that activates a stop order, called the *electing sale*, is not the effective sale for this type of odd-lot transaction. The electing sale is a round-lot transaction that takes place at a price at or through the memorandum price. The effective sale is the first transaction following the electing sale. Sample odd-lot stop order executions are listed in the table on page 478.

Open sell-stop orders are reduced in value for forthcoming distributions, on the ex-dividend date, in a manner identical to that for round lots. However, there is no semiannual reconfirmation of orders between member organizations and specialists as is required with round-lot orders.

See also Alternative Order; Good-til-Cancelled Order; Odd-Lot Stock Execution; Orders; Short-Stop and Short-Stop-Limit Orders.

Stopping Stock. By this practice a specialist guarantees a price to a customer's order that enables the broker to try to improve on that price without fear of missing the market. (Although the expressions sound alike, stop orders and stopping stock refer to two completely dissimilar practices. The stop order is a memorandum that becomes a market order when a transaction is effected at or through the indicated price.) Under the following conditions, specialists may grant a broker the privilege of a stop, although specialists are not obligated to do so:

Sample Odd-Lot Stop Order Executions

Order	Subsequent Round-Lot Transactions*	Execution Price
Buy at 28⅞ stop	28¾, **28⅞**, 29, 29⅛	
		29⅛ (29 + ⅛)
Buy at 45¼ stop	**45¼**, 45½, 45¾, 46	
		45⅝ (45½ + ⅛)
Buy at 80 stop	79¾, **80¼**, 80¾, 81¼	
		80⅞ (80¾ + ⅛)
Sell long at 34½ stop	34⅝, **34⅜**, 34⅛, 34	34 (34⅛ − ⅛)
Sell long at 13 stop	13⅛, **13**, 13, 13⅛	12⅞ (13 − ⅛)
Sell long at 60¾ stop	61, 60⅞, **60¾**, 60⅝	
		60½ (60⅝ − ⅛)

*The electing sale is in boldface type and the effective sale is boxed.

1. The order, buy or sell, must be for a public customer's account (not a member's account).

2. The broker must ask for the stop. (The specialist is prohibited from soliciting such requests from a broker.)

3. There must be a spread of at least one-quarter point in the prevailing quotation at the time of this request. (The spread is the difference in value between the bid and offering prices.)

4. The specialist must be willing and able to trade as principal if necessary, to avoid defaulting on the guarantee. (The specialist must personally sell stock to a buyer unable to improve on price, or buy stock from a seller in a similar position, when there is no contra customer order on the book at the stopped price.)

Example: Consider the situation shown at the right. Broker A, with a market order to buy 100 shares, is informed by the specialist that the quotation is 63 to 63¼. Broker A is obliged to buy that stock offered at 63¼ or face the risk of having someone else take it. If someone else does take it, Broker A is guilty of failing to satisfy instructions at a price that was practicable of execution (missing the market).

To avoid this exposure, Broker A asks the

Stopping Stock: Broker A is stopped at 63¼. A sale on the bid at 63⅛ must certainly be to Broker A, who is now making the highest bid. But if instead, the next transaction occurs at the lowest offering prevailing, it will be from Broker X at 63¼. This, in turn, requires the specialist to furnish Broker A with 100 shares at 63¼, too.

BUY		SELL
100 - BROKER Y	**63**	
100 - BROKER-A	**1/8**	
	1/4	100 - BROKER X
	3/8	100 - BROKER Z
	1/2	

specialist to *stop* 100 shares at 63¼, that is, assure Broker A a price no worse than 63¼. In this case, assume that the specialist agrees to stop the stock at 63¼. Broker A now has an opportunity to acquire the stock more cheaply without potential financial liability. Broker A is able to bid at 63⅛, in an attempt to improve the price for the customer. (Broker A must narrow the spread in the quotation by actively competing in the trading crowd.) Now, if a seller enters the area soon afterward, Broker A will buy 100 shares at this price because this bid of 63 1/8 is the highest prevailing bid.

If another buyer arrives and purchases the stock offered at 63¼ before the seller appears, then Broker A will be stopped out and forced to pay the guaranteed price (63¼). (*Stopped out* is a term used to signify a broker had a chance to improve on price but was unable to do so.) Under the rules, a broker who is stopped is allowed one transaction to improve on the guaranteed price. If the broker cannot do better on the next sale, the order must be executed at the guaranteed price. Consequently, the customer is assured of the price of the next sale. The next sale must be at the guaranteed price or better. It cannot be worse than the guaranteed price because the specialist has someone else's stock to offer (or bid, as the case may be) at that level. If that price is better than the stopped price, it must be this customer's transaction because that broker has priority. If the price is not better, it must be at the guaranteed price because this represents the worst possible price that can occur after the privilege is extended.

Stopping stock is a privilege that subjects specialists to trading account uncertainties. It also provides specialists with an opportunity to earn floor brokerage for executing orders they would not ordinarily receive. Procedural etiquette on the trading floor dictates that when a specialist stops stock for a broker, the customer's order is given to the specialist to attempt improvement. If the specialist can do better, the specialist will write the execution report and receive the brokerage fee. But if the customer is stopped out, the specialist summons the broker to the trading crowd, allowing that member to write out the report at the guaranteed price.

This tradition serves everyone's interest because (1) the specialist has an opportunity to handle immediately executable market and limit orders and increase earned income; (2) the commission house or two-dollar broker does not waste valuable time competing in a trading crowd and is thus free to execute possibly more lucrative orders elsewhere without concern about missing the market; and (3) the customer has a good chance to gain a better price for an order without risk. In fact, this procedure works so well that experienced registered representatives realize occasionally that their customers have been stopped for more than one transaction in an effort to gain them better prices. This apparent violation of rules is overlooked by the exchange because it can only work to the advantage of the public customer. The customer is always guaranteed no worse than the price of the first transaction after receipt of the stop. The assurance is backed by the specialist's own capital and trading account. The specialist strives to do better and to keep the floor brokerage fee instead of surrendering it to the original broker, as is necessary if the order is stopped out.

See also Bid and Offer; Specialist; Ticker Tape.

Straddle. A *straddle* is a call and a put involving the same underlying security, the same expiration date, and the same exercise price. A person can either buy or write a straddle (that is, be either long a straddle or short a straddle). The order execution of a straddle normally takes place at the same time, although one leg (that is, the put side or call side) may be executed first and the other later.

Long Straddle. An example of a long straddle is the purchase of one XYZ March 40 call and the purchase of one XYZ March 40 put.

A person who buys a straddle anticipates large price fluctuation in the underlying security, but is unsure as to the direction. Through the purchase of a straddle, the investor is in a position to exercise profitably or liquidate the call side of the straddle if the underlying security increases in value, and to exercise profitably or liquidate the put side if the underlying security declines in value. Because the straddle buyer is purchasing two options, the price of the underlying security must rise or fall enough to permit the investor to recover the premiums paid for both the call and put (and commissions) before a profit may be realized.

Short straddle.

Example: An investor sells (writes) one CBA June 50 call and one CBA June 50 put.

A person who writes a straddle generally wants to earn more premium income than would be earned from writing a call or a put alone. This person anticipates relatively small price fluctuation in the underlying security. By writing a straddle, an investor is in a position to profit if one option expires worthless and the other is closed out at a price less than the combined put and call premiums received. On the other hand, should the stock rise sharply in price, the straddle writer is essentially a naked call writer and is subjected to possible infinite loss

If the underlying security both rises and falls during the life of the straddle, both the put and the call could be exercised, resulting in substantial losses for the uncovered straddle writer.

Break-Even Points. The break-even point (excluding commissions) for a straddle is the same for the buyer as the writer. Since a straddle consists of both a call and a put, there is an upside break-even point and a downside break-even point. The formulae for determining these points are:

Upside break-even	= call exercise price plus total premiums
Downside break-even	= put exercise price minus total premiums

Example: This straddle consists of one LUV May 60 call at 7 and one LUV May 60 put at 5. The upside break-even point is 72 (60 + 12), that is, the call exercise price (60) plus total premiums (7 + 5). The downside break-even point is 48 (60 – 12), that is, the put exercise price (60) minus total premiums (7 + 5.

Profit Zones. The profit zone for the straddle buyer is outside (above and below) the break-even points.

In the LUV example, the straddle buyer will profit if the underlying stock is trading above 72 or below 48 just prior to expiration date. Conversely, the straddle writer will profit if the underlying stock is trading between 72 and 48.

If LUV is selling at 75 just prior to expiration date, the call's price should be about $15 and the put worthless. The straddle buyer would liquidate the call at $15 for a profit of $800 but would lose $500 paid for the put premium. The net gain would be $300 ($800 – $500).

On the other hand, if LUV is selling at 54 just prior to expiration, the put's price should be about $6 and the call worthless. The straddle writer would close out (buy back) the put at 6 creating a loss of $100 but would earn the $700 call premium. The net gain would be $600 ($700 – $100).

See also Options.

Street Name. When securities have been bought on margin or when the customer wishes the security to be held by the broker/dealer, the securities are registered and held in the broker/dealer's own firm (or "street") name.

See also Margin Transaction.

Street-Side Settlement. *See* Cash Account.

Striking Price. *See* Exercise Price.

Student Loan Marketing Association. The Student Loan Marketing Association (SLMA,

Sallie Mae) is a U.S. government-sponsored private corporation founded in 1972. It provides liquidity to lenders engaged in the Guaranteed Student Program fostered by the Higher Education Act of 1965. Liquidity is accomplished by the following programs:

1. *Warehousing Advance Program.* This consists of making loans to qualified lending institutions using student loans, insured by the U.S. Commissioner of Education or a duly authorized state or nonprofit institutional representative, as underlying collateral.

2. *Loan Purchase Program.* This consists of purchasing insured student loans from qualified lending institutions at rates determined through negotiation. Sallie Mae obtains its capital through periodic offerings of debt obligations as well as from offerings of common stock in the company. Until July 1, 1982 debt obligations may be guaranteed as to payment of principal and interest by the Secretary of the Department of Health, Education, and Welfare (HEW) and is backed by the full faith and credit of the U.S. government, making it an exempted security.

As such, interest paid to holders is not subject to income taxation by state or municipal authorities but is fully taxable by the federal government. The common stock carries no government guarantees whatsoever and is therefore not an exempted security. Moreover, there are restrictions placed on ownership and transferability of the common stock, limiting it to eligible holders, as defined by the Secretary of HEW. Eligibility is confined to institutions or organizations that make student loans or that are parties to insuring student loans. They include colleges, universities, state agencies, national banks, financial or credit institutions (that is, federal savings and loan associations and credit unions), and some insurance companies.

Subchapter M (Internal Revenue Code).
Qualified investment companies and their stockholders are accorded favorable tax treatment under Subchapter M of the Internal Revenue Code. To realize the magnitude of this privilege, let us examine briefly the tax structure in the United States as it applies to other legal entities.

If an ordinary corporation earns a profit as a result of its activities, it must pay a federal tax based on that profit. The corporation must then distribute a substantial amount of any money remaining, in the form of dividends, to its stockholders. Failure to do so without a specific business purpose in mind for that money subjects the corporation to tax penalties. Such an accumulation of income is contrary to the tax code.

The stockholders are, in turn, liable for payment of federal tax on the dividends they receive. Dividends received by corporations owning stock in a domestic concern are taxable at the regular corporate rate, but on only 20% of the dividends received. Corporate investors enjoy an exclusion from taxes equal to 80% of those dividends.

Example: If a corporation received $1,000 in dividends last year, it is liable at the corporate tax rate for only $200 worth of those dividends. Then, that corporation must face the prospect of paying out dividends on its own after-tax income. This tax liability feature is passed on indefinitely as long as the original earnings continue to be distributed as dividends, in pyramid fashion, by subsequent investor-corporations.

When a recipient of such dividends is a unit investment trust or a management company that has qualified under Subchapter M, it may avoid tax liability completely, or, at worst, have a nominal tax bill to pay to the government. This is accomplished merely by distributing those dividends to its own stockholders and thus transferring the accompanying liability as well. The terms *conduit theory* or *pipeline theory* of investment refer to this flow-through relationship between a qualified investment company, the securities in its portfolio, and its own investors (see the following figure).

**Relationship Between Qualified Investment Company,
Its Portfolio, and Its Investors**

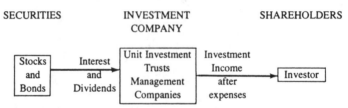

Shareholders then have an individual responsibility at their personal tax rates. However, as a result of this flow-through feature, they can also receive more money because the investment company is exempted from paying it out first in taxes on the same distribution.

Example: An industrial corporation with an investment portfolio is obliged to pay taxes at a 48% rate on 20% of dividends received. It would then be able to pay its own stockholders only $904 from $1,000 in dividend income ($1,000 − [$200 × .48]) A qualified investment company on the other hand could pay out the entire $1,000 because it has no personal tax liability when it distributes its net investment income to its shareholders.

Qualification Requirements. The Internal Revenue Service does not grant this privilege to all companies merely because they are investment companies. It is made available only to those organizations able to meet certain criteria for eligibility. The Internal Revenue Code identifies these companies as "regulated" investment companies. The more important requirements for qualification specify that such a company must meet the following criteria:

1. It must be a domestic corporation— foreign (*off-shore*) mutual funds are ineligible.

2. It must be registered with the SEC under the Investment Company Act of 1940 for the entire taxable year as a unit investment trust or management company. (To be *regulated*, an investment company must be registered, but re-

gistration in itself does not mean the organization will also be regulated.)

3. It must be diversified in its portfolio investments.

4. It must derive at least 90% of its gross income from dividends, interest, and gains from the sale of securities. (Losses from securities sales are not netted out in this computation.)

5. It must ensure that less than 30% of its gross income is derived from sales of securities held less than three months. (The purpose of these last two requirements is to provide the tax exemption to bona fide investment companies and not to speculative trading entities established specifically to circumvent the regulation.)

6. It must distribute at least 90% of its net investment income to its shareholders in the form of taxable dividends. (Net investment income considers only dividends and interest received from securities in the portfolio, less ordinary expenses. Capital gains on securities transactions are not included in this computation.)

Although the tax code prescribes distribution of at least 90%, it is common practice to pay out all the net investment income. Investment companies do so because if any net investment income is retained, it is taxed to the investment company at the ordinary corporate rates. Besides, most investors reinvest the dividends they receive anyway and pay the taxes due on them from personal savings.

Subject Market. *See* National Quotation Bureau, Inc.

Subscription Privileges (Preemptive Right). Sometimes a company gives its stockholders a preferential opportunity to purchase any new shares or bonds it offers to raise additional capital. This is called a *preemptive right* because it is offered to the stockholders before the general public has a chance to participate. To satisfy federal and stock exchange regulations, a corporation issuing rights must issue one right for each share of stock outstanding. However, the board of directors may stipulate the number of rights necessary for the purchase of one or more shares of the new stock.

Example: Four rights for one new share, three rights for two new shares, and so on.

The corporation encourages its shareholders to subscribe to the offering by pricing this new security below the price (or value) for the shares outstanding and already trading in the marketplace. This means that the privilege is a valuable one; it can be utilized by the holder or sold to someone who is anxious to take advantage of it by subscribing to this new security.

The price of the new security has an interesting effect on the market. Invariably, when the news of this financing circulates publicly, the market value of the old shares declines somewhat. This is probably due to the belief of some shareholders that the additional supply of stock will overhang the market, preventing a rise in price. Consequently, they sell their shares at prevailing values.

The price of the right itself is also of concern to owners, but its value cannot be known until it is actually distributed. As a result, there are formulas to calculate the so-called *theoretical value* of the rights.

See also Theoretical Value.

Some corporations go one step beyond issuing rights. Instead of assigning rights to owner-ship of existing shares, they link warrants to the shares of a new issue. Warrants entitle the new shareholders to purchase common stock at a future date. The difference is that warrants have a much longer life than rights, generally five to ten years.

Substantial Net Capital. *See* Financial Protection Requirements (NYSE).

Summary-Complaint Proceedings. *See* National Association of Securities Dealers.

Sundry Assets. This is a miscellaneous category, including unimproved land, prepaid expenses, deferred charges, and other items that are usually considered investments for the future. *Prepaid expenses* include payments for materials or services in advance of their receipt or use, such as early rent payments and insurance premiums. *Deferred charges* are used to "charge off major expenses, such as those incurred in the introduction of a new product or the formation of a new subsidiary company.

Example: A company spends $1 million to purchase a ten-year lease in a given year. It includes $900,000 in the sundry assets section so that the total assets section shows a decline of only $100,000 that year; that is, the company considers $900,000 of the total amount spent as an asset in terms of having a lease. The balance sheet shows cash minus $1 million and sundry assets plus $900,000. The company then reduces the $900,000 in each subsequent year for the next nine years so that it spreads out the $1 million cost for the lease over a ten-year period.

See also Balance Sheet (Assets).

Super DOT System. *DOT* is an acronym for "designated order turnaround" and was developed by the NYSE to facilitate routing of small round-lot orders. It is a message-switching system connecting member firms subscribing to this service with the trading posts on the floor of the exchange. Originally, only market orders of up to 299 shares could be entered through the system and within seconds be received at the appropriate trading post for immediate execution by the specialist. Through improvements over the years the DOT system was expanded in several stages until, in mid-1987, it could accommodate market orders of up to 2,099 shares and good-til-cancelled limit orders of up to 30,999 shares at one time for any one firm. This computerized technique enables member firms to save precious time in processing simple orders. DOT bypasses the firm's telephone clerks and eliminates the need for a commission house broker or two-dollar broker to transport that order physically and then execute it at the trading post. Transaction reports are then routed back to the originating firm through the same system. The Super DOT System also accommodates odd-lot orders of up to 99 shares separately and also when entered simultaneously with a round-lot order.

Support and Resistance Levels. Prices often move in a narrow range for a long period of time. Assume for XYZ stock that the stock moves between a low of 9 and a high of 14 for many months. This range is called the accumulation or distribution area. Levels of support and resistance are thus created. The low of 9 is considered a support level, whereas the high of 14 is considered a resistance level. The key for the technical analyst is a breakout, which is a decline through the support level or a rise through the resistance level. A decline to the support level of 9 will attract buyers eager to purchase at the appealing low price. If the stock rises to its recent high of 14, resistance to further price increases can be anticipated. Sellers skeptical of a breakout will show interest in disposing of the stock at this higher level. If XYZ stock penetrates the breakout barrier, the trend will continue (according to the technicians). Advantage can then be taken of this situation. See the following graph for a chart showing the support and resistance level pattern.

See also Double Tops and Bottoms; Head and Shoulders Patterns; Technical Analysis.

Suspense Account. This special account is created by a brokerage firm to reflect unreconciled money and securities differences on its books and records.

Swap Funds. *See* Exchange-Type Investment Company.

Swap Order. *See* Switch Order.

Swap Transaction. *See* Proceeds Sale.

Support and Resistance Levels

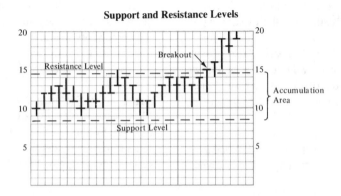

Switch. Liquidating an existing position and simultaneously reinstating a position in another futures contract of the same commodity.

Switch Order (Contingent or Swap Order). This order involves entry of a limit order to sell (buy) one stock, and when executed, entry of a limit or market order to buy (sell) another stock.

Example: These orders might be worded, "Sell long 100 OPQ Corporation at 41½ and when sold, buy 100 VBJ Corporation at 38⅞," or "Buy 100 KOK Corporation at 10⅛ and when bought, sell long 100 UVW Corporation at the market."

Some switch-order instructions are so sophisticated that they require purchase and sale of the security only if the swap can be executed with at least a three-point difference (or some other designated figure) between the transaction prices. No limit prices are actually specified, only the extent of a transaction price spread.

Syndicate. An investment banker firm interested in underwriting an issue on a guaranteed basis frequently does not have enough capital to make good on such a commitment. Even if it does have enough capital, it may be reluctant to risk it all on a single offering. Instead, it generally contacts other investment bankers to organize a group (with itself appointed as manager), to collectively ensure the legitimacy of the corporation's guarantee. These underwriting groups, commonly called *syndicates*, are traditionally formed along historic or social ties within the financial community. It is usually difficult to break into these fraternal arrangements and even more difficult for members to increase their percentage of participation within the group itself. The organizational stratum (bracket) is often fixed according to the past distribution and performance record of each investment banker in the syndicate.

Thus if a prominent investment banker has traditionally participated in syndicates with certain other well-known investment bankers, it is safe to assume that this association will continue for all future underwritings in which any one of them acts as manager. Moreover, once established as a significant distributor of securities in such offerings, that investment banker becomes recognized as a *major bracket* participant. Its name will be publicized near the top of all of the group's advertisements. The percentage of its underwriting commitment continues to rank equally with other major bracket firms. Other investment bankers in those syndicates become stereotyped as sub-major, middle, and minor bracket underwriters accordingly, depending on the amount of their participations.

Syndicate Manager. In a public offering, the underwriters draft and sign a supplementary agreement soon after the due-diligence meeting. This agreement delegates many broad powers and extra work to the *managing underwriter* (or *syndicate manager*) to help ensure success. For its additional efforts, the syndicate manager receives a special fee from the gross profit of all members of the group. It can approximate 20% of the spread, depending on the size of the issue and the amount of work involved. (The profit is technically referred to as the *underwriter's spread* and represents the difference between the price paid to the corporation and the public offering price. The spread does not appear on the red herring because it is based on the public offering price, which is not known at the time of its publication and distribution.)

Example: A debt offering shows the differential between the corporation's price and public offering price to be $8.75 per bond. The management fee is $1.75, or 20% of the spread. This leaves $7.00 per bond to be shared by each of the underwriters and the syndicate's selling group.

The syndicate manager's responsibilities include: (1) forming an underwriting group; (2) appointing a *selling group*; (3) establishing the *underwriter's retention*; (4) conducting *group sales*; (5) *stabilizing the aftermarket*; and (6) allocating *hot issues* with skill and diplomacy.

Once an underwriting group is formed, it is not necessarily a permanent entity. Commitments are continuously revised as the members ask for adjustments to reflect indications of interest they have solicited and/or accepted. Some members may drop out of the group entirely because of lack of response from their customers. Their commitment must be assumed by another investment banker or by other members of the group. The syndicate manager maintains a syndicate record book of such maneuvering.

See also Group Sales; Hot Issues; Indication of Interest; Investment Banker; SEC Rule 10b-6; Selling Group; Stabilizing the Aftermarket; Syndicate Manager; Underwriter's Retention; Underwriting; Underwriting Agreement.

Syndicate Manager. *See* Syndicate.

T

Tail. *See* Competitive Bidding (Award Ceremony).

Tax Anticipation Bill (TAB). *See* U.S. Treasury Bill.

Tear Sheet. *See* Standard & Poor's Stock Reports.

Technical Analysis. Technical analysis is the most popular method of forecasting price movements of securities. Most followers use charts that record price changes looked at in various ways over a period of time. Their methods differ, but they all subscribe to the theory that previous movements, properly interpreted, can indicate future patterns.

One point regarding technical analysis is important to all investors: If enough people *feel* that XYZ common stock is a good buy at $27 per share, it will *become* a good buy if that level is reached. The orders to purchase will cause a rise in the value of the stock independent of any basic changes in the fortunes of the company. The technical analyst is concerned with price, volume, timing, and trend. The analyst gives little consideration to those factors that are signposts to the fundamentalist. Earnings, dividends, and new product development can all be "read" in the price pattern. The technical analyst believes that all the necessary research can be gleaned from an interpretation of chart patterns. The basic belief is that what has happened in the past can forecast what will happen in the future. Compare the chartist to a doctor who specializes in cardiology: The doctor graphs the changing behavior of the heart and from it can tell what has happened. From the information in the graph, the doctor notes problems that have existed and concludes that they may well recur. The doctor can determine strength or weakness from past performance and then judge future prospects.

The chartist, too, believes in trends. Security prices tend to move in one direction for a long period of time. Interruptions occur, but an interruption is not a reversal; it may provide an outstanding opportunity for profit. Charts are best used for discovering short-term potential. They are used to select levels that may indicate an upward or downward movement, as opposed to the Dow Theory, which concerns itself with long-term movements.

Many highly regarded services follow the technical approach to market analysis. They differ sharply as to method but agree on the previously stated general premise. Instead of using charts, some services program their calculations into computers. The machine gives buy or sell signals based on the information it has been fed. The principle is the same; only the technique differs.

Technical analysis is an offshoot of statistics, and it has all the advantages and disadvantages of statistics. Its value is indicative only, not conclusive. On the other hand, it is the closest thing we have to the prediction of human behavior in the marketplace on a short-term basis.

Point and Figure Charting. One method of technical analysis is called point and figure charting. It plots market direction through significant price changes, without regard to the timing of such movements. Through a technique of posting *X*s on graph paper as prices rise and *O*s as they decline predetermined amounts, a skilled analyst can forecast anticipated price levels for an issue. A brief illustration of this technique appears in the following graph.

This chart also plots one-point price changes. Each square (not line) is a one-point unit of change. In the first vertical column, the graph shows the price declining from 79 down to 70 before the movement reverses itself and begins to rise. The second column shows a move from 71 up to 75, the third column a decline from 74 to 72, and so forth. *When* those declines and rises occur is of no importance to point and figure chartists. These technical analysts are concerned only that changes did occur and that such movements were recorded when there were significant fluctuations in daily (or weekly) high and low prices. Closing prices are not posted on these charts unless they also happen to be the high or low levels required for transcription.

Point and Figure Chart

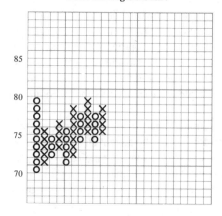

Vertical Line Charts. This charting technique is simply a series of vertical lines plotted on graph paper, showing high and low prices reached during the day (or week). The horizontal line crossing the vertical line indicates the closing price. It is the simplest charting method used by technicians.

Vertical line charts illustrate various patterns including: (1) head and shoulders patterns, which indicate upward or downward trends; (2) support and resistance levels, which show price ranges in which securities tend to remain for a period of time; (3) double tops and bottoms, which indicate major levels of supply and demand; and (4) climaxes, or breakaway patterns, which incorporate a study of volume in conjunction with a continuing price trend.

See also Advance-Decline Theory; Averages and Indexes; Digest of Earnings Reports; Double Tops and Bottoms; Dow Theory; Fundamental Analysis; Head and Shoulders Patterns; Newspaper Financial Tables; *New York Times* Market Indicators; Odd-Lot Theory; Quotations; Short Interest Theory; Standard & Poor's Stock Reports; Support and Resistance Levels; Ticker Tape.

Telephone Booths. These booths or cubicles ring the stock exchange trading rooms and are used by member organizations to (1) receive orders from their offices, (2) distribute orders to brokers for execution, and (3) transmit details of the executed orders back to their offices.

See also Trading Floor (NYSE).

Tenants by Entireties. *See* Joint Customers.

Tenants in Common (Ten in Com). *See* Joint Customers.

Tenants with Rights of Survivorship (W/R/O/S). *See* Joint Customers.

Tender Offer. A brokerage is capable of submitting securities to financial institutions acting as agents for people who seek to acquire them pursuant to a proxy statement filed with the SEC. *Tender offers*, as such proxies are known, can be successful devices for acquiring large amounts of stock without upsetting the supply/demand equilibrium in the marketplace (see the figure on page 490). The tender offer is a method often used by corporations or large institutions to effect a merger with, or gain control of, a company at reasonable cost. If an insufficient number of shares are submitted, the offeror is denied its desired objective. The offeror usually reserves the right to refuse purchase of any shares tendered; this is a valuable privilege not available in open-market transactions. Similarly, if a tender offer brings forth an overabundance of shares for sale, the offeror can accept all the shares, any portion of them, or only that particular amount specified in the proxy statement. If either of the latter two courses are chosen, the statement must also describe the manner in which tendered shares will be accepted and paid for. For instance, it can be accomplished under either of two methods:

1. *First come, first served.* Preference is given to those holders who submitted their shares for sale earlier than did other tenderees.

2. *Pro rata allocation.* Tendered shares are accepted by means of a ratio formula developed by relating the total shares submitted to the total shares desired.

Example: If a tender offer for exactly 500,000 shares resulted in stockholder submissions of 800,000 shares, the purchaser will accept $\frac{5}{8}$, or $62\frac{1}{2}\%$, of each holder's offering.

The formula for calculating the pro rata acceptance is:

$$\frac{\text{Total shares to be purchased by the company}}{\text{total shares submitted to the company}} = \text{proportion of each tenderee's shares to be accepted}$$

Tender offers may also have a significant impact on the conduct of activity in a customer's cash or margin account. From what we have already said, it should be obvious that mere submission of shares does not guarantee sale proceeds. So long as the purchaser has a right of full or partial refusal, no proceeds may be withdrawn or used for another investment. Only after official word is received about the purchaser's acceptance and payment procedures can the proceeds be applied against new commitments or used for substitution in the selling customer's account. This is the principal reason why there is still a significant amount of trading activity in the open market while the tender offer is pending. Stockholders, because they are unsure of how many shares will be accepted if tendered, often prefer to dispose of their shares at a slightly lower market price simply because an open-market contract is guaranteed to be binding for the full amount.

Tender offers also generate revenue for broker/dealers whose customers cooperate by offering their shares for sale. If the shares are accepted, the purchaser pays those firms significant fees for their help, separate and apart from proxy solicitation reimbursement expenses. This often amounts to more than a normal commission for far less work than that needed for stock exchange or usual over-the-counter transactions. There is no disadvantage to the customers. The firms deal with the purchaser on a net basis, meaning that all expenses are borne by the buyer.

Detailed Explanation of Tender Offer Illustration. Although it is important for stockholders to read the entire solicitation statement carefully before deciding whether or not to tender their shares, much valuable information about the offer can be gleaned from the title page alone. This fact is obvious from the typical newspaper announcement appearing in the figure on page 490. Let's briefly analyze that ad-

Newspaper Announcement of Tender Offer

Notice of Offer
by
¹General Development Corporation
to Purchase
up to 500,000 Shares of its Common Stock
at $7.00 Per Share

GENERAL DEVELOPMENT CORPORATION (the "Company") is offering to purchase up to 500,000 shares of its Common Stock ("Common Stock") at a price of $7.00 per share, net to the seller in cash, without deduction of brokerage commissions, any ²transfer taxes applicable to the transfer of shares directly to the Company or other expenses. Such offer is subject to all of the terms and conditions set forth in the Offer to Purchase ("Offer") and in the Letter of Transmittal. **All tenders of shares pursuant to the Offer will be irrevocable, except that shares tendered prior to January 25,** ⁴ **1974 may be withdrawn until that time.**

> ⁵ **The Offer will terminate at 5:00 P. M., New York City Time, on February 6, 1974, unless extended.**

The Company will be obligated to purchase all shares validly tendered up to 500,000. If more than 500,000 shares are tendered, the Company at its option may purchase all ⁶ or any of such additional shares, but in no event more than 1,000,000 shares. If the Company purchases less than all of the shares tendered, purchases will be made on a pro rata basis. The Offer may be extended by the Company from time to time. If the Offer is extended, shares of Common Stock tendered prior to 5:00 P. M. New York City Time on February 6, 1974 will be purchased in their entirety before additional shares ⁷ tendered during any extended period are purchased. If less than all shares tendered during any extended period are purchased, the shares will be purchased in the order tendered. All shares tendered and not purchased will be returned as soon as practicable after expiration of the Offer.

The Company will pay to any broker or dealer (including the Dealer Manager named below) who is a member of the National Association of Securities Dealers, Inc. ("NASD") or any national securities exchange, to any foreign broker or dealer who agrees to conform to the Rules of Fair Practice of the NASD or to any commercial bank ⁸ or trust company, whose name appears in the appropriate space in the Letter of Transmittal, a commission of $0.30 for each share of Common Stock tendered pursuant to such Letter of Transmittal and purchased under the Offer, not to exceed $2,500 in respect of all shares tendered by or on behalf of any single beneficial owner.

Copies of the Offer and the Letter of Transmittal may be obtained from the Depositary or the Dealer Manager. Facsimile copies of the Letter of Transmittal will be acceptable.

The Offer contains important information which should be read before tenders are made.

Depositary:

(By Hand)	(By Mail)
CHEMICAL BANK	CHEMICAL BANK
Corporate Tellers Window No. 32	Corporate Agency Division
⁹ 2nd Floor, North Building	Cooper Station
55 Water Street	P.O. Box 689
New York, New York 10041	New York, New York 10003

The Dealer Manager for the Offer is:

₁₀Goldman, Sachs & Co.

³ January 17, 1974

vertisement. The following text explains the information to which the numbers in the figure refer.

1. General Development Corporation is making a tender offer for 500,000 shares of its own common stock at $7.00 per share. That stock will then be classified as treasury stock on the company's financial records, reducing the number of shares issued and outstanding.

2. The company will pay any brokerage expense or transfer tax normally borne by a seller of securities. This will result in net proceeds for the tenderee of exactly $7.00 per share for each share purchased by the company.

3, 4. The effective date of this offering (when solicitations may legally commence) is January 17, 1974. The offer enables tenderees between January 17 and January 24, 1974, the privilege of changing their minds and withdrawing their shares from consideration. But shares on deposit after January 24 cannot be withdrawn and will be returned to sellers only if the company chooses not to purchase them.

5. The tender offer will expire at 5:00 P.M. New York City time on February 6, 1974, unless the company, at its option, chooses to extend it to some later date. Any shares not on deposit with the company's agent at that time may not be considered for purchase.

6. The company is required to accept 500,000 shares, if that many are tendered. If less than this amount are deposited, it must purchase them all. If more than this number are tendered it may, at its option, purchase as many as 1,000,000 shares at $7.00 per share. If the company chooses to purchase 500,000 or more shares, acceptance will be made on a pro rata basis. It is important to note that if these shares are tendered from a margin account in accord with that customer's request, the brokerage must continue to price that security for collateral purposes at its current market value. Because there is no assurance how many shares will be ac-

cepted, the market price is usually somewhat lower than the tender price.

7. Should the company extend its offer past the original expiration date (February 6), all shares deposited by that time will be purchased. However, any additional shares tendered thereafter may be accepted, too, but only on a first-come, first-served basis.

8. General Development will pay any qualified broker/dealer, commercial bank or trust company a solicitation fee of $.30 per share for each share it purchases, if that institution was instrumental in arranging for the tender by the underlying owner. It has also imposed a limitation on the remuneration payable to such institution acting on behalf of a single beneficial shareowner. At the scheduled rate of $.30 per share, that ceiling of $2,500 will be reached when a single owner sells 8,333 shares to the company.

9. The company has set up two depositary addresses where shares may be presented for consideration. Both are in New York City and both are locations administered by Chemical Bank.

10. The company has retained the services of Goldman, Sachs & Co., a prominent broker/dealer and investment banker, to coordinate the efforts of securities firms and banks in contacting its stockholders and soliciting tender of their shares.

Tennessee Valley Authority. Tennessee Valley Authority (TVA) obligations are authorized by Congress to promote economic development of the Tennessee River and adjacent areas. The debt created by the TVA has a senior claim on the income derived from power projects in the region that were built with the proceeds of these bond offerings. The interest paid to investors is subject to federal taxes but exempted from state and local taxes.

See also U.S. Government-Sponsored Corporation or Agency Obligation.

Term Bond. (1) These are obligations of the same issuer offered with a single interest rate and a single maturity date. Revenue bonds are usually issued in this format.

See also Serial Bond; Split Offering.

(2) Some Treasury bond issues carry a call feature in their indenture. This permits the government to redeem these bonds prior to maturity, but only five years earlier. These obligations are often referred to as *term bonds*. Their yields-to-maturity are calculated only to the call date, but it is rare to see the Treasury Department exercise its privilege. Term bonds can be identified in newspapers and offering circulars by examining the full description of the bond itself.

Example: The description of a term bond may appear as, "U.S. Treasury 4.25% due May 15th, 1989/94." The true maturity date is May 15, 1994, but the Treasury Department reserves the right to redeem this bond at face value any time between May 15, 1989 and May 15, 1994.

Theoretical Value. After a corporation announces a rights offering (*see* Preemptive Right) and before the physical distribution of these rights to subscribe, investors usually demand the determination of the *theoretical value* of this privilege. The value is "theoretical" in that no actual market for them has been established at this early date. The problem has an easy solution. Simply subtract the price of the new stock from the price of the old stock selling in the marketplace *cum rights* (with the rights attached). Then divide this difference by the number of rights necessary for one new share *plus an additional right*. The formula for calculating theoretical value is:

$$\frac{\text{market price of old stock cum rights} - \text{subscription price of new stock}}{\text{number of rights needed to buy one share} + 1} = \frac{\text{theoretical value}}{\text{of one right}}$$

Example: A corporation permits its stockholders to subscribe to one share of stock at $45 for each four shares of the stock currently owned and trading at $55 at the marketplace. Calculate as follows:

$$\text{Theoretical value} = \frac{\$55 - \$45}{4 + 1} = \frac{\$10}{5} = \$2$$

To prove the accuracy of this procedure, suppose that four "old" shares were purchased at $55 per share, at a total cost of $220 (ignoring odd-lot fees, commissions, and so on for the purpose of this illustration). If rights attached to those shares are then used to purchase one new share at $45, the total expenditure amounts to $265 ($220 + $45). However, the investor now owns five shares of that security. Therefore, the investor's average cost per share is $53 ($265 ÷ 5). Because the old stock originally cost $55 per share, the subscription privilege is worth $2.

Occasionally, the directors find it convenient to establish a subscription ratio expressed in a fashion other than in terms of one new share. They may decide to allow the purchase of two new shares for every three old shares held, or even three new shares for every five old shares held, and so on. Such an approach does not change the use of the prescribed formula. It merely adds an extra step by requiring the ratio to be translated into terms of subscription to one new share. The following examples use the prices from the previous example.

Examples:

1. If the ratio is three old shares for every two new shares:

$$\text{Theoretical value} = \frac{\$55 - \$45}{\frac{3}{2} + 1} = \frac{10}{2\frac{1}{2}} = \$4$$

2. If the ratio is five old shares for every three new shares:

$$\text{Theoretical value} = \frac{\$55 - \$45}{\frac{5}{3} + 1} = \frac{10}{2\frac{2}{3}} = \$3.75$$

The old stock begins trading in the marketplace without the subscription privilege attached to the price (ex rights—this occurs on the first business day after the rights begin trading as a separate security in the marketplace). When this happens, it signifies that preemptive rights have been physically issued and distributed and a separate, actual market value for them has been determined. At this point, *do not* add one to the subscription ratio when dividing the difference between old and new stock prices. The old stock price already reflects the reduction in value. Let us use the original figure to illustrate this point.

Example:

$$\text{Theoretical value} = \frac{\$53 \text{ old stock ex rights (``rights off'')} - \$45 \text{ new stock}}{4}$$

$$= \frac{8}{4}$$

$$= \$2$$

A preemptive right is not granted to the stockholder for an indefinite time period. The holder must act to subscribe or sell these rights, generally within thirty to sixty days after issuance. If the stockholder does not act before the deadline set by the corporation, the rights expire and are worthless.

If the stockholder receives too few rights to subscribe to a full share, the corporation normally allows him or her to "round up."

Example: A stockholder owns ten shares of stock and as a result receives ten rights. The terms of the offer allow the stockholder to subscribe to one share for each four rights. This allows the stockholder to subscribe to 2½ shares. The company normally would allow the subscription for a full three shares and charge the stockholder a small fee for the "round-up." On the other hand, if the stockholder only wanted to subscribe to two shares, the company would sell the two unused rights and forward the proceeds to the stockholder.

See also Standby Underwriting Agreement.

Third Market. These transactions are done in exchange-listed stocks by OTC, nonmember broker/dealers of that exchange who specialize in such transactions.

See also Over the Counter.

Third-Party Account. This type of brokerage account is carried in the name of a person other than a customer. The practice is prohibited by NYSE regulation.

See also Advisor's Client Account; New Account Report Form; Special Omnibus Account.

Tick. A tick is securities industry jargon for a *transaction* executed on a securities exchange.

Example: Assume that after being traded at 50, a listed stock trades at 49⅞. This is obviously lower in value than the preceding transaction. This transaction is identified as a *minus tick*. If the stock trades at 49⅞ again immediately thereafter, it is called a *zero minus tick* because, while equal to the price of the previous transaction, it is lower than the last different price that occurred.

If the next sale takes place at 50, obviously a higher price than 49⅞, it is referred to as a *plus tick*. Another sale at 50 immediately thereafter is called a *zero plus tick* because, while equal in value to the last sale, it is higher in value than the previous different-priced transaction.

Example:

50	49⅞	49⅞	50	50	50
	(minus tick)	(zero minus tick)	(plus tick)	(zero plus tick)	(zero plus tick)

See also Plus-Tick and Zero-Plus-Tick Rules.

Ticker Tape. The tape is a report of activity in each exchange-traded issue moments after execution has been completed. A technical analyst's interpretation of market trends depends on an understanding of transaction reports appearing on the stock exchange ticker tape. Experienced technicians are able to recognize changing trends by developing a feel for the market from ticker-tape readings.

Actually, the term ticker tape is something of a misnomer that stems from the original mechanical device invented and implemented in 1867 by the New York Stock Exchange to publicize transactions. Despite many technological improvements in the paper-tape system, relatively few professional broker/dealers now use it. Most member firm subscribers use an electronic display device connected to the exchange's ticker mechanism. A paper tape is used primarily by nonmember brokers and dealers as well as by wealthy individuals. Regardless of which device is used to display trades, the reporting system is called a ticker tape.

The ticker mechanism is capable of printing up to 900 characters per minute, which is about as much as the eye can recognize and the human brain can translate into understandable information. This high-speed system, introduced in 1964, resulted from an effort to display current activity in a growing marketplace dominated by high volume and rapidly changing prices. Because time and space are limited, a tape language was developed and is utilized to provide maximum transaction details.

Stock Symbols. Each issue traded on an exchange is assigned a unique letter symbol to identify that security's transactions on the ticker tape. Care is taken to ensure that this symbol has not been assigned to another issue on another exchange or has not been used for some company recently deprived of exchange trading privileges through merger, liquidation, delisting, or similar actions. To better understand how this space-conserving system operates, examine the symbols assigned to the first ten corporations that comprise the Dow Jones Industrial Average.

Corporate Title	Ticker Symbol
Allied Signal Inc.	ALD
Aluminum Company of America	AA
American Brands, Inc.	AB
American Express Company	AXP
American Telephone & Telegraph Company	T
Bethlehem Steel Corp.	BS
Chevron Corp	CHV
E.I. duPont de Nemours & Company	DD
Eastman Kodak Company	EK
Exxon Corp.	XON

Most New York or American Stock Exchange issues have one, two, or three letters assigned to them as a symbol. A few have as many as four letters, although four-letter symbols are generally used only to distinguish a preferred stock from the common stock of the same issuer or to differentiate between a voting and nonvoting class of common stock.

Example: The symbol for Monongahela Power Company is MPN, whereas its 4.40% preferred stock is MPNA. Or, Harvey Hubbell Company's Class A's symbol is HUBA, whereas its voting Class B stock has been assigned the letters HUBB. This method compares with NASDAQ's use of four-letter symbols for over-the-counter issues registered in the system and five letters (ending with a "Y") for ADRs.

When a listed company petitions the federal court system for protection from its creditors under the bankruptcy laws of the United States, this fact is disclosed on the ticker tape by the letter *Q* preceding that company's usual ticker symbol. Consequently, no securities traded on stock exchanges are assigned symbols beginning with *Q*. Thus, there is no confusion about this symbol's meaning when it appears on the tape.

Share Volume. Each depicted trade on the ticker tape is comprised of two lines of information. (Some electronic display machines illustrate the entire transaction on a single line of print.) The top line is the stock symbol; below that and to the right is the share volume and execution price. Because the typical trading unit for NYSE stocks is 100 shares, no special identification is needed to indicate a 100-share transaction. The absence of quantity means that the tape report is for a single, round-lot execution. The prints in the following example reflect 100-share trades.

Example:

T   AC

50½   27⅞

Multiple trading-unit executions show the actual quantity separated from the price by the letter *S* but ignore the zeros in the number of units. The prints in the following example are for a 200-share trade, an 800-share trade, and a trade involving 4,200 shares:

Example:

DD   BS   XON

2s160¼   8s32   42s36¼

Ten-share trading-unit stocks are recognizable on the ticker tape by means of a double *s* in vertical order between quantity and execution price. The following example illustrates reports of transactions involving stocks that trade in ten-share units.

Example:

PE pr   AB pr

1§47½   6§55

The volume totals are actually ten shares in the first illustration and sixty shares in the second. Most ten-share-unit stocks are preferred stock issues; this is shown by the letters *pr* after the company's usual ticker symbol.

Sequential Transactions. When a series of trades occurs in the same issue at the same time at the same or varying prices, the whole number of the price is dropped from the ticker prints after the initial transaction in that series; only the fractional digit and corresponding quantities appear,

in order of execution. (Unless, of course, executions occurred at a whole number price. In that case, the full price and quantities are printed.) Once again the letter *S* is used to separate data.

Example:

AA

40s 43 ¾. ¾. 2s ¾. ⅞. 5s ⅞.   10s 44

(1)   (2) (3) (4) (5)   (6)

The sequence in this example is translated as follows:
(1) 4,000 shares of Aluminum Co. of America traded at 43¾; followed by (2) 100 shares at 43¾; followed by (3) 200 shares at 43¾; followed by (4) 100 shares at 43⅞; followed by (5) 500 shares at 43⅞; followed by (6) 1,000 shares at 44.

Delayed and Volatile Transaction Prints. After completing a transaction on the trading floor of the stock exchange, it is the selling broker's responsibility to advise an exchange employee (a reporter) at that post about the terms of the execution. That clerk records the transaction data on a card and inserts the card into a scanning device that transmits impulses of what it "reads" to a ticker-tape information-collection and coordination room above the trading floor. Within a few moments, the transaction terms are published for subscribers to view throughout the United States and in several foreign countries, too.

Sometimes, either the selling broker or the reporter doesn't act promptly enough. As a result, subsequent transactions in that issue are printed before the oversight is realized. Or, perhaps the delay causes a transaction's appearance on the ticker tape to be significantly separated from the prints of other issues executed at approximately the same time. Should either of these events occur, the errant transaction is published nevertheless, but with the letters *SLD* following the ticker symbol and before the quantity and execution price. This designation is officially called a *sold sale*, and it simply means this transaction notice was delayed and is appearing out of its proper place.

Example:

CRO. SLD
    3s 12½

Closely akin to a sold sale in external semblance, but with an entirely different meaning, is a sold last sale. In order to avoid any misunderstanding, "SLD LAST SALE" is printed on the bottom line of trade information after the execution price. This expression identifies a transaction that has fluctuated volatilely, either up or down, from the last sale in that issue. Specifically, this announcement is made when a stock previously selling at 19⅞ or below trades one or more points from the last sale. If the stock previously traded at 20 or above, the "SLD LAST SALE" designation is made when the price fluctuates two or more points away from the last sale.

Example:

MAR
    913s 19½ SLD LAST SALE
IBM
    40s 248 SLD LAST SALE

The high degree of marketability experienced by exchange-listed issues makes prints of this kind an infrequent occurrence. But if a temporary inequity between supply and demand does develop, it generally occurs prior to the daily opening of that issue on the exchange. It may stem from an overnight build-up of orders relating to an important international or business announcement. When an opening price of stock falls within the categories mentioned above, the initial transaction for that day is identified by the letters *OPD* following the ticker symbol, in lieu of "SLD LAST SALE."

Example:

CB. OPD
    81 5s 10⅛

Stopped Stock. After a broker has been "stopped" by a specialist (guaranteed an execution price while attempting to improve on it), the broker has an opportunity to try for a better price. The broker does not incur personal liability if unsuccessful in this effort and another person usurps the original prevailing price. If there is no improvement over the guaranteed price available, the broker is stopped out and required to accept an execution at the figure. This transaction is characterized by the letter S set above the letter T on the second line of print following the execution price.

Example:

GM
    $50\frac{1}{4}{}^{S}_{T}$

This type of transaction is printed in its proper place on the ticker tape unless to do so might embarrass another broker who is attempting to execute an order for another customer at the same time. How can a ticker tape report embarrass another broker? Suppose, for instance, that Broker A was stopped at 27 and Broker B bought 200 shares at the market, 100 at 27 and 100 at 27⅛. Broker B's customer might claim foul play if the tape were to report these transactions as shown in our next example.

Example:

XYZ
    $27.27{}^{S}_{T}.27\frac{1}{8}$

Broker B's customer might insist that his market order should have purchased 200 shares at 27. It is difficult for a lay person to understand how someone can come in between the execution of a market order for multiple round lots. Because the ticker tape should, nevertheless, be an accurate indicator of volume and activity in each listed issue, stopped stock in these instances is printed after trading ceases for the day; akin to a sold sale but identified with the stopped stock symbol.

Bids and Offers. In a difficult market situation, such as (1) a sudden imbalance of orders, (2) a delay in the opening of a particular issue, or (3) a resumption of trading after a suspension, it is often tactically advantageous to advise viewers of prevailing conditions in order to solicit their orders. This is accomplished by printing bid and offering prices prevailing for the affected issue. In extreme circumstances, only an "indicated" quotation is disclosed. Both situations are recognizable as quotations by the letter *B* on the lower line of information. The first price given in the print is the bid; the bid is separated from the offering price by a dot.

Example:

XRX   PRD.INDICATION
 B115.118   B75.85

When-Issued or When-Distributed Stock. Soon after a listed corporation announces a forthcoming distribution of stock and before the security is actually allocated, the appropriate stock exchanges commence trading in that issue. These contracts carry no specific settlement terms until a distribution date can be ascertained; hence the name "when- issued" or "when-distributed." To distinguish these transactions from the activity in the old shares, the letters *WI* or *WD* appear in vertical order after the execution price.

Example:

LPX   SQB
 2s 19¼ $^{W}_{I}$ 41 $^{W}_{D}$

Ex Dividend, Ex Rights, Ex Warrants, or Ex Distribution. On the first day a listed security

begins trading without the value of the forthcoming cash or security distribution in its market price, the ticker tape makes that fact known by means of an identifying code after the issue's symbol. The code is:

XD	for ex dividend
XRT	for ex rights
XW	for ex warrants
XDIS	for ex distribution

The announcement appears only for the first three or four transactions in that issue. After that, it is assumed that the viewer has been adequately informed and can make intelligent interpretations of price fluctuations.

Example:

SCE.XRT   GE.XD
  19⅝   3s57¾

The Late Tape.

Conditions. There are occasions when the pace of activity on the trading floor exceeds the capacity of the ticker tape's ability to provide current information. They may occur at the opening of the exchange in the morning, or late in the afternoon at the close as traders adjust their portfolio positions, or, for that matter, at any time during the day, especially after important news is made public. New reporting procedures are then implemented into the ticker system to signify that the tape is falling behind actual trading activity; every effort is made to maintain continuous and relevant information.

Digits and volume deleted (Delete Mode 1). In the initial stage of increasing activity, when it appears that trade information is falling behind the trading floor and is likely to slip further, the announcement "DIGITS & VOLUME DELETED" is made on the ticker tape. It means only the last digit and fraction, if any, of an execution price is printed, and quantity figures for trades of less than 5,000 shares are eliminated, thus conserving space on the tape and speeding up reports. It is necessary for the tape watcher to be familiar with the issue to realize what the first digit(s) should be.

Example:

TX	S	DD
7⅞.	8⅛.	3½.

As these items appear, it is essential for the viewer's understanding to realize that *TX* is Texaco Inc. and its price is 27⅞; *S* is Sears Roebuck at 88⅛; and *DD* is E.I. duPont de Nemours at 163½. There are two important exceptions to this procedure, however. Both require complete price prints, although digits are otherwise deleted: (1) an opening transaction is always announced with its full terms; and (2) an execution price ending in a zero is always printed in its entirety (for instance, 20½ is not depicted as 0½). When conditions permit, normal reporting procedures are employed following the announcement, "DIGITS & VOLUME RESUMED."

Repeat prices omitted. If the ticker tape should fall further behind trading activity, the words "REPEAT PRICES OMITTED" are published. From that point on until the tape is clear again, sequential repeat transactions at the same price are dropped from the tape. This practice conserves valuable space and time and avoids printing a string of transactions all at the same time and price, a condition typical of active issues and active markets. Here, too, accurate daily volume figures are properly recorded and maintained by the exchange.

Minimum price changes omitted. Under exceptional circumstances the ticker tape can begin running behind actual floor executions by a considerable amount of time (that is, ten minutes or more). To provide for timely dissemination of important price changes, the Consolidate Tape Association (CTA) has programmed the system to omit trades in each issue unless they are more than one-eighth point, up or down, from the preceding transaction in that same issue. When those conditions develop and this mode is implemented, the words "MINIMUM PRICE CHANGES OMITTED" are published by the CTA. Although this technique may remain in effect until the tape lateness is cleared, all volume and price information is nevertheless captured by the high-speed Consolidated Tape System and is published by commercial vendors (that is, Associated Press, Fitch Investors Service) for public consumption.

See also Consolidated Tape System.

Time Deposit. In this type of account, the owner has committed funds to a bank for an extended period of time in exchange for payment of interest. The time period is generally fixed somewhere from three months to one year but has also been known to continue as long as seven years. Banks that solicit these accounts must pay fixed interest for the life of the agreement at a rate slightly higher than short-term rates that prevail when the deposit is accepted.

See also Certificate of Deposit (CD); Demand Deposit; Savings Deposit.

Time of Trading. *See* Listed Option.

Time Value. This amount, called *time value* or *extrinsic value*, is the amount by which the market price of an option exceeds the amount that could be realized if the option were exercised and the underlying commodity liquidated; that is, the excess amount over intrinsic value that an option buyer is willing to pay.

Example: A stock is selling at 57, and the January 60 call is trading at 4½. The January 60 call option is out-of-the-money. Therefore, it has no intrinsic value. Since the option is selling for 4½, it does have time value due to the time remaining until the expiration date. Thus the sum of zero (for the intrinsic value) and 4½ (for the time value) equals the price of the option.

If an XYZ August 70 put is trading for 6 and

the stock price is 68, the option is two points in-the-money. Its intrinsic value of $200 and time value of $400 equal the option price of $600. As the expiration date approaches, the time value decreases so that in the days just prior to expiration the option trades very close to the intrinsic value.

See also Evaluating Options; In-, and Out-of-the-Money; Intrinsic Value.

Tombstone. When a public offering (underwriting) commences, the syndicate manager often publicizes this fact by advertising in one or more newspapers and periodicals. It is a nondescript notice because, by law, any written document that can be construed as a solicitation to purchase a registered security must be accompanied by a prospectus. The lackluster nature of this advertisement inspired its industry name, *tombstone*. Nevertheless, this nonsales-oriented announcement, whose copy must contain no exaggeration, elaboration, or solicitation, presents useful information to a knowledgeable reader. Examine the typical tombstone on page 000. The items have been numbered to facilitate your inspection of this tombstone.

1. This is an SEC-mandated hedge clause advising readers that this advertisement is not a solicitation and that a prospectus is available for such purpose.

2. This is the aggregate par value of these debt instruments and is not the offering or current market value.

3. The full description of this issue reflects interest rate, maturity date, and the fact that both principal and interest payments are guaranteed, if necessary, by another and much larger corporate entity. These bonds are also debentures with no specific claim on particular assets of either company in the event of a catastrophic failure.

4. Interest payments totalling 9.25% of par value ($92.50 per $1,000) will be paid each year

until maturity: $46.25 will be disbursed each February and August first.

5. The offering price is fixed at 99.50% of par value ($995 per $1,000) plus interest accruable from February 1, 1976 to settlement date of the transaction.

6. This is a caveat advising the reader that this security may be offered by a particular underwriter only in states in which that firm is registered to act as a broker/dealer and only in compliance with the "blue sky" laws of that state.

7. The syndicate manager's name always appears at the top of the list of underwriters in any tombstone advertisement.

8. The principal underwriters of this issue then appear in alphabetical order but subdivided into brackets of financial responsibility for marketing this issue. (Horizontal lines have been drawn by the author to help the less experienced reader identify these groupings.) The *major bracket* underwriters at the top of the list have each committed themselves to bear greater financial liability to the issuer for failure to sell the bonds than a *sub-major bracket* firm just below them—and certainly greater than any *minor bracket* underwriter at the bottom of the listing. In large syndicates the names of small underwriters may not even be published in the advertisement. Selling group participant names never appear in a tombstone regardless of syndicate size.

9. This is the effective date, the earliest date on which the public offering may commence.

See also Effective Date; Syndicate; Syndicate Manager; Twenty-Day Cooling-Off Period; Underwriting.

Total Volume. This column in the listed stock and bond tables shows total shares of stocks traded (omitting the last two zeros) and the total par value of bonds traded (omitting the last three zeros).

See also News Paper Financial Tables.

Trading Authorization. The registered representative must obtain the name and occupation of any person(s) with authority to create activity in a customer's account before accepting instructions from someone other than the customer. In instances where orders are given by an intermediary, a trading authorization form (power of attorney) must be signed by the customer *prior* to purchase or sale of any security.

Most firms recommend use of either a limited or full authorization form specifically designed for securities transactions (see the following figures) in preference to a standard power-of-attorney document, which is couched in general terminology. The limited trading authorization permits the designee to create purchase and sale activity in the customer's account, while the full authorization also permits withdrawal of money and/or securities from the account.

See also Discretionary Account; Registered Representative (Responsibilities).

Trading Floor (NYSE). Most orders in NYSE-listed stocks received by a member organization are executed on the trading floor of the New York Stock Exchange. Exceptions often occur when either (1) the stock is listed on more than one registered exchange in the United States, and a member organization with comparable privileges elsewhere has chosen instead to execute the order on that exchange; (2) the stock is an inactively traded preferred issue or one of the few existing guaranteed equities (a stock whose dividend payments are assured by the promise of a corporation other than the issuer of that security) appearing on a special list of stocks exempted from this requirement by the exchange; (3) the quantity and/or terms of the order are such that the equilibrium between supply and demand would be dramatically upset and the NYSE has given its approval to execute it over the counter; (4) the customer is situated outside of the United States and wants to buy or sell that security before or after the normal hours of trading on the NYSE; or (5) after inquiry on the floor of the NYSE, the member firm finds the customer's interest can best be served by it acting as agent in an over-the-counter transaction.

Otherwise, orders to buy or sell listed stock are transmitted to the trading floor of the NYSE for execution by means of (1) telephone; (2) teletype; or (3) automated machinery approved by the NYSE and installed on the trading floor.

Trading Rooms. The *floor* is actually comprised of three trading rooms (see the figure on page 504). Each of the areas is connected by short passageways on the same level, making it relatively easy for a member to walk from room to room to execute orders. The three trading rooms are as follows:

1. The *main room* is where most of the listed stocks on the exchange have been assigned trading privileges.

2. The *garage* is a nickname assigned to a smaller trading area positioned next to the main room. It was built to facilitate trading when space became a major consideration years ago.

3. The *blue room* is a nickname assigned to an even smaller trading area on the other side of the main room (see the figure on page 504). Opened in the late 1960s when the volume of activity necessitated further expansion of physical facilities, it is so named because of its colorful, attractive decor.

4. The *bond room* is a trading area where debt issues listed on the exchange have been assigned trading privileges.

The assignment of trading privileges in any of these rooms is not related to the quality of a particular issue. The designation is made primarily because of space considerations, and reassignments to not occur to meet changing conditions. Each of the rooms enjoys comparable mechanical and electronic conveniences for use in the transaction of business on the floor.

TRADING AUTHORIZATION LIMITED TO PURCHASES AND SALES OF SECURITIES AND COMMODITIES

Gentlemen:

The undersigned hereby authorizes .... (whose signature appears below) as his agent and attorney in fact to buy, sell (including short sales) and trade in stocks, bonds and any other securities and/or commodities and/or contracts relating to the same on margin or otherwise in accordance with your terms and conditions for the undersigned's account and risk and in the undersigned's name, or number on your books. The undersigned hereby agrees to indemnify and hold you harmless from and to pay you promptly on demand any and all losses arising therefrom or debit balance due thereon.

In all such purchases, sales or trades you are authorized to follow the instructions of .... in every respect concerning the undersigned's account with you; and he is authorized to act for the undersigned and in the undersigned's behalf in the same manner and with the same force and effect as the undersigned might or could do with respect to such purchases, sales or trades as well as with respect to all other things necessary or incidental to the furtherance or conduct of such purchases, sales or trades.

The undersigned hereby ratifies and confirms any and all transactions with you heretofore or hereafter made by the aforesaid agent or for the undersigned's account.

This authorization and indemnity is in addition to (and in no way limits or restricts) any rights which you may have under any other agreement or agreements between the undersigned and your firm.

This authorization and indemnity is also a continuing one and shall remain in full force and effect until revoked by the undersigned by a written notice addressed to you and delivered to your office at ...., but such revocation shall not affect any liability in any way resulting from transactions initiated prior to such revocation. This authorization and indemnity shall enure to the benefit of your present firm and of any successor firm or firms irrespective of any change or changes at any time in the personnel thereof for any cause whatsoever, and of the assigns of your present firm or any successor firm.

Dated, ...

....
       (City)   (State)

Very truly yours,

....

SIGNATURE OF AUTHORIZED AGENT:

....

FULL TRADING AUTHORIZATION WITH PRIVILEGE TO WITHDRAW MONEY AND/OR SECURITIES

To ....
          (Name of Firm Addressed)

....
          (Address of Firm Addressed)

Gentlemen:

    The undersigned hereby authorizes .... (whose signature appears below) as his agent and attorney in fact to buy, sell (including short sales) and trade in stocks, bonds and any other securities and/or commodities and/or contracts relating to the same on margin or otherwise in accordance with your terms and conditions for the undersigned's account and risk and in the undersigned's name, or number on your books. The undersigned hereby agrees to indemnify and hold you harmless from and to pay you promptly on demand any and all losses arising therefrom or debit balance due thereon.

    You are authorized to follow the instructions of Mr. .... in every respect concerning the undersigned's account with you, and make deliveries of securities and payment of moneys to him or as he may order and direct. In all matters and things aforementioned, as well as in all other things necessary or incidental to the furtherance or conduct of the account of the undersigned, the aforesaid agent and attorney in fact is authorized to act for the undersigned and in the undersigned's behalf in the same manner and with the same force and effect as the undersigned might or could do.

    The undersigned hereby ratifies and confirms any and all transactions with you heretofore or hereafter made by the aforesaid agent or for the undersigned's account.

    This authorization and indemnity is in addition to (and in no way limits or restricts) any rights which you may have under any other agreement or agreements between the undersigned and your firm.

    This authorization and indemnity is also a continuing one and shall remain in full force and effect until revoked by the undersigned by a written notice addressed to you and delivered to your office at ...., but such revocation shall not affect any liability in any way resulting from transactions initiated prior to such revocation. This authorization and indemnity shall enure to the benefit of your present firm and of any successor firm or firms irrespective of any change or changes at any time in the personnel thereof for any cause whatsoever, and of the assigns of your present firm or any successor firm.

Dated, ...

....
      (City)   (State)

                             Very truly yours,

....
          Witness

SIGNATURE OF AUTHORIZED AGENT:

....

Trading Posts. Transactions in the three rooms where listed stock activity occurs are consummated at specific locations known as *trading posts* (see the figure on page 504). With one exception, the 23 trading posts on the floor of the NYSE are seven-foot-high horseshoe-shaped structures with an outside circumference ranging from 31 to 76 feet, depending on location.

"Telephone Booths." Ringing the perimeter of the trading rooms are booths or cubicles for use by the member organizations and from which they (1) receive orders transmitted from their offices; (2) distribute such orders to members of the stock exchange for execution; and (3) transmit back to their offices the details of executed orders and pertinent trading information.

Within the confines of existing space limitations, members may rent from the NYSE as many of these locations, strategically positioned in the various trading rooms, as they deem necessary to carry on their business. These areas are uniformly referred to as *telephone booths*, even though the firm may use a teletype machine or another automated device for its purposes.

The booths are staffed with clerks employed by the renting firm to ensure that (1) the orders received on the floor are in proper form for execution; and (2) they are disseminated to the appropriate stock exchange members for execution.

See also Bid and Offer; Order Transmission; Order Ticket; Super DOT System.

Trading Flat. *See* Bond Interest.

Trading Market. *See* National Quotation Bureau, Inc.

Trading Plus Accrued Interest. *See* Bond Interest.

Trading Post. Each of these twenty-three locations on the floor of the NYSE is a seven-foot-

high, horseshoe-shaped structure with an outside circumference of from 31 to 76 feet. The one exception is a table-like structure, Post 30, in the garage, where most inactive preferred stocks are traded in multiples of ten shares. The posts have been replaced by a round structure with a lot of electronics display.

See also Trading Floor (NYSE).

Trading Ring. *See* Corporate Bond Transaction.

Trading Variations. With few exceptions (principally for subscription rights), trading variations in each equity security listed on the NYSE are reflected in eighths of a dollar ($.125 or 12½¢). Stocks and warrants are always represented by valuations reflected in *dollars and cents,* so for these issues

⅛ point	=	12½¢ per share
¼ point	=	25¢ per share
⅜ point	=	37½¢ per share
½ point	=	50¢ per share
⅝ point	=	62½¢ per share
¾ point	=	75¢ per share
⅞ point	=	87½¢ per share
1 point	=	$1.00 per share

Bonds, on the other hand, are generally reflected as *percentages of face value* ($1,000); so for most of those issues

⅛ point	=	$ 1.25 per bond	(⅛% of $1000)
¼ point	=	$ 2.50 per bond	(¼% of $1000)
⅜ point	=	$ 3.75 per bond	(⅜% of $1000)
½ point	=	$ 5.00 per bond	(½% of $1000)
⅝ point	=	$ 6.25 per bond	(⅝% of $1000)
¾ point	=	$ 7.50 per bond	(¾% of $1000)
⅞ point	=	$ 8.75 per bond	(⅞% of $1000)
1 point	=	$10.00 per bond	(1% of $1000)

Transfer. The Transfer Section of a brokerage is responsible for reregistering securities into a

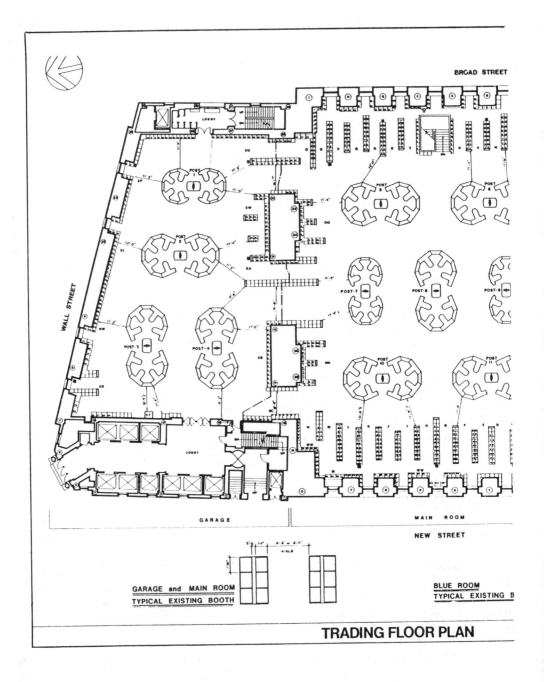

TRADING FLOOR PLAN

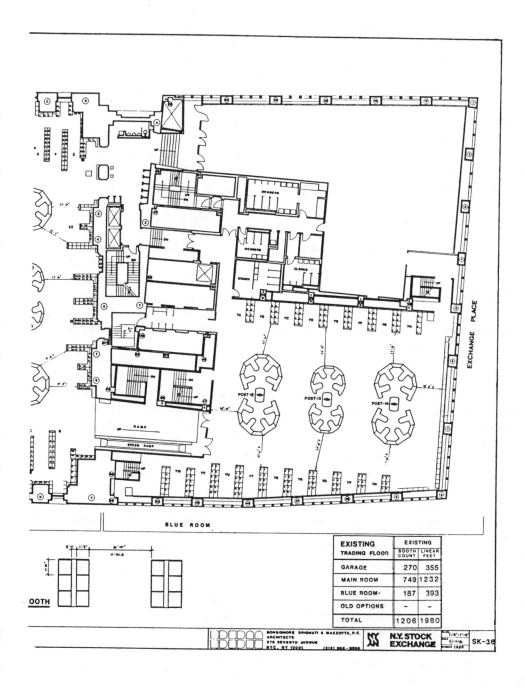

BLUE ROOM

EXISTING	EXISTING	
TRADING FLOOR	BOOTH COUNT	LINEAR FEET
GARAGE	270	355
MAIN ROOM	749	1232
BLUE ROOM	187	393
OLD OPTIONS	–	–
TOTAL	1206	1980

N.Y. STOCK EXCHANGE

SK-36

more desirable title of ownership and/or certificate denomination. This is accomplished by submitting the old certificate to the issuing corporation or to its authorized agent, accompanied by written instructions as to the type of change required. (Relatively few corporations reregister their own securities. Most use the specialized services of a commercial bank to act as transfer agent.) Transfer is completed when the corporation or its agent cancels the old certificate, issues a new one, adjusts its ownership records accordingly, and returns the new document to the same brokerage firm. Due to the potential for error in this detailed process, many corporations preferably appoint two separate organizations to handle the necessary chores; one to facilitate reregistration and the other to adjust the company's record of ownership. The concern responsible for cancelling the old certificate and issuing a new one is called a *transfer agent*. The party responsible for adjusting the ownership record and ensuring that the transfer agent issues the same total quantity cancelled is called a *registrar*.

Normally registered securities received by a firm are reregistered into either firm name, for segregation purposes, or into customer name, for safekeeping or delivery purposes, per instruction from the Margin Department or the Box Section. (Bearer certificates; that is, securities without an owner's name imprinted on the face of the documents or recorded on the issuer's books are fungible instruments. They are, therefore, immediately placed into segregation or rehypothecation, as the case may be.) Exceptions occur only in the case of securities sold soon after purchase or for delivery to a customer's agent bank or broker versus payment (C.O.D. transaction).

As a general rule, the Margin Department will not authorize registration of a security into customer name unless (1) it was a fully paid certificate in a cash account; (2) the customer did not owe the firm delivery of another security whose sale was pending; or (3) the margin ac-

count (if the security was in a margin account) had no debit balance or a debit that was fully protected by other securities in the account. If the third situation prevails, then, once reregistered into customer name, the security will be delivered to the customer or transferred from the margin account to a cash account and placed into safekeeping.

It is a bad business to practice to segregate or hypothecate securities registered in the name of someone else, even though those certificates may be fully negotiable. Serious problems arise if the issuing corporation pays a dividend/interest or distributes an important communication to the holders whose names and addresses appear on its records. That distribution will obviously go to persons or brokers who legally disposed of their financial interest in the company some time ago. Any dividend or interest payment, in particular, must then be claimed by the rightful owner, entailing a lot of unnecessary paperwork, at best.

If securities are in proper form for delivery but the available denominations are all wrong, the brokerage must request from the company's agent the right-sized pieces to make good delivery to the contra firm. It is to the firm's financial advantage to anticipate these problems in the original reregistration and request frequently needed denominations at that time.

Example:

If a brokerage firm receives a total of 1,000 shares registered in various names and wants to transfer them into its own name, it is probably wiser to do so by requesting several certificates in denominations such as the following:

1 × 500 =	500
3 × 100 =	300
2 × 50 =	100
2 × 25 =	50
4 × 10 =	40
2 × 5 =	10
	1,000 shares

Otherwise, if the Transfer Section opts for an easy registration of 1,000 shares in a single piece, the firm will be hard pressed to make prompt delivery unless it sells all 1,000 shares at the same time, and to the same contra party.

Denomination consideration is not a serious concern when deliveries between member firms are arranged via a national securities depository. The problem then belongs to the depository. However, when a firm deals directly with other firms or its own customers, its Transfer Section's good judgment is essential for efficient management of firm assets.

See also Broker/Dealer Organization (Cashiering Department); Registrar; Segregation; Reregistering Securities.

Transferable Form. For brokers, dealers, and depositories, *transferable form* means that the certificates must meet the specifications for good delivery outlined in the New York Stock Exchange Constitution or in the NASD Uniform Practice Code, as the case may be.

Transfer Tax. *See* Securities Exchange Act of 1934 (Section 28).

Treasury Securities. *See* Certificate of Indebtedness; Series EE Bond; Series HH Bond; U.S. Treasury Bill; U.S. Treasury Bond; U.S. Treasury Note.

Trustee. *See* Fiduciary Accounts.

Trust Indenture Act of 1939. Although separate and distinct, this Act was enacted as an amendment to the Securities Act of 1933. It provides additional protections for public investors. The basis for its passage was the discovery by Congress that the 1933 Act did not safeguard the rights of investors in debt securities after the public offering was completed. Moreover, it found that purchasers of issues exempted from the registration requirements often did not even have the minimum protections accorded to investors in offerings required to be registered with the SEC.

Consequently, the Trust Indenture Act of 1939 (1) integrated its own requirements with those of the 1933 Act for debt issues registered under that law and (2) imposed unique requirements for issuers of public or private debt securities exempted from provisions of the 1933 Act.

Generally, the terms of the 1939 Act extend to issuers of any debt security with a principal amount of $5 million or more. The issuer of a debt security subject to this law must appoint one or more trustees responsible for ensuring that the terms of the indenture are scrupulously adhered to by all parties to the agreement. At least one of those trustees must be a corporation empowered with authority to act as a fiduciary and must be subject to supervision or examination by a governmental body or agency. It must also have a combined capital surplus of at least $150,000. The trustees cannot have "conflicting interests" and must provide an annual report to the SEC reaffirming their continued qualifications to serve in this capacity. (The term, "conflicting interests," is meticulously explained in the law itself. Broadly defined, the term means that the trustees may not be prejudiced, economically or otherwise, toward any party in its administration of the loan arrangement.)

See also Indenture Registration; Securities Act of 1933.

Twelve-Month Trend (NYSE). *See New York Times* Market Indicators.

Twenty-Day Cooling-Off Period. If the SEC has not sent an issuing corporation a deficiency letter by the twentieth calendar day after the filing of a registration statement, the statement becomes effective. This period is called the *twenty-day cooling-off period.* On the other hand, the effective date can be delayed merely because the SEC is unable to properly examine the pertinent information within the twenty-day period. The commission then notifies the issuer that its workload has overwhelmed the staff's capability to perform its function. In the busy underwriting years of 1960 and 1961, for example, it was not uncommon for issuers of securities to encounter four- to six-month delays for this reason. Unfortunately, there wasn't much they could do except wait, and by the time their registration statements were allowed to become effective, market conditions had changed dramatically.

The following activities take place during the twenty-day cooling-off period: (1) A preliminary underwriting agreement must be arranged for full guarantee, best-efforts, or all-or-none offering. (2) A *syndicate* of underwriters must be formed. (3) Customers must be contacted for *indications of interest.* (4) Customers must be sent a *preliminary prospectus* (red herring) to solicit indications of interest.

Two-Dollar Broker. Members standing ready, willing, and able to execute orders in any security for any organization, are called *two-dollar brokers.* The origin of that title dates back many years when freelance activity earned these members a flat $2 for each 100-share order executed. Now two-dollar brokers receive a fee, known as *floor brokerage*, that is fully negotiated according to execution difficulty and often by the price of the security.

Some members earn their livelihood acting as independent brokers executing orders for firms in need of assistance any time during the trading day. Commission house brokers with available time can also accommodate other member firms by executing some of their orders and charging them floor brokerage for this service.

Example: When one of Prudential Bache members executes an order for Prudential Bache Inc., that person is acting as their commission house broker. But if this member were to execute an order for Josephthal & Co. during the day, Josephthal classifies that person as a two-dollar broker and the fee charged would be earned in behalf of Prudential Bache Inc.

See also Commission House Broker.

U

U-4 Form. *See* Registration of Personnel (NYSE).

Uncovered Call Options. *See* Option Strategies.

Underlying Security. This security is subject to being purchased or sold on exercise of an option. The exchanges at present have generally uniform standards governing the selection and maintenance of underlying securities for options trading. A few of the basic listing requirements are as follows: (1) a minimum of 7 million shares owned by the public; (2) a minimum of 6,000 shareholders; (3) a trading volume of at least 2.4 million shares per year in the preceding calendar year on all markets on which the underlying security is traded; (4) a market price at least $10 per share each business day of the three calendar months preceding the date of selection; (5) a company aggregate net income after taxes of at least $1 million during the preceding eight financial accounting quarters.

See also Listed Options; Options.

Underwriter. An underwriter, as described in the Securities Act of 1933, may be broadly subclassified as "voluntary" or "involuntary."

A *voluntary underwriter* is an individual or an organization that purchases a security from an issuer or affiliated person and subsequently reoffers it for public sale under a registration statement that has become effective.

An *involuntary underwriter* is an individual or an organization that purchases an unregistered security and subsequently offers it in a public distribution without benefit of an effective registration statement. Such parties, officially identified as *statutory underwriters*, are subject to fine and/or imprisonment as a result. Brokerage firms can be considered to be statutory underwriters even if they merely act as agent for a customer in a public distribution of securities not exempted under the Securities Act of 1933 or pursuant to SEC Rule 144.

See also SEC Rule 144; Securities Act of 1933.

Underwriters Agreement.

For Corporate Securities. The formal contract between the investment bankers and the corporation is officially signed the evening before, or on the morning of, the effective date. At this time, too, the final terms and prices are established. This contract is immediately filed with the SEC and becomes part of the registration statement via amendment.

The agreement for underwriting of corporate securities is customarily signed *severally but not jointly*. This means that while the investment bankers sign the contract collectively, they limit their individual liability to the corporation only to that portion of the issue they have personally agreed to purchase. As a result, any underwriter able to market its own commitment cannot be held financially accountable to the issuer for the inabilities of its co-underwriters.

However, this scheme for limiting financial liability does not extend to the purchaser's protections granted under the Securities Act of 1933. The purchaser who can prove that an omission or misrepresentation of material fact caused investment loss on that offering can bring suit for recovery from any and all parties whose names appear voluntarily in the prospectus, whether or not the purchase was made from that underwriter. This limiting relationship is also referred to as a *divided account*, or even occasionally as a *western account*.

For Municipal Bonds. Most municipal bond offerings, on the other hand, are underwritten *severally and jointly*. In other words, each underwriter has full financial responsibility to the issuing state of municipality for the inability of fellow participants to sell those bonds to their customers. This type of relationship is known as *united account,* or *eastern account* to differentiate it from the corporate syndicate arrangements.

Underwriter's Retention. The syndicate manager must decide how much of each investment banker firm's commitment will be made available to the underwriter for distribution to its customers. The manager withholds part of each member's commitment (1) to allocate to the selling group and (2) to have available for institutional purchasers, who deal in substantial quantities. In this respect, the syndicate manager's responsibility is a touchy one. The manager must coordinate an all-out sales effort and, at the same time, diplomatically juggle requests from members of the syndicate, selling group, and large buyers. If the underwriter's retention percentage is set too high for an offering that becomes very popular, the selling group and big institutions are dissatisfied with their inability to acquire sufficient quantities. If it is set too low, the underwriters are unhappy. They reason that if they must assume financial responsibility for a poor

deal, they should enjoy the benefits of popular distributions by satisfying their own customers first.

A typical retention for participating underwriters is approximately 75%. This means that each underwriter can personally decide on customer allocations for 75% of the financial commitment to the corporation. The manager decides on the other 25%.

See also Spread; Syndicate.

A syndicate manager withholds a portion of each underwriter's share of the distribution. Part of this is offered to institutional purchasers in behalf of the underwriters, out of a common pool (referred to in slang as a *pot*) created for this purpose. Most institutions normally buy in sizable amounts and prefer dealing with only one underwriter in executing transactions for their portfolios. It is more convenient and economical for them to contract with the manager to buy 50,000 shares from the pot than to do business with ten different members of the syndicate and buy 5,000 shares from each one. Such a purchaser can designate one or more specific underwriters for monetary credit on this transaction. If no such designation is made, all underwriters will benefit pro rata.

Group sales also serve as a useful barometer and a profitable sales tool for the underwriters. The most stimulating news from a syndicate manager is a simple announcement that, "The pot is clean!" It is indicative of institutional demand for this issue; it inspires the underwriters and the selling group members to sell out their participations quickly. The smaller, sometimes hesitant, investors generally follow suit.

See also Syndicate.

Underwriting. Within the twenty-day period prior to the anticipated effective date, the officers of the corporation work to finalize arrangements to implement the public offering. They can attempt the distribution themselves if they have the necessary expertise and are willing to assume the financial risk, but generally this does not happen. Instead, even prior to the time a registration statement is prepared, the corporation's officials contract with an investment banker to assist in the offering through a procedure known as *underwriting*. This means that the investment banker guarantees the corporation its money by agreement to purchase this issue and reoffer it publicly at a price somewhat higher than that paid to the corporation. This is called a *firm commitment underwriting*. Thus the issuer's risk of failure is eliminated and is assumed by the investment banker

Example: The underwriter may guarantee the corporation $28.25 per share of stock, while attempting to sell it publicly at a fixed price of $29.50. If successful, the underwriter earns a gross profit of $1.25 per share. However, if it is unable to market it at $29.50, it must still pay the corporation $28.25 on the closing date of their contract.

See also All-or-None Offering; Best-Efforts Offering; Investment Banker; Standby Underwriting Agreement; Underwriter; Underwriting Agreement.

About a week after the effective date and commencement of the offering, the corporation and the underwriters settle up the terms of their contract. In return for the actual certificates, which the syndicate manager distributes to underwriting and selling groups, these investment bankers complete payment of the money specified in the underwriting agreement. They must do so even though the offering may not yet be completed, or even profitable. Unfortunately, that is the business risk assumed by an investment banker on an underwriting of securities.

See also Due-Diligence Meeting; Investment Banker; Syndicate.

Undivided Account. *See* Eastern (Undivided Account.

Uniform Application for Securities and Com- modities **Industry Representative and/or Agent.** *See* Registration of Personnel (NYSE).

Uniform Gifts to Minors Acts (UGMA). These state laws regarding accounts and assets gifted to minors provide for the appointment of a properly qualified custodian. In this connection it is important to remember that the UGMA permits only one person to serve as custodian for each minor for any securities account or issuable certificate. Joint custodians or accounts for the benefit of two or more minors designated jointly have no legal standing under the UGMA. Donors of money or securities in this account appoint the custodian and in doing so give up any personal ownership of those assets. The assets cannot be reclaimed or borrowed by the donor for any reason whatsoever. Nor can the custodian or minor lend or give those securities to someone during the minor's incumbency. Moreover, donors should refrain from appointing themselves as custodian. It is illegal to do so under the UGMA if the securities are in bearer form, and such action carries potentially adverse tax consequences if they are in registered form. For if the donor dies before the minor reaches the age of majority, the IRS will value those securities as part of the donor's assets for estate-tax purposes. Custodians serving under the UGMA are prohibited from dealing in margin accounts or from hypothecating securities belonging to the minor. However, only the custodian is empowered to buy and sell securities in this account, including the privilege of exercising or selling subscription rights when deemed appropriate to the minor's interest. In fact, should the custodian choose to do so, personal funds may be temporarily loaned to the minor to enable the account to "round up" to the next highest share on such subscriptions. In all instances investment decisions may be influenced by state law prevailing in the minor's domicile. The minor's state of residency has jurisdiction in the conduct of accounts under the UGMA. Tax liability for realized profits and losses stemming from transactions in this account, as well as for dividend and interest payments received from investments, is the ultimate responsibility of the minor. Consequently, the custodian must ensure that a full accounting is made annually to the person preparing the minor's tax returns—if any return need be filed at all. The custodian is precluded from charging a fee for these agency services unless the custodian is also acting as a court-appointed guardian for the minor. When the minor reaches the age of majority (18-21 years as state law may dictate), the custodial arrangement is legally and automatically terminated. Previously defined minors can then reregister those securities in their own name individually, without charge, simply by providing the transfer agent with proof of age. The former minor now has full power and authority over any and all assets in the account.

See also Fiduciary Accounts; Prudent Man.

Uniform Practice Code (UPC). The Uniform Practice Code (UPC) is concerned with the mechanics of executing and completing securities transactions between NASD members. The purpose of this code is to enable members of the NASD to work with each other using high standards of business practice. The code is delineated in a comprehensive manual whose guidelines provide members of the NASD with a means of avoiding or reducing controversy in their dealings with each other. What few disputes and misunderstandings do develop are quickly resolved by the national or district Uniform Practice Committees. The national Uniform Practice Committee has further authority to issue and interpret rulings to make trading customs and techniques consistent throughout the industry.

The terms of this code have jurisdiction in member-to-member transactions accomplished over the counter but not necessarily in member-customer relationships. For instance, many people erroneously believe that NASD standards for member-to-member transactions involving delivery units and close-out procedures or contracts in default are exactly the same for broker-to-customer dealings. Member organizations proceeding on that assumption may very well end up in court defending themselves against (1) customer litigation and/or (2) SEC suits for violation of certain federal laws that sometimes require somewhat different treatment for customers.

The code is also inapplicable to transactions involving securities exempted under Section 3a(12) of the Securities Exchange Act of 1934 (including U.S. government and some federal agency obligations), unless the participating broker/dealers choose to be subject to its terms for each particular transaction. (The UPC does not directly encompass transactions in state and municipal securities, although the contract settlement procedures of the Municipal Securities Rulemaking Board are fundamentally similar to the UPC.)

In general, the NASD's Uniform Practice Code affords a person with substantial insight into the entire securities industry because procedures found therein are basically identical to those of the national securities exchanges as well.

See also Bond Interest; Close-Out Procedures; Confirmations (Comparisons); Delivery Dates; Dividend Distributions; Due Bills and Due Bill Checks; Good Delivery of Securities; Mark to the Market; National Association of Securities Dealers; Rejections and Reclamations.

Unincorporated Associations. This category of brokerage customer includes partnerships, charitable organizations, schools, churches, hospitals, and those hedge funds that are not corporations. (A hedge fund is a well-capitalized investment partnership formed for the purpose of trading securities. The name is derived from a technique often used by such groups of establishing long positions and short positions in different stocks of companies competing in the same industry, thereby supposedly hedging their commitment.) A registered representative must make a searching inquiry into the names, occupations, and business affiliations of all people with an interest in any investment partnership, club, or hedge fund. Compliance with exchange rules concerning written authorizations from employers, duplicate copies of activity, and NASD free-riding limitations must also be observed.

If a Partner Dies. In the event of the death of a partner in this form of organization, reference must be made to the group's official agreement for information about (1) distributing assets from the account; and (2) further transactions in behalf of that organization. If the agreement does not provide for such a situation, or if the brokerage firm does not have on file the agreement signed by all of the participants, it is wise not to permit withdrawals of money or securities from this account without advice from legal counsel. Purchases of securities or any new commitment also would be risky under these circumstances. However, sales or other liquidating transactions on instruction from surviving partners are usually acceptable so long as the account is capable of making a good delivery to satisfy such sale. This latter activity is considered proper because it tends to conserve the assets in the account, eliminating further market risk pending resolution of the problem. In no event should the proceeds be distributed until legal counsel has given its approval.

Cash Account. The following documents are required for cash accounts of unincorporated associations: (1) new account report form; (2) a certified copy of the constitution, partnership agreement, or bylaws authorizing transactions in securities; and (3) a certified copy of a resolution of the governing body authorizing specific

people to act in its behalf (*see* Corporate Accounts).

Margin Account. The following documents are required for margin accounts of unincorporated associations: (1) new account report form; (2) a certified copy of the constitution, partnership agreement, or bylaws authorizing transactions in securities on a credit or margin basis; (3) a certified copy of a resolution of the governing body authorizing specific people to act in its behalf (*see* Corporate Accounts); (4) customer's agreement; (5) loan-consent agreement; and (6) a signed credit agreement.

Unincorporated investment clubs fall into this category and require similar documentation and supervision. Because of complex legal ramifications, registered representatives are cautioned against providing any investment club with advice about organization or operation. The principals should be referred to their own counsel and the National Association of Investment Clubs (NAIC), 300 Washington Boulevard Building, Detroit, Michigan 48226.

See also Corporate Accounts; Credit Agreement; Customer's Agreement; Loan-Consent Agreement; New Account Report Form; Partnership.

Unit of Trading. *See* Options.

United Account. *See* Underwriting Agreement.

Unit Investment Trust Company. This type of investment company is a financial institution organized under a trust indenture rather than a corporate charter. The difference between the trust and the corporate approaches is legal in nature and is distinguishable solely by the manner of administration. Otherwise, they may be considered identical in most other respects.

Example: (1) A corporation's activities are supervised by a board of directors elected by the shareholders, whereas investment trust activities are administered by a body of trustees who appoint their own successors; (2) a corporation may issue redeemable or nonredeemable shares of stock in exchange for capital, whereas an investment trust may issue only redeemable shares of beneficial interest (SBI) to represent an undivided participation in a unit of specified securities.

There are two forms of common trust agreements—fixed and participating (*see* Fixed Trust; Participating Trust).

See also Face-Amount Certificate Company; Investment Company; Management Company.

Unit Refund Annuity. *See* Annuity Contract.

U.S. Government-Sponsored Corporation or Agency Obligations. Some securities are not direct obligations of the U.S. government but enjoy federal sponsorship or guarantees to some extent. The major agencies in this category are: (1) Banks for Cooperatives (Co-op); (2) Federal Home Loan Banks (FHLB); (3) Federal Intermediate Credit Banks (FICB), (4) Federal Land Banks (FLB), (5) Federal National Mortgage Association (FNMA, Fannie Mae), (6) Government National Mortgage Association (GNMA, Ginnie Mae), (7) Tennessee Valley Authority (TVA), (8) U.S. Postal Service, and (9) Student Loan Marketing Association (SLMA, Sallie Mae). See these entries for further information on guarantees and taxability.

See also Marketable Security; Nonmarketable Security.

U.S. Postal Service. The Post Office Department was reorganized as an independent entity in 1971 and is now known as the U.S. Postal Service. Its founding legislation authorizes it to issue debt securities (not to exceed $10 billion) to finance capital expenditures and conduct operations of a postal system within the United States. These securities may be guaranteed as to payment of principal and interest by the U.S. government if petitioned to by the Postal Service and if the Secretary of the Treasury deems it in the public interest to do so. The initial offering of 6⅞% debentures due February 1, 1997 does not carry such guarantees, although it is widely assumed that the Postal Service's obligations offer an implied, if not actual, guarantee. Interest received by the holders of these bonds is taxable by the federal government but exempted from state and local taxes.

See also U.S. Government-Sponsored Corporation or Agency Obligation.

U.S. Treasury Bill. U.S. Treasury bills (T bills) are bearer obligations with maturities ranging up to one year. The Federal Reserve, as agent for the Treasury Department, issues three-month and six-month bills at a weekly auction. *Year bills*, bills with maturities of one-year, are generally issued at a monthly auction. The amount of issue, the timing of auctions, and bill maturities may vary as needs of the Treasury dictate. Treasury bills are designed for corporate and institutional investment purposes in denominations ranging from $10,000 to $1 million per bill. Their yields are computed in the same way as corporate bond yields.

Occasionally, the Federal Reserve will issue *tax anticipation bills* (*TABs*), which are designed to encourage corporate investors. These bills mature several days after a tax payment date (such as April 15 or June 15) but are accepted at face value in payment of taxes. This arrangement gives the corporate investor several extra days' interest.

Treasury bills do not pay a fixed rate of interest. There is no preset rate associated with them in any way. All Treasury bills are issued, and subsequently traded, at a discount from face value. The extent of the reduced purchase price determines the rate of return. The difference between the purchase cost (discounted from face value) and the redemption proceeds at maturity (face value) establishes the rate of interest received on this investment. The discount earned on a Treasury bill is taxed as ordinary interest income. If it is sold before maturity, any trading gain or loss is taxed as a capital gain or loss.

Treasury bills are the only U.S. government securities always quoted and traded at a percentage discount of face value. Therefore, their bid and asked prices always distinguish them from other government obligations.

Example: A typical quotation for a six-month bill may appear in this form:

Bid	Asked
4.85% discount	4.66% discount

Note that the bid is a *numerically* higher percentage than the asked, which is indicative of a price reflected in terms of a discount from face value. The larger discount is really a lower *dollar price*. If you buy the bill in the preceding example at the asked price and redeem it at maturity, the yield (rate of return) on your original investment is 4.66% (calculated at an annual rate).

See also Certificate of Indebtedness; Marketable Security; U.S. Treasury Bill; U.S. Treasury Bond; U.S. Treasury Note; Yield.

U.S. Treasury Bond. U.S. Treasury bonds may be in registered or bearer form at the preference of the investor. They may be issued with any maturity, but they customarily range from 5 to 35 years in duration. These obligations carry a fixed interest rate and are issued, quoted, and traded as a percentage of their face value. They are offered in denominations of $500 up to $1 million in value. The typical face value is

$1,000, however. Their yields are computed in the same way as corporate bond yields.

Example: A quotation for a Treasury bond with a 3.50% interest rate and a twenty-year maturity appears in this form:

Bid	Asked	Current Yield	Yield-to-Maturity
74¾	75¼	4.65%	5.55%

There are two special types of Treasury bonds. *Term bonds* are redeemable by the Treasury before maturity, but only five years earlier. *Flower bonds*, not issued since 1971, can be redeemed by heirs of large estates at face value to satisfy estate tax obligations—even if the face amount is significantly lower than the bonds' fair market value.

See also Flower Bond; Marketable Security; Term Bond; U.S. Treasury Bill; U.S. Treasury Note; Yield.

U.S. Treasury Note. U.S. Treasury notes are debt obligations of the federal government issued in registered or bearer form in denominations of $1,000 up to $500 million. Treasury notes are issued with maturities of more than one year and up to ten years in duration. Carrying a fixed rate of interest, they are issued, quoted, and traded as a percentage of their face value. Their yields are computed in the same way as corporate bond yields.

Example: The bid and asked prices of a five-year Treasury note with a 7.50% interest rate appear in this form:

Bid	Asked	Current Yield	Yield-to-Maturity
105¼	105½	7.11%	6.20%

Most Treasury notes are owned by commercial banks, federal reserve banks, U.S. government agencies and trust funds. These notes permit such groups to arrange their portfolios with coupons and maturities spaced over a limited period of years. This provides them with automatic liquidity and attractive average yields.

515

See also Marketable Security; U.S. Treasury Bill; U.S. Treasury Bond; Yield.

U.S. Government Securities. As the issuer of U.S. government securities, the Treasury Department faces the same financial problems confronted by most corporate finance officers today. The Treasury Department's responsibility is primarily to pay for the cost of operating the government. In this regard, the Treasury Department is authorized to issue both marketable and nonmarketable securities. There is no question about the government's ability to repay any borrowing because of its unlimited powers of taxation; therefore, credit rating is not a consideration. From the investor's vantage point, however, the interest received from these securities is only partially free from taxation. Interest from U.S. government securities is exempted from state taxation but subject to full taxation as ordinary income by the federal government itself.

The Treasury issues two types of securities: marketable and nonmarketable. *Nonmarketable securities* or savings bonds, include the well-known Series EE and Series HH bonds. They are considered nonmarketable because they are sold directly to, and are redeemed by, the holder. They do not trade freely in the open market. *Marketable securities*, which trade freely in the marketplace, include Treasury bills (less than one-year maturities), certificates of indebtedness, Treasury notes, (one- to ten-year maturities), and Treasury bonds (5- to 35-year maturities).

Other government securities are issued not by the Treasury, but by government-sponsored corporations and agents.

See also Marketable Security; Nonmarketable Security; U.S. Government-Sponsored Corporation or Agency Obligation; U.S. Treasury Bill; U.S. Treasury Bond; U.S. Treasury Note.

V

Variable Annuity. In this type of annuity, the life insurance company makes periodic distributions to the annuitant during his or her lifetime. However, those payments vary in amount according to the investment performance of equity securitics (mainly common stocks) in a special portfolio created for such contracts with the insurance company's reserves. The theory behind this approach is that, in the long run, a carefully managed portfolio of common stocks will tend to keep pace with the cost of living. This will offset fluctuations in the purchasing power of the dollar. Variable annuity payments should increase in inflationary times and decline during deflationary periods. But, the insurance company cannot guarantee that this will always be true in this plan or in any future market situation. Therefore, an obvious and important difference between the fixed and variable annuity is that with a fixed contract, investment risk is borne by the insurance company; with the variable contract, investment risk is borne by the subscriber.

The variable annuity is subject to scrutiny by the SEC because of investor reliance on fluctuating equity values in its special portfolio. It is this feature that attracts our attention. Because it does not have this feature, the fixed annuity is subject to the exclusive jurisdiction of state insurance commissioners.

Deposits invested in a variable annuity are used to acquire fractional participations in a legal entity created by the insurance company and operated as a unit investment trust. It is similar in function to a mutual fund plan company. It is

also registered as an investment company with the SEC. The insurance industry calls each such arrangement a *separate account*. The separate account is formed as an individual entity to avoid jeopardizing the assets of the parent company and other affiliated companies. The principal assets of a separate account are shares in a mutual fund organized and managed by the same insurance company. The mutual fund is the organization that actually invests in the common stock portfolio. However, the annuitant's participation in the separate account provides an indirect interest that is dependent on the investment performance of those securities (see the following figure).

Relationships of Insurance Company and Annuity to the Separate Account and Mutual Fund

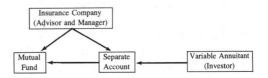

The annuitant's fractional participation purchases in a separate account are not expressed in terms of dollars invested but rather in terms of accumulation units. An *accumulation unit* is an accounting symbol that indicates the value of the separate account's reserves (net assets) during the deposit period. Each contribution by the annuitant is used to purchase these accumulation units. The value of the accumulation units varies daily relative to the investment results of the

517

mutual fund in which the separate account, in turn, is invested. The dollar value of the subscriber's variable annuity at any time is therefore determined by multiplying the number of accumulation units purchased by the current value of one unit.

Example: If you have purchased thus far in your variable annuity program 137.00321 units, and each unit today is calculated to be worth $12.153252, the dollar value of your annuity is the product of these two numbers, or approximately $1,665.03.

Variable Contracts. *See* Rules of Fair Practice (Section 29).

Velocity (of Money). The number of times a dollar changes hands in one year. Given a fixed money supply, increased velocity is usually a sign to the Federal Reserve that an increase in the money supply is needed.

See also Multiplier Effect of Credit Power.

Venture Capital Company. The objective of this type of investment company is to invest in new or underdeveloped companies. They specialize by investing solely in new corporations and/or fledgling industries.

See also Management Company.

Vertical Line Chart. *See* Technical Analysis.

Vertical Spread. *See* Option Strategies (Spreads).

Volatility. A measurement of the price movement of a security during a specific period.

Voluntary-Accumulation Plan. This plan is an informal investment program that provides customers with the ability and facility to purchase modest quantities of mutual fund shares at their option. At the same time, it enables shareholders to enjoy certain benefits of service normally available only for substantial securities investors.

The plan is established with a minimum amount of money or number of shares of that fund, as prescribed by the company or its underwriter. A typical plan account may be started with $250 or $500, or perhaps 100 shares. Future deposits are made at any time as long as they meet a nominal payment schedule set, once again, by the company or its underwriter. This minimum amount, whether it is due monthly, quarterly, annually, or at some other set interval is usually $50 to $100.

A commercial bank is appointed to act as administrator of the plan in order to accomplish all bookkeeping and act as depository for investor monies and fund shares. It is usually the same bank used by the mutual fund itself for protection of the fund's monies and portfolio securities, as required by federal law. When the investor mails in each deposit, the bank deducts a standard $.50 or $1 processing fee and purchases from the underwriter as many full and/or fractional shares of the fund as possible with the balance. The price paid for the shares is determined by the net established offering price using the forward-pricing technique previously described. Instead of registering and delivering these shares, however, the bank holds and accumulates them in this form of open account. Fractional shares are normally calculated to 1/10,000 of a share (four decimal places), although some custodians calculate to only three decimal places. Of course, if they so request, the investors can take delivery of the full shares they own at any time, provided they leave the minimum amount necessary for continuation of the voluntary plan.

Advantages and Services.

Self-explanatory advantages. There are advantages and services gained by subscribing to a voluntary accumulation plan. Certain of them require no explanation: (1) professional management; (2) diversification of investment portfolio; (3) ease of operation of investment; (4) dollar-cost averaging; (5) ability to purchase full and/or fractional shares with each deposit; and (6) advantageous breakpoint privileges on purchases.

Automatic reinvestment of distributions. If and when the mutual fund makes a distribution of dividends or capital gains to its shareholders, participants in the voluntary-accumulation plan may elect to have such distributions reinvested for them automatically in more full and/or fractional shares. To encourage participants to do so, mutual funds often permit this acquisition at net asset value rather than at a loaded offering price. That privilege is not offered by all the mutual funds. Some companies require reinvested dividend purchases at the loaded offering price; only capital gains distributions can be plowed back into the fund at net asset value.

Note that there is no *obligation* to reinvest any distributions. All payments can be taken by the shareholder in the form of cash. Be aware, too, that whether the investor opts for automatic reinvestment or takes the distribution in cash, the shareholder is liable for the appropriate federal tax in this distribution in the year in which the dividend or capital gain is paid by the fund.

Redemption. Mutual funds must be continuously prepared to repurchase shares from holders who request them to do so. Shareholders in the voluntary-accumulation plan are privileged to redeem any or all of their shares merely on written notice to the custodial bank. Their accounts will be readjusted to reflect the reduction or withdrawal from the plan based on the next established net asset value following receipt of notice by the bank and transmission to the underwriter.

Conversion. Several mutual funds are participants in a "family" of funds. That is, several funds, each with a different objective, are managed by the same executive group. They allow shareholders whose personal circumstances may have changed over the years to exchange their shares for comparable value in another fund from that group having an objective more closely attuned to the investor's revised needs. The swap is accomplished at net asset value with a nominal charge of $5 or $10, levied merely to cover the paperwork expense. Thus, the customer saves sales charges on the liquidation and repurchase. However, this convenience does not circumvent, or even defer, the investor's tax liability to the federal government on this capital transaction.

Automatic withdrawal. Many mutual funds permit shareholders to turn their accumulation program into an automatic withdrawal service. Written instructions must be given to the custodian bank to either: (1) hold all dividend distributions in the form of cash and supplement withdrawals, if necessary, with full and/or fractional share liquidations to meet dollar payments when required; or (2) automatically reinvest dividends in more shares at net asset value, then liquidate as many full and/or fractional shares as necessary to meet each withdrawal payment at the time intervals specified (that is, monthly, quarterly, or annually).

Hopefully, the value of accumulated holdings will appreciate more rapidly than the rate at which redemptions take place. Otherwise, in time, the shares in this account will be exhausted and the program terminated. To forestall this, most investment companies offering this privilege insist on minimum initial value of $7,500 or $10,000 in the account and discourage annual withdrawals in excess of 6% of the total. Withdrawal amounts can be adjusted up or down from time to time.

Automatic withdrawal privileges are also available to investors making sufficient single-payment deposits in shares of that fund. Withdrawal programs are not restricted to accumulation planholders.

See also Contractual-Periodic Payment Plan; Mutual Fund.

Voluntary Association. This form of business dates back to medieval England and involves a partnership with continuing existence but unlimited financial liability. The NYSE was originally a voluntary association.

See also New York Stock Exchange, Inc.

Voluntary Underwriter. *See* Underwriter.

Voting Privilege. This is the right, associated with the ownership of common stock, to decide on matters of essential interest in the affairs of a corporation.

See also Common Stock; Proxy.

Voting Trust. If a corporation experiences an extended period of poor operating results, a dissident group may form with the intent of ousting company management. However, they soon discover that deterioration has been extensive and that their plans for recovery are, of necessity, very long term. If successful in a proxy contest, they do not want to risk their own removal from office after only one year. Therefore, the dissidents ask the stockholders to deposit their shares into a *voting trust* established by them for the

purpose of gaining control of the company. After appointing a commercial bank to act as trustee, the dissidents authorize the bank to issue *voting trust certificates* (*VTCs*) in exchange for the stock deposited.

The stockholders who deposit the shares and accept a VTC in exchange retain title to any and all privileges normally granted to stockholders *except the right to vote*. They must relinquish the voting privilege for the duration of the trust. (Although voting trusts are subject to state regulation, they generally survive for extended periods, frequently as long as ten years.) The investors who surrender their stock for a VTC cannot recover their certificates until the trust is dissolved by its creators. They do not, however, lose the marketability associated with their original security investment. Consequently, two separate markets for these securities are established, one for the VTC and one for the common stock that was not tendered to the dissidents. The two securities are not readily interchangeable after the initial appeal.

Voting Trust Certificate (VTC). *See* Voting Trust.

W

Warehousing. The SEC prohibits *warehousing*—an arrangement whereby a sale is made between a broker/dealer and a customer (or another broker/dealer) that carries a provison for repurchase on a future date at a preset price. Establishing an artificially fixed price in advance of, and without respect to, conditions prevailing at the time constitutes a deceptive practice. It countermands the principles of a free and open market for securities and can also violate margin requirements adopted under Regulations G, T, or U.

See also Manipulation of Security Prices and Deceptive Devices; Regulation G; Regulation T; Regulation U.

Warrants. Some corporations attempting to raise capital through issuance of securities make these offerings attractive by attaching warrants to the new securities. To stimulate investor interest, they structure it as a package deal rather than tie the subscription rights to the old certificates. A warrant gives its holder a *long-term* privilege to subscribe to common stock; shares are specifically reserved for this potentiality by the corporation. (This reserve comes from authorized but unissued stock or even treasury stock earmarked for this purpose.) A warrant normally has an expiration date set five to ten years after date of issuance. Some warrants, however, expire after a longer interval, and a few, called *perpetual warrants*, never expire.

Each warrant can be used to subscribe to one or more shares of stock, as determined by the corporation's board of directors. The number of warrants attached to each certificate offered is also determined by the board after it considers what must be done to attract capital investment. Longer-term warrants often provide for changes in subscription price and conditions every few years. This provides the opportunity to speculate or trade in them as the underlying stock appreciates or merely fluctuates in price.

Compared to a right, a warrant's subscription price at the time of the original offering is higher than the current market price of the underlying stock. In terms of market value, at its initial offering, a warrant is mathematically worthless. Its appeal is strictly speculative, based on the possibility of a higher percentage gain within its effective lifetime.

The opportunity to acquire warrants at no additional cost with the purchase of another valuable security issued by the corporation: (1) entices speculators to risk their capital and (2) affords the corporation an opportunity to raise long-term funds at reasonable cost. This attachment is a very effective way to "sweeten" a somewhat speculative offering of securities and make it more palatable for prospective investors.

See also Subscription Privilege (Preemptive Right).

Wash Sale. (1) For regulatory purposes, the purchase and sale of the same security at the same time and price without any real change of ownership. This practice is outlawed under Section 10 of the Securities Exchange Act of 1934.

See also Manipulation of Security Prices and Deceptive Devices.

Western (Divided) Account. In the *Western* or *divided* account, each member of the underwriting group is responsible only for its own participation, with no liability for other members' unsold securities. This type of account is typical for corporate offerings where all the securities are identical (same coupon, same price, same maturity) and thus all equally attractive (or unattractive). Western accounts are sometimes seen in an offering of municipal *term bonds* (where all bonds in the issue carry the same coupon rate and maturation date). Other municipal bonds are generally offered through an Eastern, or undivided, account.

See also Eastern (Undivided) Account; Underwriting Agreement.

When-Issued or When-Distributed Contract. A when-issued or when-distributed contract differs from other contracts in that the securities involved in the transaction do not yet exist. Sometimes, a corporation makes an official announcement of intent to issue certificates in the future. Trading in these securities often begins immediately after the announcement. If the corporation changes its mind or alters the terms and conditions of the security, all contracts are cancelled.

Delivery of the certificates is due on a date to be determined some time in the future by the Uniform Practice Committee of the NASD. If the committee does not make the declaration, the seller may deliver the certificates when available after giving the purchasing firm one business day's notice of intention to do so.

The delivery date (settlement) may be indefinite or long delayed. During this period, the price of a when-issued or when-distributed security may fluctuate widely from the original contract price, thus making one party to the transaction unsecured and jeopardizing its capital position as a result.

Example:

Broker A buys a when-issued security at $60
Current market price = $80

Broker A is unsecured by $20 per share. Because the market price has improved significantly from the original trade value and because the settlement date will be extended past a regular-way contract, Broker A will ask Broker B for $20 per share as a good faith deposit.

Or,

Broker B sells a when-issued security at $80
Current market price = $60

Broker B is unsecured by $20 per share. Because the market price has declined significantly from the original trade value and because the settlement date will be extended past a regular-way contract, Broker B will ask Broker A for $20 per share as a good faith deposit. Each demand for a good faith deposit is known as a mark to the market.

See also Cash Contract; Delivery Dates; Delivery-Option Contract; Regular-Way Contract.

A *when-issued (WI)/when-distributed (WD)* contract therefore calls for settlement sometime in the future, on a date to be determined by the NYSE. These contracts relate only to securities that have not yet been distributed to stockholders by the issuing corporation. The certificates can arise from bonds to be issued in payment for another company's securities in a merger proposition or from exchange offers of stock or convertible bonds for a new issue of a straight debt security.

Trading in these new securities often commences immediately on agreement by management of the corporations but before final arrangements are made for physical delivery. Therefore, these transactions are effected literally on a when-, as-, and if-issued basis for settlement. Should distribution arrangements be altered or terminated by the issuers, all pending trading contracts must be cancelled immediately, including contingent profits and losses. The credit department of a brokerage firm will, therefore, withhold any profits, losses, and contingent transaction fees from customers who trade in and out of when-issued/when-distributed contracts before the final terms are validated.

See also Cash Contract; Corporate Bond Transaction; Next-Day Contract; Regular-Way Contract; Seller's-Option Contract.

Withholding. This failure by a broker/dealer to make a bona fide distribution of a hot issue, thus encouraging demand at a premium price, is a violation of the NASD Rules of Fair Practice.

See also Hot Issue.

Window Settlement. *See* Comparison Procedures (Over-the-Counter Physical Comparison).

Wire Room *See* Broker/Dealer Organization (Order Department).

Working Capital. The relationship between current assets and current liabilities is quite important. After all, it is certainly necessary for a corporation to be able to keep current on its obligations. At a minimum, there should be an excess of current assets over current liabilities. This excess, called *working capital*, represents the amount of money that would be left from the current assets if all current liabilities were paid off. This important figure is derived by subtracting current liabilities from current assets:

Working capital = current assets − current liabilities

A company's ability to meet its obligations is measured, at least in part, by the amount of its working capital. Working capital is also known as *net working capital* or *net current assets*.

Example:

Assets

Cash	$ 75,000
Marketable securities	150,000
Accounts receivable	375,000
Inventory	+ 400,000
Total current assets	$1,000,000

Liabilities

Accounts payable	$200,000
Accrued expenses	150,000
Accrued taxes	50,000
	+
Total current liabilities	$400,000

For this corporation:

Working capital = current assets − current liabilities
= $1,000,000 − $400,000
= $600,000

See also Balance Sheet.

Workout Market. *See* National Quotation Bureau, Inc.

Write-Out. By means of this exchange floor procedure, specialists are allowed to buy stock for themselves from a customer's offering in their books, or sell from their accounts to a customer's bid. They must, however, allow the broker who entered the order to execute and "write out" the confirmation of the transaction and earn the contingent brokerage fee.

See also Specialist.

Writer of an Option. This person initially sells an option contract, thus creating a short option position.

See also Buyer of an Option; Options.

Writing Put Options. *See* Option Strategies.

World Bank. *See* International Bank for Reconstruction and Development.

Y

Yellow Sheet. *See* National Quotation Bureau, Inc.

Yield. The purchaser of a debt security wants to invest capital generally for one reason—the rate of return earned by this money. The rate of return on capital is commonly referred to as *yield*. The concept of yield has different meanings for different investors, according to their purposes and objectives. In the securities industry, three types of yields are important:

1. *Nominal yield* is the annual rate of interest specified in the indenture.

2. *Current yield* is a calculation of yield based on the nominal interest rate and the actual market price of the bond.

3. *Yield-to-maturity* is a calculation similar to that for current yield, but it also takes into account the time remaining to maturity.

See also Current Yield; Nominal Yield; Yield-to-Maturity.

Yield on Common Stock. To determine current yield, divide a security's annual dividends (or coupons) by its current market price.

$$\text{Current yield} = \frac{\text{Annual dividend rate}}{\text{Market price}}$$

Generally speaking, companies with greater prospects for growth have lower yields, because growth companies usually reinvest most of their earnings in their own businesses.

Example: A common stock has a current market price of 42 and pays annual dividends of $1.80. Its current yield is 4.3%, calculated thus:

$$\text{Current yield} = \frac{\$1.80}{42} = 0.043 \text{ or } 4.3\%$$

Yield-to-Maturity. Because most bonds trade not at par but at a discount or premium, comparing nominal yields does not enable investors to make valid investment decisions. Yield-to-maturity, another way of looking at a bondholder's return on invested capital, is a more sophisticated approach to the subject of yield. It is used by institutional investors and portfolio managers who supervise pools of capital on a long-term, semipermanent basis. It is also used by professional securities traders as an accurate means of identifying the relative worth of a particular bond.

Yield-to-Maturity is an average rate of return in consideration of a bond's: (1) interest rate; (2) current price; and (3) number of years remaining until maturity.

Because a corporation is expected to repay holders the face value of their bonds at maturity, yield-to-maturity requires the (1) *pro rata accumulation* of the capital gain to be realized on redemption, if the bond is acquired below face value (discount), (2) *pro rata amortization* of the capital loss to be incurred on redemption, if the bond is acquired above face value (premium).

Rule-of-Thumb Formula. There is a simple rule-of-thumb method used for calculating a bond's yield-to-maturity. It is inaccurate for professional use, and it becomes increasingly so with longer-term maturities. yet it is satisfactory as an introduction to the subject.

When a bond is trading at a *discount* (below face value): (1) *compute* the capital gain if the bond is held to maturity; (2) *equally allocate* the capital gain to be established at maturity over the remaining years of the life of the bond; (3) *add* this annual appreciation to the annual interest distribution; (4) *average* the redemption proceeds and the acquisition cost; and (5) *divide* the total by the average of the redemption proceeds and the acquisition cost.

Example: If a 6% debenture is purchased for $975 and matures in exactly 10 years, its yield-to-maturity is calculated as follows:

1. $1,000 redemption price
   − 975 current market price

   $ 25 gain to be realized if held to maturity

2. $25 gain ÷ 10-year life = $2.50 per year gain

3. $ 2.50 annual capital gain
   + 60.00 annual interest at 6%

   $62.50

4.
redemption proceeds		acquisition cost
$1,000	+	$975

   $$\frac{\$1,000 \;+\; \$975}{2} = \$987.50$$

5. $62.50 ÷ $987.50 = .06329
   yield-to-maturity = 6.33%

When a bond is trading at a *premium* (above face value): (1) *compute* the loss if bond is held to maturity; (2) *equally amortize* the capital loss to be established at maturity over the remaining years of life of the bond; (3) *subtract* this annual depreciation from the annual interest distribution; (4) *average* the redemption proceeds and the acquisition cost; (5) *divide* the remainder by the average of the redemption proceeds and the acquisition cost.

Example: If a 7.5% debenture is purchased

for $1,036.25 and matures in exactly four years, its yield-to-maturity is calculated as follows:

1. $1,036.25 current market price
   −1,000.00 redemption price

   $ 36.25 loss to be realized if held to maturity

2. $26.25 loss ÷ 4-year life = $9.06 per year loss

3. $75.00 annual interest in 7.5%
   − 9.06 annual deduction

   $65.94

4.
redemption proceeds		acquisition cost
$1,000	+	$1,036.25

   $$\frac{\$1,000 \;+\; \$1,036.25}{2} = \$1,018.13$$

5. $65.94 ÷ $1,018.13 = .06476
   yield-to-maturity = 6.48%

Alternate Method. A somewhat more accurate method to calculate yield-to-maturity is similar, but with two important changes: (1) The annual accumulation (amortization) is subtracted (added) from (to) the redemption proceeds before averaging yields based on acquisition cost and redemption proceeds. (2) Each equation is calculated separately in decimal form and converted to a percentage figure only in the final analysis. The result is somewhat more accurate than the rule-of-thumb method, but still not precise enough for the professional. (This alternate method is used to provide yield figures in the widely used, monthly *Bond Guide* published by Standard & Poor's Corporation.)

When a bond is trading at a *discount* (below face value): (1) *compute* the capital gain if bond is held to maturity: (2) *equally allocate* the capital gain to be established at maturity over the remaining years of life of the bond; (3) *add* this annual appreciation to the annual interest distribution; (4) *divide* that total by the current price of the bond; (5) *divide* that same total by the redemption proceeds minus the annual capital gain; (6) *average* the sum of the two division results in steps 4 and 5.

Example: For a 6% debenture selling at 97.50 and maturing in exactly ten years, the yield-to-maturity is calculated as follows:

1. $1,000 redemption price
   − 975 current market price

   $ 25 gain to be realized if held to maturity

2. $25 gain ÷ 10-year life = $2.50 per year gain

3. $ 2.50 annual capital gain
   + 60.00 annual interest

   $62.50

4. $62.50 ÷ $975 (current price) = .06410

5. $62.50 ÷ $997.50 ($1,000 redemption proceeds − $2.50 annual gain) = .06266

6. $$\frac{.06410 + .06266}{2} = \frac{.12676}{2} = .06338$$

   yield-to-maturity = 6.34%

When a bond is trading at a *premium* (above face value): (1) *compute* the loss if bond is held to maturity; (2) *equally allocate* the capital loss to be established at maturity over the remaining years of life of the bond; (3) *subtract* the annual depreciation from the annual interest distribution; (4) *divide* that total by the current price of the bond; (5) *divide* that same total by the redemption proceeds plus the annual capital loss; (6) *average* the sum of the two division results in steps 4 and 5.

Example: For a 7.5% debenture selling at 103⅝, maturing in exactly four years, the yield-to-maturity is calculated as follows:

1. $1,036.25 current market price
   −1,000.00 redemption price

   $ 36.25 loss to be realized if held to maturity

2. $36.25 loss ÷ 4-year life = $9.06 per year loss

3. $75.00 annual interest
   − 9.06 annual capital loss

   $65.94

4. $65.94 ÷ $1,036.25 (current price) = .06363

5. $65.94 ÷ $1,009.06 ($1,000 redemption proceeds + $9.06 annual loss) = .06535

6. $$\frac{.06363 + .06535}{2} = \frac{.12898}{2} = .06449$$

   yield-to-maturity = 6.45%

Professional Method. The most reliable method for determining yields-to-maturity recognizes that the capital gain or loss does not accrue in equal annual installments. It considers such accumulation or amortization as if reinvested at the coupon rate and applies these sums to the basic principles of coupon rates, acquisition price, and exact period of time until maturity.

The mathematical formula is complicated and impractical for ordinary use even by professionals, especially in view of the almost unlimited combination of variables in the basic principles. Fortunately, however, the calculations for the most frequently found coupons, maturities, and yields-to-maturity have been printed and are sold by the Financial Publishing Company in a book of bond tables. An example of one such table, for a 6.5% coupon rate, is shown on page 527. Note that the market value is 100.00 across the entire row marked 6.50 under the column headed yield-to-maturity. As the prices above that row rise, the yield-to-maturity decreases. On the other hand, as the prices below that row decrease, the yield-to-maturity increases.

The yields-to-maturity in this table are expressed in "basis points." A *basis point* equals .01%, or 1/100%, of $1,000 — or ten cents.

Example: A yield-to-maturity of 4.20 equals 4.20%. The difference between 4.20 and 4.40 is twenty basis points.

Bond tables like the one shown may be used as a ready reference for: (1) *finding the yield-to-maturity*, if you know the coupon rate, current price, and remaining years and months to date of maturation; and (2) *finding market value*, if you know the coupon rate, yield-to-maturity, and remaining years and months to date of maturation.

Example of Finding the Yield-to-Maturity Directly: With a coupon rate of 6.50%, a bond selling at 81 and due to mature in exactly fourteen years, has a yield-to-maturity of 8.90% according to the table. In the table, for a 6.50% coupon rate, glance down the column labeled 14 years and 0 months until you reach a price of 81. Then look across, under the column headed yield-to-maturity.

Example of Finding the Market Value Directly: The market value of a bond with a 6.50% coupon rate and a yield-to-maturity of 7.80%, due to mature in eleven years and six months, is 90.25 according to the table. Glance down the yield column to 7.80%. Look right, across this line, to the point where it intersects the column headed 11-6.

Example of Finding the Needed Data by Interpolating: Although reading from the bond table is simple enough, the tables show yields only in increments of ten or twenty basis points and market values that are not divisible by eighths (the usual trading variation). This presents a problem in finding the yield-to-maturity of a bond selling at a price between entries, such as a bond selling at 101½ and due to mature in twelve years and six months. Nor is it helpful in finding the market value of a bond selling at a 7.23 basis and due to mature in exactly eleven years.

Bond Table, 6.50% Coupon Rate, 10 Years, 6 Months to 14 Years to Maturity.

Years and Months Prior to Maturity

Yield-to-Maturity	10-6	11-0	11-6	12-0	12-6	13-0	13-6	14-0
4.00	121.26	122.07	122.87	123.64	124.40	125.15	125.88	126.60
4.20	119.37	120.10	120.81	121.51	122.19	122.86	123.52	124.16
4.40	117.51	118.16	118.79	119.42	120.03	120.62	121.21	121.78
4.60	115.68	116.26	116.82	117.37	117.91	118.44	118.95	119.45
4.80	113.89	114.40	114.89	115.37	115.84	116.30	116.75	117.19
5.00	112.14	112.57	113.00	113.41	113.82	114.21	114.60	114.97
5.20	110.42	110.79	111.15	111.50	111.84	112.17	112.50	112.82
5.40	108.73	109.03	103.33	109.62	109.91	110.18	110.45	110.71
5.60	107.07	107.32	107.56	107.79	108.01	108.23	108.45	108.65
5.80	105.45	105.63	105.82	105.99	106.16	106.33	106.49	106.65
6.00	103.85	103.98	104.11	104.23	104.35	104.47	104.58	104.69
6.10	103.07	103.17	103.27	103.37	103.46	103.55	103.64	103.73
6.20	102.29	102.37	102.44	102.51	102.58	102.65	102.72	102.78
6.30	101.52	101.57	101.62	101.67	101.71	101.76	101.80	101.84
6.40	100.76	100.78	100.81	100.83	100.85	100.87	100.89	100.92
6.50	100.00	100.00	100.00	100.00	100.00	100.00	100.00	100.00
6.60	99.25	99.23	99.20	99.18	99.16	99.14	99.12	99.10
6.70	98.51	98.46	98.41	98.37	98.32	98.28	98.24	98.20
6.80	97.77	97.70	97.63	97.57	97.50	97.44	97.38	97.32
6.90	97.05	96.95	96.86	96.77	96.69	96.60	96.52	96.45
7.00	96.33	96.21	96.09	95.99	95.88	95.78	95.68	95.58
7.10	95.61	95.47	95.34	95.21	95.08	94.96	94.84	94.73
7.20	94.90	94.74	94.59	94.44	94.29	94.15	94.02	93.89
7.30	94.20	94.02	93.85	93.68	93.51	93.36	93.20	93.06
7.40	93.51	93.31	93.11	92.92	92.74	92.57	92.40	92.24
7.50	92.82	92.60	92.38	92.18	91.98	91.79	91.60	91.42
7.60	92.14	91.90	91.66	91.44	91.22	91.01	90.81	90.62
7.70	91.47	91.20	90.95	90.71	90.48	90.25	90.04	89.83
7.80	90.80	90.52	90.25	89.99	89.74	89.50	89.27	89.04
7.90	90.13	89.84	89.55	89.27	89.01	88.75	88.50	88.27

8.00	89.48	89.16	88.86	88.56	88.28	88.01	87.75	87.50
8.10	88.83	88.49	88.17	87.86	87.57	87.28	87.01	86.75
8.20	88.18	87.83	87.50	87.17	86.86	86.56	86.27	86.00
8.30	87.55	87.18	86.83	86.49	86.16	85.85	85.55	85.26
8.40	86.91	86.53	86.16	85.81	85.47	85.14	84.83	84.53
8.50	86.29	85.89	85.50	85.14	84.78	84.44	84.12	83.81
8.60	85.67	85.25	84.85	84.47	84.10	83.75	83.42	83.09
8.70	85.05	84.62	84.21	83.81	83.43	83.07	82.72	82.39
8.80	84.44	84.00	83.57	83.16	82.77	82.40	82.04	81.69
8.90	83.84	83.38	82.94	82.52	82.11	81.73	81.36	81.00
9.00	83.24	82.77	82.32	81.88	81.46	81.07	80.69	80.32
9.10	82.65	82.16	81.70	81.25	80.82	80.41	80.02	79.65
9.20	82.07	81.56	81.08	80.62	80.19	79.77	79.37	78.98
9.30	81.48	80.97	80.48	80.01	79.56	79.13	78.72	78.33
9.40	80.91	80.38	79.88	79.39	78.93	78.50	78.08	77.68
9.50	80.34	79.80	79.28	78.79	78.32	77.87	77.44	77.03
9.60	79.77	79.22	78.69	78.19	77.71	77.25	76.81	76.40
9.70	79.21	78.65	78.11	77.60	77.11	76.64	76.19	75.77
9.80	78.66	78.08	77.53	77.01	76.51	76.03	75.58	75.15
9.90	78.11	77.52	76.96	76.43	75.92	75.44	74.97	74.53
10.00	77.56	76.96	76.39	75.85	75.34	74.84	74.37	73.93
10.20	76.49	75.87	75.28	74.72	74.19	73.68	73.20	72.74
10.40	75.43	74.79	74.19	73.61	73.06	72.54	72.04	71.57
10.60	74.40	73.74	73.11	72.52	71.96	71.42	70.91	70.43
10.80	73.38	72.70	72.06	71.45	70.88	70.33	69.81	69.32
11.00	72.38	71.69	71.03	70.41	69.82	69.26	68.73	68.23
11.20	71.40	70.69	70.02	69.38	68.78	68.21	67.67	67.16
11.40	70.44	69.71	69.03	68.38	67.77	67.19	66.64	66.12
11.60	69.49	68.75	68.06	67.40	66.77	66.18	65.63	65.10
11.80	68.56	67.81	67.10	66.43	65.80	65.20	64.64	64.11
12.00	67.65	66.89	66.17	65.49	64.85	64.24	63.67	63.13

Numbers inside this bond table are market values.

Z

Zero Coupon. This is a debt security that makes no periodic payments but that is sold at a deep discount from face value. The holder receives no periodic payments, only the full face amount at maturity.

For tax purposes, the prorated difference between the discounted price and the face value is to be included in the holder's return each year, even though no payments are in fact made.

The most popular type of zero security is the zero coupon bond. This bond may be issued by corporations, who need only pay back the full face value at a future date and are not burdened with periodic principal and interest payments. The bonds may also be created by brokerage firms, which strip the coupons from conventional bonds (usually a government securities) and sell the coupons and principal separately.

Zero coupon mortgages work pretty much the same way: The holder receives no periodic payments, just full face value at maturity.

Zero securities are most useful as investments for providing a future payment—such as a college tuition bill.

Because zero's do not make interest payments, they are considered a relatively volatile type of bond, compared with bonds that make periodic payments. When interest rates rise, zero's drop in value more sharply than interest-paying bonds; similarly, when rates drop, zero's rise in value more quickly.

Zero Plus Tick. *See* Plus-Tick Rule.

Zero-Plus-Tick Rule. *See* Plus-Tick and Zero-Plus-Tick Rules.